JOSS WHEDON

Andi **Watson** • Dan **Brereton** • Christopher **Golden** • Joe **Bennett** • Cliff **Richards**

Buffy the vampire slayer™

LEGACY EDITION BOOK TWO

Published by

BOOM! STUDIOS

Collection Designer
Scott Newman

Additional Art by
Jeff Matsuda, **Randy Green**, **Chrstian Zanier**,
Jon Sibal, and **Tim Townsend**

Original Series Editor
Scott Allie

Legacy Edition Assistant Editor
Gavin Gronenthal

Legacy Edition Associate Editor
Jonathan Manning

Legacy Edition Editor
Jeanine Schaefer

Special Thanks to
Sierra Hahn, **Becca J. Sadowski**,
and **Nicole Spiegel** & **Carol Roeder**

Originally published by
Dark Horse Comics

Ross Richie CEO & Founder
Joy Huffman CFO
Matt Gagnon Editor-in-Chief
Filip Sablik President, Publishing & Marketing
Stephen Christy President, Development
Lance Kreiter Vice President, Licensing & Merchandising
Arune Singh Vice President, Marketing
Bryce Carlson Vice President, Editorial & Creative Strategy
Kate Henning Director, Operations
Spencer Simpson Director, Sales
Scott Newman Manager, Production Design
Elyse Strandberg Manager, Finance
Sierra Hahn Executive Editor
Jeanine Schaefer Executive Editor
Dafna Pleban Senior Editor
Shannon Watters Senior Editor
Eric Harburn Senior Editor
Matthew Levine Editor
Sophie Philips-Roberts Associate Editor
Amanda LaFranco Associate Editor
Jonathan Manning Associate Editor
Gavin Gronenthal Assistant Editor

Gwen Waller Assistant Editor
Allyson Gronowitz Assistant Editor
Ramiro Portnoy Assistant Editor
Shelby Netschke Editorial Assistant
Michelle Ankley Design Coordinator
Marie Krupina Production Designer
Grace Park Production Designer
Chelsea Roberts Production Designer
Samantha Knapp Production Design Assistant
José Meza Live Events Lead
Stephanie Hocutt Digital Marketing Lead
Esther Kim Marketing Coordinator
Cat O'Grady Digital Marketing Coordinator
Breanna Sarpy Live Events Coordinator
Amanda Lawson Marketing Assistant
Holly Aitchison Digital Sales Coordinator
Morgan Perry Retail Sales Coordinator
Megan Christopher Operations Coordinator
Rodrigo Hernandez Operations Coordinator
Zipporah Smith Operations Assistant
Jason Lee Senior Accountant
Sabrina Lesin Accounting Assistant

BUFFY THE VAMPIRE SLAYER LEGACY EDITION BOOK
TWO, August 2020. Published by BOOM! Studios, a division
of Boom Entertainment, Inc. Buffy the Vampire Slayer ™ &
© 2020 Twentieth Century Fox Film Corporation. All rights
reserved. Originally published in single magazine form
as BUFFY THE VAMPIRE SLAYER No. 11-19, "Stinger," "Play
with Fire," "The Latest Craze," "Bad Dog," "Killing Time," ™ &
© 1999-2000 Twentieth Century Fox Film Corporation. All
rights reserved. BOOM! Studios™ and the BOOM! Studios
logo are trademarks of Boom Entertainment, Inc., registered
in various countries and categories. All characters, events,
and institutions depicted herein are fictional. Any similarity
between any of the names, characters, persons, events,
and/or institutions in this publication to actual names,
characters, and persons, whether living or dead, events, and/
or institutions is unintended and purely coincidental. BOOM!
Studios does not read or accept unsolicited submissions of
ideas, stories, or artwork.

BOOM! Studios, 5670 Wilshire Boulevard, Suite 400,
Los Angeles, CA 90036-5679. Printed in China. First Printing.

ISBN: 978-1-68415-533-0, eISBN: 978-1-64144-699-0

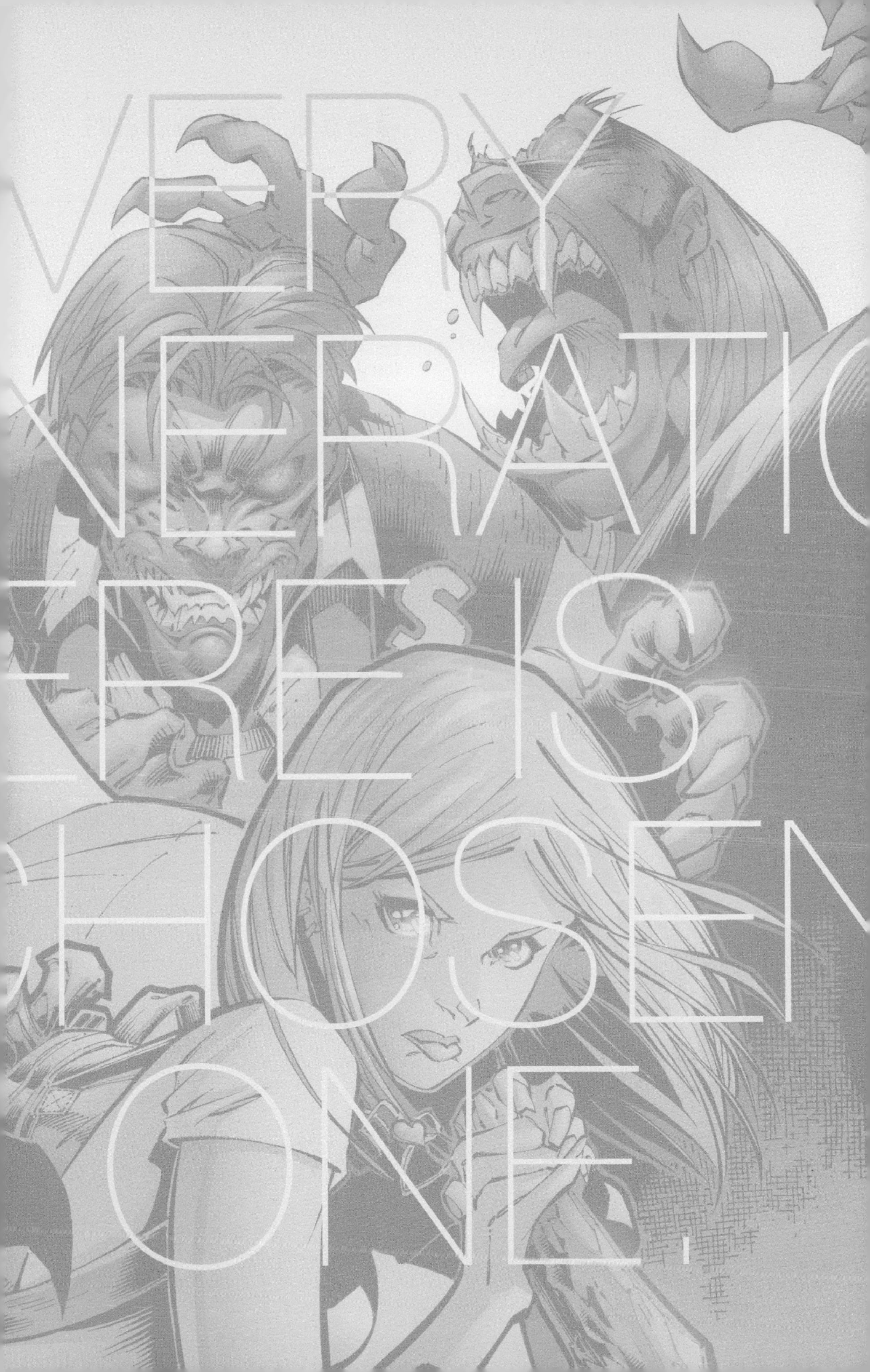
VERY
NERATI
RE IS
HOSE
ONE.

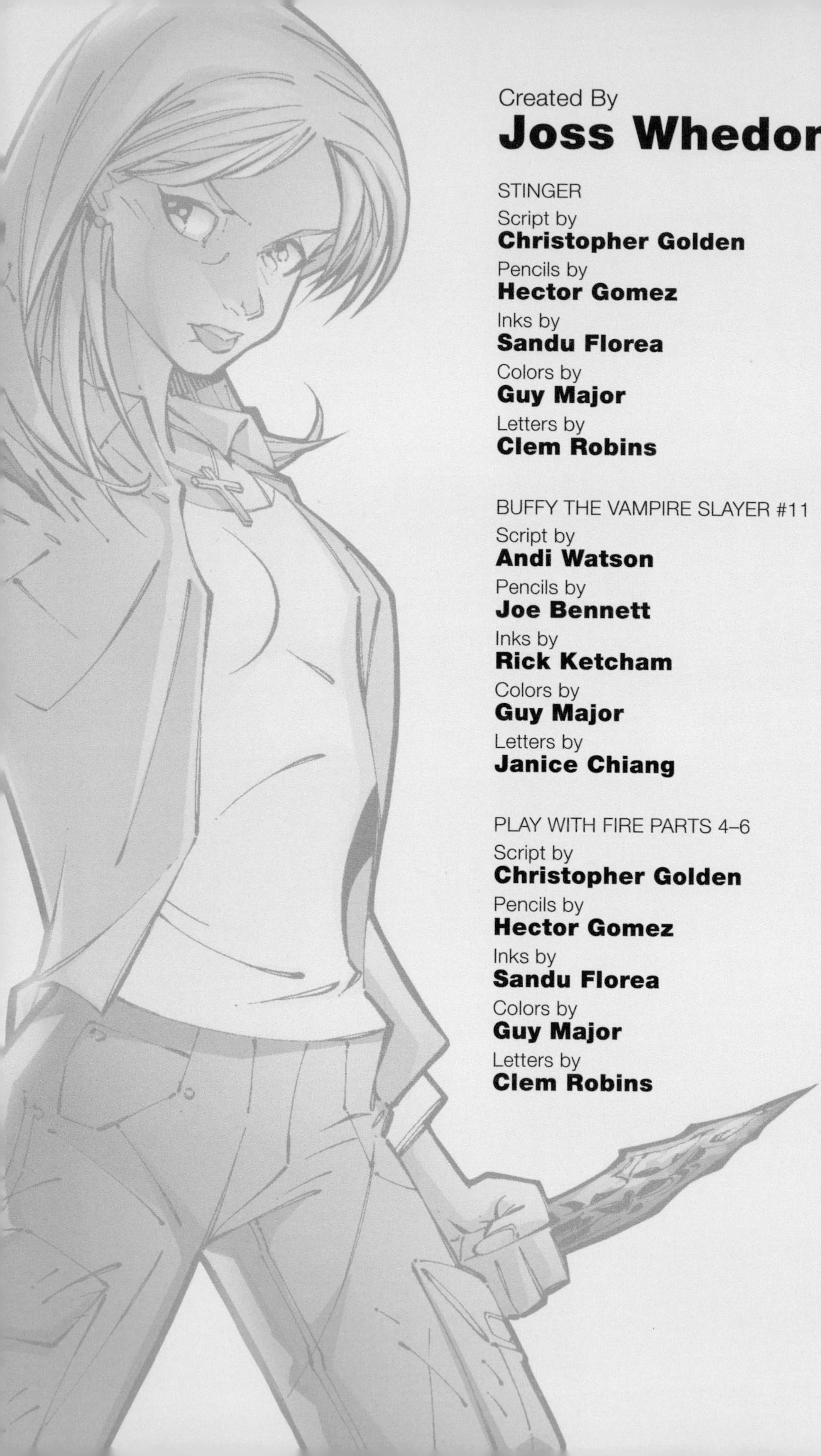

Created By
Joss Whedon

STINGER
Script by
Christopher Golden
Pencils by
Hector Gomez
Inks by
Sandu Florea
Colors by
Guy Major
Letters by
Clem Robins

BUFFY THE VAMPIRE SLAYER #11
Script by
Andi Watson
Pencils by
Joe Bennett
Inks by
Rick Ketcham
Colors by
Guy Major
Letters by
Janice Chiang

PLAY WITH FIRE PARTS 4–6
Script by
Christopher Golden
Pencils by
Hector Gomez
Inks by
Sandu Florea
Colors by
Guy Major
Letters by
Clem Robins

BUFFY THE VAMPIRE SLAYER #12
Script by
Christopher Golden
Pencils by
Christian Zanier
Inks by
Andy Owens
Colors by
Guy Major
Letters by
Janice Chiang

THE LATEST CRAZE
Script by
Christopher Golden
& Thomas E. Sniegoski
Pencils by
Cliff Richards
Inks by
Joe Pimentel
Colors by
Guy Major
Letters by
Clem Robins

BAD DOG
Script by
Doug Petrie
Pencils by
Ryan Sook
Inks by
Tim Goodyear
Colors by
Guy Major
Letters by
Pat Brosseau

BUFFY THE VAMPIRE SLAYER #13
Script by
Andi Watson
Pencils by
Cliff Richards
Inks by
Joe Pimentel
Colors by
Guy Major
Letters by
Amador Cisneros

BUFFY THE VAMPIRE SLAYER #14–16
Script by
Andi Watson
Pencils by
Cliff Richards
& Christian Zanier (Issue 16)
Background Assists by
Marvin Mariano
& Draxhall Jump (Issue 16)
Inks by
Joe Pimentel
with **Curtis P. Arnold**,
Jason Minor,
& Andy Owens (Issue 16)
Colors by
Guy Major
Letters by
Amador Cisneros

KILLING TIME
Script by
Douglas Petrie
Pencils by
Cliff Richards
Inks by
Joe Pimentel
Colors by
Guy Major
Letters by
Amador Cisneros

BUFFY THE VAMPIRE SLAYER #17–19
Script by
Andi Watson
Pencils by
Cliff Richards
Inks by
Joe Pimentel
Colors by
Guy Major
Letters by
Amador Cisneros

Cover by
Nimit Malavia

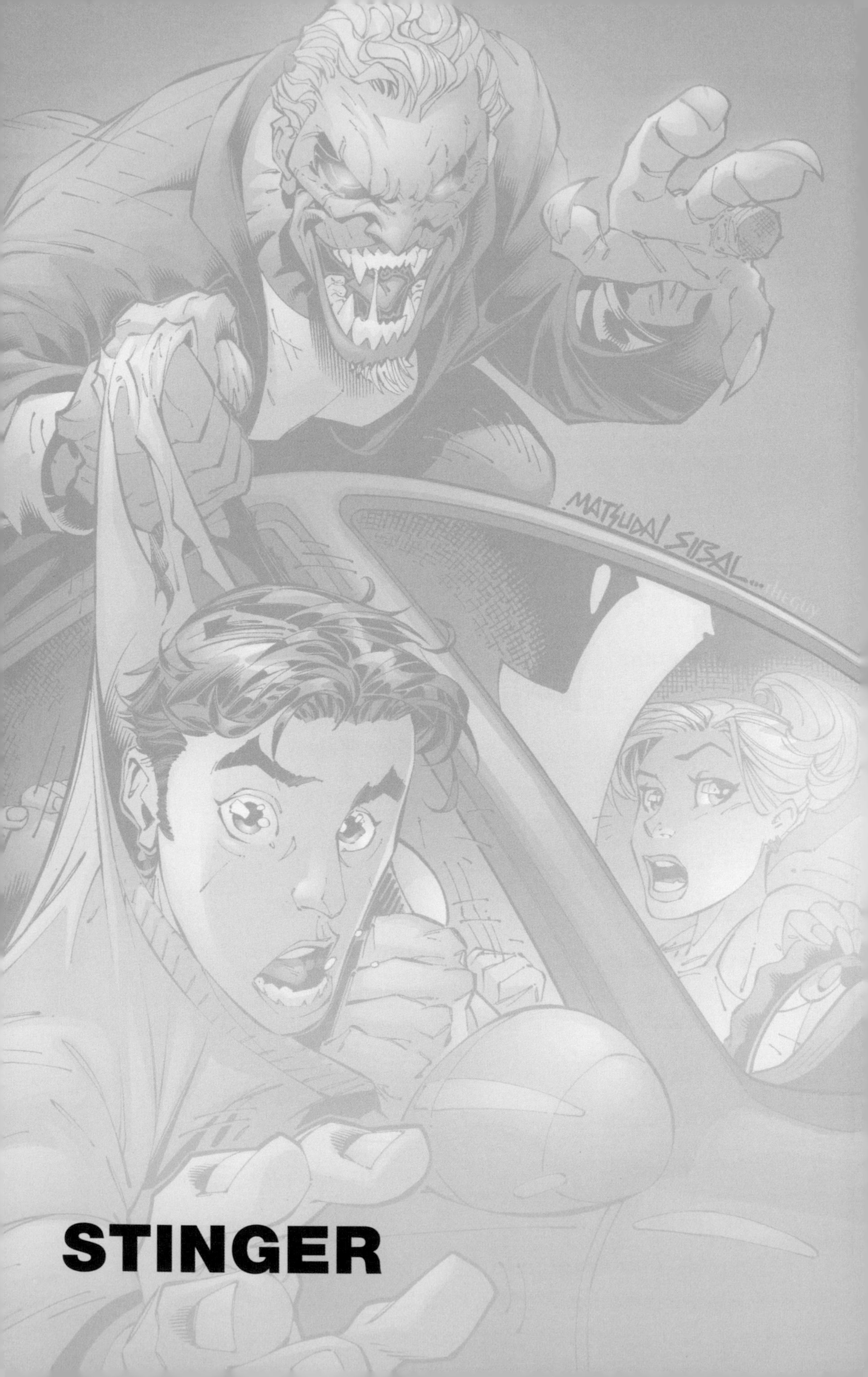
MATSUDA/SIBAL...

STINGER

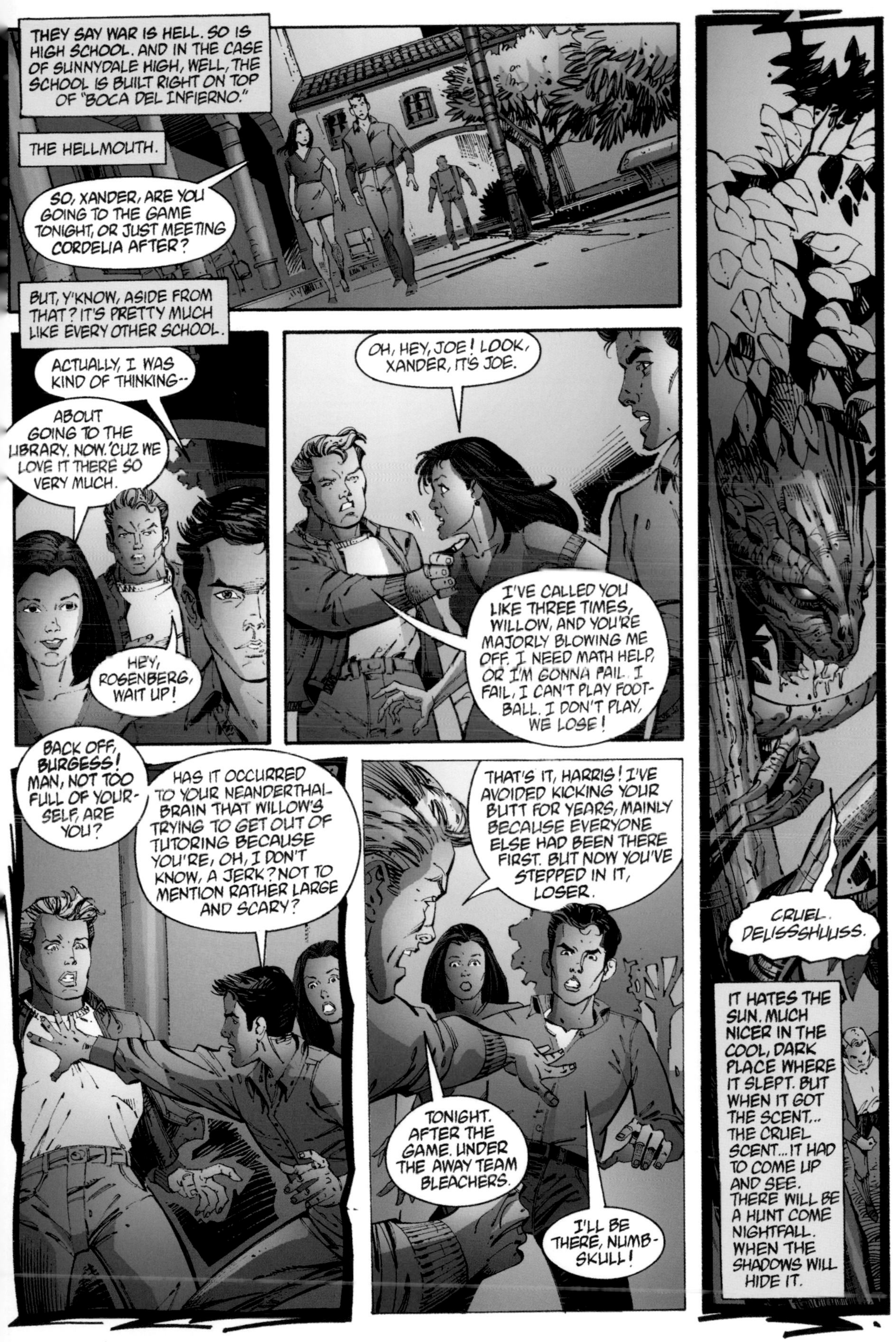
THEY SAY WAR IS HELL. SO IS HIGH SCHOOL. AND IN THE CASE OF SUNNYDALE HIGH, WELL, THE SCHOOL IS BUILT RIGHT ON TOP OF "BOCA DEL INFIERNO."
THE HELLMOUTH.
SO, XANDER, ARE YOU GOING TO THE GAME TONIGHT, OR JUST MEETING CORDELIA AFTER?
BUT, Y'KNOW, ASIDE FROM THAT? IT'S PRETTY MUCH LIKE EVERY OTHER SCHOOL.
ACTUALLY, I WAS KIND OF THINKING--
ABOUT GOING TO THE LIBRARY. NOW. 'CUZ WE LOVE IT THERE SO VERY MUCH.
HEY, ROSENBERG, WAIT UP!
OH, HEY, JOE! LOOK, XANDER, IT'S JOE.
I'VE CALLED YOU LIKE THREE TIMES, WILLOW, AND YOU'RE MAJORLY BLOWING ME OFF. I NEED MATH HELP, OR I'M GONNA FAIL. I FAIL, I CAN'T PLAY FOOT-BALL. I DON'T PLAY, WE LOSE!
CRUEL. DELISSSHUUSS.
BACK OFF, BURGESS! MAN, NOT TOO FULL OF YOUR-SELF, ARE YOU?
HAS IT OCCURRED TO YOUR NEANDERTHAL-BRAIN THAT WILLOW'S TRYING TO GET OUT OF TUTORING BECAUSE YOU'RE, OH, I DON'T KNOW, A JERK? NOT TO MENTION RATHER LARGE AND SCARY?
THAT'S IT, HARRIS! I'VE AVOIDED KICKING YOUR BUTT FOR YEARS, MAINLY BECAUSE EVERYONE ELSE HAD BEEN THERE FIRST. BUT NOW YOU'VE STEPPED IN IT, LOSER.
TONIGHT. AFTER THE GAME. UNDER THE AWAY TEAM BLEACHERS.
I'LL BE THERE, NUMB-SKULL!
IT HATES THE SUN. MUCH NICER IN THE COOL, DARK PLACE WHERE IT SLEPT. BUT WHEN IT GOT THE SCENT... THE CRUEL SCENT... IT HAD TO COME UP AND SEE. THERE WILL BE A HUNT COME NIGHTFALL. WHEN THE SHADOWS WILL HIDE IT.

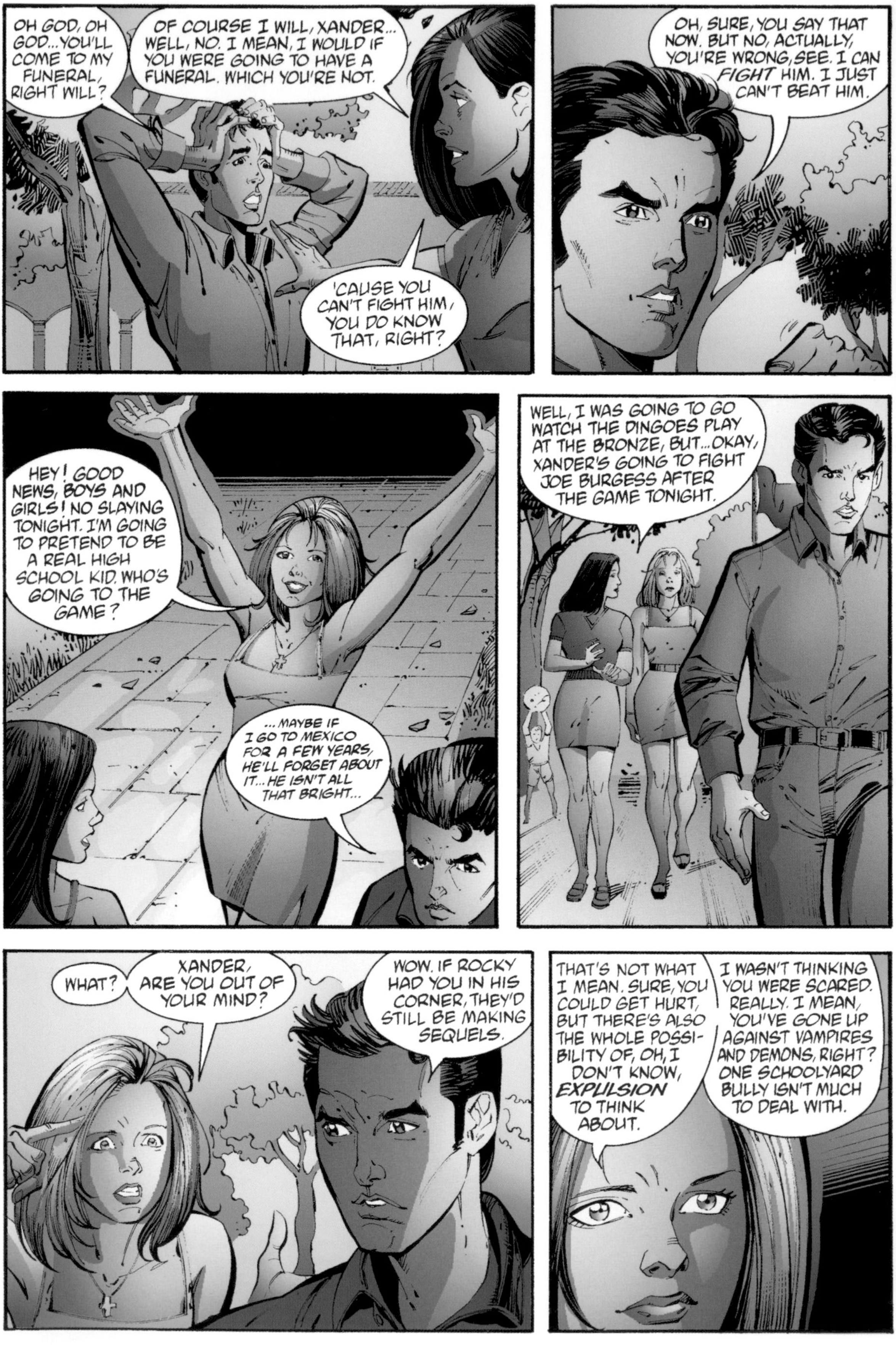
OH GOD, OH GOD...YOU'LL COME TO MY FUNERAL, RIGHT WILL?
OF COURSE I WILL, XANDER... WELL, NO. I MEAN, I WOULD IF YOU WERE GOING TO HAVE A FUNERAL. WHICH YOU'RE NOT.
'CAUSE YOU CAN'T FIGHT HIM, YOU DO KNOW THAT, RIGHT?
OH, SURE, YOU SAY THAT NOW. BUT NO, ACTUALLY, YOU'RE WRONG, SEE. I CAN FIGHT HIM. I JUST CAN'T BEAT HIM.
HEY! GOOD NEWS, BOYS AND GIRLS! NO SLAYING TONIGHT. I'M GOING TO PRETEND TO BE A REAL HIGH SCHOOL KID. WHO'S GOING TO THE GAME?
...MAYBE IF I GO TO MEXICO FOR A FEW YEARS, HE'LL FORGET ABOUT IT...HE ISN'T ALL THAT BRIGHT...
WELL, I WAS GOING TO GO WATCH THE DINGOES PLAY AT THE BRONZE, BUT...OKAY, XANDER'S GOING TO FIGHT JOE BURGESS AFTER THE GAME TONIGHT.
WHAT?
XANDER, ARE YOU OUT OF YOUR MIND?
WOW. IF ROCKY HAD YOU IN HIS CORNER, THEY'D STILL BE MAKING SEQUELS.
THAT'S NOT WHAT I MEAN. SURE, YOU COULD GET HURT, BUT THERE'S ALSO THE WHOLE POSSI-BILITY OF, OH, I DON'T KNOW, EXPULSION TO THINK ABOUT.
I WASN'T THINKING YOU WERE SCARED. REALLY. I MEAN, YOU'VE GONE UP AGAINST VAMPIRES AND DEMONS, RIGHT? ONE SCHOOLYARD BULLY ISN'T MUCH TO DEAL WITH.

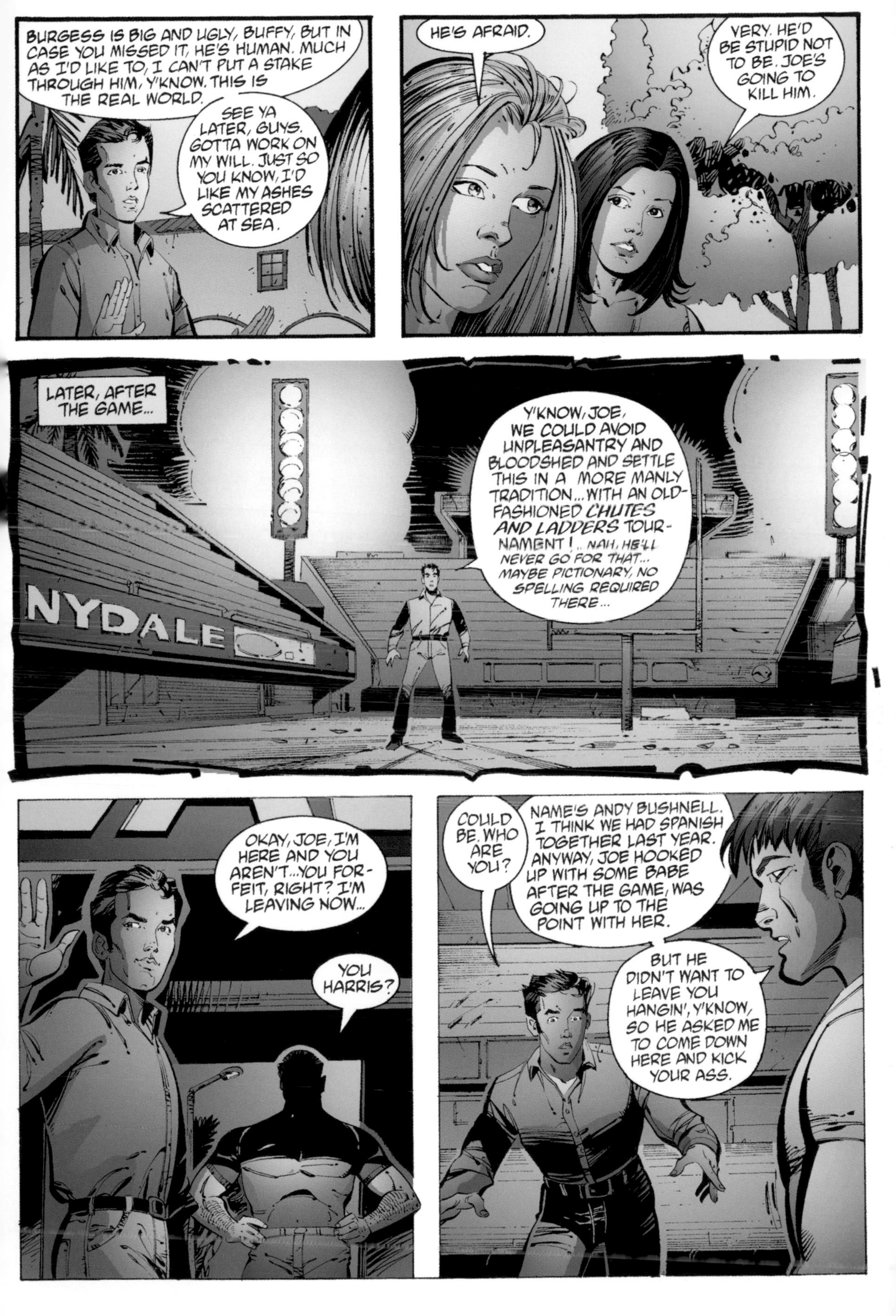
BURGESS IS BIG AND UGLY, BUFFY, BUT IN CASE YOU MISSED IT, HE'S HUMAN. MUCH AS I'D LIKE TO, I CAN'T PUT A STAKE THROUGH HIM, Y'KNOW. THIS IS THE REAL WORLD.
SEE YA LATER, GUYS. GOTTA WORK ON MY WILL. JUST SO YOU KNOW, I'D LIKE MY ASHES SCATTERED AT SEA.
HE'S AFRAID.
VERY. HE'D BE STUPID NOT TO BE. JOE'S GOING TO KILL HIM.
LATER, AFTER THE GAME...
Y'KNOW, JOE, WE COULD AVOID UNPLEASANTRY AND BLOODSHED AND SETTLE THIS IN A MORE MANLY TRADITION... WITH AN OLD-FASHIONED CHUTES AND LADDERS TOURNAMENT! ...NAH, HE'LL NEVER GO FOR THAT... MAYBE PICTIONARY, NO SPELLING REQUIRED THERE...
NYDALE
OKAY, JOE, I'M HERE AND YOU AREN'T...YOU FORFEIT, RIGHT? I'M LEAVING NOW...
YOU HARRIS?
COULD BE. WHO ARE YOU?
NAME'S ANDY BUSHNELL. I THINK WE HAD SPANISH TOGETHER LAST YEAR. ANYWAY, JOE HOOKED UP WITH SOME BABE AFTER THE GAME, WAS GOING UP TO THE POINT WITH HER.
BUT HE DIDN'T WANT TO LEAVE YOU HANGIN', Y'KNOW, SO HE ASKED ME TO COME DOWN HERE AND KICK YOUR ASS.

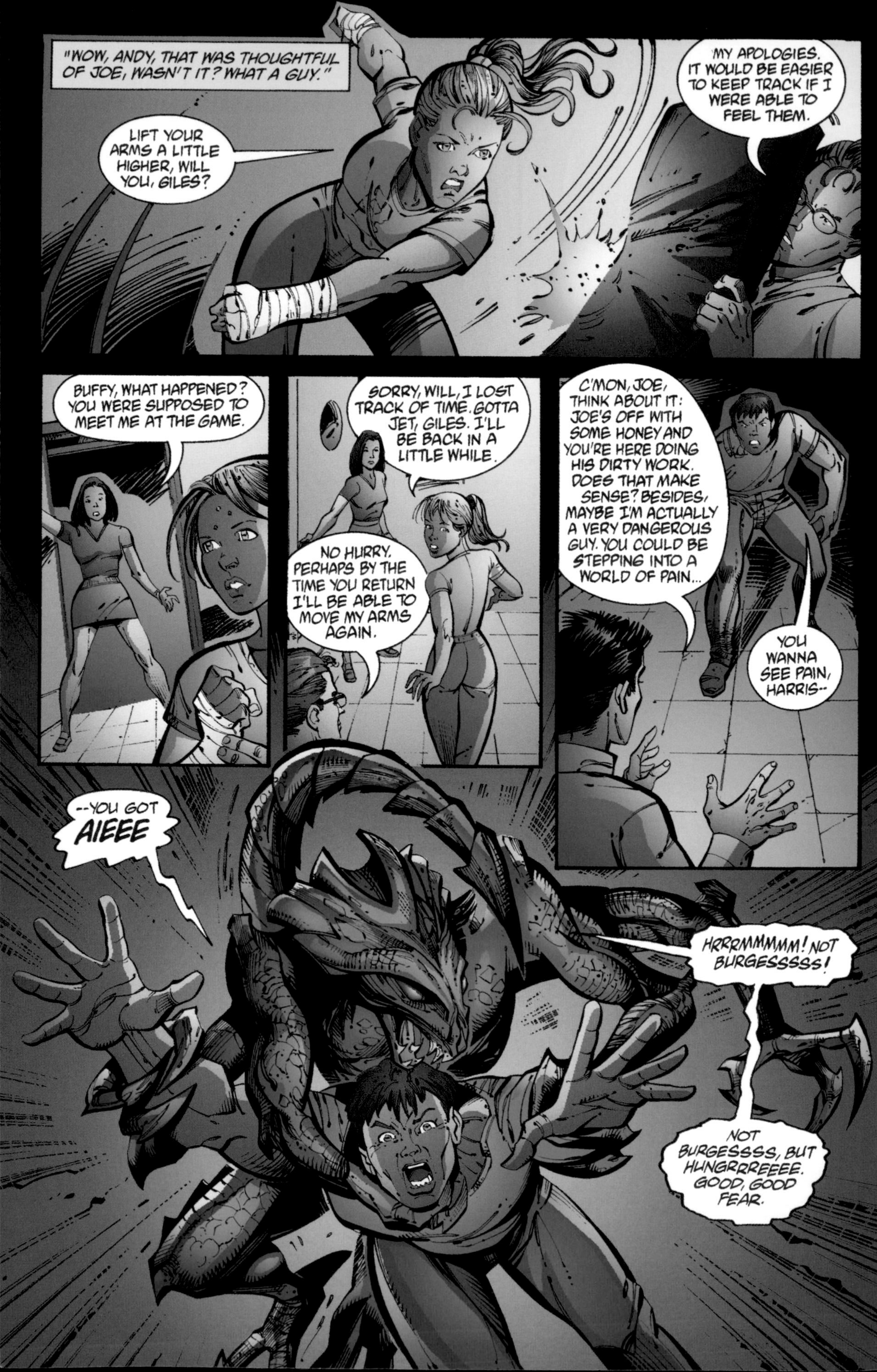
"WOW, ANDY, THAT WAS THOUGHTFUL OF JOE, WASN'T IT? WHAT A GUY."
LIFT YOUR ARMS A LITTLE HIGHER, WILL YOU, GILES?
MY APOLOGIES. IT WOULD BE EASIER TO KEEP TRACK IF I WERE ABLE TO FEEL THEM.
BUFFY, WHAT HAPPENED? YOU WERE SUPPOSED TO MEET ME AT THE GAME.
SORRY, WILL, I LOST TRACK OF TIME. GOTTA JET, GILES. I'LL BE BACK IN A LITTLE WHILE.
NO HURRY. PERHAPS BY THE TIME YOU RETURN I'LL BE ABLE TO MOVE MY ARMS AGAIN.
C'MON, JOE, THINK ABOUT IT: JOE'S OFF WITH SOME HONEY AND YOU'RE HERE DOING HIS DIRTY WORK. DOES THAT MAKE SENSE? BESIDES, MAYBE I'M ACTUALLY A VERY DANGEROUS GUY. YOU COULD BE STEPPING INTO A WORLD OF PAIN...
YOU WANNA SEE PAIN, HARRIS--
--YOU GOT AIEEE
HRRRMMMMM! NOT BURGESSSS!
NOT BURGESSSS, BUT HUNGRRREEEE. GOOD, GOOD FEAR.

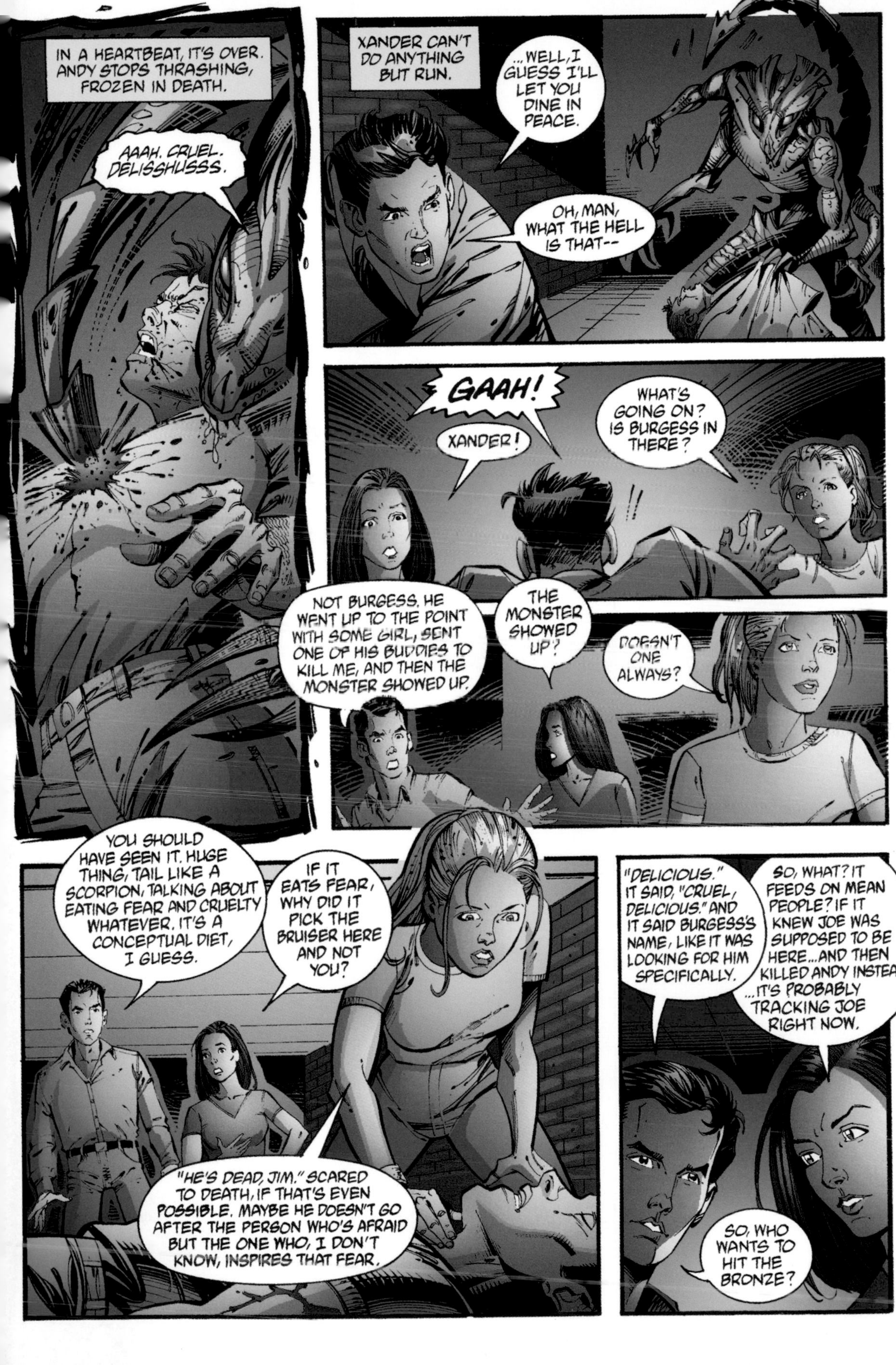
IN A HEARTBEAT, IT'S OVER. ANDY STOPS THRASHING, FROZEN IN DEATH.
AAAH. CRUEL. DELISSHUSSS.
XANDER CAN'T DO ANYTHING BUT RUN.
...WELL, I GUESS I'LL LET YOU DINE IN PEACE.
OH, MAN, WHAT THE HELL IS THAT--
GAAH!
XANDER!
WHAT'S GOING ON? IS BURGESS IN THERE?
NOT BURGESS. HE WENT UP TO THE POINT WITH SOME GIRL, SENT ONE OF HIS BUDDIES TO KILL ME, AND THEN THE MONSTER SHOWED UP.
THE MONSTER SHOWED UP?
DOESN'T ONE ALWAYS?
YOU SHOULD HAVE SEEN IT. HUGE THING, TAIL LIKE A SCORPION, TALKING ABOUT EATING FEAR AND CRUELTY WHATEVER. IT'S A CONCEPTUAL DIET, I GUESS.
IF IT EATS FEAR, WHY DID IT PICK THE BRUISER HERE AND NOT YOU?
"HE'S DEAD, JIM." SCARED TO DEATH, IF THAT'S EVEN POSSIBLE. MAYBE HE DOESN'T GO AFTER THE PERSON WHO'S AFRAID BUT THE ONE WHO, I DON'T KNOW, INSPIRES THAT FEAR.
"DELICIOUS." IT SAID, "CRUEL, DELICIOUS." AND IT SAID BURGESS'S NAME, LIKE IT WAS LOOKING FOR HIM SPECIFICALLY.
SO, WHAT? IT FEEDS ON MEAN PEOPLE? IF IT KNEW JOE WAS SUPPOSED TO BE HERE...AND THEN KILLED ANDY INSTEAD ...IT'S PROBABLY TRACKING JOE RIGHT NOW.
SO, WHO WANTS TO HIT THE BRONZE?

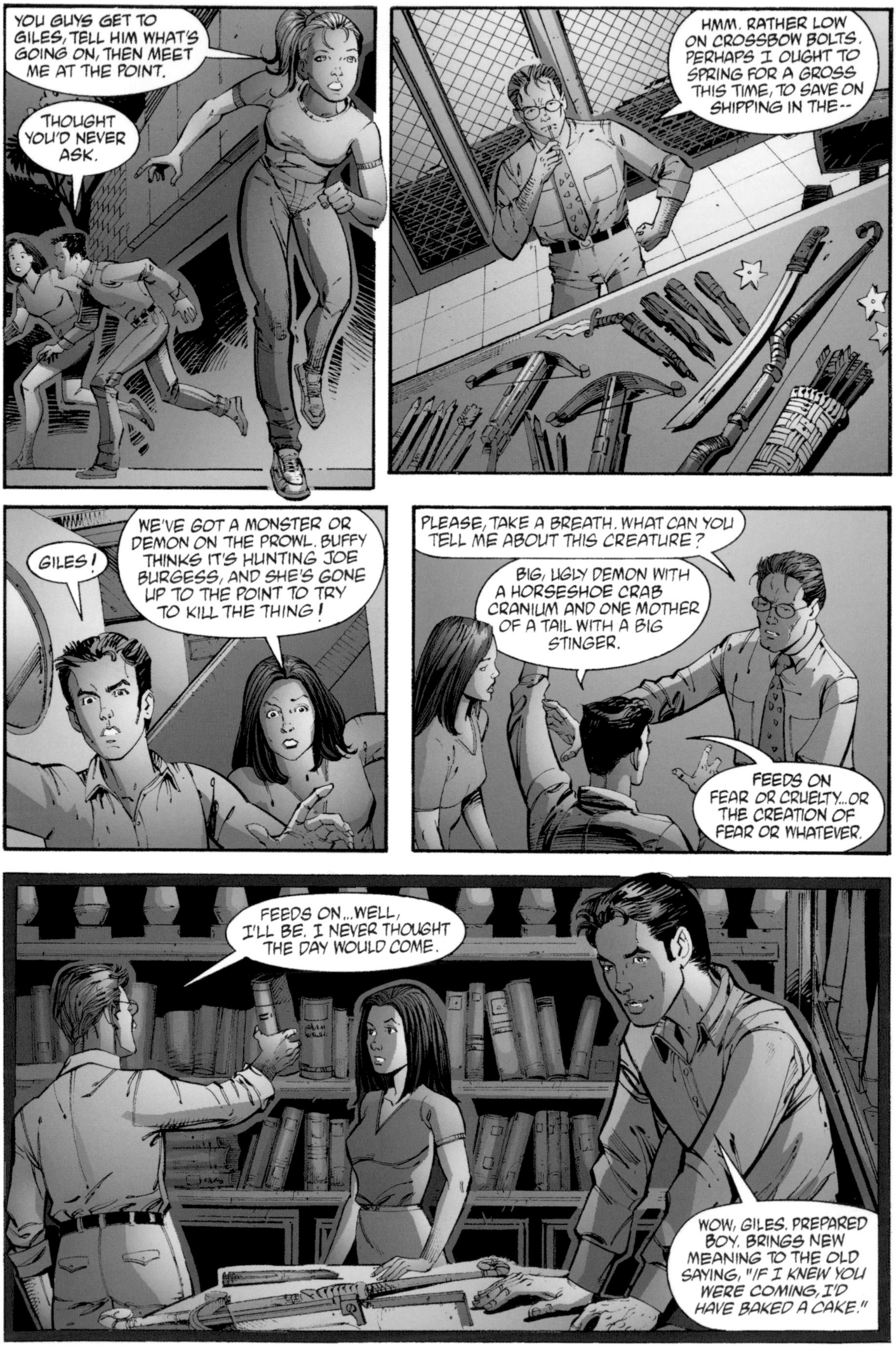
YOU GUYS GET TO GILES, TELL HIM WHAT'S GOING ON, THEN MEET ME AT THE POINT.
THOUGHT YOU'D NEVER ASK.
HMM. RATHER LOW ON CROSSBOW BOLTS. PERHAPS I OUGHT TO SPRING FOR A GROSS THIS TIME, TO SAVE ON SHIPPING IN THE--
GILES!
WE'VE GOT A MONSTER OR DEMON ON THE PROWL. BUFFY THINKS IT'S HUNTING JOE BURGESS, AND SHE'S GONE UP TO THE POINT TO TRY TO KILL THE THING!
PLEASE, TAKE A BREATH. WHAT CAN YOU TELL ME ABOUT THIS CREATURE?
BIG, UGLY DEMON WITH A HORSESHOE CRAB CRANIUM AND ONE MOTHER OF A TAIL WITH A BIG STINGER.
FEEDS ON FEAR OR CRUELTY...OR THE CREATION OF FEAR OR WHATEVER.
FEEDS ON...WELL, I'LL BE. I NEVER THOUGHT THE DAY WOULD COME.
WOW, GILES. PREPARED BOY. BRINGS NEW MEANING TO THE OLD SAYING, "IF I KNEW YOU WERE COMING, I'D HAVE BAKED A CAKE."

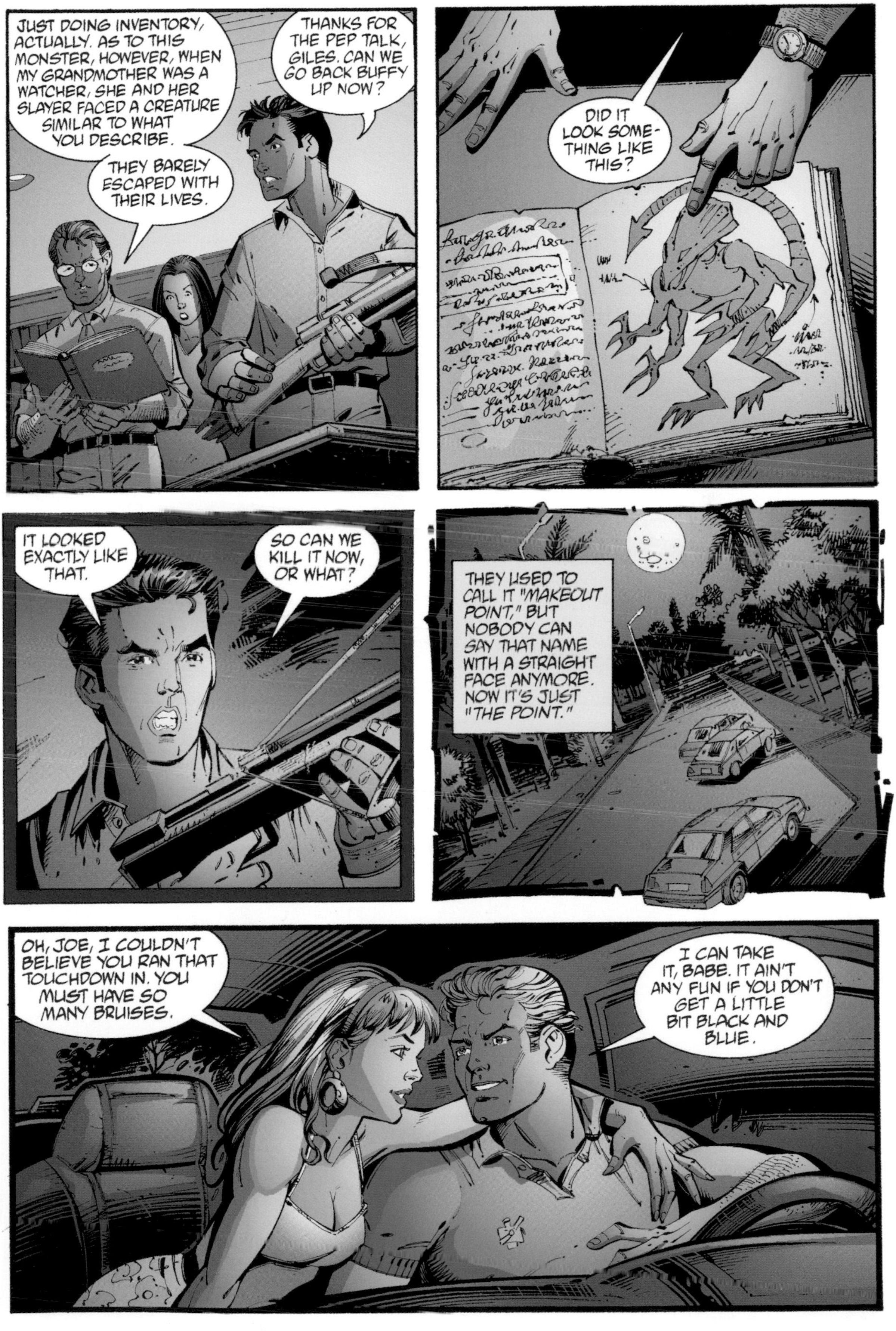
JUST DOING INVENTORY, ACTUALLY. AS TO THIS MONSTER, HOWEVER, WHEN MY GRANDMOTHER WAS A WATCHER, SHE AND HER SLAYER FACED A CREATURE SIMILAR TO WHAT YOU DESCRIBE.
THEY BARELY ESCAPED WITH THEIR LIVES.
THANKS FOR THE PEP TALK, GILES. CAN WE GO BACK BUFFY UP NOW?
DID IT LOOK SOMETHING LIKE THIS?
IT LOOKED EXACTLY LIKE THAT.
SO CAN WE KILL IT NOW, OR WHAT?
THEY USED TO CALL IT "MAKEOUT POINT," BUT NOBODY CAN SAY THAT NAME WITH A STRAIGHT FACE ANYMORE. NOW IT'S JUST "THE POINT."
OH, JOE, I COULDN'T BELIEVE YOU RAN THAT TOUCHDOWN IN. YOU MUST HAVE SO MANY BRUISES.
I CAN TAKE IT, BABE. IT AIN'T ANY FUN IF YOU DON'T GET A LITTLE BIT BLACK AND BLUE.

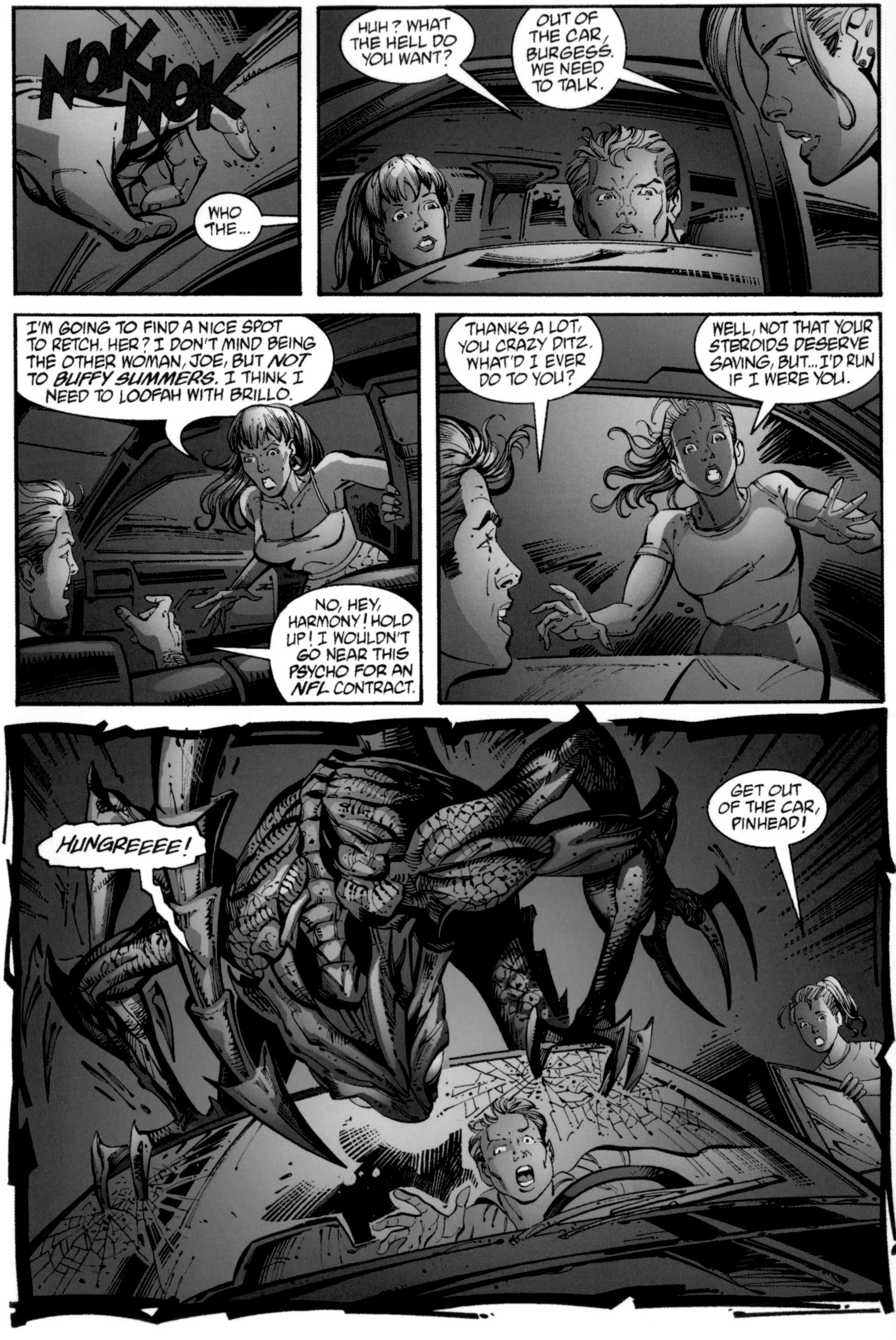
NOK NOK
WHO THE...
HUH? WHAT THE HELL DO YOU WANT?
OUT OF THE CAR, BURGESS. WE NEED TO TALK.
I'M GOING TO FIND A NICE SPOT TO RETCH. HER? I DON'T MIND BEING THE OTHER WOMAN, JOE, BUT NOT TO BUFFY SUMMERS. I THINK I NEED TO LOOFAH WITH BRILLO.
NO, HEY, HARMONY! HOLD UP! I WOULDN'T GO NEAR THIS PSYCHO FOR AN NFL CONTRACT.
THANKS A LOT, YOU CRAZY DITZ. WHAT'D I EVER DO TO YOU?
WELL, NOT THAT YOUR STEROIDS DESERVE SAVING, BUT... I'D RUN IF I WERE YOU.
HUNGREEEE!
GET OUT OF THE CAR, PINHEAD!

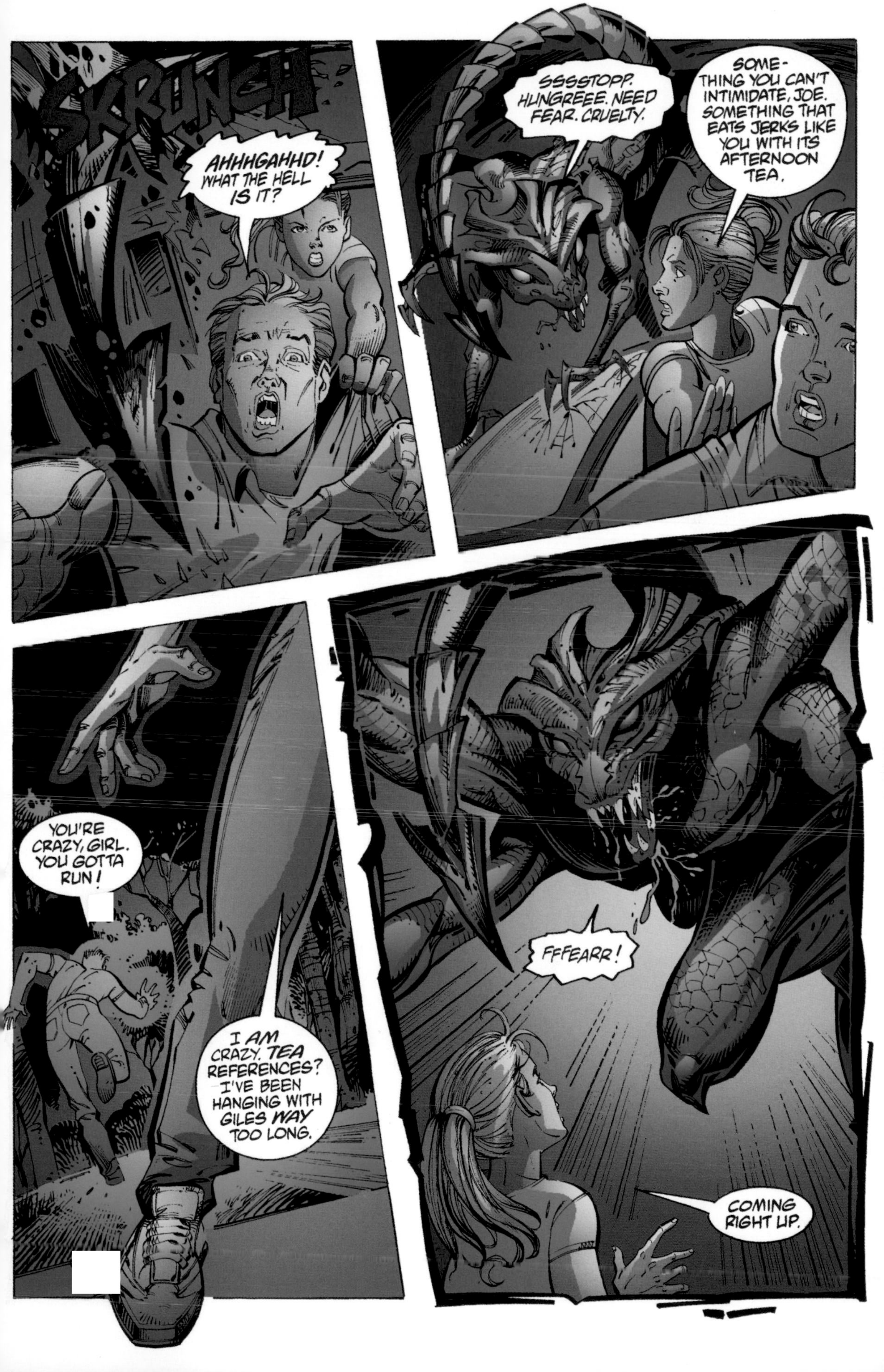
SKRUNCH
AHHHGAHHD! WHAT THE HELL IS IT?
SSSSTOPP. HUNGREEE. NEED FEAR. CRUELTY.
SOME-THING YOU CAN'T INTIMIDATE, JOE. SOMETHING THAT EATS JERKS LIKE YOU WITH ITS AFTERNOON TEA.
YOU'RE CRAZY, GIRL. YOU GOTTA RUN!
I AM CRAZY. TEA REFERENCES? I'VE BEEN HANGING WITH GILES WAY TOO LONG.
FFFEARR!
COMING RIGHT UP.

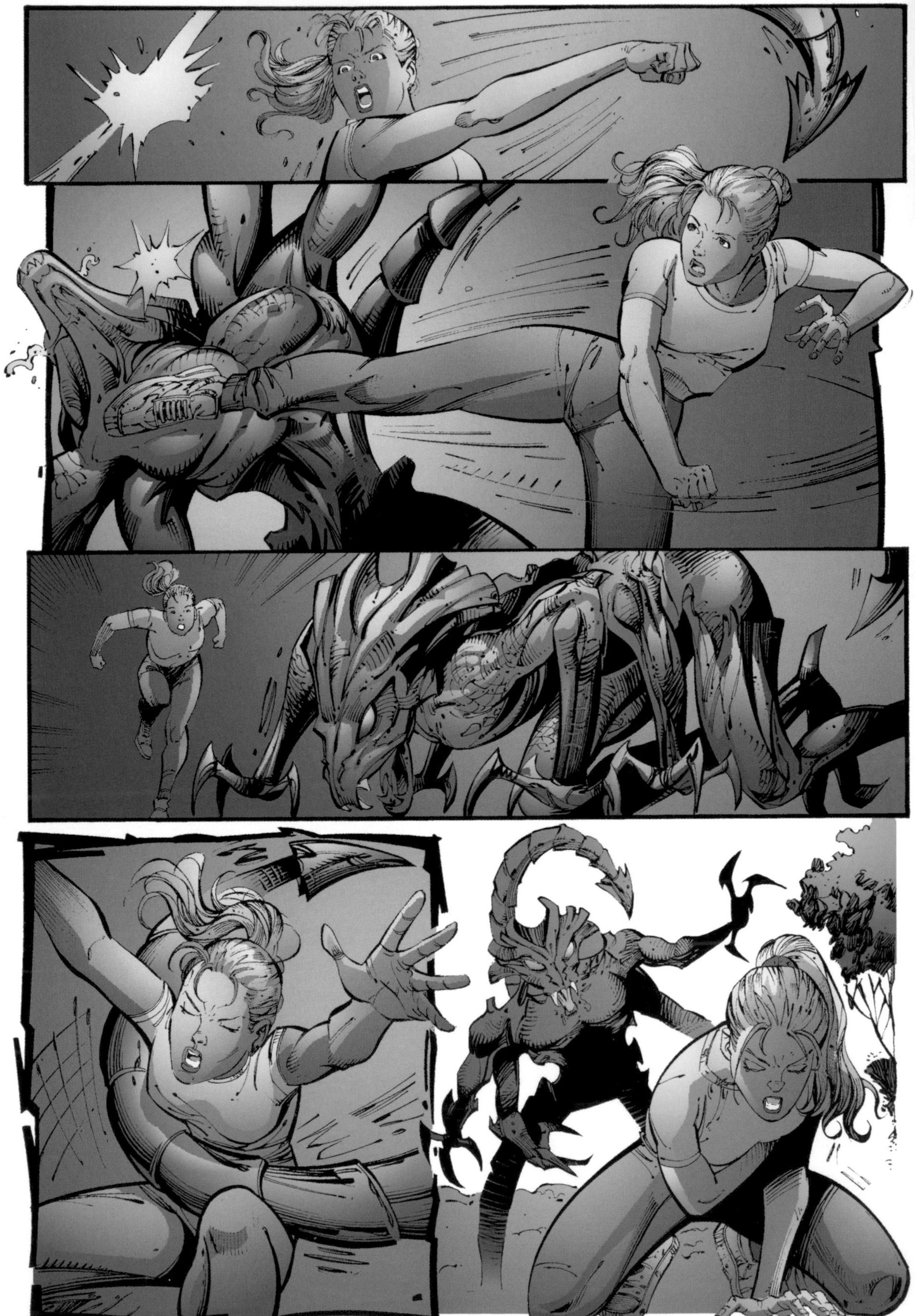

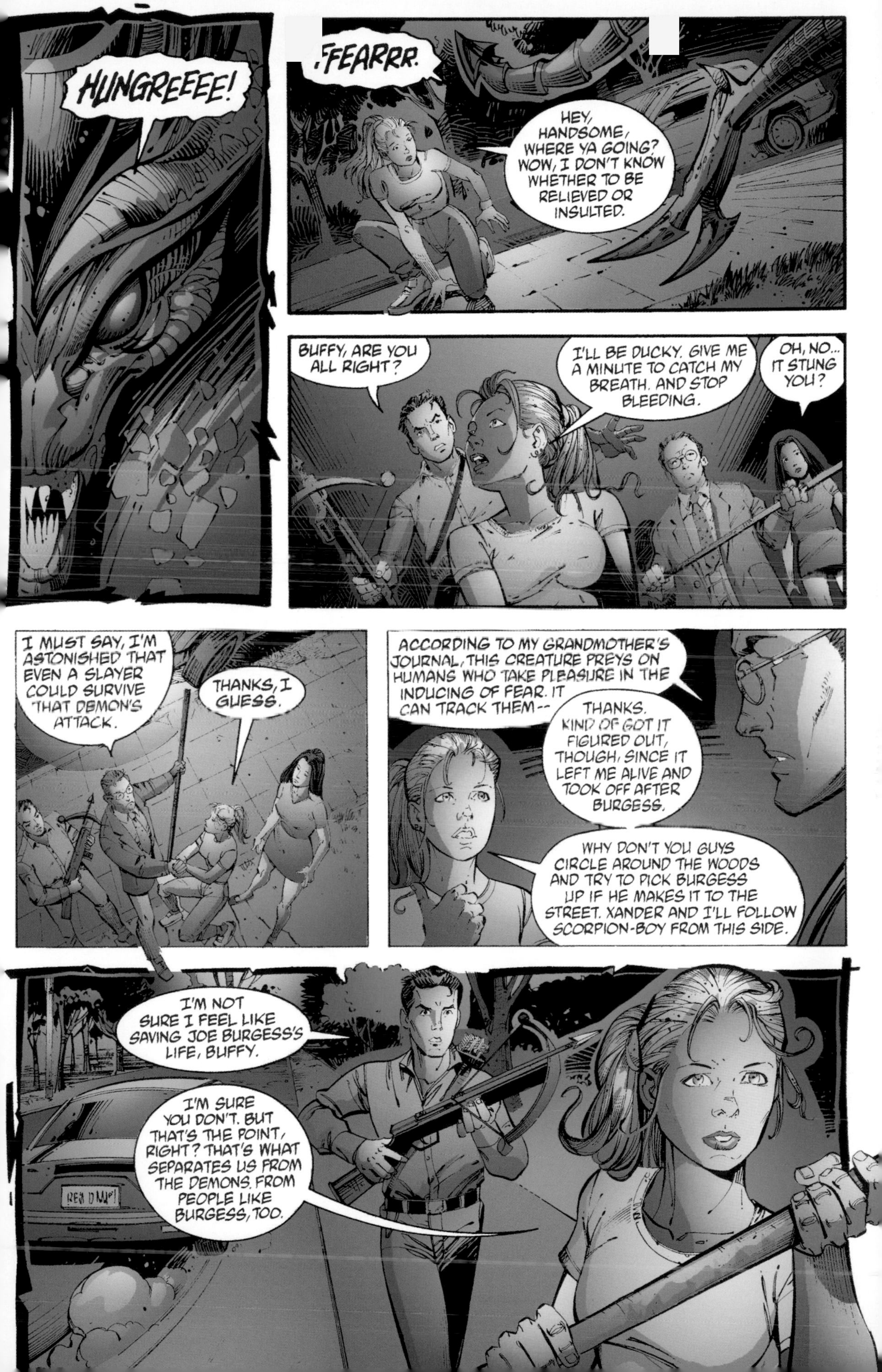
HUNGREEEE!
FEARRR.
HEY, HANDSOME, WHERE YA GOING? WOW, I DON'T KNOW WHETHER TO BE RELIEVED OR INSULTED.
BUFFY, ARE YOU ALL RIGHT?
I'LL BE DUCKY. GIVE ME A MINUTE TO CATCH MY BREATH. AND STOP BLEEDING.
OH, NO... IT STUNG YOU?
I MUST SAY, I'M ASTONISHED THAT EVEN A SLAYER COULD SURVIVE THAT DEMON'S ATTACK.
THANKS, I GUESS.
ACCORDING TO MY GRANDMOTHER'S JOURNAL, THIS CREATURE PREYS ON HUMANS WHO TAKE PLEASURE IN THE INDUCING OF FEAR. IT CAN TRACK THEM--
THANKS. KIND OF GOT IT FIGURED OUT, THOUGH, SINCE IT LEFT ME ALIVE AND TOOK OFF AFTER BURGESS.
WHY DON'T YOU GUYS CIRCLE AROUND THE WOODS AND TRY TO PICK BURGESS UP IF HE MAKES IT TO THE STREET. XANDER AND I'LL FOLLOW SCORPION-BOY FROM THIS SIDE.
I'M NOT SURE I FEEL LIKE SAVING JOE BURGESS'S LIFE, BUFFY.
I'M SURE YOU DON'T. BUT THAT'S THE POINT, RIGHT? THAT'S WHAT SEPARATES US FROM THE DEMONS. FROM PEOPLE LIKE BURGESS, TOO.

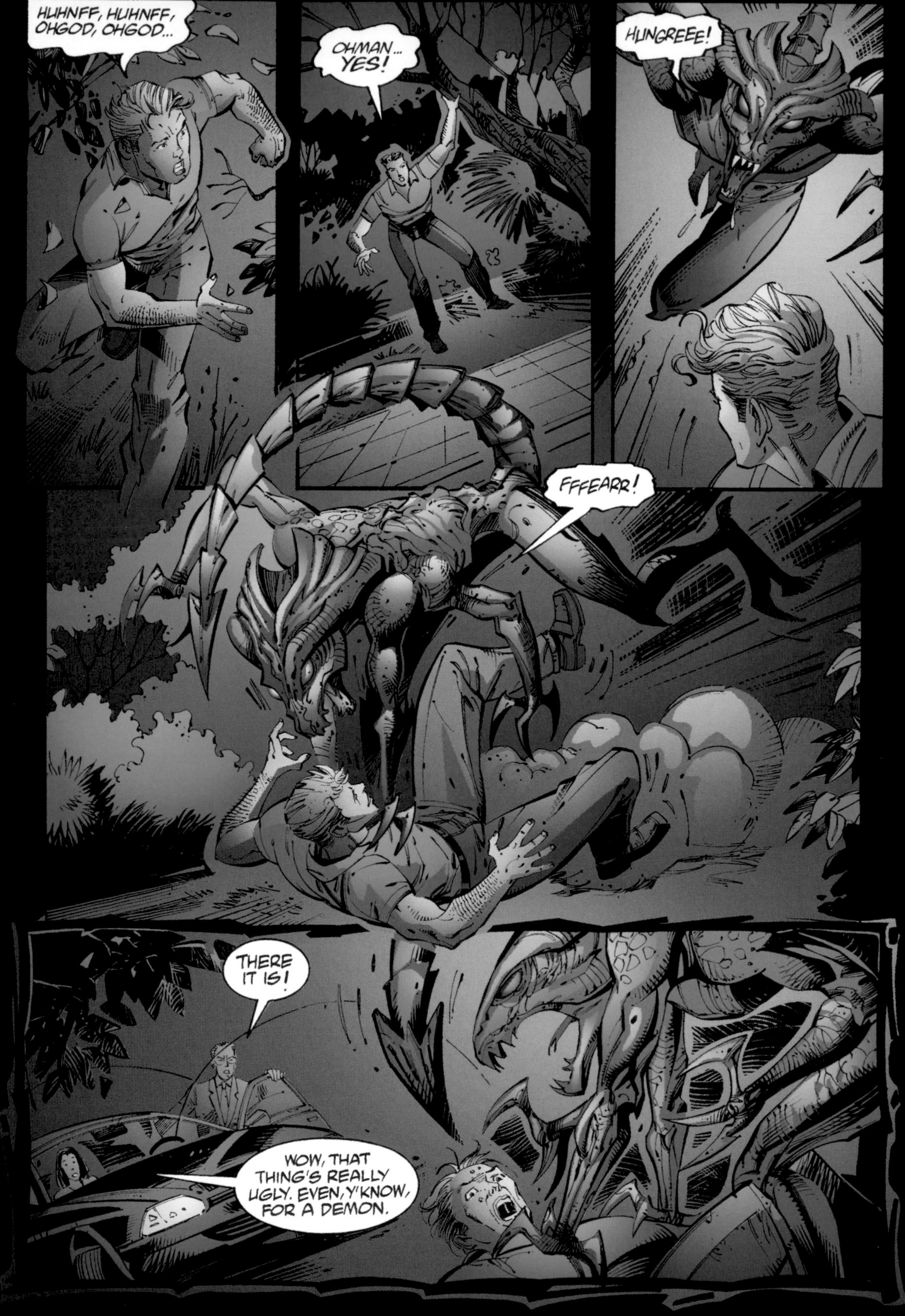
HUHNFF, HUHNFF, OHGOD, OHGOD...
OHMAN... YES!
HUNGREEE!
FFFEARR!
THERE IT IS!
WOW, THAT THING'S REALLY UGLY. EVEN, Y'KNOW, FOR A DEMON.

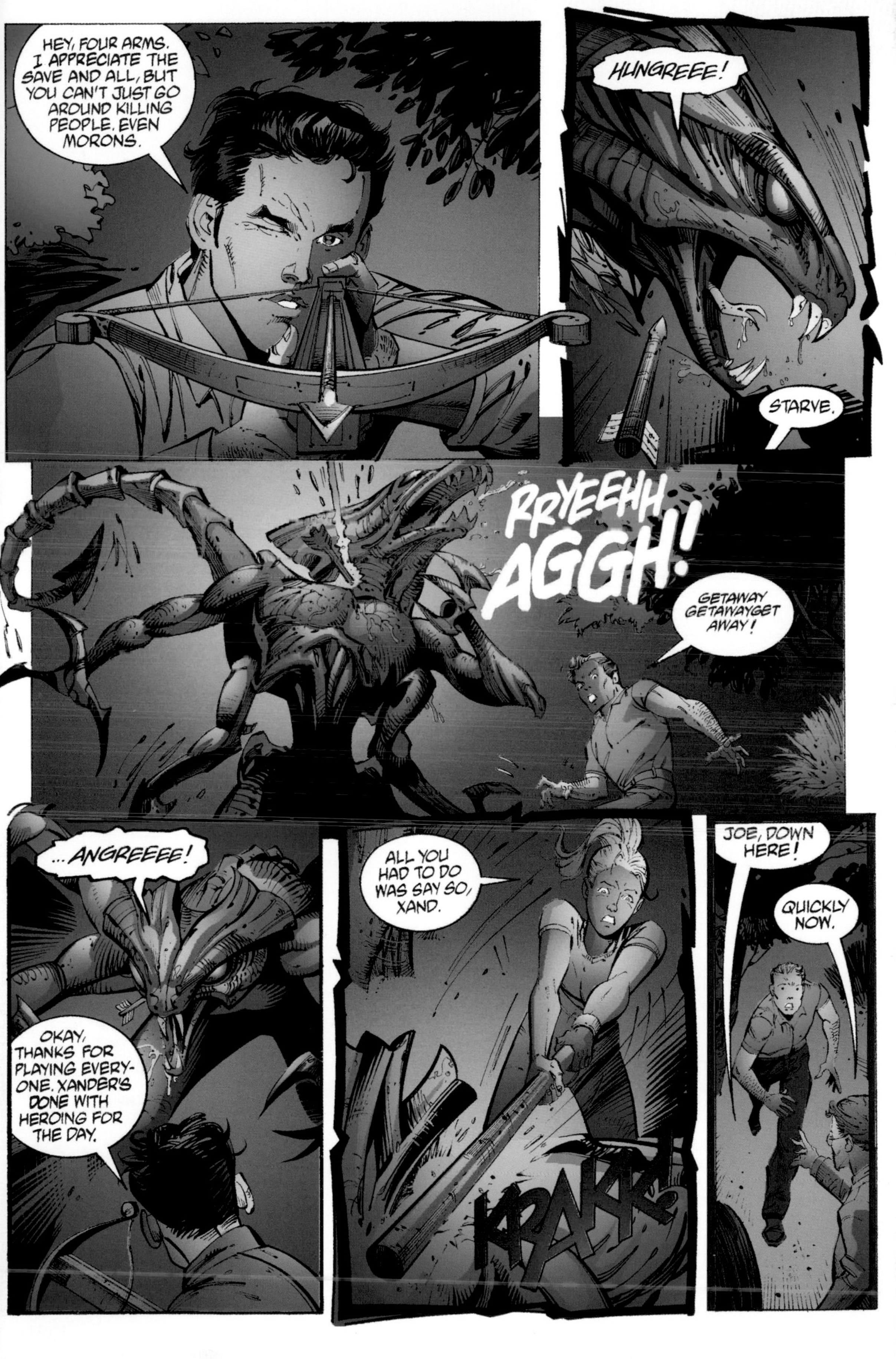
HEY, FOUR ARMS. I APPRECIATE THE SAVE AND ALL, BUT YOU CAN'T JUST GO AROUND KILLING PEOPLE. EVEN MORONS.
HUNGREEE!
STARVE.
RRYEEHH AGGH!
GETAWAY GETAWAYGET AWAY!
...ANGREEEE!
OKAY, THANKS FOR PLAYING EVERY-ONE. XANDER'S DONE WITH HEROING FOR THE DAY.
ALL YOU HAD TO DO WAS SAY SO, XAND.
KRAKK!
JOE, DOWN HERE!
QUICKLY NOW.

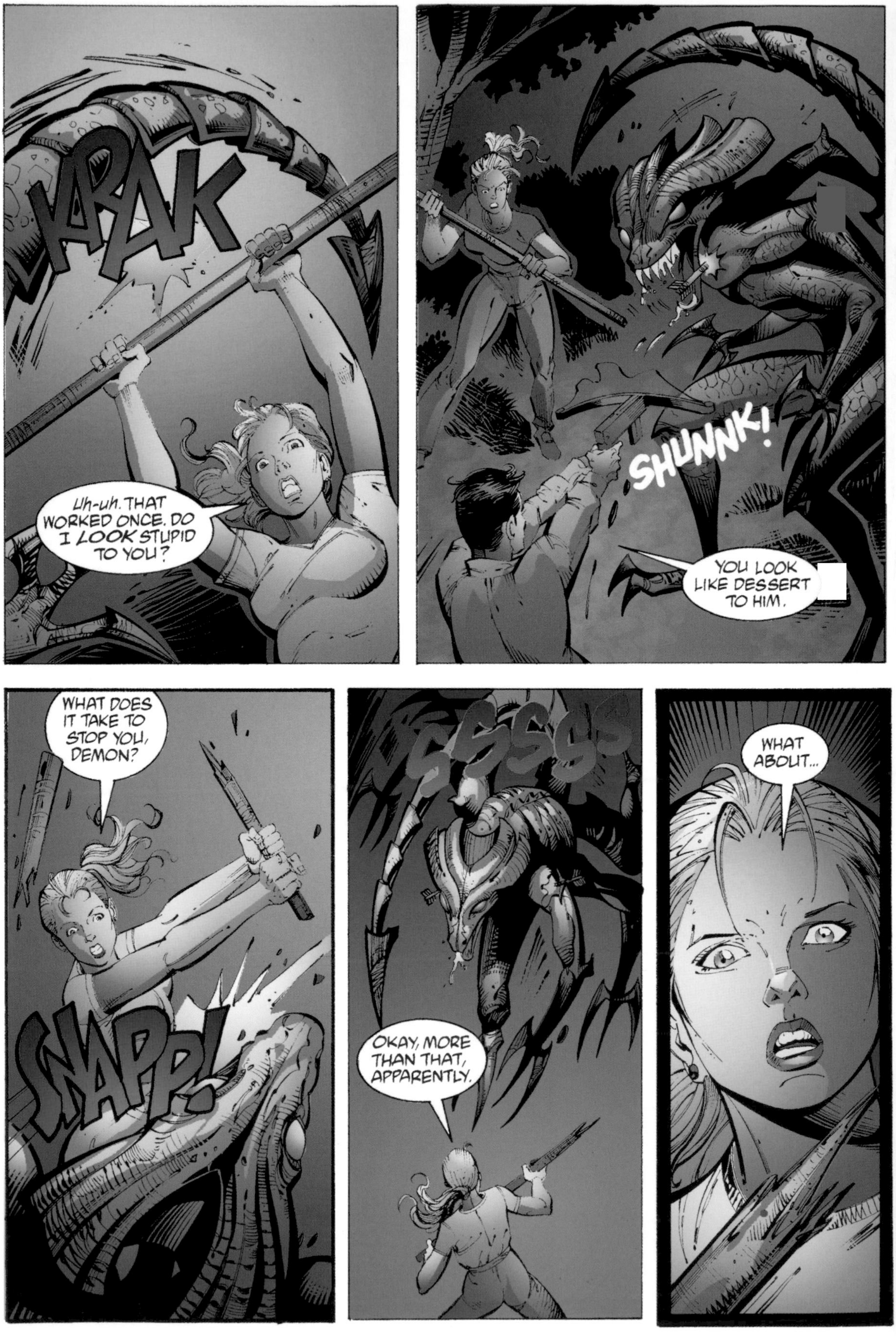
KRAK
Uh-uh. THAT WORKED ONCE. DO I LOOK STUPID TO YOU?
SHUNNK!
YOU LOOK LIKE DESSERT TO HIM.
WHAT DOES IT TAKE TO STOP YOU, DEMON?
SNAPP!
SSSSS
OKAY, MORE THAN THAT, APPARENTLY.
WHAT ABOUT...

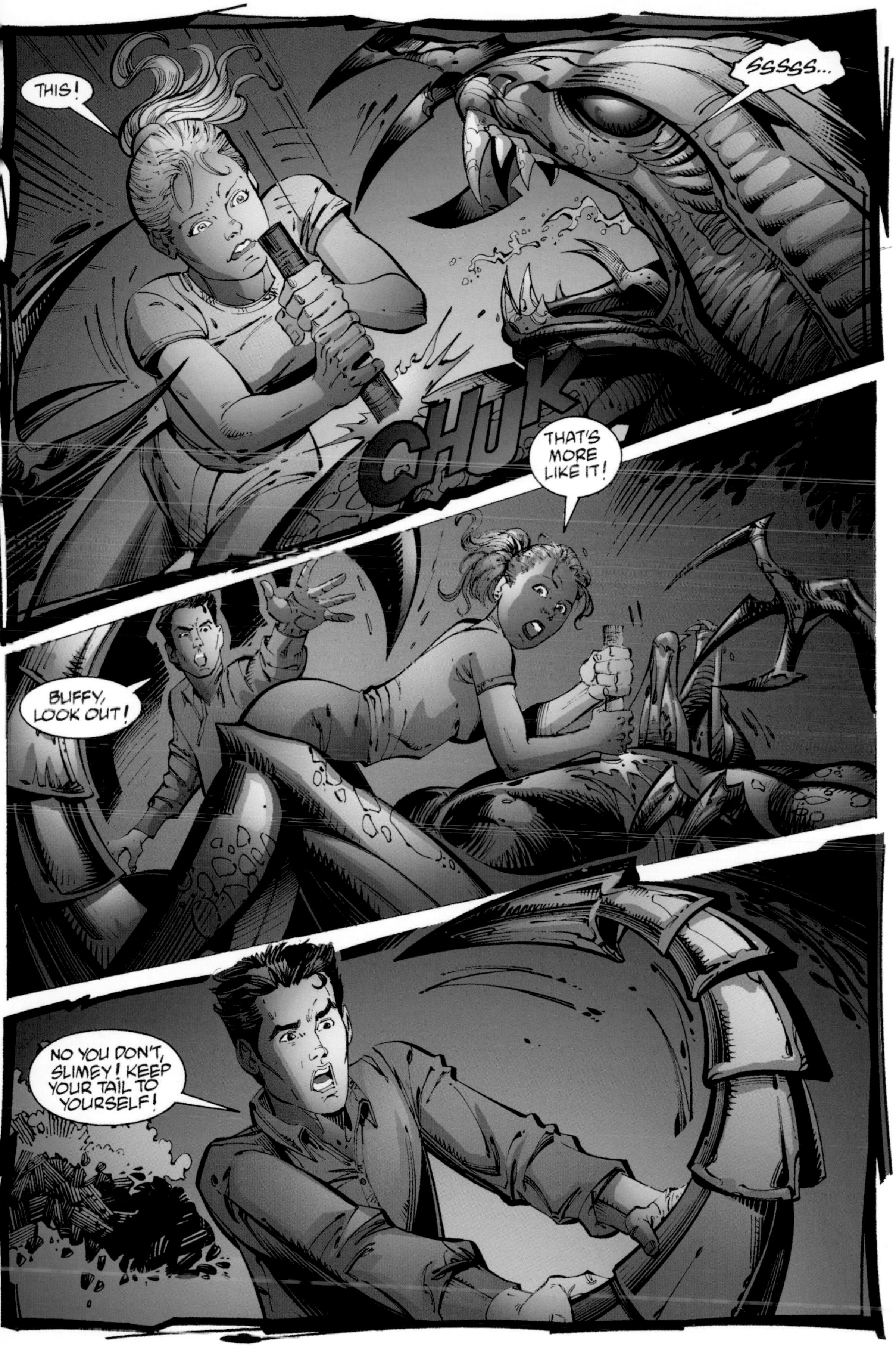
THIS!
SSSSS...
CHUK
THAT'S MORE LIKE IT!
BUFFY, LOOK OUT!
NO YOU DON'T, SLIMEY! KEEP YOUR TAIL TO YOURSELF!

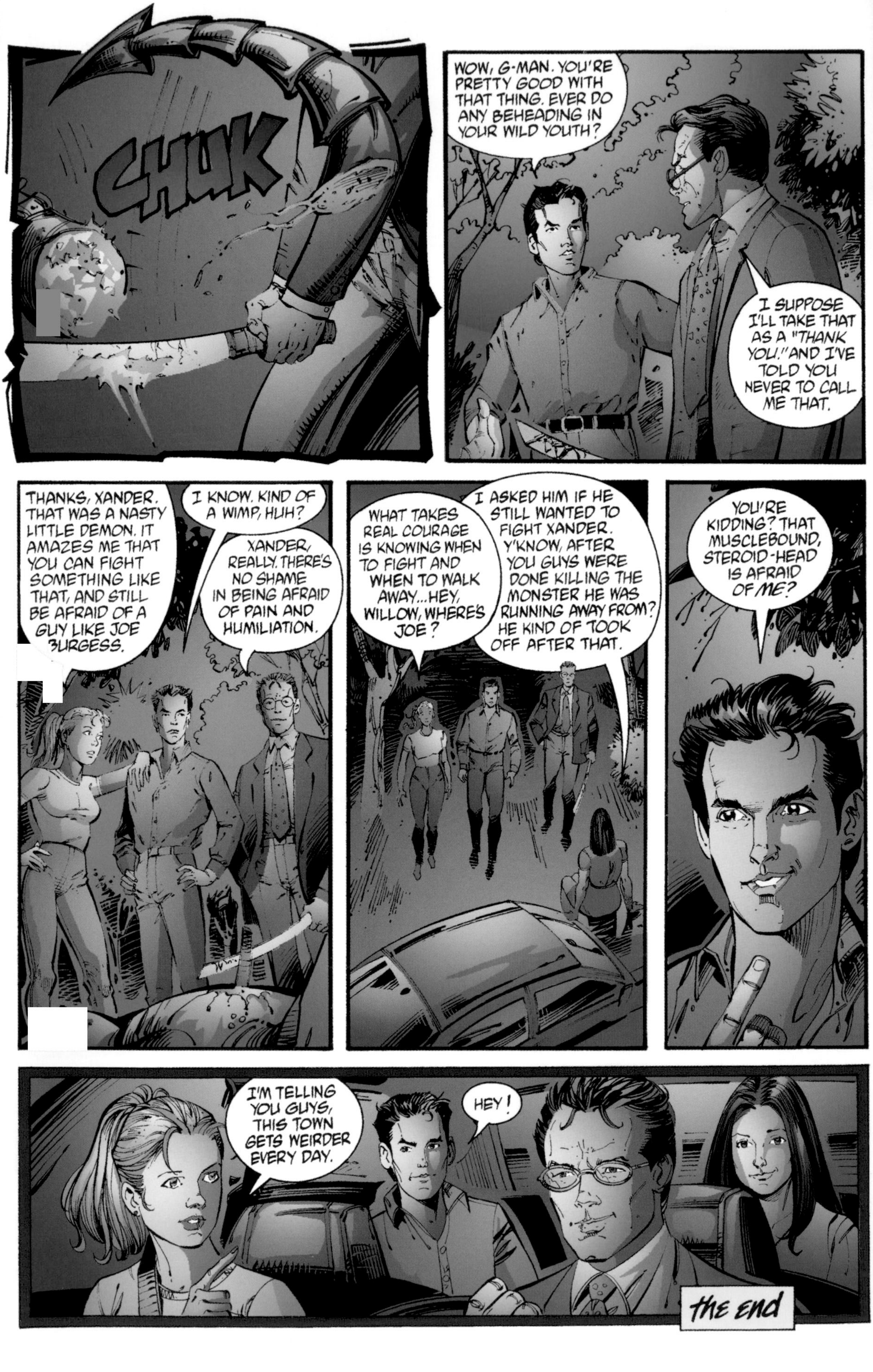
CHUK
WOW, G-MAN. YOU'RE PRETTY GOOD WITH THAT THING. EVER DO ANY BEHEADING IN YOUR WILD YOUTH?
I SUPPOSE I'LL TAKE THAT AS A "THANK YOU." AND I'VE TOLD YOU NEVER TO CALL ME THAT.
THANKS, XANDER. THAT WAS A NASTY LITTLE DEMON. IT AMAZES ME THAT YOU CAN FIGHT SOMETHING LIKE THAT, AND STILL BE AFRAID OF A GUY LIKE JOE BURGESS.
I KNOW. KIND OF A WIMP, HUH?
XANDER, REALLY. THERE'S NO SHAME IN BEING AFRAID OF PAIN AND HUMILIATION.
WHAT TAKES REAL COURAGE IS KNOWING WHEN TO FIGHT AND WHEN TO WALK AWAY...HEY, WILLOW, WHERE'S JOE?
I ASKED HIM IF HE STILL WANTED TO FIGHT XANDER. Y'KNOW, AFTER YOU GUYS WERE DONE KILLING THE MONSTER HE WAS RUNNING AWAY FROM? HE KIND OF TOOK OFF AFTER THAT.
YOU'RE KIDDING? THAT MUSCLEBOUND, STEROID-HEAD IS AFRAID OF ME?
I'M TELLING YOU GUYS, THIS TOWN GETS WEIRDER EVERY DAY.
HEY!
THE END

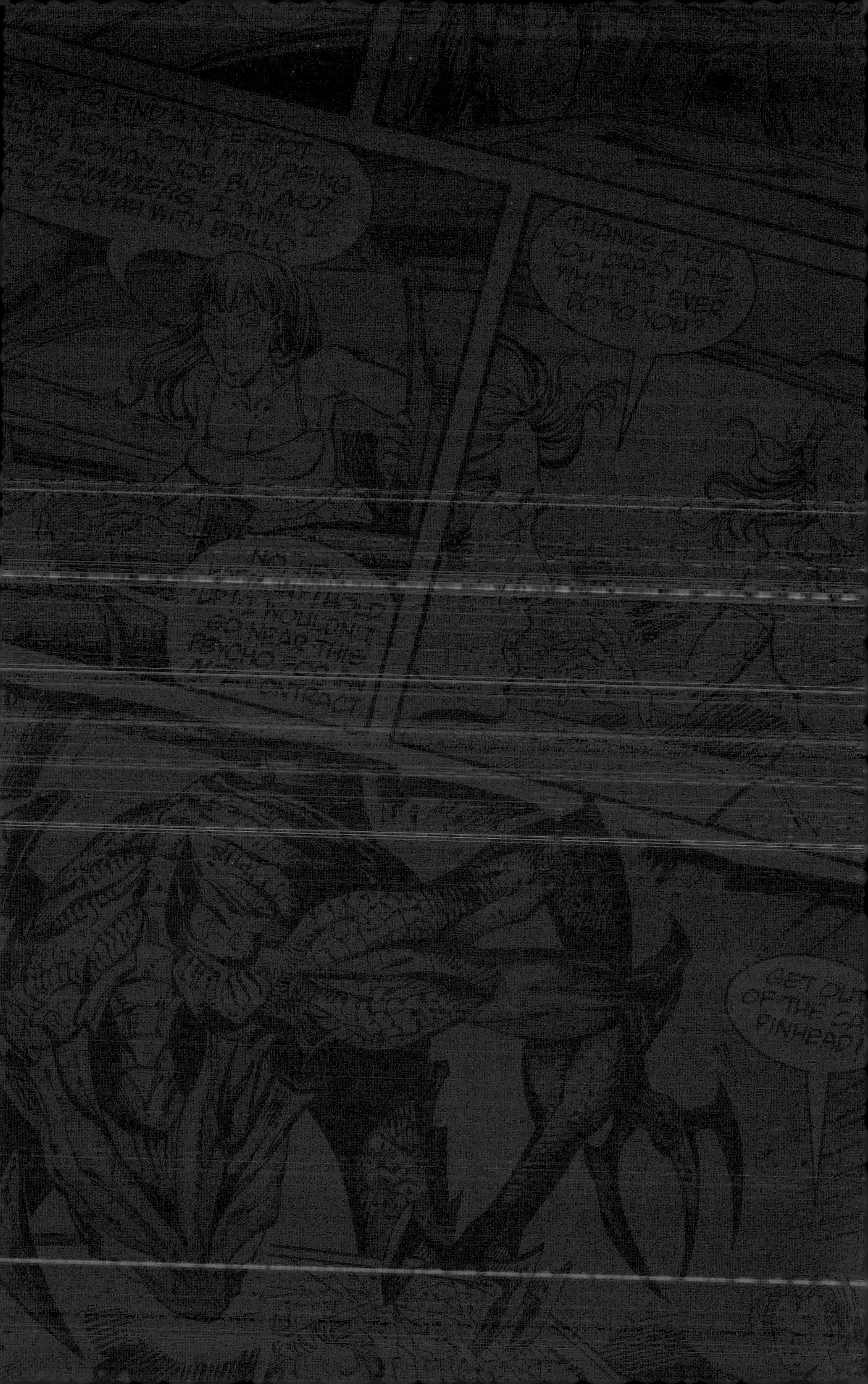
THANKS A LOT, YOU CRAZY ... WHAT'D I EVER DO TO YOU?
... WOULDN'T GO NEAR THIS PSYCHO ... CONTRACT
GET OUT OF THE ... PINHEAD!

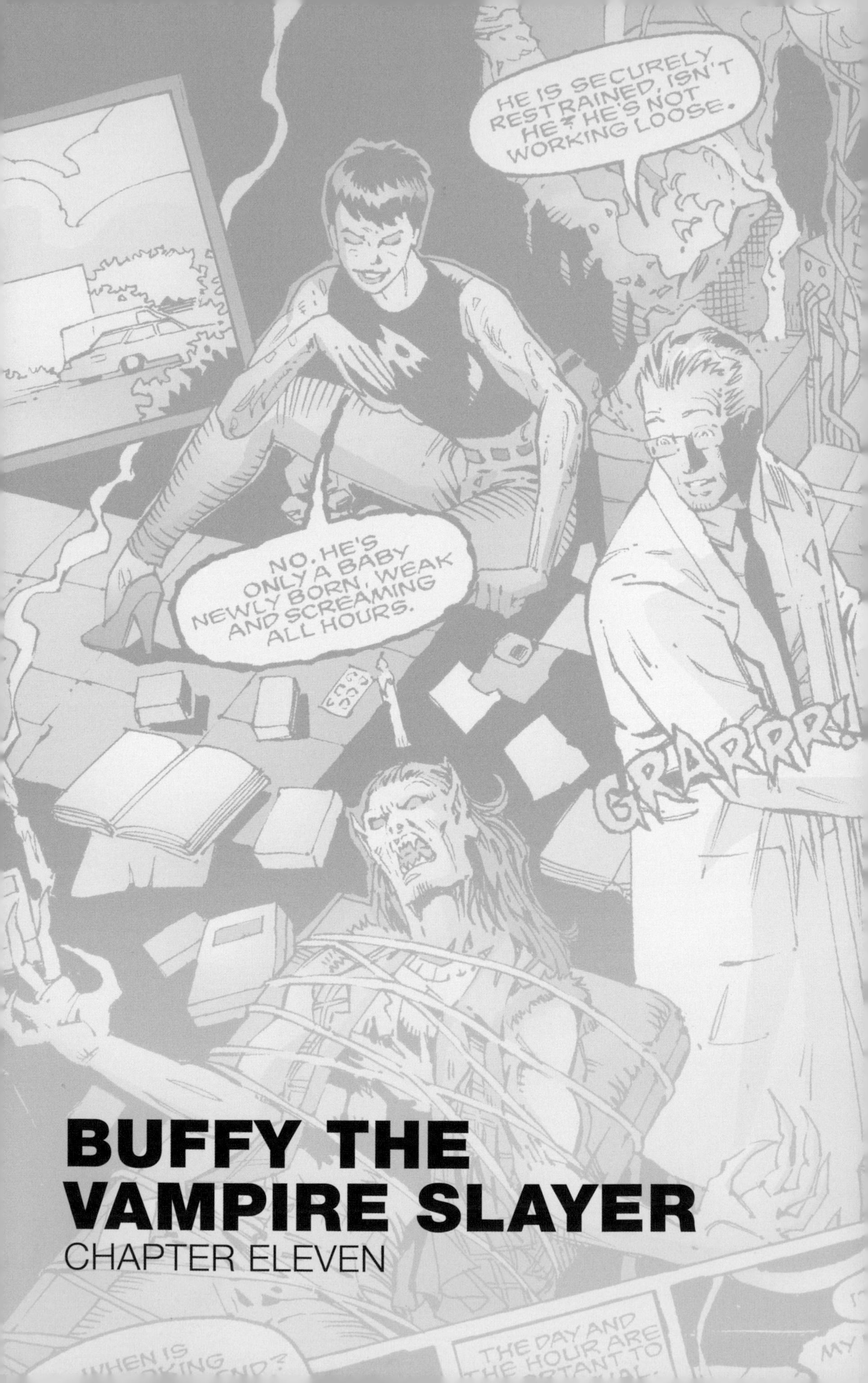
HE IS SECURELY RESTRAINED, ISN'T HE? HE'S NOT WORKING LOOSE.
NO. HE'S ONLY A BABY NEWLY BORN, WEAK AND SCREAMING ALL HOURS.
GRARRR!

BUFFY THE VAMPIRE SLAYER

CHAPTER ELEVEN

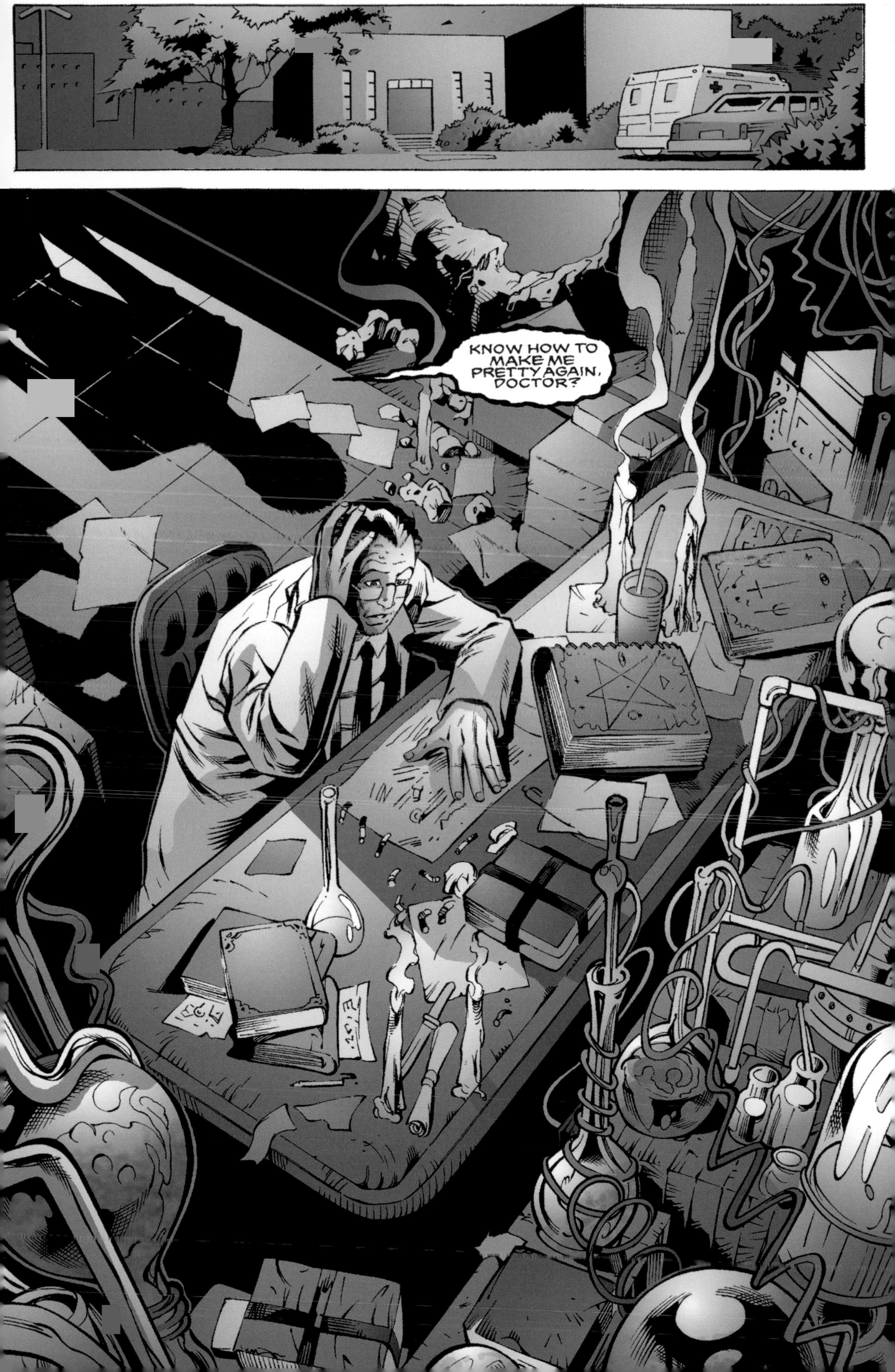
KNOW HOW TO MAKE ME PRETTY AGAIN, DOCTOR?

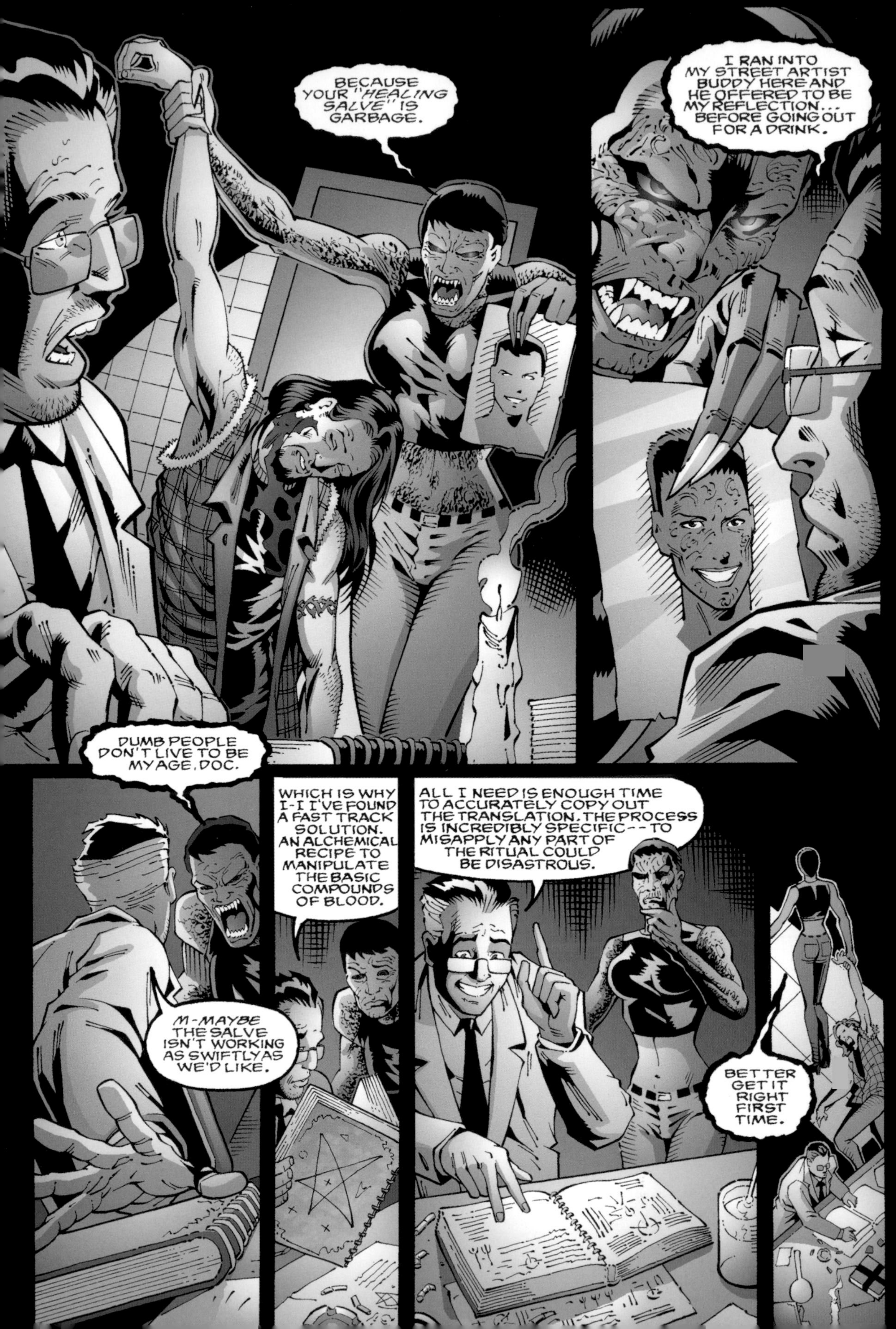
BECAUSE YOUR "HEALING SALVE" IS GARBAGE.
I RAN INTO MY STREET ARTIST BUDDY HERE AND HE OFFERED TO BE MY REFLECTION... BEFORE GOING OUT FOR A DRINK.
DUMB PEOPLE DON'T LIVE TO BE MY AGE, DOC.
M-MAYBE THE SALVE ISN'T WORKING AS SWIFTLY AS WE'D LIKE.
WHICH IS WHY I-I I'VE FOUND A FAST TRACK SOLUTION. AN ALCHEMICAL RECIPE TO MANIPULATE THE BASIC COMPOUNDS OF BLOOD.
ALL I NEED IS ENOUGH TIME TO ACCURATELY COPY OUT THE TRANSLATION. THE PROCESS IS INCREDIBLY SPECIFIC-- TO MISAPPLY ANY PART OF THE RITUAL COULD BE DISASTROUS.
BETTER GET IT RIGHT FIRST TIME.

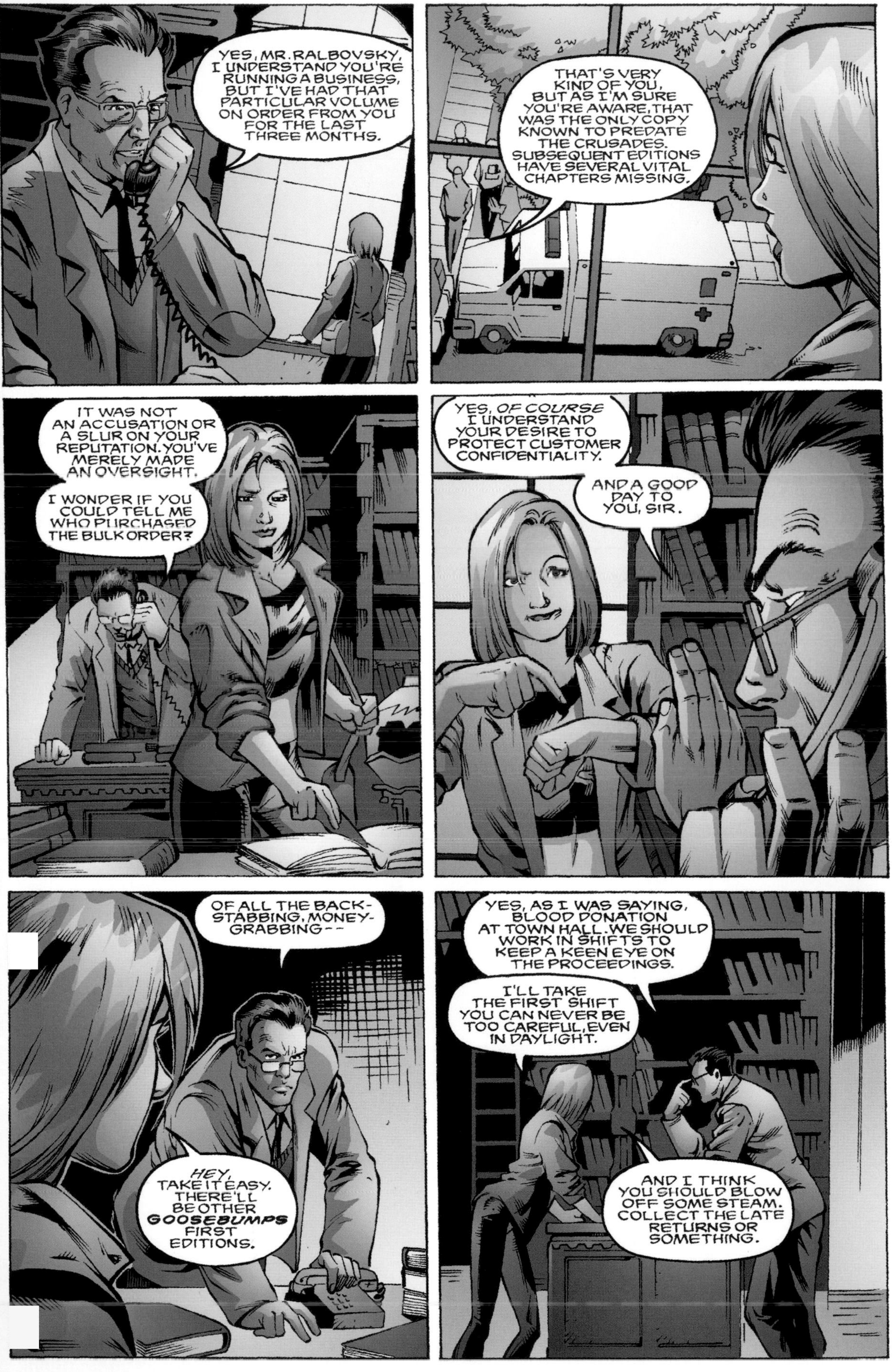
YES, MR. RALBOVSKY, I UNDERSTAND YOU'RE RUNNING A BUSINESS, BUT I'VE HAD THAT PARTICULAR VOLUME ON ORDER FROM YOU FOR THE LAST THREE MONTHS.
THAT'S VERY KIND OF YOU, BUT AS I'M SURE YOU'RE AWARE, THAT WAS THE ONLY COPY KNOWN TO PREDATE THE CRUSADES. SUBSEQUENT EDITIONS HAVE SEVERAL VITAL CHAPTERS MISSING.
IT WAS NOT AN ACCUSATION OR A SLUR ON YOUR REPUTATION. YOU'VE MERELY MADE AN OVERSIGHT.
I WONDER IF YOU COULD TELL ME WHO PURCHASED THE BULK ORDER?
YES, OF COURSE I UNDERSTAND YOUR DESIRE TO PROTECT CUSTOMER CONFIDENTIALITY.
AND A GOOD DAY TO YOU, SIR.
OF ALL THE BACK-STABBING, MONEY-GRABBING--
HEY, TAKE IT EASY. THERE'LL BE OTHER GOOSEBUMPS FIRST EDITIONS.
YES, AS I WAS SAYING, BLOOD DONATION AT TOWN HALL. WE SHOULD WORK IN SHIFTS TO KEEP A KEEN EYE ON THE PROCEEDINGS.
I'LL TAKE THE FIRST SHIFT. YOU CAN NEVER BE TOO CAREFUL, EVEN IN DAYLIGHT.
AND I THINK YOU SHOULD BLOW OFF SOME STEAM. COLLECT THE LATE RETURNS OR SOMETHING.

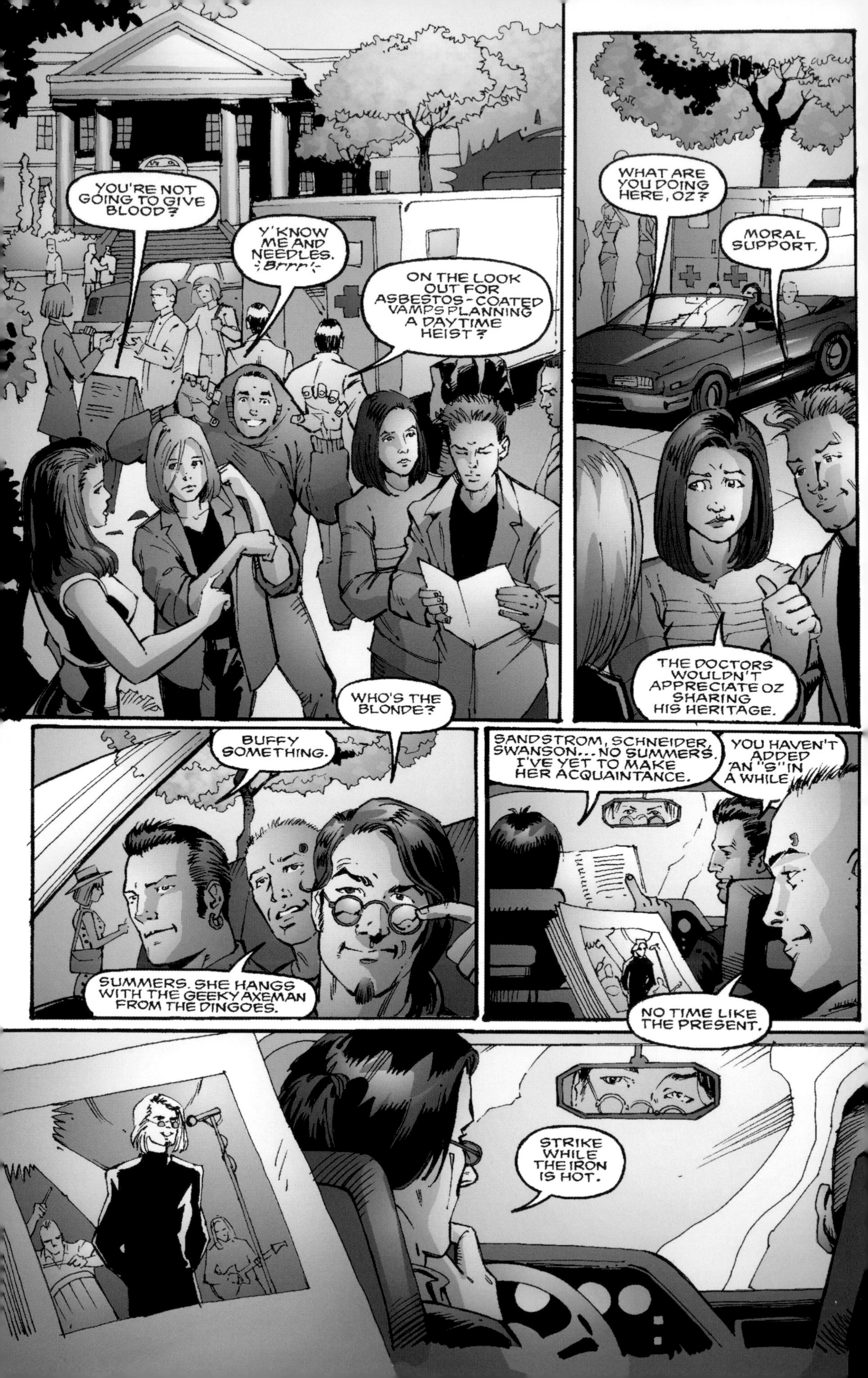
YOU'RE NOT GOING TO GIVE BLOOD?
Y'KNOW ME AND NEEDLES. Brrr!
ON THE LOOK OUT FOR ASBESTOS-COATED VAMPS PLANNING A DAYTIME HEIST?
WHAT ARE YOU DOING HERE, OZ?
MORAL SUPPORT.
THE DOCTORS WOULDN'T APPRECIATE OZ SHARING HIS HERITAGE.
WHO'S THE BLONDE?
BUFFY SOMETHING.
SUMMERS. SHE HANGS WITH THE GEEKY AXEMAN FROM THE DINGOES.
SANDSTROM, SCHNEIDER, SWANSON... NO SUMMERS. I'VE YET TO MAKE HER ACQUAINTANCE.
YOU HAVEN'T ADDED AN "S" IN A WHILE
NO TIME LIKE THE PRESENT.
STRIKE WHILE THE IRON IS HOT.

WE'RE CALLED DOUBLE-CROSS AND WE'RE HEADLINING THE BRONZE TONIGHT. CATCH US NOW, BEFORE WE'RE ALL OVER MTV.

BUFFY SUMMERS, RIGHT? I DON'T THINK WE'VE EVER MET.

LET ME GUESS, THE LEAD SINGER OF DOUBLE-CROSS?

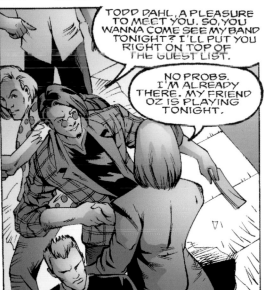

TODD DAHL, A PLEASURE TO MEET YOU. SO, YOU WANNA COME SEE MY BAND TONIGHT? I'LL PUT YOU RIGHT ON TOP OF THE GUEST LIST.

NO PROBS. I'M ALREADY THERE. MY FRIEND OZ IS PLAYING TONIGHT.

THAT'S RIGHT. DINGOES ARE WARMING UP FOR US.

SO YOU'LL BE HOT WHEN I HIT THE STAGE?

IF THE A/C'S WRECKED.

DAHL, TODD?

THAT'S MY CALL. SEE YOU TONIGHT.

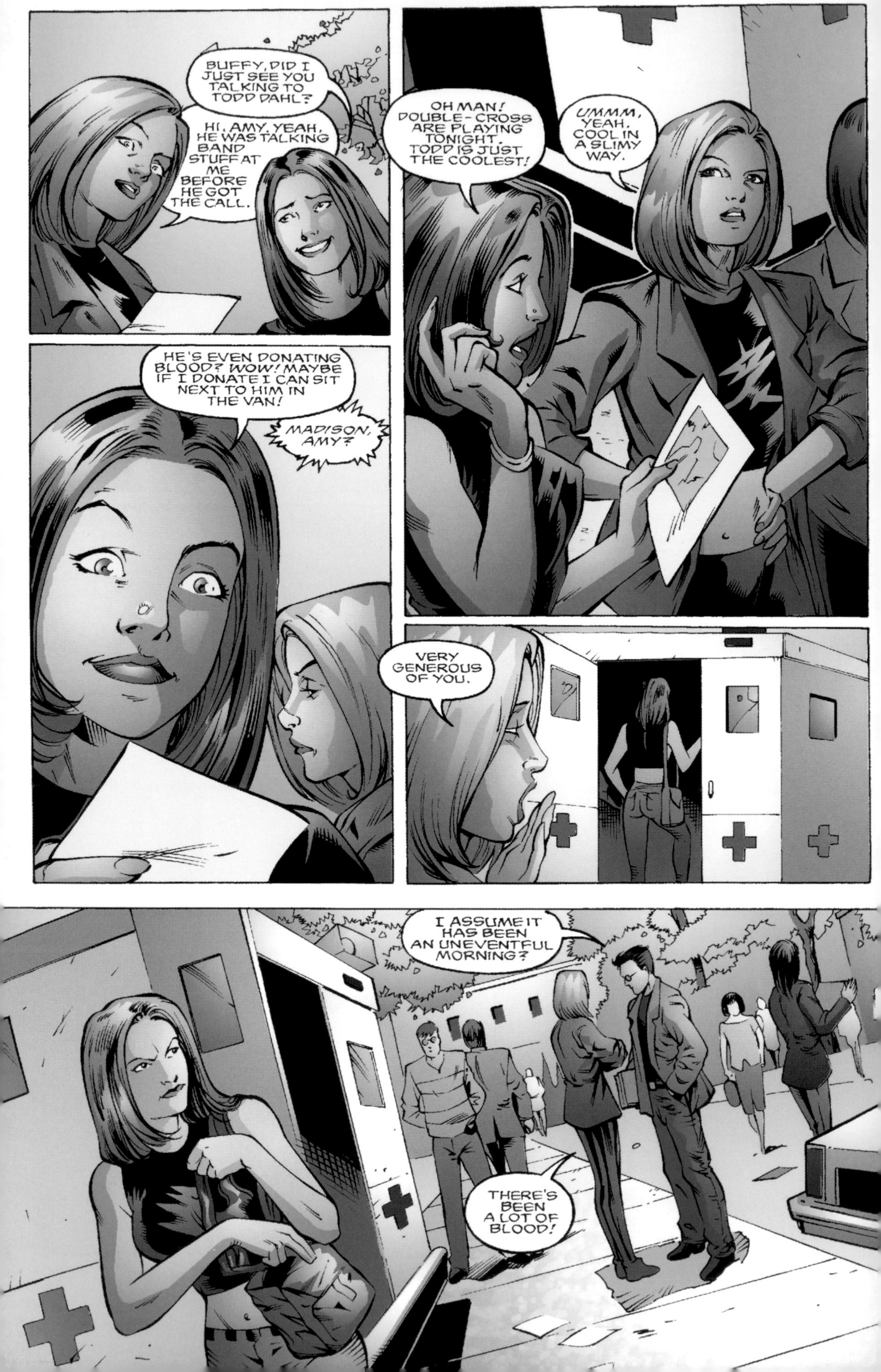
BUFFY, DID I JUST SEE YOU TALKING TO TODD DAHL?
HI, AMY. YEAH, HE WAS TALKING BAND STUFF AT ME BEFORE HE GOT THE CALL.
OH MAN! DOUBLE-CROSS ARE PLAYING TONIGHT. TODD IS JUST THE COOLEST!
UMMM, YEAH. COOL IN A SLIMY WAY.
HE'S EVEN DONATING BLOOD? WOW! MAYBE IF I DONATE I CAN SIT NEXT TO HIM IN THE VAN!
MADISON, AMY?
VERY GENEROUS OF YOU.
I ASSUME IT HAS BEEN AN UNEVENTFUL MORNING?
THERE'S BEEN A LOT OF BLOOD!

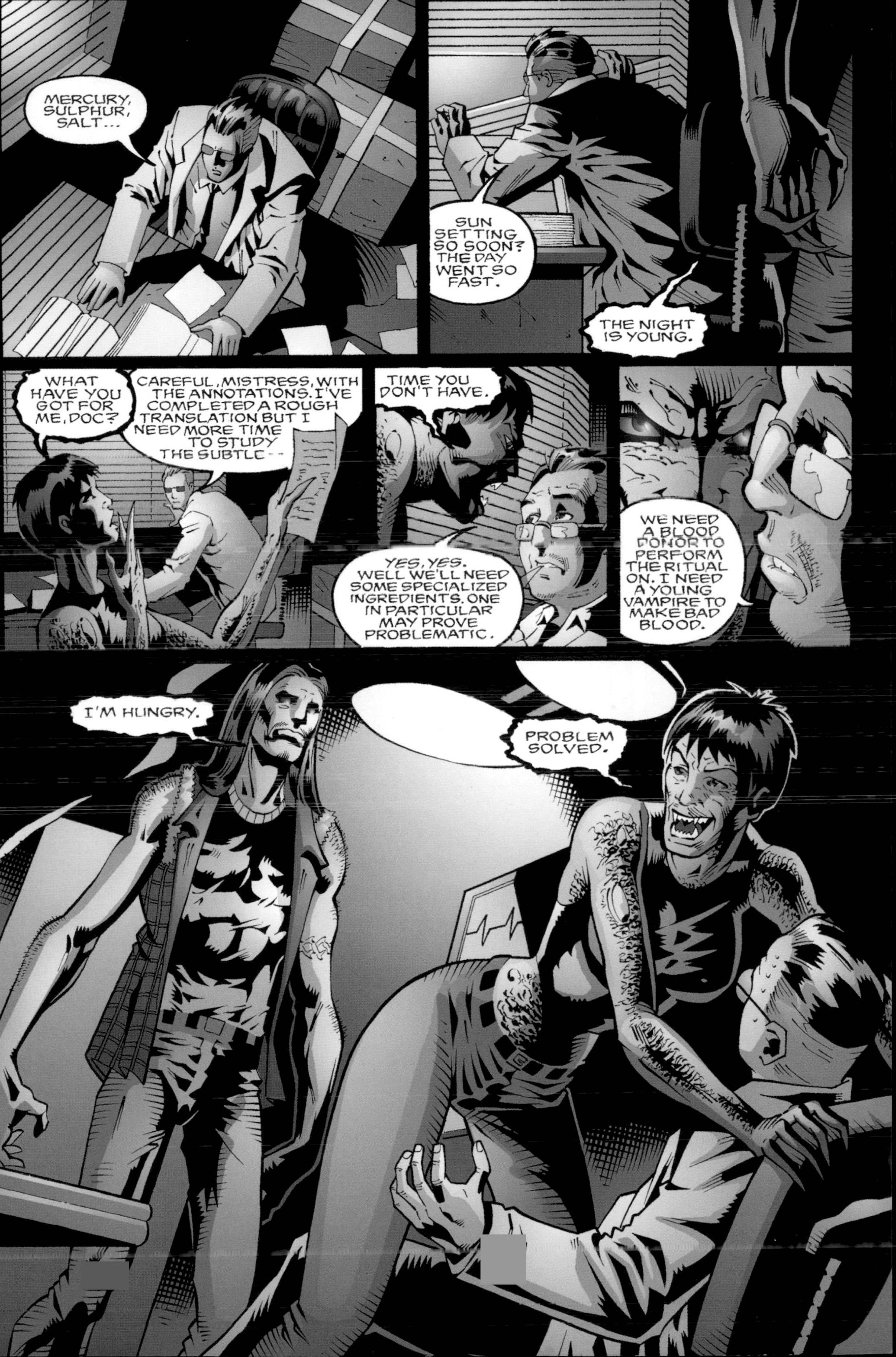
MERCURY, SULPHUR, SALT...
SUN SETTING SO SOON? THE DAY WENT SO FAST.
THE NIGHT IS YOUNG.
WHAT HAVE YOU GOT FOR ME, DOC?
CAREFUL, MISTRESS, WITH THE ANNOTATIONS. I'VE COMPLETED A ROUGH TRANSLATION BUT I NEED MORE TIME TO STUDY THE SUBTLE--
TIME YOU DON'T HAVE.
YES, YES. WELL WE'LL NEED SOME SPECIALIZED INGREDIENTS. ONE IN PARTICULAR MAY PROVE PROBLEMATIC.
WE NEED A BLOOD DONOR TO PERFORM THE RITUAL ON. I NEED A YOUNG VAMPIRE TO MAKE BAD BLOOD.
I'M HUNGRY.
PROBLEM SOLVED.

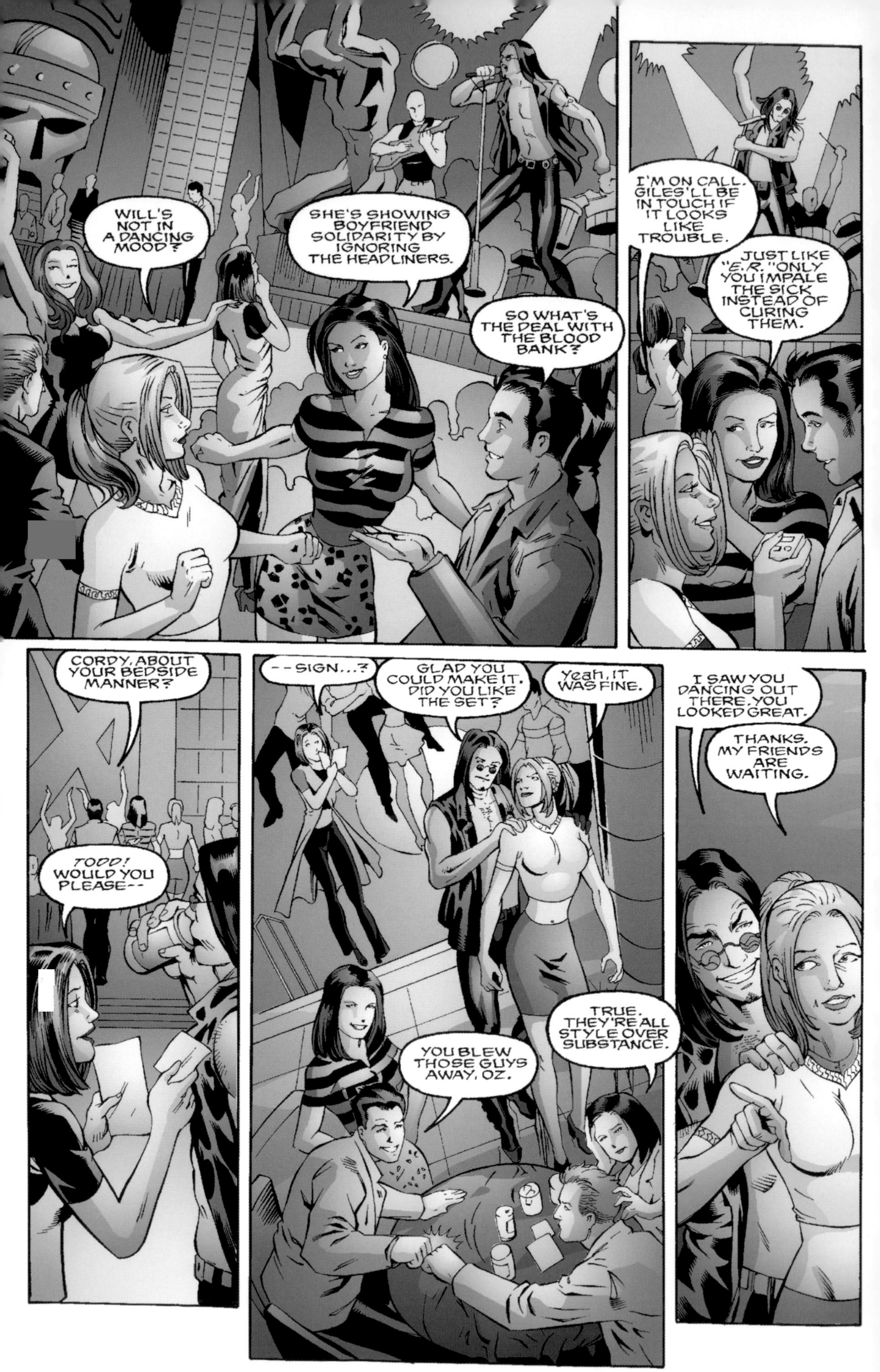

WILL'S NOT IN A DANCING MOOD?
SHE'S SHOWING BOYFRIEND SOLIDARITY BY IGNORING THE HEADLINERS.
SO WHAT'S THE DEAL WITH THE BLOOD BANK?
I'M ON CALL. GILES'LL BE IN TOUCH IF IT LOOKS LIKE TROUBLE.
JUST LIKE "E.R." ONLY YOU IMPALE THE SICK INSTEAD OF CURING THEM.
CORDY, ABOUT YOUR BEDSIDE MANNER?
TODD! WOULD YOU PLEASE--
--SIGN...?
GLAD YOU COULD MAKE IT. DID YOU LIKE THE SET?
Yeah, IT WAS FINE.
YOU BLEW THOSE GUYS AWAY, OZ.
TRUE. THEY'RE ALL STYLE OVER SUBSTANCE.
I SAW YOU DANCING OUT THERE. YOU LOOKED GREAT.
THANKS. MY FRIENDS ARE WAITING.

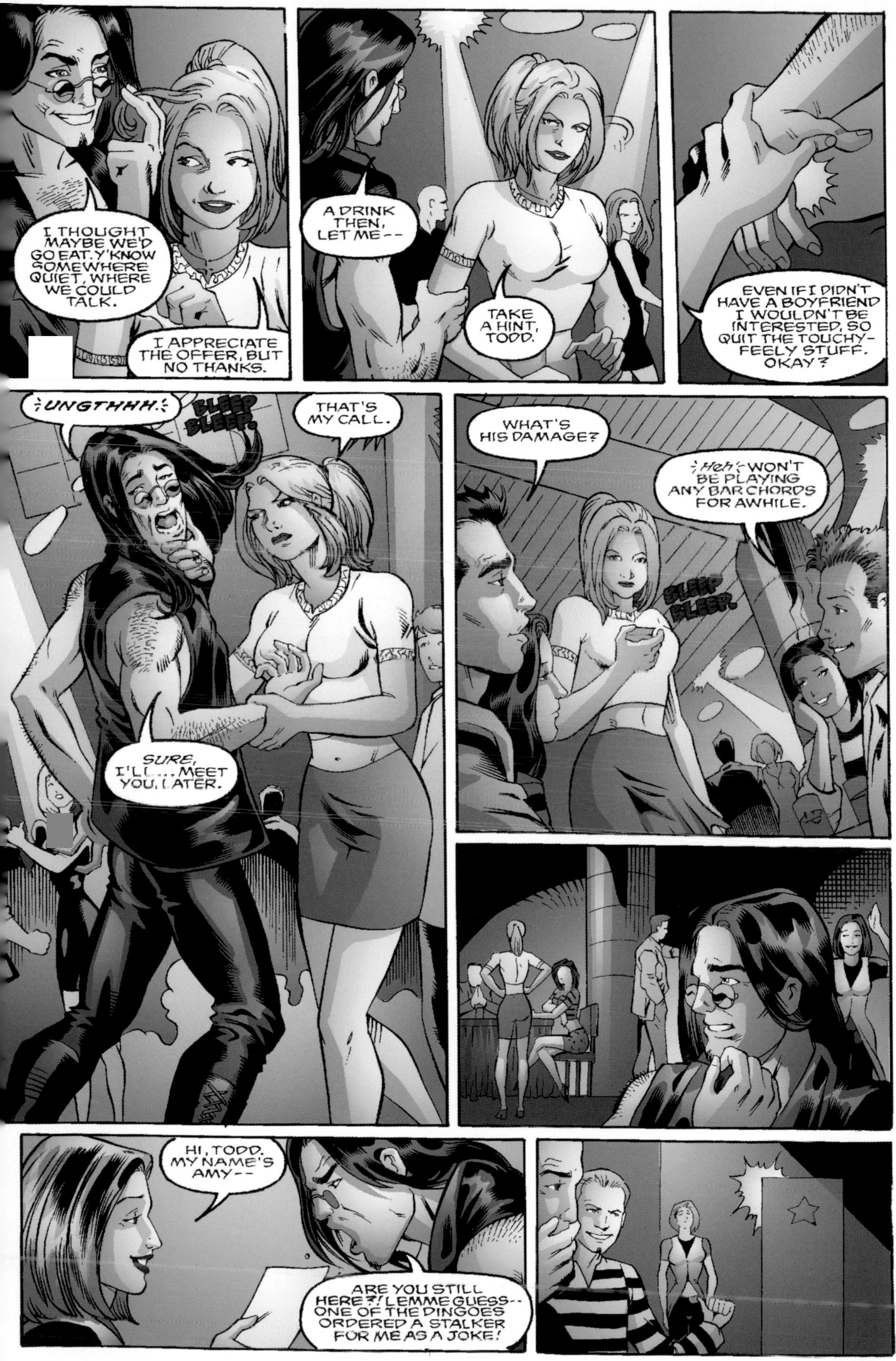
I THOUGHT MAYBE WE'D GO EAT. Y'KNOW SOMEWHERE QUIET, WHERE WE COULD TALK.
I APPRECIATE THE OFFER, BUT NO THANKS.
A DRINK THEN, LET ME--
TAKE A HINT, TODD.
EVEN IF I DIDN'T HAVE A BOYFRIEND I WOULDN'T BE INTERESTED, SO QUIT THE TOUCHY-FEELY STUFF. OKAY?
UNGTHHH.
BLEEP BLEEP.
THAT'S MY CALL.
SURE, I'LL... MEET YOU, LATER.
WHAT'S HIS DAMAGE?
Heh -WON'T BE PLAYING ANY BAR CHORDS FOR AWHILE.
BLEEP BLEEP.
HI, TODD. MY NAME'S AMY--
ARE YOU STILL HERE?! LEMME GUESS-- ONE OF THE DINGOES ORDERED A STALKER FOR ME AS A JOKE!

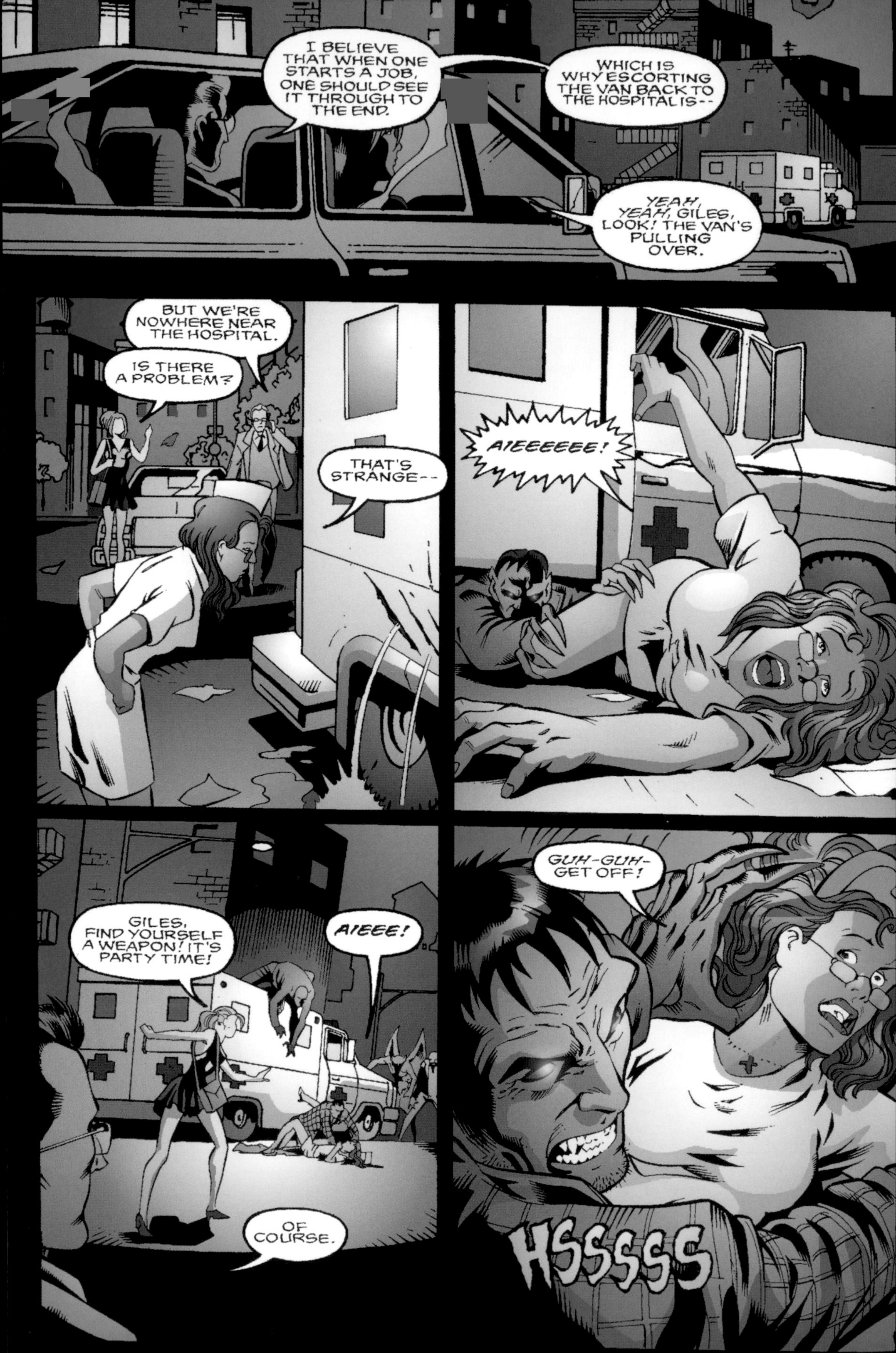
I BELIEVE THAT WHEN ONE STARTS A JOB, ONE SHOULD SEE IT THROUGH TO THE END.
WHICH IS WHY ESCORTING THE VAN BACK TO THE HOSPITAL IS--
YEAH, YEAH, GILES, LOOK! THE VAN'S PULLING OVER.
BUT WE'RE NOWHERE NEAR THE HOSPITAL.
IS THERE A PROBLEM?
THAT'S STRANGE--
AIEEEEEEE!
GILES, FIND YOURSELF A WEAPON! IT'S PARTY TIME!
AIEEE!
OF COURSE.
GUH-GUH-GET OFF!
HSSSSS

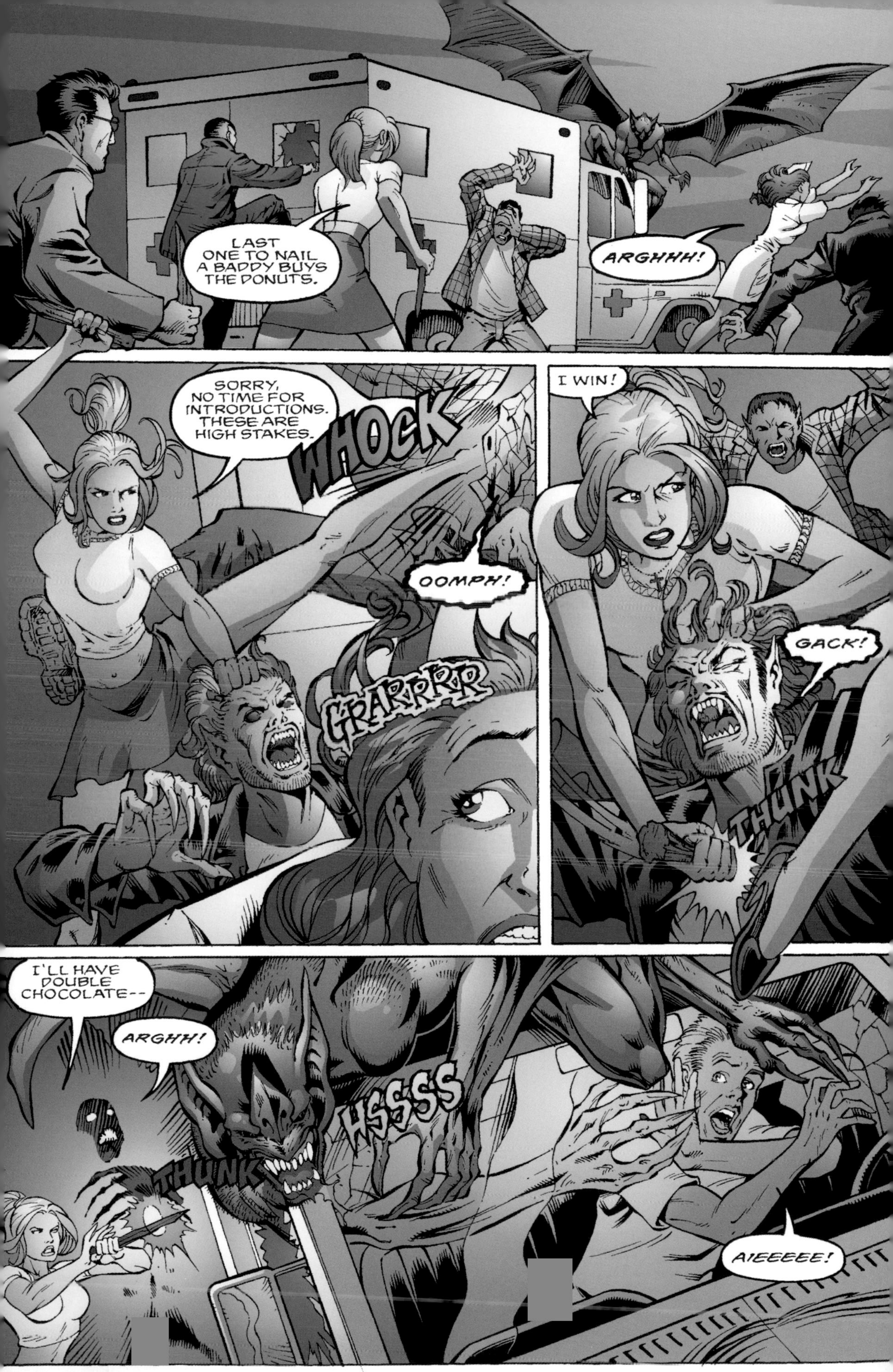
LAST ONE TO NAIL A BADDY BUYS THE DONUTS.
ARGHHH!
SORRY, NO TIME FOR INTRODUCTIONS. THESE ARE HIGH STAKES.
WHOCK
OOMPH!
GRARRRR
I WIN!
GACK!
THUNK
I'LL HAVE DOUBLE CHOCOLATE--
ARGHH!
HSSSS
THUNK
AIEEEEE!

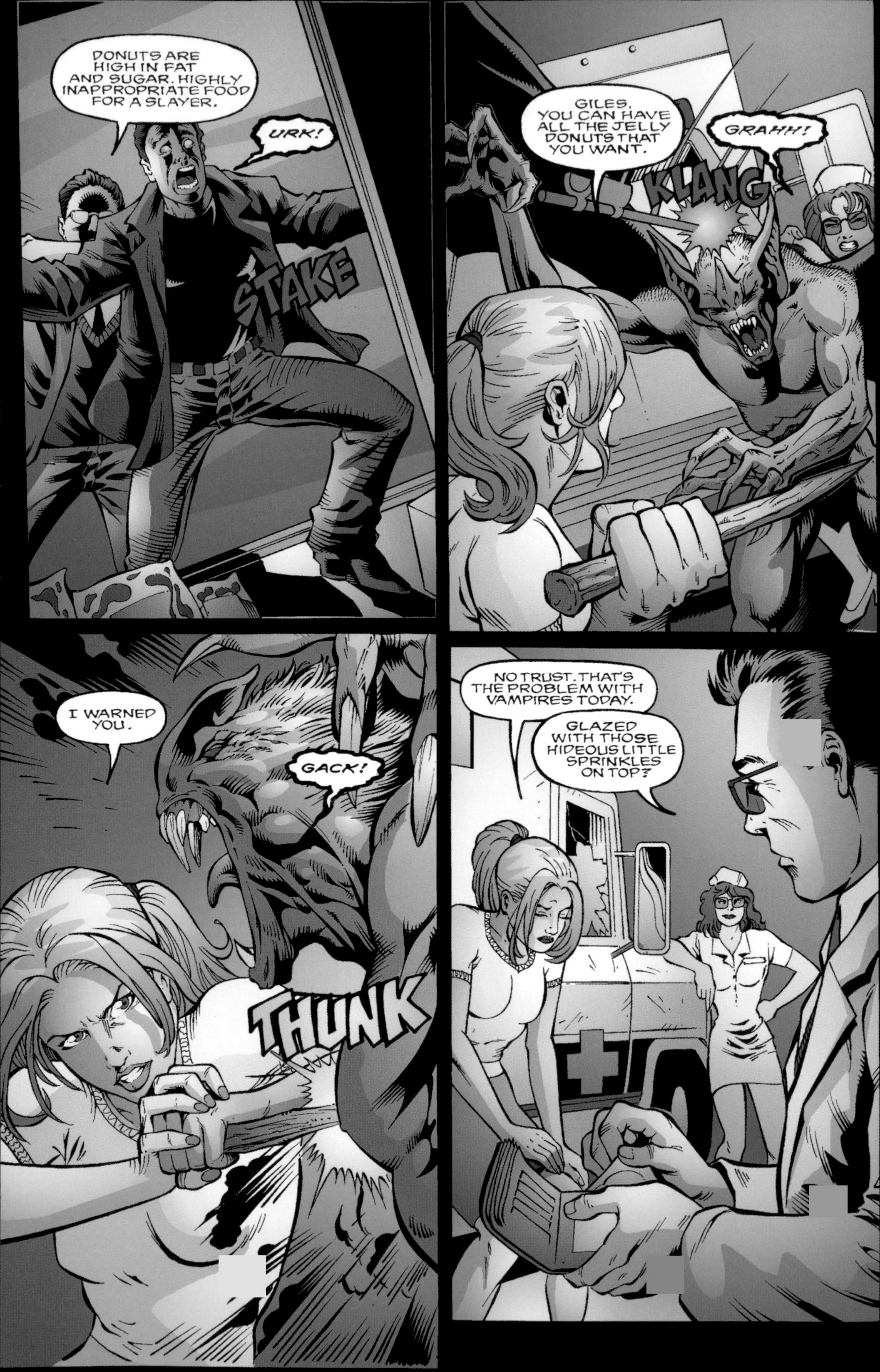
DONUTS ARE HIGH IN FAT AND SUGAR. HIGHLY INAPPROPRIATE FOOD FOR A SLAYER.
URK!
STAKE
GILES, YOU CAN HAVE ALL THE JELLY DONUTS THAT YOU WANT.
GRAHH!
KLANG
I WARNED YOU.
GACK!
THUNK
NO TRUST. THAT'S THE PROBLEM WITH VAMPIRES TODAY.
GLAZED WITH THOSE HIDEOUS LITTLE SPRINKLES ON TOP?

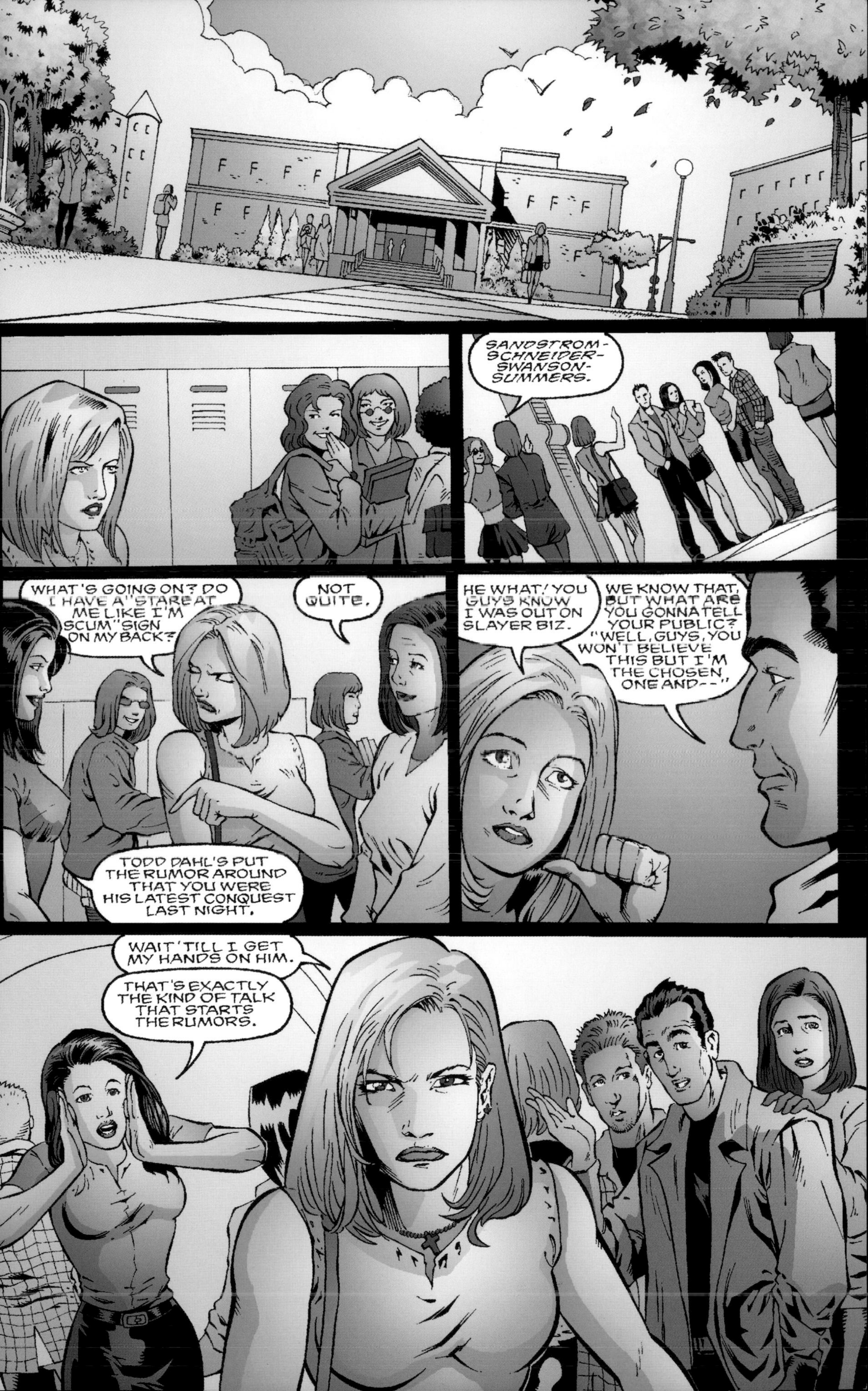

SANDSTROM-SCHNEIDER-SWANSON-SUMMERS.
WHAT'S GOING ON? DO I HAVE A "STARE AT ME LIKE I'M SCUM" SIGN ON MY BACK?
NOT QUITE.
TODD DAHL'S PUT THE RUMOR AROUND THAT YOU WERE HIS LATEST CONQUEST LAST NIGHT.
HE WHAT! YOU GUYS KNOW I WAS OUT ON SLAYER BIZ.
WE KNOW THAT, BUT WHAT ARE YOU GONNA TELL YOUR PUBLIC? "WELL, GUYS, YOU WON'T BELIEVE THIS BUT I'M THE CHOSEN ONE AND--"
WAIT 'TILL I GET MY HANDS ON HIM.
THAT'S EXACTLY THE KIND OF TALK THAT STARTS THE RUMORS.

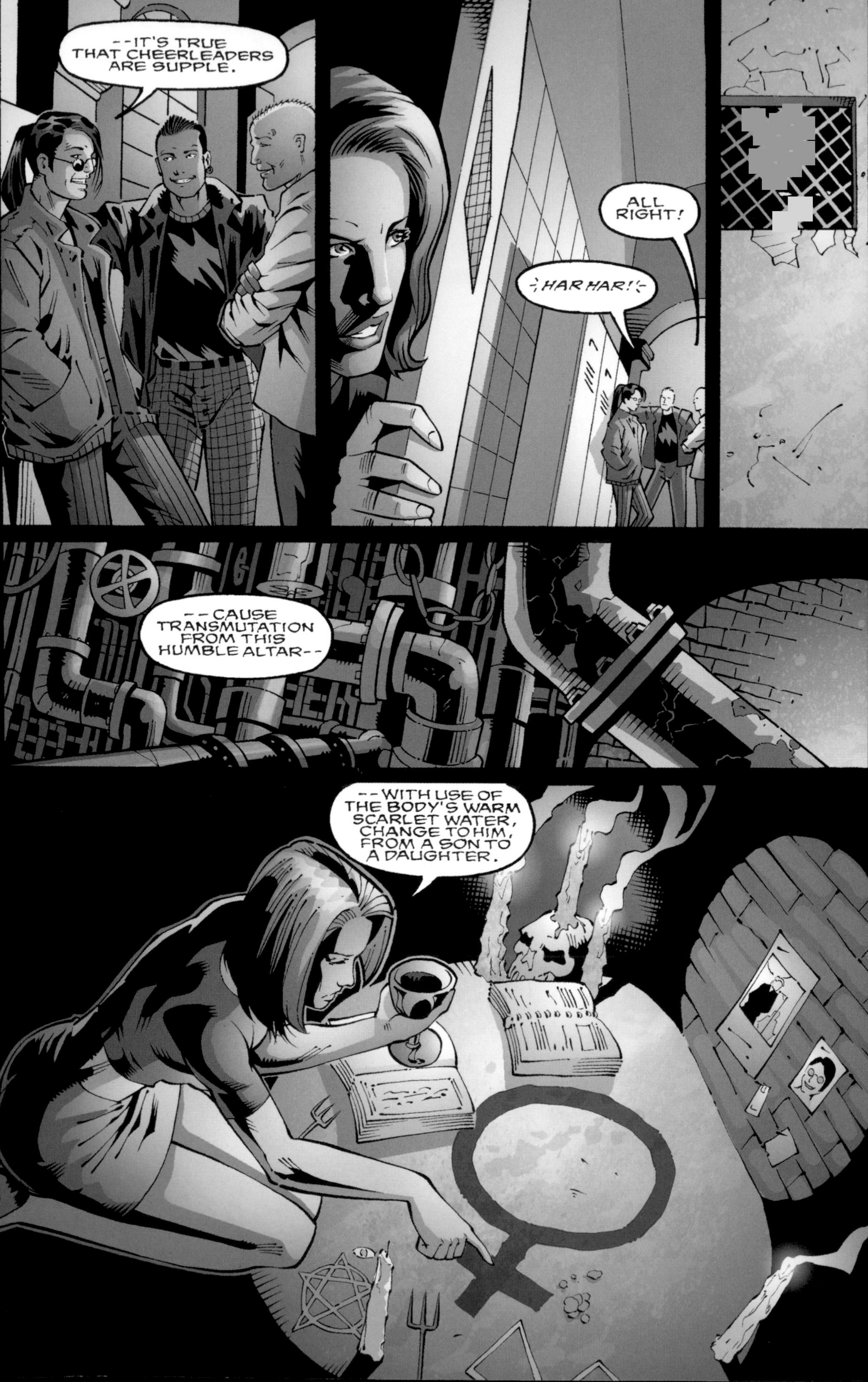
--IT'S TRUE THAT CHEERLEADERS ARE SUPPLE.
ALL RIGHT!
HAR HAR!
--CAUSE TRANSMUTATION FROM THIS HUMBLE ALTAR--
--WITH USE OF THE BODY'S WARM SCARLET WATER, CHANGE TO HIM, FROM A SON TO A DAUGHTER.

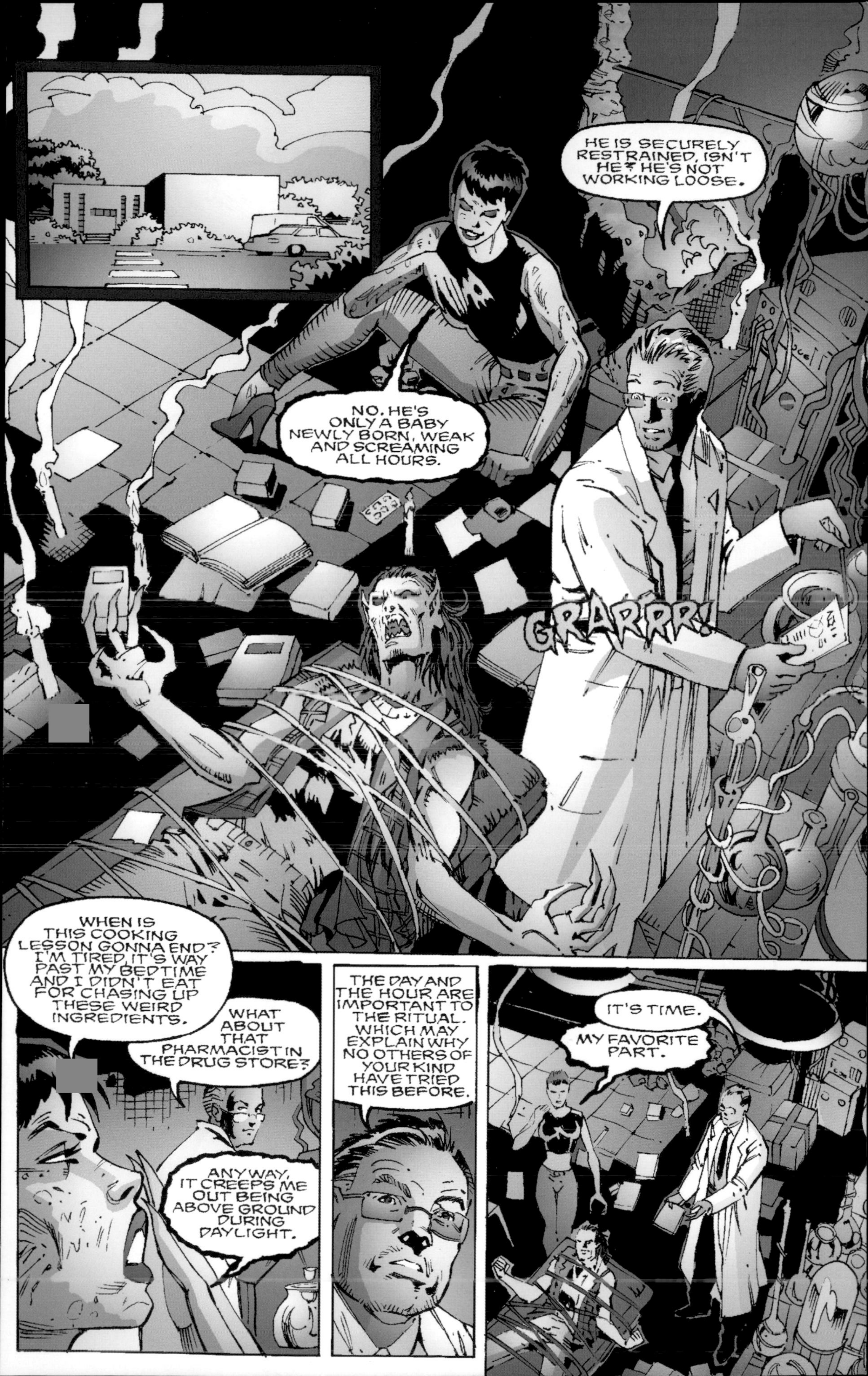
HE IS SECURELY RESTRAINED, ISN'T HE? HE'S NOT WORKING LOOSE.
NO. HE'S ONLY A BABY NEWLY BORN, WEAK AND SCREAMING ALL HOURS.
GRARRR!
WHEN IS THIS COOKING LESSON GONNA END? I'M TIRED. IT'S WAY PAST MY BEDTIME AND I DIDN'T EAT FOR CHASING UP THESE WEIRD INGREDIENTS.
WHAT ABOUT THAT PHARMACIST IN THE DRUG STORE?
ANYWAY, IT CREEPS ME OUT BEING ABOVE GROUND DURING DAYLIGHT.
THE DAY AND THE HOUR ARE IMPORTANT TO THE RITUAL. WHICH MAY EXPLAIN WHY NO OTHERS OF YOUR KIND HAVE TRIED THIS BEFORE.
IT'S TIME.
MY FAVORITE PART.

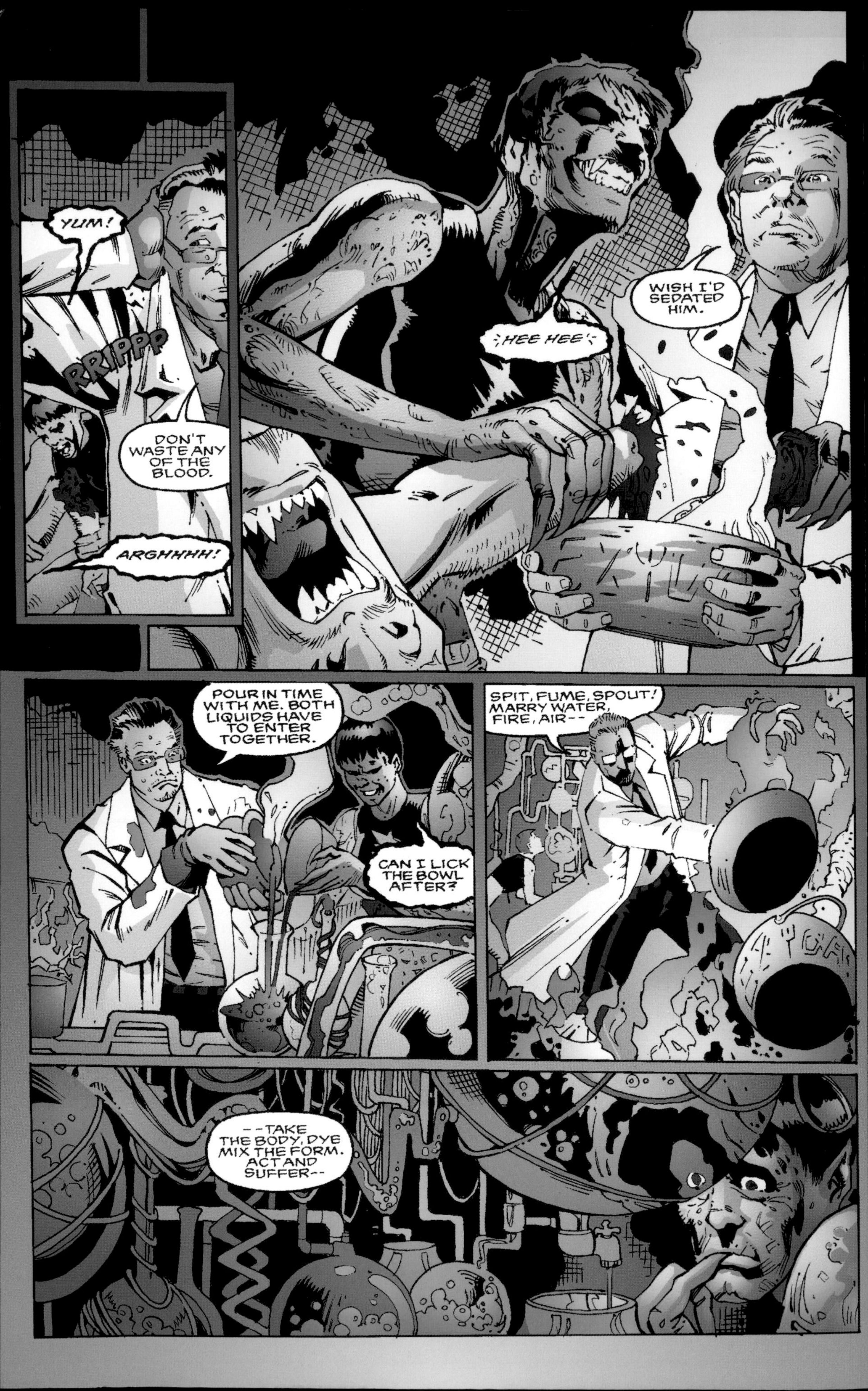

YUM!
RRIPPP
DON'T WASTE ANY OF THE BLOOD.
ARGHHHH!
HEE HEE
WISH I'D SEDATED HIM.
POUR IN TIME WITH ME. BOTH LIQUIDS HAVE TO ENTER TOGETHER.
CAN I LICK THE BOWL AFTER?
SPIT, FUME, SPOUT! MARRY WATER, FIRE, AIR--
--TAKE THE BODY, DYE MIX THE FORM. ACT AND SUFFER--

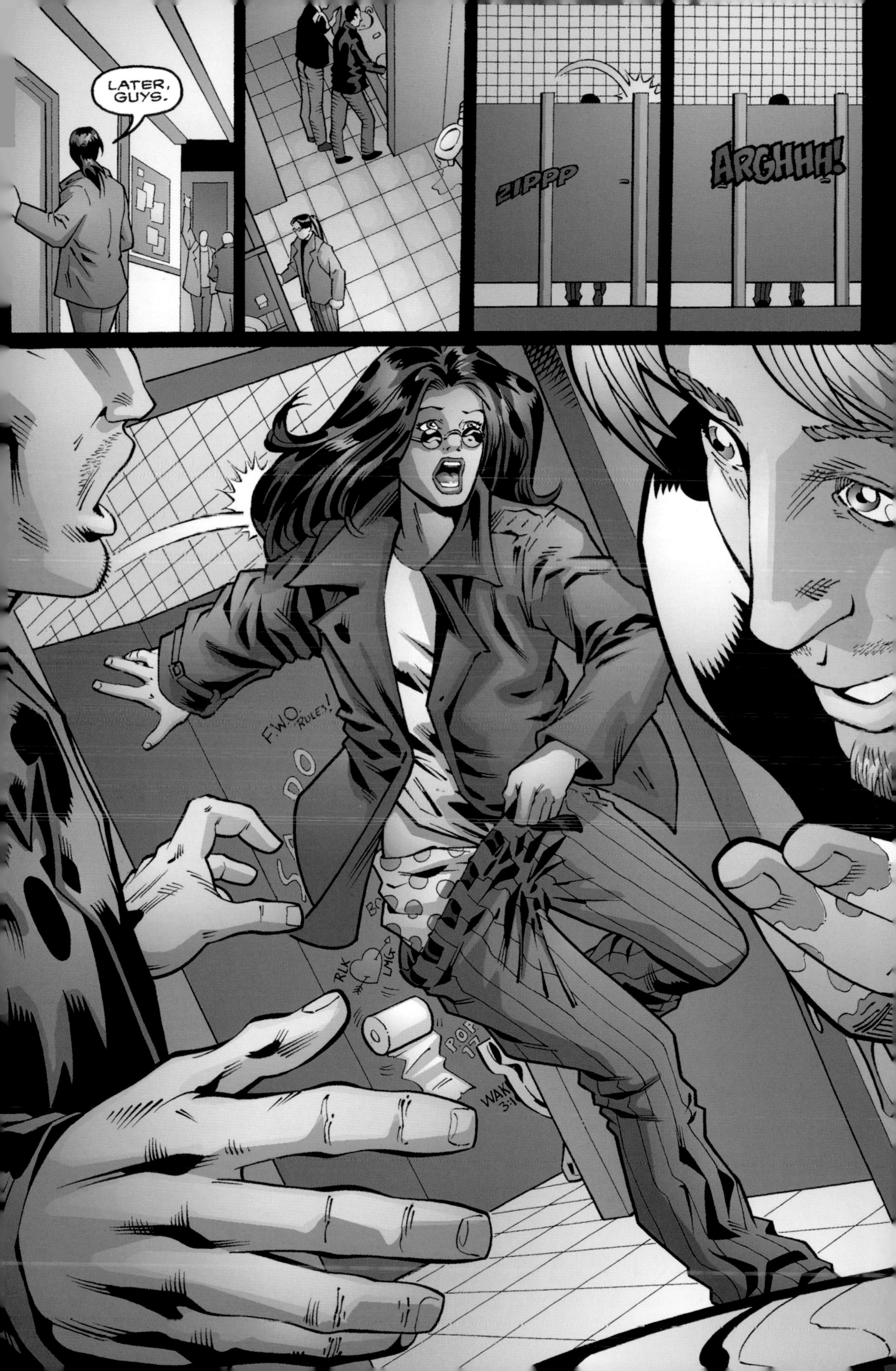
LATER, GUYS.
ZIPPP
ARGHHH!
F.W.O. RULES!
RLK
LMG
WAK 3:1

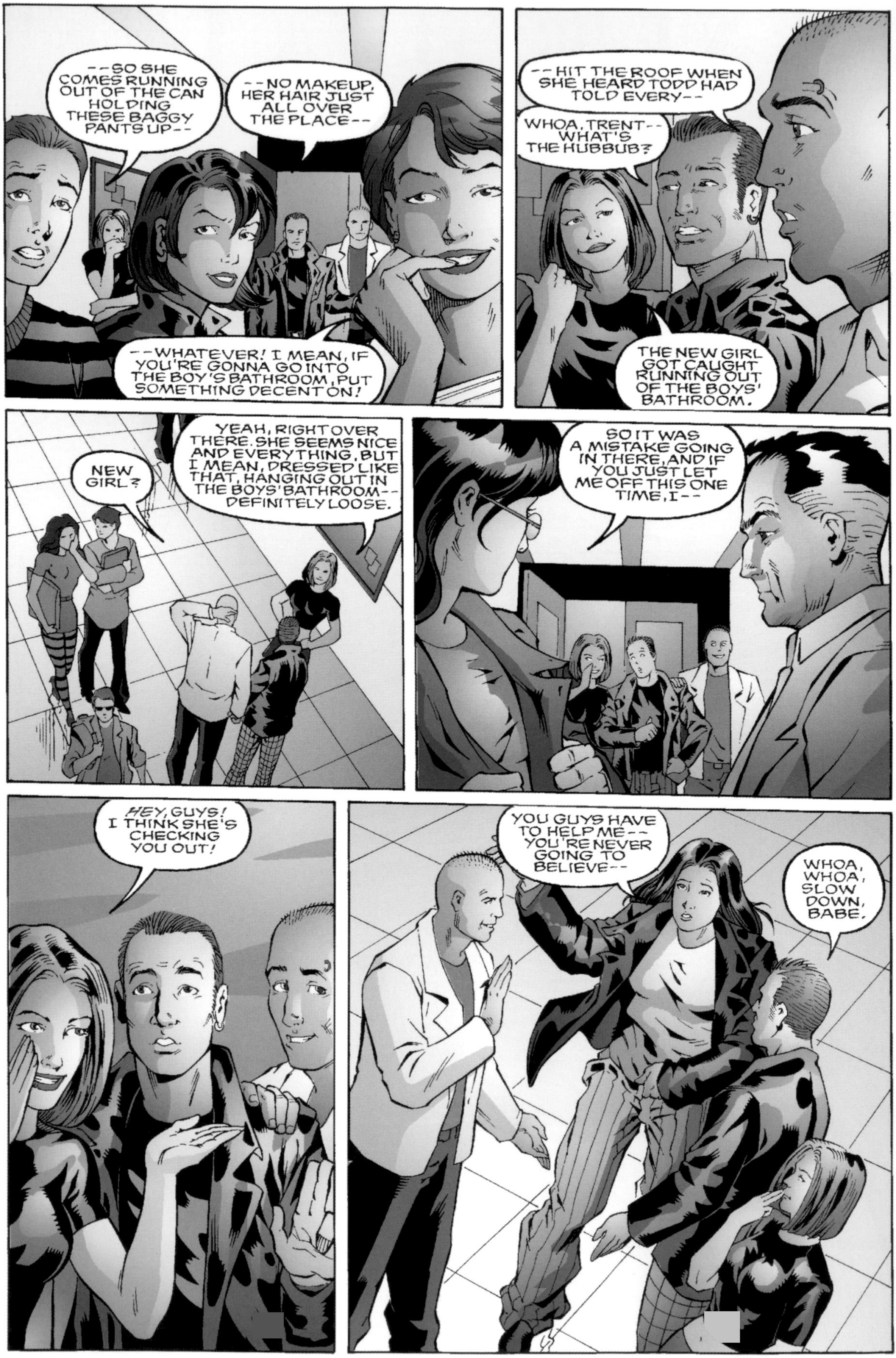
--SO SHE COMES RUNNING OUT OF THE CAN HOLDING THESE BAGGY PANTS UP--
--NO MAKEUP, HER HAIR JUST ALL OVER THE PLACE--
--WHATEVER! I MEAN, IF YOU'RE GONNA GO INTO THE BOY'S BATHROOM, PUT SOMETHING DECENT ON!
--HIT THE ROOF WHEN SHE HEARD TODD HAD TOLD EVERY--
WHOA, TRENT--WHAT'S THE HUBBUB?
THE NEW GIRL GOT CAUGHT RUNNING OUT OF THE BOYS' BATHROOM.
NEW GIRL?
YEAH, RIGHT OVER THERE. SHE SEEMS NICE AND EVERYTHING, BUT I MEAN, DRESSED LIKE THAT, HANGING OUT IN THE BOYS' BATHROOM--DEFINITELY LOOSE.
SO IT WAS A MISTAKE GOING IN THERE, AND IF YOU JUST LET ME OFF THIS ONE TIME, I--
HEY, GUYS! I THINK SHE'S CHECKING YOU OUT!
YOU GUYS HAVE TO HELP ME--YOU'RE NEVER GOING TO BELIEVE--
WHOA, WHOA, SLOW DOWN, BABE.

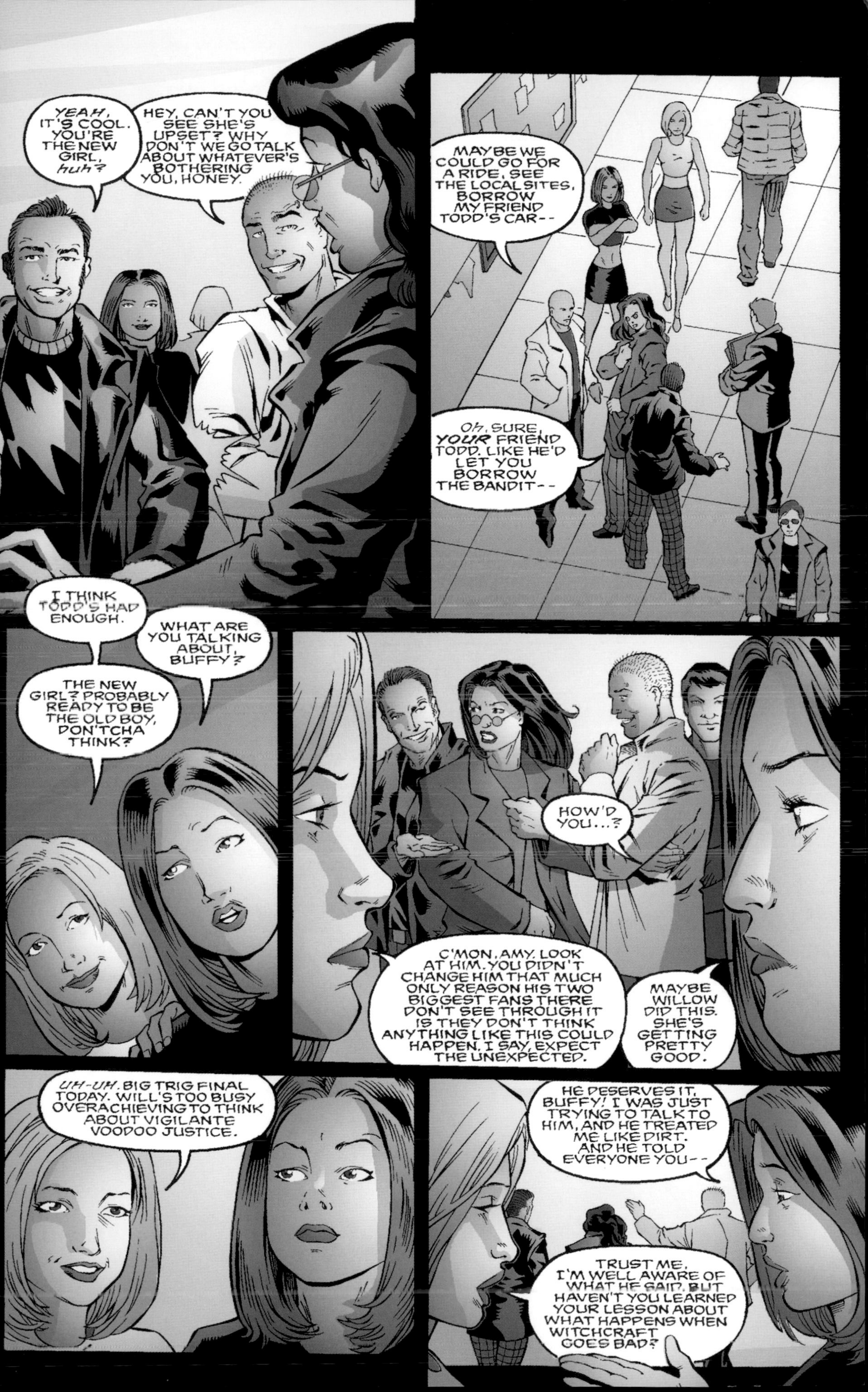

YEAH, IT'S COOL. YOU'RE THE NEW GIRL, huh?
HEY, CAN'T YOU SEE SHE'S UPSET? WHY DON'T WE GO TALK ABOUT WHATEVER'S BOTHERING YOU, HONEY.
MAYBE WE COULD GO FOR A RIDE, SEE THE LOCAL SITES, BORROW MY FRIEND TODD'S CAR--
Oh, SURE, YOUR FRIEND TODD. LIKE HE'D LET YOU BORROW THE BANDIT--
I THINK TODD'S HAD ENOUGH.
WHAT ARE YOU TALKING ABOUT, BUFFY?
THE NEW GIRL? PROBABLY READY TO BE THE OLD BOY, DON'TCHA THINK?
HOW'D YOU...?
C'MON, AMY. LOOK AT HIM. YOU DIDN'T CHANGE HIM THAT MUCH. ONLY REASON HIS TWO BIGGEST FANS THERE DON'T SEE THROUGH IT IS THEY DON'T THINK ANYTHING LIKE THIS COULD HAPPEN. I SAY, EXPECT THE UNEXPECTED.
MAYBE WILLOW DID THIS. SHE'S GETTING PRETTY GOOD.
UH-UH. BIG TRIG FINAL TODAY. WILL'S TOO BUSY OVERACHIEVING TO THINK ABOUT VIGILANTE VOODOO JUSTICE.
HE DESERVES IT, BUFFY! I WAS JUST TRYING TO TALK TO HIM, AND HE TREATED ME LIKE DIRT. AND HE TOLD EVERYONE YOU--
TRUST ME, I'M WELL AWARE OF WHAT HE SAID. BUT HAVEN'T YOU LEARNED YOUR LESSON ABOUT WHAT HAPPENS WHEN WITCHCRAFT GOES BAD?

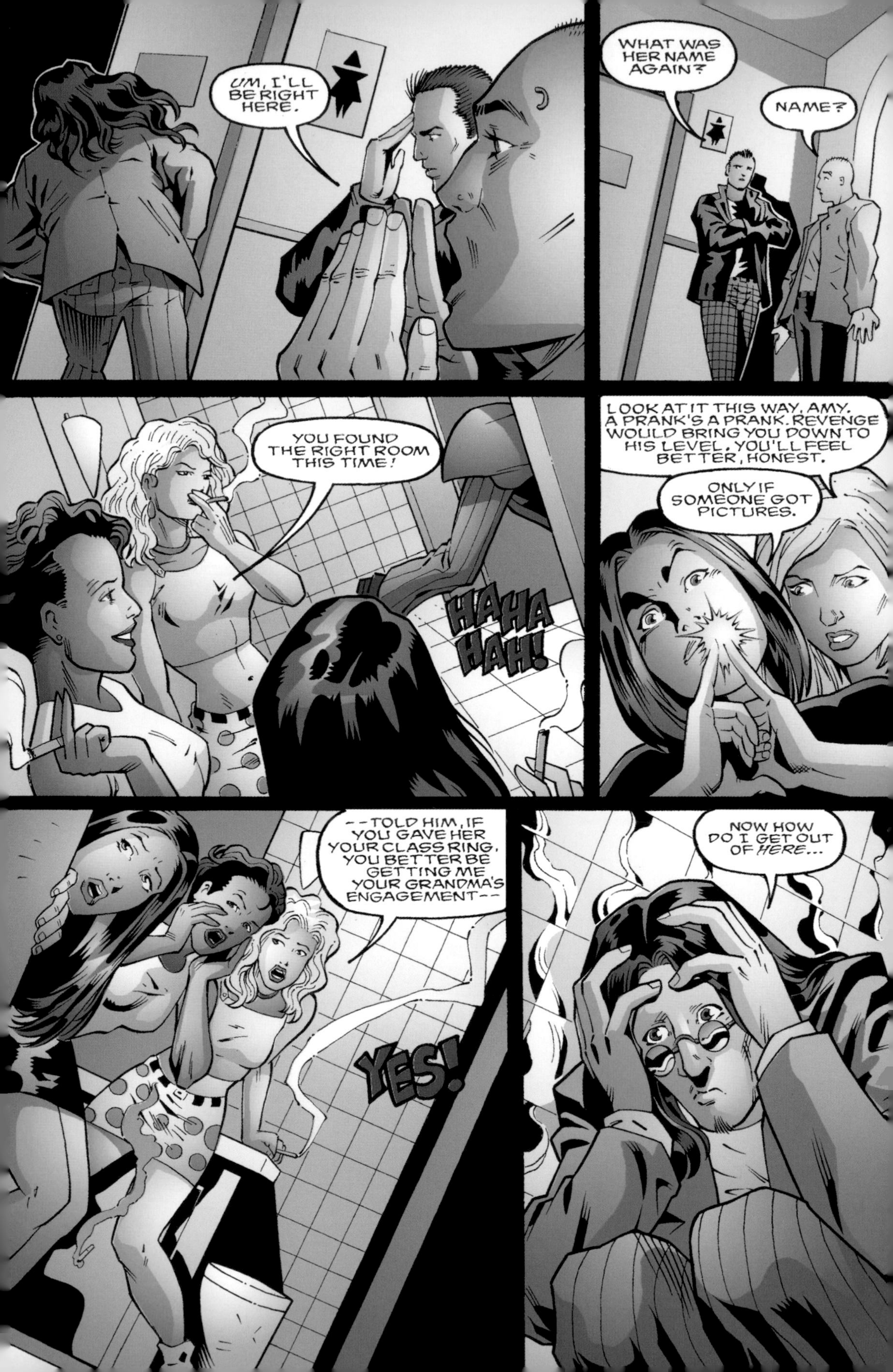
UM, I'LL BE RIGHT HERE.
WHAT WAS HER NAME AGAIN?
NAME?
YOU FOUND THE RIGHT ROOM THIS TIME!
HAHAHAH!
LOOK AT IT THIS WAY, AMY. A PRANK'S A PRANK. REVENGE WOULD BRING YOU DOWN TO HIS LEVEL. YOU'LL FEEL BETTER, HONEST.
ONLY IF SOMEONE GOT PICTURES.
--TOLD HIM, IF YOU GAVE HER YOUR CLASS RING, YOU BETTER BE GETTING ME YOUR GRANDMA'S ENGAGEMENT--
YES!
NOW HOW DO I GET OUT OF HERE...

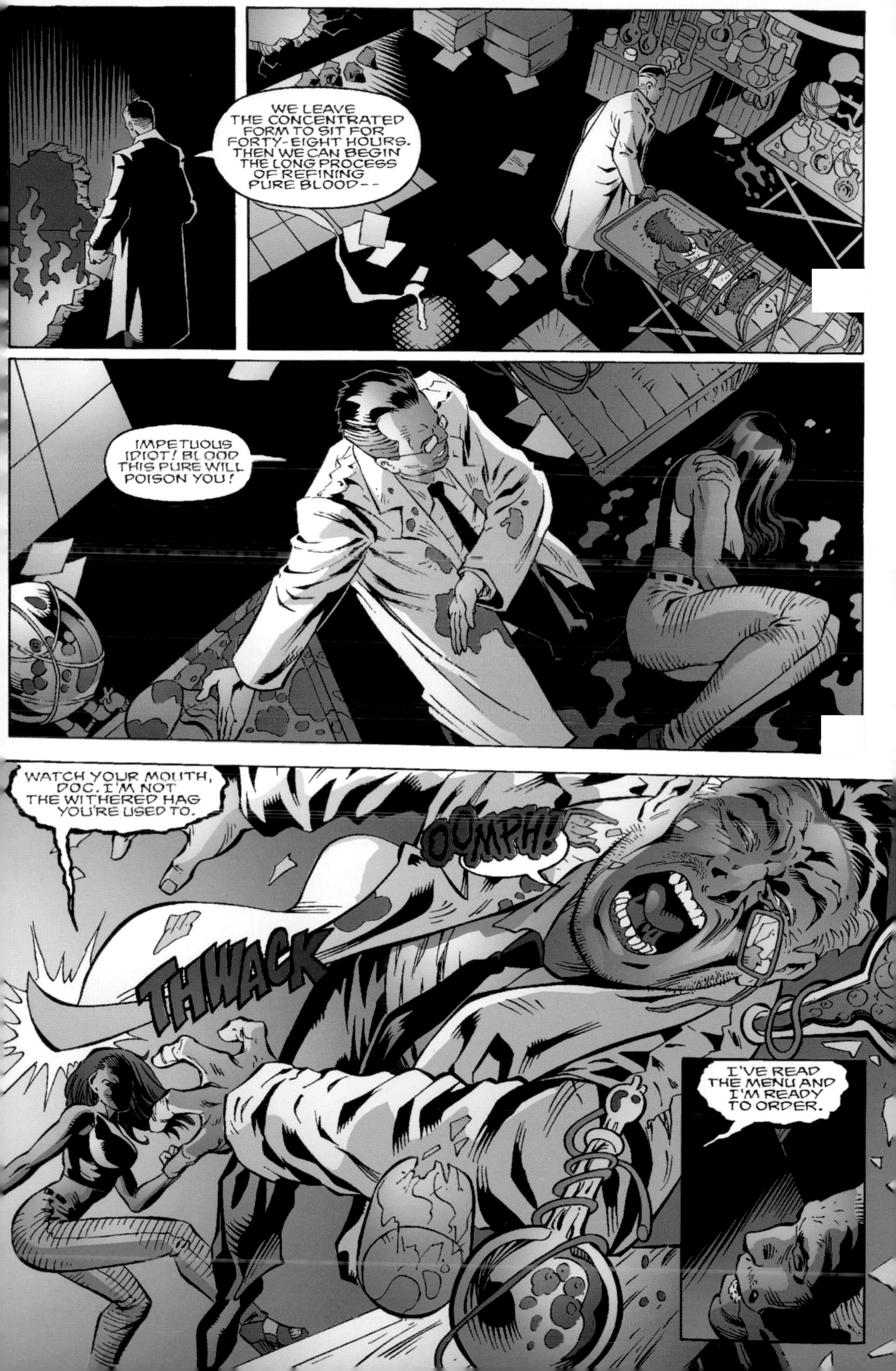
WE LEAVE THE CONCENTRATED FORM TO SIT FOR FORTY-EIGHT HOURS. THEN WE CAN BEGIN THE LONG PROCESS OF REFINING PURE BLOOD--
IMPETUOUS IDIOT! BLOOD THIS PURE WILL POISON YOU!
WATCH YOUR MOUTH, DOC. I'M NOT THE WITHERED HAG YOU'RE USED TO.
OOMPH!
THWACK
I'VE READ THE MENU AND I'M READY TO ORDER.

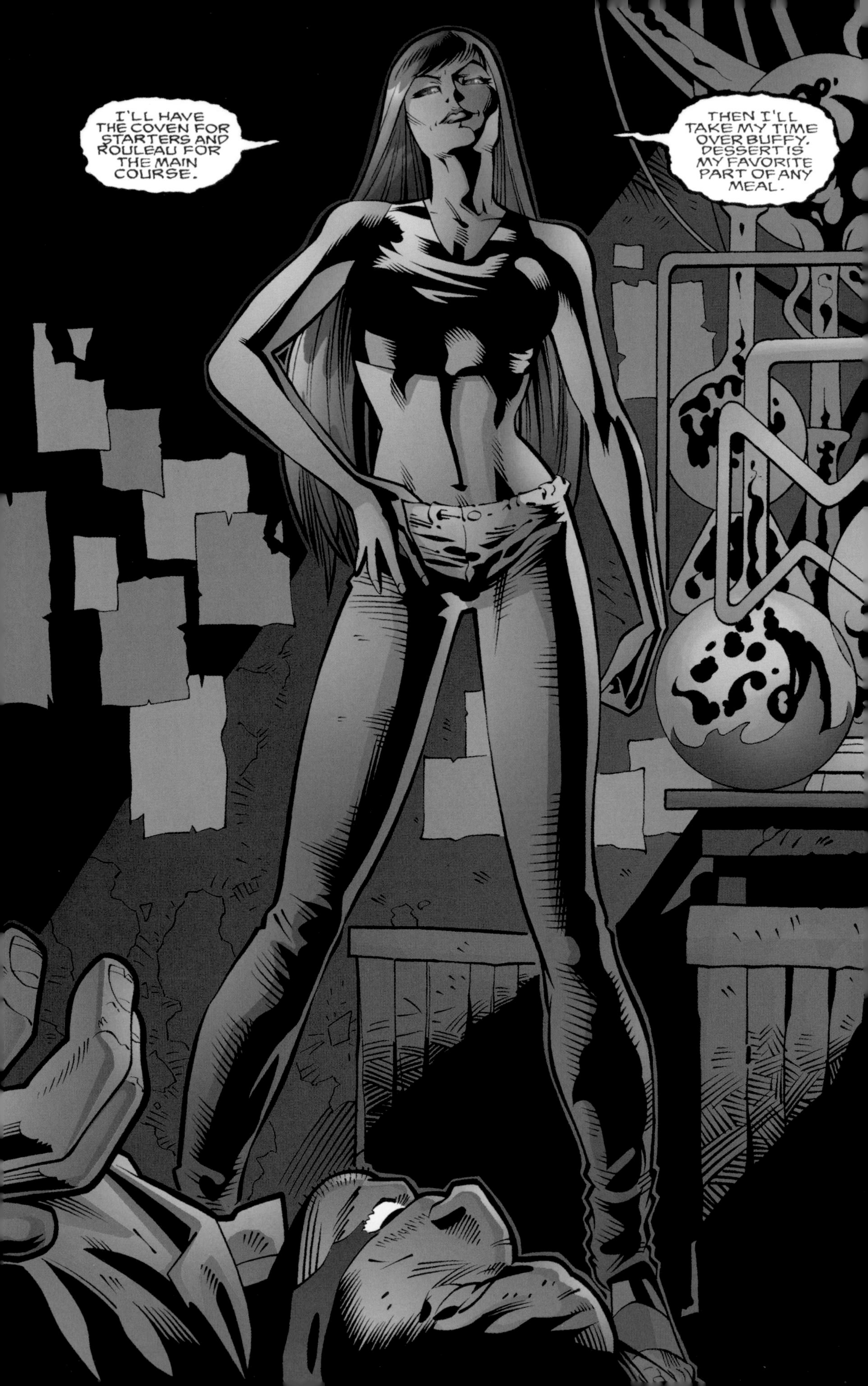
I'LL HAVE THE COVEN FOR STARTERS AND ROULEAU FOR THE MAIN COURSE.
THEN I'LL TAKE MY TIME OVER BUFFY. DESSERT IS MY FAVORITE PART OF ANY MEAL.

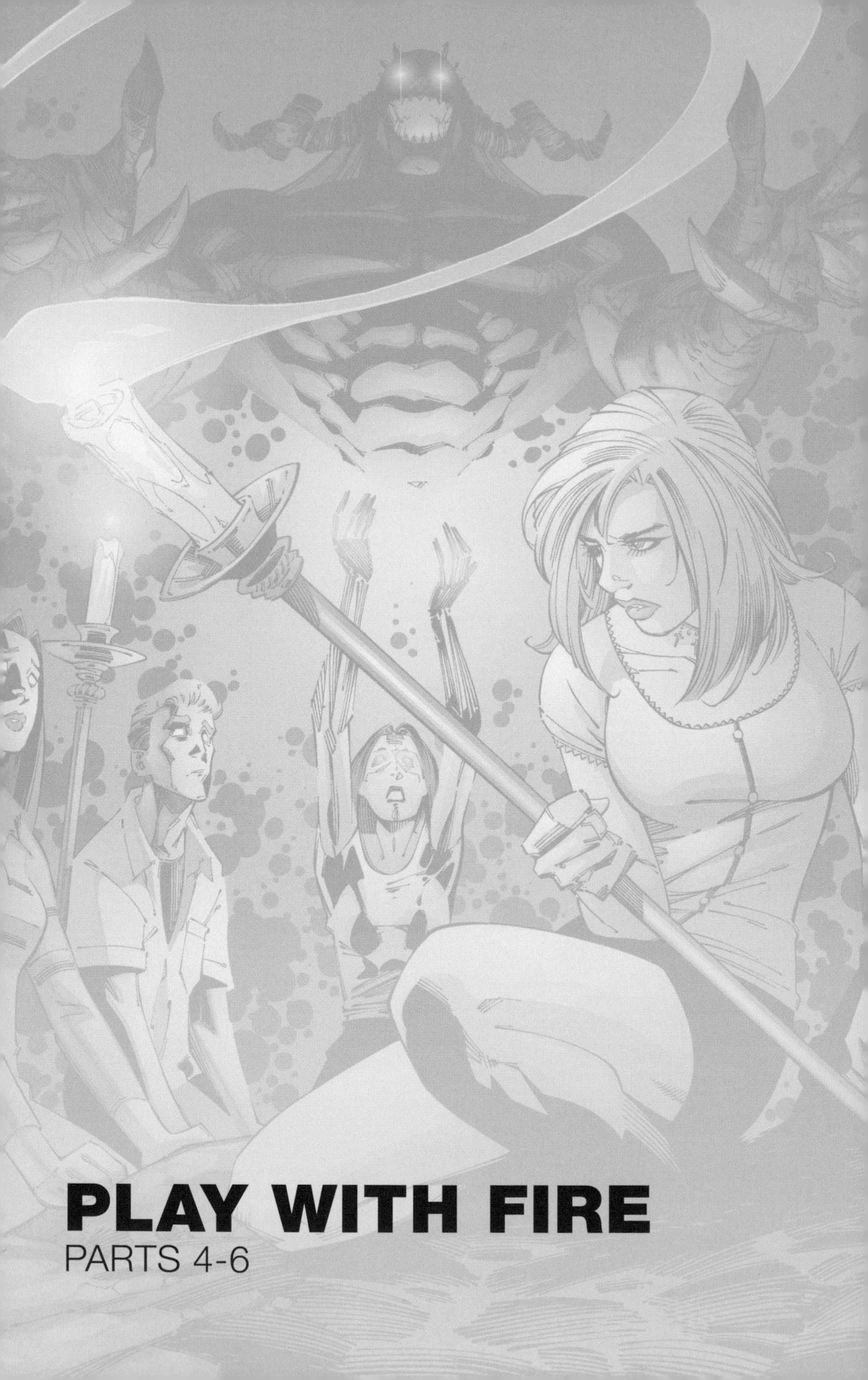

PLAY WITH FIRE

PARTS 4-6

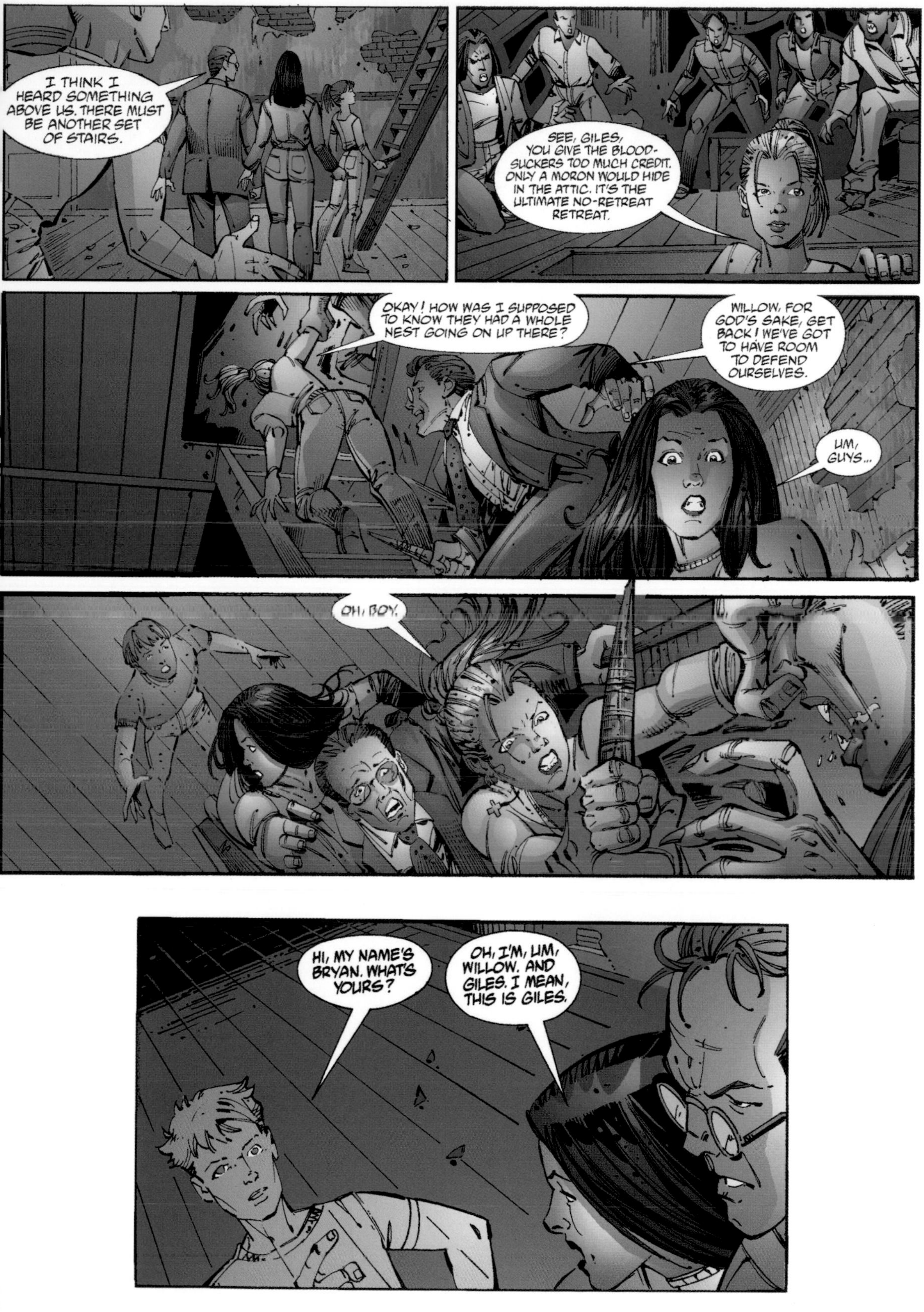
I THINK I HEARD SOMETHING ABOVE US. THERE MUST BE ANOTHER SET OF STAIRS.
SEE, GILES, YOU GIVE THE BLOOD-SUCKERS TOO MUCH CREDIT. ONLY A MORON WOULD HIDE IN THE ATTIC. IT'S THE ULTIMATE NO-RETREAT RETREAT.
OKAY! HOW WAS I SUPPOSED TO KNOW THEY HAD A WHOLE NEST GOING ON UP THERE?
WILLOW, FOR GOD'S SAKE, GET BACK! WE'VE GOT TO HAVE ROOM TO DEFEND OURSELVES.
UM, GUYS...
OH, BOY.
HI, MY NAME'S BRYAN. WHAT'S YOURS?
OH, I'M, UM, WILLOW. AND GILES. I MEAN, THIS IS GILES.

HEY, WILL! COULD WE FLIRT WITH THE GHOST-BOY WHEN WE'RE DONE FIGHTING FOR OUR LIVES, PLEASE? I COULD USE A LITTLE--HEY!

IT'S SO NICE TO HAVE SOME HUMAN COMPANY. IT'S BEEN QUITE SOME TIME SINCE--

OH, EXCUSE ME.

IT ISN'T THAT I'M AGAINST SOCIALIZING, SEE...

I WASN'T FLIRTING.

OH, WOW, I'M SORRY. I'M PROBABLY BEING A DISTRACTION. IT'S JUST BEEN SO LONG...

I'M BEING RUDE, AREN'T I? YOU GUYS WOULD PROBABLY LIKE SOME HELP.

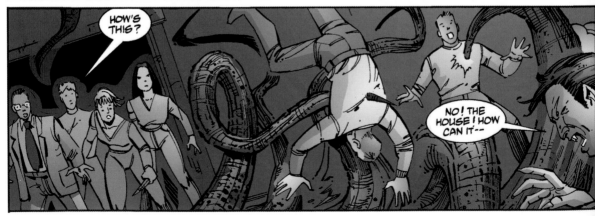

HOW'S THIS?

NO! THE HOUSE! HOW CAN IT--

THAT WAS NOT BAD, ACTUALLY. ≷COUGH COUGH≷ THANKS FOR THE HELP. MAYBE I CAN ACTUALLY GET HOME IN TIME TO STUDY FOR THAT TRIG TEST NOW.

I'M SORRY, BUT I DON'T THINK I CAN LET YOU LEAVE.

"IT WAS THE SPRING OF '88. I WAS SIXTEEN. A BUNCH OF US HAD STARTED TO DABBLE IN MAGIC AND STUFF. I THOUGHT IT WOULD BE COOL IF WE TRIED TO RAISE A DEMON.

"I DON'T THINK WE RAISED ANYTHING, BUT WE DID SOMETHING TO THE HOUSE, BROUGHT IT TO LIFE SOMEHOW.

"THE OTHERS ALL GOT AWAY. THEY DIDN'T EVEN LOOK BACK. THE HOUSE HAD ME--TOOK ME AND MADE ME A PART OF IT."

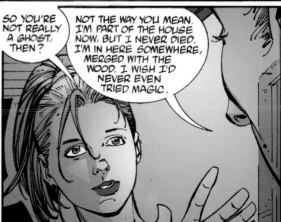

SO YOU'RE NOT REALLY A GHOST, THEN?

NOT THE WAY YOU MEAN. I'M PART OF THE HOUSE NOW, BUT I NEVER DIED. I'M IN HERE SOMEWHERE, MERGED WITH THE WOOD. I WISH I'D NEVER EVEN TRIED MAGIC.

THAT SOUNDS A LOT LIKE YOUR CUE, WILLOW. THINK YOU CAN GET HIM OUT?

WELL, SINCE YOU ASKED--

NO.

WE CAN'T BE CERTAIN HE'S TELLING THE TRUTH ABOUT ANY OF THIS.

BUT...WHAT IF HE IS, AND WE JUST LEAVE HIM HERE? I'D NEVER BE ABLE TO SLEEP AGAIN, GILES.

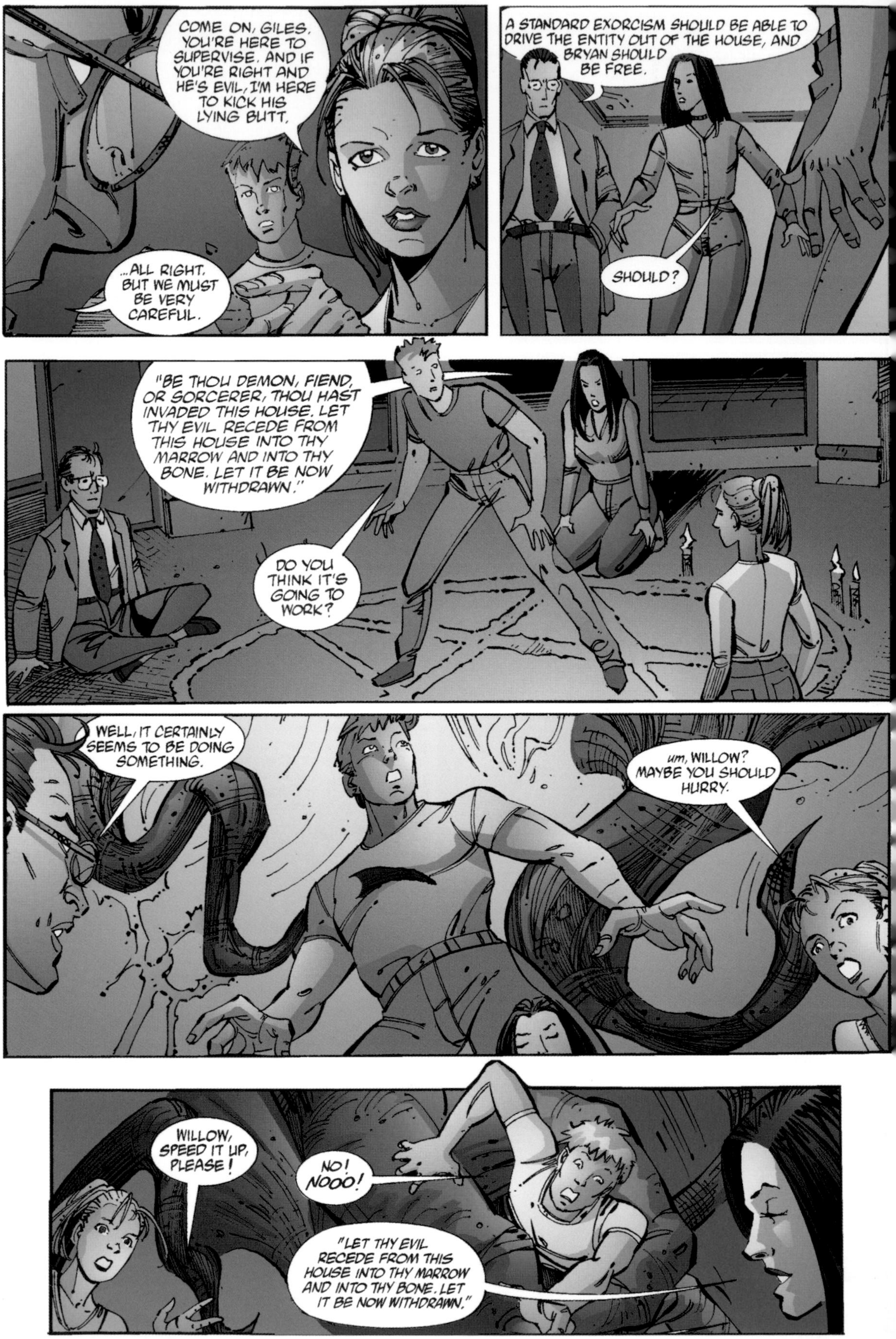
COME ON, GILES. YOU'RE HERE TO SUPERVISE. AND IF YOU'RE RIGHT AND HE'S EVIL, I'M HERE TO KICK HIS LYING BUTT.
...ALL RIGHT. BUT WE MUST BE VERY CAREFUL.
A STANDARD EXORCISM SHOULD BE ABLE TO DRIVE THE ENTITY OUT OF THE HOUSE, AND BRYAN SHOULD BE FREE.
SHOULD?
"BE THOU DEMON, FIEND, OR SORCERER, THOU HAST INVADED THIS HOUSE. LET THY EVIL RECEDE FROM THIS HOUSE INTO THY MARROW AND INTO THY BONE. LET IT BE NOW WITHDRAWN."
DO YOU THINK IT'S GOING TO WORK?
WELL, IT CERTAINLY SEEMS TO BE DOING SOMETHING.
um, WILLOW? MAYBE YOU SHOULD HURRY.
WILLOW, SPEED IT UP, PLEASE!
NO! NOOO!
"LET THY EVIL RECEDE FROM THIS HOUSE INTO THY MARROW AND INTO THY BONE. LET IT BE NOW WITHDRAWN."

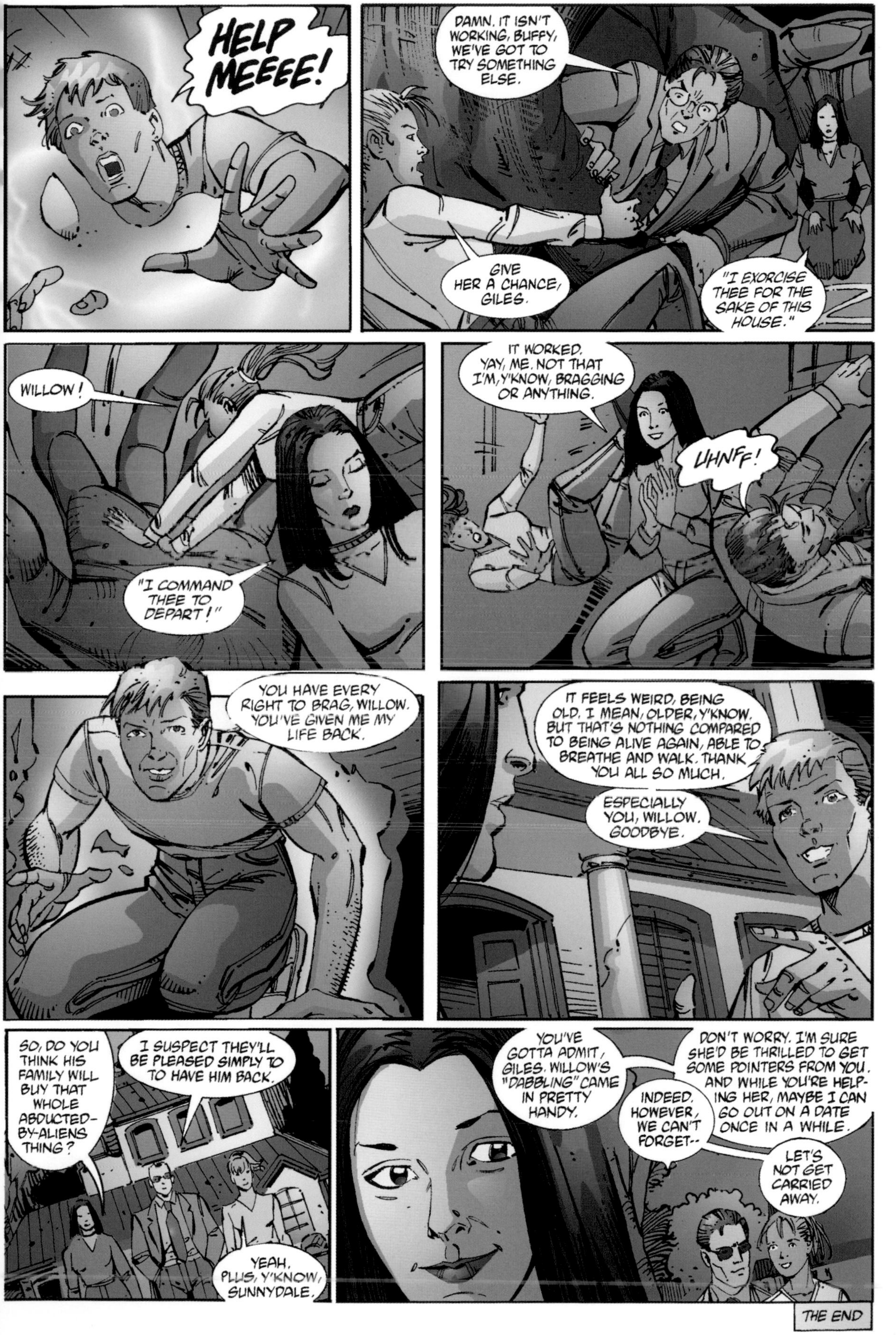
HELP MEEEE!
DAMN. IT ISN'T WORKING, BUFFY, WE'VE GOT TO TRY SOMETHING ELSE.
GIVE HER A CHANCE, GILES.
"I EXORCISE THEE FOR THE SAKE OF THIS HOUSE."
WILLOW!
"I COMMAND THEE TO DEPART!"
IT WORKED. YAY, ME. NOT THAT I'M, Y'KNOW, BRAGGING OR ANYTHING.
UHNFF!
YOU HAVE EVERY RIGHT TO BRAG, WILLOW. YOU'VE GIVEN ME MY LIFE BACK.
IT FEELS WEIRD, BEING OLD. I MEAN, OLDER, Y'KNOW. BUT THAT'S NOTHING COMPARED TO BEING ALIVE AGAIN, ABLE TO BREATHE AND WALK. THANK YOU ALL SO MUCH.
ESPECIALLY YOU, WILLOW. GOODBYE.
SO, DO YOU THINK HIS FAMILY WILL BUY THAT WHOLE ABDUCTED-BY-ALIENS THING?
I SUSPECT THEY'LL BE PLEASED SIMPLY TO TO HAVE HIM BACK.
YEAH, PLUS, Y'KNOW, SUNNYDALE.
YOU'VE GOTTA ADMIT, GILES. WILLOW'S "DABBLING" CAME IN PRETTY HANDY.
INDEED. HOWEVER, WE CAN'T FORGET--
DON'T WORRY. I'M SURE SHE'D BE THRILLED TO GET SOME POINTERS FROM YOU. AND WHILE YOU'RE HELPING HER, MAYBE I CAN GO OUT ON A DATE ONCE IN A WHILE.
LET'S NOT GET CARRIED AWAY.
THE END

BUFFY THE VAMPIRE SLAYER
CHAPTER TWELVE

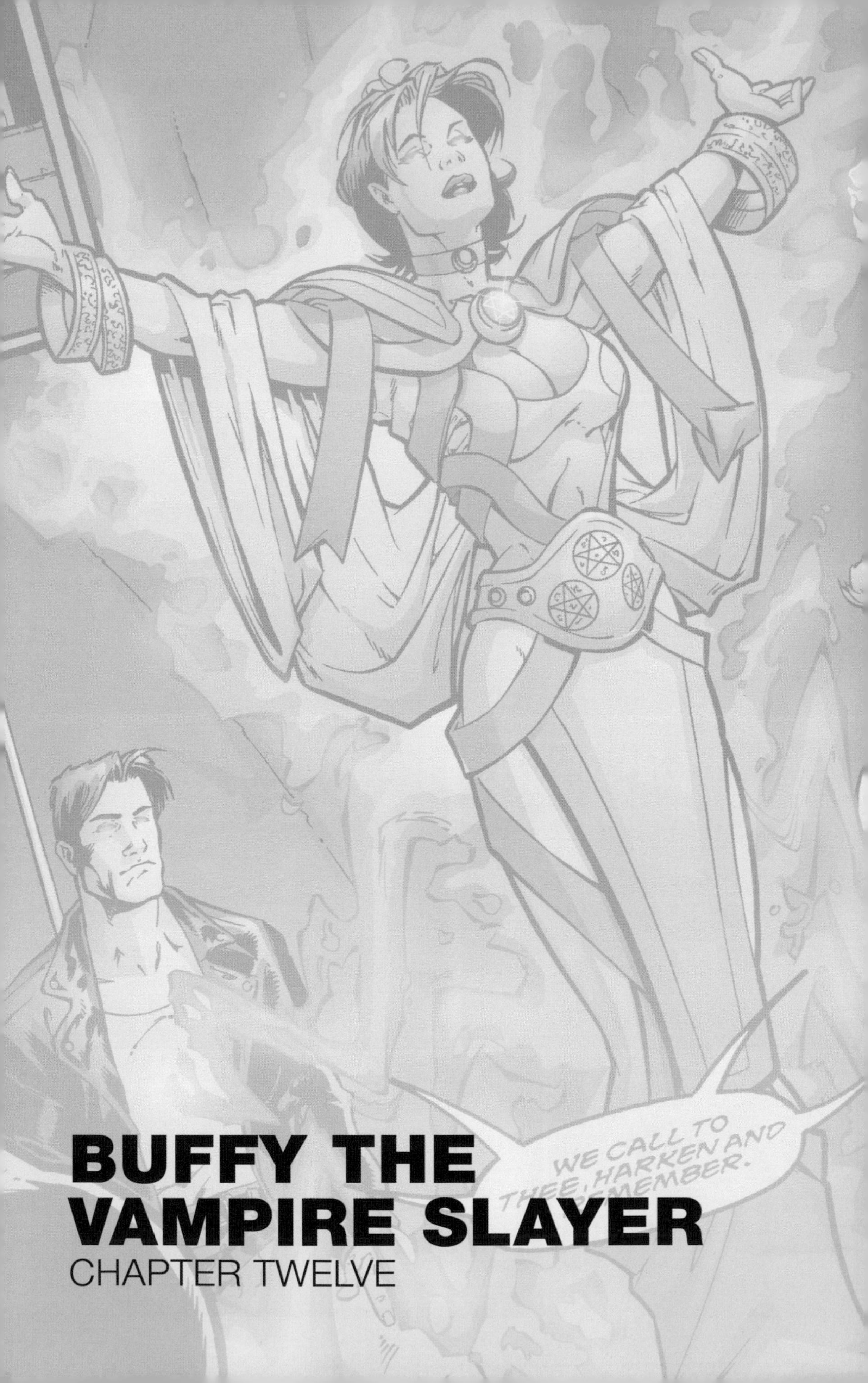
WE CALL TO THEE, HARKEN AND

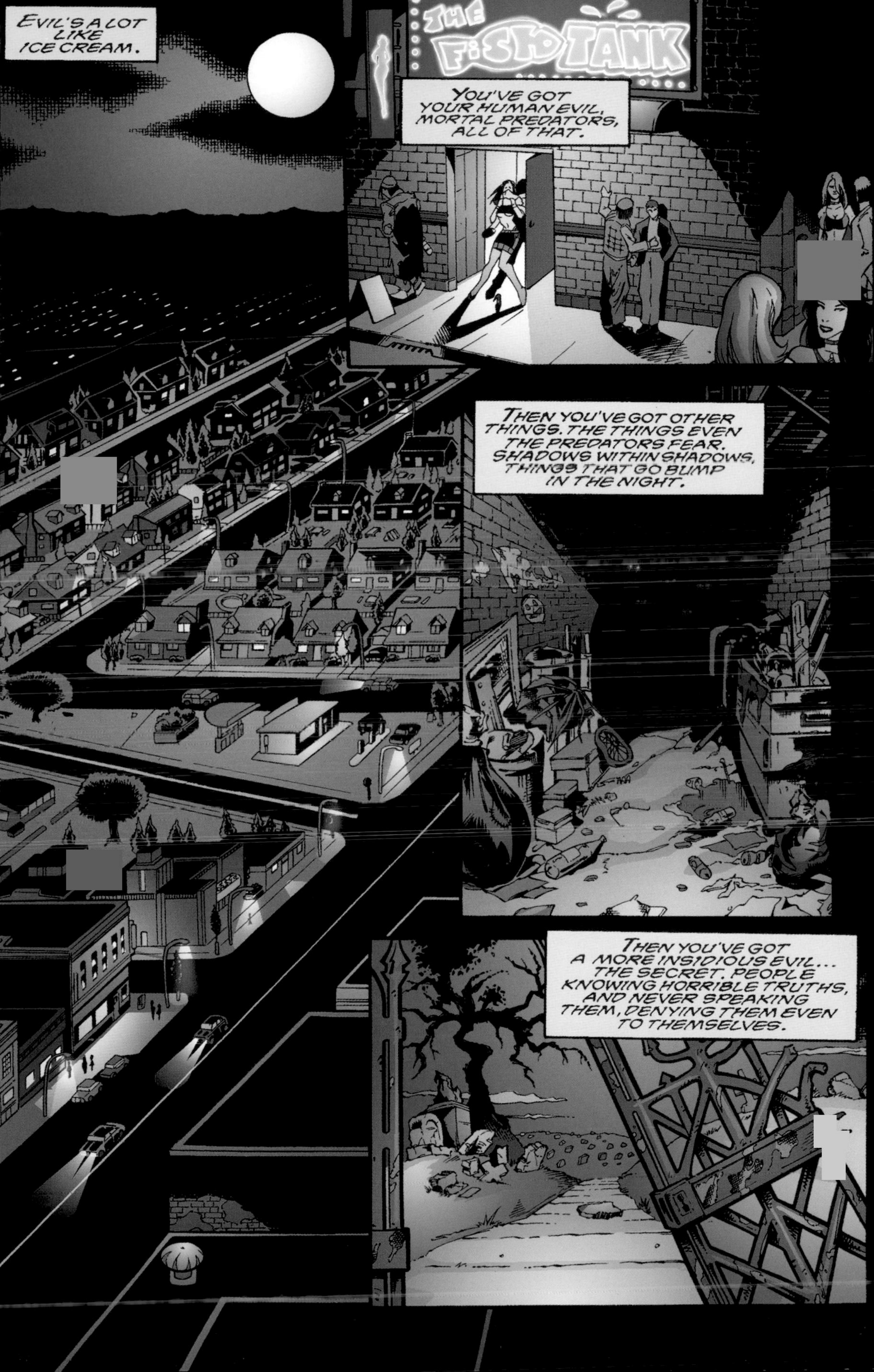
EVIL'S A LOT LIKE ICE CREAM.
THE FISH TANK
YOU'VE GOT YOUR HUMAN EVIL, MORTAL PREDATORS, ALL OF THAT.
THEN YOU'VE GOT OTHER THINGS. THE THINGS EVEN THE PREDATORS FEAR. SHADOWS WITHIN SHADOWS, THINGS THAT GO BUMP IN THE NIGHT.
THEN YOU'VE GOT A MORE INSIDIOUS EVIL... THE SECRET. PEOPLE KNOWING HORRIBLE TRUTHS, AND NEVER SPEAKING THEM, DENYING THEM EVEN TO THEMSELVES.

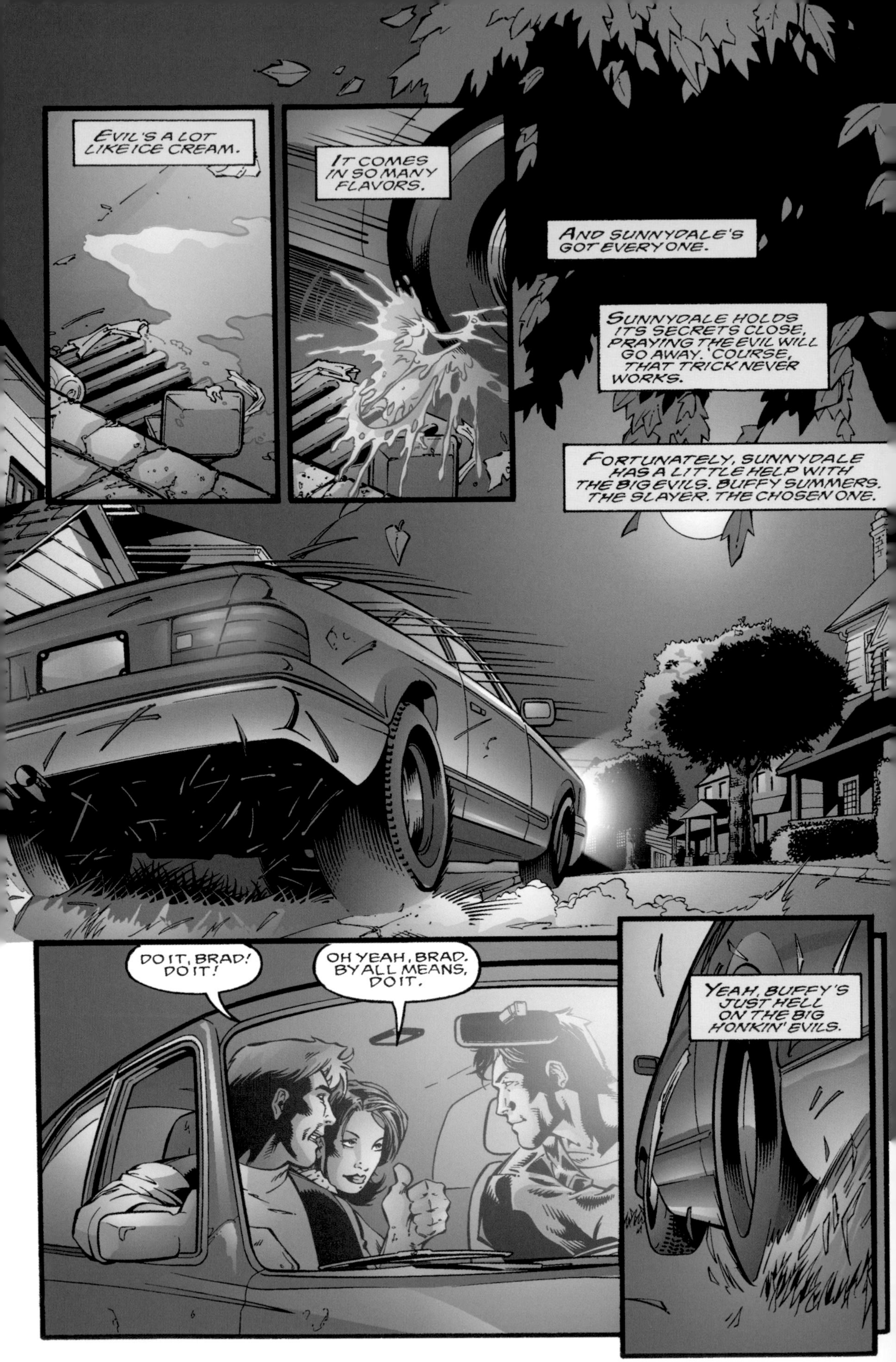
EVIL'S A LOT LIKE ICE CREAM.
IT COMES IN SO MANY FLAVORS.
AND SUNNYDALE'S GOT EVERY ONE.
SUNNYDALE HOLDS ITS SECRETS CLOSE, PRAYING THE EVIL WILL GO AWAY. 'COURSE, THAT TRICK NEVER WORKS.
FORTUNATELY, SUNNYDALE HAS A LITTLE HELP WITH THE BIG EVILS. BUFFY SUMMERS. THE SLAYER. THE CHOSEN ONE.
DO IT, BRAD! DO IT!
OH YEAH, BRAD. BY ALL MEANS, DO IT.
YEAH. BUFFY'S JUST HELL ON THE BIG HONKIN' EVILS.

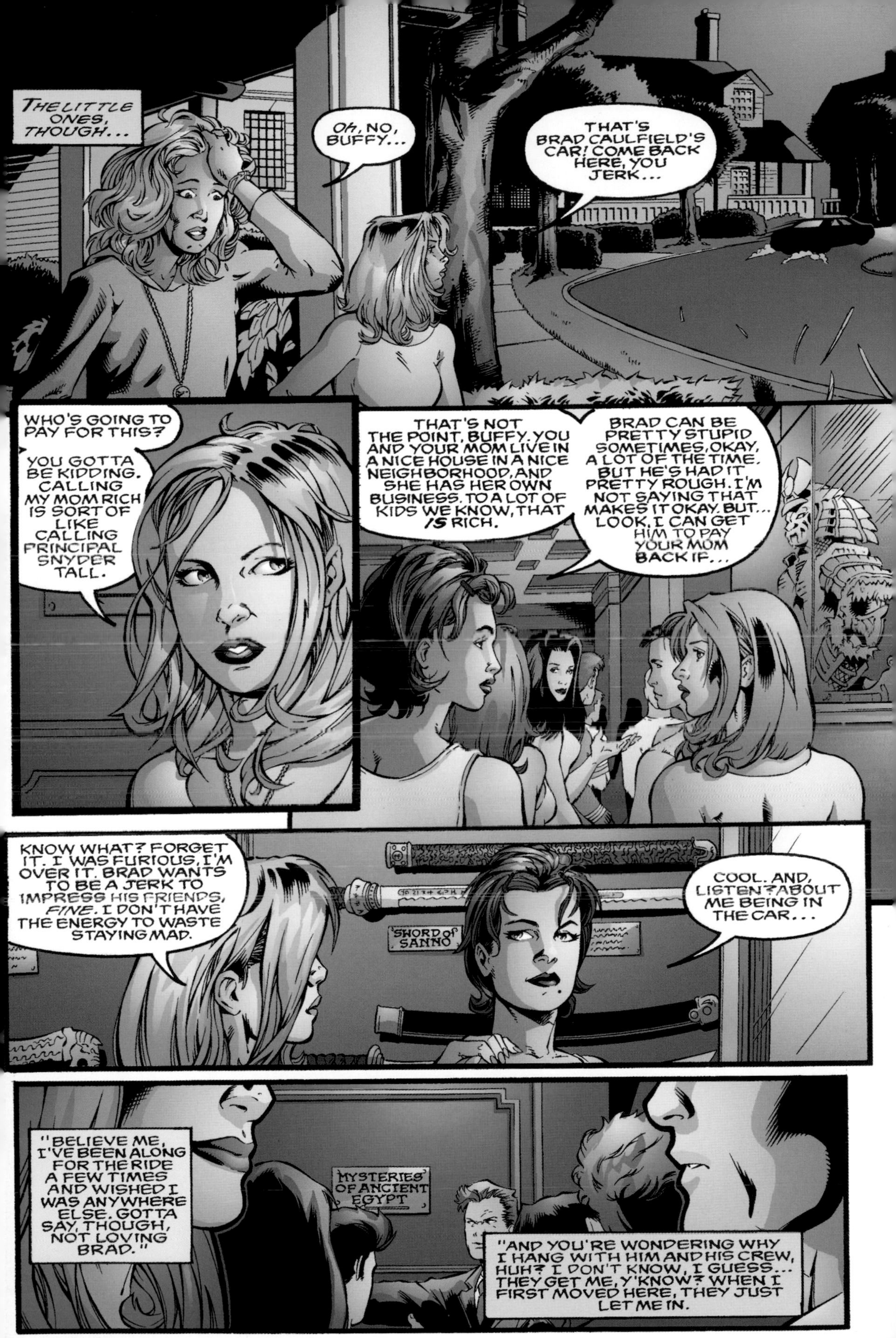
THE LITTLE ONES, THOUGH...
OH, NO, BUFFY...
THAT'S BRAD CAULFIELD'S CAR! COME BACK HERE, YOU JERK...
WHO'S GOING TO PAY FOR THIS?
YOU GOTTA BE KIDDING. CALLING MY MOM RICH IS SORT OF LIKE CALLING PRINCIPAL SNYDER TALL.
THAT'S NOT THE POINT, BUFFY. YOU AND YOUR MOM LIVE IN A NICE HOUSE IN A NICE NEIGHBORHOOD, AND SHE HAS HER OWN BUSINESS. TO A LOT OF KIDS WE KNOW, THAT *IS* RICH.
BRAD CAN BE PRETTY STUPID SOMETIMES, OKAY, A LOT OF THE TIME. BUT HE'S HAD IT PRETTY ROUGH. I'M NOT SAYING THAT MAKES IT OKAY. BUT... LOOK, I CAN GET HIM TO PAY YOUR MOM BACK IF...
KNOW WHAT? FORGET IT. I WAS FURIOUS, I'M OVER IT. BRAD WANTS TO BE A JERK TO IMPRESS HIS FRIENDS, *FINE*. I DON'T HAVE THE ENERGY TO WASTE STAYING MAD.
SWORD OF SANNO
COOL. AND, LISTEN? ABOUT ME BEING IN THE CAR...
"BELIEVE ME, I'VE BEEN ALONG FOR THE RIDE A FEW TIMES AND WISHED I WAS ANYWHERE ELSE. GOTTA SAY, THOUGH, NOT LOVING BRAD."
MYSTERIES OF ANCIENT EGYPT
"AND YOU'RE WONDERING WHY I HANG WITH HIM AND HIS CREW, HUH? I DON'T KNOW, I GUESS... THEY GET ME, Y'KNOW? WHEN I FIRST MOVED HERE, THEY JUST LET ME IN.

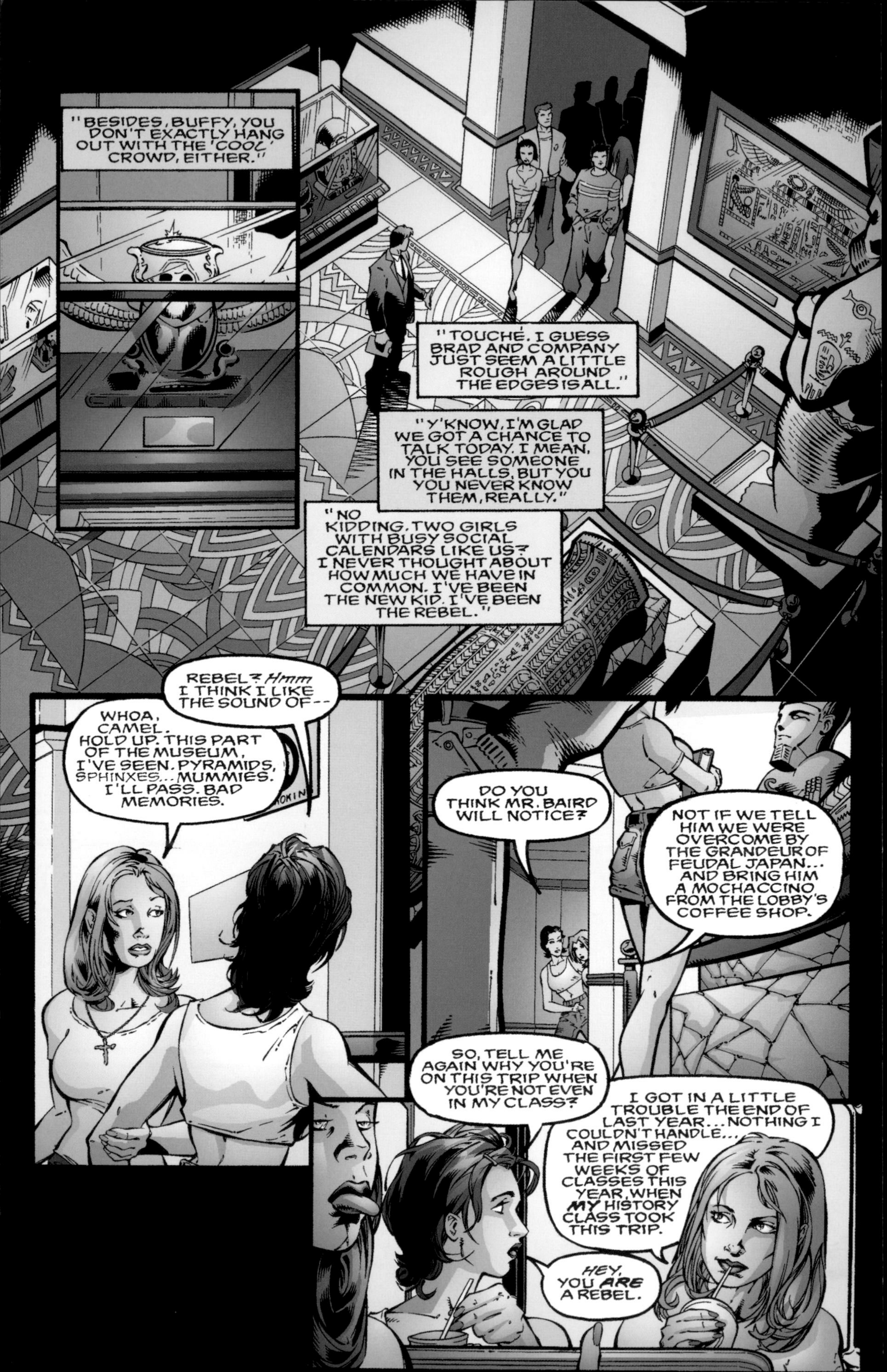
"BESIDES, BUFFY, YOU DON'T EXACTLY HANG OUT WITH THE 'COOL' CROWD, EITHER."
"TOUCHÉ. I GUESS BRAD AND COMPANY JUST SEEM A LITTLE ROUGH AROUND THE EDGES IS ALL."
"Y'KNOW, I'M GLAD WE GOT A CHANCE TO TALK TODAY. I MEAN, YOU SEE SOMEONE IN THE HALLS, BUT YOU YOU NEVER KNOW THEM, REALLY."
"NO KIDDING. TWO GIRLS WITH BUSY SOCIAL CALENDARS LIKE US? I NEVER THOUGHT ABOUT HOW MUCH WE HAVE IN COMMON. I'VE BEEN THE NEW KID. I'VE BEEN THE REBEL."
REBEL? *Hmm* I THINK I LIKE THE SOUND OF--
WHOA, CAMEL. HOLD UP. THIS PART OF THE MUSEUM, I'VE SEEN. PYRAMIDS, SPHINXES... MUMMIES. I'LL PASS. BAD MEMORIES.
DO YOU THINK MR. BAIRD WILL NOTICE?
NOT IF WE TELL HIM WE WERE OVERCOME BY THE GRANDEUR OF FEUDAL JAPAN... AND BRING HIM A MOCHACCINO FROM THE LOBBY'S COFFEE SHOP.
SO, TELL ME AGAIN WHY YOU'RE ON THIS TRIP WHEN YOU'RE NOT EVEN IN MY CLASS?
I GOT IN A LITTLE TROUBLE THE END OF LAST YEAR... NOTHING I COULDN'T HANDLE... AND MISSED THE FIRST FEW WEEKS OF CLASSES THIS YEAR, WHEN ***MY*** HISTORY CLASS TOOK THIS TRIP.
*HEY, YOU **ARE** A REBEL.*

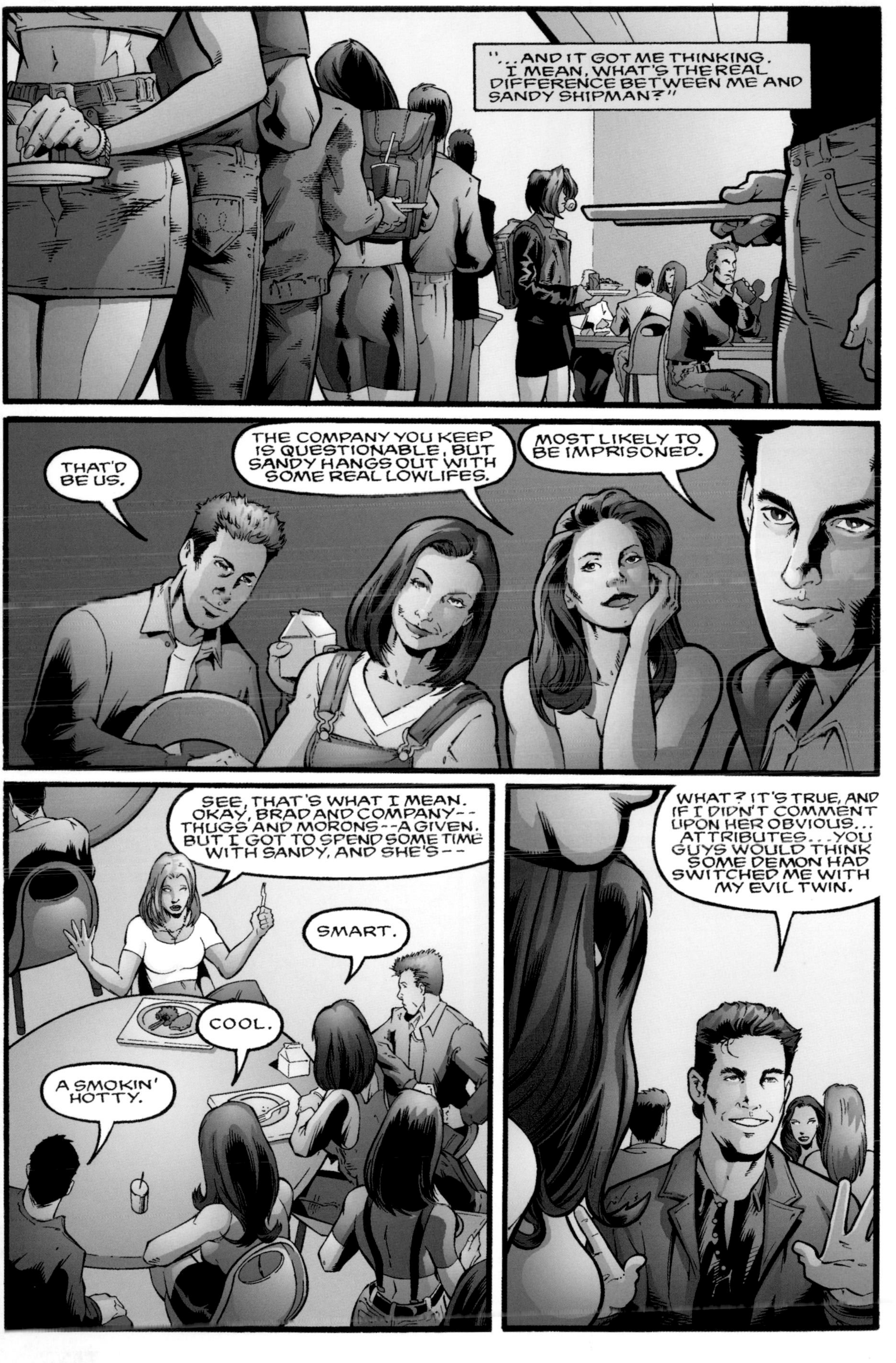
"...AND IT GOT ME THINKING. I MEAN, WHAT'S THE REAL DIFFERENCE BETWEEN ME AND SANDY SHIPMAN?"
THAT'D BE US.
THE COMPANY YOU KEEP IS QUESTIONABLE, BUT SANDY HANGS OUT WITH SOME REAL LOWLIFES.
MOST LIKELY TO BE IMPRISONED.
SEE, THAT'S WHAT I MEAN. OKAY, BRAD AND COMPANY-- THUGS AND MORONS--A GIVEN. BUT I GOT TO SPEND SOME TIME WITH SANDY, AND SHE'S--
SMART.
COOL.
A SMOKIN' HOTTY.
WHAT? IT'S TRUE, AND IF I DIDN'T COMMENT UPON HER OBVIOUS... ATTRIBUTES... YOU GUYS WOULD THINK SOME DEMON HAD SWITCHED ME WITH MY EVIL TWIN.

SANDY'S REALLY NICE, BUFFY. NOTHING LIKE THOSE CAVEMEN SHE HANGS OUT WITH. BUT IT'S SORT OF WELL, CAVEGIRL BY ASSOCIATION, Y'KNOW?

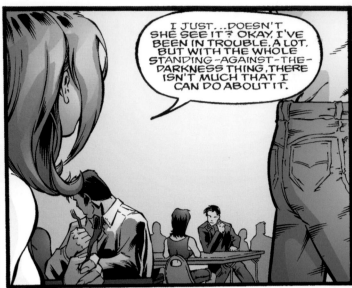

I JUST...DOESN'T SHE SEE IT? OKAY, I'VE BEEN IN TROUBLE, A LOT, BUT WITH THE WHOLE STANDING-AGAINST-THE-DARKNESS THING, THERE ISN'T MUCH THAT I CAN DO ABOUT IT.

SANDY'S BEEN HANGING WITH THOSE GUYS EVER SINCE SHE MOVED HERE. I CAN'T CHANGE MY LIFE, BUT *SHE* COULD CHANGE HERS.

"SHE'S GOT SO MUCH GOING FOR HER, DOESN'T SHE SEE THAT THEY'RE DRAGGING HER DOWN?"

WHICH I GUESS MEANS THAT, WITH YOUR BAD-GIRL REP AND ALL, HANGING OUT WITH US IS KINDA LIKE DRAGGING YOU *UP*, HUH?

Xander...

AND THEY SAY *I* HAVE NO TACT.

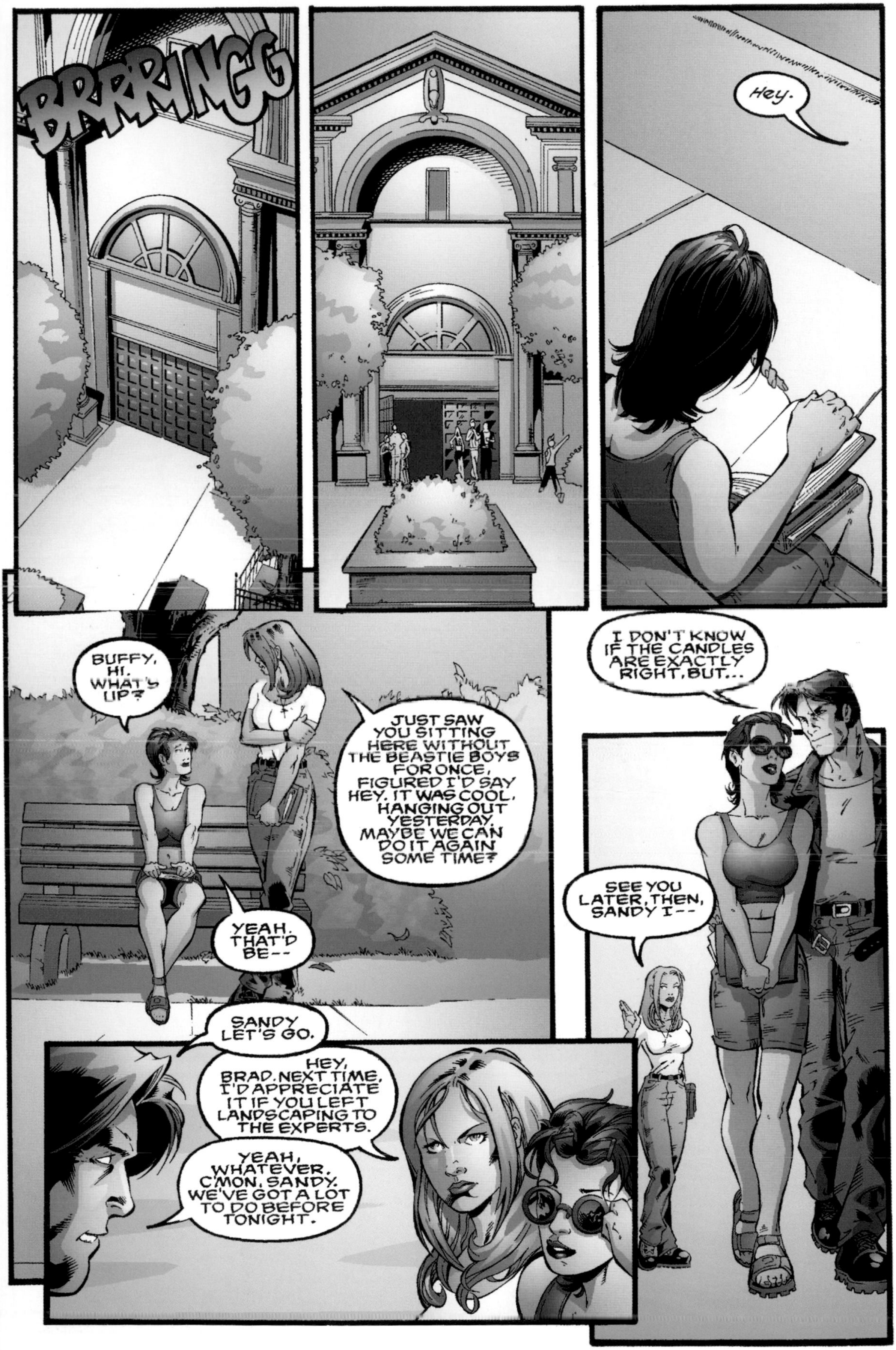
BRRRINGG
Hey.
BUFFY, HI. WHAT'S UP?
JUST SAW YOU SITTING HERE WITHOUT THE BEASTIE BOYS FOR ONCE, FIGURED I'D SAY HEY. IT WAS COOL, HANGING OUT YESTERDAY. MAYBE WE CAN DO IT AGAIN SOME TIME?
YEAH. THAT'D BE--
SANDY LET'S GO.
HEY, BRAD. NEXT TIME, I'D APPRECIATE IT IF YOU LEFT LANDSCAPING TO THE EXPERTS.
YEAH, WHATEVER. C'MON, SANDY. WE'VE GOT A LOT TO DO BEFORE TONIGHT.
I DON'T KNOW IF THE CANDLES ARE EXACTLY RIGHT, BUT...
SEE YOU LATER, THEN, SANDY I--

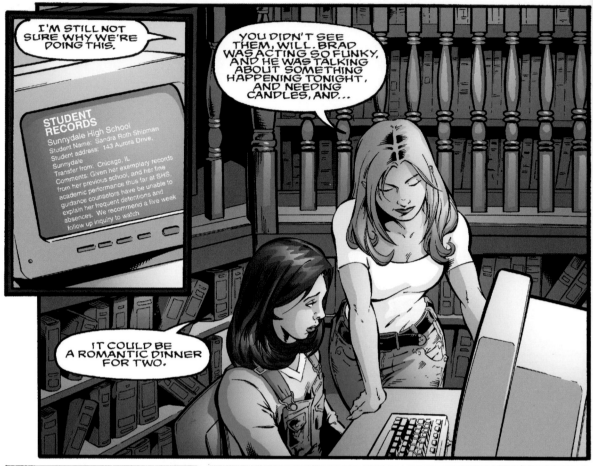

I'M STILL NOT SURE WHY WE'RE DOING THIS.

YOU DIDN'T SEE THEM, WILL. BRAD WAS ACTING SO FUNKY, AND HE WAS TALKING ABOUT SOMETHING HAPPENING TONIGHT, AND NEEDING CANDLES, AND...

STUDENT RECORDS
Sunnydale High School
Student Name: Sandra Roth Shipman
Student address: 143 Aurora Drive, Sunnydale
Transfer from: Chicago, IL
Comments: Given her exemplary records from her previous school, and her fine academic performance thus far at SHS, guidance counselors have been unable to explain her frequent detentions and absences. We recommend a five week follow up inquiry to watch

IT COULD BE A ROMANTIC DINNER FOR TWO.

YES, BUFFY. I REALLY MUST PROTEST. DON'T YOU THINK YOU'RE OVERREACTING A BIT?

I FIND THE IDEA THAT BRAD IS SOMEHOW USING THE BLACK ARTS TO FORCE SANDY TO BE WITH HIM A BIT FAR-FETCHED. THERE ISN'T A SINGLE SHRED OF EVIDENCE TO SUPPORT THE IDEA.

YOU SAID YOURSELF IT WAS KIND OF FREAKY THAT SOMEONE LIKE SANDY WOULD HANG WITH THOSE GUYS OF HER OWN FREE WILL.

I DON'T BELIEVE I USED THE WORD "FREAKY," BUT STILL, YOU HAVE NO EVIDENCE OF ANYTHING OUT OF THE ORDINARY AT WORK HERE.

STUDENT RECORDS
Sunnydale High School
Student Name: Sandra Roth Shipman
Student address: 143 Auror... Sunnydale
Transfer from: Chicago, IL
Comments: Given her exemp... from her previous school, and her fi... ...ce thus far at SHS, guidance ...be unable to explain her ...sences. We ...quiry to watch

I WILL. AFTER TONIGHT.

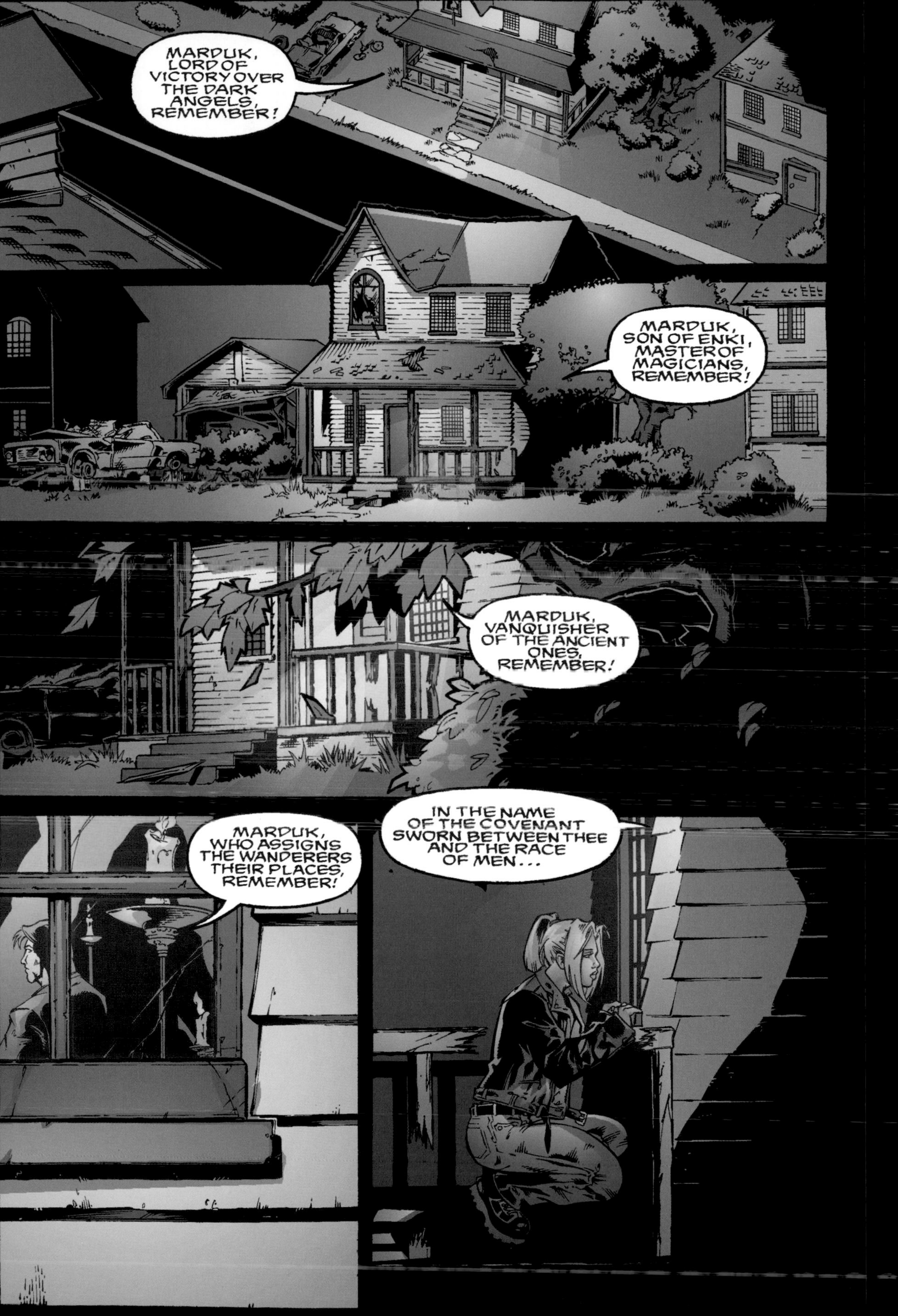
MARDUK, LORD OF VICTORY OVER THE DARK ANGELS, REMEMBER!
MARDUK, SON OF ENKI, MASTER OF MAGICIANS, REMEMBER!
MARDUK, VANQUISHER OF THE ANCIENT ONES, REMEMBER!
MARDUK, WHO ASSIGNS THE WANDERERS THEIR PLACES, REMEMBER!
IN THE NAME OF THE COVENANT SWORN BETWEEN THEE AND THE RACE OF MEN...

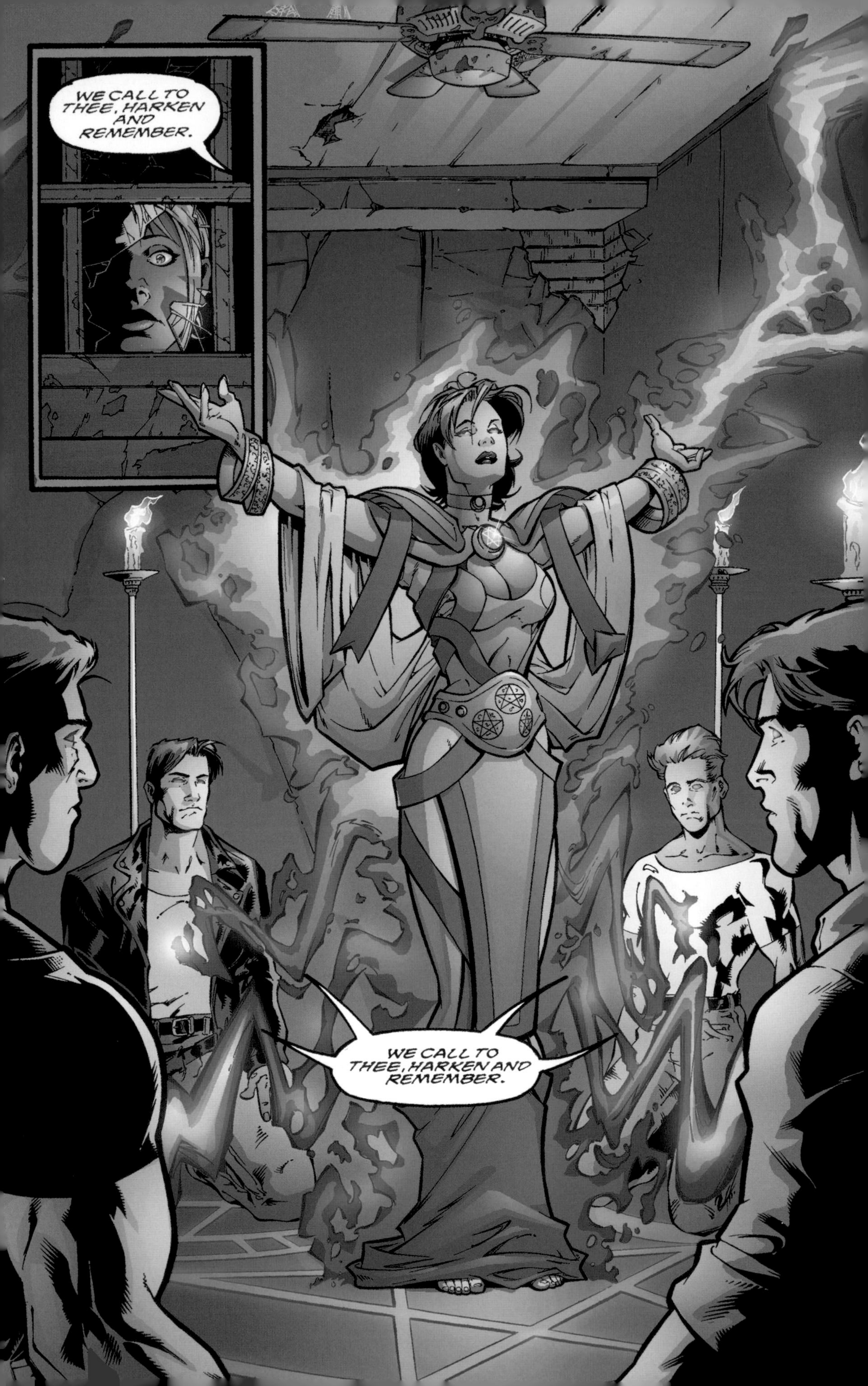
WE CALL TO THEE, HARKEN AND REMEMBER.
WE CALL TO THEE, HARKEN AND REMEMBER.

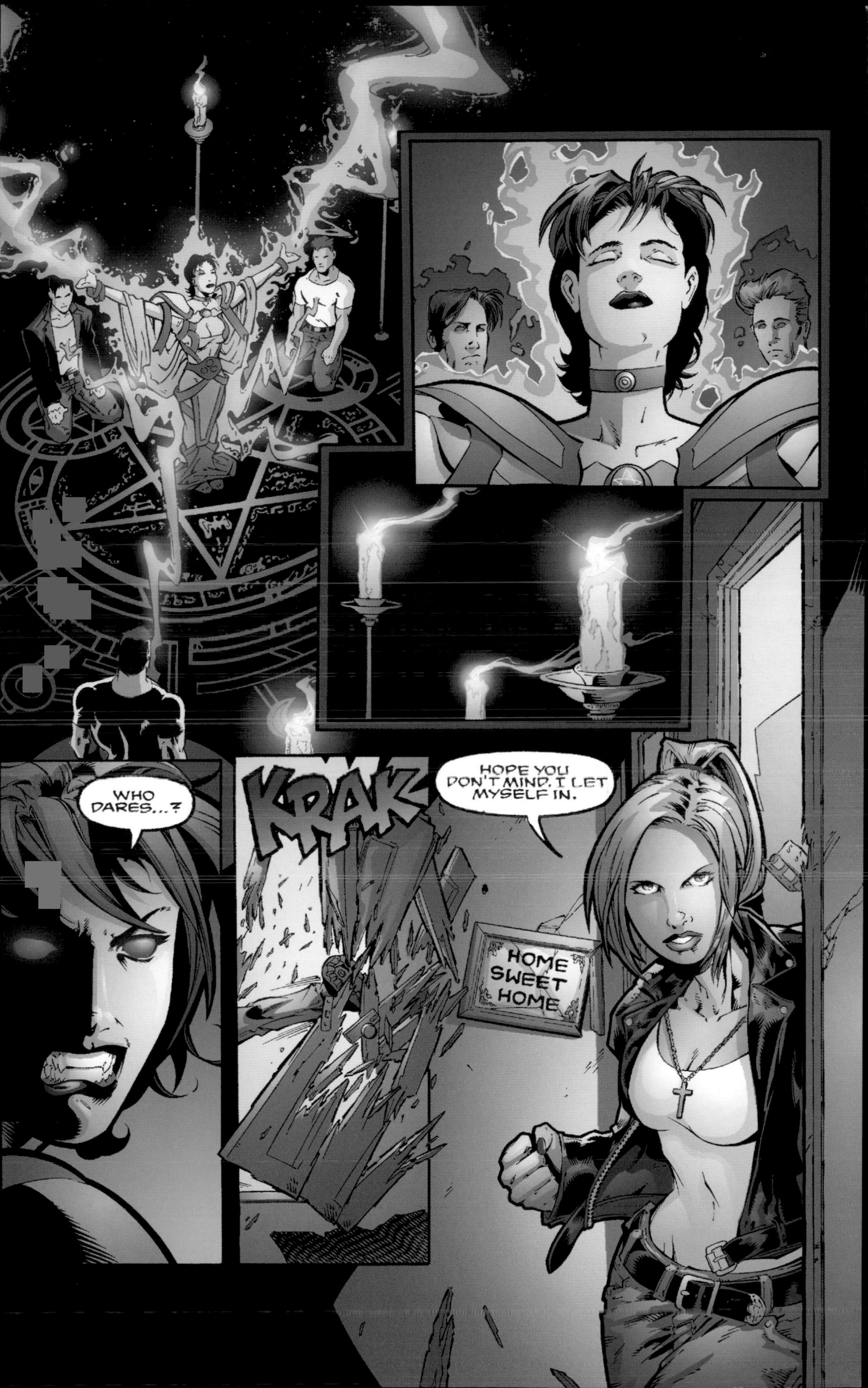
WHO DARES...?
KRAK
HOPE YOU DON'T MIND. I LET MYSELF IN.
HOME SWEET HOME

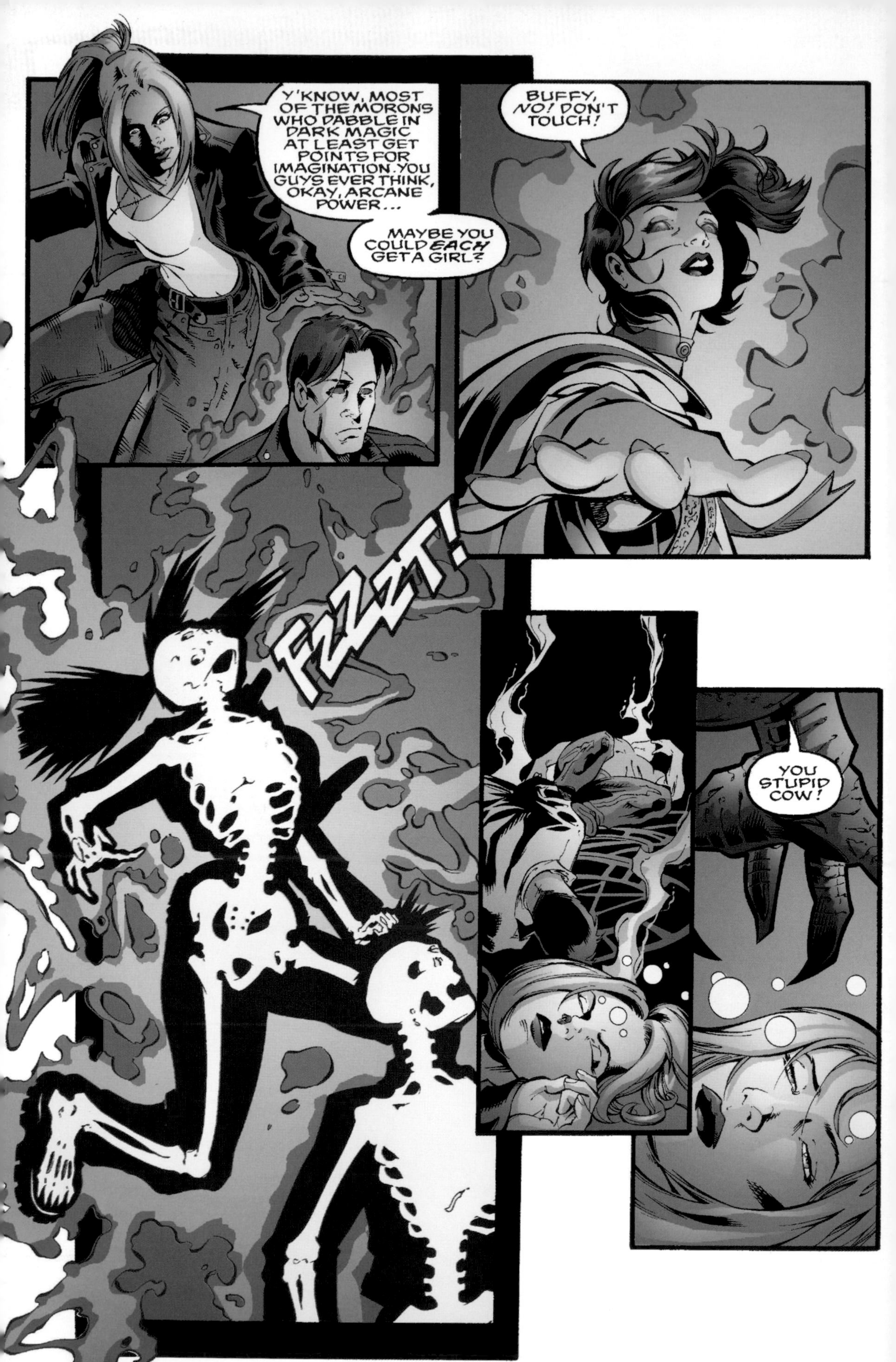

Y'KNOW, MOST OF THE MORONS WHO DABBLE IN DARK MAGIC AT LEAST GET POINTS FOR IMAGINATION. YOU GUYS EVER THINK, OKAY, ARCANE POWER...
MAYBE YOU COULD *EACH* GET A GIRL?
BUFFY, *NO!* DON'T TOUCH!
FZZZT!
YOU STUPID COW!

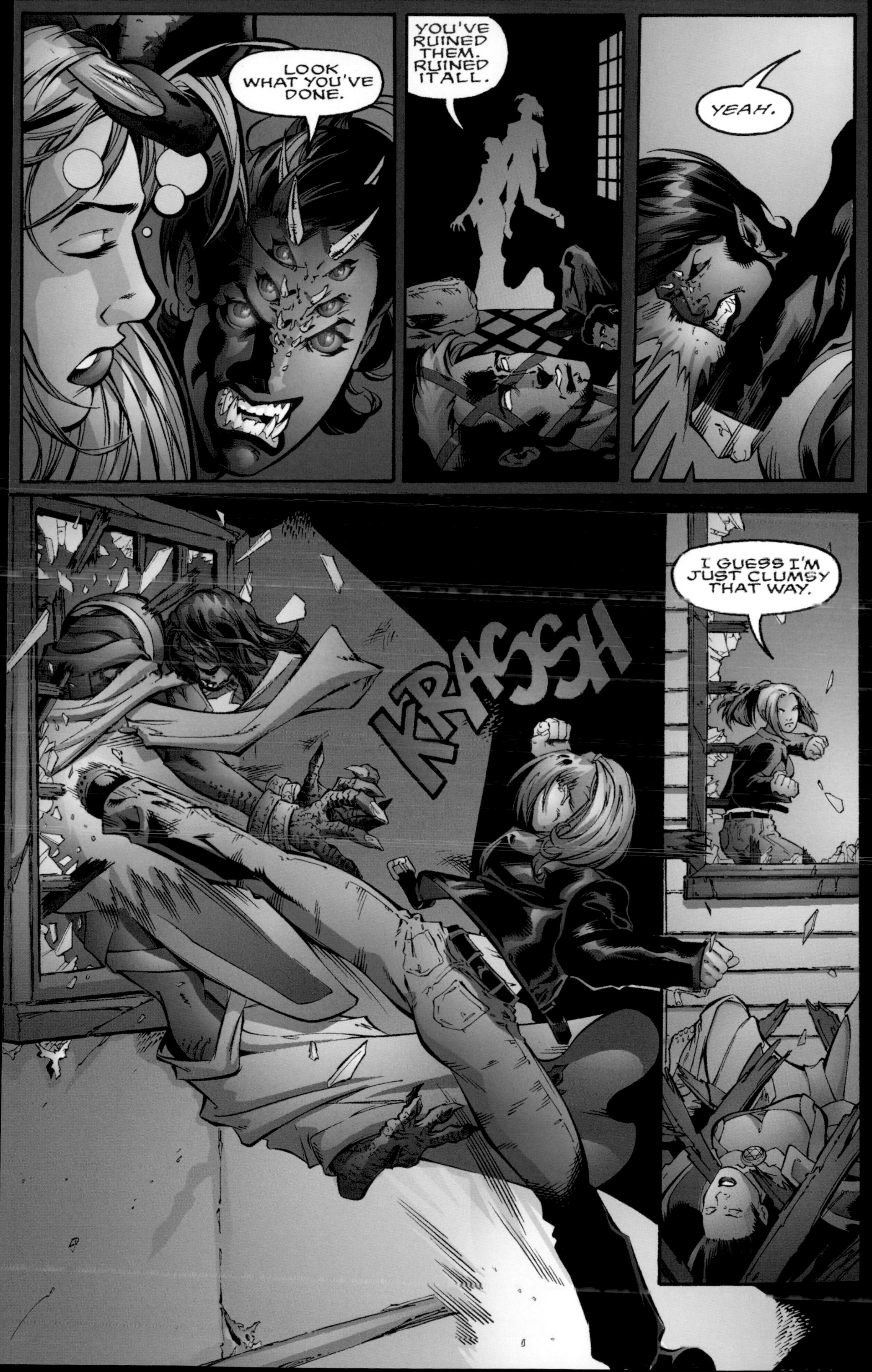
LOOK WHAT YOU'VE DONE.
YOU'VE RUINED THEM. RUINED IT ALL.
YEAH.
KRASSH
I GUESS I'M JUST CLUMSY THAT WAY.

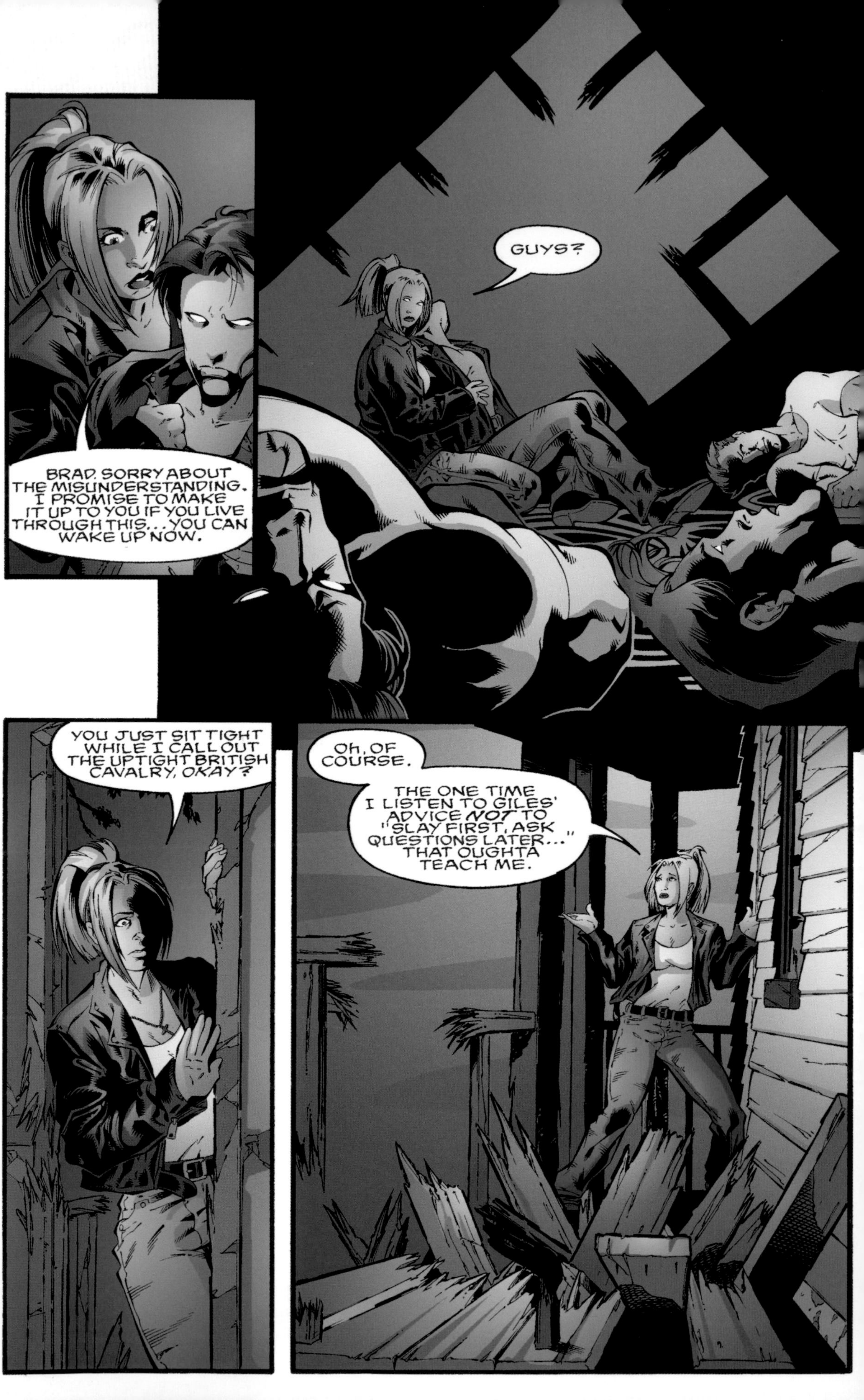
GUYS?
BRAD. SORRY ABOUT THE MISUNDERSTANDING. I PROMISE TO MAKE IT UP TO YOU IF YOU LIVE THROUGH THIS... YOU CAN WAKE UP NOW.
YOU JUST SIT TIGHT WHILE I CALL OUT THE UPTIGHT BRITISH CAVALRY, OKAY?
OH, OF COURSE.
THE ONE TIME I LISTEN TO GILES' ADVICE NOT TO "SLAY FIRST, ASK QUESTIONS LATER..." THAT OUGHTA TEACH ME.

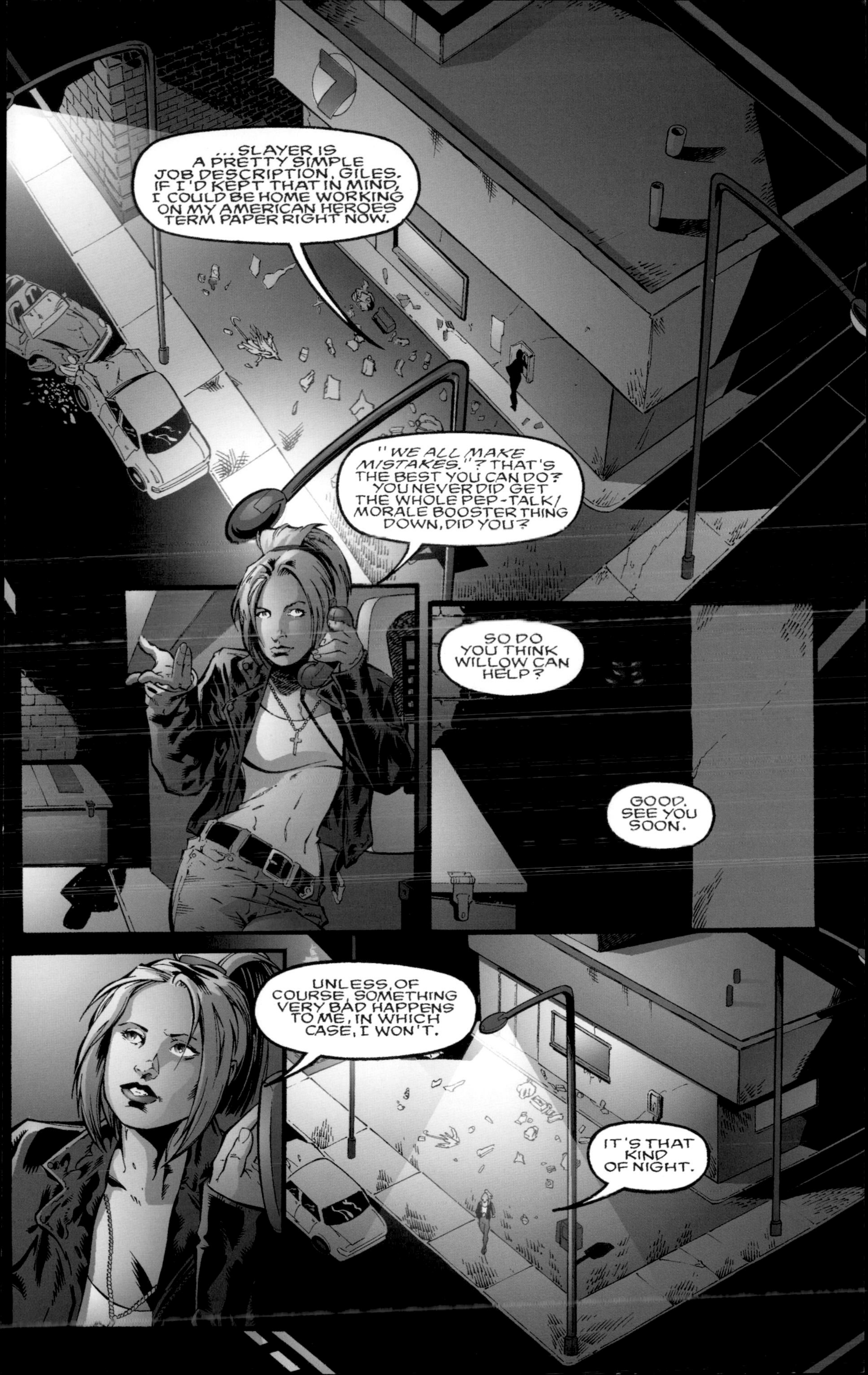
...SLAYER IS A PRETTY SIMPLE JOB DESCRIPTION, GILES. IF I'D KEPT THAT IN MIND, I COULD BE HOME WORKING ON MY AMERICAN HEROES TERM PAPER RIGHT NOW.
"WE ALL MAKE MISTAKES."? THAT'S THE BEST YOU CAN DO? YOU NEVER DID GET THE WHOLE PEP-TALK/ MORALE BOOSTER THING DOWN, DID YOU?
SO DO YOU THINK WILLOW CAN HELP?
GOOD. SEE YOU SOON.
UNLESS, OF COURSE, SOMETHING VERY BAD HAPPENS TO ME, IN WHICH CASE, I WON'T.
IT'S THAT KIND OF NIGHT.

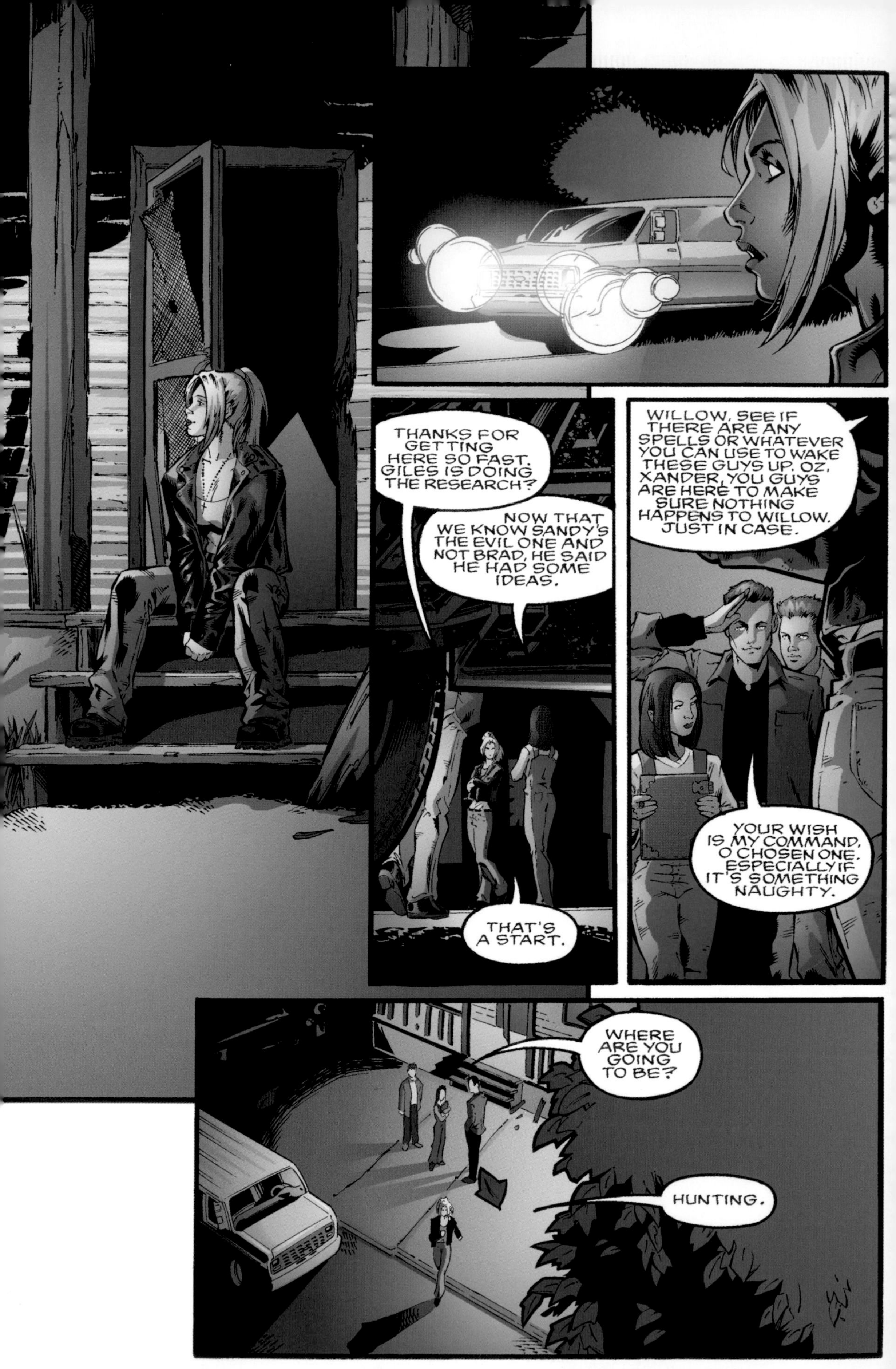
THANKS FOR GETTING HERE SO FAST. GILES IS DOING THE RESEARCH?
NOW THAT WE KNOW SANDY'S THE EVIL ONE AND NOT BRAD, HE SAID HE HAD SOME IDEAS.
THAT'S A START.
WILLOW, SEE IF THERE ARE ANY SPELLS OR WHATEVER YOU CAN USE TO WAKE THESE GUYS UP. OZ, XANDER, YOU GUYS ARE HERE TO MAKE SURE NOTHING HAPPENS TO WILLOW. JUST IN CASE.
YOUR WISH IS MY COMMAND, O CHOSEN ONE. ESPECIALLY IF IT'S SOMETHING NAUGHTY.
WHERE ARE YOU GOING TO BE?
HUNTING.

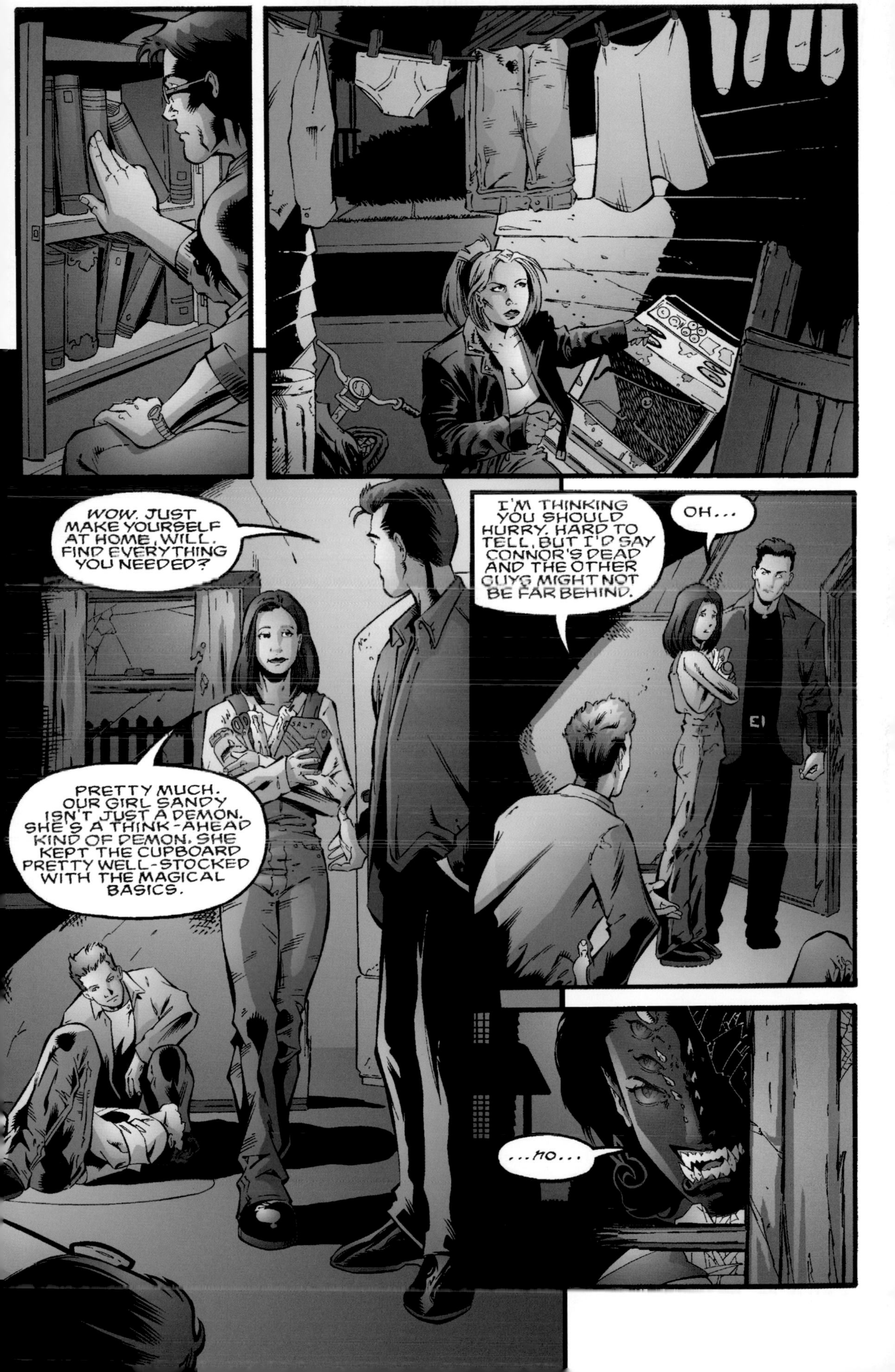
WOW. JUST MAKE YOURSELF AT HOME, WILL. FIND EVERYTHING YOU NEEDED?
PRETTY MUCH. OUR GIRL SANDY ISN'T JUST A DEMON. SHE'S A THINK-AHEAD KIND OF DEMON. SHE KEPT THE CUPBOARD PRETTY WELL-STOCKED WITH THE MAGICAL BASICS.
I'M THINKING YOU SHOULD HURRY. HARD TO TELL, BUT I'D SAY CONNOR'S DEAD AND THE OTHER GUYS MIGHT NOT BE FAR BEHIND.
OH...
SALT
...NO...

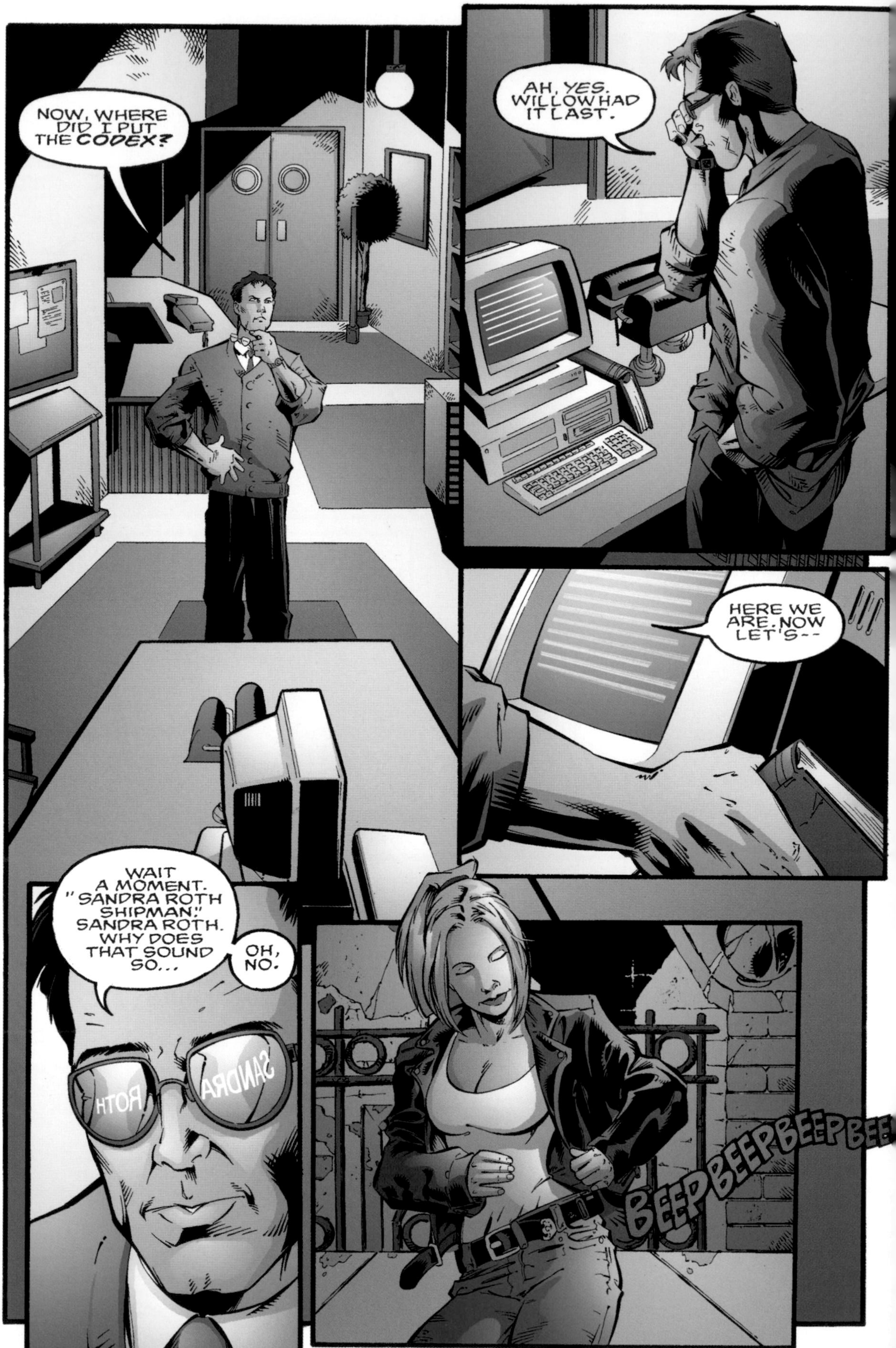

NOW, WHERE DID I PUT THE CODEX?
AH, YES. WILLOW HAD IT LAST.
HERE WE ARE. NOW LET'S--
WAIT A MOMENT. "SANDRA ROTH SHIPMAN." SANDRA ROTH. WHY DOES THAT SOUND SO...
OH, NO.
SANDRA ROTH
BEEPBEEPBEEPBEE

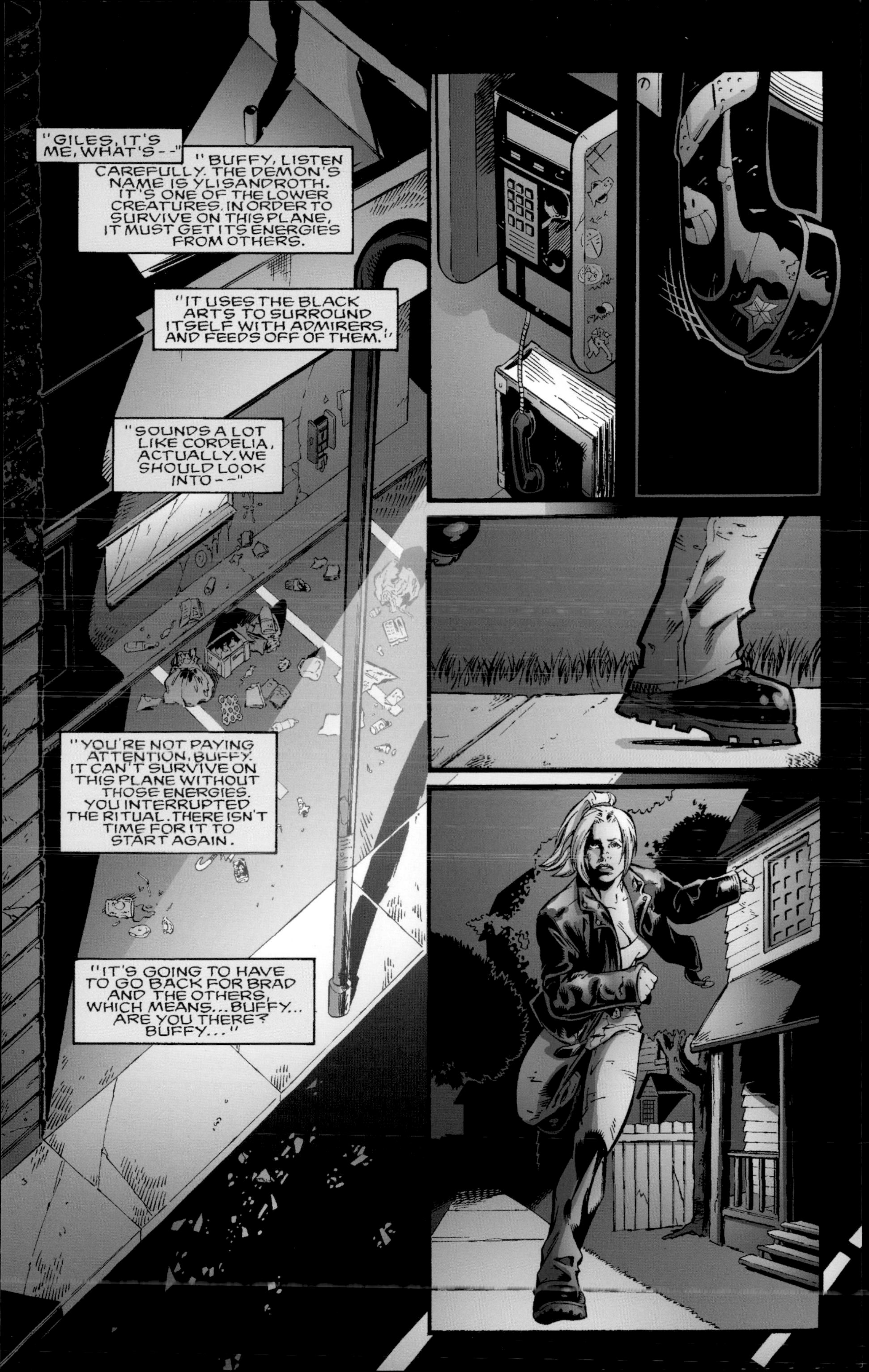
"GILES, IT'S ME, WHAT'S--"
"BUFFY, LISTEN CAREFULLY. THE DEMON'S NAME IS YLISANDROTH. IT'S ONE OF THE LOWER CREATURES. IN ORDER TO SURVIVE ON THIS PLANE, IT MUST GET ITS ENERGIES FROM OTHERS.
"IT USES THE BLACK ARTS TO SURROUND ITSELF WITH ADMIRERS, AND FEEDS OFF OF THEM."
"SOUNDS A LOT LIKE CORDELIA, ACTUALLY. WE SHOULD LOOK INTO--"
"YOU'RE NOT PAYING ATTENTION, BUFFY. IT CAN'T SURVIVE ON THIS PLANE WITHOUT THOSE ENERGIES. YOU INTERRUPTED THE RITUAL. THERE ISN'T TIME FOR IT TO START AGAIN.
"IT'S GOING TO HAVE TO GO BACK FOR BRAD AND THE OTHERS, WHICH MEANS... BUFFY... ARE YOU THERE? BUFFY..."

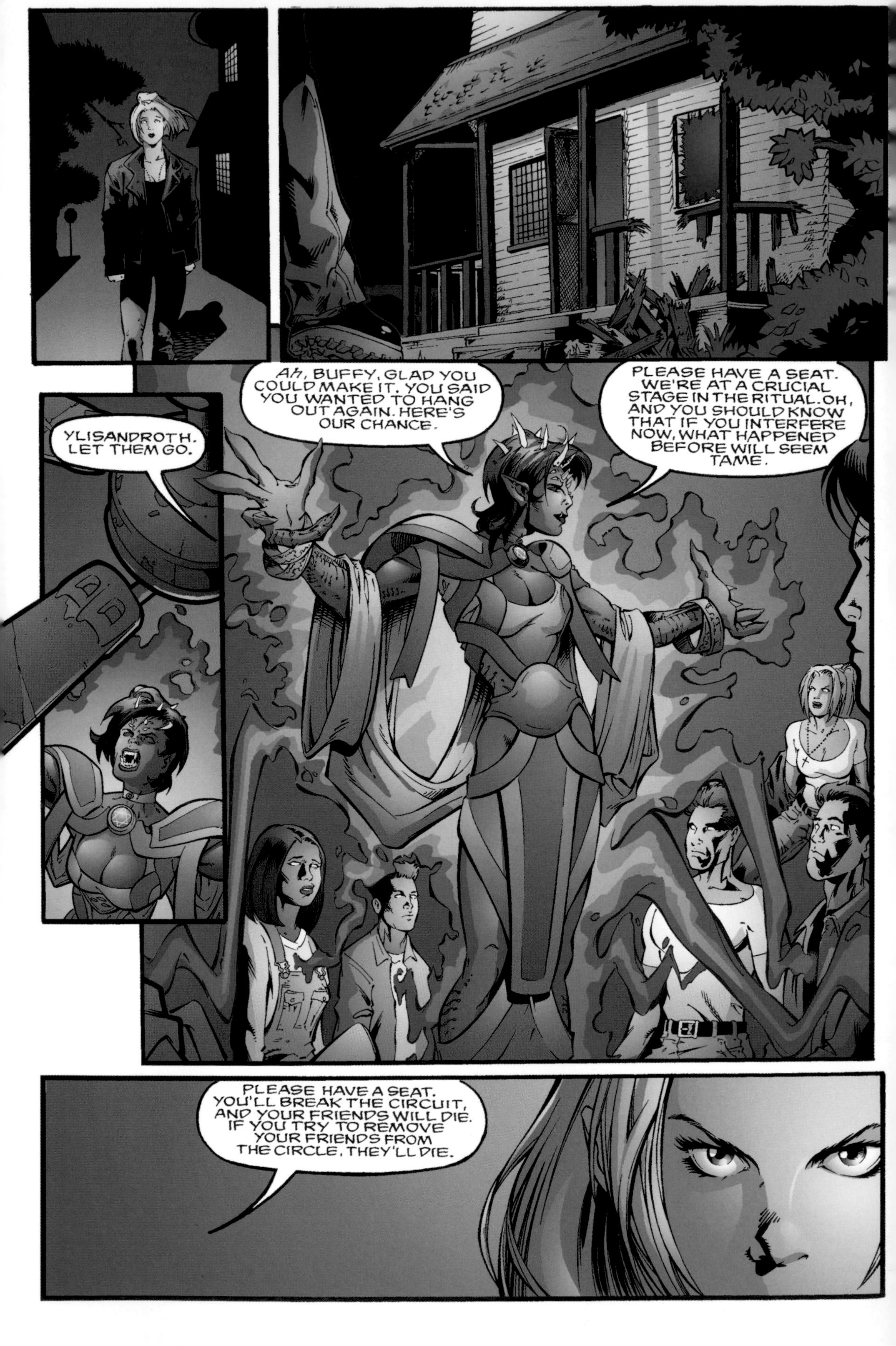
YLISANDROTH. LET THEM GO.
Ah, BUFFY, GLAD YOU COULD MAKE IT. YOU SAID YOU WANTED TO HANG OUT AGAIN. HERE'S OUR CHANCE.
PLEASE HAVE A SEAT. WE'RE AT A CRUCIAL STAGE IN THE RITUAL. OH, AND YOU SHOULD KNOW THAT IF YOU INTERFERE NOW, WHAT HAPPENED BEFORE WILL SEEM TAME.
PLEASE HAVE A SEAT. YOU'LL BREAK THE CIRCUIT, AND YOUR FRIENDS WILL DIE. IF YOU TRY TO REMOVE YOUR FRIENDS FROM THE CIRCLE, THEY'LL DIE.

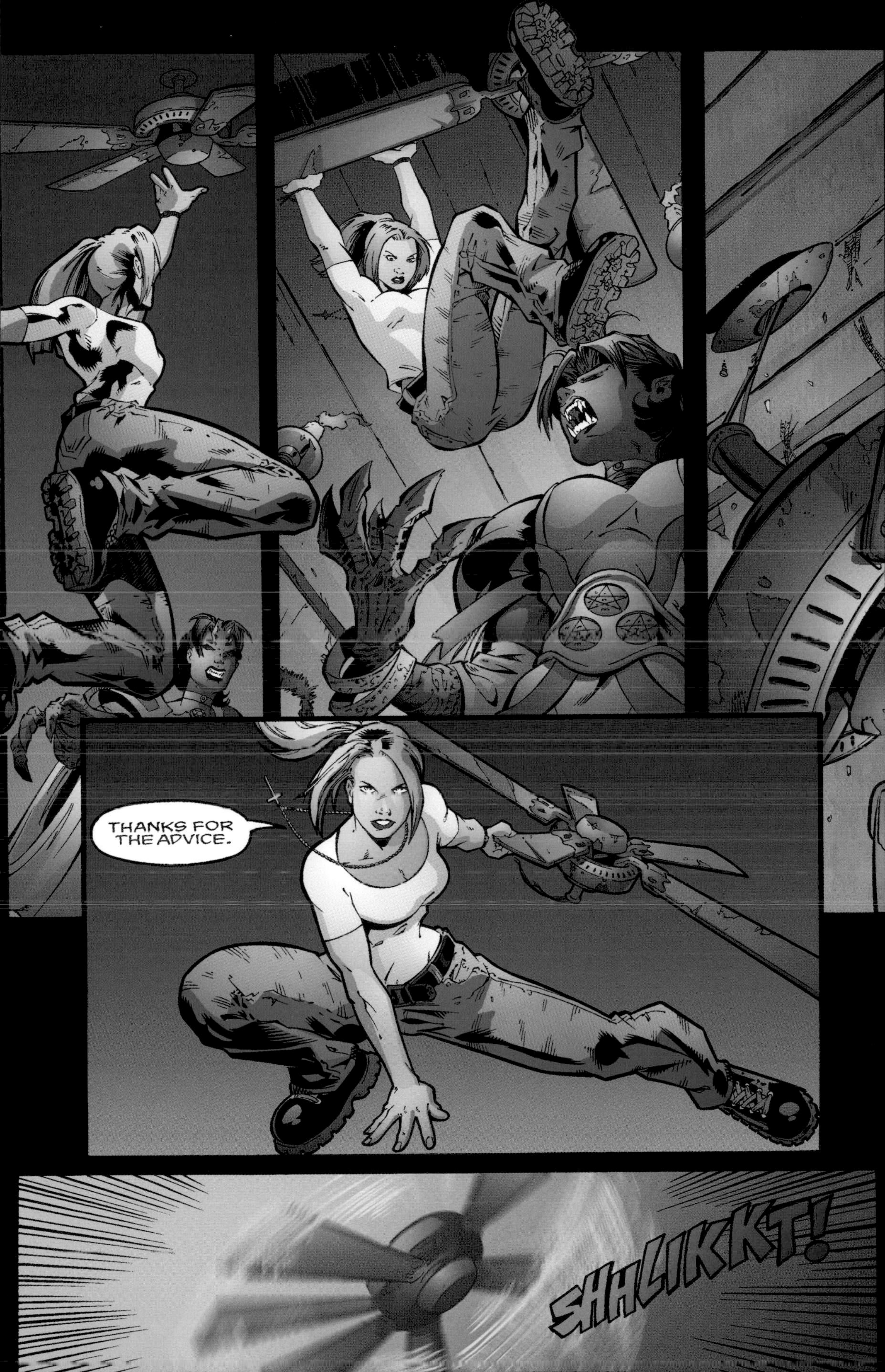
THANKS FOR THE ADVICE.
SHHLIKKT!

HEY, YOU SCRUBS, WAIT UP!

NO WAY, DUDE!

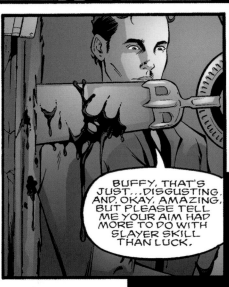

BUFFY, THAT'S JUST...DISGUSTING. AND, OKAY, AMAZING, BUT PLEASE TELL ME YOUR AIM HAD MORE TO DO WITH SLAYER SKILL THAN LUCK.

SO, I GUESS CONNOR WASN'T DEAD AFTER ALL.

OR ISN'T ANYMORE. YOU NEVER KNOW WITH THIS SORT OF THING.

WELL, I GUESS THAT'S THE LAST TIME I'LL STICK MY NOSE INTO SOMEONE ELSE'S BUSINESS.

OR NOT.

SO...

WHO WANTS ICE CREAM?

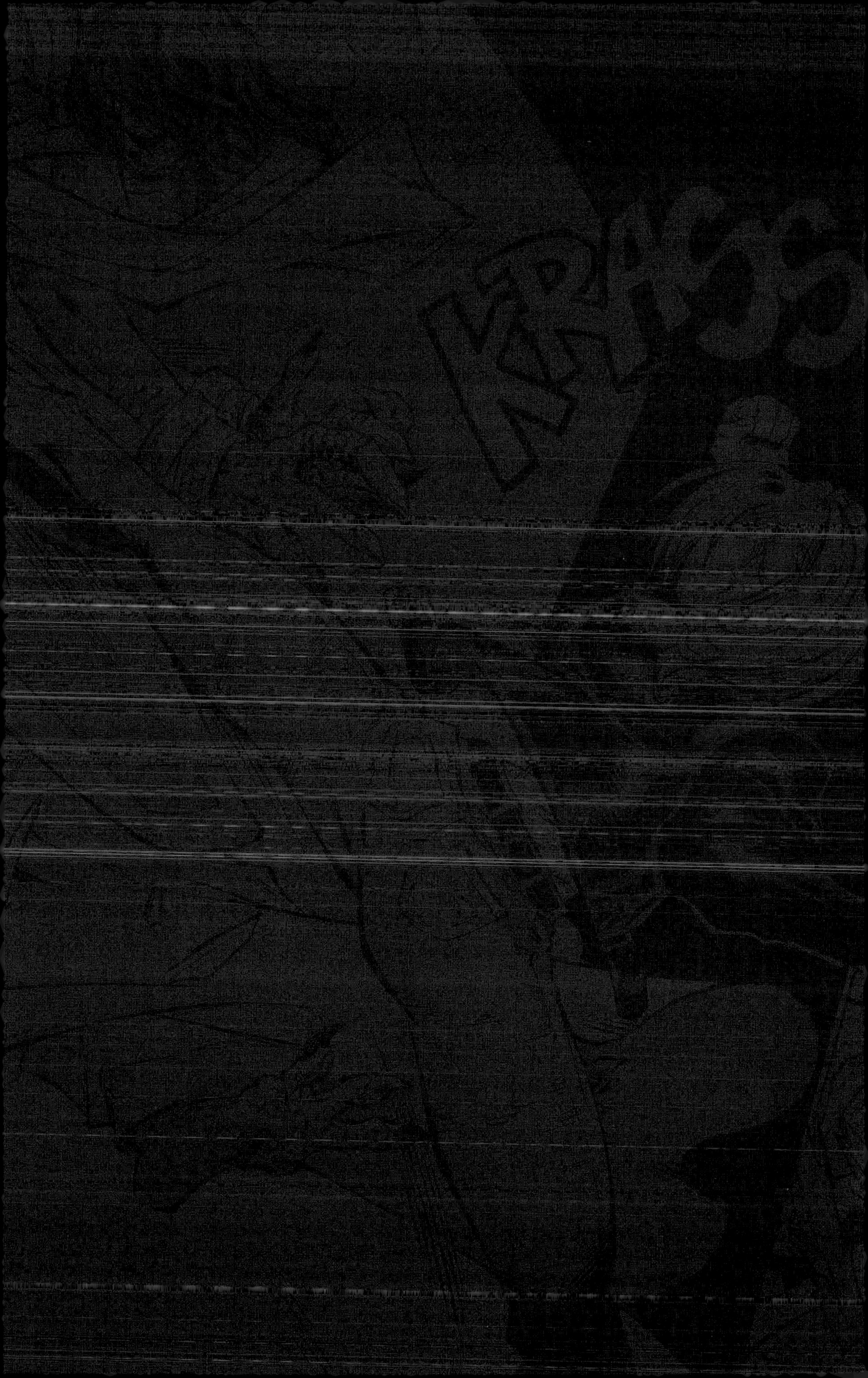

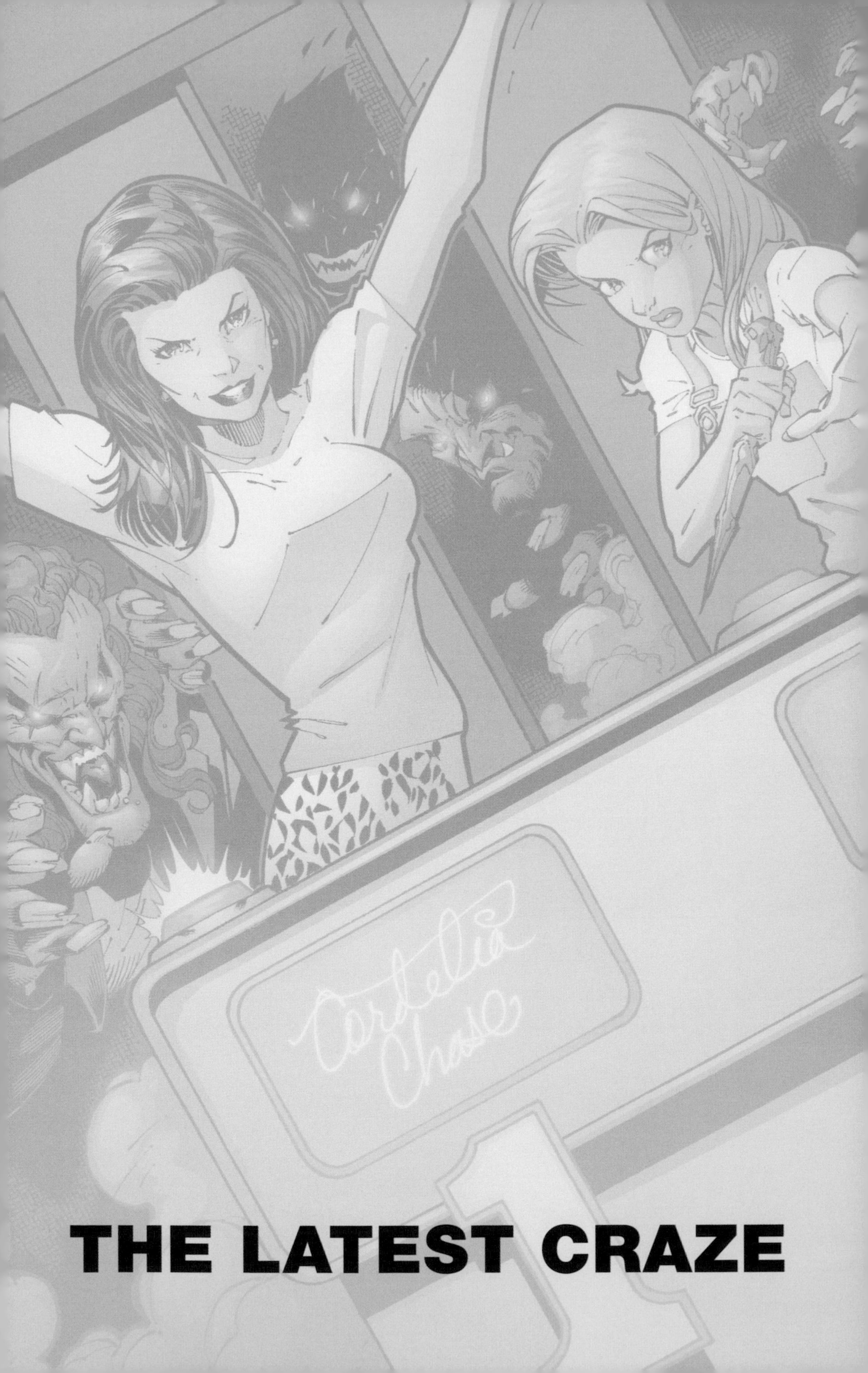
Cordelia Chase

THE LATEST CRAZE

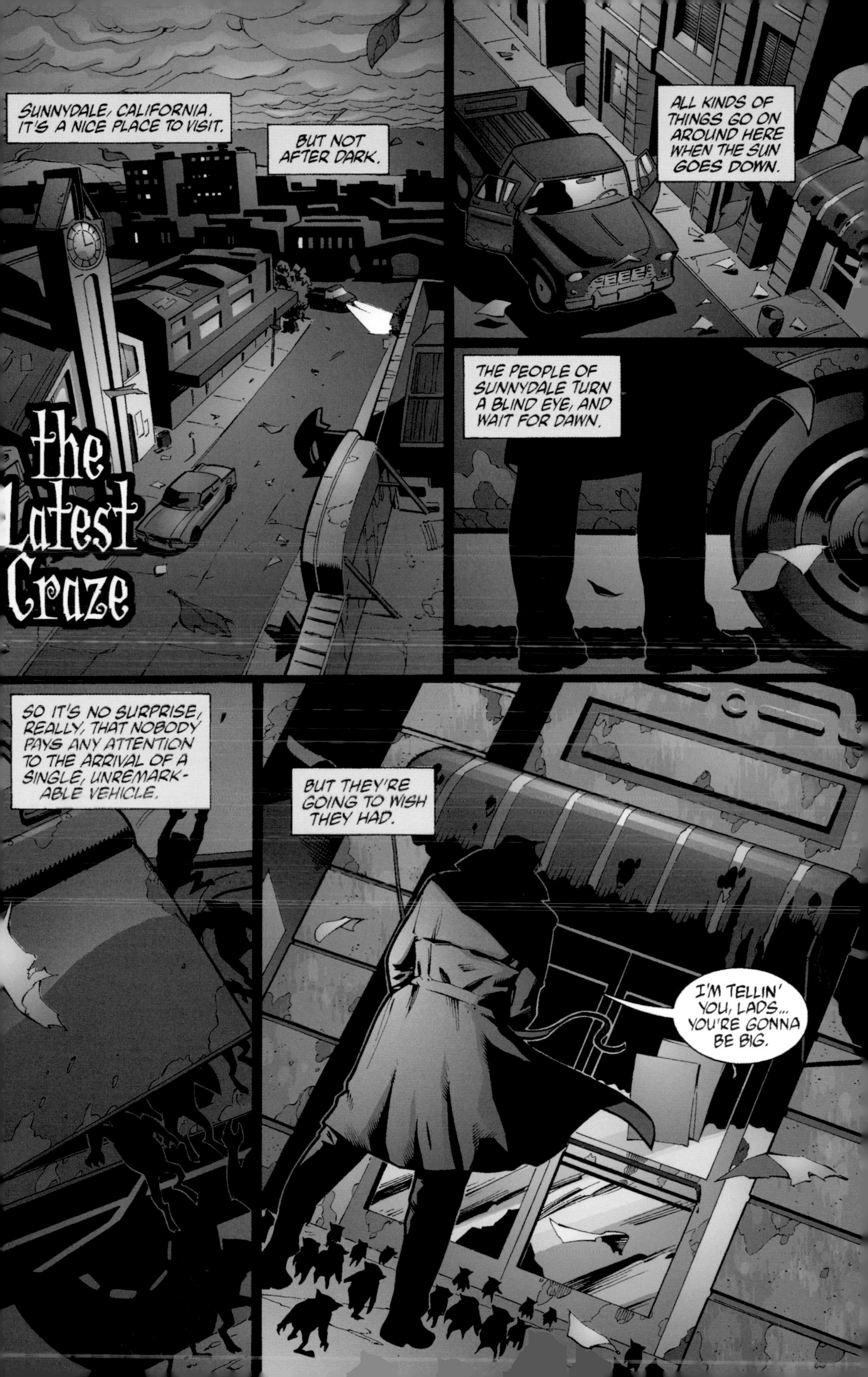
SUNNYDALE, CALIFORNIA. IT'S A NICE PLACE TO VISIT.
BUT NOT AFTER DARK.
the Latest Craze
ALL KINDS OF THINGS GO ON AROUND HERE WHEN THE SUN GOES DOWN.
THE PEOPLE OF SUNNYDALE TURN A BLIND EYE, AND WAIT FOR DAWN.
SO IT'S NO SURPRISE, REALLY, THAT NOBODY PAYS ANY ATTENTION TO THE ARRIVAL OF A SINGLE, UNREMARK-ABLE VEHICLE.
BUT THEY'RE GOING TO WISH THEY HAD.
I'M TELLIN' YOU, LADS... YOU'RE GONNA BE BIG.

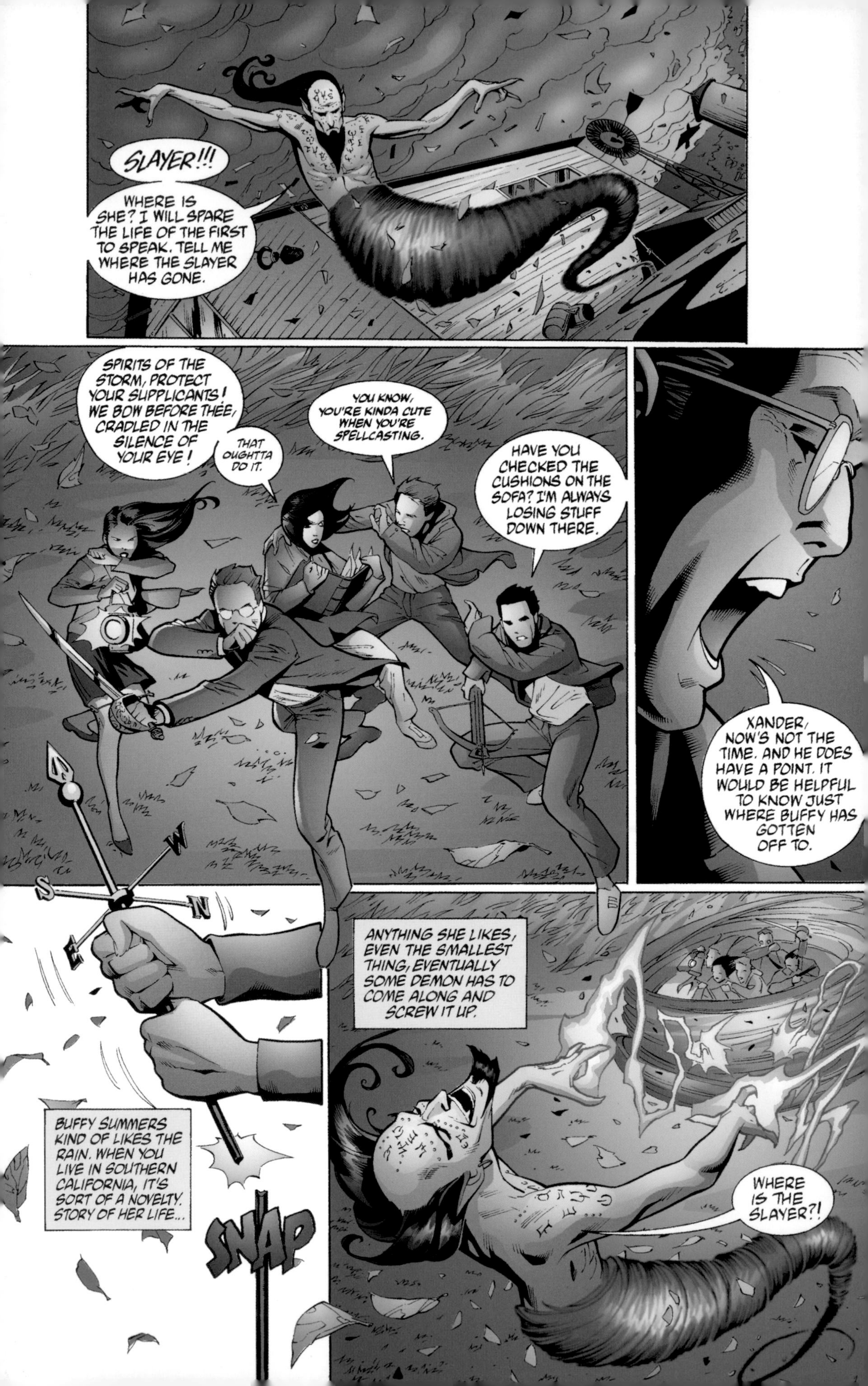
SLAYER!!!
WHERE IS SHE? I WILL SPARE THE LIFE OF THE FIRST TO SPEAK. TELL ME WHERE THE SLAYER HAS GONE.
SPIRITS OF THE STORM, PROTECT YOUR SUPPLICANTS! WE BOW BEFORE THEE, CRADLED IN THE SILENCE OF YOUR EYE!
THAT OUGHTTA DO IT.
YOU KNOW, YOU'RE KINDA CUTE WHEN YOU'RE SPELLCASTING.
HAVE YOU CHECKED THE CUSHIONS ON THE SOFA? I'M ALWAYS LOSING STUFF DOWN THERE.
XANDER, NOW'S NOT THE TIME. AND HE DOES HAVE A POINT. IT WOULD BE HELPFUL TO KNOW JUST WHERE BUFFY HAS GOTTEN OFF TO.
S
W
N
E
BUFFY SUMMERS KIND OF LIKES THE RAIN. WHEN YOU LIVE IN SOUTHERN CALIFORNIA, IT'S SORT OF A NOVELTY. STORY OF HER LIFE...
SNAP
ANYTHING SHE LIKES, EVEN THE SMALLEST THING, EVENTUALLY SOME DEMON HAS TO COME ALONG AND SCREW IT UP.
WHERE IS THE SLAYER?!

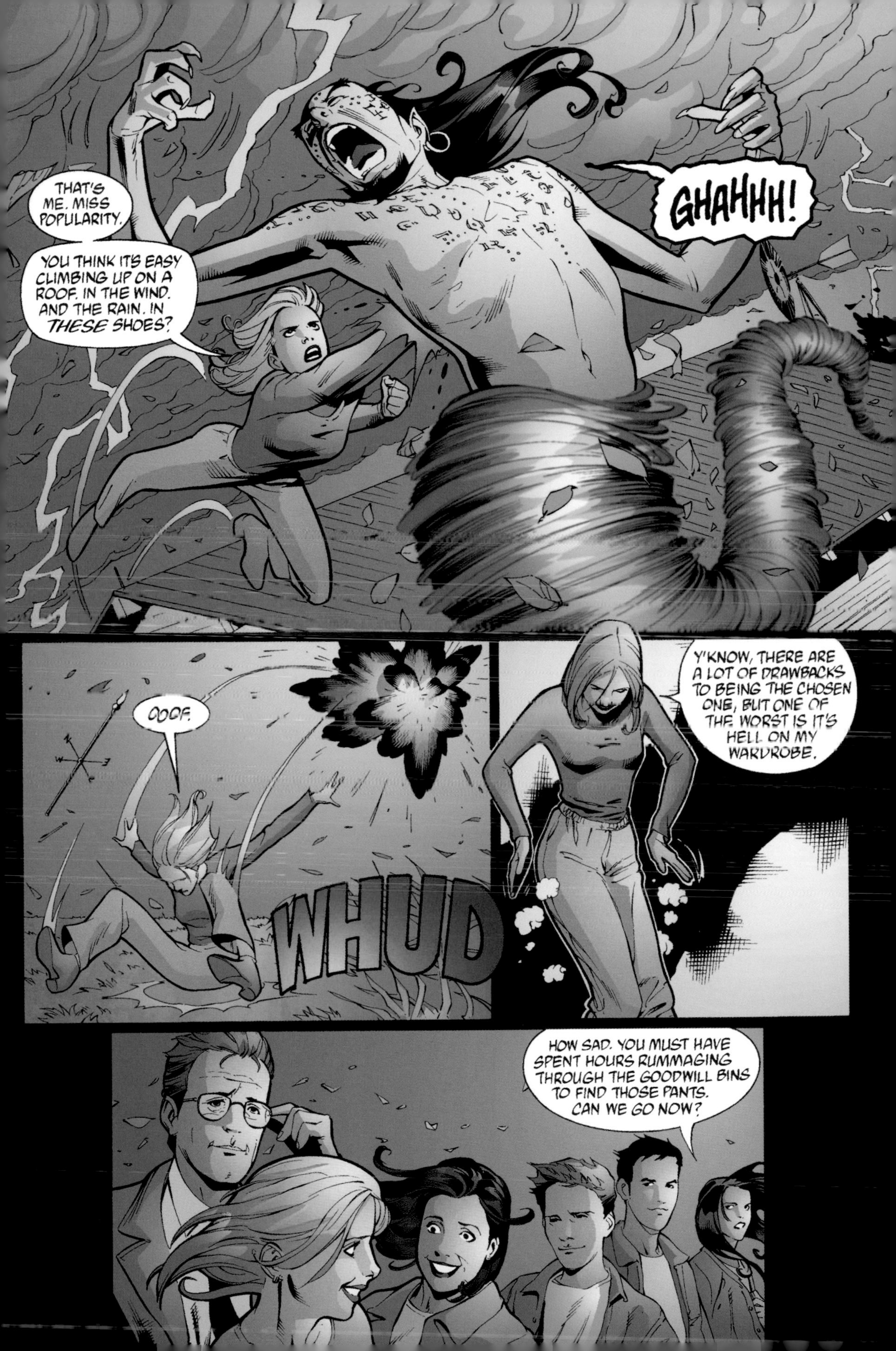
THAT'S ME. MISS POPULARITY.
YOU THINK IT'S EASY CLIMBING UP ON A ROOF. IN THE WIND. AND THE RAIN. IN *THESE* SHOES?
GHAHHH!
OOOF.
WHUD
Y'KNOW, THERE ARE A LOT OF DRAWBACKS TO BEING THE CHOSEN ONE, BUT ONE OF THE WORST IS IT'S HELL ON MY WARDROBE.
HOW SAD. YOU MUST HAVE SPENT HOURS RUMMAGING THROUGH THE GOODWILL BINS TO FIND THOSE PANTS. CAN WE GO NOW?

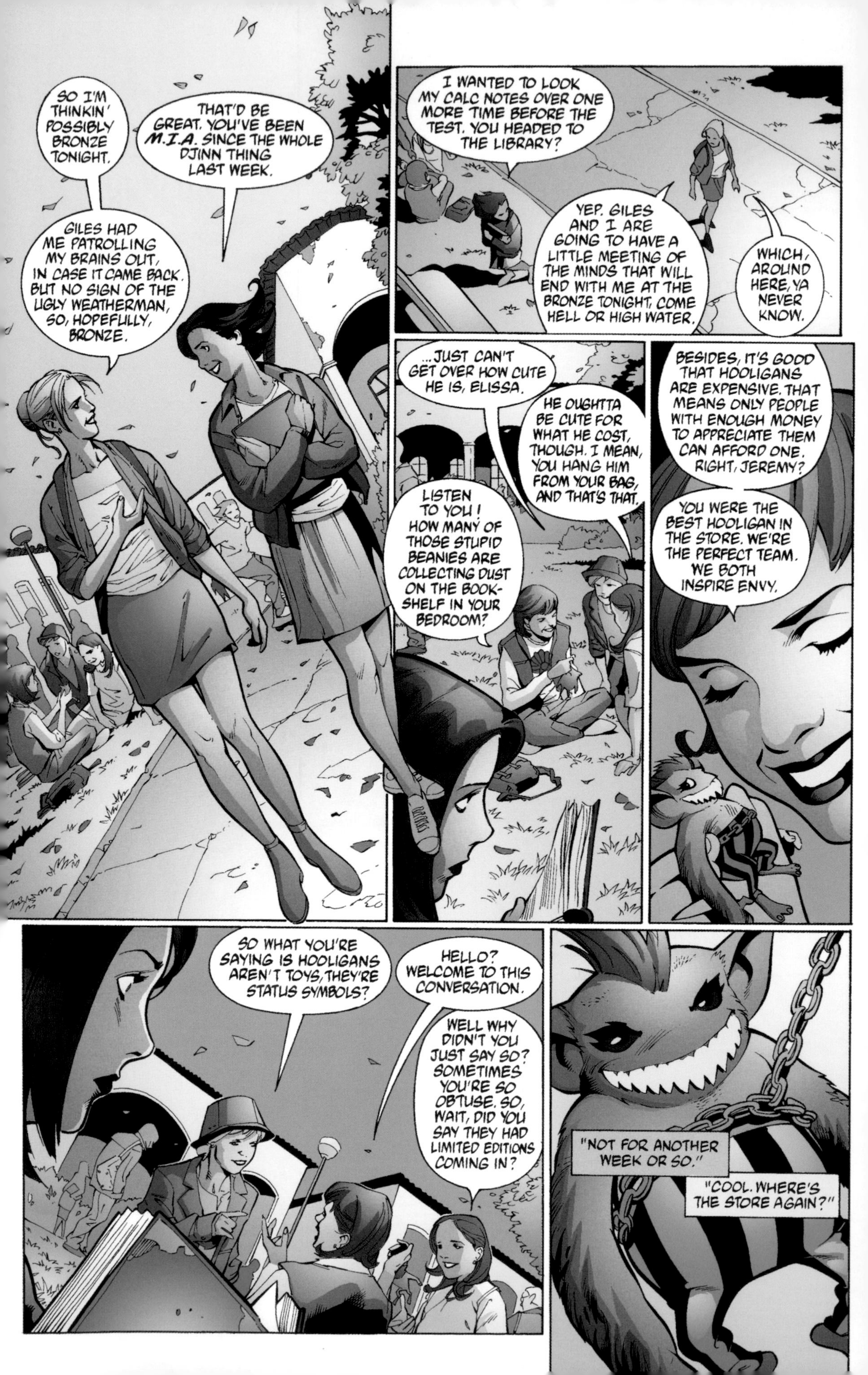
SO I'M THINKIN' POSSIBLY BRONZE TONIGHT.
THAT'D BE GREAT. YOU'VE BEEN M.I.A. SINCE THE WHOLE DJINN THING LAST WEEK.
GILES HAD ME PATROLLING MY BRAINS OUT, IN CASE IT CAME BACK. BUT NO SIGN OF THE UGLY WEATHERMAN, SO, HOPEFULLY, BRONZE.
I WANTED TO LOOK MY CALC NOTES OVER ONE MORE TIME BEFORE THE TEST. YOU HEADED TO THE LIBRARY?
YEP. GILES AND I ARE GOING TO HAVE A LITTLE MEETING OF THE MINDS THAT WILL END WITH ME AT THE BRONZE TONIGHT, COME HELL OR HIGH WATER.
WHICH, AROUND HERE, YA NEVER KNOW.
...JUST CAN'T GET OVER HOW CUTE HE IS, ELISSA.
HE OUGHTTA BE CUTE FOR WHAT HE COST, THOUGH. I MEAN, YOU HANG HIM FROM YOUR BAG, AND THAT'S THAT.
LISTEN TO YOU! HOW MANY OF THOSE STUPID BEANIES ARE COLLECTING DUST ON THE BOOK-SHELF IN YOUR BEDROOM?
BESIDES, IT'S GOOD THAT HOOLIGANS ARE EXPENSIVE. THAT MEANS ONLY PEOPLE WITH ENOUGH MONEY TO APPRECIATE THEM CAN AFFORD ONE. RIGHT, JEREMY?
YOU WERE THE BEST HOOLIGAN IN THE STORE. WE'RE THE PERFECT TEAM. WE BOTH INSPIRE ENVY.
SO WHAT YOU'RE SAYING IS HOOLIGANS AREN'T TOYS, THEY'RE STATUS SYMBOLS?
HELLO? WELCOME TO THIS CONVERSATION.
WELL WHY DIDN'T YOU JUST SAY SO? SOMETIMES YOU'RE SO OBTUSE. SO, WAIT, DID YOU SAY THEY HAD LIMITED EDITIONS COMING IN?
"NOT FOR ANOTHER WEEK OR SO."
"COOL. WHERE'S THE STORE AGAIN?"

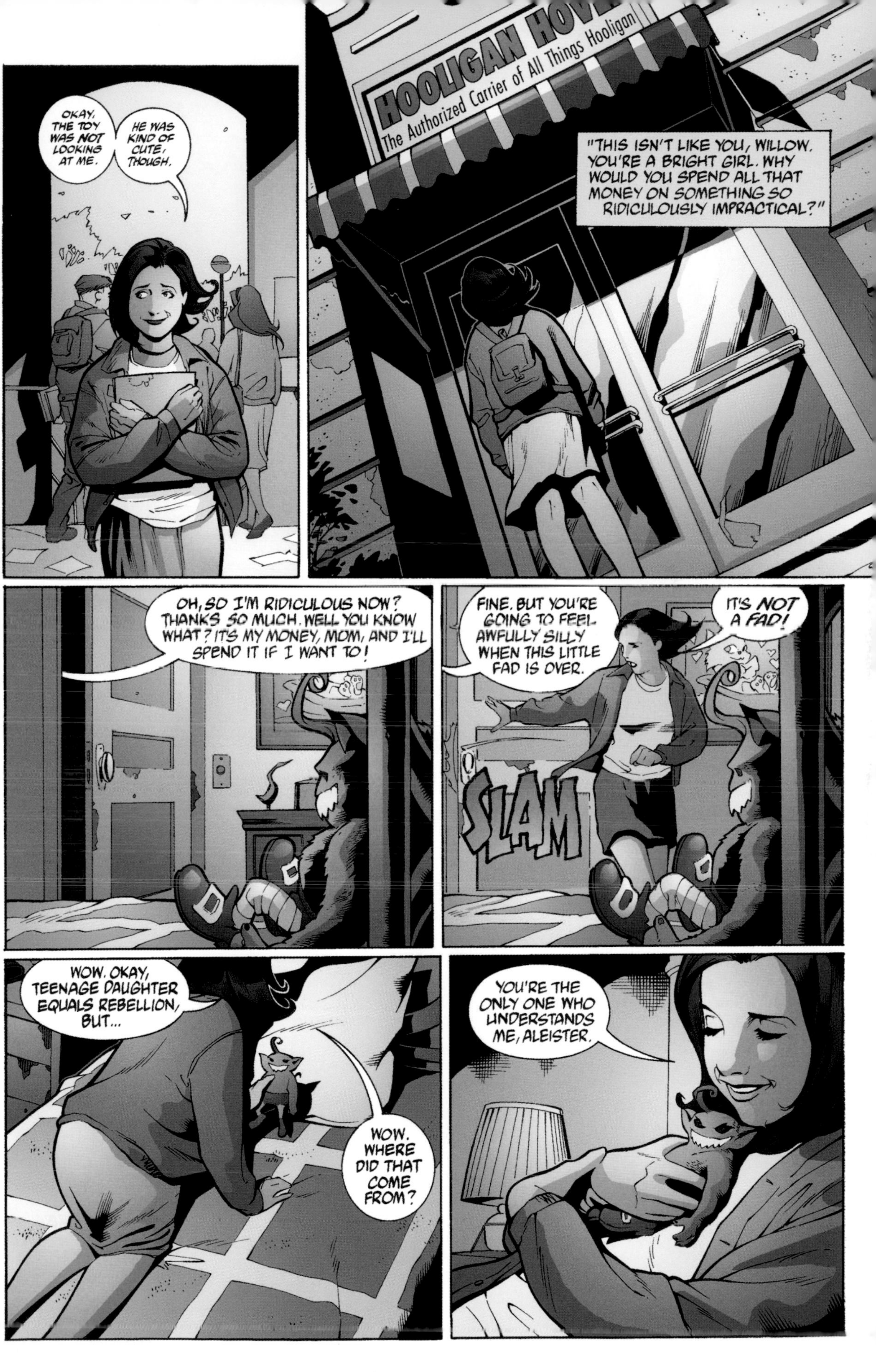
OKAY, THE TOY WAS NOT LOOKING AT ME.
HE WAS KIND OF CUTE, THOUGH.
HOOLIGAN HOV
The Authorized Carrier of All Things Hooligan
"THIS ISN'T LIKE YOU, WILLOW. YOU'RE A BRIGHT GIRL. WHY WOULD YOU SPEND ALL THAT MONEY ON SOMETHING SO RIDICULOUSLY IMPRACTICAL?"
OH, SO I'M RIDICULOUS NOW? THANKS SO MUCH. WELL YOU KNOW WHAT? IT'S MY MONEY, MOM, AND I'LL SPEND IT IF I WANT TO!
FINE. BUT YOU'RE GOING TO FEEL AWFULLY SILLY WHEN THIS LITTLE FAD IS OVER.
IT'S NOT A FAD!
SLAM
WOW. OKAY, TEENAGE DAUGHTER EQUALS REBELLION, BUT...
WOW. WHERE DID THAT COME FROM?
YOU'RE THE ONLY ONE WHO UNDERSTANDS ME, ALEISTER.

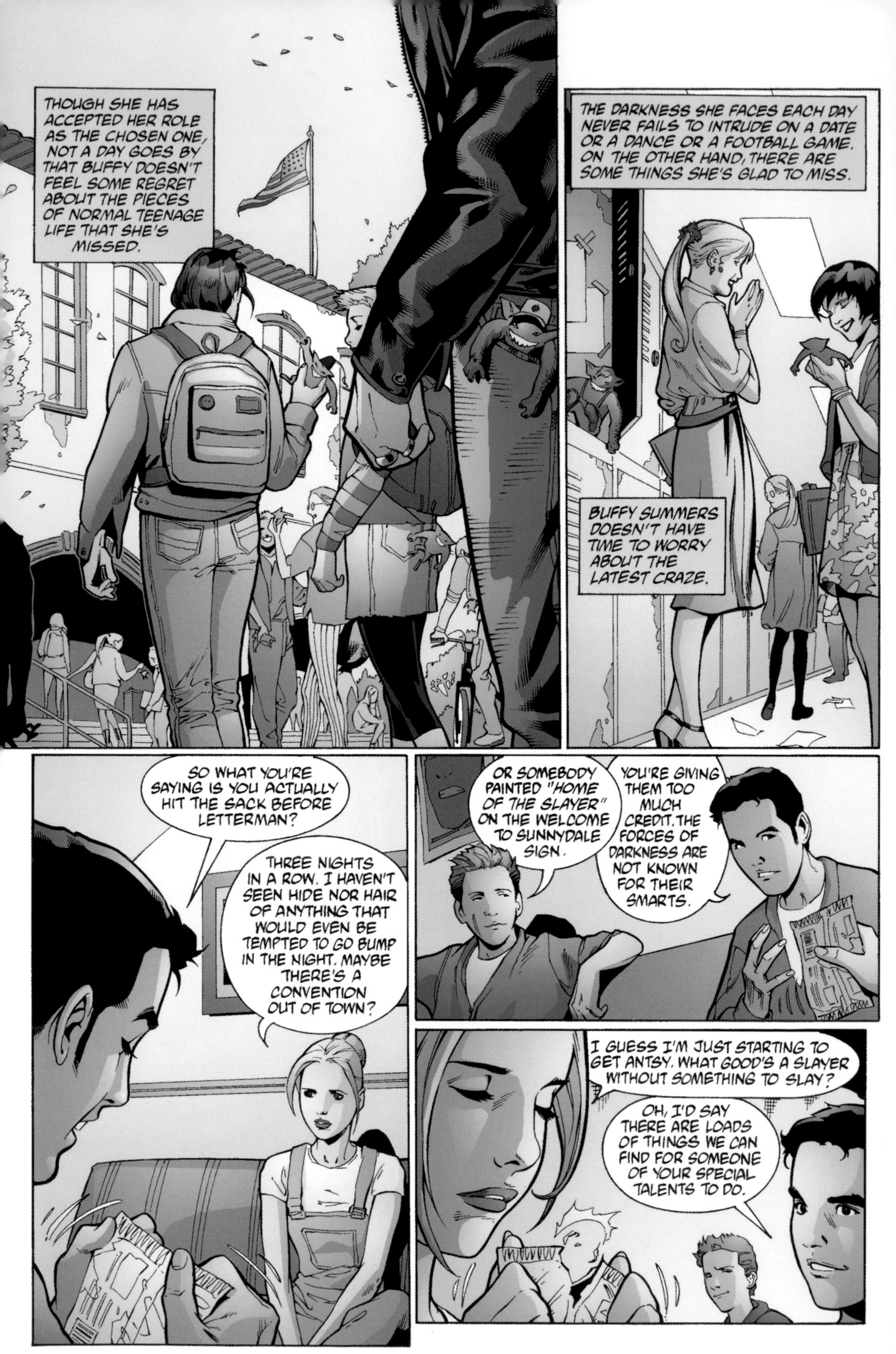
THOUGH SHE HAS ACCEPTED HER ROLE AS THE CHOSEN ONE, NOT A DAY GOES BY THAT BUFFY DOESN'T FEEL SOME REGRET ABOUT THE PIECES OF NORMAL TEENAGE LIFE THAT SHE'S MISSED.
THE DARKNESS SHE FACES EACH DAY NEVER FAILS TO INTRUDE ON A DATE OR A DANCE OR A FOOTBALL GAME. ON THE OTHER HAND, THERE ARE SOME THINGS SHE'S GLAD TO MISS.
BUFFY SUMMERS DOESN'T HAVE TIME TO WORRY ABOUT THE LATEST CRAZE.
SO WHAT YOU'RE SAYING IS YOU ACTUALLY HIT THE SACK BEFORE LETTERMAN?
THREE NIGHTS IN A ROW. I HAVEN'T SEEN HIDE NOR HAIR OF ANYTHING THAT WOULD EVEN BE TEMPTED TO GO BUMP IN THE NIGHT. MAYBE THERE'S A CONVENTION OUT OF TOWN?
OR SOMEBODY PAINTED "HOME OF THE SLAYER" ON THE WELCOME TO SUNNYDALE SIGN.
YOU'RE GIVING THEM TOO MUCH CREDIT. THE FORCES OF DARKNESS ARE NOT KNOWN FOR THEIR SMARTS.
I GUESS I'M JUST STARTING TO GET ANTSY. WHAT GOOD'S A SLAYER WITHOUT SOMETHING TO SLAY?
OH, I'D SAY THERE ARE LOADS OF THINGS WE CAN FIND FOR SOMEONE OF YOUR SPECIAL TALENTS TO DO.

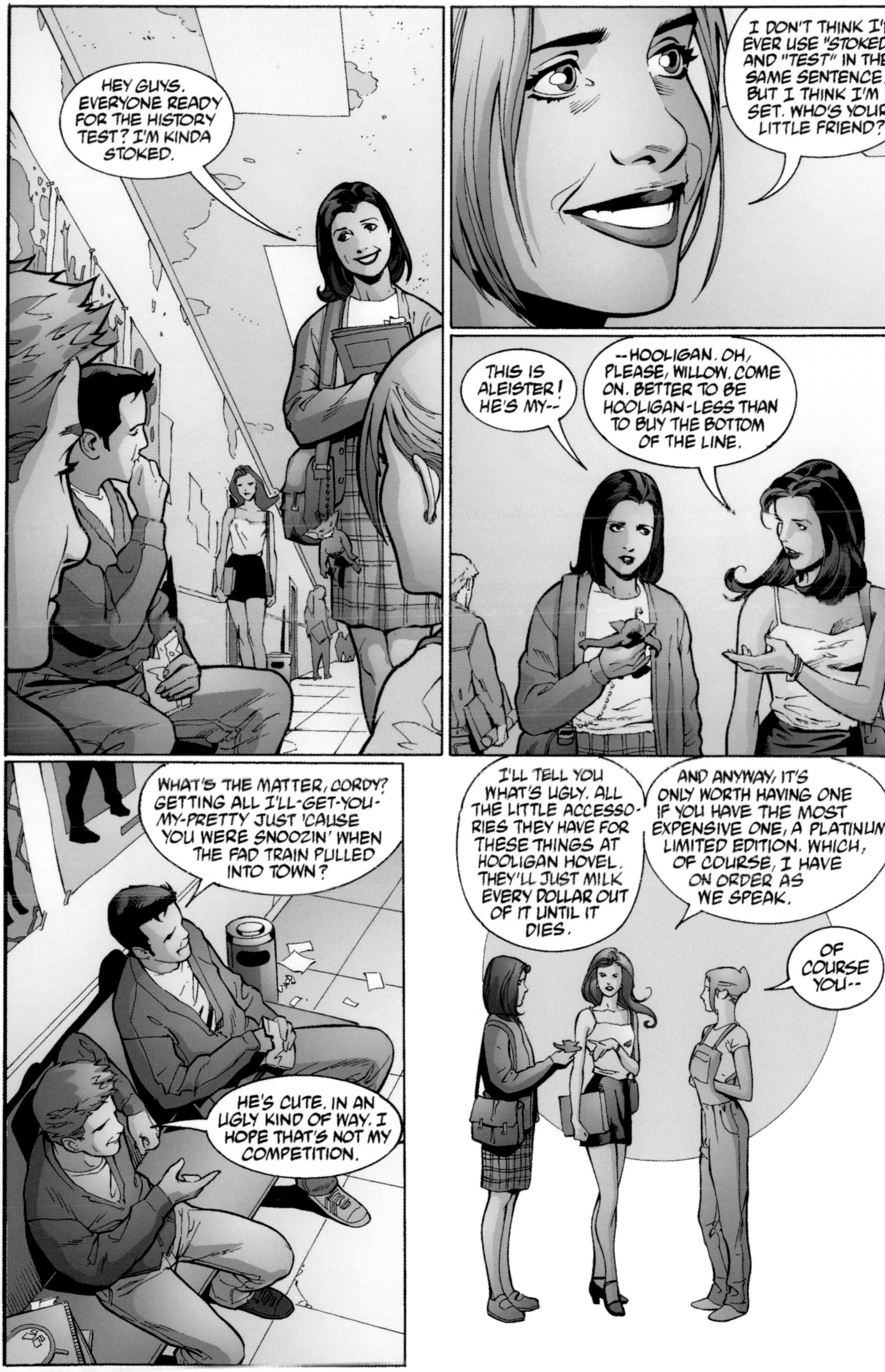
HEY GUYS. EVERYONE READY FOR THE HISTORY TEST? I'M KINDA STOKED.
I DON'T THINK I'D EVER USE "STOKED" AND "TEST" IN THE SAME SENTENCE, BUT I THINK I'M SET. WHO'S YOUR LITTLE FRIEND?
THIS IS ALEISTER! HE'S MY--
--HOOLIGAN. OH, PLEASE, WILLOW. COME ON. BETTER TO BE HOOLIGAN-LESS THAN TO BUY THE BOTTOM OF THE LINE.
WHAT'S THE MATTER, CORDY? GETTING ALL I'LL-GET-YOU-MY-PRETTY JUST 'CAUSE YOU WERE SNOOZIN' WHEN THE FAD TRAIN PULLED INTO TOWN?
HE'S CUTE, IN AN UGLY KIND OF WAY. I HOPE THAT'S NOT MY COMPETITION.
I'LL TELL YOU WHAT'S UGLY. ALL THE LITTLE ACCESSORIES THEY HAVE FOR THESE THINGS AT HOOLIGAN HOVEL. THEY'LL JUST MILK EVERY DOLLAR OUT OF IT UNTIL IT DIES.
AND ANYWAY, IT'S ONLY WORTH HAVING ONE IF YOU HAVE THE MOST EXPENSIVE ONE, A PLATINUM LIMITED EDITION. WHICH, OF COURSE, I HAVE ON ORDER AS WE SPEAK.
OF COURSE YOU--

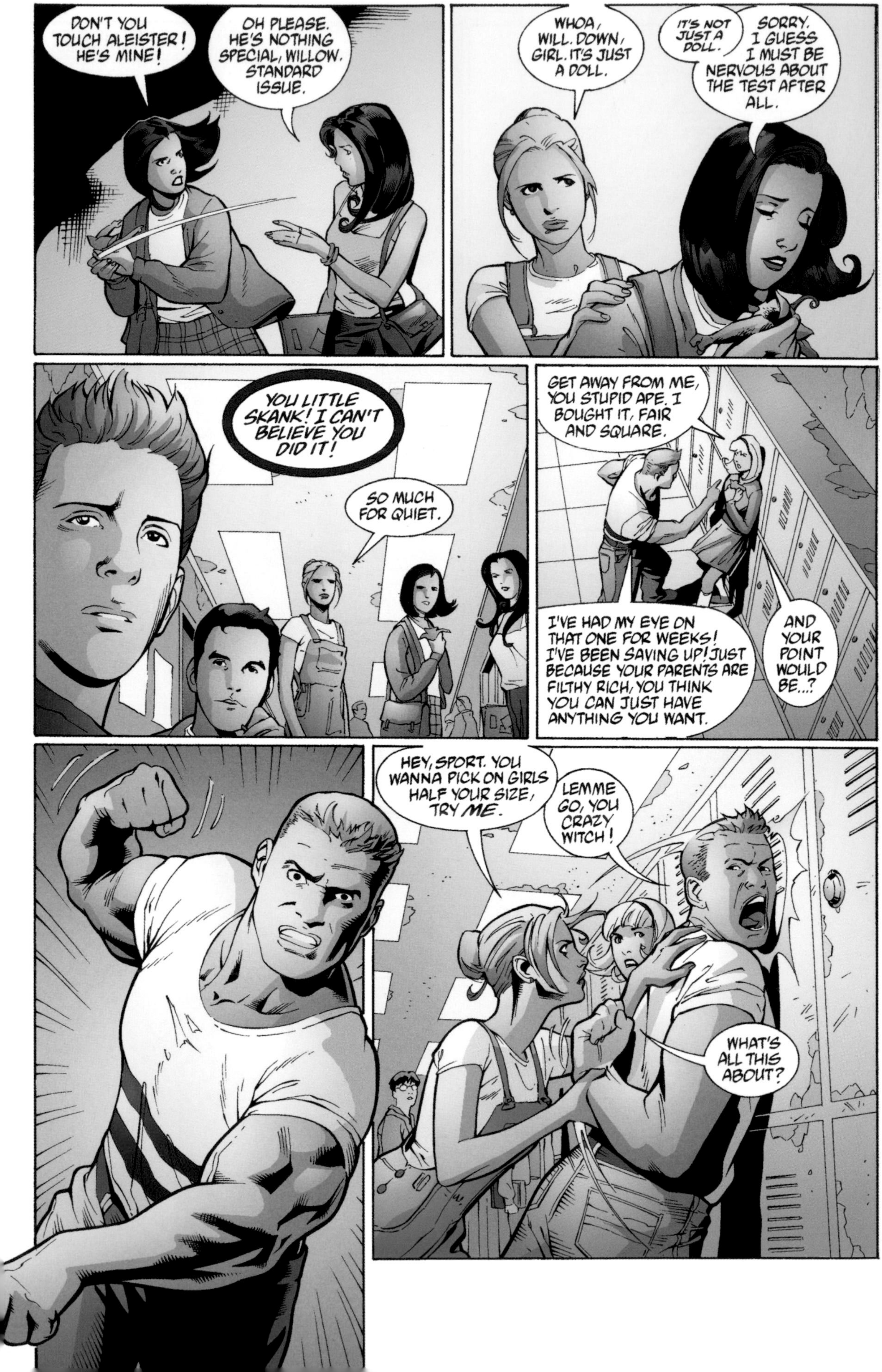
DON'T YOU TOUCH ALEISTER! HE'S MINE!
OH PLEASE. HE'S NOTHING SPECIAL, WILLOW. STANDARD ISSUE.
WHOA, WILL. DOWN, GIRL. IT'S JUST A DOLL.
SORRY. I GUESS I MUST BE NERVOUS ABOUT THE TEST AFTER ALL.
IT'S NOT JUST A DOLL.
YOU LITTLE SKANK! I CAN'T BELIEVE YOU DID IT!
SO MUCH FOR QUIET.
GET AWAY FROM ME, YOU STUPID APE. I BOUGHT IT, FAIR AND SQUARE.
I'VE HAD MY EYE ON THAT ONE FOR WEEKS! I'VE BEEN SAVING UP! JUST BECAUSE YOUR PARENTS ARE FILTHY RICH, YOU THINK YOU CAN JUST HAVE ANYTHING YOU WANT.
AND YOUR POINT WOULD BE...?
HEY, SPORT. YOU WANNA PICK ON GIRLS HALF YOUR SIZE, TRY ME.
LEMME GO, YOU CRAZY WITCH!
WHAT'S ALL THIS ABOUT?

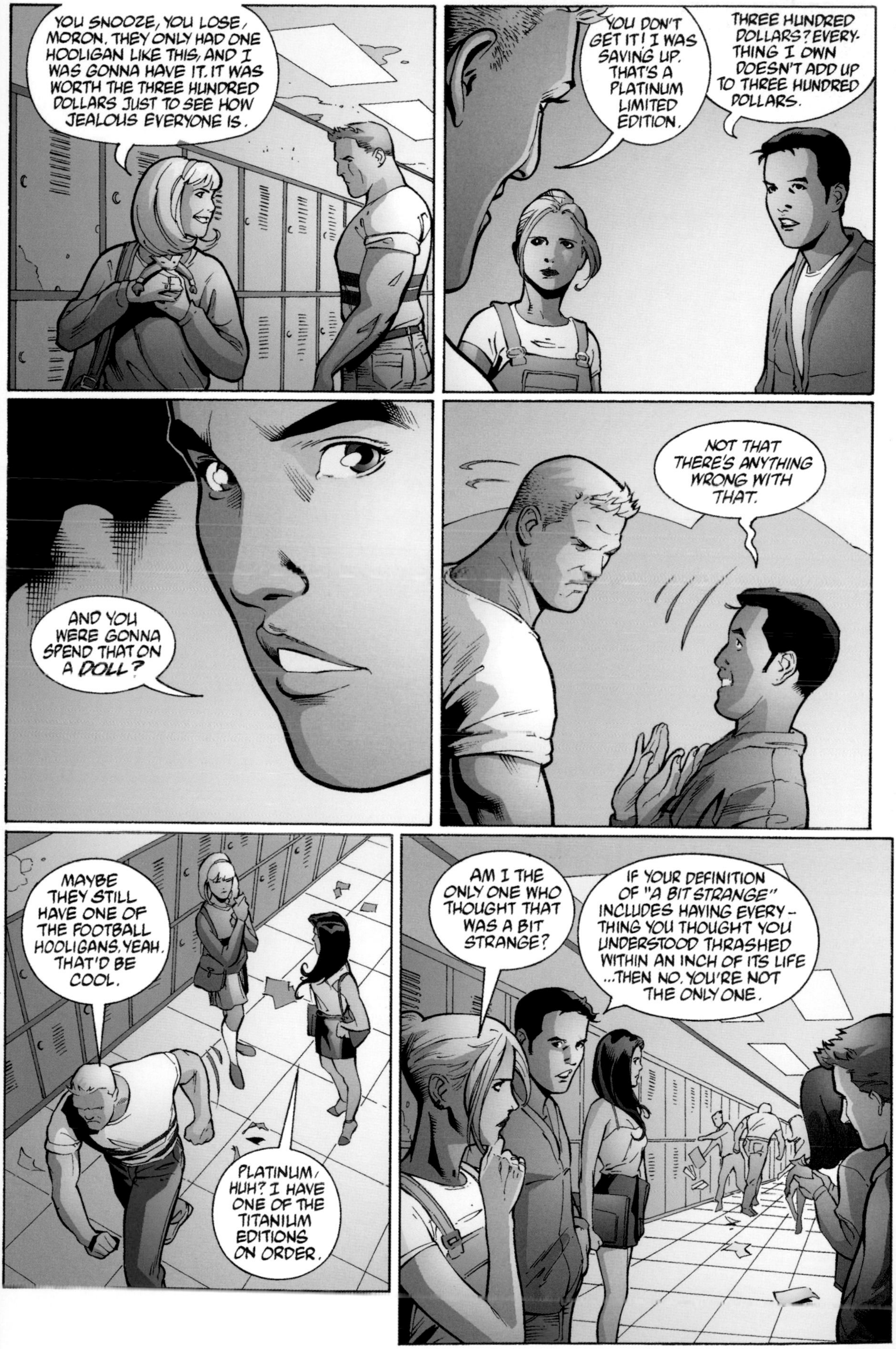
YOU SNOOZE, YOU LOSE, MORON. THEY ONLY HAD ONE HOOLIGAN LIKE THIS, AND I WAS GONNA HAVE IT. IT WAS WORTH THE THREE HUNDRED DOLLARS JUST TO SEE HOW JEALOUS EVERYONE IS.
YOU DON'T GET IT! I WAS SAVING UP. THAT'S A PLATINUM LIMITED EDITION.
THREE HUNDRED DOLLARS? EVERYTHING I OWN DOESN'T ADD UP TO THREE HUNDRED DOLLARS.
AND YOU WERE GONNA SPEND THAT ON A DOLL?
NOT THAT THERE'S ANYTHING WRONG WITH THAT.
MAYBE THEY STILL HAVE ONE OF THE FOOTBALL HOOLIGANS. YEAH. THAT'D BE COOL.
PLATINUM, HUH? I HAVE ONE OF THE TITANIUM EDITIONS ON ORDER.
AM I THE ONLY ONE WHO THOUGHT THAT WAS A BIT STRANGE?
IF YOUR DEFINITION OF "A BIT STRANGE" INCLUDES HAVING EVERYTHING YOU THOUGHT YOU UNDERSTOOD THRASHED WITHIN AN INCH OF ITS LIFE ...THEN NO. YOU'RE NOT THE ONLY ONE.

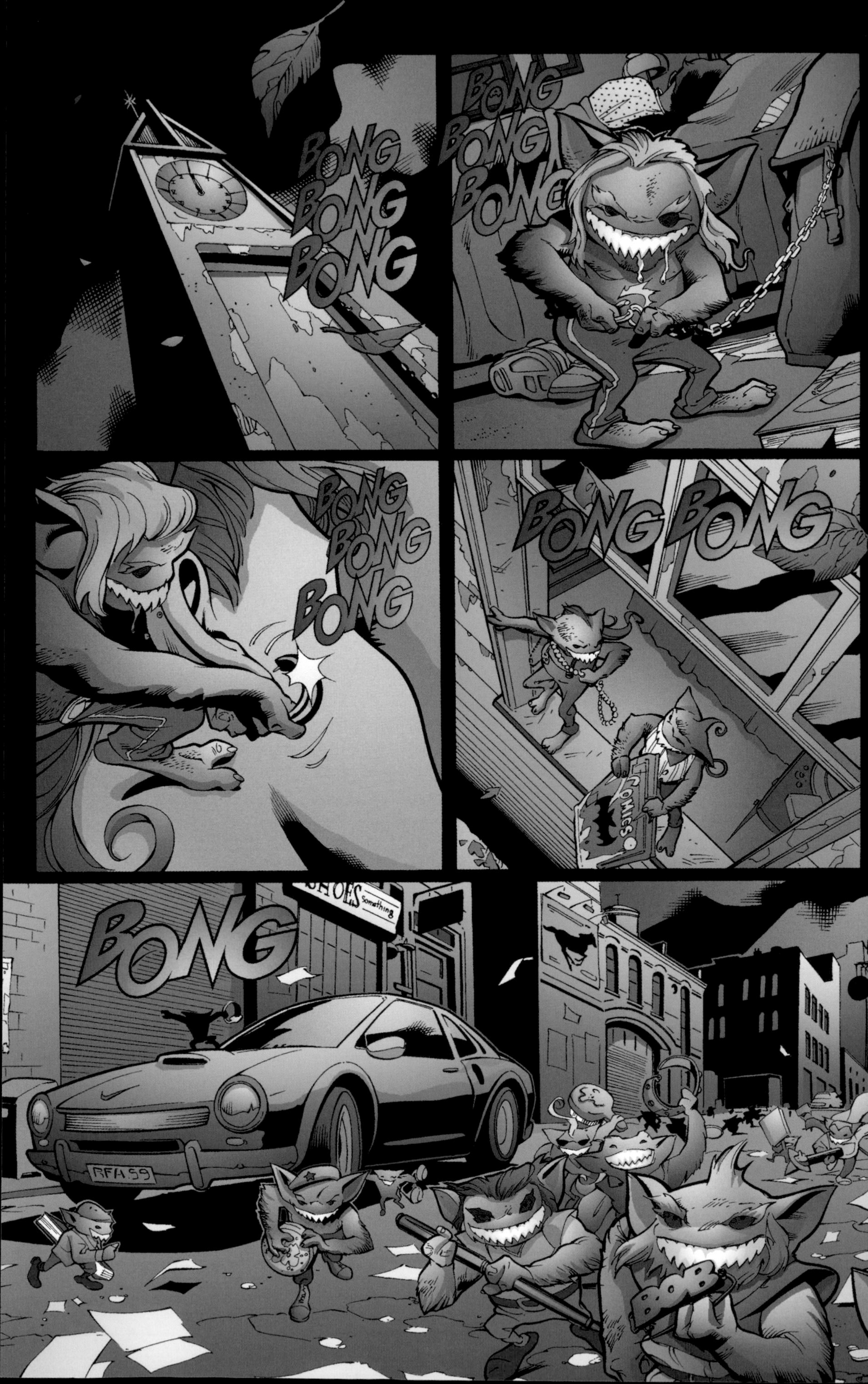
BONG
BONG
BONG
BONG
BONG
BONG
BONG
BONG
BONG
BONG
BONG
COMICS
BONG
SHOES
Something
RFA 59
BOB

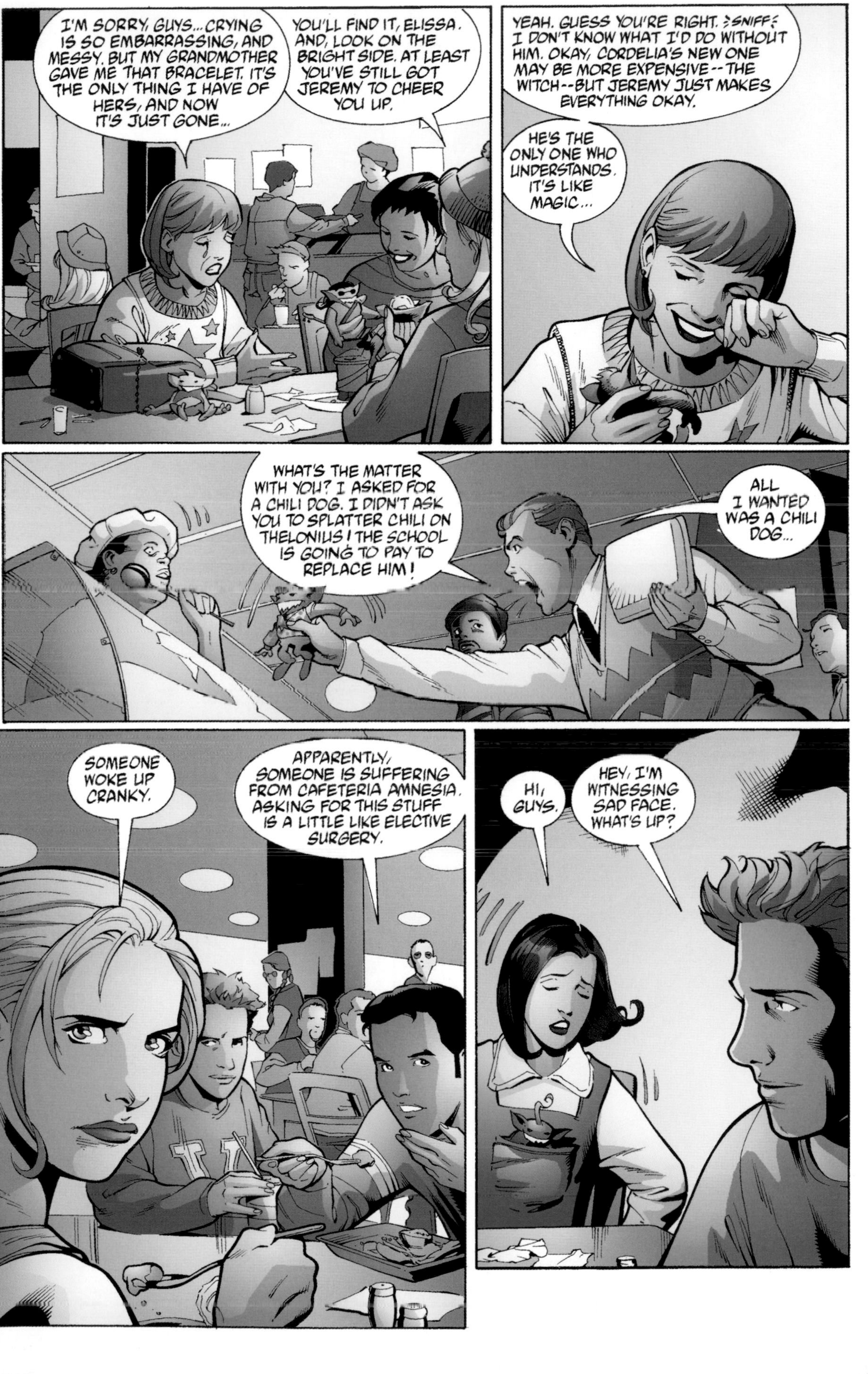
I'M SORRY, GUYS... CRYING IS SO EMBARRASSING, AND MESSY. BUT MY GRANDMOTHER GAVE ME THAT BRACELET. IT'S THE ONLY THING I HAVE OF HERS, AND NOW IT'S JUST GONE...
YOU'LL FIND IT, ELISSA. AND, LOOK ON THE BRIGHT SIDE. AT LEAST YOU'VE STILL GOT JEREMY TO CHEER YOU UP.
YEAH. GUESS YOU'RE RIGHT. >SNIFF< I DON'T KNOW WHAT I'D DO WITHOUT HIM. OKAY, CORDELIA'S NEW ONE MAY BE MORE EXPENSIVE--THE WITCH--BUT JEREMY JUST MAKES EVERYTHING OKAY.
HE'S THE ONLY ONE WHO UNDERSTANDS. IT'S LIKE MAGIC...
WHAT'S THE MATTER WITH YOU? I ASKED FOR A CHILI DOG. I DIDN'T ASK YOU TO SPLATTER CHILI ON THELONIUS! THE SCHOOL IS GOING TO PAY TO REPLACE HIM!
ALL I WANTED WAS A CHILI DOG...
SOMEONE WOKE UP CRANKY.
APPARENTLY, SOMEONE IS SUFFERING FROM CAFETERIA AMNESIA. ASKING FOR THIS STUFF IS A LITTLE LIKE ELECTIVE SURGERY.
HI, GUYS.
HEY, I'M WITNESSING SAD FACE. WHAT'S UP?

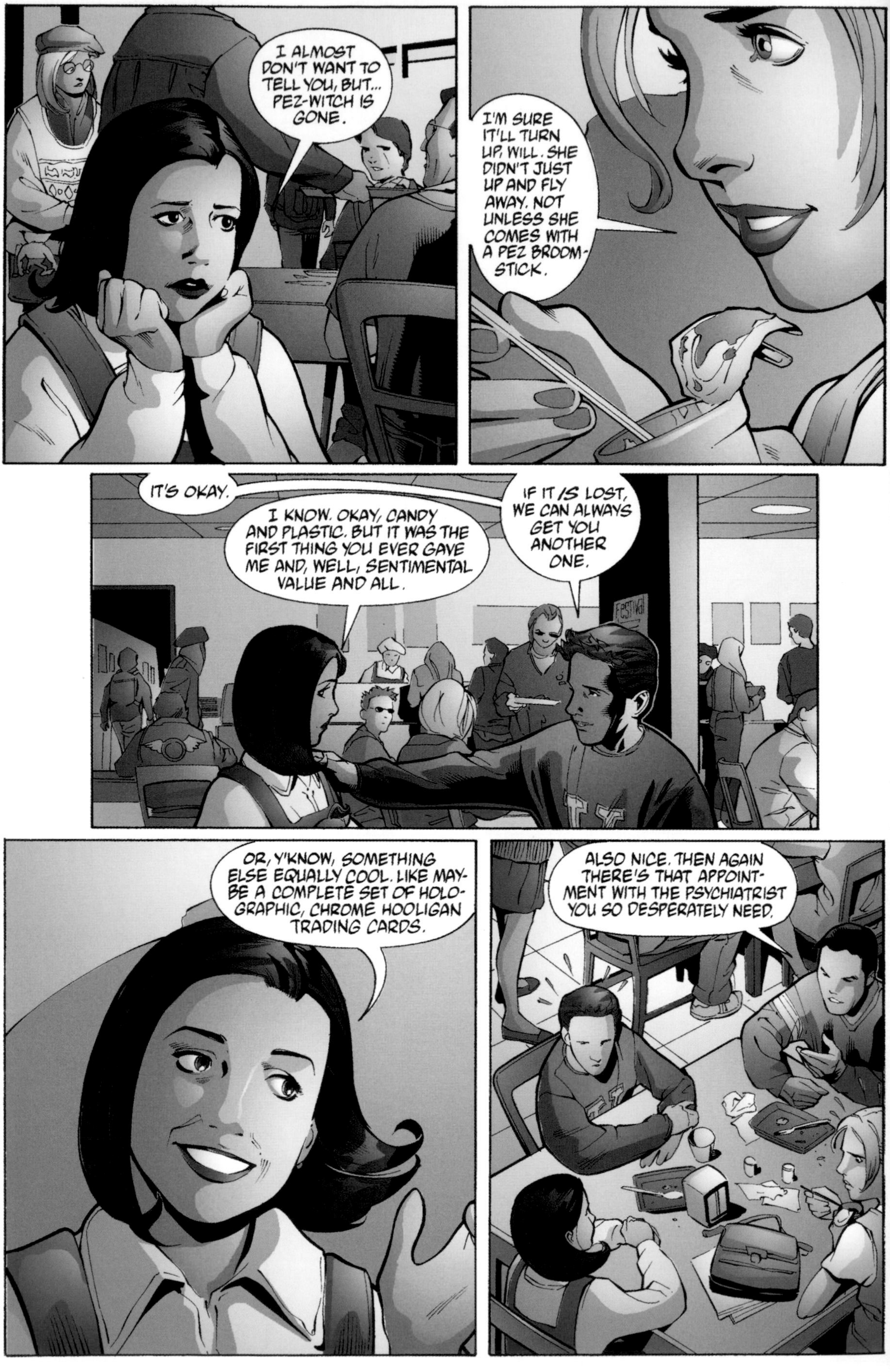
I ALMOST DON'T WANT TO TELL YOU, BUT... PEZ-WITCH IS GONE.
I'M SURE IT'LL TURN UP, WILL. SHE DIDN'T JUST UP AND FLY AWAY. NOT UNLESS SHE COMES WITH A PEZ BROOM-STICK.
IT'S OKAY.
I KNOW. OKAY, CANDY AND PLASTIC. BUT IT WAS THE FIRST THING YOU EVER GAVE ME AND, WELL, SENTIMENTAL VALUE AND ALL.
IF IT IS LOST, WE CAN ALWAYS GET YOU ANOTHER ONE.
OR, Y'KNOW, SOMETHING ELSE EQUALLY COOL. LIKE MAY-BE A COMPLETE SET OF HOLO-GRAPHIC, CHROME HOOLIGAN TRADING CARDS.
ALSO NICE. THEN AGAIN THERE'S THAT APPOINT-MENT WITH THE PSYCHIATRIST YOU SO DESPERATELY NEED.

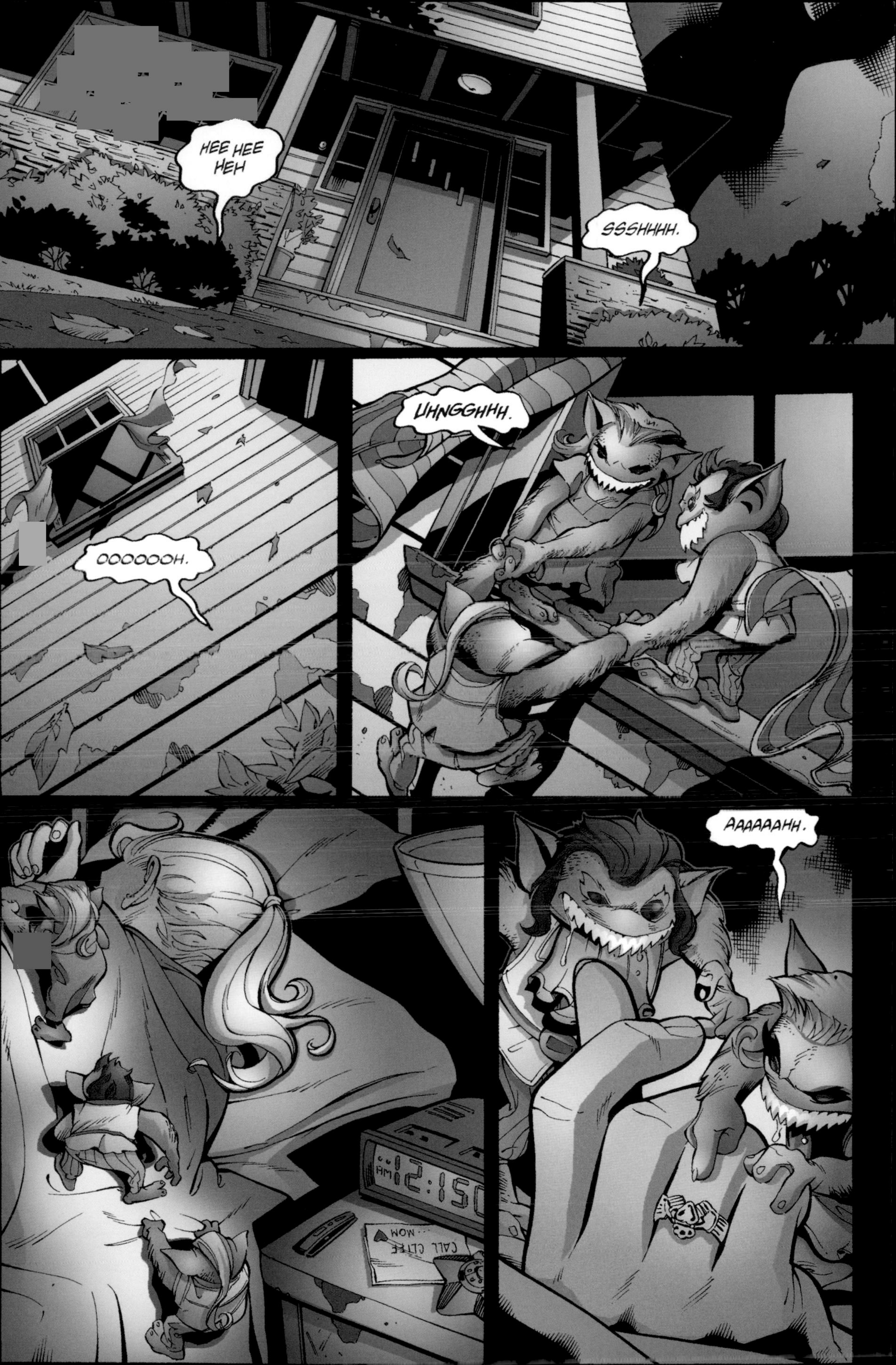
HEE HEE HEH
SSSHHHH.
OOOOOOH.
UHNGGHHH.
AAAAAAH.

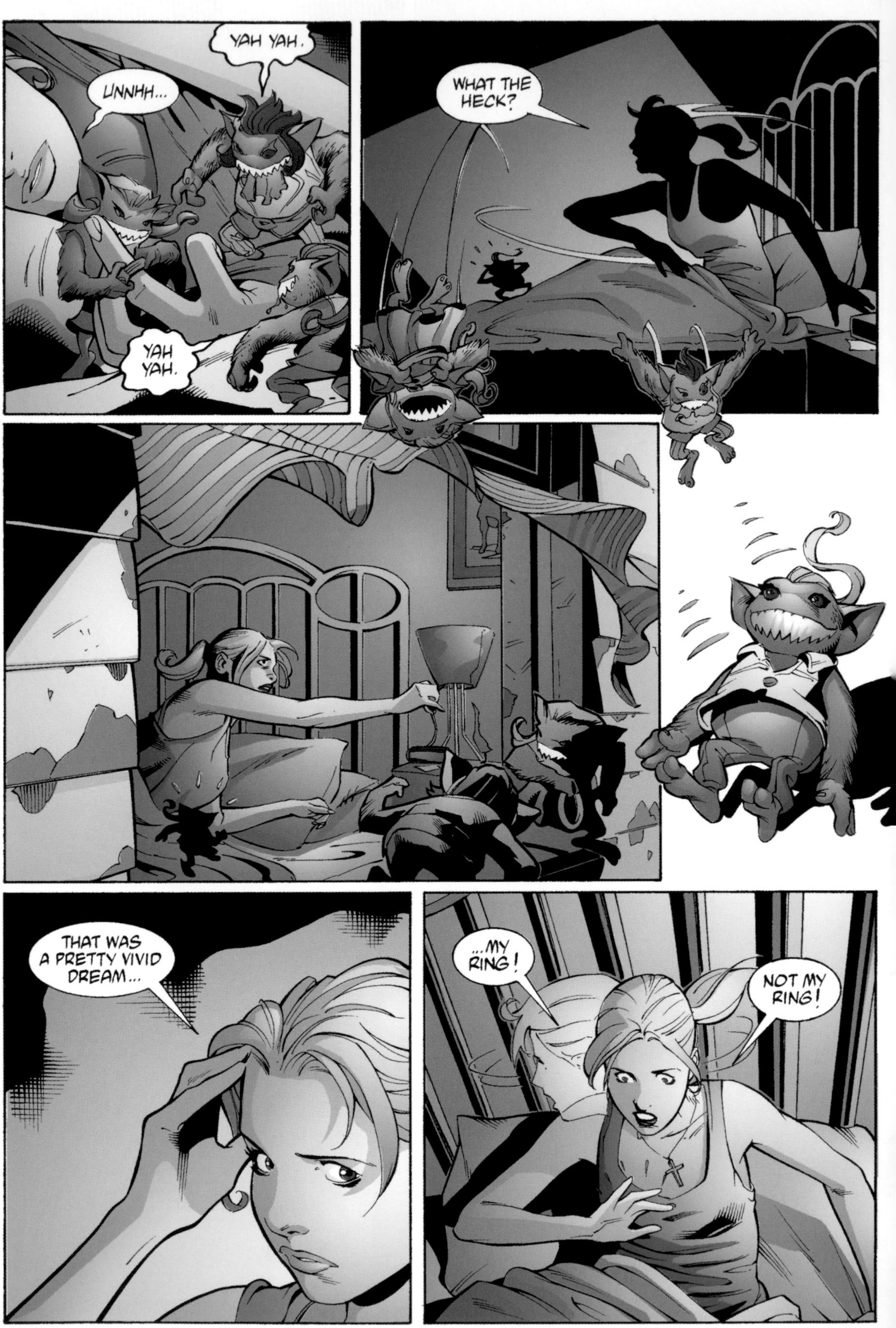

YAH YAH.
UNNHH...
YAH YAH.
WHAT THE HECK?
THAT WAS A PRETTY VIVID DREAM...
...MY RING!
NOT MY RING!

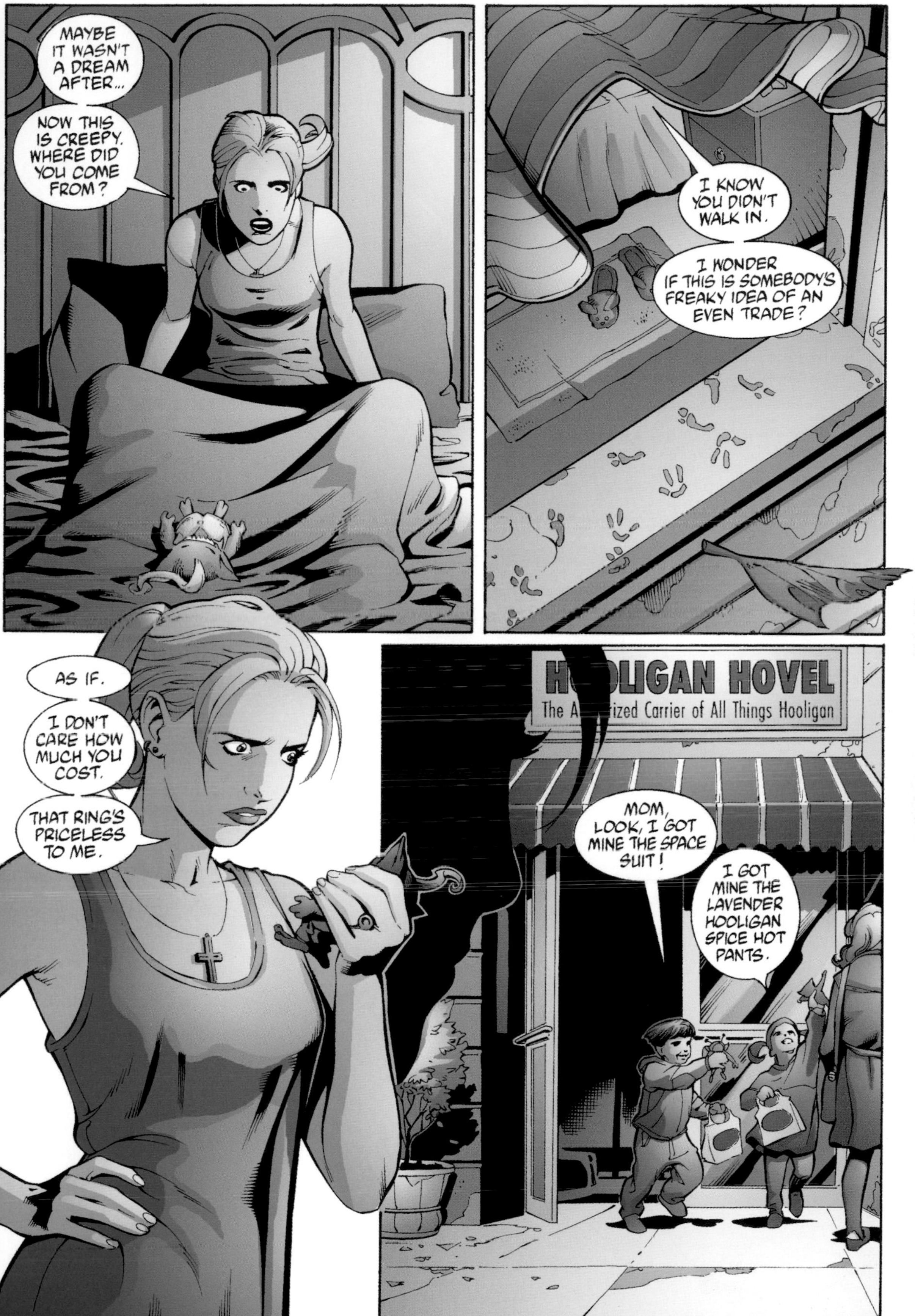
MAYBE IT WASN'T A DREAM AFTER...
NOW THIS IS CREEPY. WHERE DID YOU COME FROM?
I KNOW YOU DIDN'T WALK IN.
I WONDER IF THIS IS SOMEBODY'S FREAKY IDEA OF AN EVEN TRADE?
AS IF.
I DON'T CARE HOW MUCH YOU COST.
THAT RING'S PRICELESS TO ME.
HOOLIGAN HOVEL
The A rized Carrier of All Things Hooligan
MOM, LOOK, I GOT MINE THE SPACE SUIT!
I GOT MINE THE LAVENDER HOOLIGAN SPICE HOT PANTS.

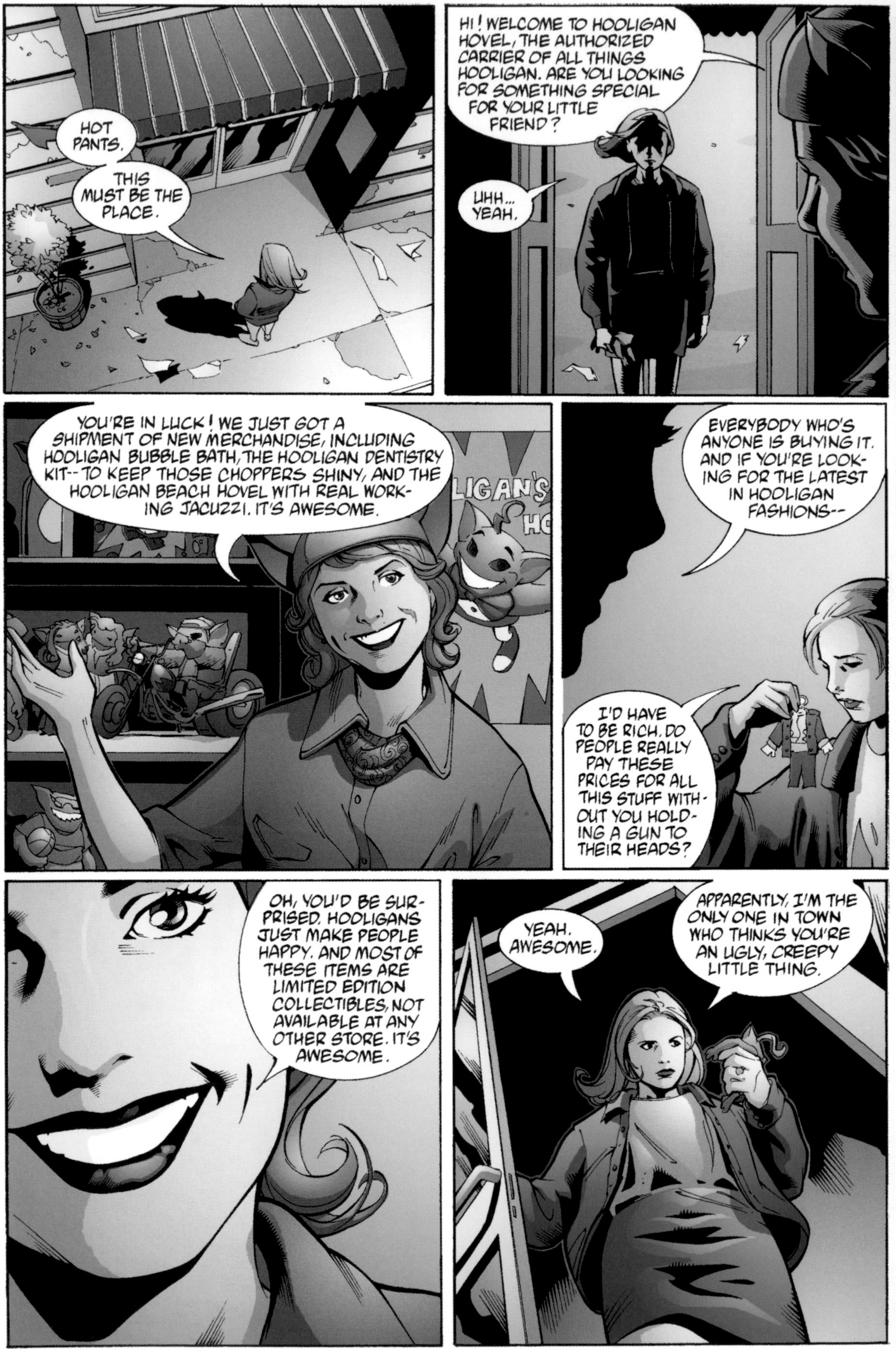
HOT PANTS.
THIS MUST BE THE PLACE.
HI! WELCOME TO HOOLIGAN HOVEL, THE AUTHORIZED CARRIER OF ALL THINGS HOOLIGAN. ARE YOU LOOKING FOR SOMETHING SPECIAL FOR YOUR LITTLE FRIEND?
UHH... YEAH.
YOU'RE IN LUCK! WE JUST GOT A SHIPMENT OF NEW MERCHANDISE, INCLUDING HOOLIGAN BUBBLE BATH, THE HOOLIGAN DENTISTRY KIT-- TO KEEP THOSE CHOPPERS SHINY, AND THE HOOLIGAN BEACH HOVEL WITH REAL WORKING JACUZZI. IT'S AWESOME.
LIGAN'S
HO
EVERYBODY WHO'S ANYONE IS BUYING IT. AND IF YOU'RE LOOKING FOR THE LATEST IN HOOLIGAN FASHIONS--
I'D HAVE TO BE RICH. DO PEOPLE REALLY PAY THESE PRICES FOR ALL THIS STUFF WITHOUT YOU HOLDING A GUN TO THEIR HEADS?
OH, YOU'D BE SURPRISED. HOOLIGANS JUST MAKE PEOPLE HAPPY. AND MOST OF THESE ITEMS ARE LIMITED EDITION COLLECTIBLES, NOT AVAILABLE AT ANY OTHER STORE. IT'S AWESOME.
YEAH. AWESOME.
APPARENTLY, I'M THE ONLY ONE IN TOWN WHO THINKS YOU'RE AN UGLY, CREEPY LITTLE THING.

OKAY, HAVE AN AWESOME DAY! THANKS FOR STOPPING BY HOOLIGAN HOVEL, THE AUTHORIZED CARRIER OF ALL THINGS HOOLIGAN!

YOU CAN COME OUT NOW, BOSS. SHE'S GONE. I DIDN'T THINK SHE WAS MEAN, THOUGH. I THOUGHT SHE WAS KIND OF NICE. SHE HAD A CUTE HOOLIGAN...

WOULD YOU CEASE YOUR INANE PRATTLING, AND GET BACK TO STOCKING THE SHELVES?!

SURE THING, MR. RAYNE, RIGHT AWAY.

DON'T TOUCH MY HOOLIGAN, YOU FREAK! YOU WANT ONE, BUY ONE!

HOOLIGAN NIGHT
BRING YOUR HOOLIGAN DRINKS 1/2 PRICE

WOULD YOU BELIEVE AURA DOESN'T EVEN HAVE A HOOLIGAN?

SHE'S A CULTURAL CRIPPLE. SHE'S STILL TRYING TO KEEP THAT KEYCHAIN THING ALIVE.

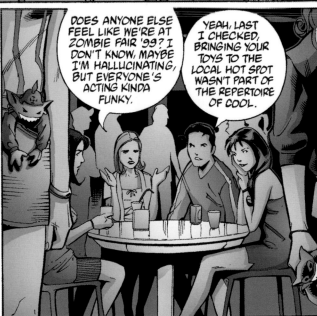

DOES ANYONE ELSE FEEL LIKE WE'RE AT ZOMBIE FAIR '99? I DON'T KNOW, MAYBE I'M HALLUCINATING, BUT EVERYONE'S ACTING KINDA FUNKY.

YEAH, LAST I CHECKED, BRINGING YOUR TOYS TO THE LOCAL HOT SPOT WASN'T PART OF THE REPERTOIRE OF COOL.

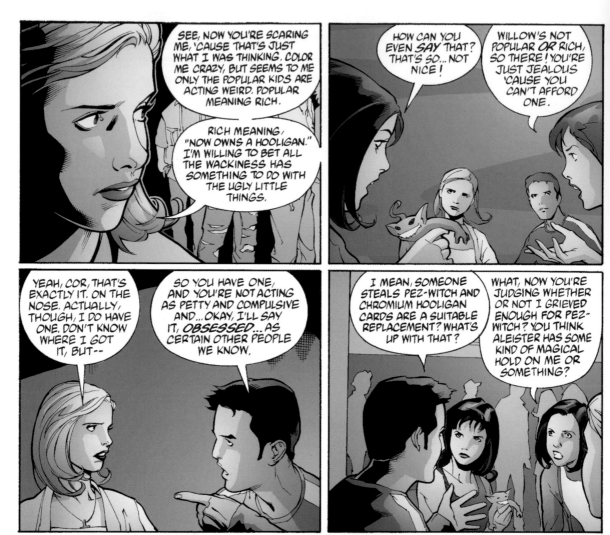

SEE, NOW YOU'RE SCARING ME, 'CAUSE THAT'S JUST WHAT I WAS THINKING. COLOR ME CRAZY, BUT SEEMS TO ME ONLY THE POPULAR KIDS ARE ACTING WEIRD. POPULAR MEANING RICH.

RICH MEANING, "NOW OWNS A HOOLIGAN." I'M WILLING TO BET ALL THE WACKINESS HAS SOMETHING TO DO WITH THE UGLY LITTLE THINGS.

HOW CAN YOU EVEN *SAY* THAT? THAT'S SO... NOT NICE!

WILLOW'S NOT POPULAR *OR* RICH, SO THERE! YOU'RE JUST JEALOUS 'CAUSE YOU CAN'T AFFORD ONE.

YEAH, COR, THAT'S EXACTLY IT. ON THE NOSE. ACTUALLY, THOUGH, I DO HAVE ONE. DON'T KNOW WHERE I GOT IT, BUT--

SO YOU HAVE ONE, AND YOU'RE NOT ACTING AS PETTY AND COMPULSIVE AND... OKAY, I'LL SAY IT, *OBSESSED*... AS CERTAIN OTHER PEOPLE WE KNOW.

I MEAN, SOMEONE STEALS PEZ-WITCH AND CHROMIUM HOOLIGAN CARDS ARE A SUITABLE REPLACEMENT? WHAT'S UP WITH THAT?

WHAT, NOW YOU'RE JUDGING WHETHER OR NOT I GRIEVED ENOUGH FOR PEZ-WITCH? YOU THINK ALEISTER HAS SOME KIND OF MAGICAL HOLD ON ME OR SOMETHING?

THAT'S RIDICULOUS! BUFFY HAS A HOOLIGAN, AND SHE'S BEEN WHINING ABOUT LOSING THAT CHEAP LITTLE RING ANGEL GAVE HER EVER SINCE WE GOT IN HERE.

I WAS GONNA SAY THAT.

TRUE, BUT BUFFY'S ALSO THE SLAYER. IF THESE THINGS *ARE* MAKING EVERYONE ACT FREAKY, MAYBE THEY CAN'T AFFECT HER.

PRETTY MUCH. YEP.

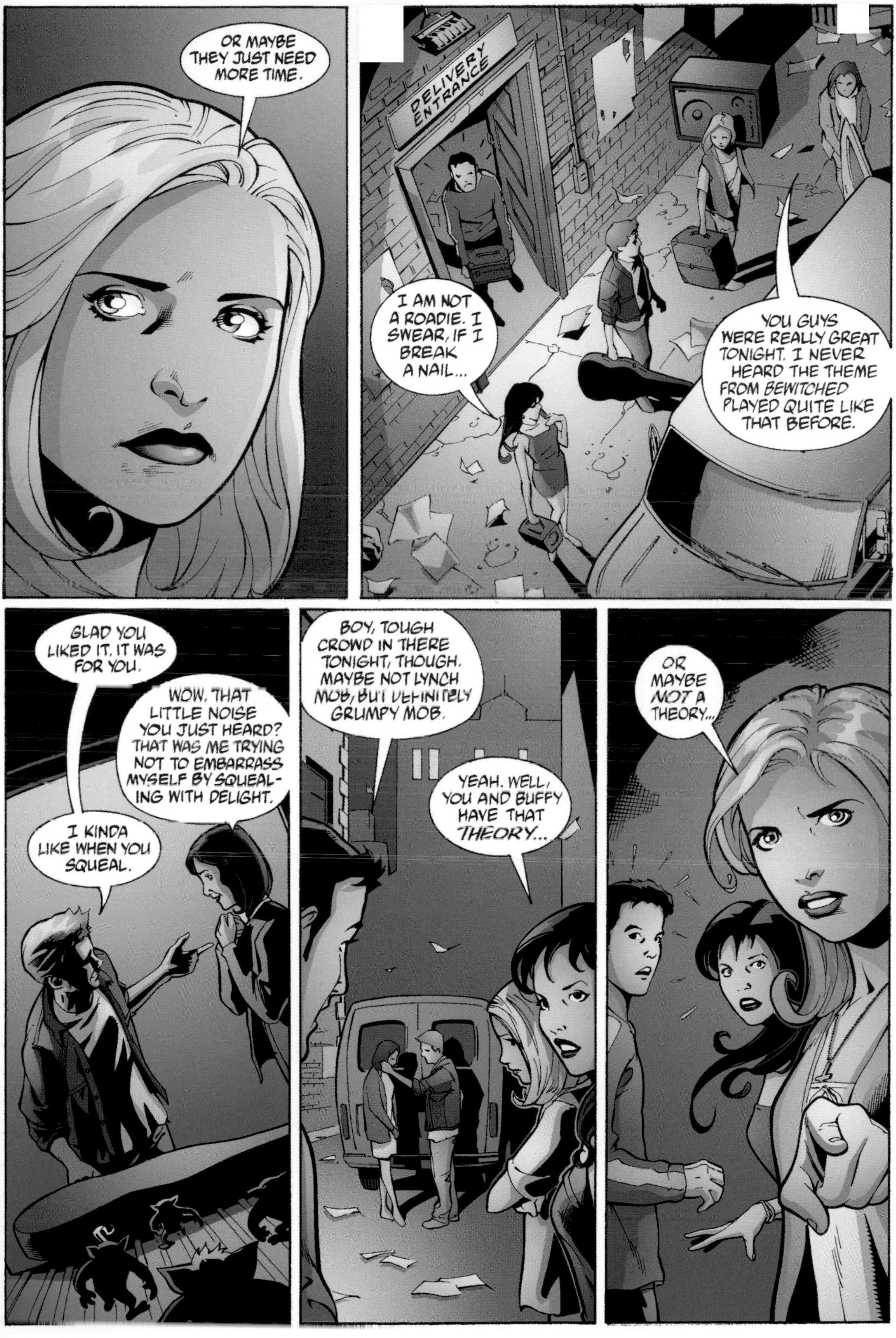

OR MAYBE THEY JUST NEED MORE TIME.
DELIVERY ENTRANCE
I AM NOT A ROADIE. I SWEAR, IF I BREAK A NAIL...
YOU GUYS WERE REALLY GREAT TONIGHT. I NEVER HEARD THE THEME FROM BEWITCHED PLAYED QUITE LIKE THAT BEFORE.
GLAD YOU LIKED IT. IT WAS FOR YOU.
WOW. THAT LITTLE NOISE YOU JUST HEARD? THAT WAS ME TRYING NOT TO EMBARRASS MYSELF BY SQUEALING WITH DELIGHT.
I KINDA LIKE WHEN YOU SQUEAL.
BOY, TOUGH CROWD IN THERE TONIGHT, THOUGH. MAYBE NOT LYNCH MOB, BUT DEFINITELY GRUMPY MOB.
YEAH. WELL, YOU AND BUFFY HAVE THAT THEORY...
OR MAYBE NOT A THEORY...

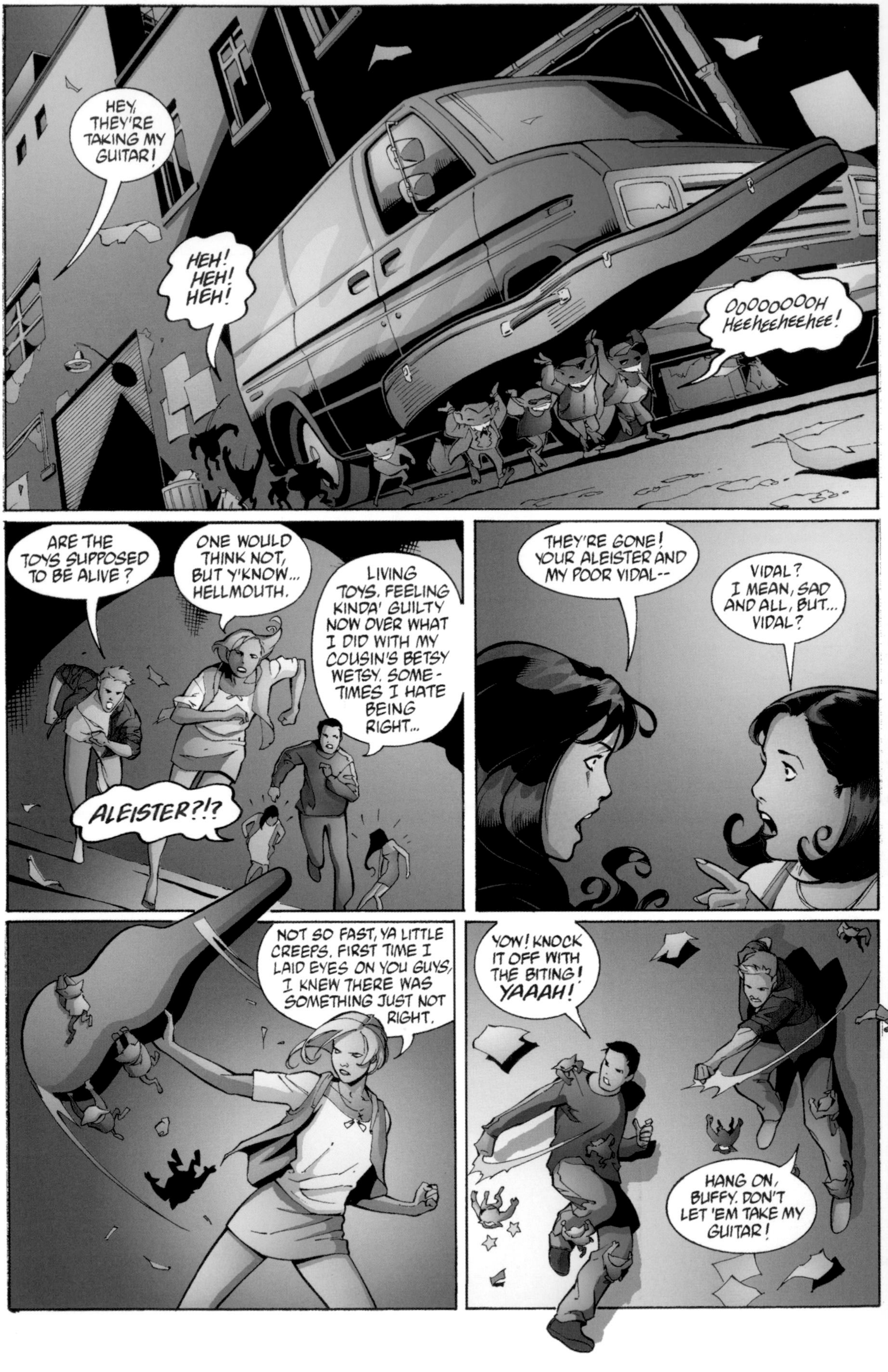
HEY, THEY'RE TAKING MY GUITAR!
HEH! HEH! HEH!
OOOOOOOOH Heeheeheehee!
ARE THE TOYS SUPPOSED TO BE ALIVE?
ONE WOULD THINK NOT, BUT Y'KNOW... HELLMOUTH.
LIVING TOYS. FEELING KINDA' GUILTY NOW OVER WHAT I DID WITH MY COUSIN'S BETSY WETSY. SOMETIMES I HATE BEING RIGHT...
ALEISTER?!?
THEY'RE GONE! YOUR ALEISTER AND MY POOR VIDAL--
VIDAL? I MEAN, SAD AND ALL, BUT... VIDAL?
NOT SO FAST, YA LITTLE CREEPS. FIRST TIME I LAID EYES ON YOU GUYS, I KNEW THERE WAS SOMETHING JUST NOT RIGHT.
YOW! KNOCK IT OFF WITH THE BITING! YAAAH!
HANG ON, BUFFY. DON'T LET 'EM TAKE MY GUITAR!

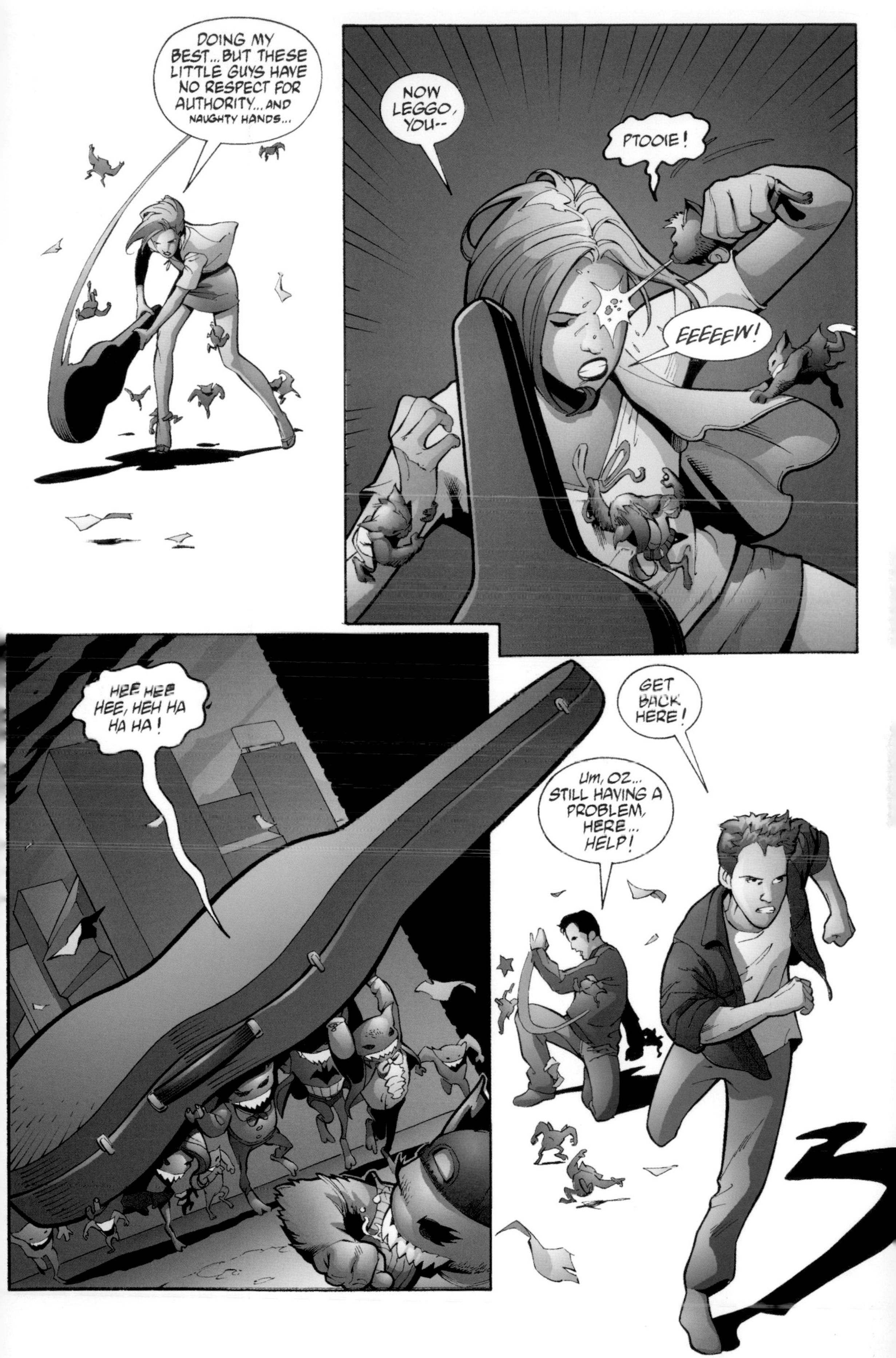
DOING MY BEST... BUT THESE LITTLE GUYS HAVE NO RESPECT FOR AUTHORITY... AND NAUGHTY HANDS...
NOW LEGGO, YOU--
PTOOIE!
EEEEEW!
HEE HEE HEE, HEH HA HA HA!
GET BACK HERE!
UM, OZ... STILL HAVING A PROBLEM, HERE... HELP!

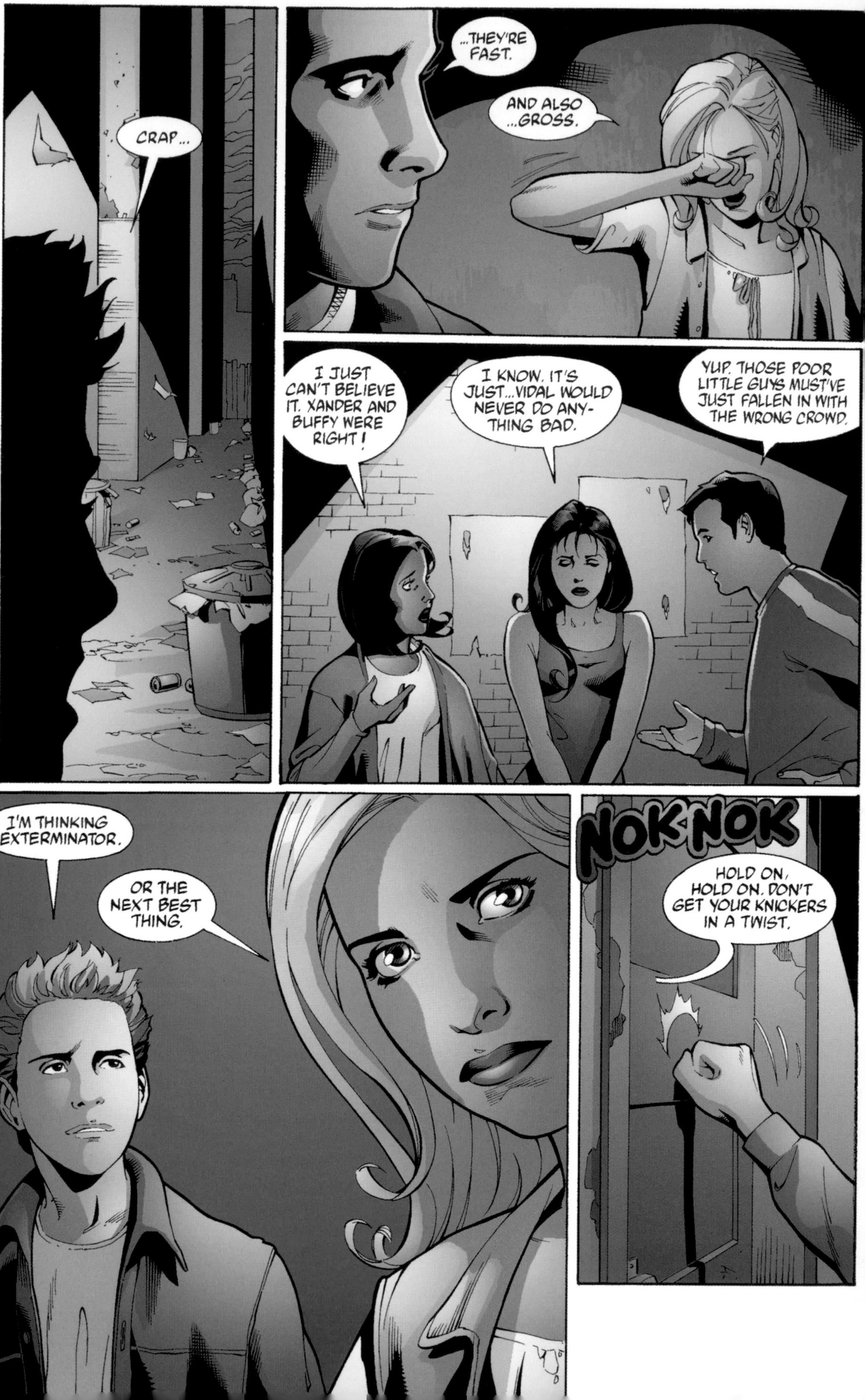
CRAP...
...THEY'RE FAST.
AND ALSO ...GROSS.
I JUST CAN'T BELIEVE IT. XANDER AND BUFFY WERE RIGHT!
I KNOW. IT'S JUST...VIDAL WOULD NEVER DO ANYTHING BAD.
YUP. THOSE POOR LITTLE GUYS MUST'VE JUST FALLEN IN WITH THE WRONG CROWD.
I'M THINKING EXTERMINATOR.
OR THE NEXT BEST THING.
NOK NOK
HOLD ON, HOLD ON. DON'T GET YOUR KNICKERS IN A TWIST.

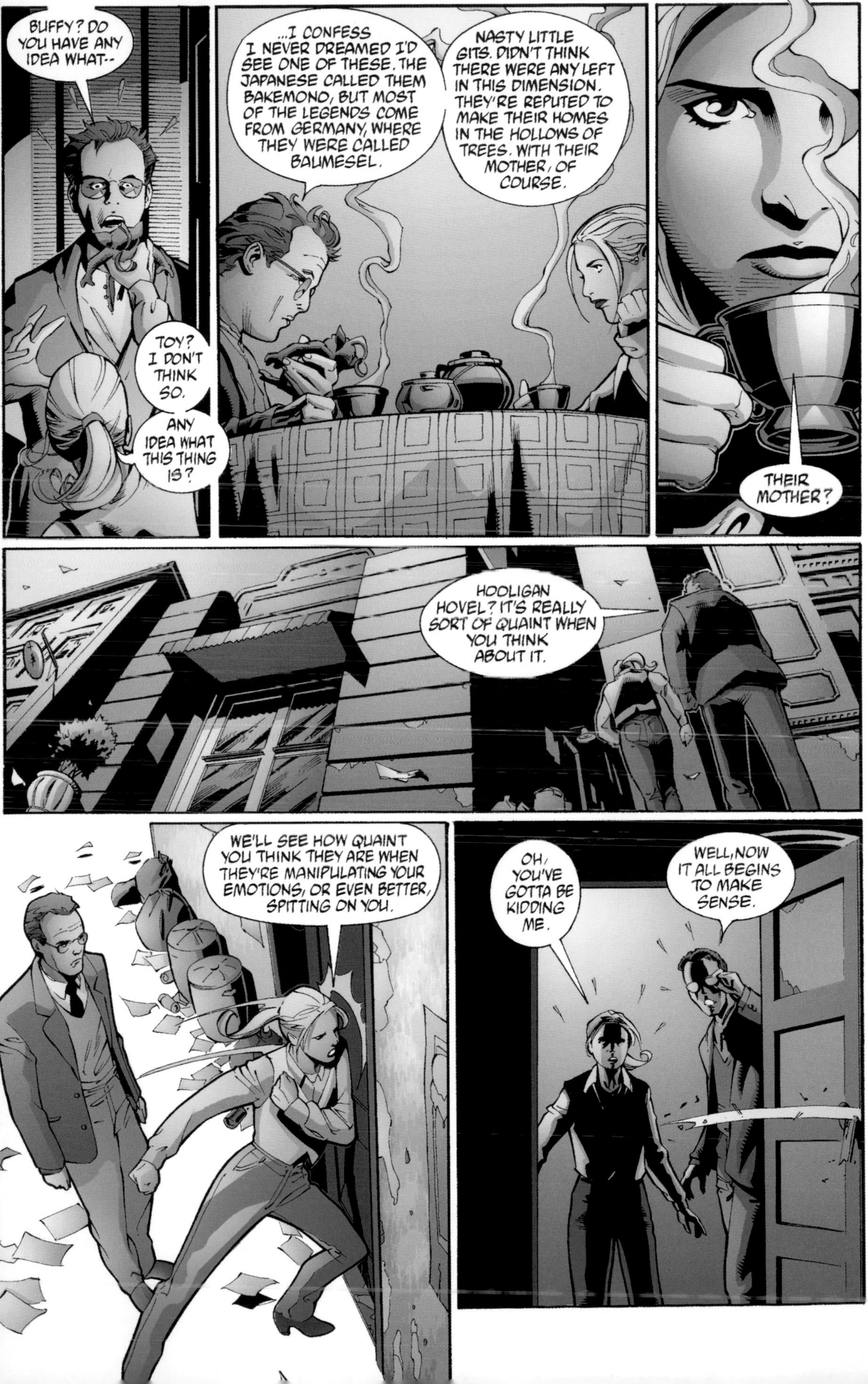
BUFFY? DO YOU HAVE ANY IDEA WHAT--
TOY? I DON'T THINK SO.
ANY IDEA WHAT THIS THING IS?
...I CONFESS I NEVER DREAMED I'D SEE ONE OF THESE. THE JAPANESE CALLED THEM BAKEMONO, BUT MOST OF THE LEGENDS COME FROM GERMANY, WHERE THEY WERE CALLED BAUMESEL.
NASTY LITTLE GITS. DIDN'T THINK THERE WERE ANY LEFT IN THIS DIMENSION. THEY'RE REPUTED TO MAKE THEIR HOMES IN THE HOLLOWS OF TREES. WITH THEIR MOTHER, OF COURSE.
THEIR MOTHER?
HOOLIGAN HOVEL? IT'S REALLY SORT OF QUAINT WHEN YOU THINK ABOUT IT.
WE'LL SEE HOW QUAINT YOU THINK THEY ARE WHEN THEY'RE MANIPULATING YOUR EMOTIONS, OR EVEN BETTER, SPITTING ON YOU.
OH, YOU'VE GOTTA BE KIDDING ME.
WELL, NOW IT ALL BEGINS TO MAKE SENSE.

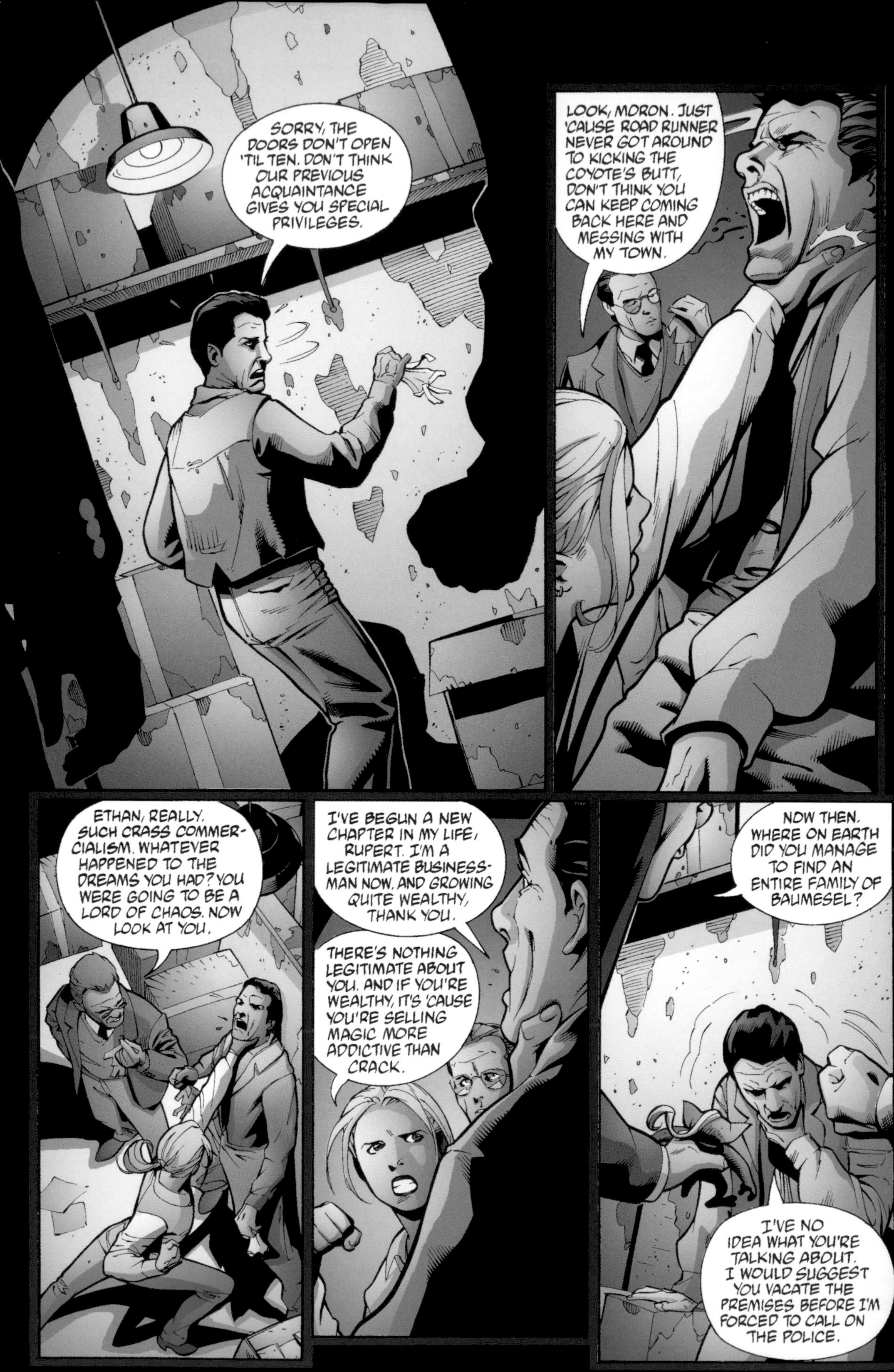
SORRY, THE DOORS DON'T OPEN 'TIL TEN. DON'T THINK OUR PREVIOUS ACQUAINTANCE GIVES YOU SPECIAL PRIVILEGES.
LOOK, MORON. JUST 'CAUSE ROAD RUNNER NEVER GOT AROUND TO KICKING THE COYOTE'S BUTT, DON'T THINK YOU CAN KEEP COMING BACK HERE AND MESSING WITH MY TOWN.
ETHAN, REALLY. SUCH CRASS COMMERCIALISM. WHATEVER HAPPENED TO THE DREAMS YOU HAD? YOU WERE GOING TO BE A LORD OF CHAOS. NOW LOOK AT YOU.
I'VE BEGUN A NEW CHAPTER IN MY LIFE, RUPERT. I'M A LEGITIMATE BUSINESSMAN NOW, AND GROWING QUITE WEALTHY, THANK YOU.
THERE'S NOTHING LEGITIMATE ABOUT YOU. AND IF YOU'RE WEALTHY, IT'S 'CAUSE YOU'RE SELLING MAGIC MORE ADDICTIVE THAN CRACK.
NOW THEN. WHERE ON EARTH DID YOU MANAGE TO FIND AN ENTIRE FAMILY OF BAUMESEL?
I'VE NO IDEA WHAT YOU'RE TALKING ABOUT. I WOULD SUGGEST YOU VACATE THE PREMISES BEFORE I'M FORCED TO CALL ON THE POLICE.

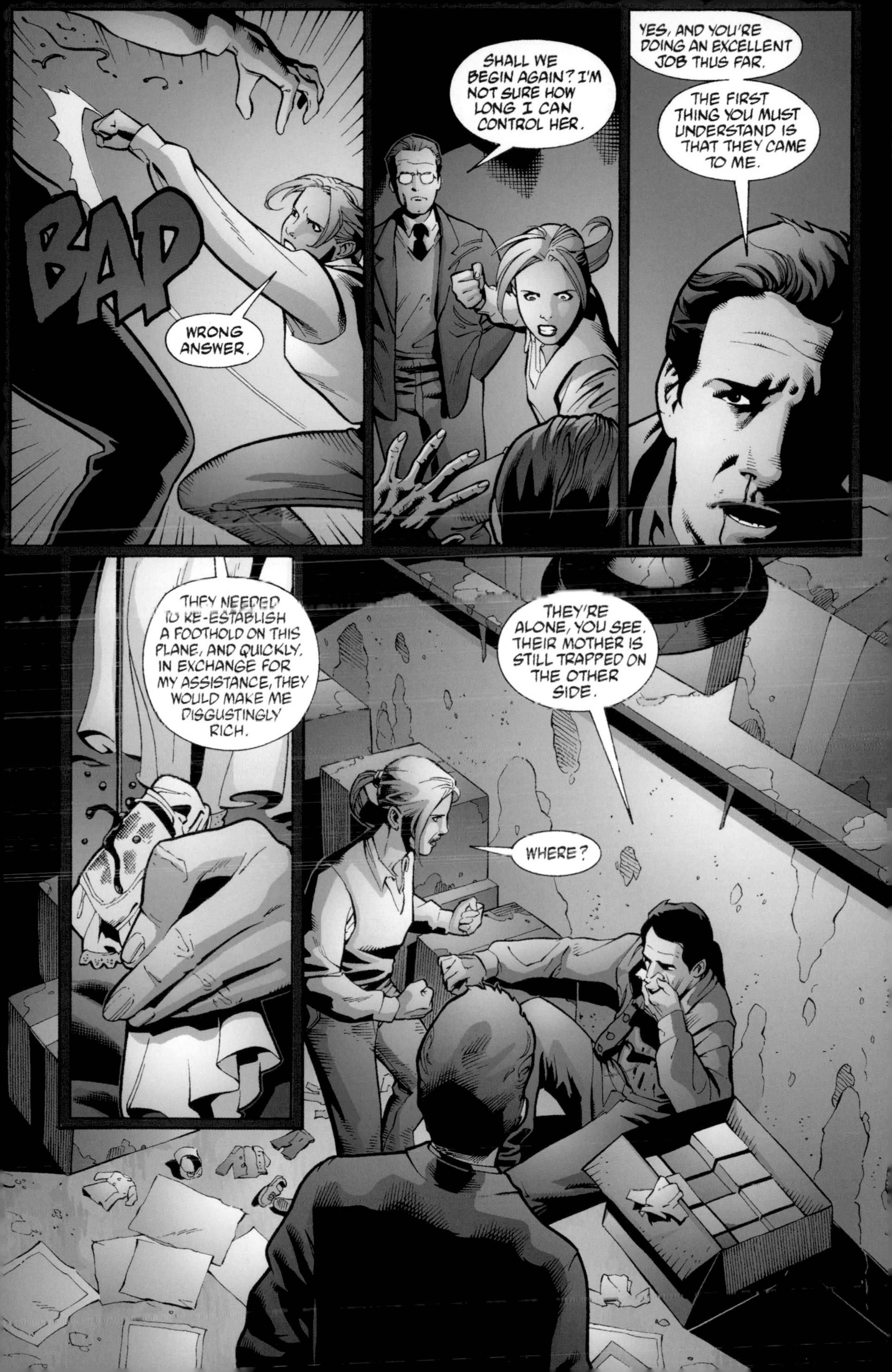
BAP
WRONG ANSWER.
SHALL WE BEGIN AGAIN? I'M NOT SURE HOW LONG I CAN CONTROL HER.
YES, AND YOU'RE DOING AN EXCELLENT JOB THUS FAR.
THE FIRST THING YOU MUST UNDERSTAND IS THAT THEY CAME TO ME.
THEY NEEDED TO RE-ESTABLISH A FOOTHOLD ON THIS PLANE, AND QUICKLY. IN EXCHANGE FOR MY ASSISTANCE, THEY WOULD MAKE ME DISGUSTINGLY RICH.
THEY'RE ALONE, YOU SEE. THEIR MOTHER IS STILL TRAPPED ON THE OTHER SIDE.
WHERE?

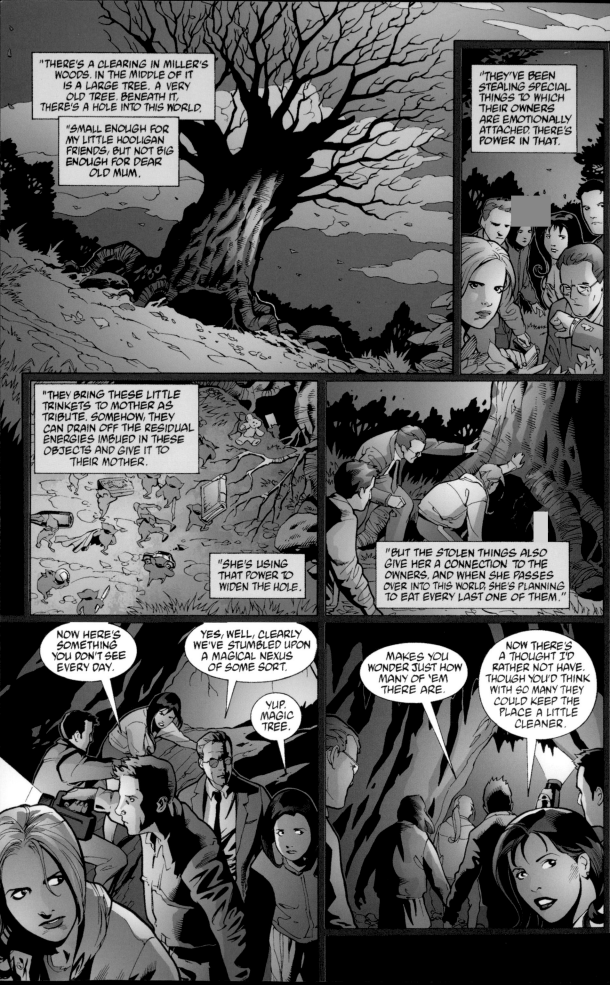

"THERE'S A CLEARING IN MILLER'S WOODS. IN THE MIDDLE OF IT IS A LARGE TREE. A VERY OLD TREE. BENEATH IT, THERE'S A HOLE INTO THIS WORLD.

"SMALL ENOUGH FOR MY LITTLE HOOLIGAN FRIENDS, BUT NOT BIG ENOUGH FOR DEAR OLD MUM.

"THEY'VE BEEN STEALING SPECIAL THINGS TO WHICH THEIR OWNERS ARE EMOTIONALLY ATTACHED. THERE'S POWER IN THAT.

"THEY BRING THESE LITTLE TRINKETS TO MOTHER AS TRIBUTE. SOMEHOW, THEY CAN DRAIN OFF THE RESIDUAL ENERGIES IMBUED IN THESE OBJECTS AND GIVE IT TO THEIR MOTHER.

"SHE'S USING THAT POWER TO WIDEN THE HOLE.

"BUT THE STOLEN THINGS ALSO GIVE HER A CONNECTION TO THE OWNERS, AND WHEN SHE PASSES OVER INTO THIS WORLD, SHE'S PLANNING TO EAT EVERY LAST ONE OF THEM."

NOW HERE'S SOMETHING YOU DON'T SEE EVERY DAY.

YES, WELL, CLEARLY WE'VE STUMBLED UPON A MAGICAL NEXUS OF SOME SORT.

YUP. MAGIC TREE.

MAKES YOU WONDER JUST HOW MANY OF 'EM THERE ARE.

NOW THERE'S A THOUGHT I'D RATHER NOT HAVE. THOUGH YOU'D THINK WITH SO MANY THEY COULD KEEP THE PLACE A LITTLE CLEANER.

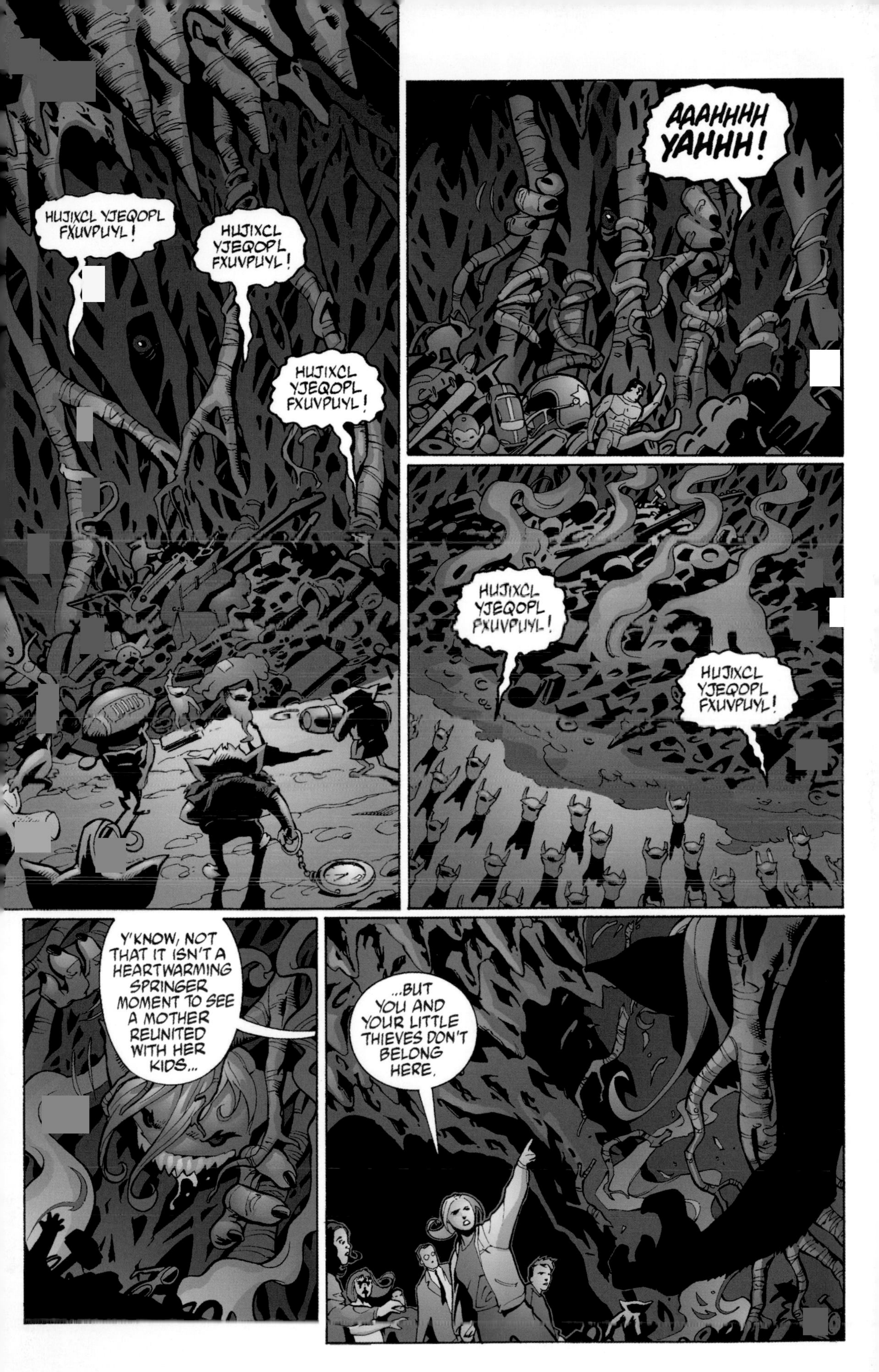
HUJIXCL YJEQOPL FXUVPUYL!
HUJIXCL YJEQOPL FXUVPUYL!
HUJIXCL YJEQOPL FXUVPUYL!
AAAHHHH YAHHH!
HUJIXCL YJEQOPL FXUVPUYL!
HUJIXCL YJEQOPL FXUVPUYL!
Y'KNOW, NOT THAT IT ISN'T A HEARTWARMING SPRINGER MOMENT TO SEE A MOTHER REUNITED WITH HER KIDS...
...BUT YOU AND YOUR LITTLE THIEVES DON'T BELONG HERE.

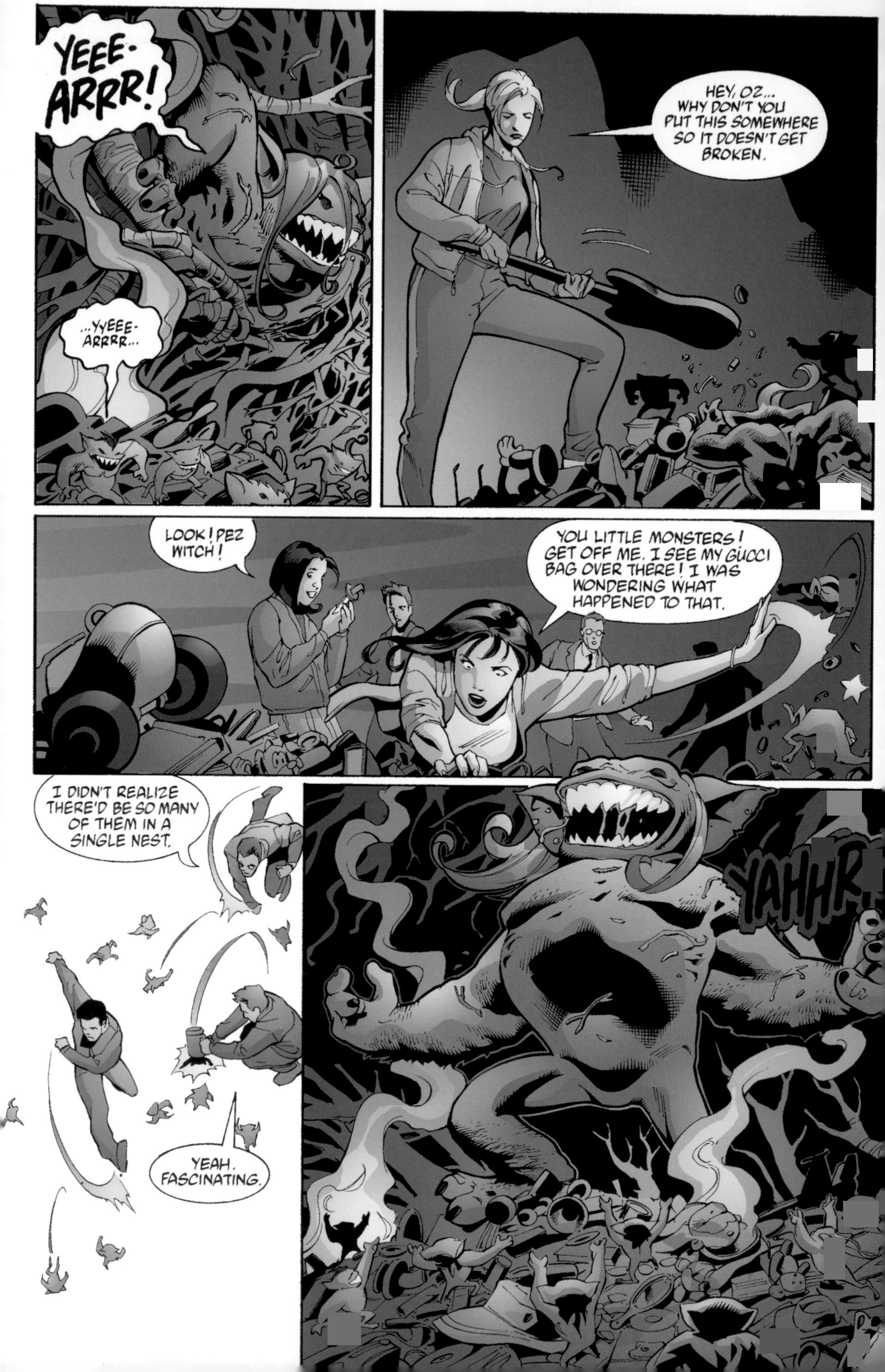
YEEE-ARRR!
...YYEEE-ARRRR...
HEY, OZ... WHY DON'T YOU PUT THIS SOMEWHERE SO IT DOESN'T GET BROKEN.
LOOK! PEZ WITCH!
YOU LITTLE MONSTERS! GET OFF ME. I SEE MY GUCCI BAG OVER THERE! I WAS WONDERING WHAT HAPPENED TO THAT.
I DIDN'T REALIZE THERE'D BE SO MANY OF THEM IN A SINGLE NEST.
YEAH. FASCINATING.
YAHHR!

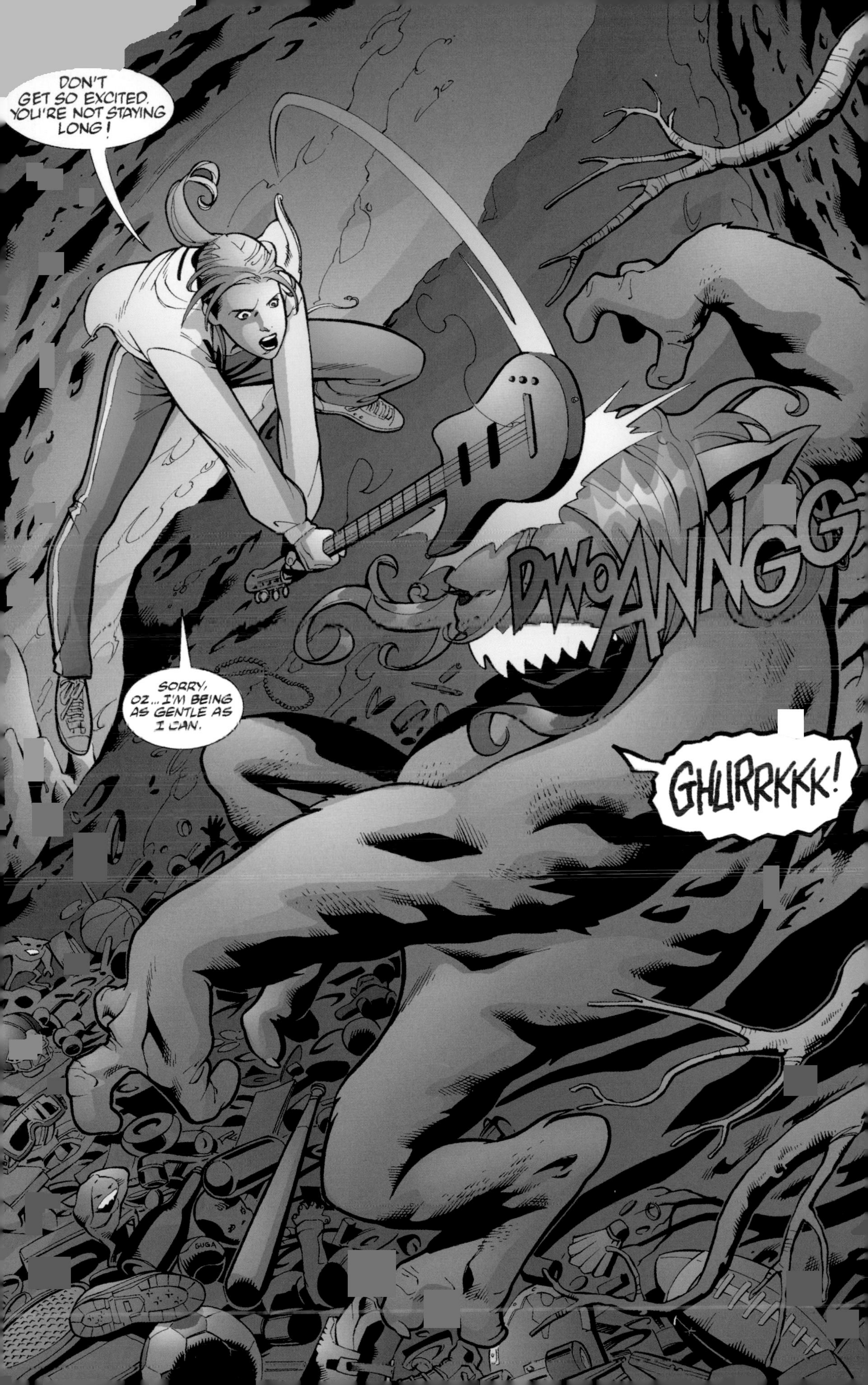
DON'T GET SO EXCITED. YOU'RE NOT STAYING LONG!
DWOANNGG
SORRY, OZ... I'M BEING AS GENTLE AS I CAN.
GHURRKKK!

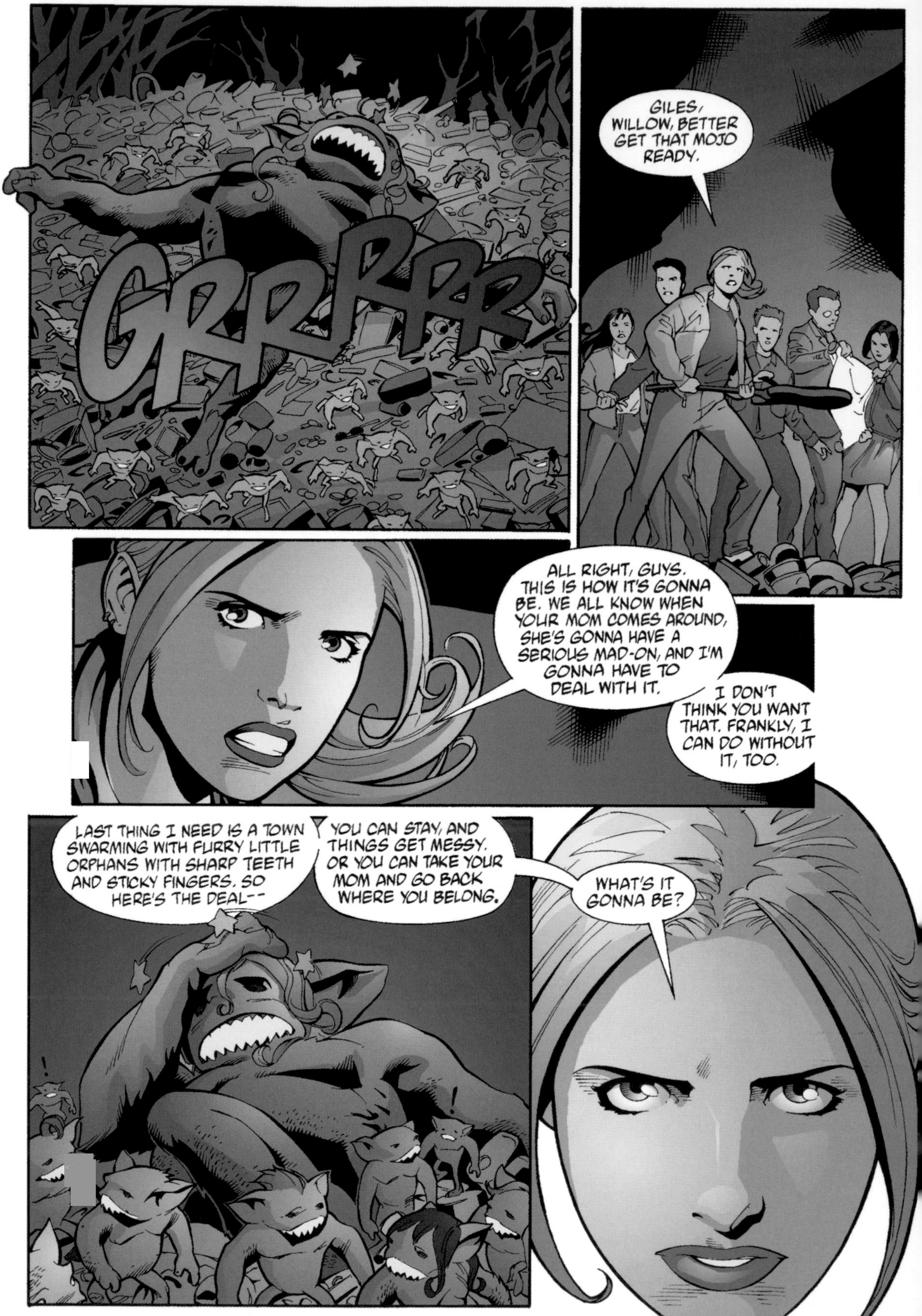
GRRRRR
GILES, WILLOW, BETTER GET THAT MOJO READY.
ALL RIGHT, GUYS. THIS IS HOW IT'S GONNA BE. WE ALL KNOW WHEN YOUR MOM COMES AROUND, SHE'S GONNA HAVE A SERIOUS MAD-ON, AND I'M GONNA HAVE TO DEAL WITH IT.
I DON'T THINK YOU WANT THAT. FRANKLY, I CAN DO WITHOUT IT, TOO.
LAST THING I NEED IS A TOWN SWARMING WITH FURRY LITTLE ORPHANS WITH SHARP TEETH AND STICKY FINGERS. SO HERE'S THE DEAL--
YOU CAN STAY, AND THINGS GET MESSY. OR YOU CAN TAKE YOUR MOM AND GO BACK WHERE YOU BELONG.
WHAT'S IT GONNA BE?
!
!

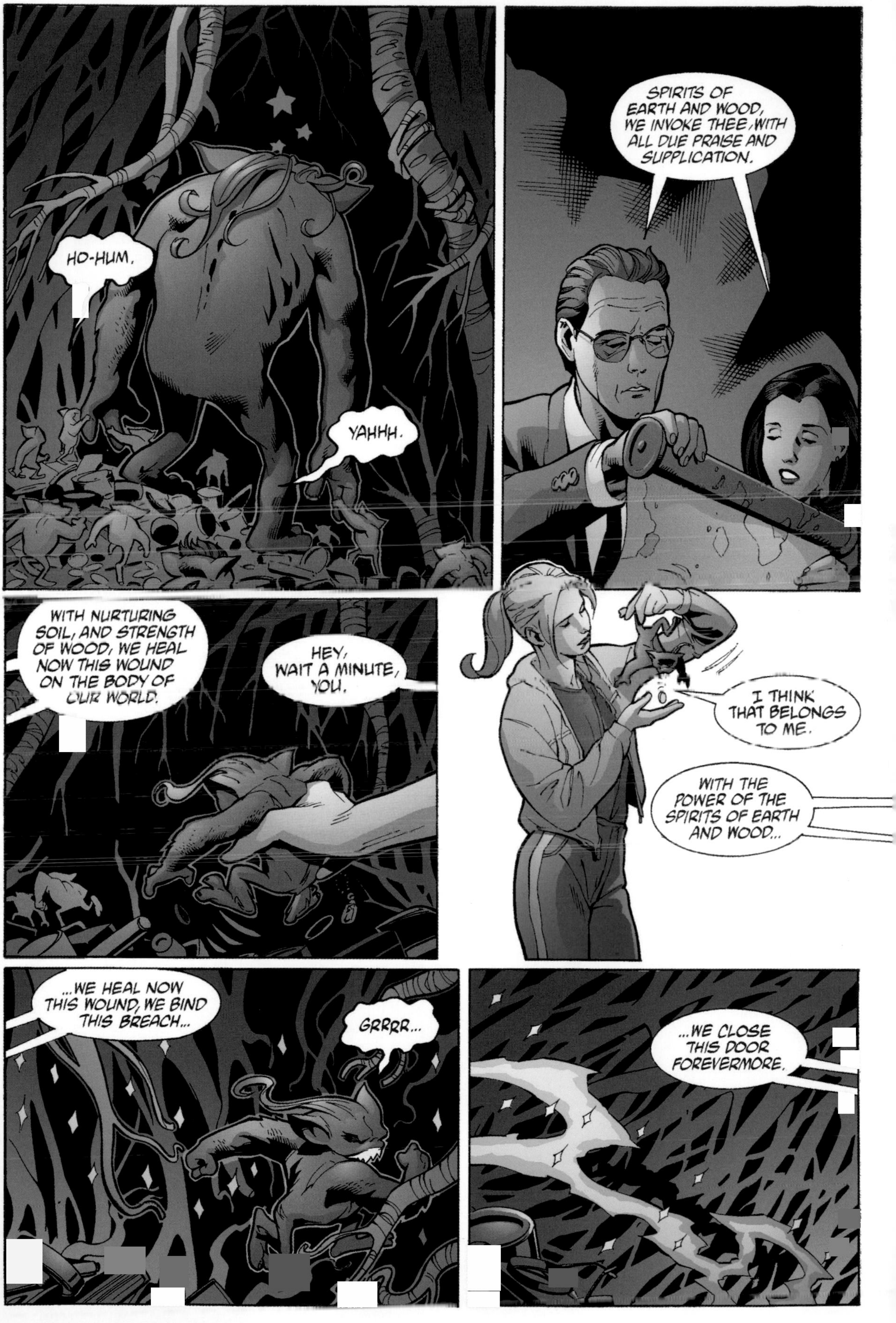
HO-HUM.
YAHHH.
SPIRITS OF EARTH AND WOOD, WE INVOKE THEE, WITH ALL DUE PRAISE AND SUPPLICATION.
WITH NURTURING SOIL, AND STRENGTH OF WOOD, WE HEAL NOW THIS WOUND ON THE BODY OF OUR WORLD.
HEY, WAIT A MINUTE, YOU.
I THINK THAT BELONGS TO ME.
WITH THE POWER OF THE SPIRITS OF EARTH AND WOOD...
...WE HEAL NOW THIS WOUND, WE BIND THIS BREACH...
GRRRR...
...WE CLOSE THIS DOOR FOREVERMORE.

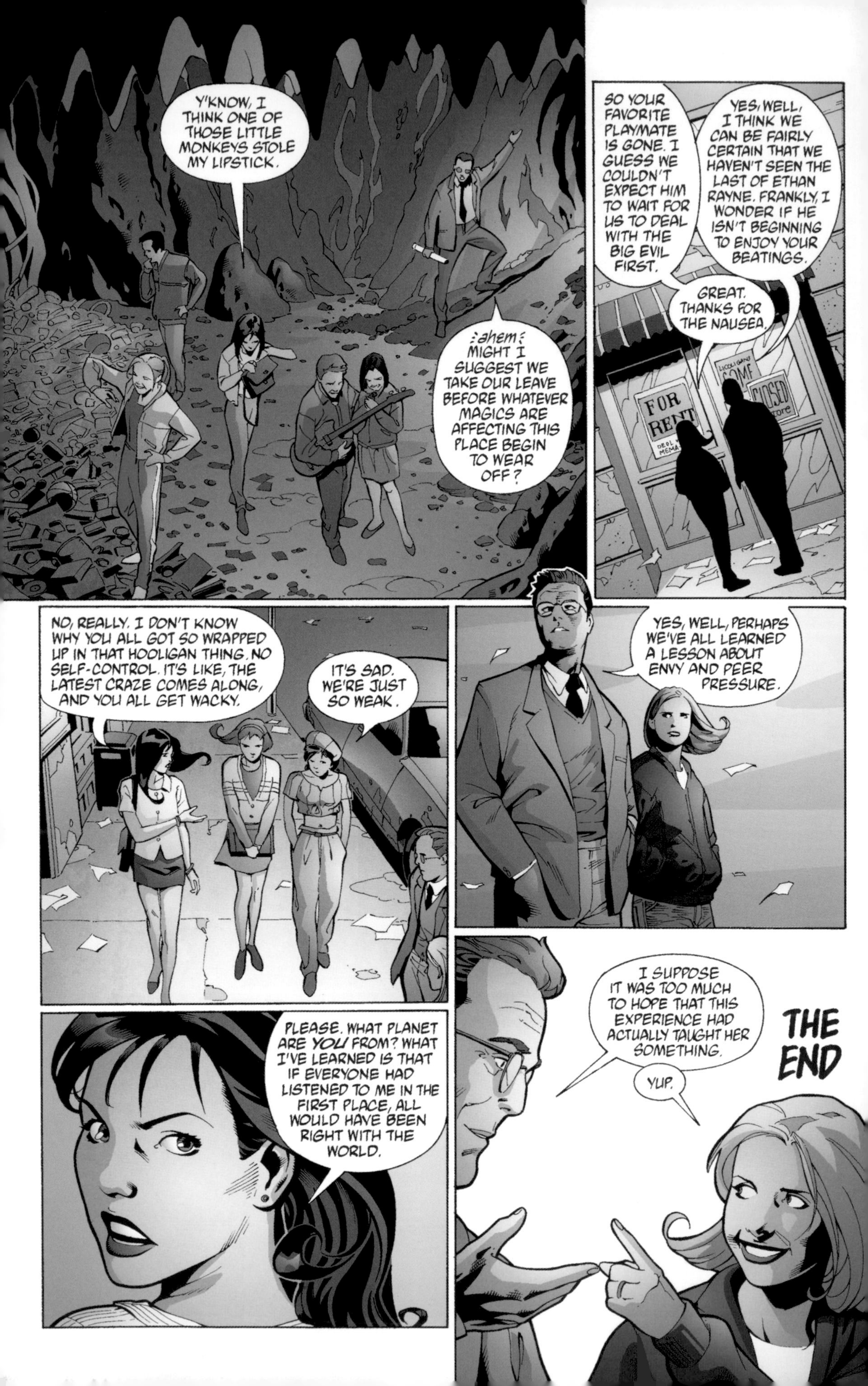
Y'KNOW, I THINK ONE OF THOSE LITTLE MONKEYS STOLE MY LIPSTICK.
:ahem: MIGHT I SUGGEST WE TAKE OUR LEAVE BEFORE WHATEVER MAGICS ARE AFFECTING THIS PLACE BEGIN TO WEAR OFF?
SO YOUR FAVORITE PLAYMATE IS GONE. I GUESS WE COULDN'T EXPECT HIM TO WAIT FOR US TO DEAL WITH THE BIG EVIL FIRST.
YES, WELL, I THINK WE CAN BE FAIRLY CERTAIN THAT WE HAVEN'T SEEN THE LAST OF ETHAN RAYNE. FRANKLY, I WONDER IF HE ISN'T BEGINNING TO ENJOY YOUR BEATINGS.
GREAT. THANKS FOR THE NAUSEA.
FOR RENT
CLOSED
NO, REALLY. I DON'T KNOW WHY YOU ALL GOT SO WRAPPED UP IN THAT HOOLIGAN THING. NO SELF-CONTROL. IT'S LIKE, THE LATEST CRAZE COMES ALONG, AND YOU ALL GET WACKY.
IT'S SAD. WE'RE JUST SO WEAK.
YES, WELL, PERHAPS WE'VE ALL LEARNED A LESSON ABOUT ENVY AND PEER PRESSURE.
PLEASE. WHAT PLANET ARE YOU FROM? WHAT I'VE LEARNED IS THAT IF EVERYONE HAD LISTENED TO ME IN THE FIRST PLACE, ALL WOULD HAVE BEEN RIGHT WITH THE WORLD.
I SUPPOSE IT WAS TOO MUCH TO HOPE THAT THIS EXPERIENCE HAD ACTUALLY TAUGHT HER SOMETHING.
YUP.
THE END

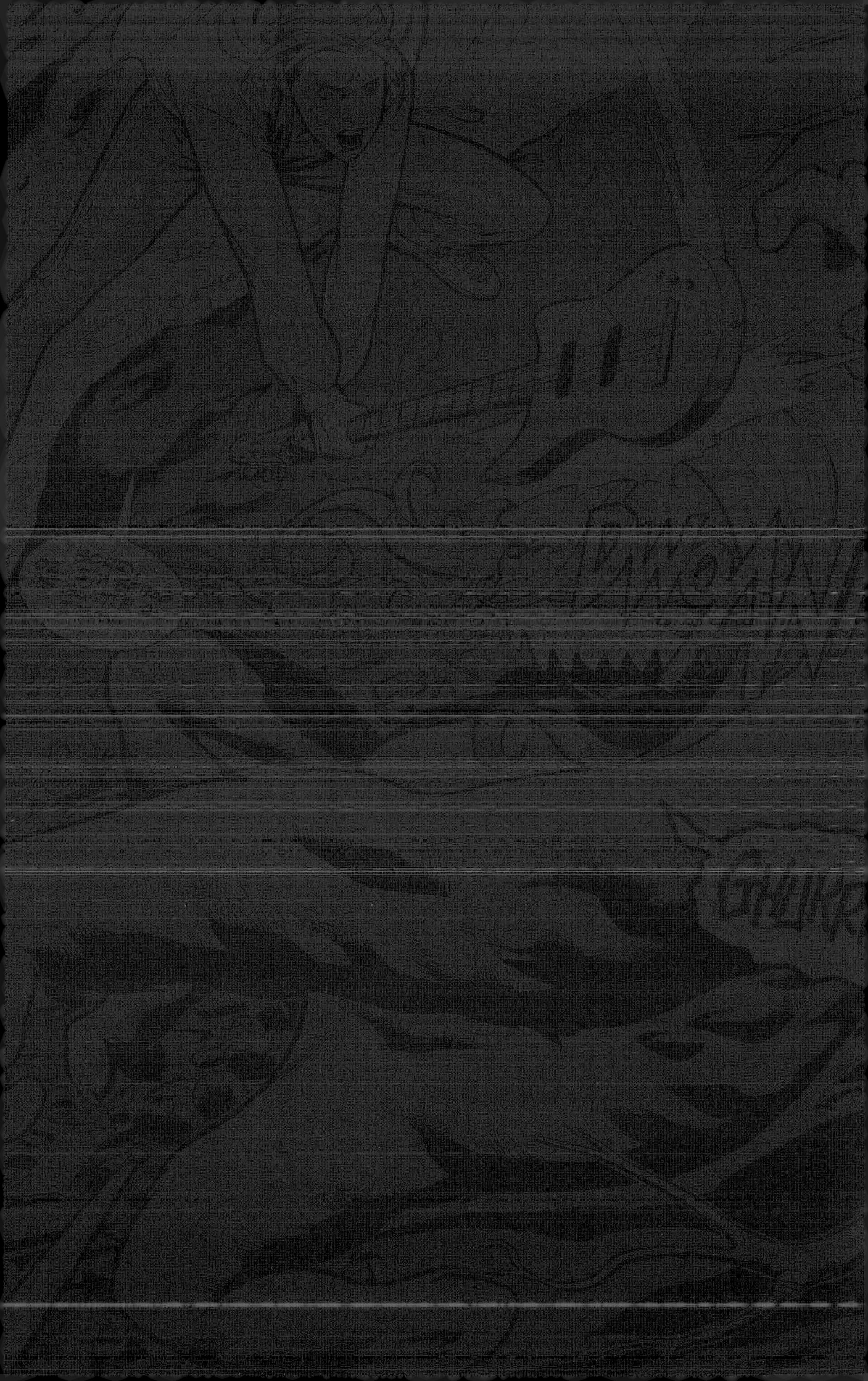

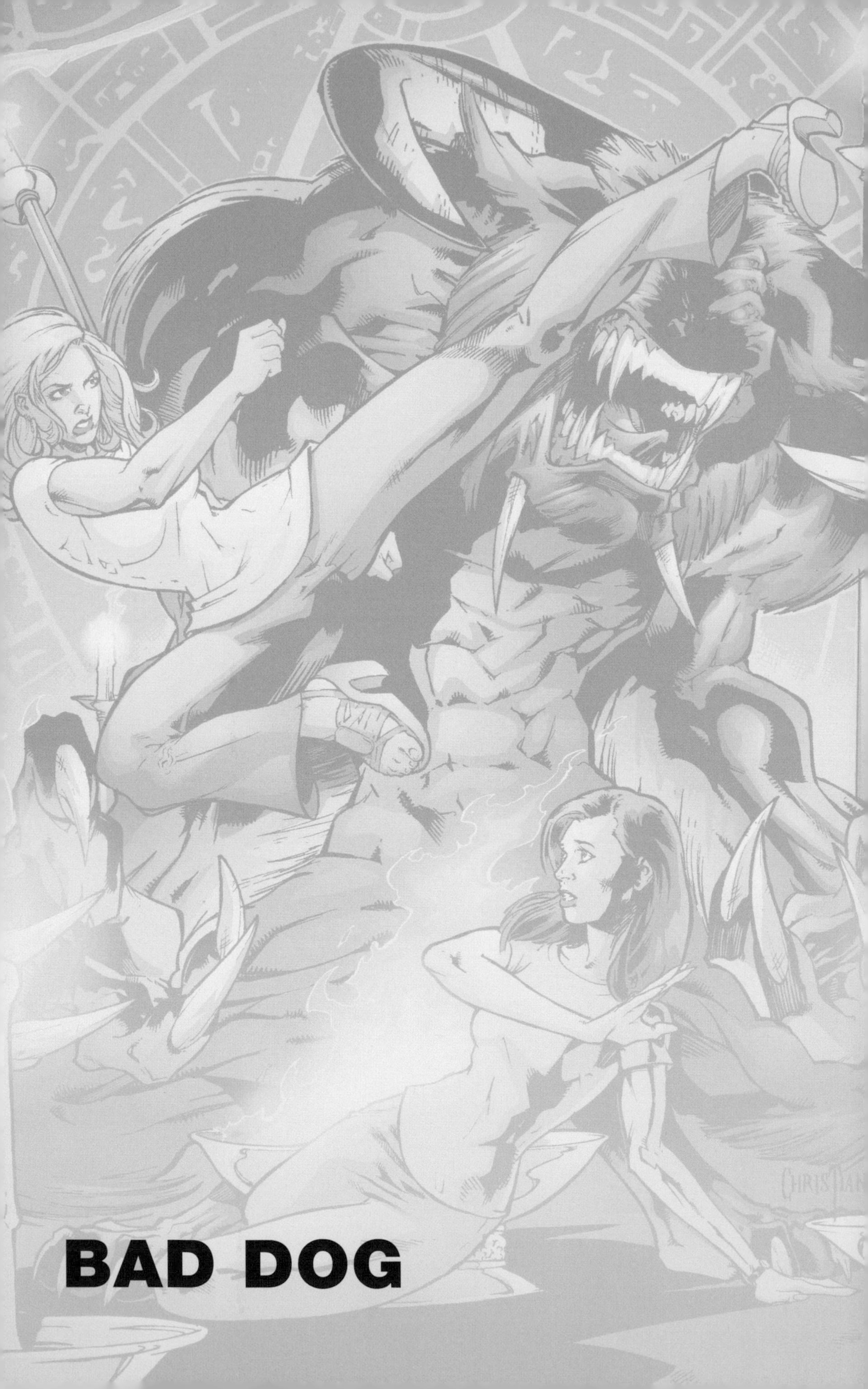

BAD DOG

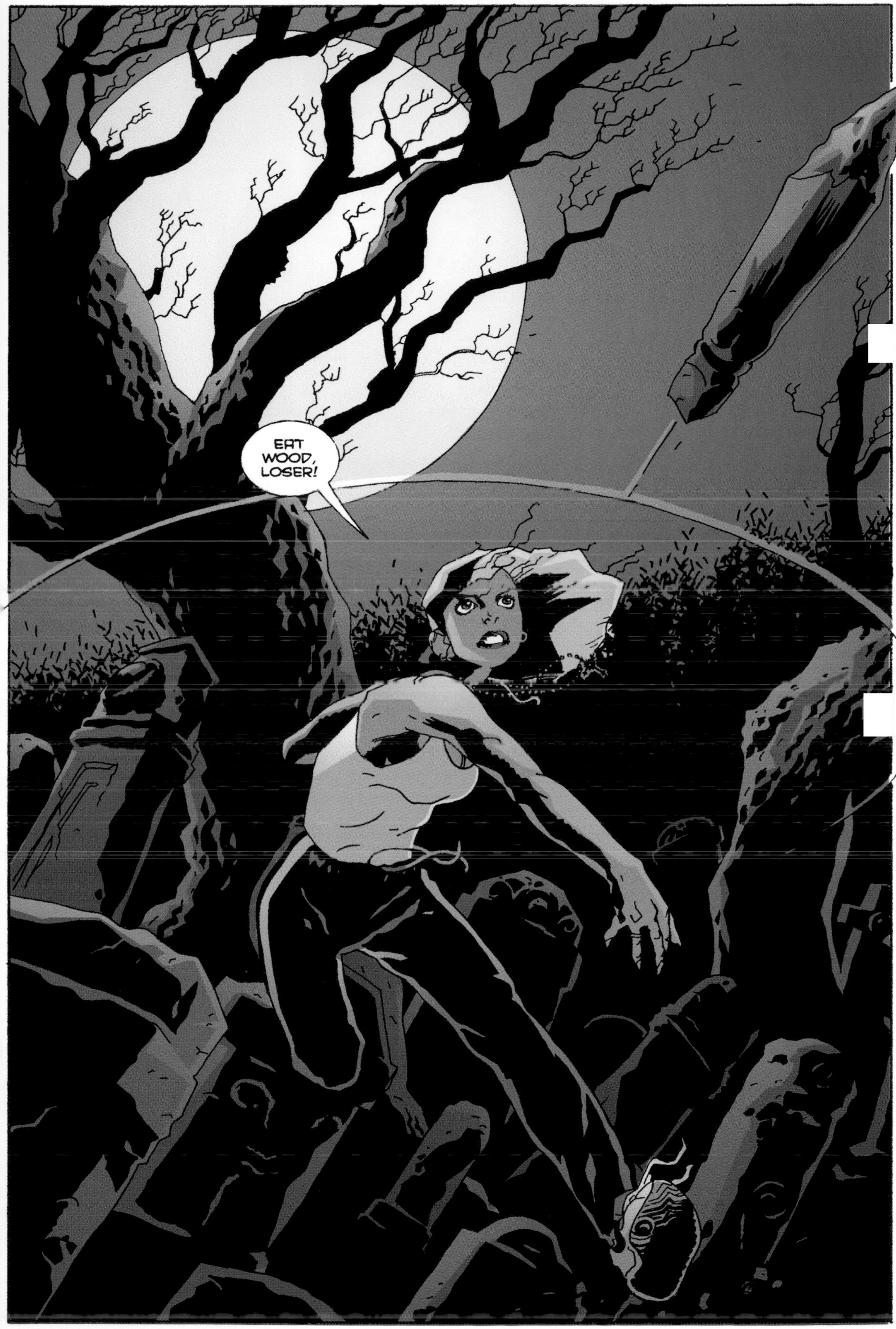
EAT WOOD, LOSER!

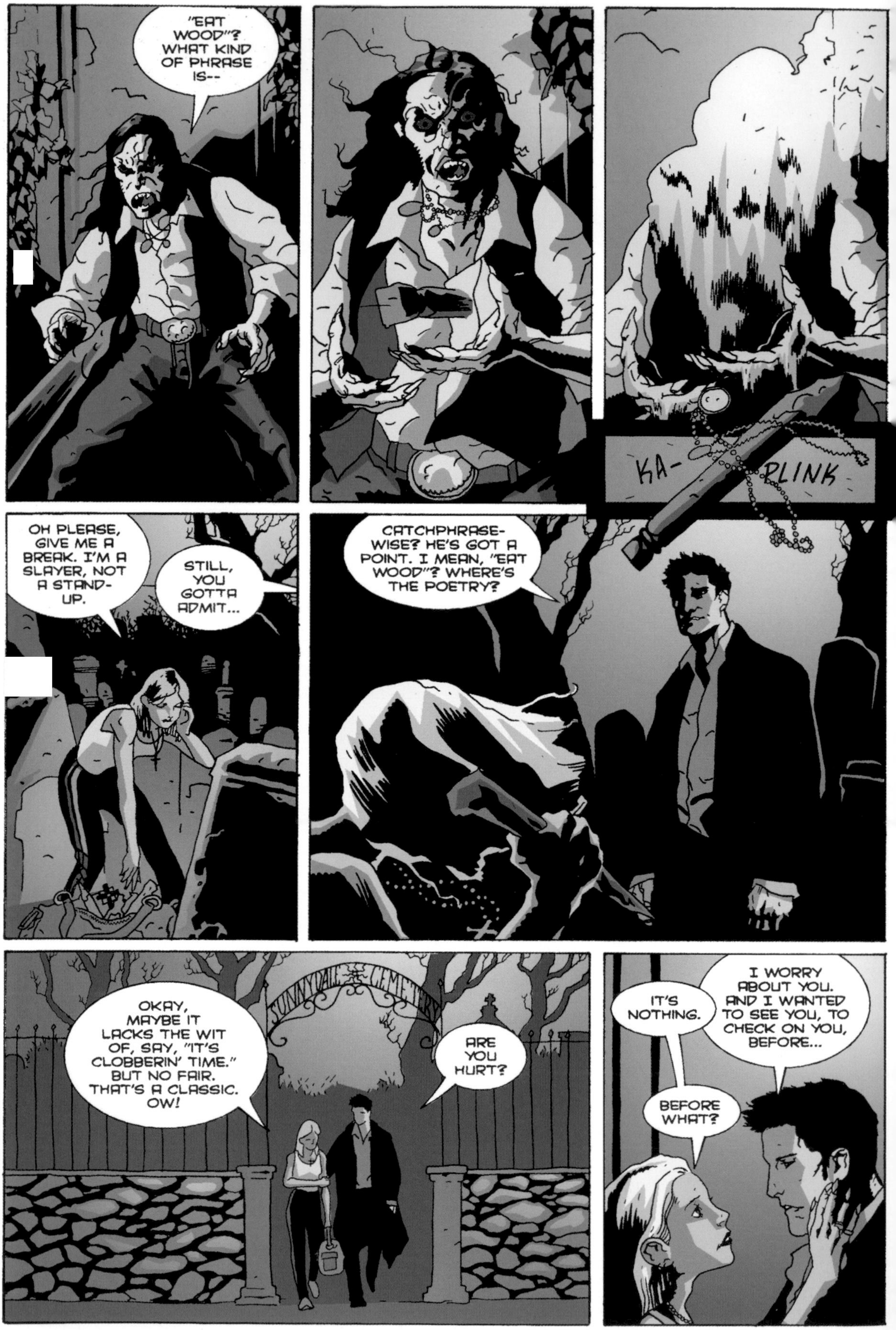
"EAT WOOD"? WHAT KIND OF PHRASE IS--
KA-PLINK
OH PLEASE, GIVE ME A BREAK. I'M A SLAYER, NOT A STAND-UP.
STILL, YOU GOTTA ADMIT...
CATCHPHRASE-WISE? HE'S GOT A POINT. I MEAN, "EAT WOOD"? WHERE'S THE POETRY?
SUNNYDALE CEMETERY
OKAY, MAYBE IT LACKS THE WIT OF, SAY, "IT'S CLOBBERIN' TIME." BUT NO FAIR. THAT'S A CLASSIC. OW!
ARE YOU HURT?
IT'S NOTHING.
I WORRY ABOUT YOU. AND I WANTED TO SEE YOU, TO CHECK ON YOU, BEFORE...
BEFORE WHAT?

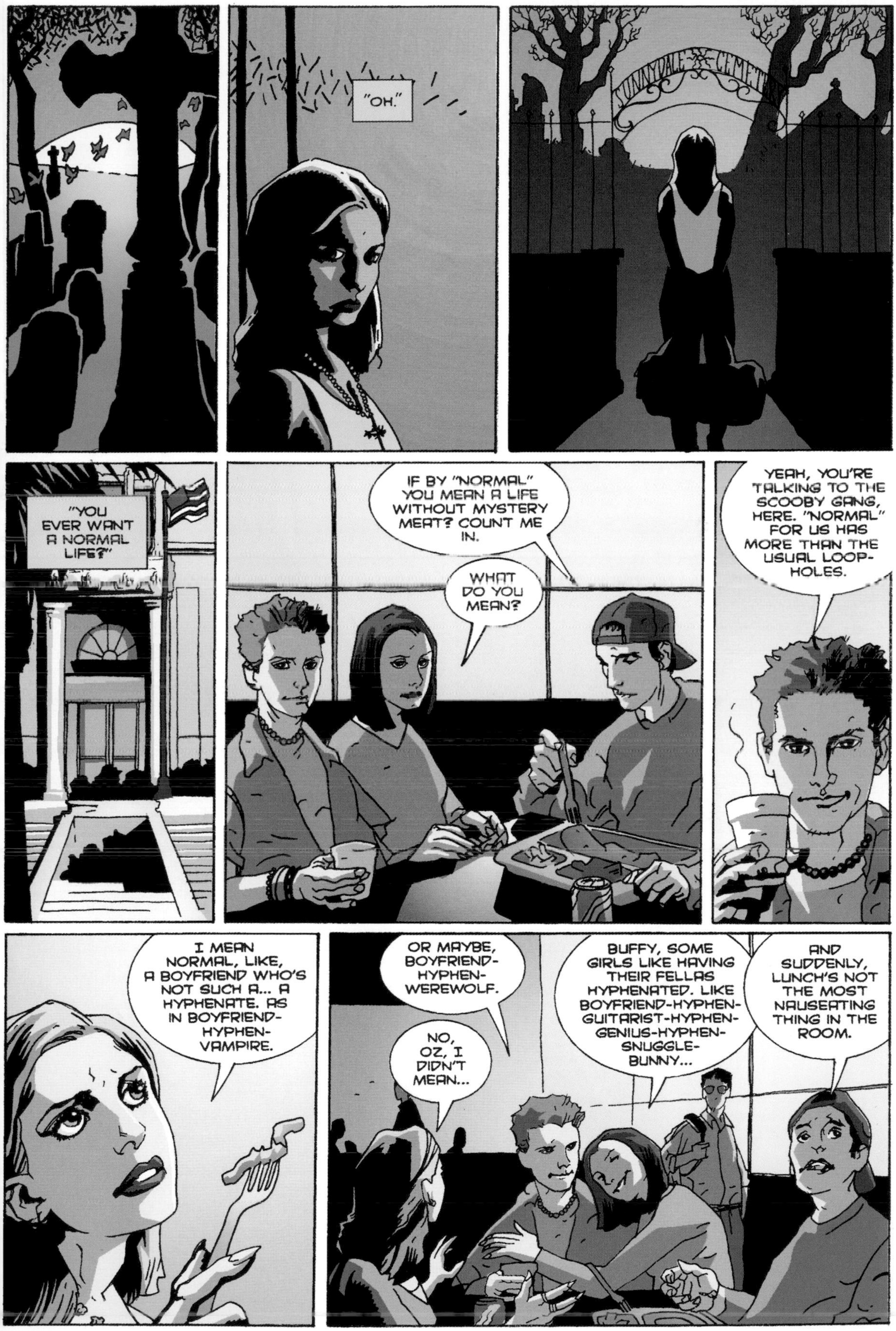
"OH."
"YOU EVER WANT A NORMAL LIFE?"
IF BY "NORMAL" YOU MEAN A LIFE WITHOUT MYSTERY MEAT? COUNT ME IN.
WHAT DO YOU MEAN?
YEAH, YOU'RE TALKING TO THE SCOOBY GANG, HERE. "NORMAL" FOR US HAS MORE THAN THE USUAL LOOP-HOLES.
I MEAN NORMAL, LIKE, A BOYFRIEND WHO'S NOT SUCH A... A HYPHENATE. AS IN BOYFRIEND-HYPHEN-VAMPIRE.
OR MAYBE, BOYFRIEND-HYPHEN-WEREWOLF.
NO, OZ, I DIDN'T MEAN...
BUFFY, SOME GIRLS LIKE HAVING THEIR FELLAS HYPHENATED. LIKE BOYFRIEND-HYPHEN-GUITARIST-HYPHEN-GENIUS-HYPHEN-SNUGGLE-BUNNY...
AND SUDDENLY, LUNCH'S NOT THE MOST NAUSEATING THING IN THE ROOM.

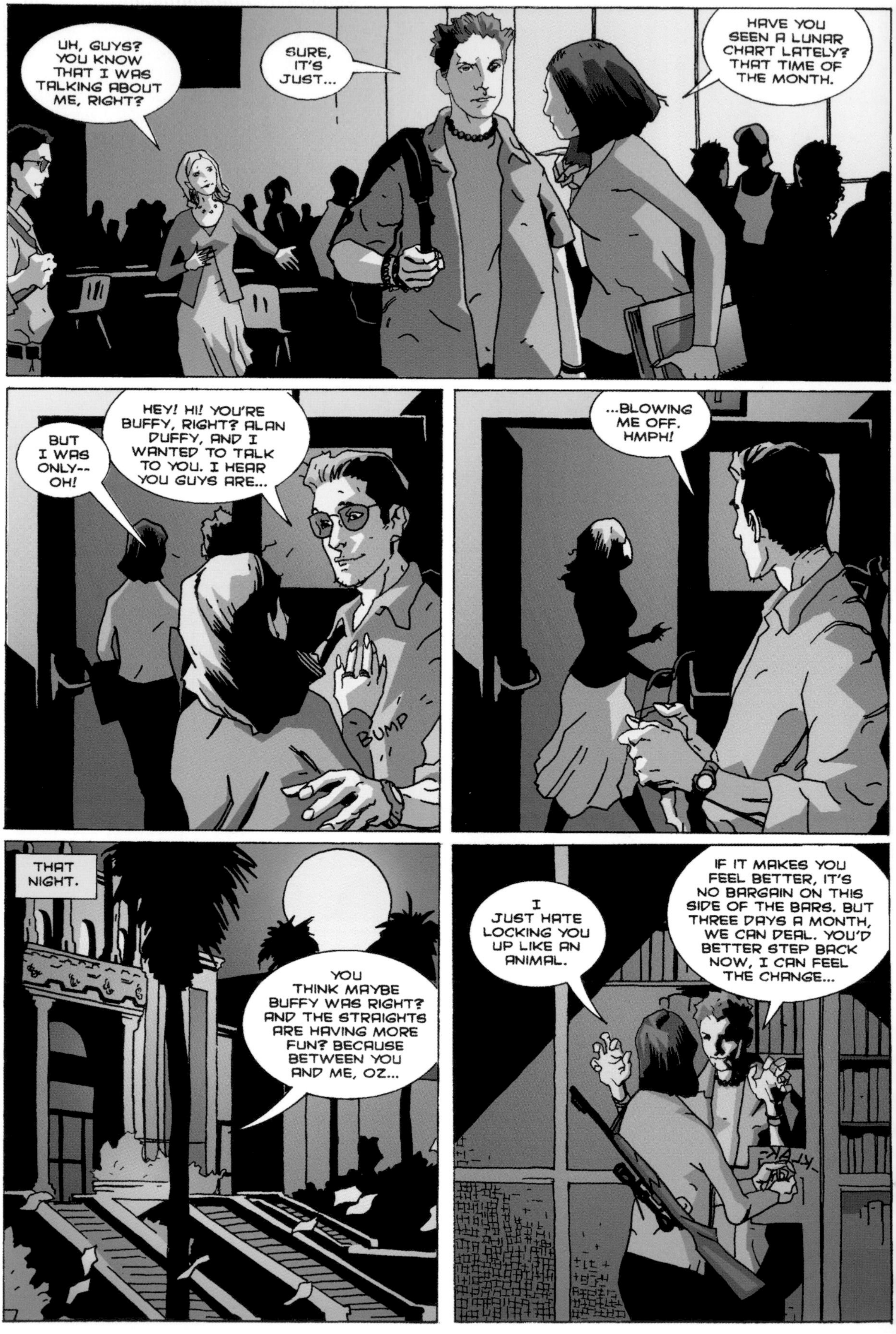
UH, GUYS? YOU KNOW THAT I WAS TALKING ABOUT ME, RIGHT?
SURE, IT'S JUST...
HAVE YOU SEEN A LUNAR CHART LATELY? THAT TIME OF THE MONTH.
BUT I WAS ONLY-- OH!
HEY! HI! YOU'RE BUFFY, RIGHT? ALAN DUFFY, AND I WANTED TO TALK TO YOU. I HEAR YOU GUYS ARE...
BUMP
...BLOWING ME OFF. HMPH!
THAT NIGHT.
YOU THINK MAYBE BUFFY WAS RIGHT? AND THE STRAIGHTS ARE HAVING MORE FUN? BECAUSE BETWEEN YOU AND ME, OZ...
I JUST HATE LOCKING YOU UP LIKE AN ANIMAL.
IF IT MAKES YOU FEEL BETTER, IT'S NO BARGAIN ON THIS SIDE OF THE BARS. BUT THREE DAYS A MONTH, WE CAN DEAL. YOU'D BETTER STEP BACK NOW, I CAN FEEL THE CHANGE...

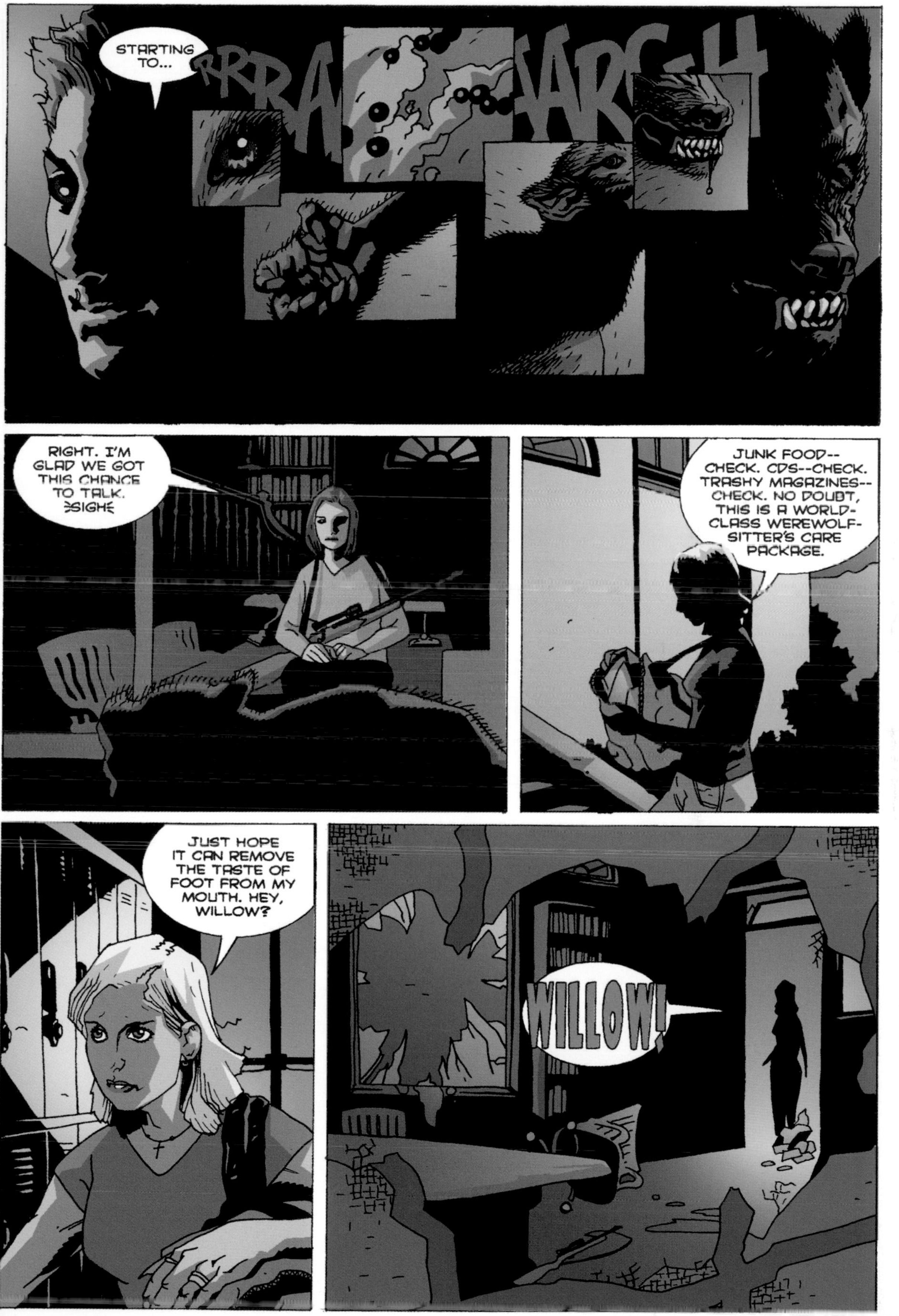

STARTING TO...
RRRA
ARG-H
RIGHT. I'M GLAD WE GOT THIS CHANCE TO TALK. ≷SIGH≷
JUNK FOOD-- CHECK. CDS--CHECK. TRASHY MAGAZINES-- CHECK. NO DOUBT, THIS IS A WORLD-CLASS WEREWOLF-SITTER'S CARE PACKAGE.
JUST HOPE IT CAN REMOVE THE TASTE OF FOOT FROM MY MOUTH. HEY, WILLOW?
WILLOW!

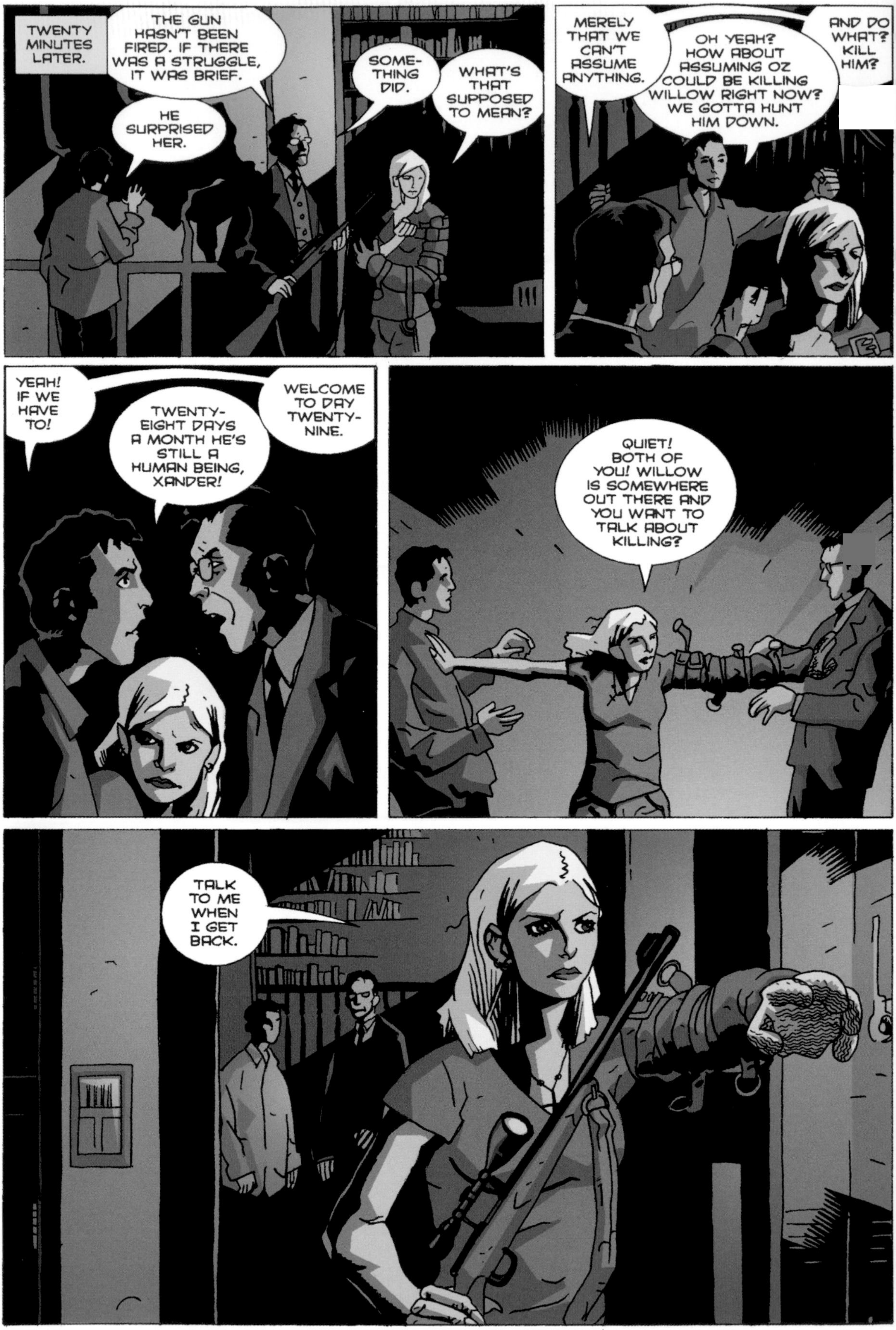
TWENTY MINUTES LATER.
THE GUN HASN'T BEEN FIRED. IF THERE WAS A STRUGGLE, IT WAS BRIEF.
HE SURPRISED HER.
SOMETHING DID.
WHAT'S THAT SUPPOSED TO MEAN?
MERELY THAT WE CAN'T ASSUME ANYTHING.
OH YEAH? HOW ABOUT ASSUMING OZ COULD BE KILLING WILLOW RIGHT NOW? WE GOTTA HUNT HIM DOWN.
AND DO WHAT? KILL HIM?
YEAH! IF WE HAVE TO!
TWENTY-EIGHT DAYS A MONTH HE'S STILL A HUMAN BEING, XANDER!
WELCOME TO DAY TWENTY-NINE.
QUIET! BOTH OF YOU! WILLOW IS SOMEWHERE OUT THERE AND YOU WANT TO TALK ABOUT KILLING?
TALK TO ME WHEN I GET BACK.

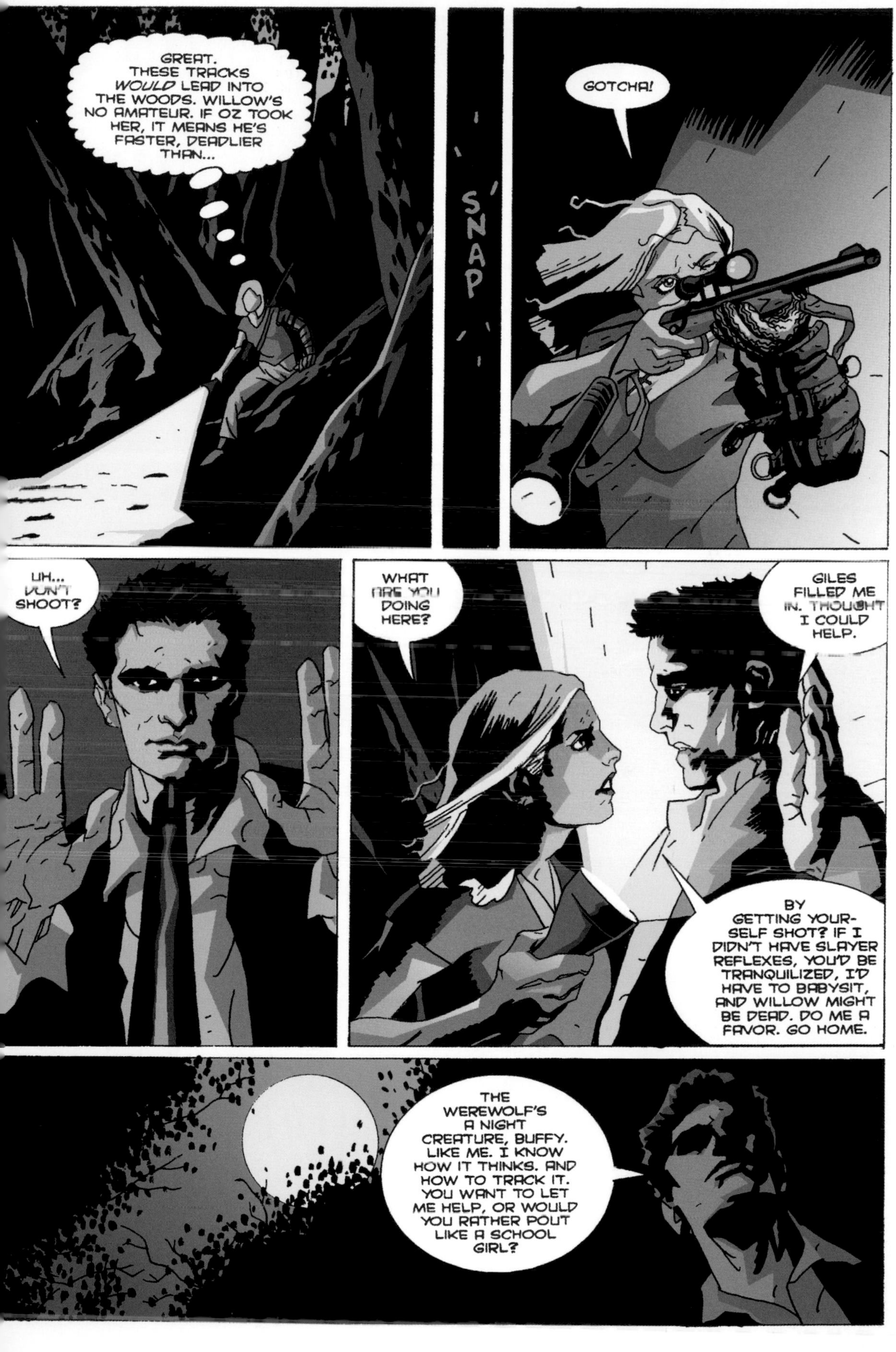
GREAT. THESE TRACKS WOULD LEAD INTO THE WOODS. WILLOW'S NO AMATEUR. IF OZ TOOK HER, IT MEANS HE'S FASTER, DEADLIER THAN...
SNAP
GOTCHA!
UH... DON'T SHOOT?
WHAT ARE YOU DOING HERE?
GILES FILLED ME IN. THOUGHT I COULD HELP.
BY GETTING YOURSELF SHOT? IF I DIDN'T HAVE SLAYER REFLEXES, YOU'D BE TRANQUILIZED, I'D HAVE TO BABYSIT, AND WILLOW MIGHT BE DEAD. DO ME A FAVOR. GO HOME.
THE WEREWOLF'S A NIGHT CREATURE, BUFFY. LIKE ME. I KNOW HOW IT THINKS. AND HOW TO TRACK IT. YOU WANT TO LET ME HELP, OR WOULD YOU RATHER POUT LIKE A SCHOOL GIRL?

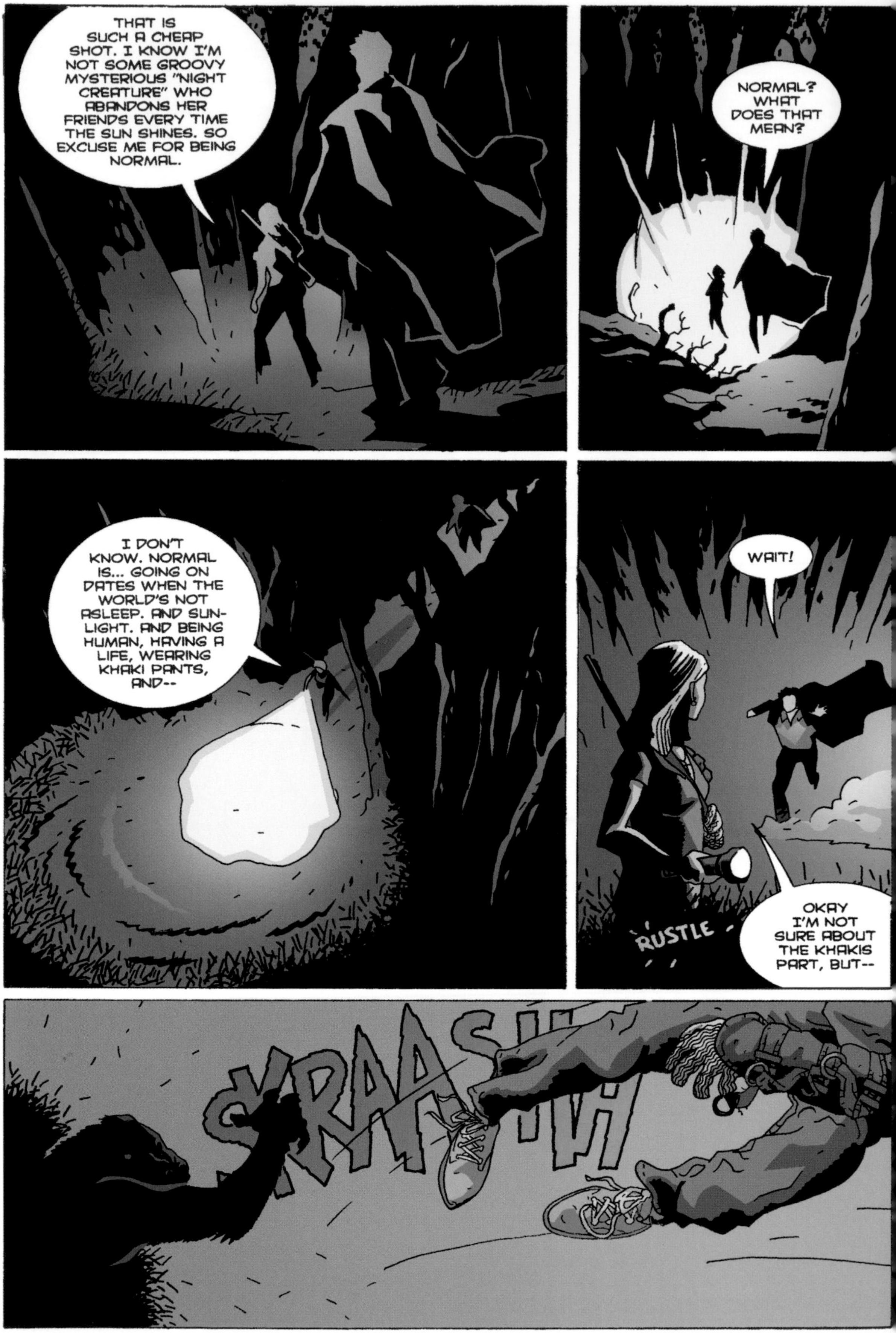

THAT IS SUCH A CHEAP SHOT. I KNOW I'M NOT SOME GROOVY MYSTERIOUS "NIGHT CREATURE" WHO ABANDONS HER FRIENDS EVERY TIME THE SUN SHINES. SO EXCUSE ME FOR BEING NORMAL.
NORMAL? WHAT DOES THAT MEAN?
I DON'T KNOW. NORMAL IS... GOING ON DATES WHEN THE WORLD'S NOT ASLEEP. AND SUN-LIGHT. AND BEING HUMAN, HAVING A LIFE, WEARING KHAKI PANTS, AND--
WAIT!
RUSTLE
OKAY I'M NOT SURE ABOUT THE KHAKIS PART, BUT--
SKRAASHH

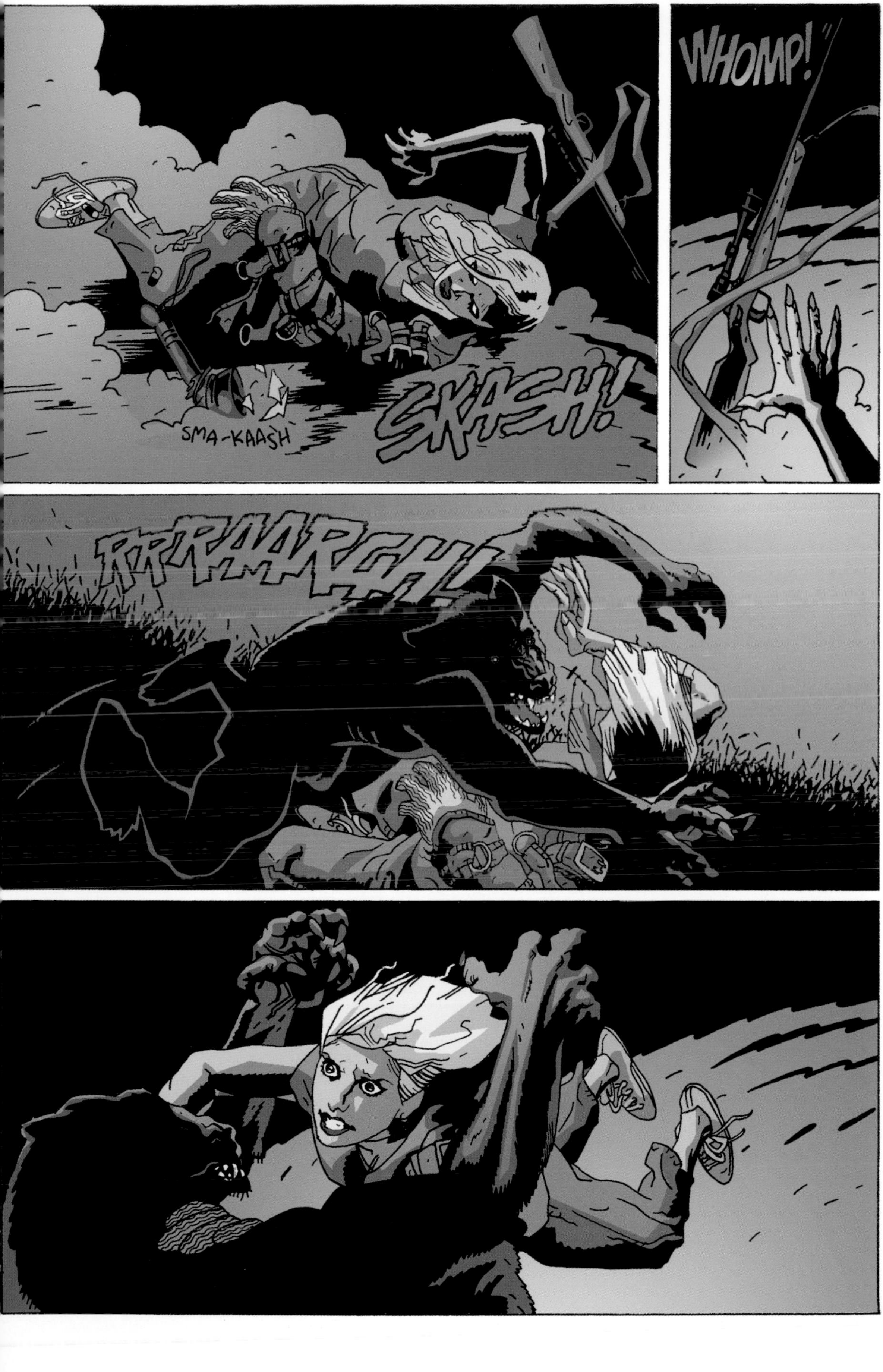
SMA-KAASH
SKASH!
WHOMP!
RRRAARGH!

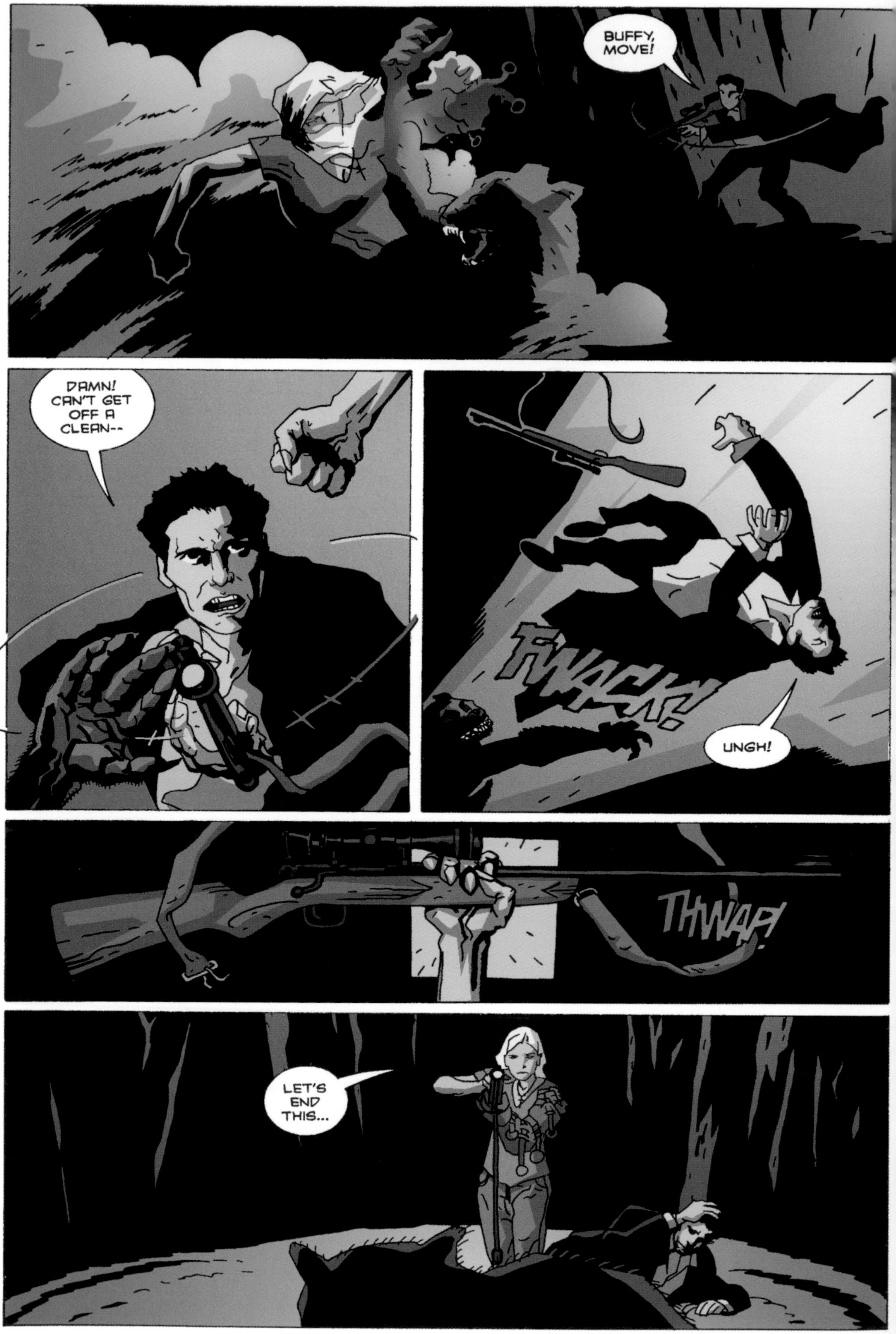

BUFFY, MOVE!
DAMN! CAN'T GET OFF A CLEAN--
FWACK!
UNGH!
THWAP!
LET'S END THIS...

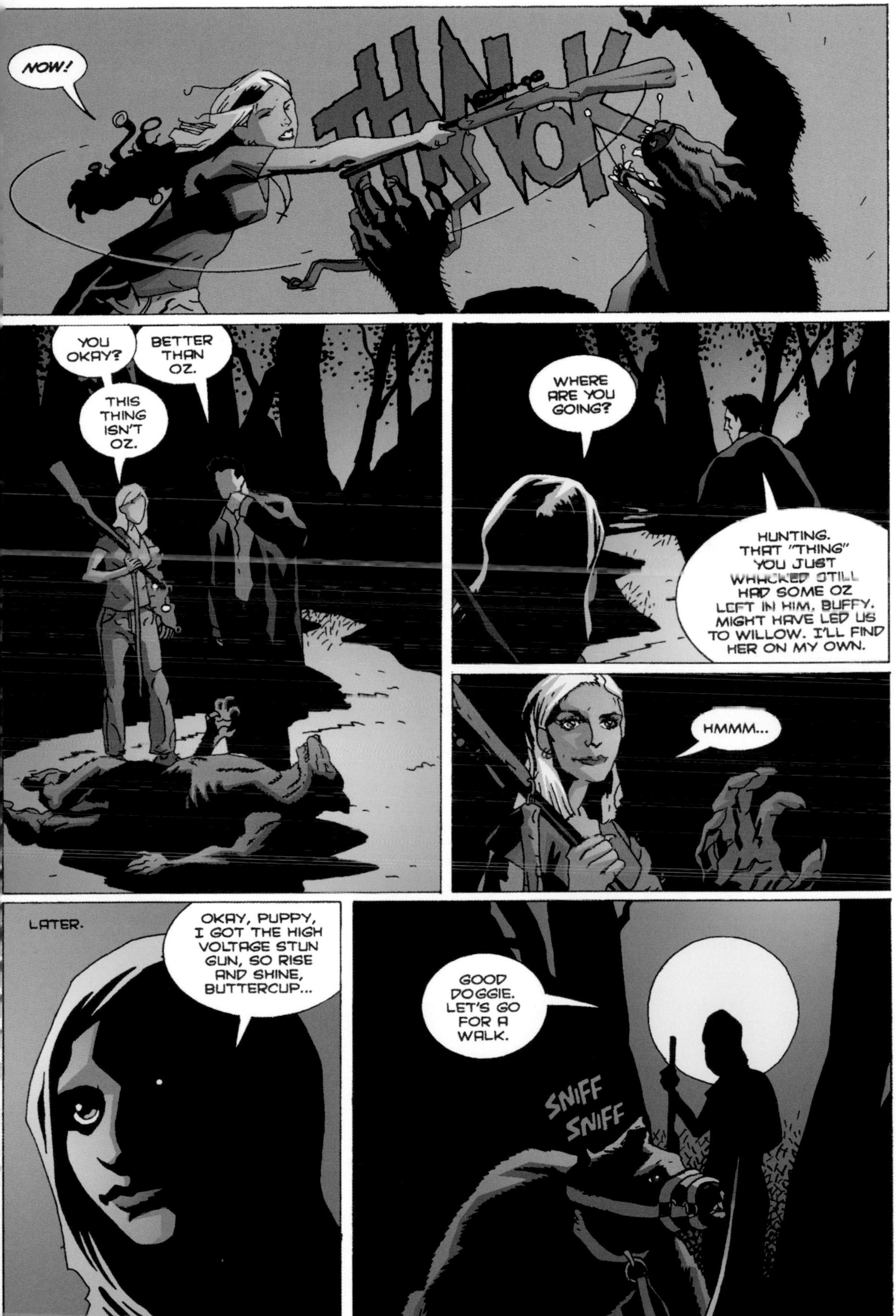
NOW!
THUNK
THWOK
YOU OKAY?
BETTER THAN OZ.
THIS THING ISN'T OZ.
WHERE ARE YOU GOING?
HUNTING. THAT "THING" YOU JUST WHACKED STILL HAD SOME OZ LEFT IN HIM, BUFFY. MIGHT HAVE LED US TO WILLOW. I'LL FIND HER ON MY OWN.
HMMM...
LATER.
OKAY, PUPPY, I GOT THE HIGH VOLTAGE STUN GUN, SO RISE AND SHINE, BUTTERCUP...
GOOD DOGGIE. LET'S GO FOR A WALK.
SNIFF SNIFF

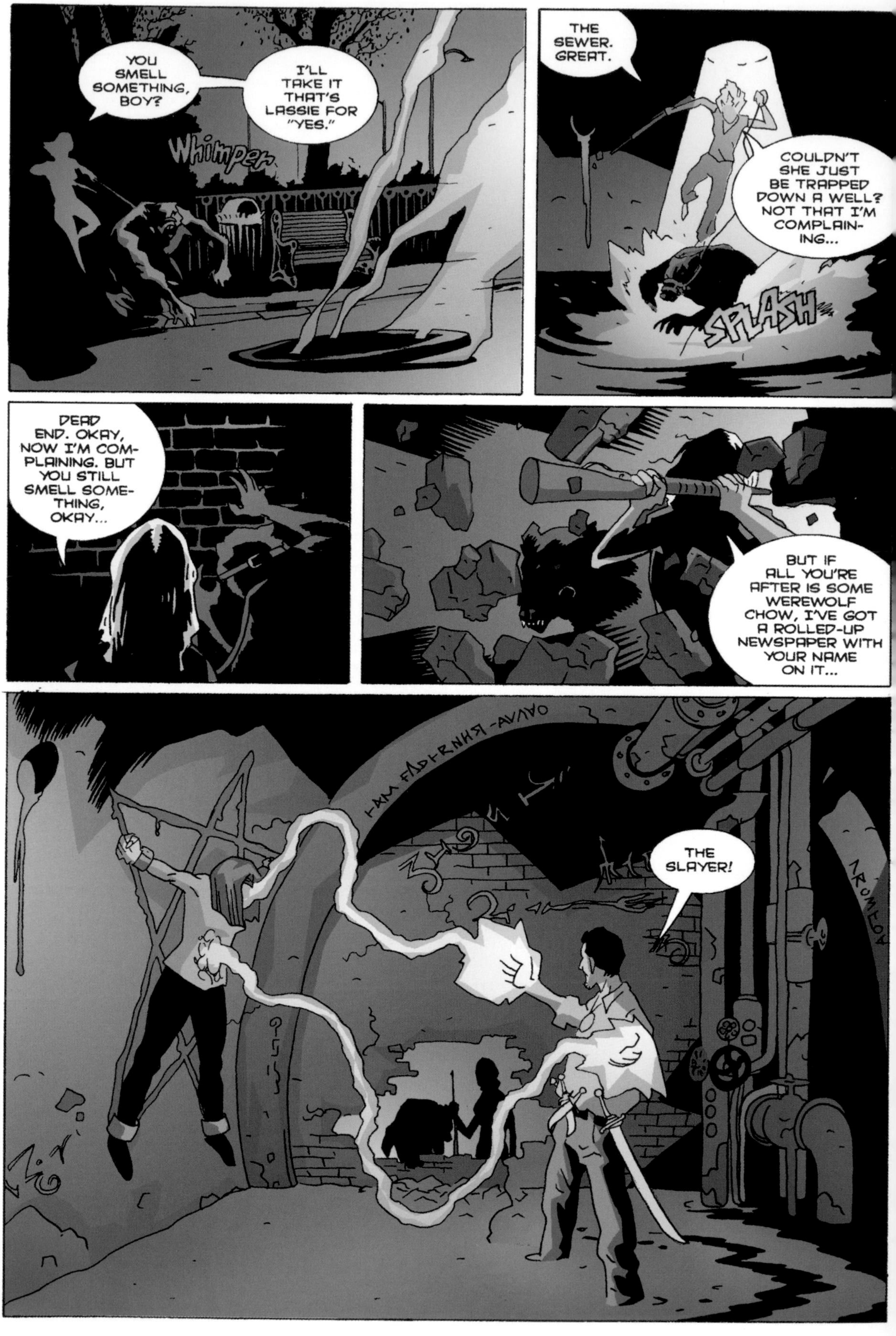
YOU SMELL SOMETHING, BOY?
I'LL TAKE IT THAT'S LASSIE FOR "YES."
Whimper
THE SEWER. GREAT.
COULDN'T SHE JUST BE TRAPPED DOWN A WELL? NOT THAT I'M COMPLAINING...
SPLASH
DEAD END. OKAY, NOW I'M COMPLAINING. BUT YOU STILL SMELL SOMETHING, OKAY...
BUT IF ALL YOU'RE AFTER IS SOME WEREWOLF CHOW, I'VE GOT A ROLLED-UP NEWSPAPER WITH YOUR NAME ON IT...
THE SLAYER!

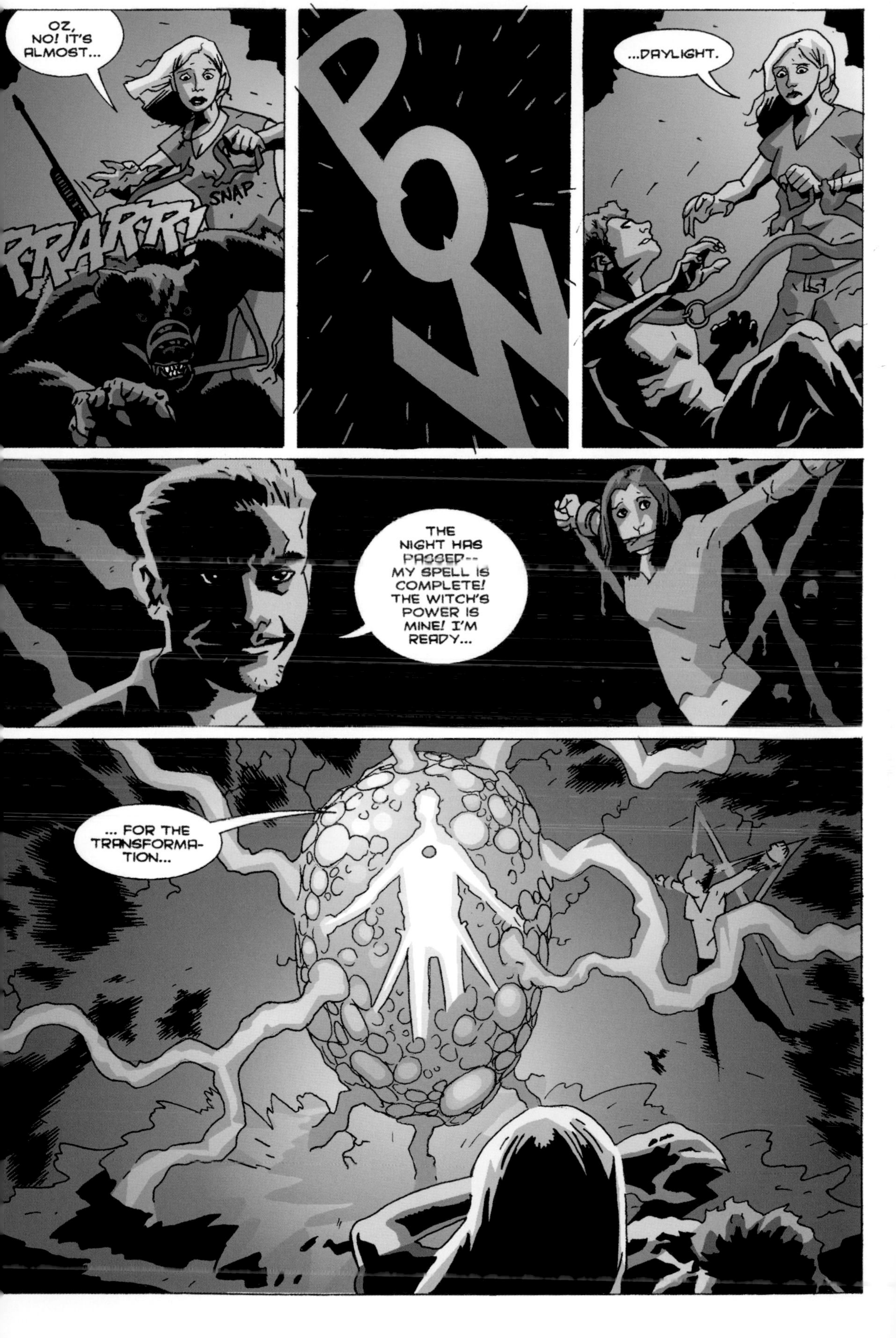
OZ, NO! IT'S ALMOST...
SNAP
PRARR!
POW
...DAYLIGHT.
THE NIGHT HAS PASSED-- MY SPELL IS COMPLETE! THE WITCH'S POWER IS MINE! I'M READY...
... FOR THE TRANSFORMATION...

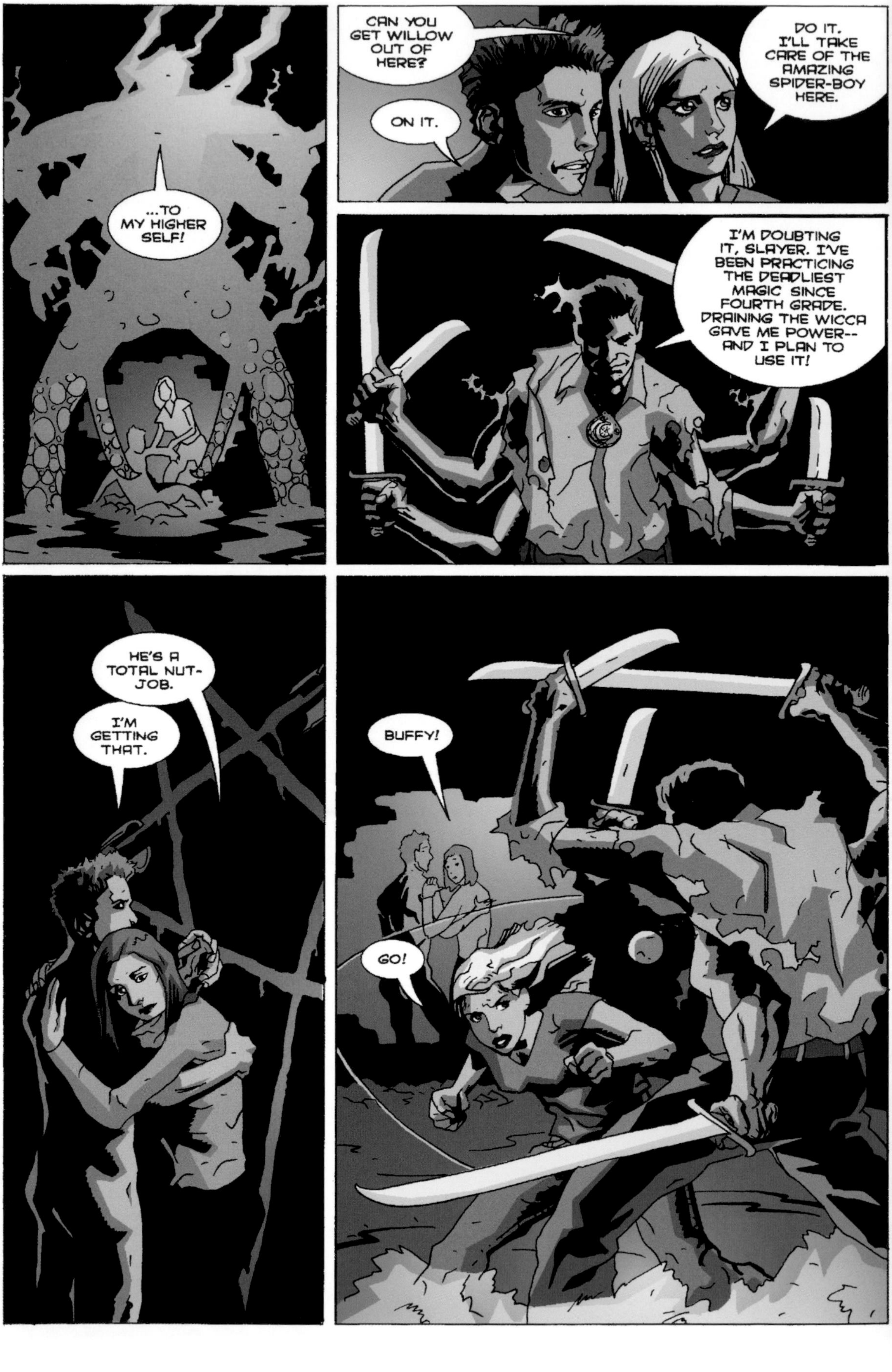
...TO MY HIGHER SELF!
CAN YOU GET WILLOW OUT OF HERE?
ON IT.
DO IT. I'LL TAKE CARE OF THE AMAZING SPIDER-BOY HERE.
I'M DOUBTING IT, SLAYER. I'VE BEEN PRACTICING THE DEADLIEST MAGIC SINCE FOURTH GRADE. DRAINING THE WICCA GAVE ME POWER-- AND I PLAN TO USE IT!
HE'S A TOTAL NUT-JOB.
I'M GETTING THAT.
BUFFY!
GO!

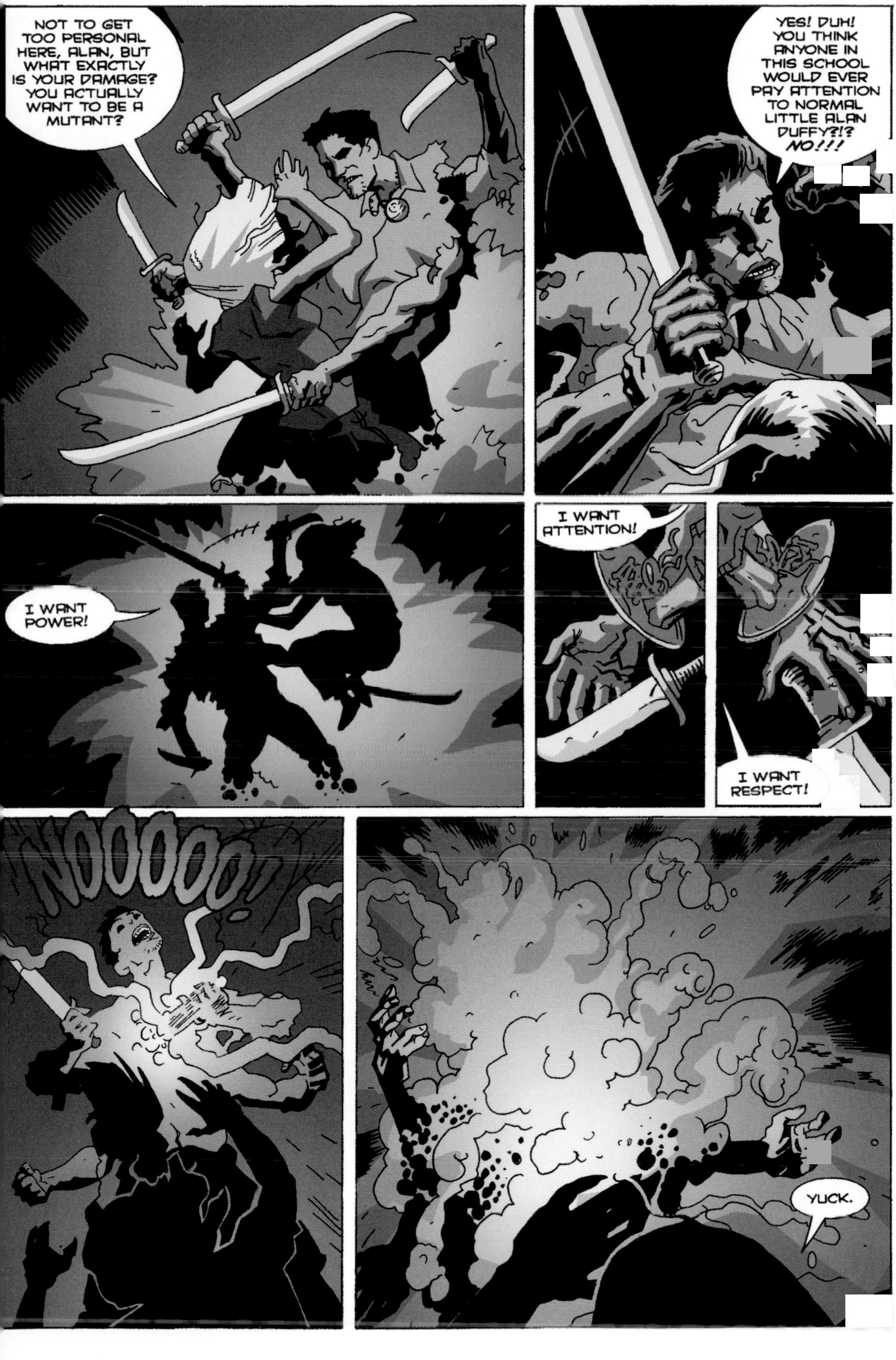
NOT TO GET TOO PERSONAL HERE, ALAN, BUT WHAT EXACTLY IS YOUR DAMAGE? YOU ACTUALLY WANT TO BE A MUTANT?
YES! DUH! YOU THINK ANYONE IN THIS SCHOOL WOULD EVER PAY ATTENTION TO NORMAL LITTLE ALAN DUFFY?!? NO!!!
I WANT POWER!
I WANT ATTENTION!
I WANT RESPECT!
NOOOOO!
YUCK.

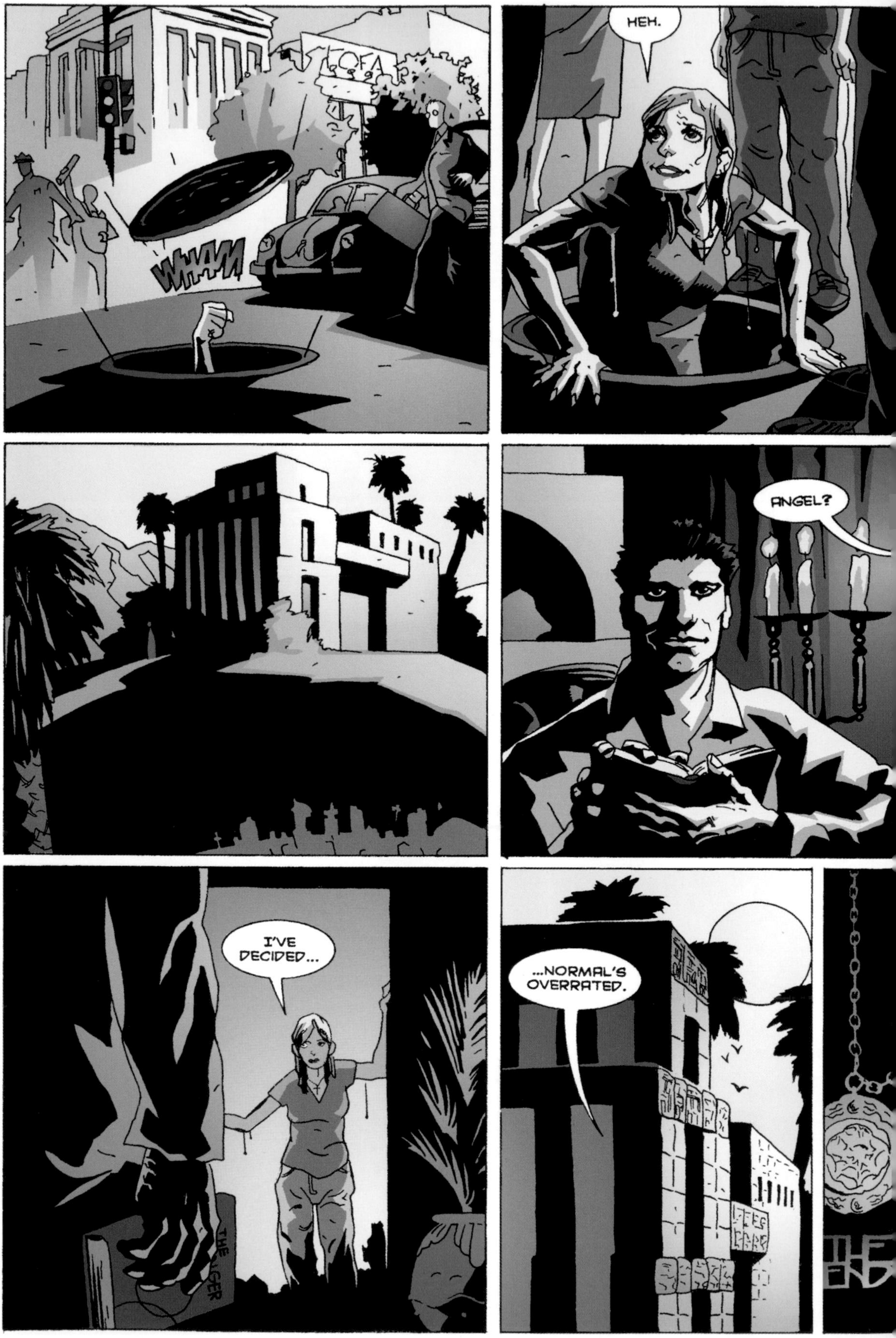
WHAM
HEH.
ANGEL?
I'VE DECIDED...
...NORMAL'S OVERRATED.
THE END

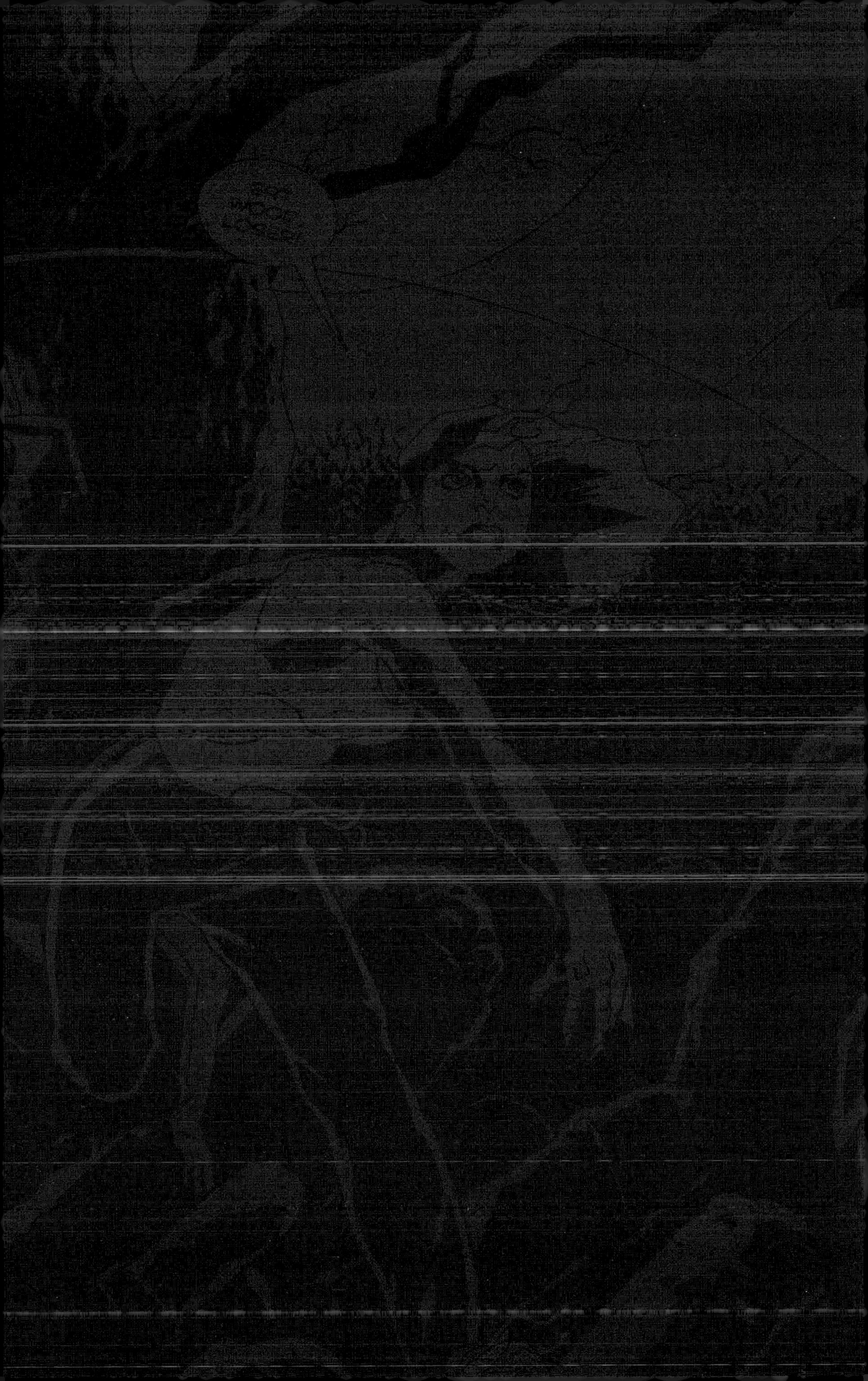

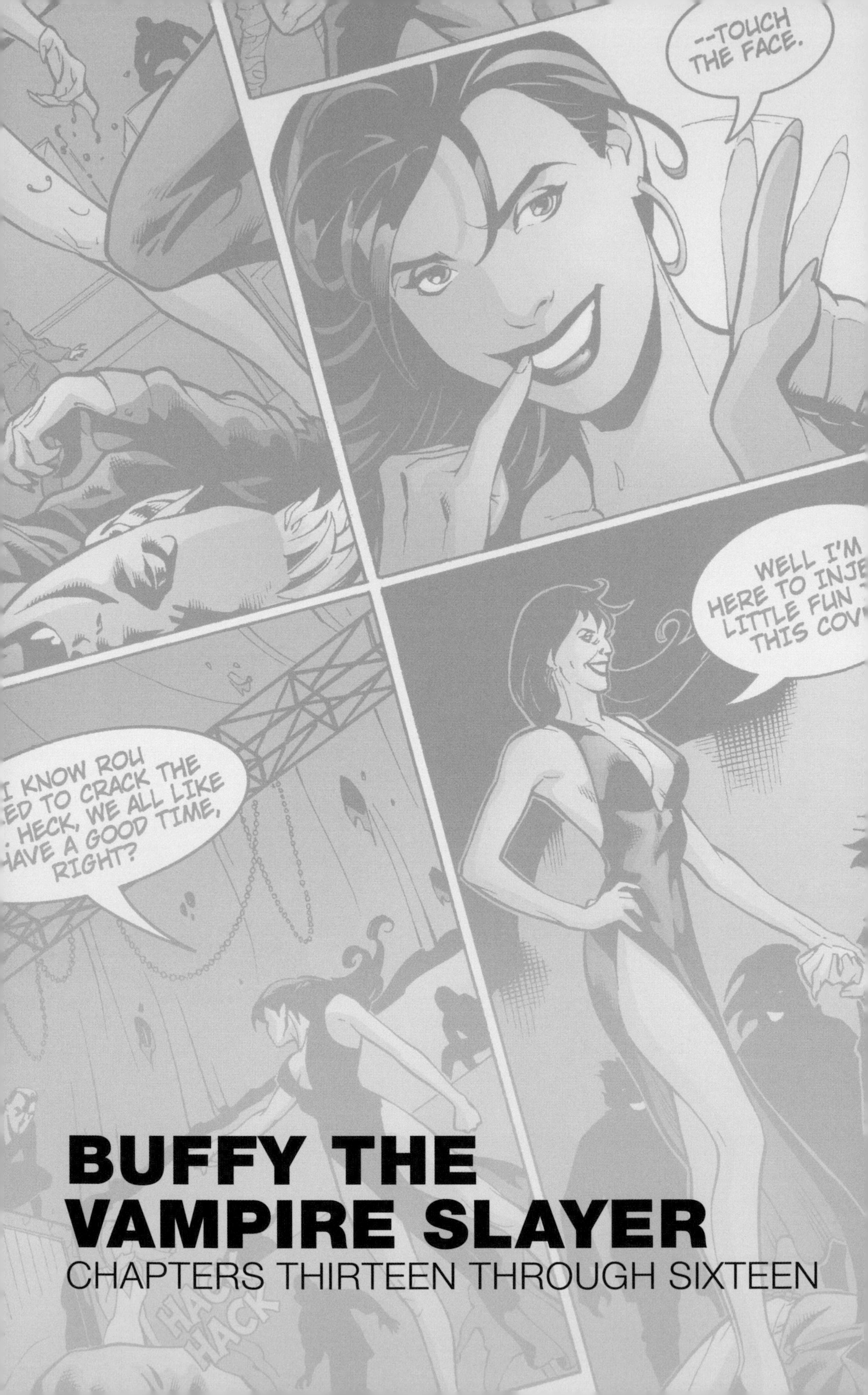
--TOUCH THE FACE.

BUFFY THE VAMPIRE SLAYER

CHAPTERS THIRTEEN THROUGH SIXTEEN

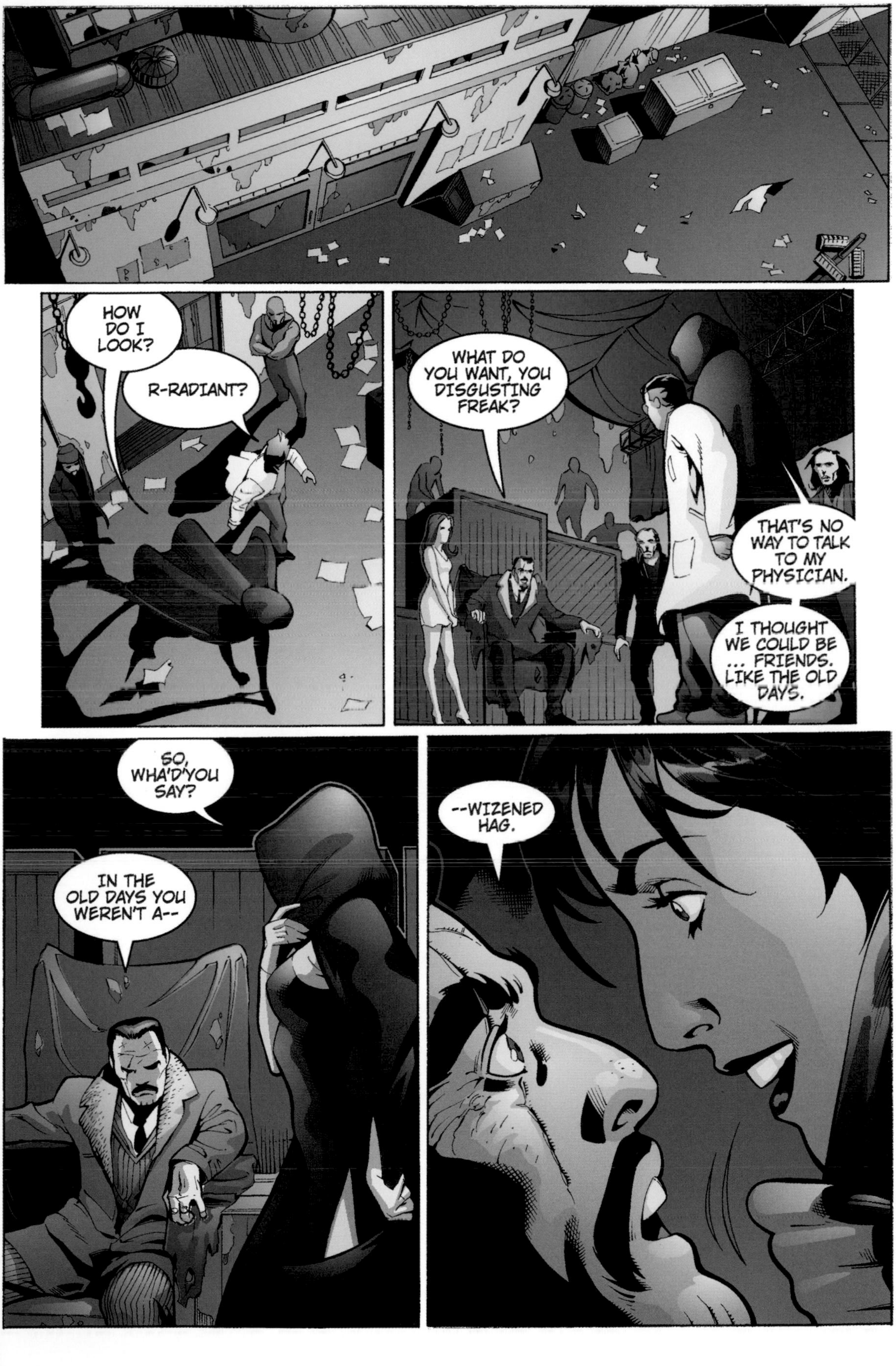
HOW DO I LOOK?
R-RADIANT?
WHAT DO YOU WANT, YOU DISGUSTING FREAK?
THAT'S NO WAY TO TALK TO MY PHYSICIAN.
I THOUGHT WE COULD BE ... FRIENDS. LIKE THE OLD DAYS.
SO, WHA'D'YOU SAY?
IN THE OLD DAYS YOU WEREN'T A--
--WIZENED HAG.

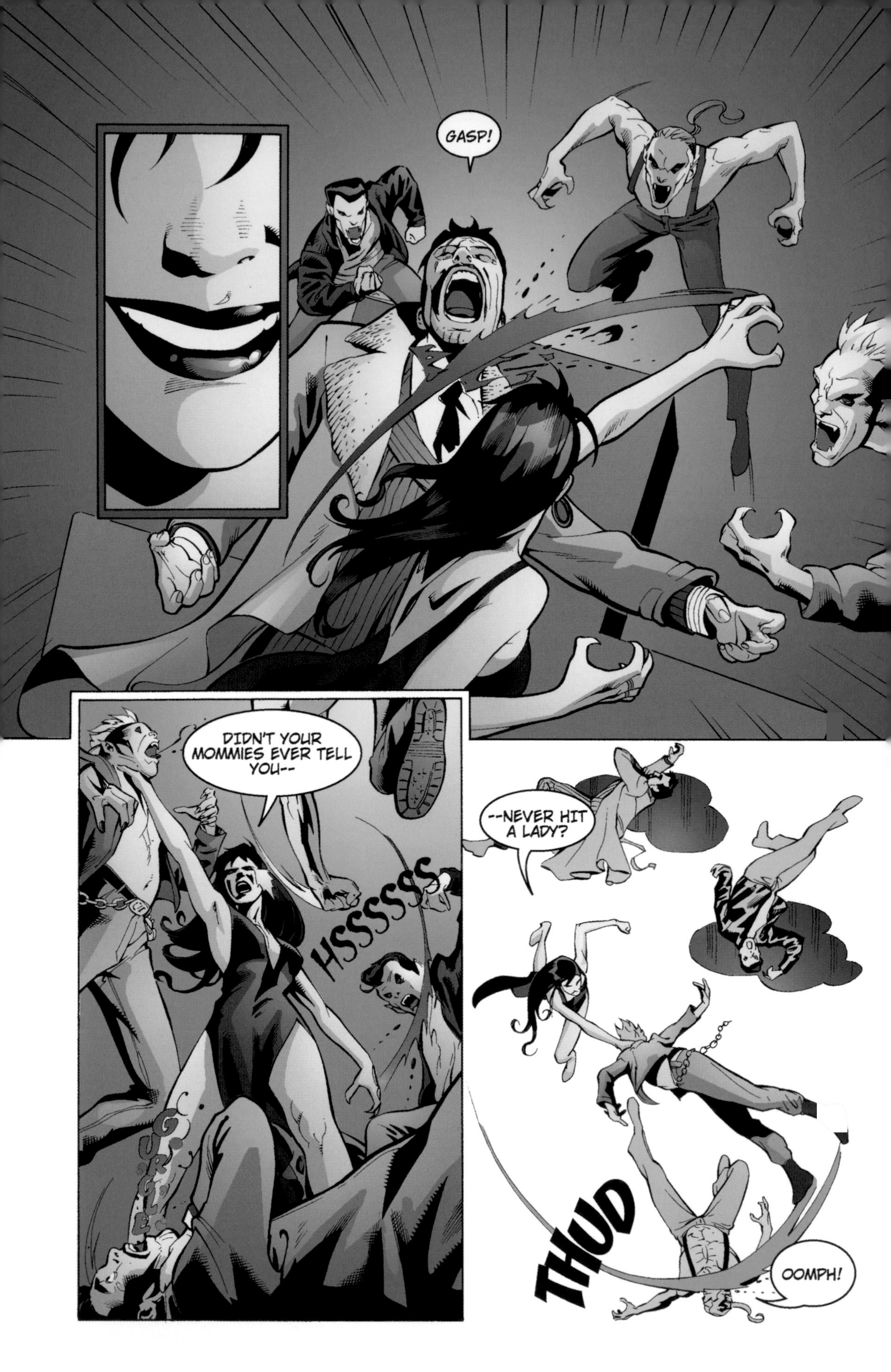
GASP!
DIDN'T YOUR MOMMIES EVER TELL YOU--
HSSSSSS
GURGLE
--NEVER HIT A LADY?
THUD
OOMPH!

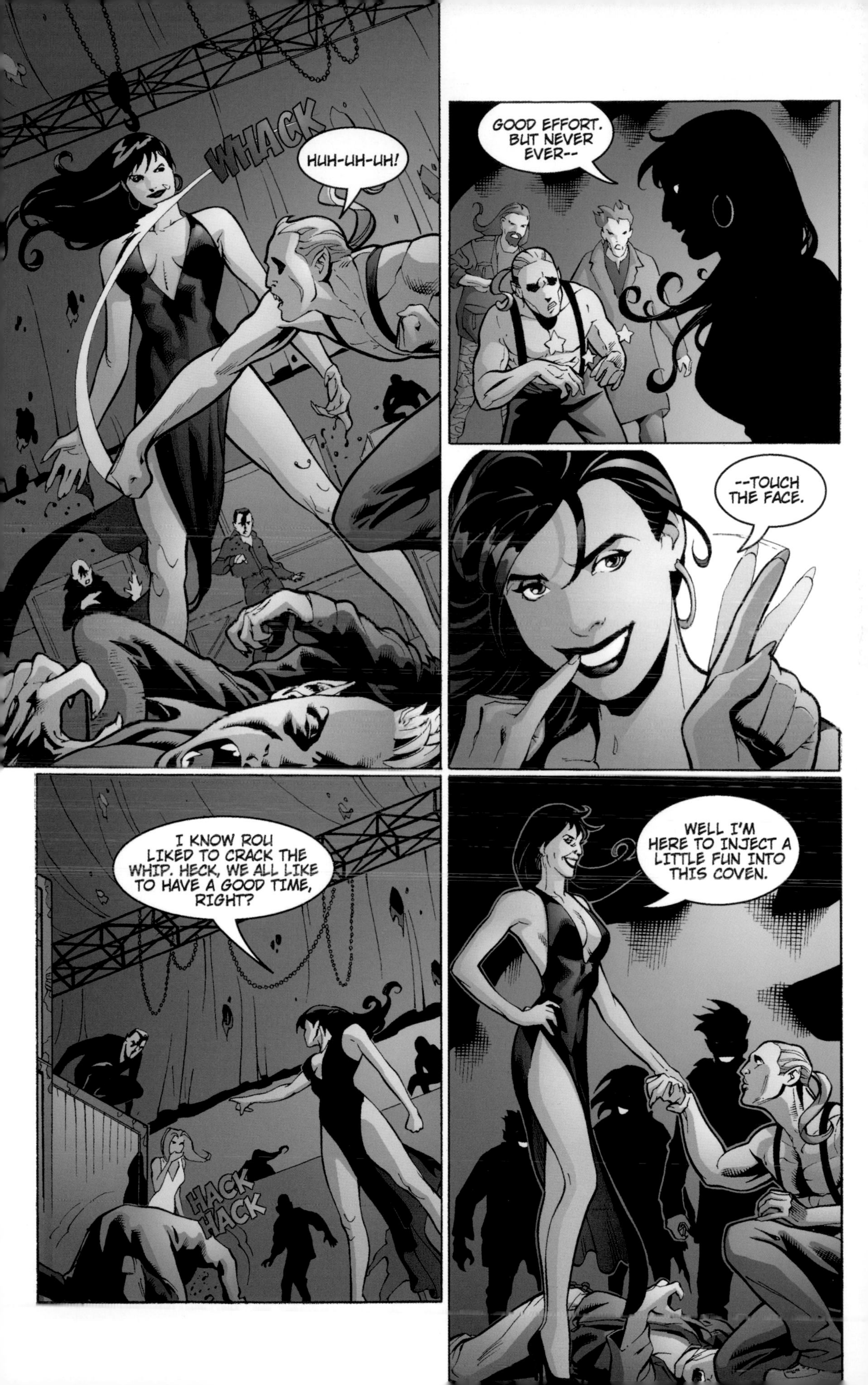
WHACK
HUH-UH-UH!
GOOD EFFORT. BUT NEVER EVER--
--TOUCH THE FACE.
I KNOW ROU LIKED TO CRACK THE WHIP. HECK, WE ALL LIKE TO HAVE A GOOD TIME, RIGHT?
HACK HACK
WELL I'M HERE TO INJECT A LITTLE FUN INTO THIS COVEN.

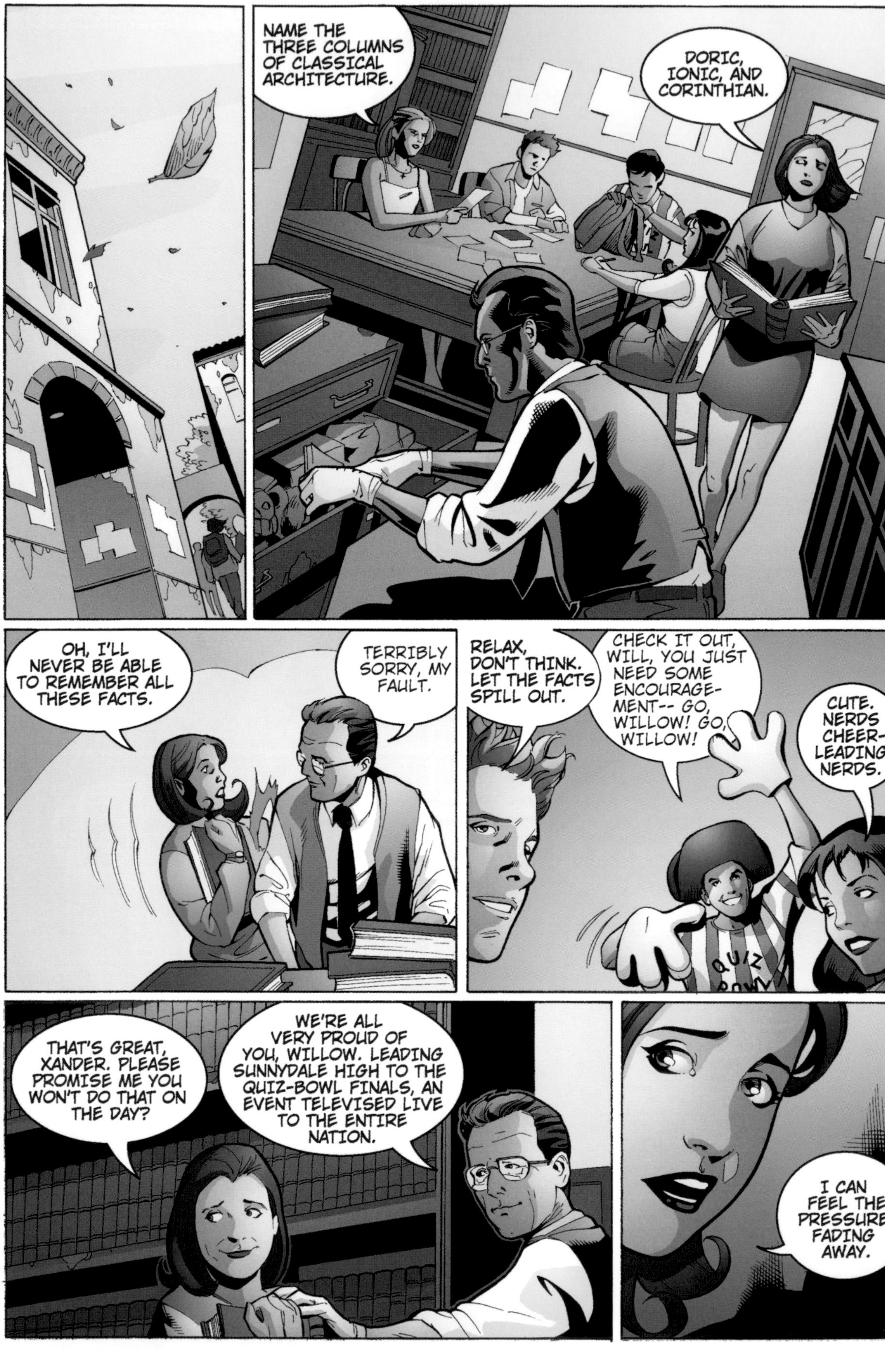
NAME THE THREE COLUMNS OF CLASSICAL ARCHITECTURE.
DORIC, IONIC, AND CORINTHIAN.
OH, I'LL NEVER BE ABLE TO REMEMBER ALL THESE FACTS.
TERRIBLY SORRY, MY FAULT.
RELAX, DON'T THINK. LET THE FACTS SPILL OUT.
CHECK IT OUT, WILL, YOU JUST NEED SOME ENCOURAGE-MENT-- GO, WILLOW! GO, WILLOW!
CUTE. NERDS CHEER-LEADING NERDS.
THAT'S GREAT, XANDER. PLEASE PROMISE ME YOU WON'T DO THAT ON THE DAY?
WE'RE ALL VERY PROUD OF YOU, WILLOW. LEADING SUNNYDALE HIGH TO THE QUIZ-BOWL FINALS, AN EVENT TELEVISED LIVE TO THE ENTIRE NATION.
I CAN FEEL THE PRESSURE FADING AWAY.

S'CUSE ME, IT'S ON P.B.S. A GUARANTEED AUDIENCE OF TWO, MAYBE THREE, LOSERS!

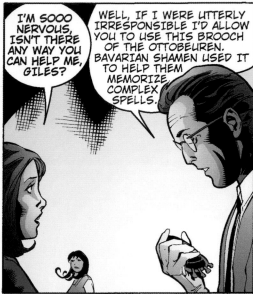

I'M SOOO NERVOUS, ISN'T THERE ANY WAY YOU CAN HELP ME, GILES?

WELL, IF I WERE UTTERLY IRRESPONSIBLE I'D ALLOW YOU TO USE THIS BROOCH OF THE OTTOBEUREN. BAVARIAN SHAMEN USED IT TO HELP THEM MEMORIZE COMPLEX SPELLS.

EWW, IT MAKES THE JOAN RIVERS COLLECTION LOOK TASTEFUL.

IT IS ALSO THE ONLY ONE OF ITS KIND. MAKING IT TOO PRECIOUS FOR GREASY FINGERS.

WE'RE UP AGAINST HORTON MILITARY ACADEMY. SIX-TIME WINNERS WITH A WEAKNESS FOR GUNPLAY AND STA-PREST UNIFORMS.

THE FINAL'S NOT 'TIL FRIDAY. YOU STILL HAVE A WHOLE WEEK TO BONE UP.

AND THERE'S LYLE, MILO, AND SARAH ON THE TEAM.

YEAH, THERE'S LYLE, WILL.

SO, WHAT'S THE DEAL WITH LYLE?

LYLE, AS IN "SCI-FI LYLE"?

WELL, LYLE'S... FRIENDLY.

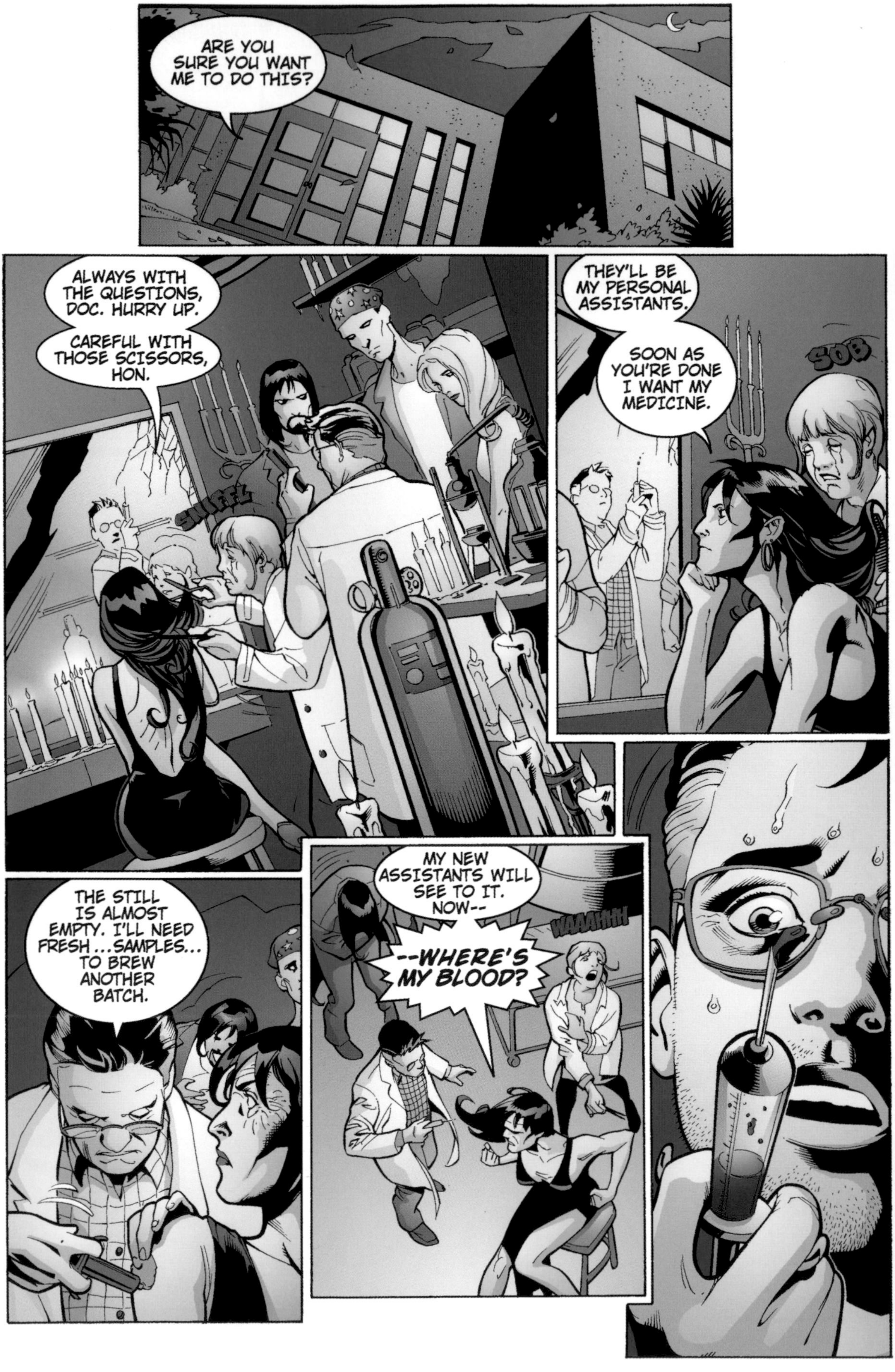
ARE YOU SURE YOU WANT ME TO DO THIS?
ALWAYS WITH THE QUESTIONS, DOC. HURRY UP.
CAREFUL WITH THOSE SCISSORS, HON.
SNIFFL
THEY'LL BE MY PERSONAL ASSISTANTS.
SOON AS YOU'RE DONE I WANT MY MEDICINE.
SOB
THE STILL IS ALMOST EMPTY. I'LL NEED FRESH ...SAMPLES... TO BREW ANOTHER BATCH.
MY NEW ASSISTANTS WILL SEE TO IT. NOW--
WAAAHHH
--WHERE'S MY BLOOD?

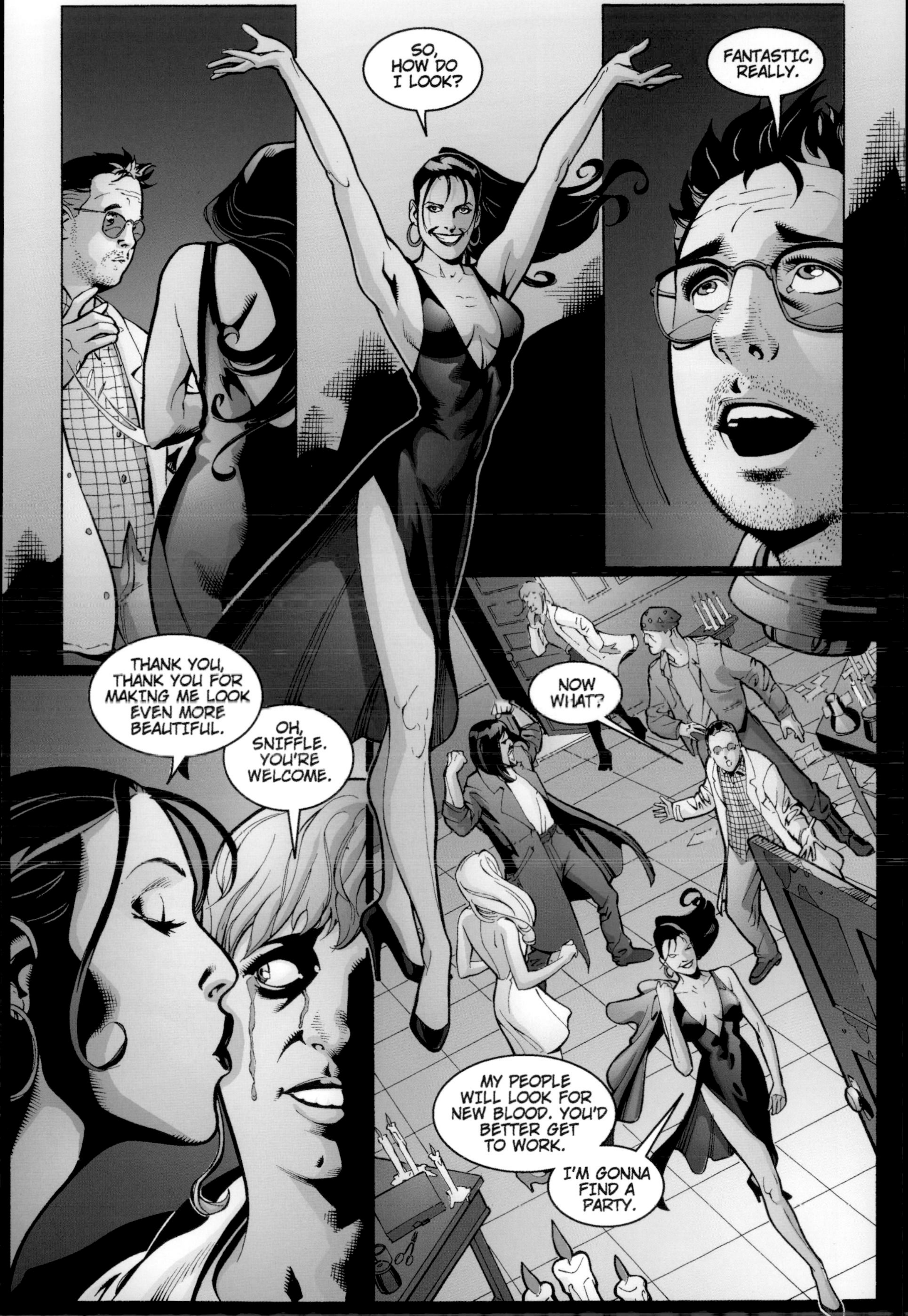

SO, HOW DO I LOOK?
FANTASTIC, REALLY.
THANK YOU, THANK YOU FOR MAKING ME LOOK EVEN MORE BEAUTIFUL.
OH, SNIFFLE. YOU'RE WELCOME.
NOW WHAT?
MY PEOPLE WILL LOOK FOR NEW BLOOD. YOU'D BETTER GET TO WORK.
I'M GONNA FIND A PARTY.

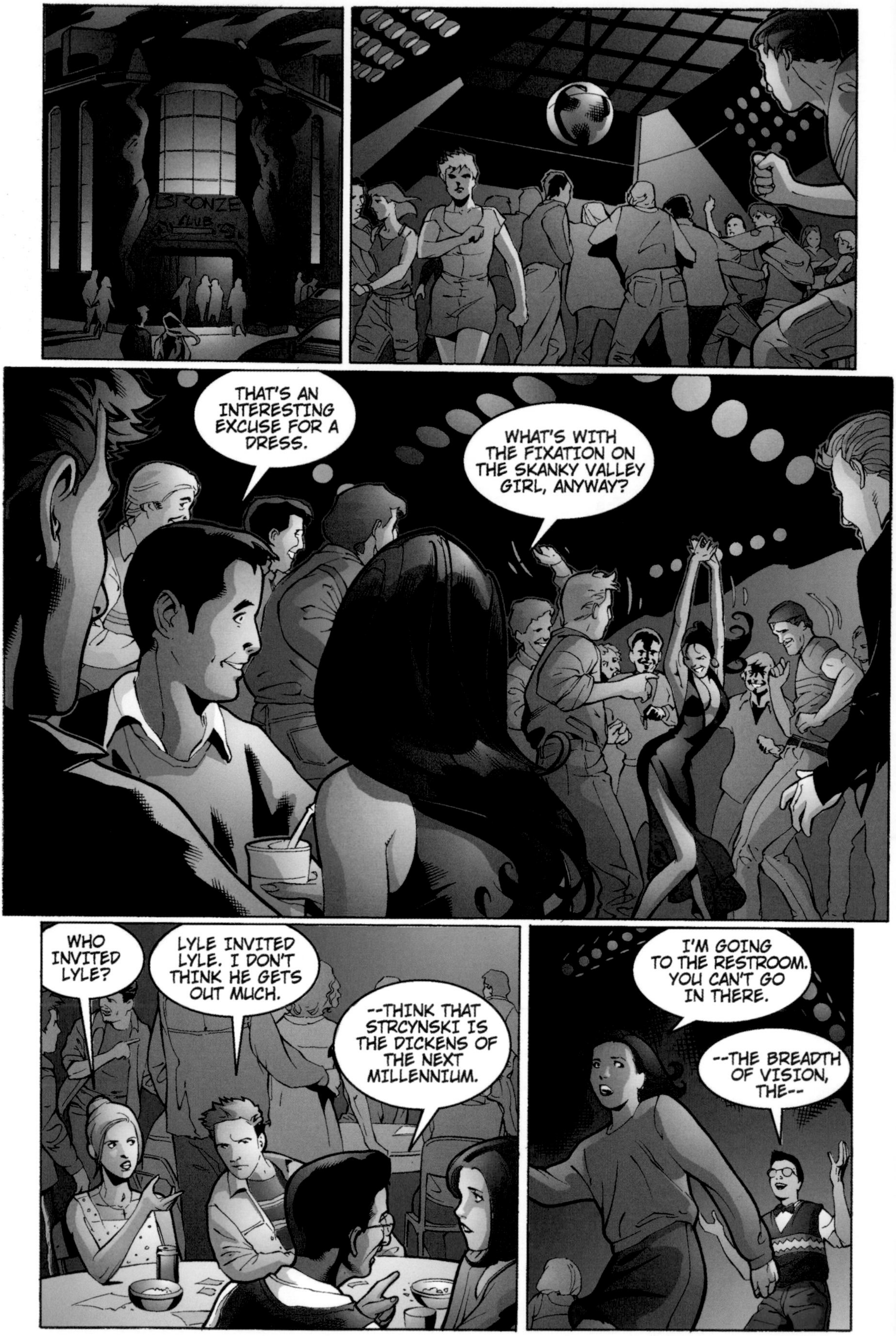
BRONZE
THAT'S AN INTERESTING EXCUSE FOR A DRESS.
WHAT'S WITH THE FIXATION ON THE SKANKY VALLEY GIRL, ANYWAY?
WHO INVITED LYLE?
LYLE INVITED LYLE. I DON'T THINK HE GETS OUT MUCH.
--THINK THAT STRCYNSKI IS THE DICKENS OF THE NEXT MILLENNIUM.
I'M GOING TO THE RESTROOM. YOU CAN'T GO IN THERE.
--THE BREADTH OF VISION, THE--

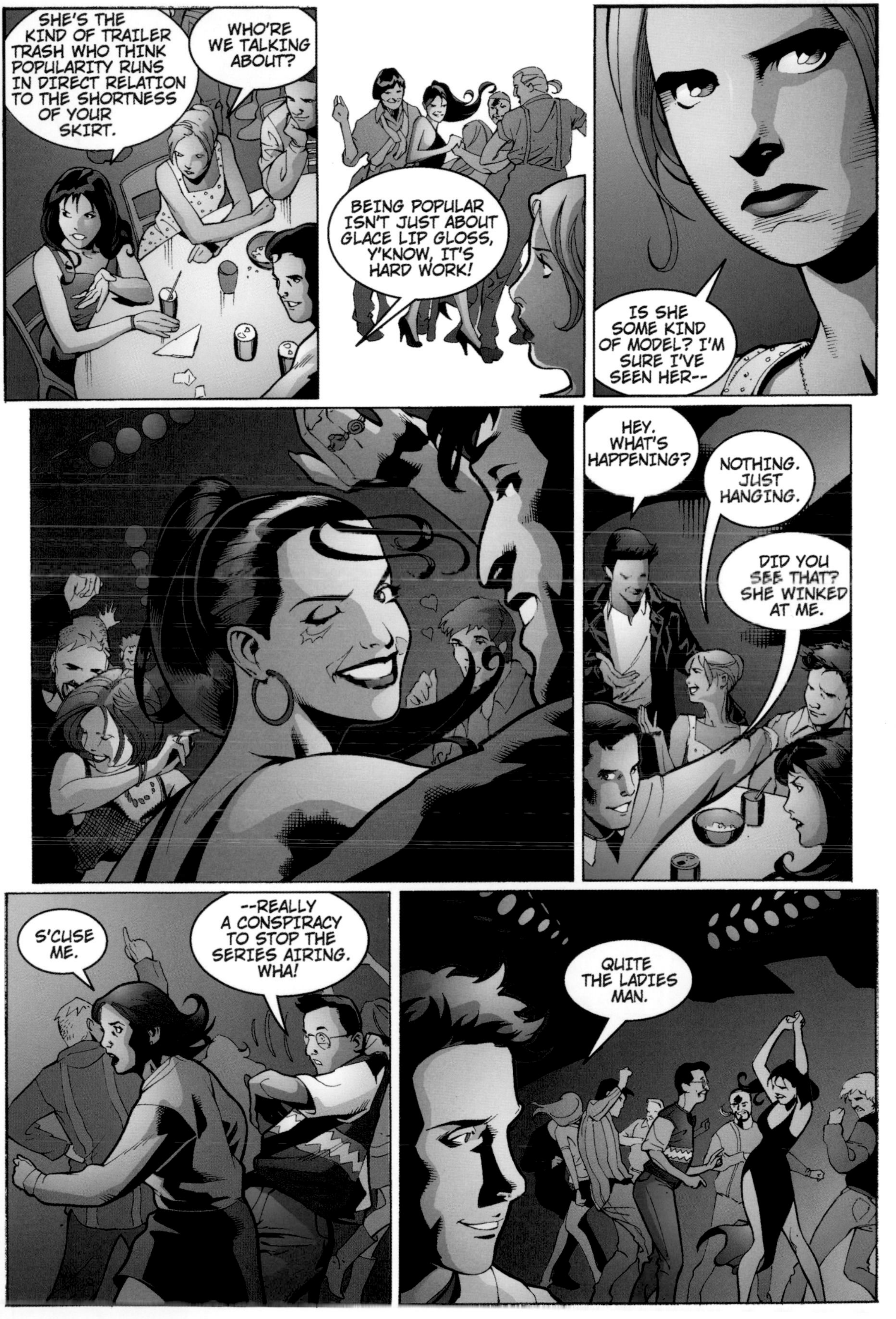
SHE'S THE KIND OF TRAILER TRASH WHO THINK POPULARITY RUNS IN DIRECT RELATION TO THE SHORTNESS OF YOUR SKIRT.
WHO'RE WE TALKING ABOUT?
BEING POPULAR ISN'T JUST ABOUT GLACE LIP GLOSS, Y'KNOW, IT'S HARD WORK!
IS SHE SOME KIND OF MODEL? I'M SURE I'VE SEEN HER--
HEY. WHAT'S HAPPENING?
NOTHING. JUST HANGING.
DID YOU SEE THAT? SHE WINKED AT ME.
S'CUSE ME.
--REALLY A CONSPIRACY TO STOP THE SERIES AIRING. WHA!
QUITE THE LADIES MAN.

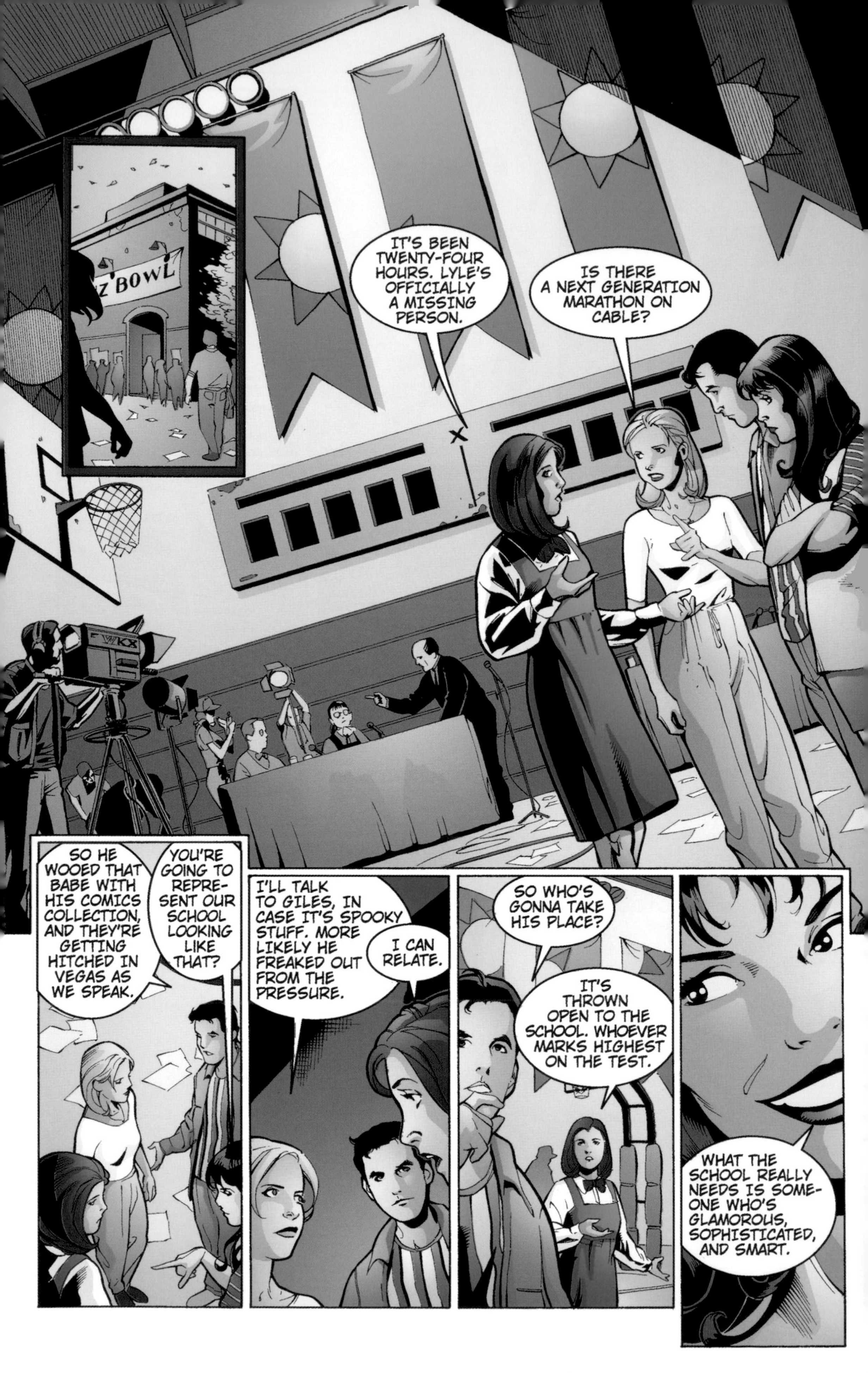
IT'S BEEN TWENTY-FOUR HOURS. LYLE'S OFFICIALLY A MISSING PERSON.
IS THERE A NEXT GENERATION MARATHON ON CABLE?
SO HE WOOED THAT BABE WITH HIS COMICS COLLECTION, AND THEY'RE GETTING HITCHED IN VEGAS AS WE SPEAK.
YOU'RE GOING TO REPRE-SENT OUR SCHOOL LOOKING LIKE THAT?
I'LL TALK TO GILES, IN CASE IT'S SPOOKY STUFF. MORE LIKELY HE FREAKED OUT FROM THE PRESSURE.
I CAN RELATE.
SO WHO'S GONNA TAKE HIS PLACE?
IT'S THROWN OPEN TO THE SCHOOL. WHOEVER MARKS HIGHEST ON THE TEST.
WHAT THE SCHOOL REALLY NEEDS IS SOME-ONE WHO'S GLAMOROUS, SOPHISTICATED, AND SMART.

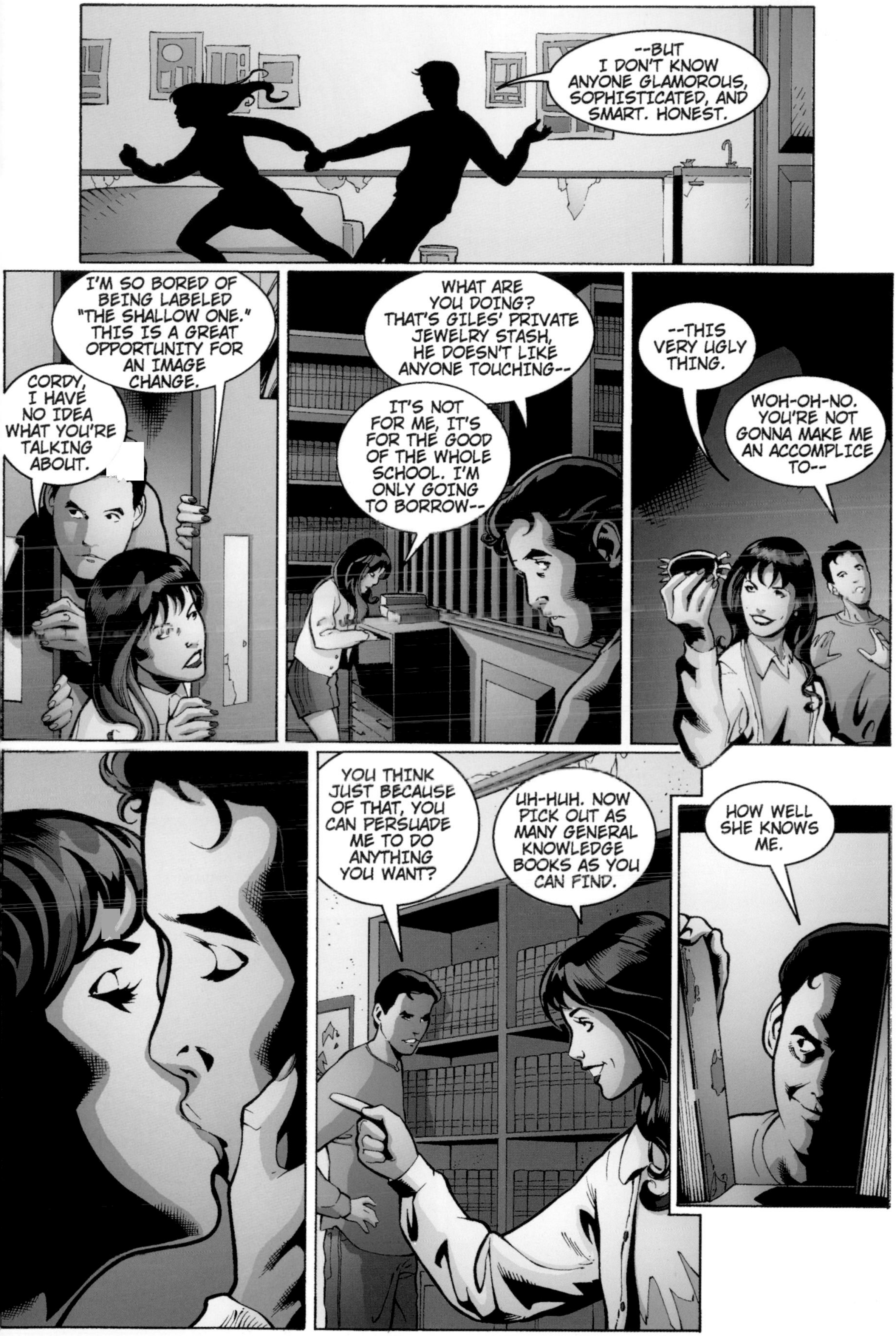
--BUT I DON'T KNOW ANYONE GLAMOROUS, SOPHISTICATED, AND SMART. HONEST.
I'M SO BORED OF BEING LABELED "THE SHALLOW ONE." THIS IS A GREAT OPPORTUNITY FOR AN IMAGE CHANGE.
CORDY, I HAVE NO IDEA WHAT YOU'RE TALKING ABOUT.
WHAT ARE YOU DOING? THAT'S GILES' PRIVATE JEWELRY STASH, HE DOESN'T LIKE ANYONE TOUCHING--
IT'S NOT FOR ME, IT'S FOR THE GOOD OF THE WHOLE SCHOOL. I'M ONLY GOING TO BORROW--
--THIS VERY UGLY THING.
WOH-OH-NO. YOU'RE NOT GONNA MAKE ME AN ACCOMPLICE TO--
YOU THINK JUST BECAUSE OF THAT, YOU CAN PERSUADE ME TO DO ANYTHING YOU WANT?
UH-HUH. NOW PICK OUT AS MANY GENERAL KNOWLEDGE BOOKS AS YOU CAN FIND.
HOW WELL SHE KNOWS ME.

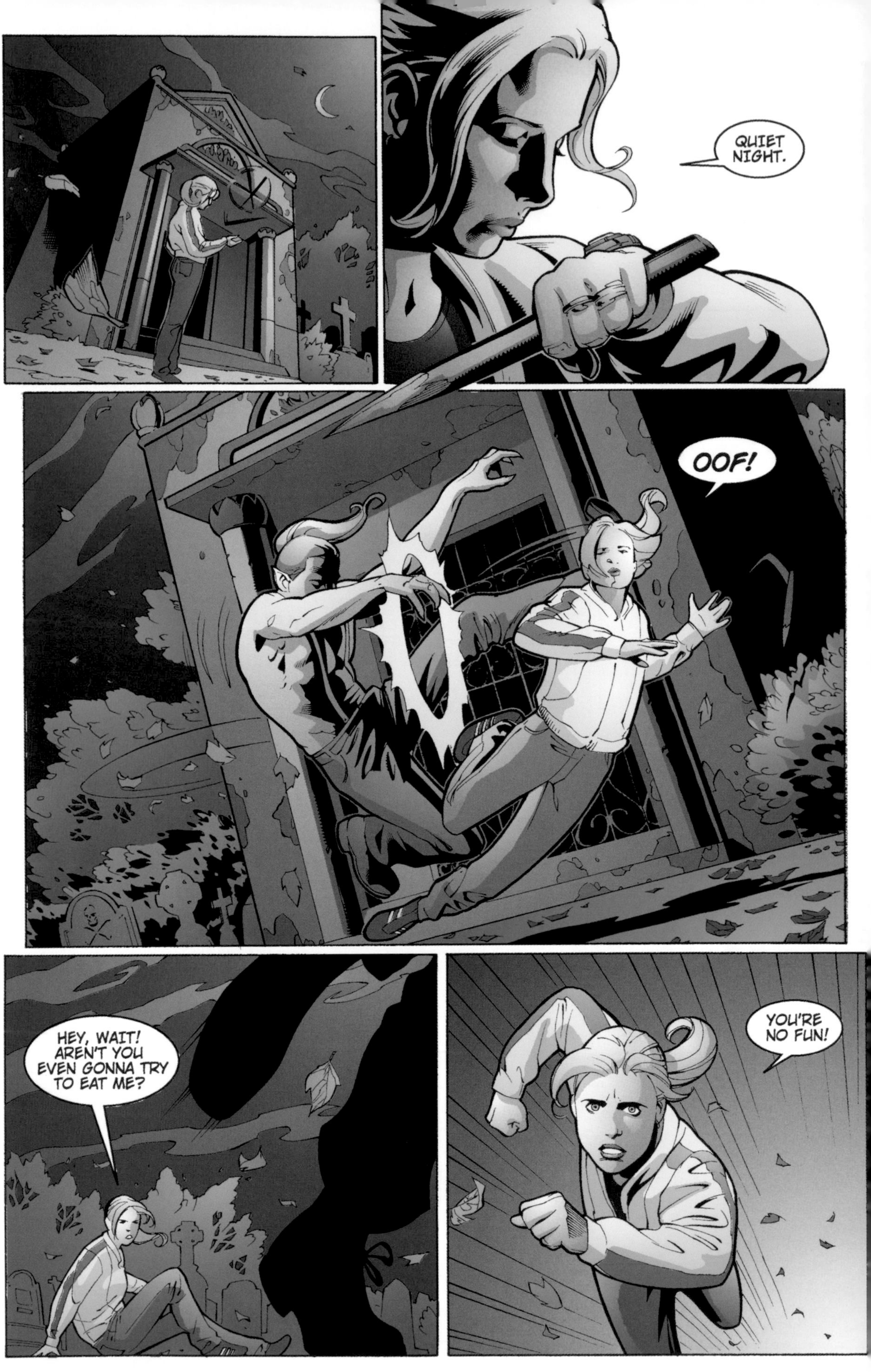
QUIET NIGHT.
OOF!
HEY, WAIT! AREN'T YOU EVEN GONNA TRY TO EAT ME?
YOU'RE NO FUN!

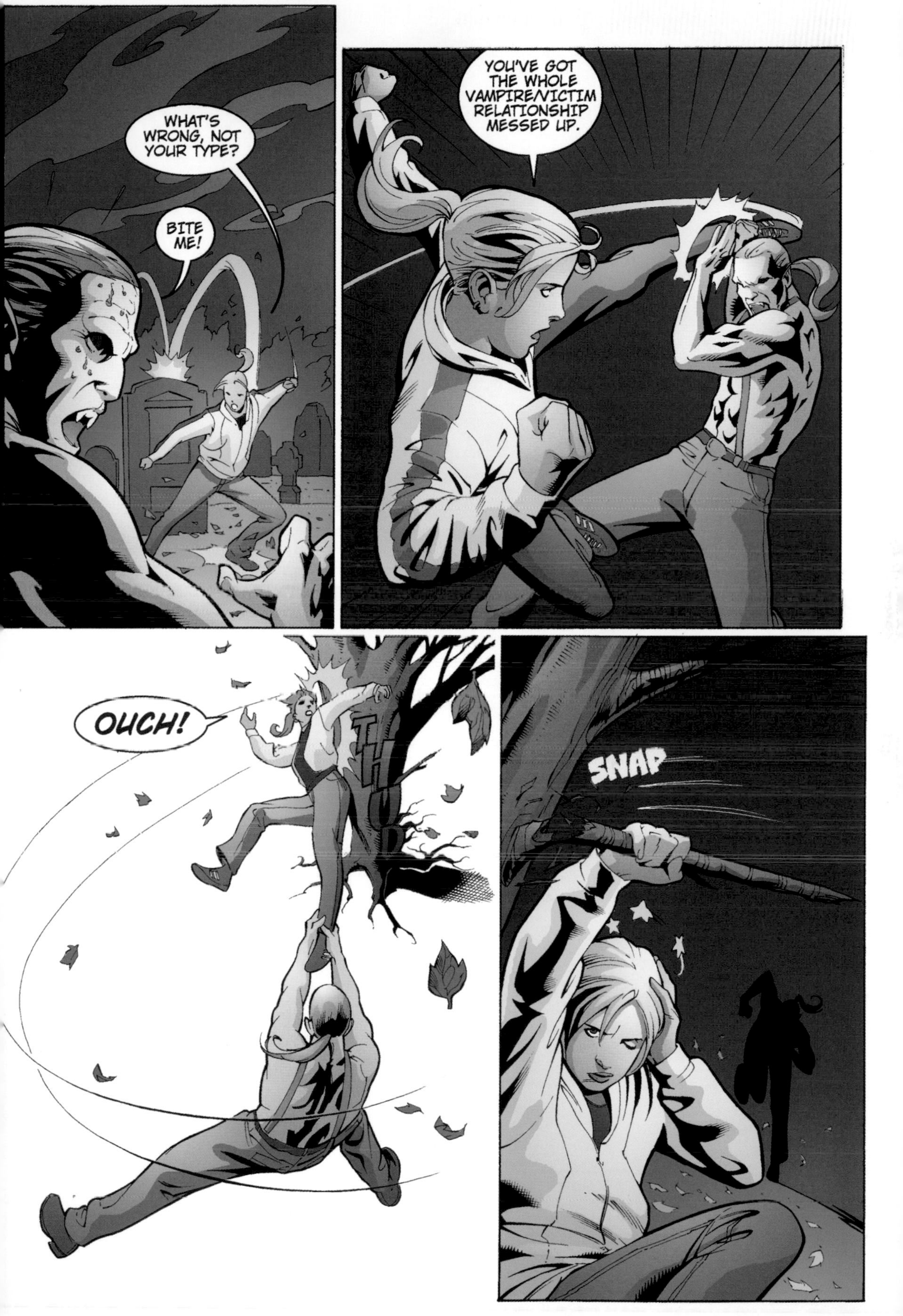
WHAT'S WRONG, NOT YOUR TYPE?
BITE ME!
YOU'VE GOT THE WHOLE VAMPIRE/VICTIM RELATIONSHIP MESSED UP.
OUCH!
THUD
SNAP

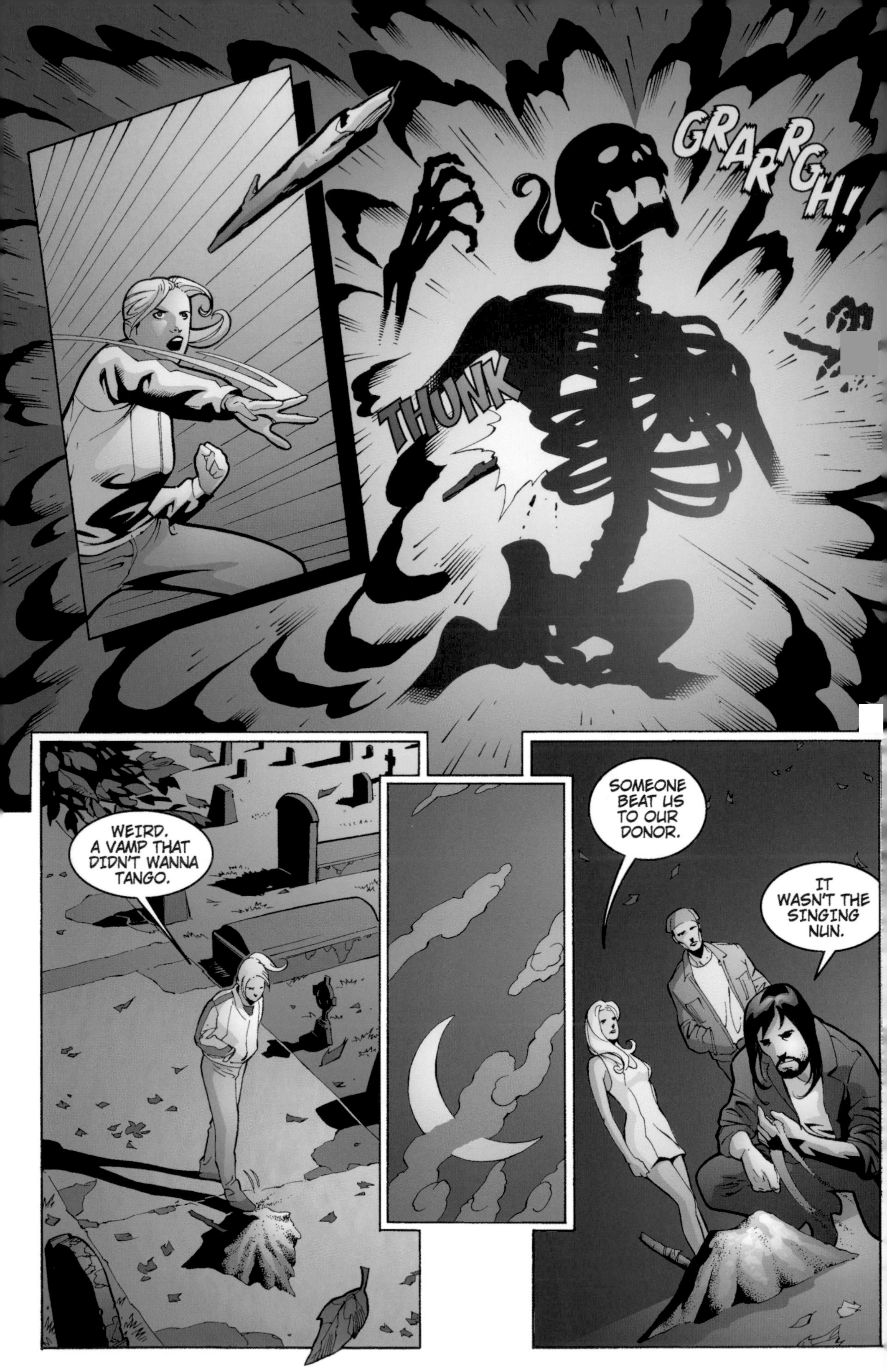

GRARRGH!
THUNK
WEIRD. A VAMP THAT DIDN'T WANNA TANGO.
SOMEONE BEAT US TO OUR DONOR.
IT WASN'T THE SINGING NUN.

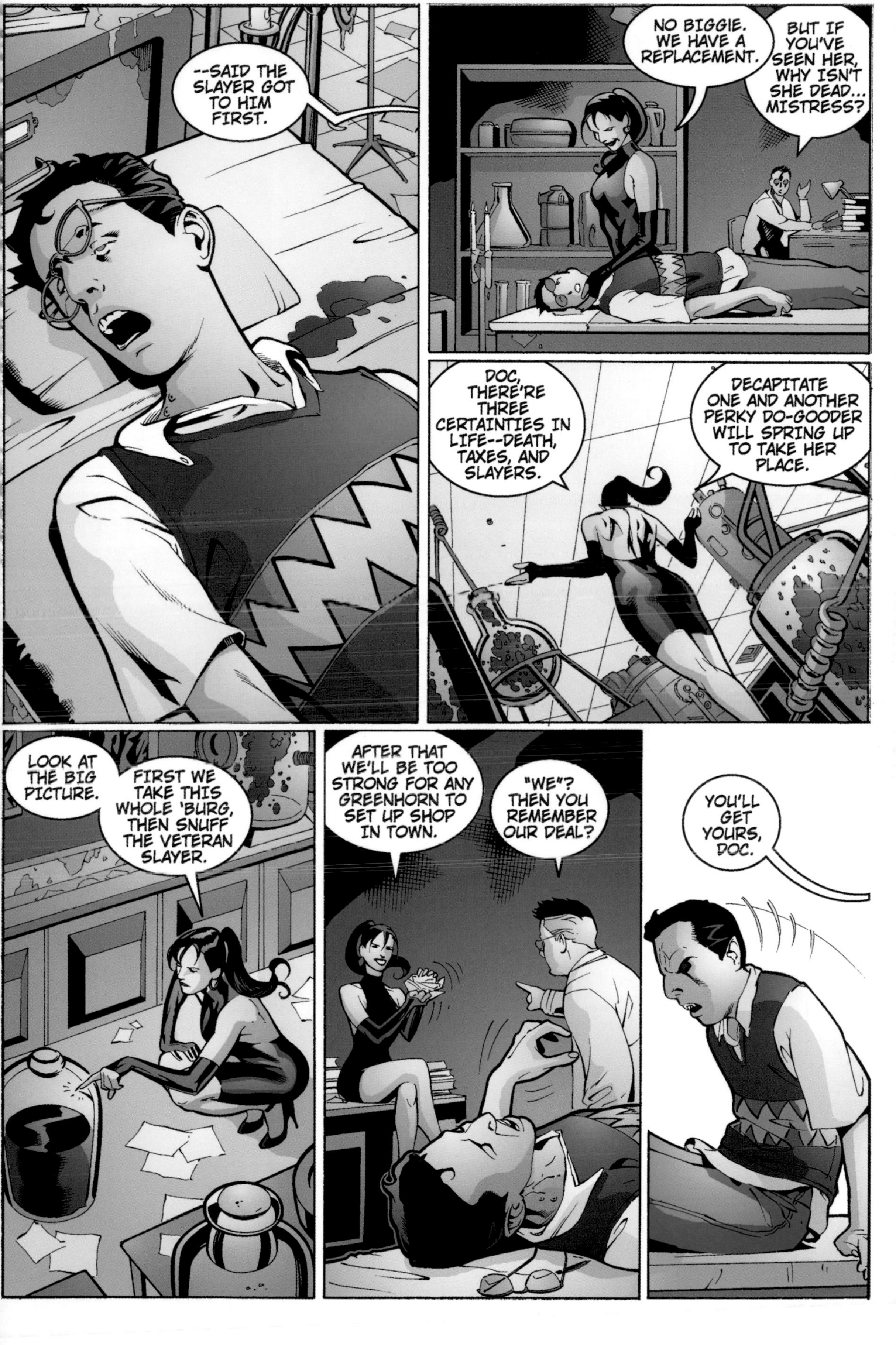
--SAID THE SLAYER GOT TO HIM FIRST.
NO BIGGIE. WE HAVE A REPLACEMENT.
BUT IF YOU'VE SEEN HER, WHY ISN'T SHE DEAD... MISTRESS?
DOC, THERE'RE THREE CERTAINTIES IN LIFE--DEATH, TAXES, AND SLAYERS.
DECAPITATE ONE AND ANOTHER PERKY DO-GOODER WILL SPRING UP TO TAKE HER PLACE.
LOOK AT THE BIG PICTURE.
FIRST WE TAKE THIS WHOLE 'BURG, THEN SNUFF THE VETERAN SLAYER.
AFTER THAT WE'LL BE TOO STRONG FOR ANY GREENHORN TO SET UP SHOP IN TOWN.
"WE"? THEN YOU REMEMBER OUR DEAL?
YOU'LL GET YOURS, DOC.

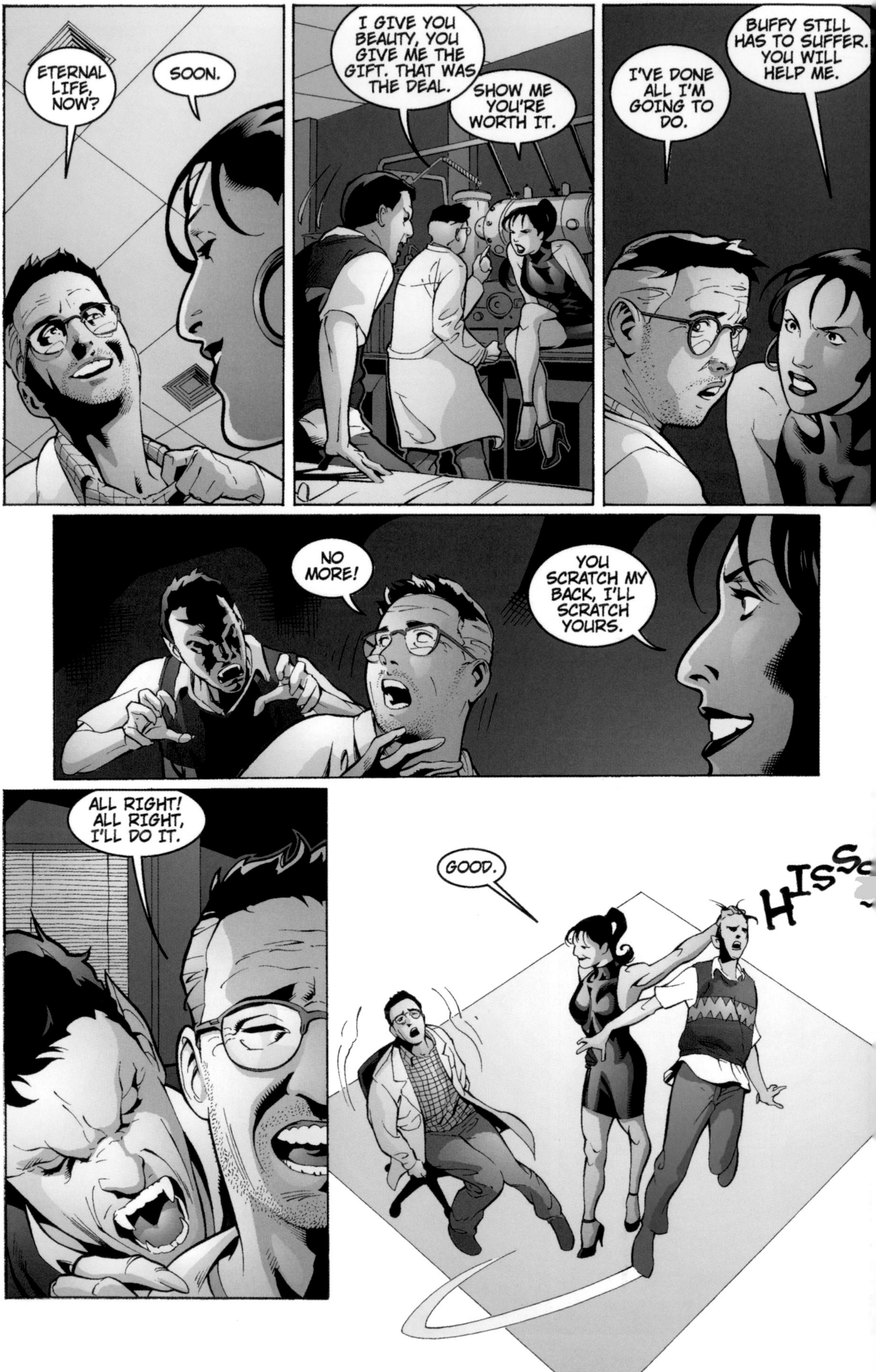
ETERNAL LIFE, NOW?
SOON.
I GIVE YOU BEAUTY, YOU GIVE ME THE GIFT. THAT WAS THE DEAL.
SHOW ME YOU'RE WORTH IT.
I'VE DONE ALL I'M GOING TO DO.
BUFFY STILL HAS TO SUFFER. YOU WILL HELP ME.
NO MORE!
YOU SCRATCH MY BACK, I'LL SCRATCH YOURS.
ALL RIGHT! ALL RIGHT, I'LL DO IT.
GOOD.
HISSS

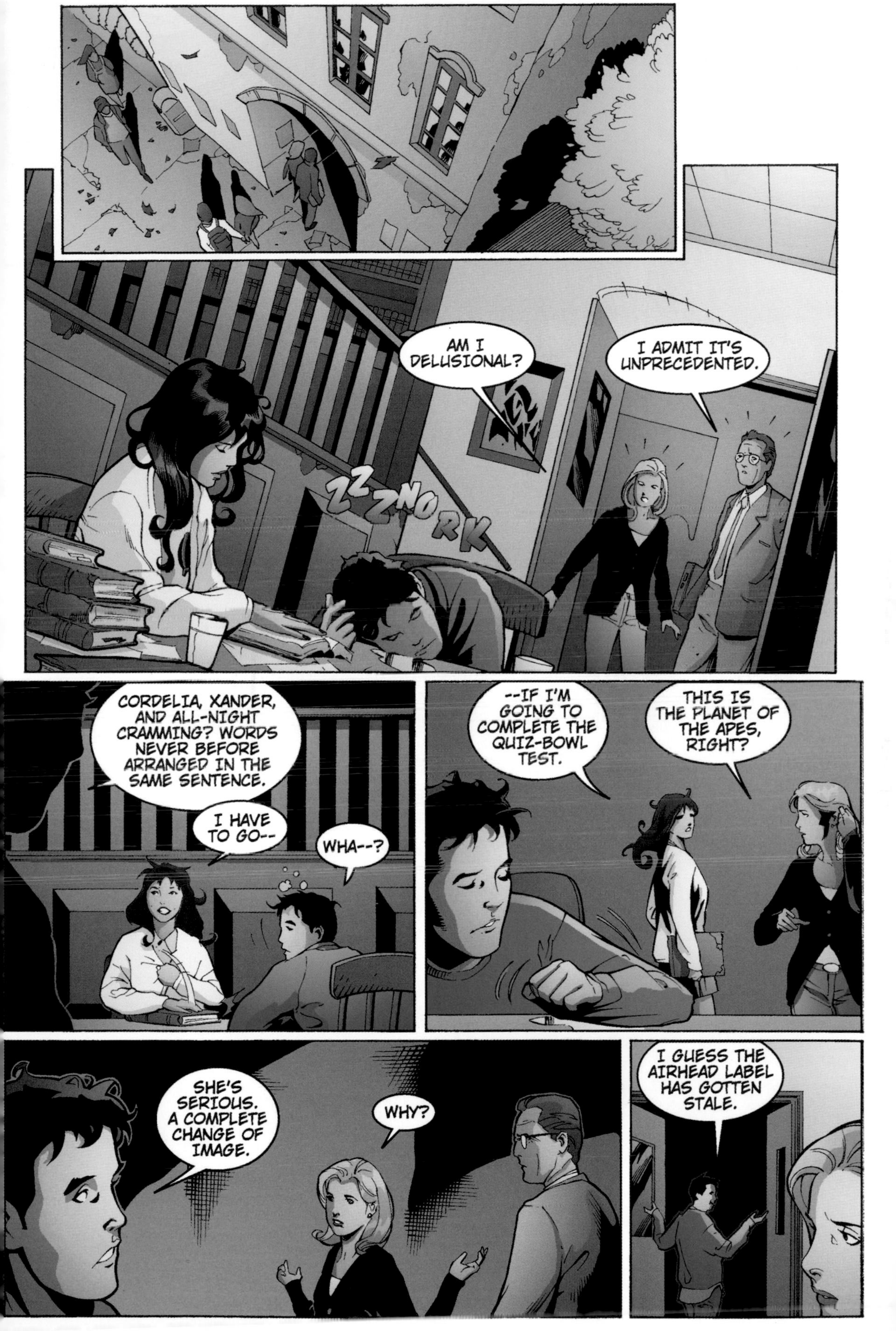
AM I DELUSIONAL?
I ADMIT IT'S UNPRECEDENTED.
ZZZNORK
CORDELIA, XANDER, AND ALL-NIGHT CRAMMING? WORDS NEVER BEFORE ARRANGED IN THE SAME SENTENCE.
I HAVE TO GO--
WHA--?
--IF I'M GOING TO COMPLETE THE QUIZ-BOWL TEST.
THIS IS THE PLANET OF THE APES, RIGHT?
SHE'S SERIOUS. A COMPLETE CHANGE OF IMAGE.
WHY?
I GUESS THE AIRHEAD LABEL HAS GOTTEN STALE.

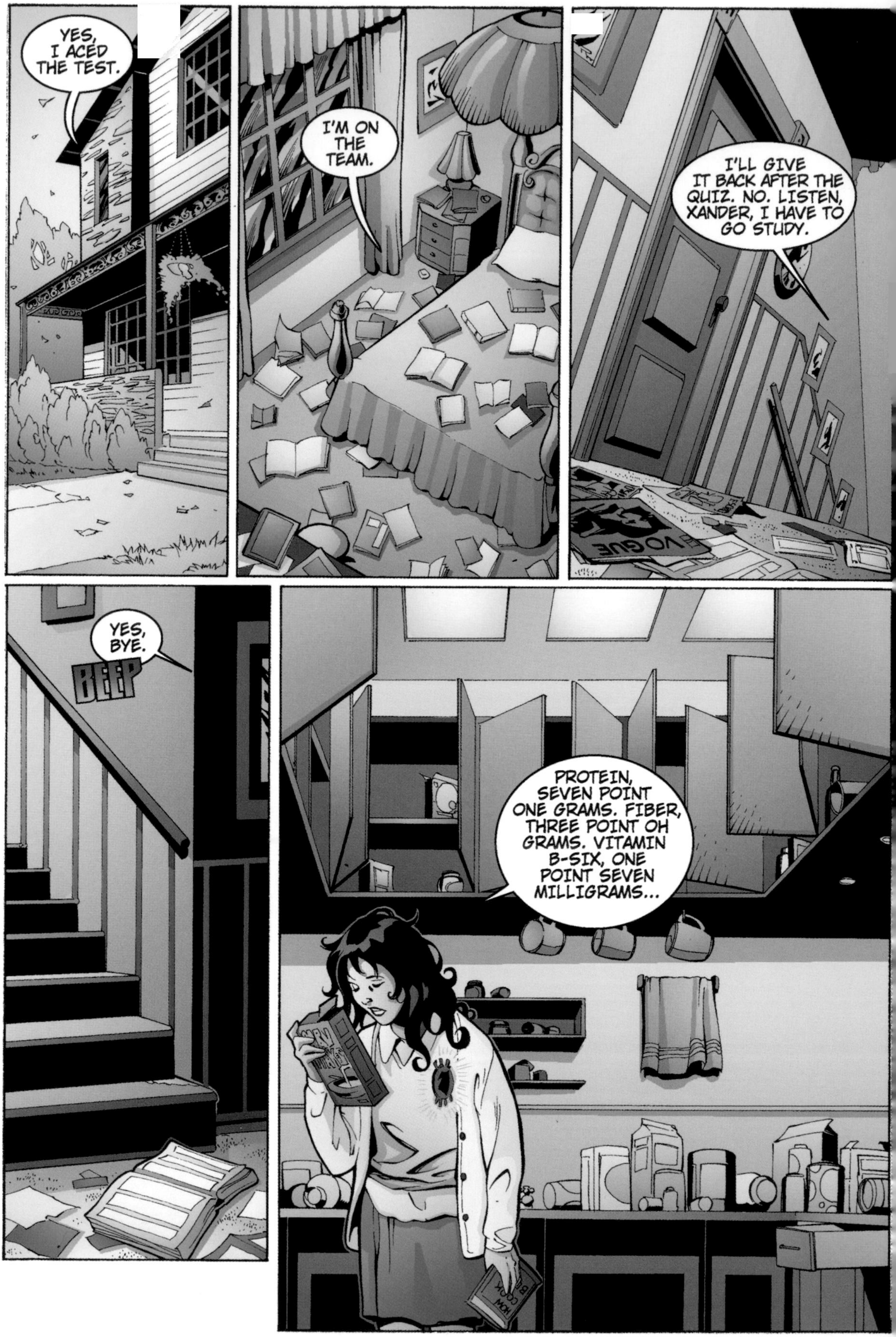
YES, I ACED THE TEST.
I'M ON THE TEAM.
I'LL GIVE IT BACK AFTER THE QUIZ. NO. LISTEN, XANDER, I HAVE TO GO STUDY.
VOGUE
YES, BYE.
BEEP
PROTEIN, SEVEN POINT ONE GRAMS. FIBER, THREE POINT OH GRAMS. VITAMIN B-SIX, ONE POINT SEVEN MILLIGRAMS...

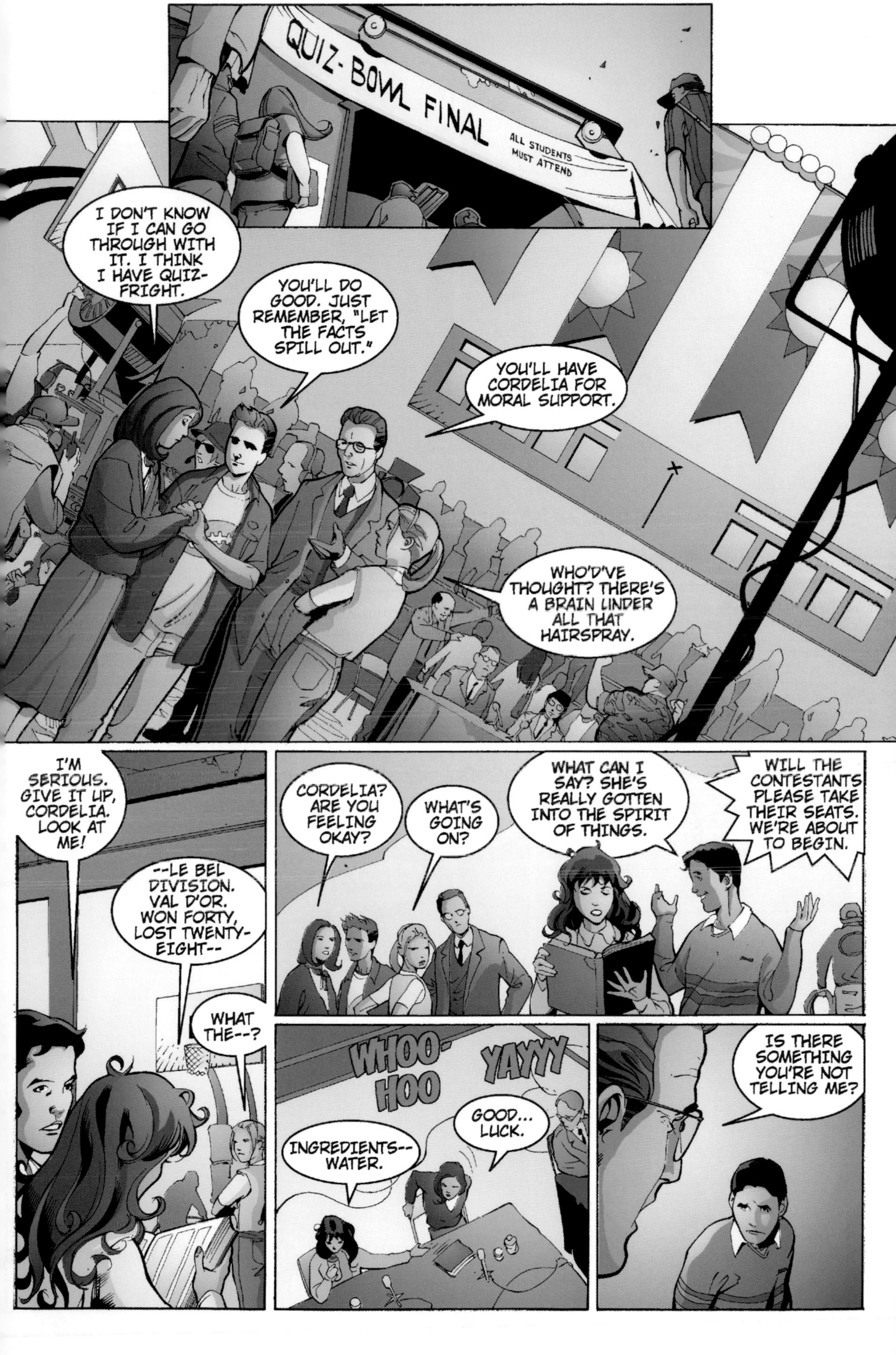
QUIZ-BOWL FINAL
ALL STUDENTS MUST ATTEND
I DON'T KNOW IF I CAN GO THROUGH WITH IT. I THINK I HAVE QUIZ-FRIGHT.
YOU'LL DO GOOD. JUST REMEMBER, "LET THE FACTS SPILL OUT."
YOU'LL HAVE CORDELIA FOR MORAL SUPPORT.
WHO'D'VE THOUGHT? THERE'S A BRAIN UNDER ALL THAT HAIRSPRAY.
I'M SERIOUS. GIVE IT UP, CORDELIA. LOOK AT ME!
--LE BEL DIVISION. VAL D'OR. WON FORTY, LOST TWENTY-EIGHT--
WHAT THE--?
CORDELIA? ARE YOU FEELING OKAY?
WHAT'S GOING ON?
WHAT CAN I SAY? SHE'S REALLY GOTTEN INTO THE SPIRIT OF THINGS.
WILL THE CONTESTANTS PLEASE TAKE THEIR SEATS. WE'RE ABOUT TO BEGIN.
WHOO-HOO
YAYYY
INGREDIENTS--WATER.
GOOD... LUCK.
IS THERE SOMETHING YOU'RE NOT TELLING ME?

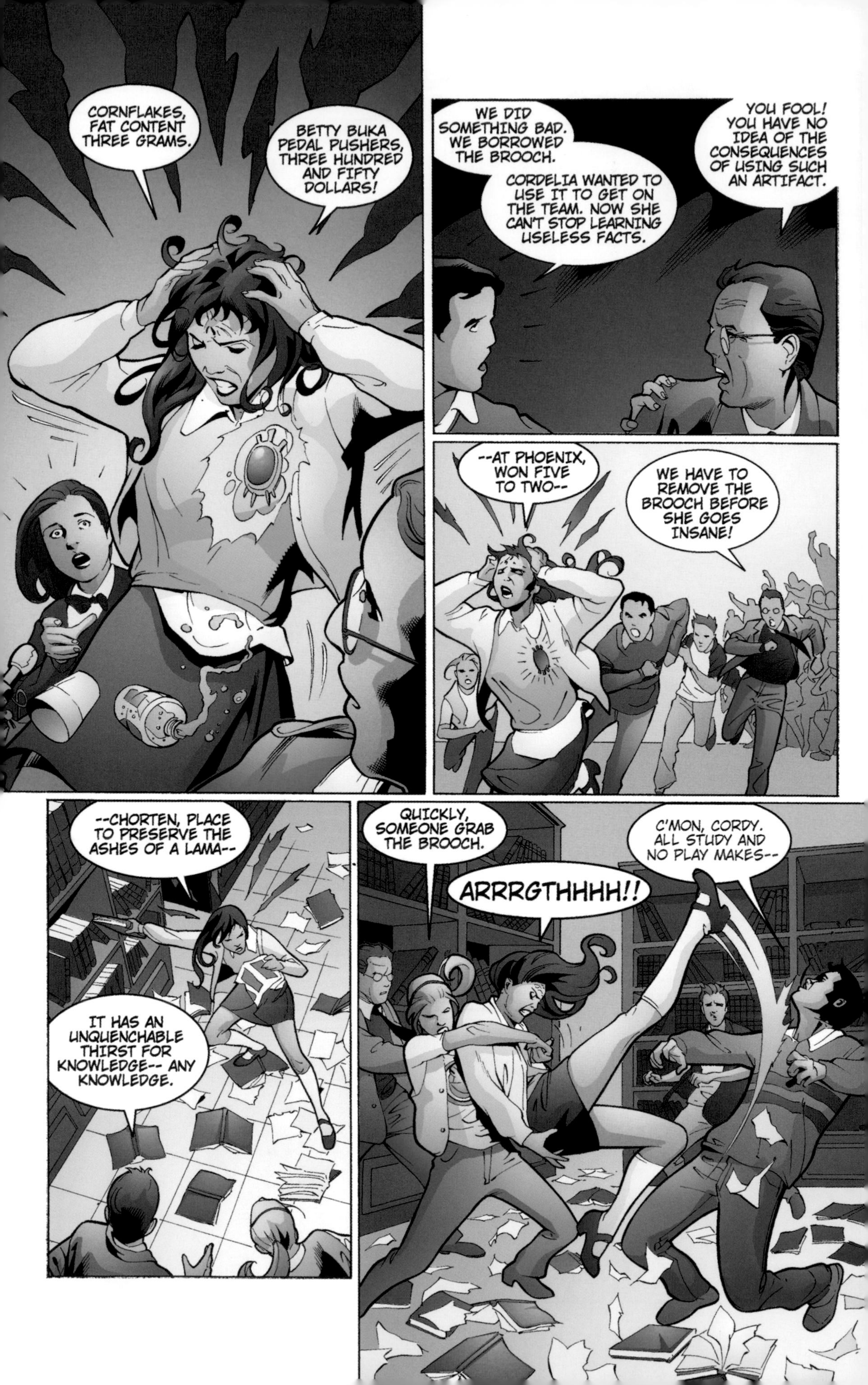
CORNFLAKES, FAT CONTENT THREE GRAMS.
BETTY BUKA PEDAL PUSHERS, THREE HUNDRED AND FIFTY DOLLARS!
WE DID SOMETHING BAD. WE BORROWED THE BROOCH.
CORDELIA WANTED TO USE IT TO GET ON THE TEAM. NOW SHE CAN'T STOP LEARNING USELESS FACTS.
YOU FOOL! YOU HAVE NO IDEA OF THE CONSEQUENCES OF USING SUCH AN ARTIFACT.
--AT PHOENIX, WON FIVE TO TWO--
WE HAVE TO REMOVE THE BROOCH BEFORE SHE GOES INSANE!
--CHORTEN, PLACE TO PRESERVE THE ASHES OF A LAMA--
IT HAS AN UNQUENCHABLE THIRST FOR KNOWLEDGE-- ANY KNOWLEDGE.
QUICKLY, SOMEONE GRAB THE BROOCH.
ARRRGTHHHH!!
C'MON, CORDY. ALL STUDY AND NO PLAY MAKES--

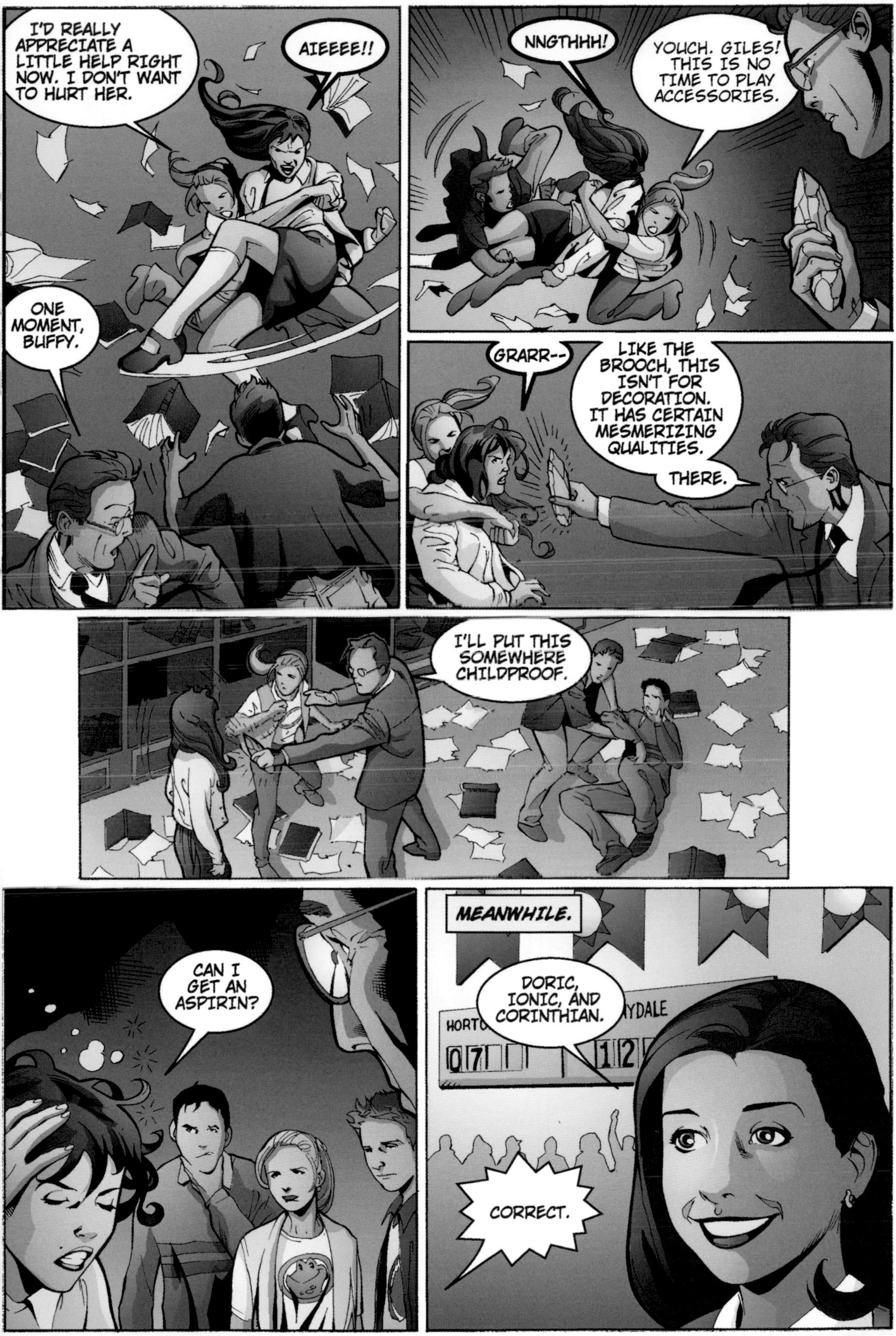
I'D REALLY APPRECIATE A LITTLE HELP RIGHT NOW. I DON'T WANT TO HURT HER.
AIEEEE!!
ONE MOMENT, BUFFY.
NNGTHHH!
YOUCH. GILES! THIS IS NO TIME TO PLAY ACCESSORIES.
GRARR--
LIKE THE BROOCH, THIS ISN'T FOR DECORATION. IT HAS CERTAIN MESMERIZING QUALITIES.
THERE.
I'LL PUT THIS SOMEWHERE CHILDPROOF.
CAN I GET AN ASPIRIN?
MEANWHILE.
DORIC, IONIC, AND CORINTHIAN.
CORRECT.

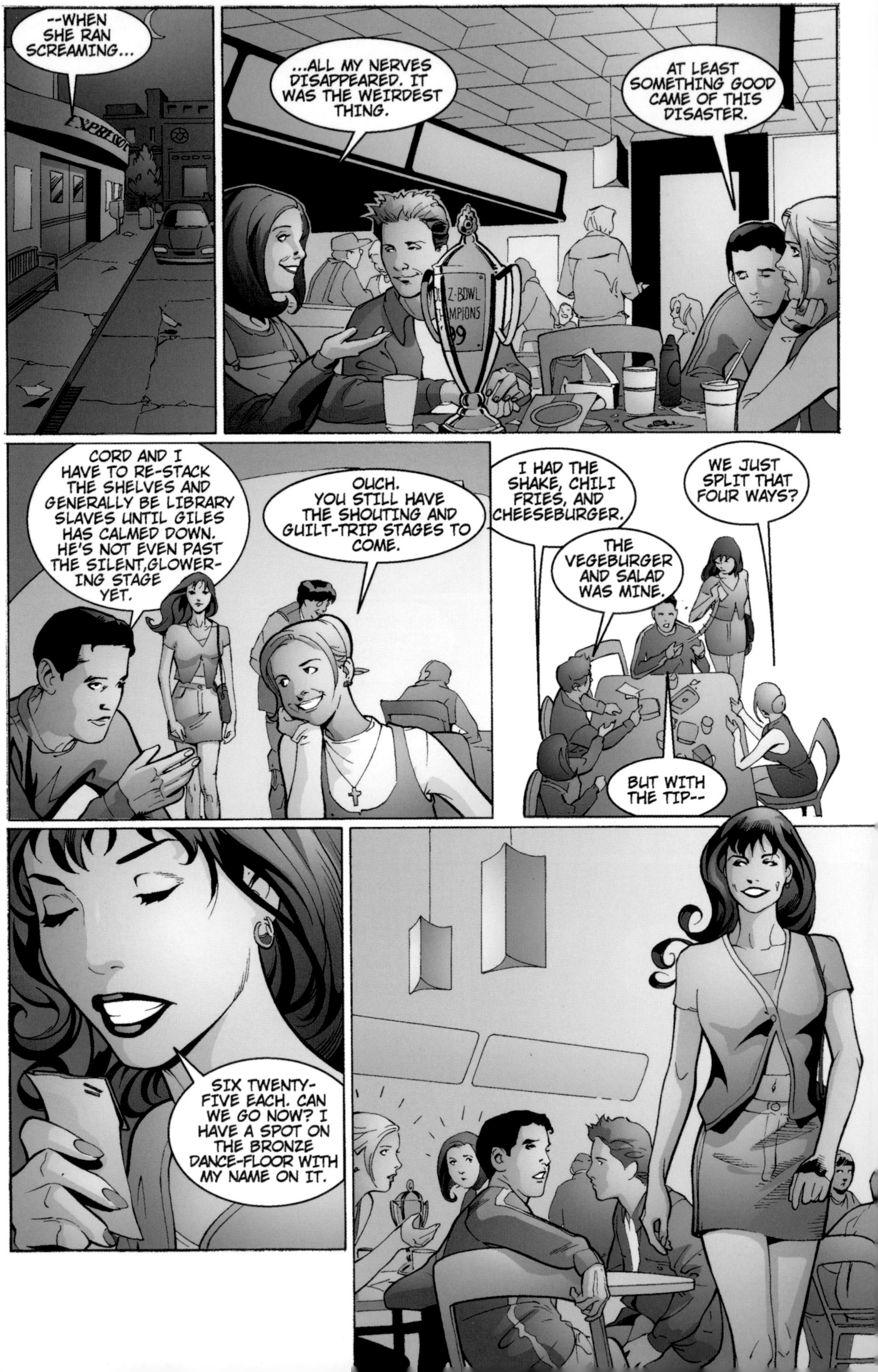
--WHEN SHE RAN SCREAMING...
...ALL MY NERVES DISAPPEARED. IT WAS THE WEIRDEST THING.
AT LEAST SOMETHING GOOD CAME OF THIS DISASTER.
Z-BOWL CHAMPIONS 99
CORD AND I HAVE TO RE-STACK THE SHELVES AND GENERALLY BE LIBRARY SLAVES UNTIL GILES HAS CALMED DOWN. HE'S NOT EVEN PAST THE SILENT, GLOWERING STAGE YET.
OUCH. YOU STILL HAVE THE SHOUTING AND GUILT-TRIP STAGES TO COME.
I HAD THE SHAKE, CHILI FRIES, AND CHEESEBURGER.
THE VEGEBURGER AND SALAD WAS MINE.
WE JUST SPLIT THAT FOUR WAYS?
BUT WITH THE TIP--
SIX TWENTY-FIVE EACH. CAN WE GO NOW? I HAVE A SPOT ON THE BRONZE DANCE-FLOOR WITH MY NAME ON IT.

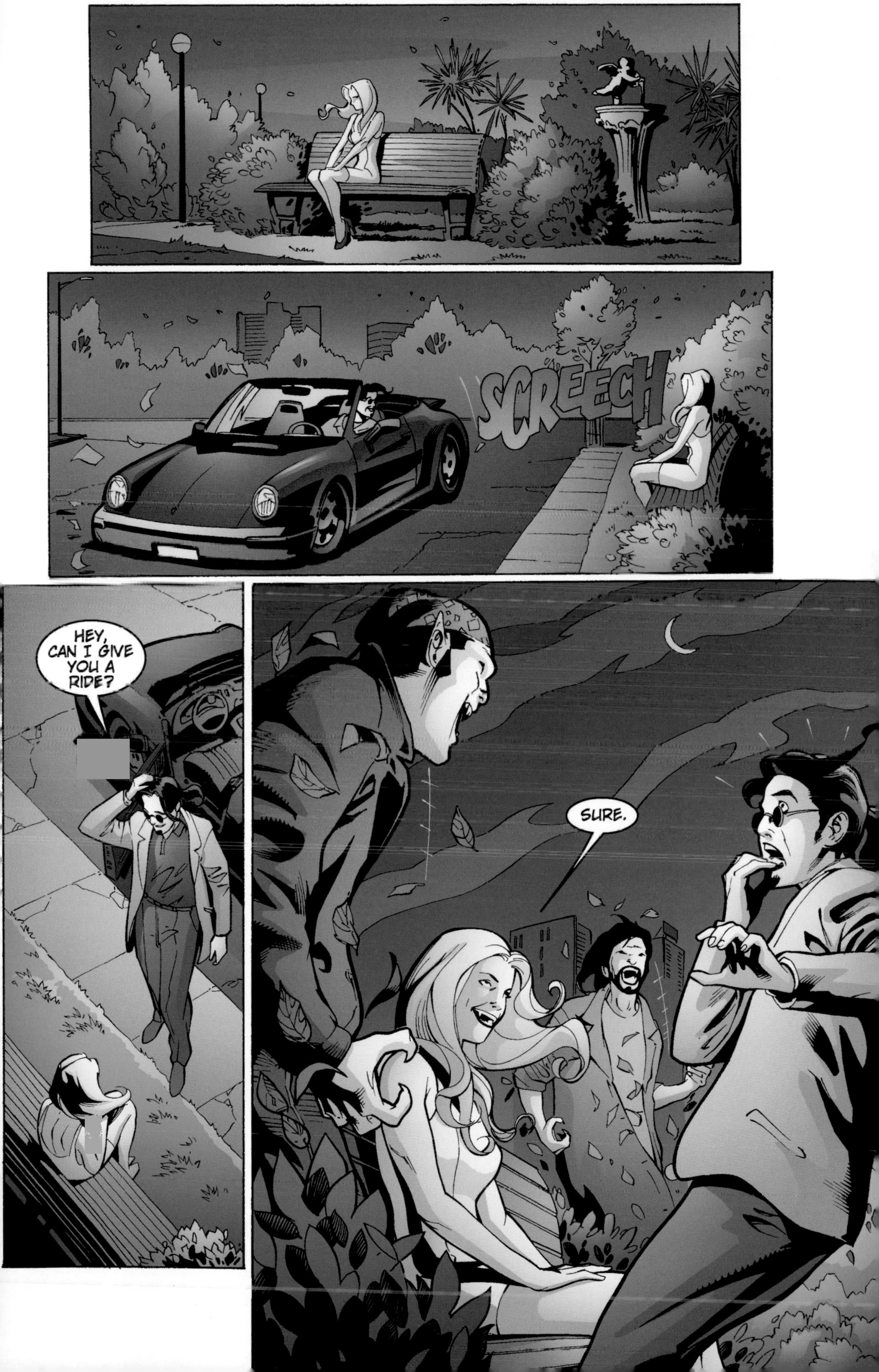
SCREECH
HEY, CAN I GIVE YOU A RIDE?
SURE.

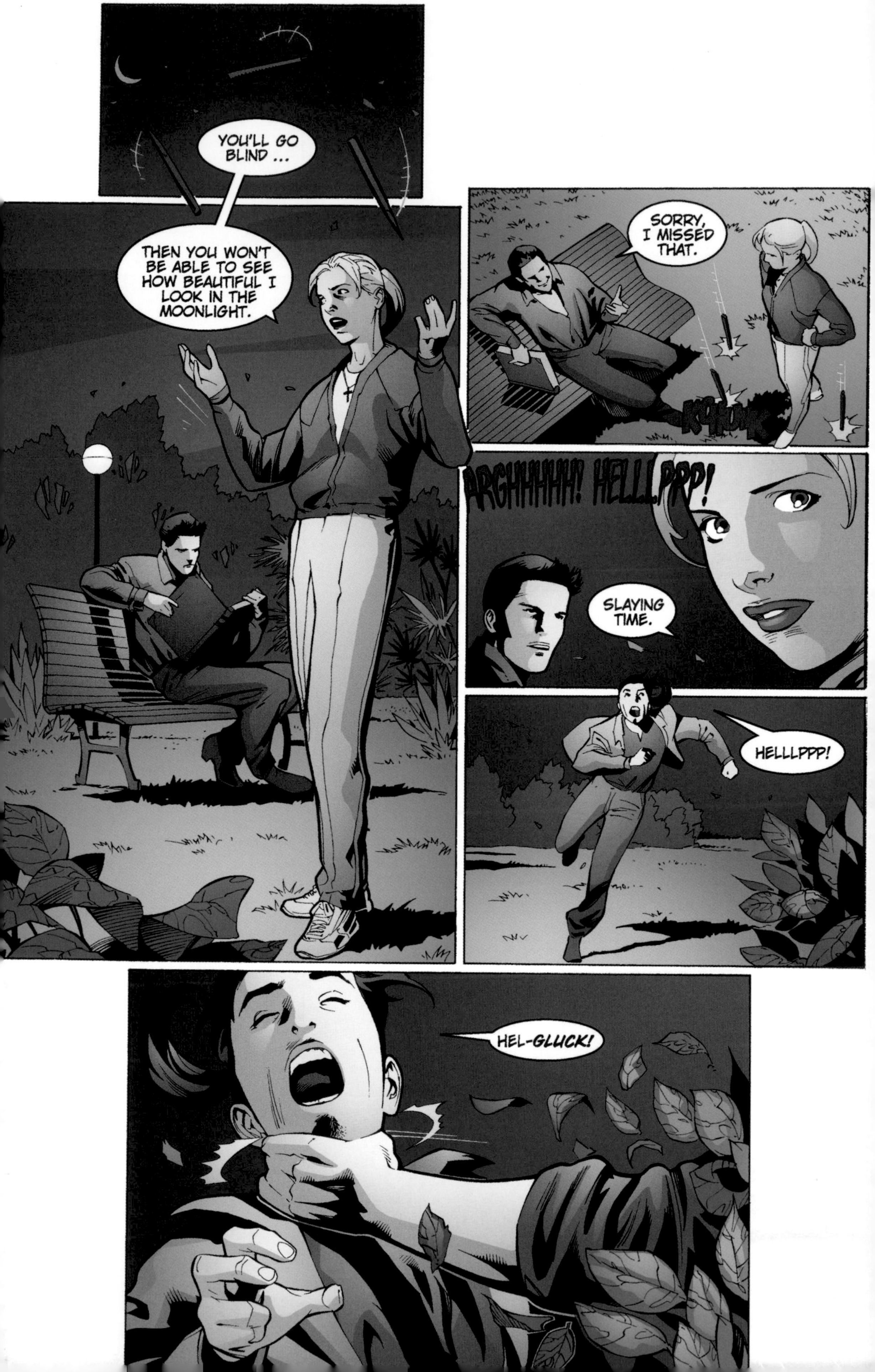

YOU'LL GO BLIND ...
THEN YOU WON'T BE ABLE TO SEE HOW BEAUTIFUL I LOOK IN THE MOONLIGHT.
SORRY, I MISSED THAT.
KCHUNK
ARGHHHHH! HELLLPRP!
SLAYING TIME.
HELLLPPP!
HEL-*GLUCK!*

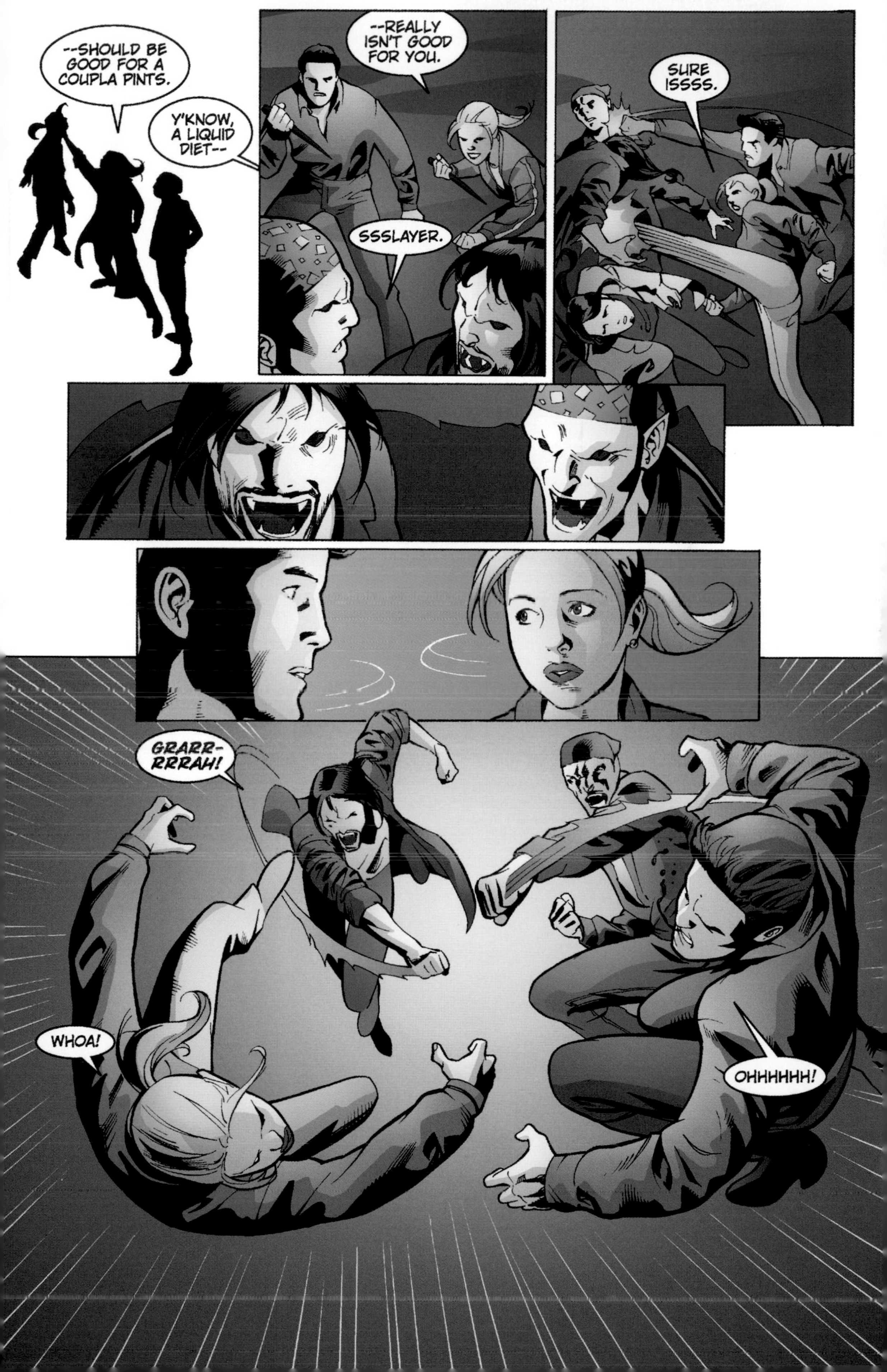
--SHOULD BE GOOD FOR A COUPLA PINTS.
Y'KNOW, A LIQUID DIET--
--REALLY ISN'T GOOD FOR YOU.
SSSLAYER.
SURE ISSSS.
GRARR-RRRAH!
WHOA!
OHHHHHH!

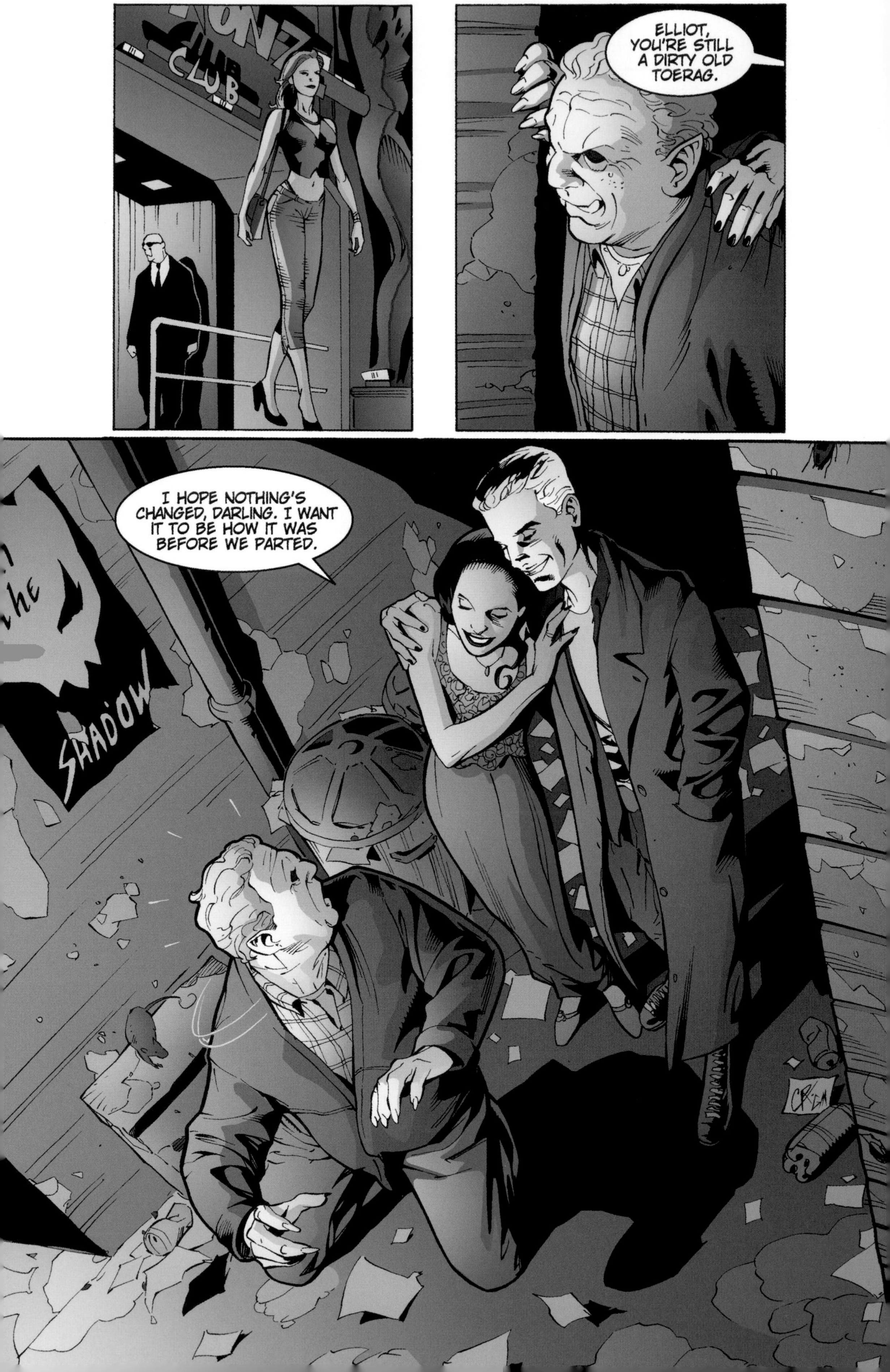
CLUB
ELLIOT, YOU'RE STILL A DIRTY OLD TOERAG.
I HOPE NOTHING'S CHANGED, DARLING. I WANT IT TO BE HOW IT WAS BEFORE WE PARTED.
SHADOW

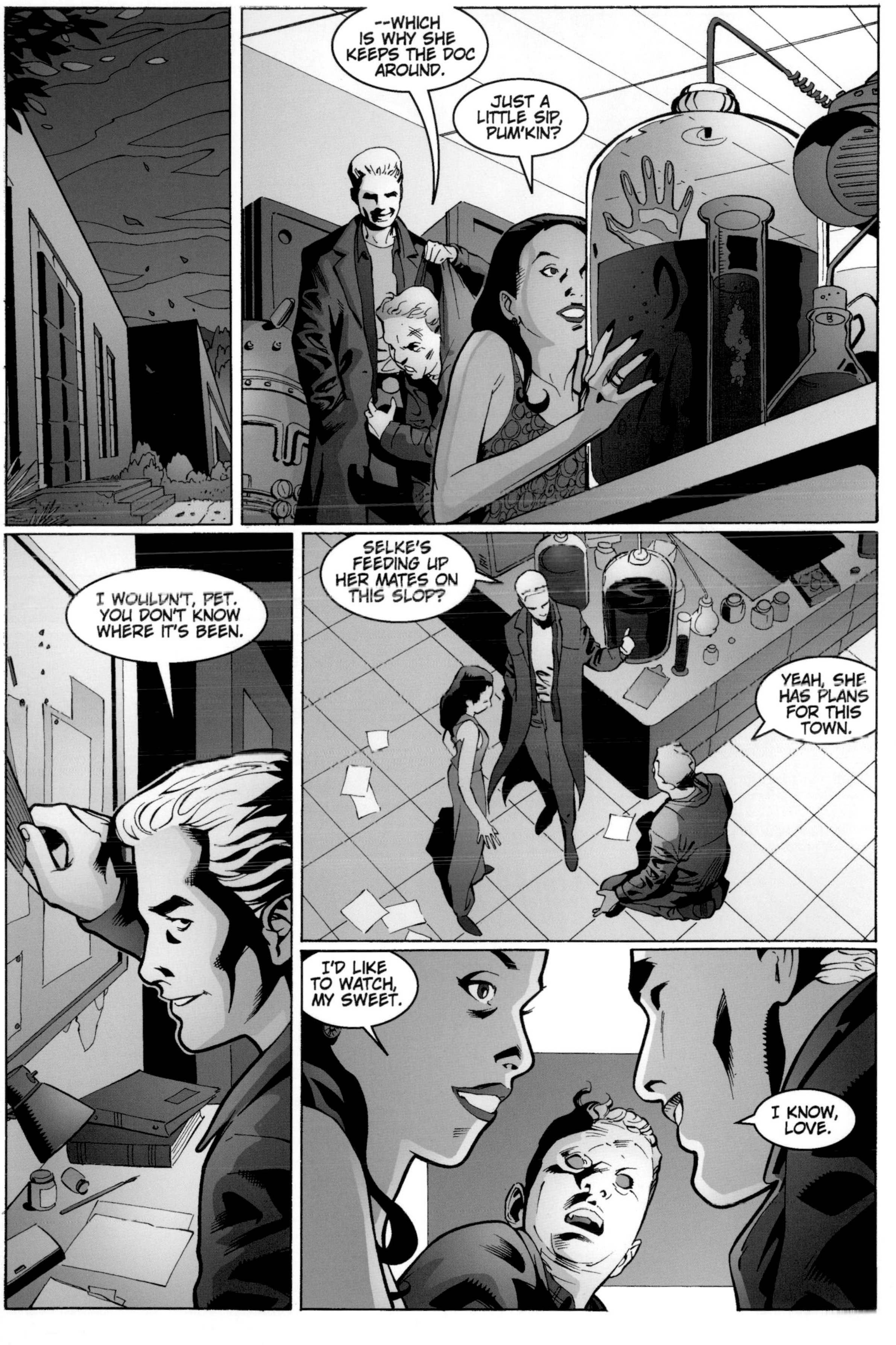
--WHICH IS WHY SHE KEEPS THE DOC AROUND.
JUST A LITTLE SIP, PUM'KIN?
I WOULDN'T, PET. YOU DON'T KNOW WHERE IT'S BEEN.
SELKE'S FEEDING UP HER MATES ON THIS SLOP?
YEAH, SHE HAS PLANS FOR THIS TOWN.
I'D LIKE TO WATCH, MY SWEET.
I KNOW, LOVE.

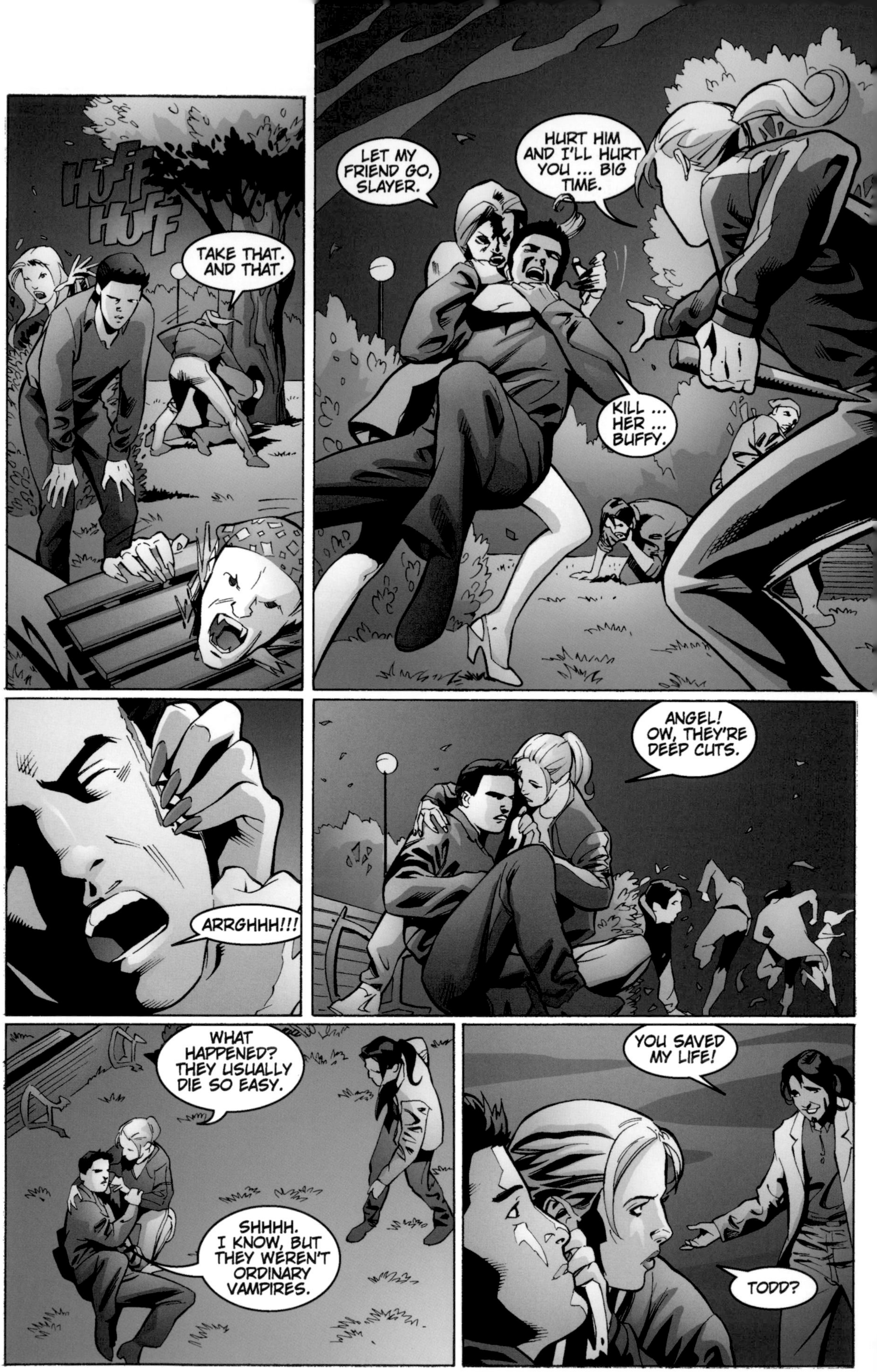
HUFF HUFF
TAKE THAT. AND THAT.
LET MY FRIEND GO, SLAYER.
HURT HIM AND I'LL HURT YOU ... BIG TIME.
KILL ... HER ... BUFFY.
ARRGHHH!!!
ANGEL! OW, THEY'RE DEEP CUTS.
WHAT HAPPENED? THEY USUALLY DIE SO EASY.
SHHHH. I KNOW, BUT THEY WEREN'T ORDINARY VAMPIRES.
YOU SAVED MY LIFE!
TODD?

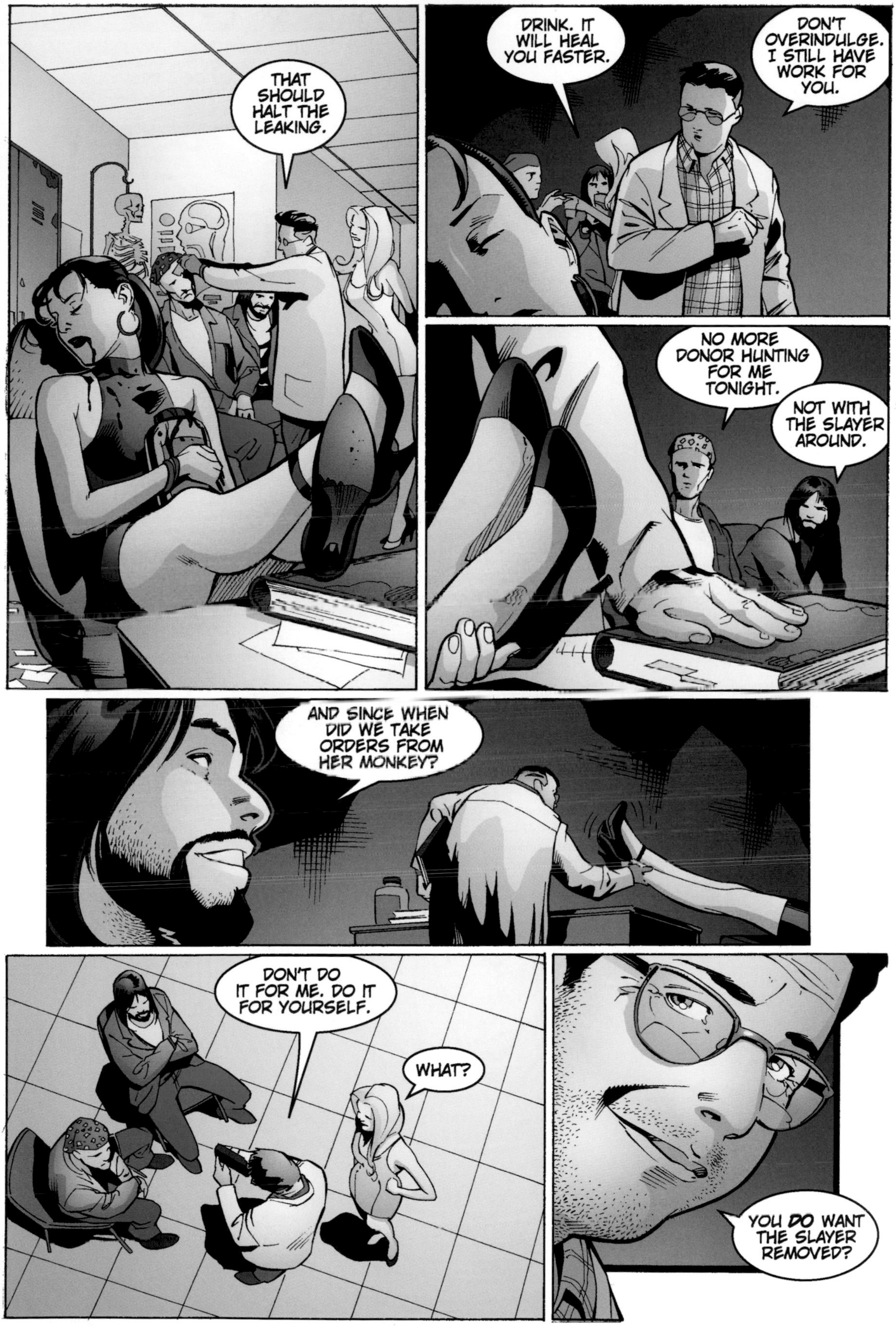
THAT SHOULD HALT THE LEAKING.
DRINK. IT WILL HEAL YOU FASTER.
DON'T OVERINDULGE. I STILL HAVE WORK FOR YOU.
NO MORE DONOR HUNTING FOR ME TONIGHT.
NOT WITH THE SLAYER AROUND.
AND SINCE WHEN DID WE TAKE ORDERS FROM HER MONKEY?
DON'T DO IT FOR ME. DO IT FOR YOURSELF.
WHAT?
YOU *DO* WANT THE SLAYER REMOVED?

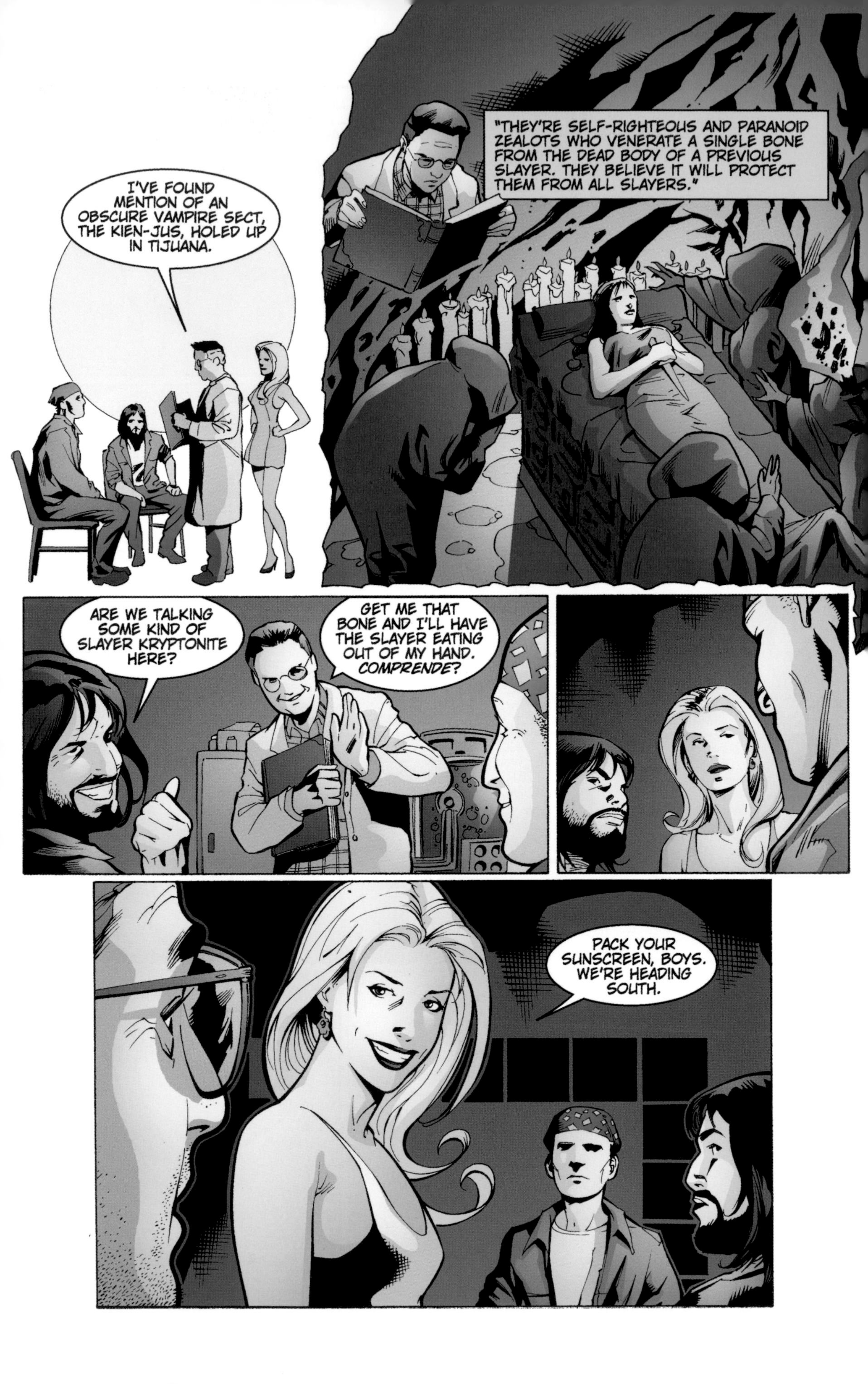
I'VE FOUND MENTION OF AN OBSCURE VAMPIRE SECT, THE KIEN-JUS, HOLED UP IN TIJUANA.
"THEY'RE SELF-RIGHTEOUS AND PARANOID ZEALOTS WHO VENERATE A SINGLE BONE FROM THE DEAD BODY OF A PREVIOUS SLAYER. THEY BELIEVE IT WILL PROTECT THEM FROM ALL SLAYERS."
ARE WE TALKING SOME KIND OF SLAYER KRYPTONITE HERE?
GET ME THAT BONE AND I'LL HAVE THE SLAYER EATING OUT OF MY HAND. *COMPRENDE?*
PACK YOUR SUNSCREEN, BOYS. WE'RE HEADING SOUTH.

--FELT LIKE TEN ROUNDS WITH A HEAVYWEIGHT. BUT WITH MORE BITING!

THIS IS A MOST PERPLEXING DEVELOPMENT.

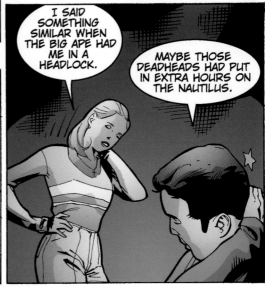

I SAID SOMETHING SIMILAR WHEN THE BIG APE HAD ME IN A HEADLOCK.

MAYBE THOSE DEADHEADS HAD PUT IN EXTRA HOURS ON THE NAUTILUS.

THEY WERE NOT YOUR COMMON OR GARDEN VAMPS.

SUPER-SUCKERS IN SUNNYDALE?

NEVER A DULL MOMENT.

THIS IS UNPRECEDENTED. I TRUST ANGEL IS MAKING INQUIRIES OF THE UNDERWORLD?

UH-HUH. I ONLY HOPE THESE FREAKS ARE A ONCE-ONLY DEAL.

BUFFY, HI. CAN WE TALK?

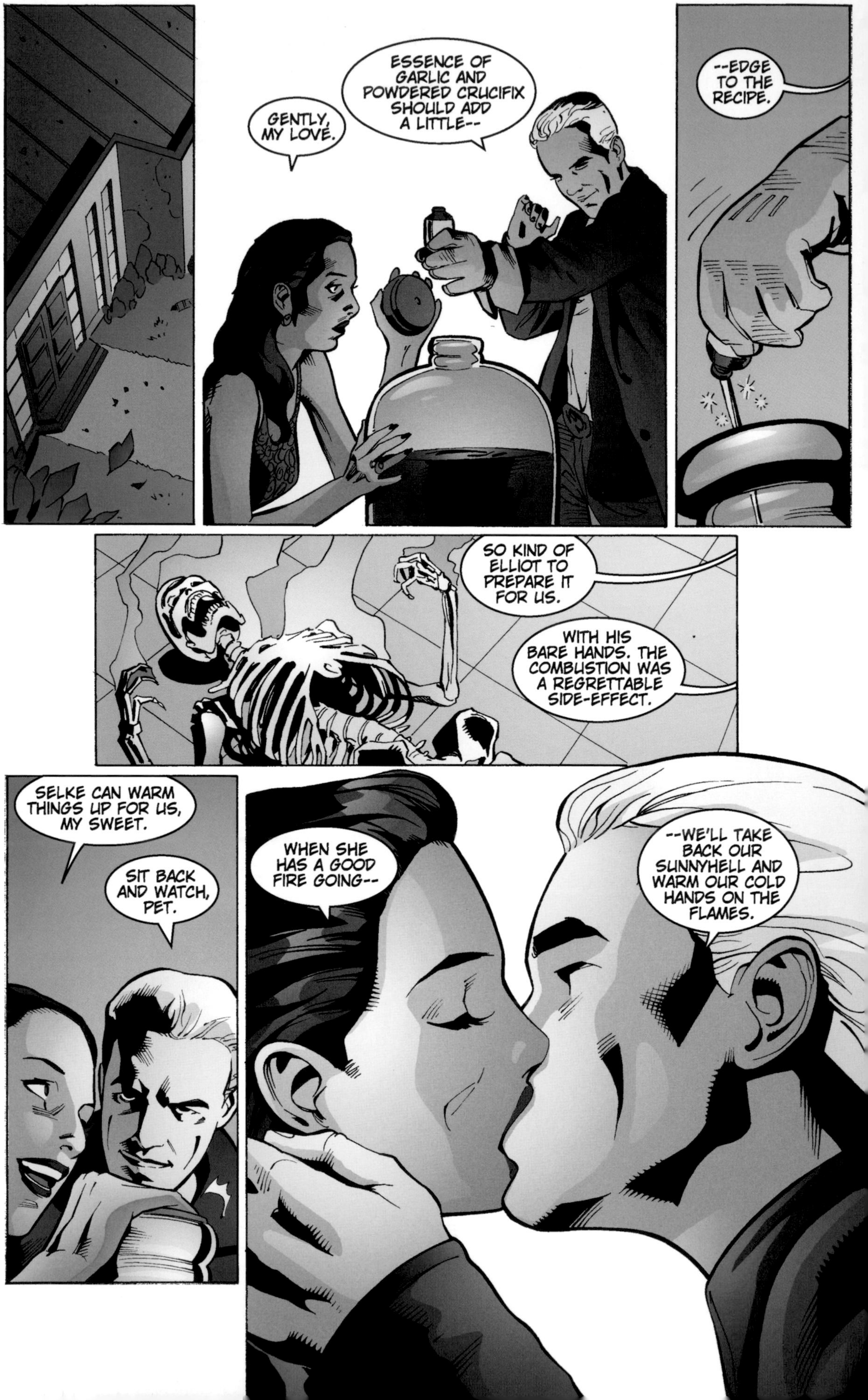
GENTLY, MY LOVE.
ESSENCE OF GARLIC AND POWDERED CRUCIFIX SHOULD ADD A LITTLE--
--EDGE TO THE RECIPE.
SO KIND OF ELLIOT TO PREPARE IT FOR US.
WITH HIS BARE HANDS. THE COMBUSTION WAS A REGRETTABLE SIDE-EFFECT.
SELKE CAN WARM THINGS UP FOR US, MY SWEET.
SIT BACK AND WATCH, PET.
WHEN SHE HAS A GOOD FIRE GOING--
--WE'LL TAKE BACK OUR SUNNYHELL AND WARM OUR COLD HANDS ON THE FLAMES.

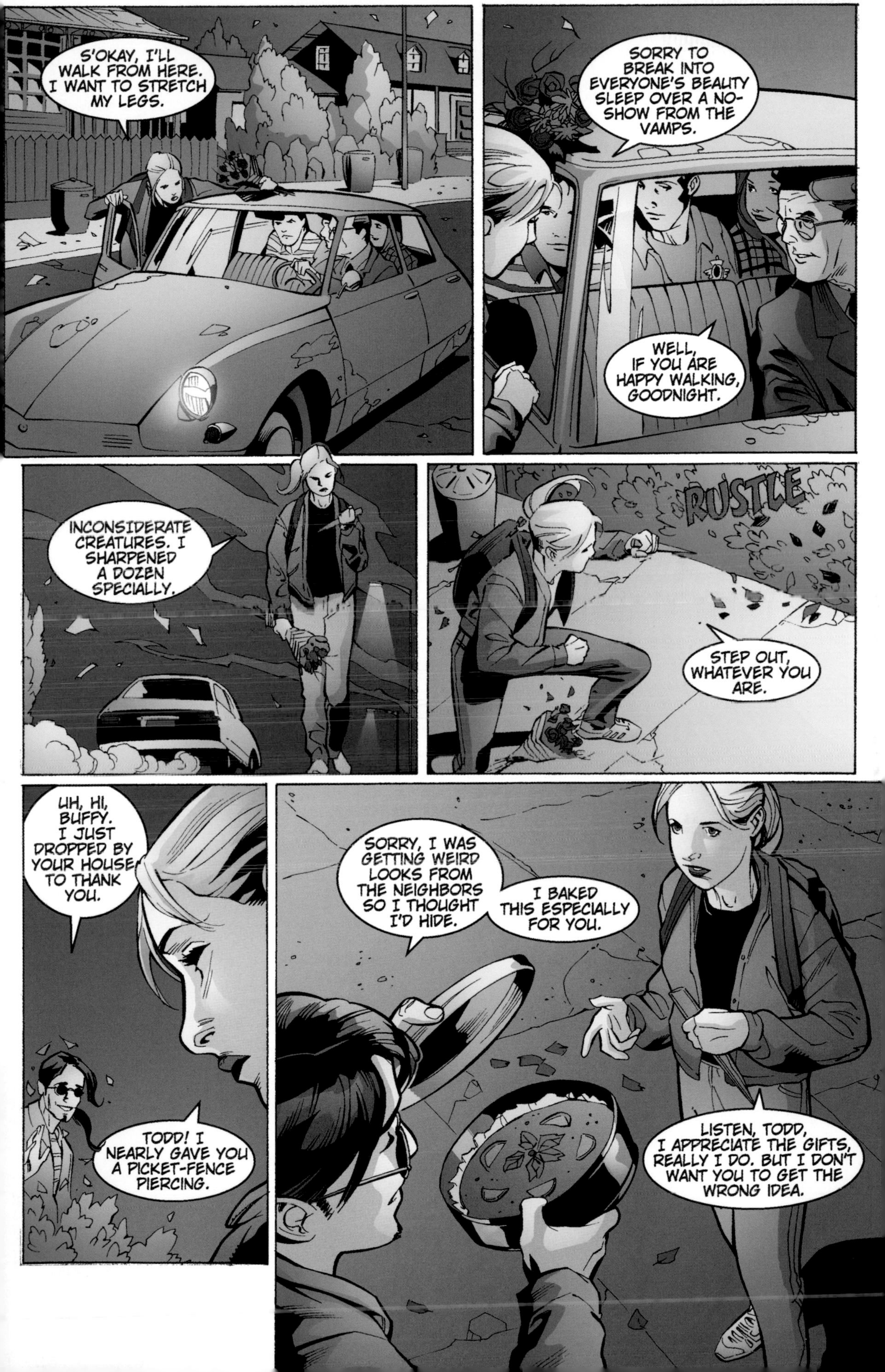
S'OKAY, I'LL WALK FROM HERE. I WANT TO STRETCH MY LEGS.
SORRY TO BREAK INTO EVERYONE'S BEAUTY SLEEP OVER A NO-SHOW FROM THE VAMPS.
WELL, IF YOU ARE HAPPY WALKING, GOODNIGHT.
INCONSIDERATE CREATURES. I SHARPENED A DOZEN SPECIALLY.
RUSTLE
STEP OUT, WHATEVER YOU ARE.
UH, HI, BUFFY. I JUST DROPPED BY YOUR HOUSE TO THANK YOU.
TODD! I NEARLY GAVE YOU A PICKET-FENCE PIERCING.
SORRY, I WAS GETTING WEIRD LOOKS FROM THE NEIGHBORS SO I THOUGHT I'D HIDE.
I BAKED THIS ESPECIALLY FOR YOU.
LISTEN, TODD, I APPRECIATE THE GIFTS, REALLY I DO. BUT I DON'T WANT YOU TO GET THE WRONG IDEA.

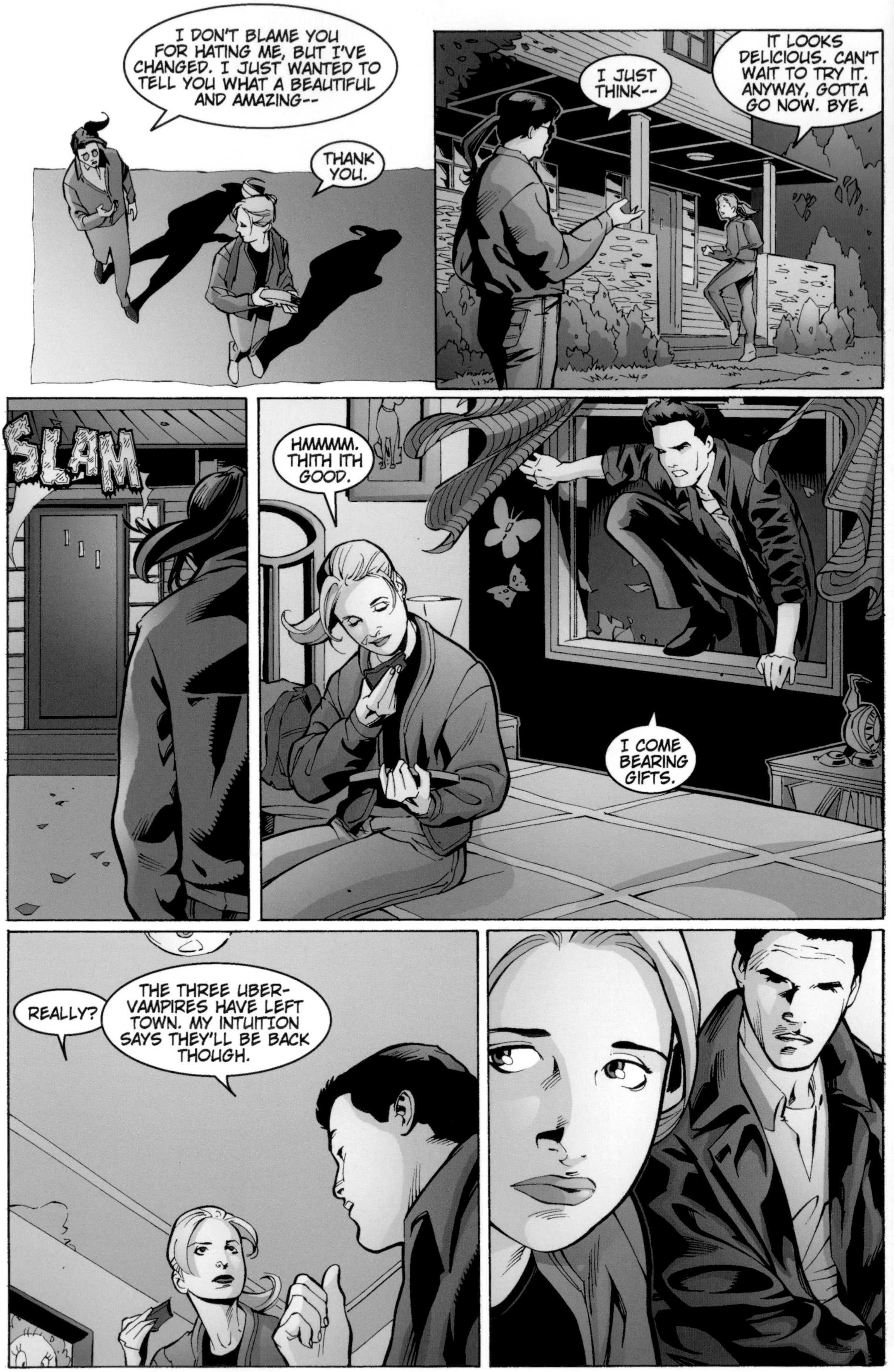
I DON'T BLAME YOU FOR HATING ME, BUT I'VE CHANGED. I JUST WANTED TO TELL YOU WHAT A BEAUTIFUL AND AMAZING--
THANK YOU.
I JUST THINK--
IT LOOKS DELICIOUS. CAN'T WAIT TO TRY IT. ANYWAY, GOTTA GO NOW. BYE.
SLAM
HMMMM. THITH ITH GOOD.
I COME BEARING GIFTS.
REALLY?
THE THREE UBER-VAMPIRES HAVE LEFT TOWN. MY INTUITION SAYS THEY'LL BE BACK THOUGH.

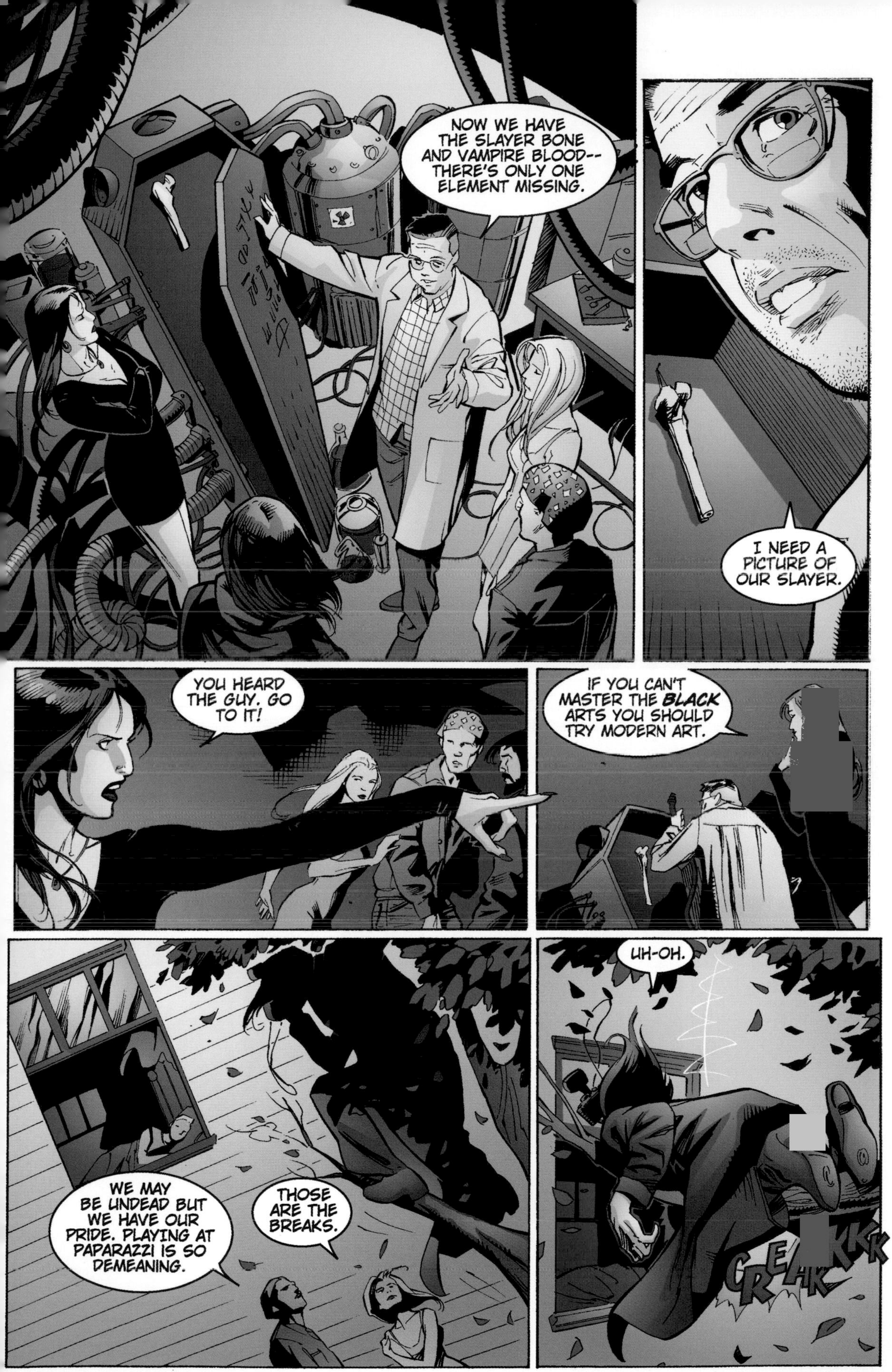
NOW WE HAVE THE SLAYER BONE AND VAMPIRE BLOOD-- THERE'S ONLY ONE ELEMENT MISSING.
I NEED A PICTURE OF OUR SLAYER.
YOU HEARD THE GUY. GO TO IT!
IF YOU CAN'T MASTER THE *BLACK* ARTS YOU SHOULD TRY MODERN ART.
WE MAY BE UNDEAD BUT WE HAVE OUR PRIDE. PLAYING AT PAPARAZZI IS SO DEMEANING.
THOSE ARE THE BREAKS.
UH-OH.

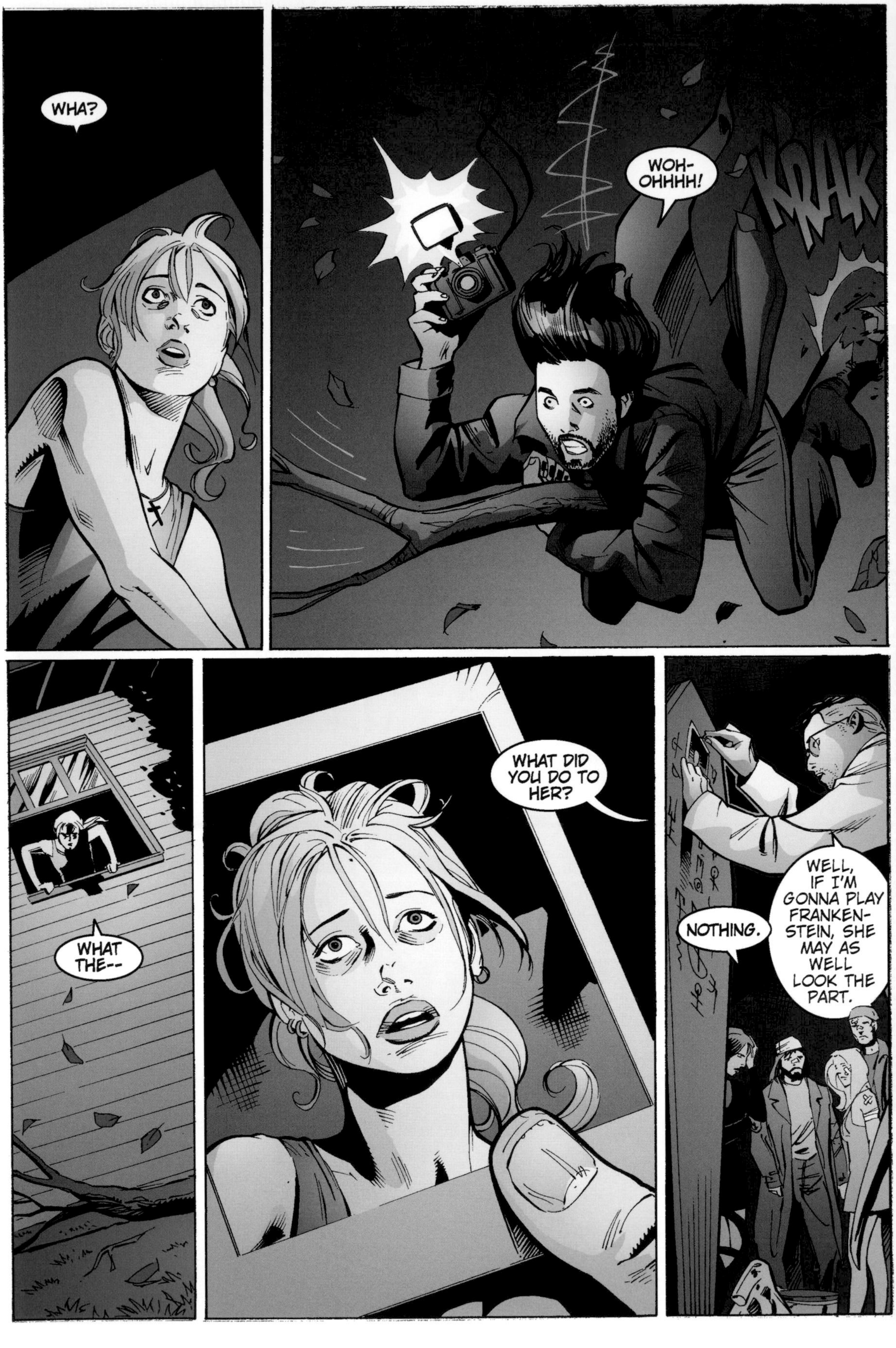
WHA?
WOH-OHHHH!
KRAK
WHAT THE--
WHAT DID YOU DO TO HER?
NOTHING.
WELL, IF I'M GONNA PLAY FRANKEN-STEIN, SHE MAY AS WELL LOOK THE PART.

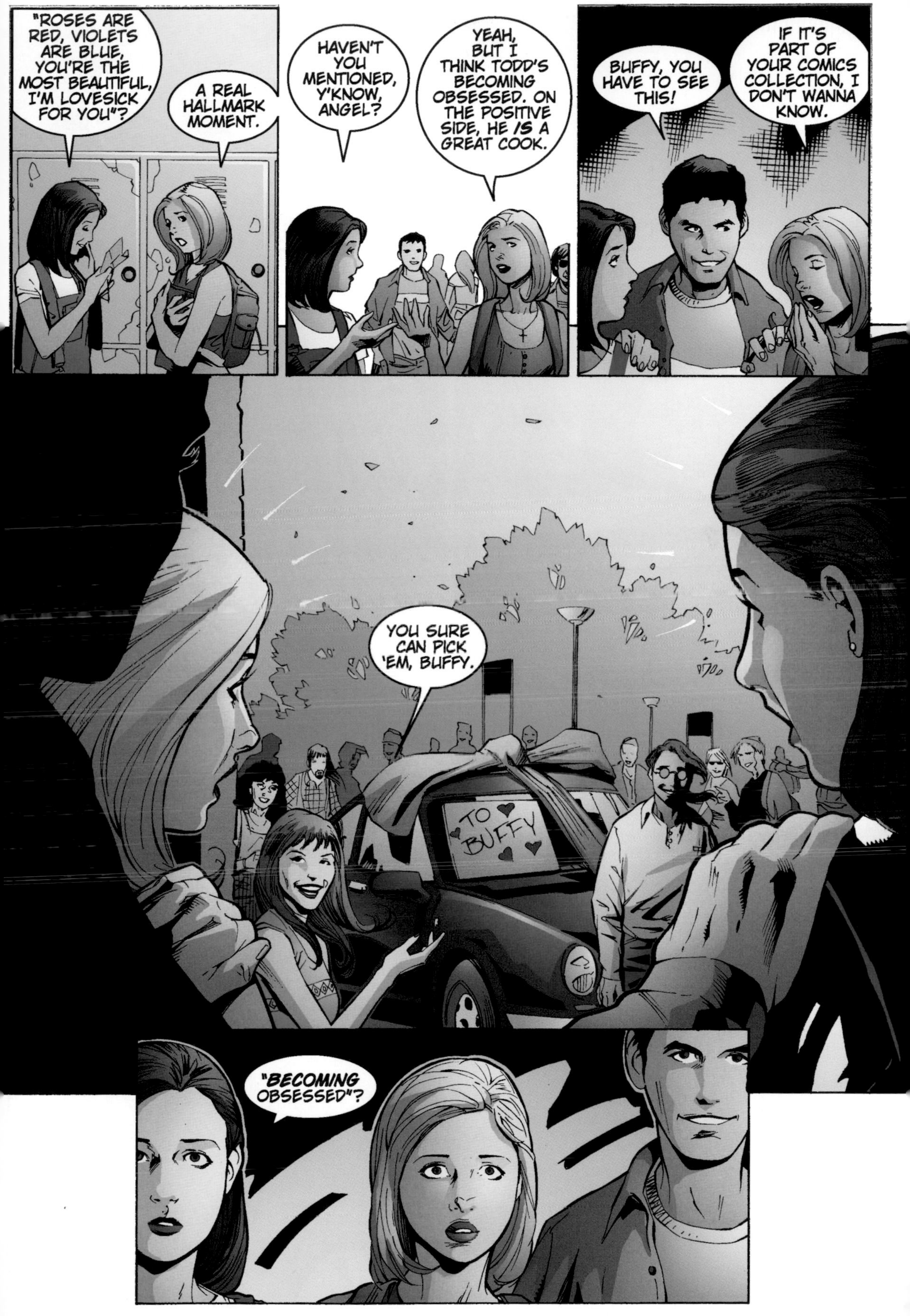
"ROSES ARE RED, VIOLETS ARE BLUE, YOU'RE THE MOST BEAUTIFUL, I'M LOVESICK FOR YOU"?
A REAL HALLMARK MOMENT.
HAVEN'T YOU MENTIONED, Y'KNOW, ANGEL?
YEAH, BUT I THINK TODD'S BECOMING OBSESSED. ON THE POSITIVE SIDE, HE IS A GREAT COOK.
BUFFY, YOU HAVE TO SEE THIS!
IF IT'S PART OF YOUR COMICS COLLECTION, I DON'T WANNA KNOW.
YOU SURE CAN PICK 'EM, BUFFY.
TO BUFFY
"BECOMING OBSESSED"?

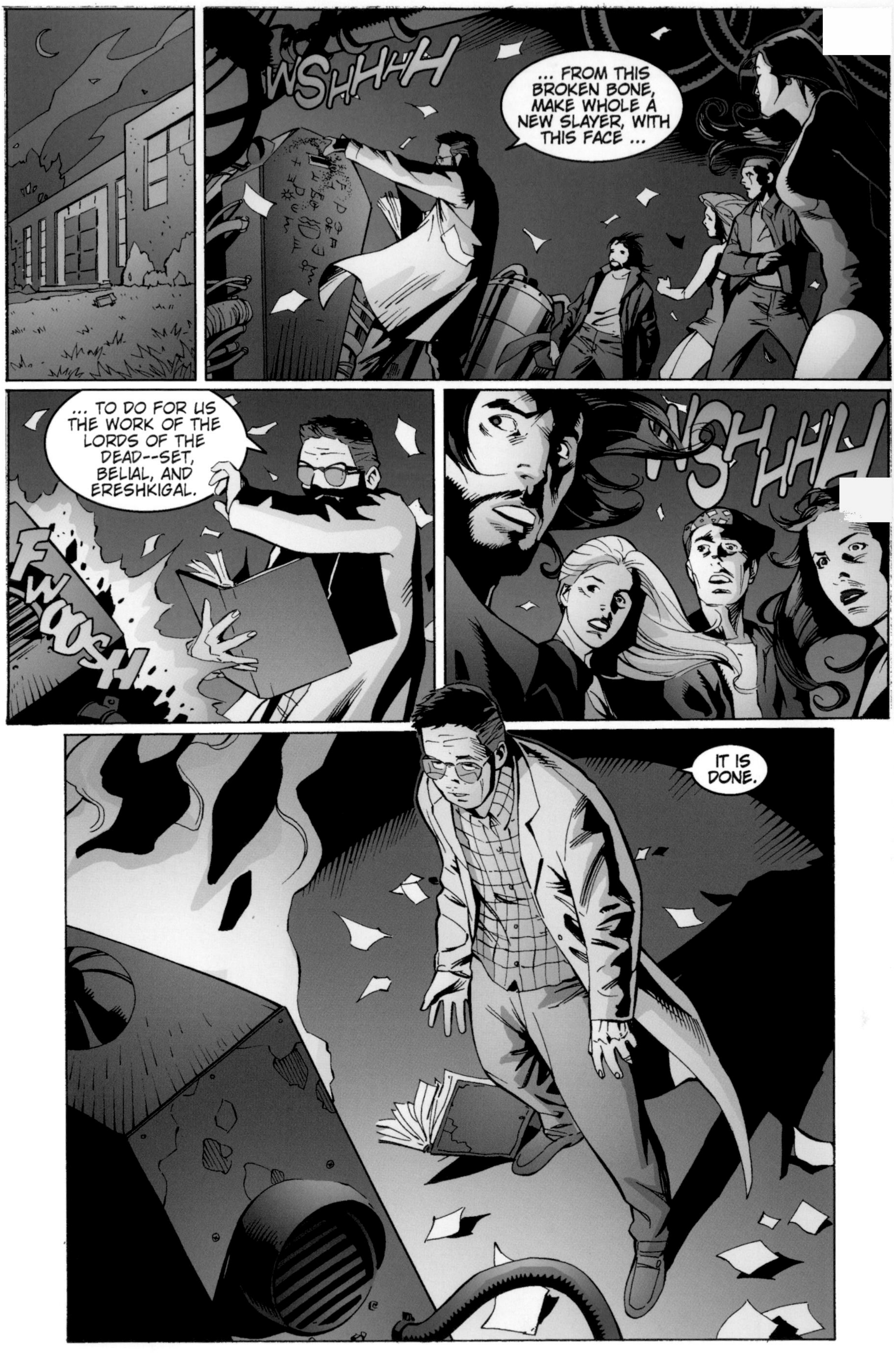
WSHHHH
... FROM THIS BROKEN BONE, MAKE WHOLE A NEW SLAYER, WITH THIS FACE ...
... TO DO FOR US THE WORK OF THE LORDS OF THE DEAD--SET, BELIAL, AND ERESHKIGAL.
FWOOSH
WSHHHH
IT IS DONE.

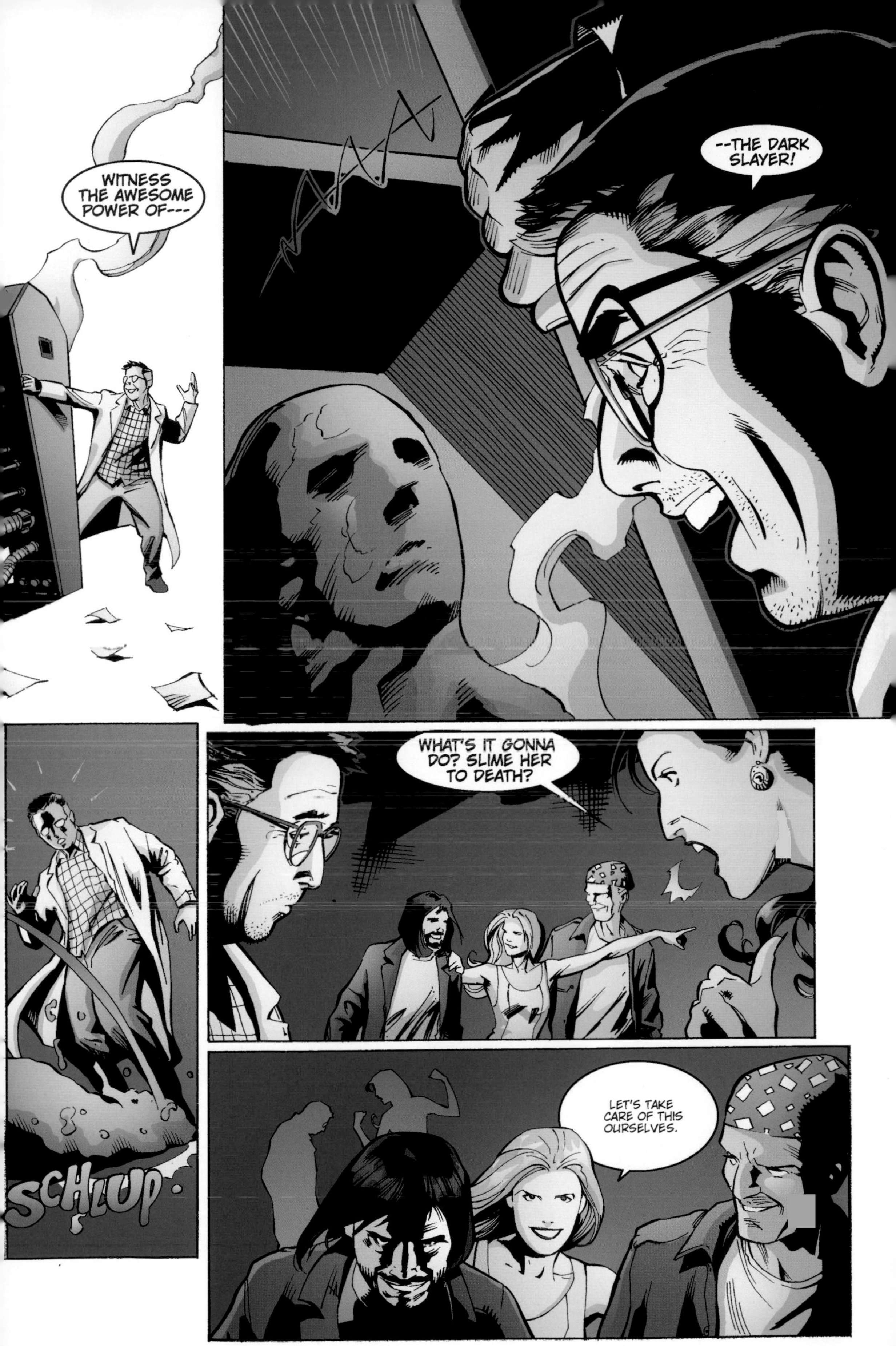
WITNESS THE AWESOME POWER OF---
--THE DARK SLAYER!
SCHLUP
WHAT'S IT GONNA DO? SLIME HER TO DEATH?
LET'S TAKE CARE OF THIS OURSELVES.

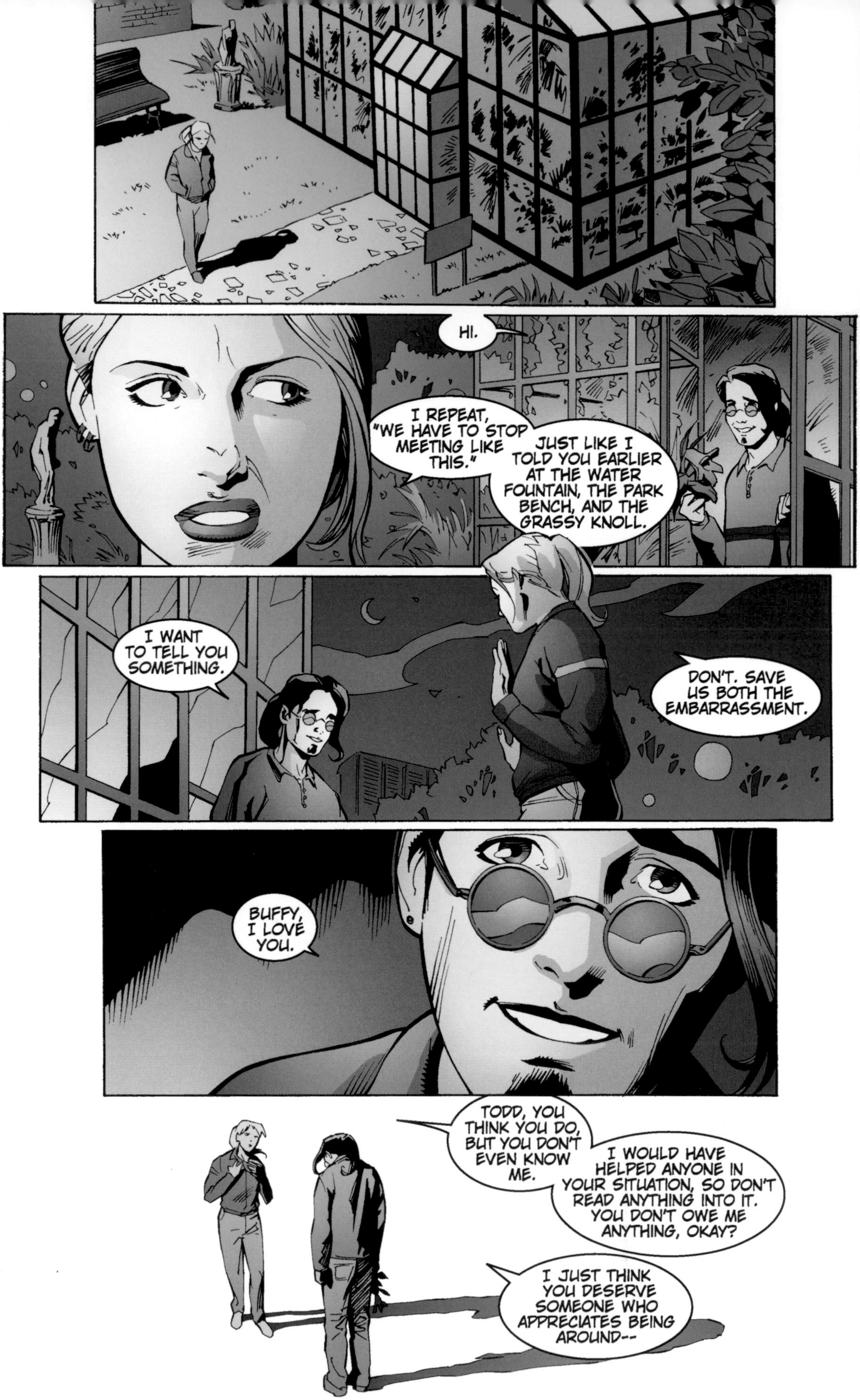
HI.
I REPEAT, "WE HAVE TO STOP MEETING LIKE THIS."
JUST LIKE I TOLD YOU EARLIER AT THE WATER FOUNTAIN, THE PARK BENCH, AND THE GRASSY KNOLL.
I WANT TO TELL YOU SOMETHING.
DON'T. SAVE US BOTH THE EMBARRASSMENT.
BUFFY, I LOVE YOU.
TODD, YOU THINK YOU DO, BUT YOU DON'T EVEN KNOW ME.
I WOULD HAVE HELPED ANYONE IN YOUR SITUATION, SO DON'T READ ANYTHING INTO IT. YOU DON'T OWE ME ANYTHING, OKAY?
I JUST THINK YOU DESERVE SOMEONE WHO APPRECIATES BEING AROUND--

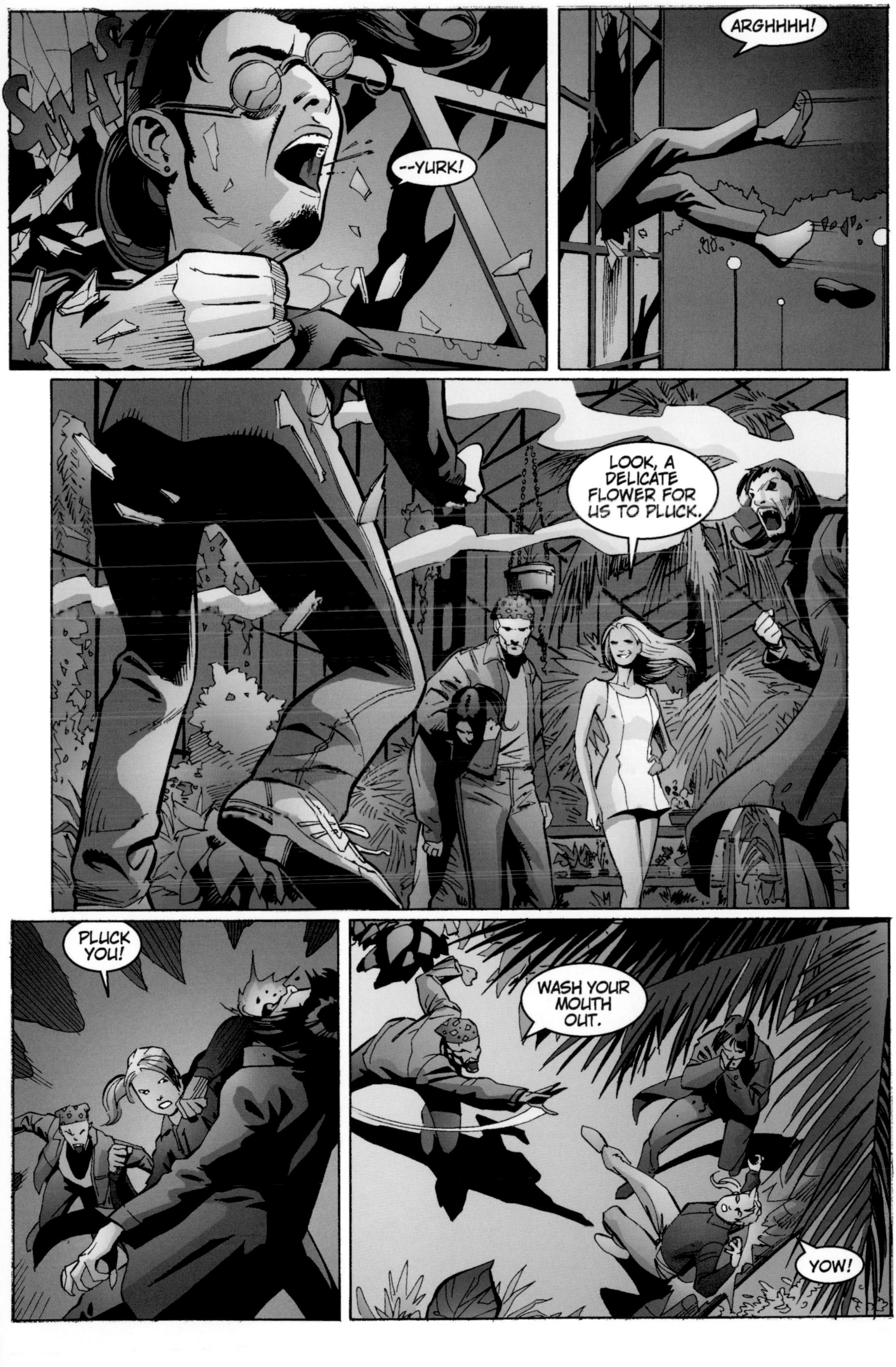
SMASH
--YURK!
ARGHHHH!
LOOK, A DELICATE FLOWER FOR US TO PLUCK.
PLUCK YOU!
WASH YOUR MOUTH OUT.
YOW!

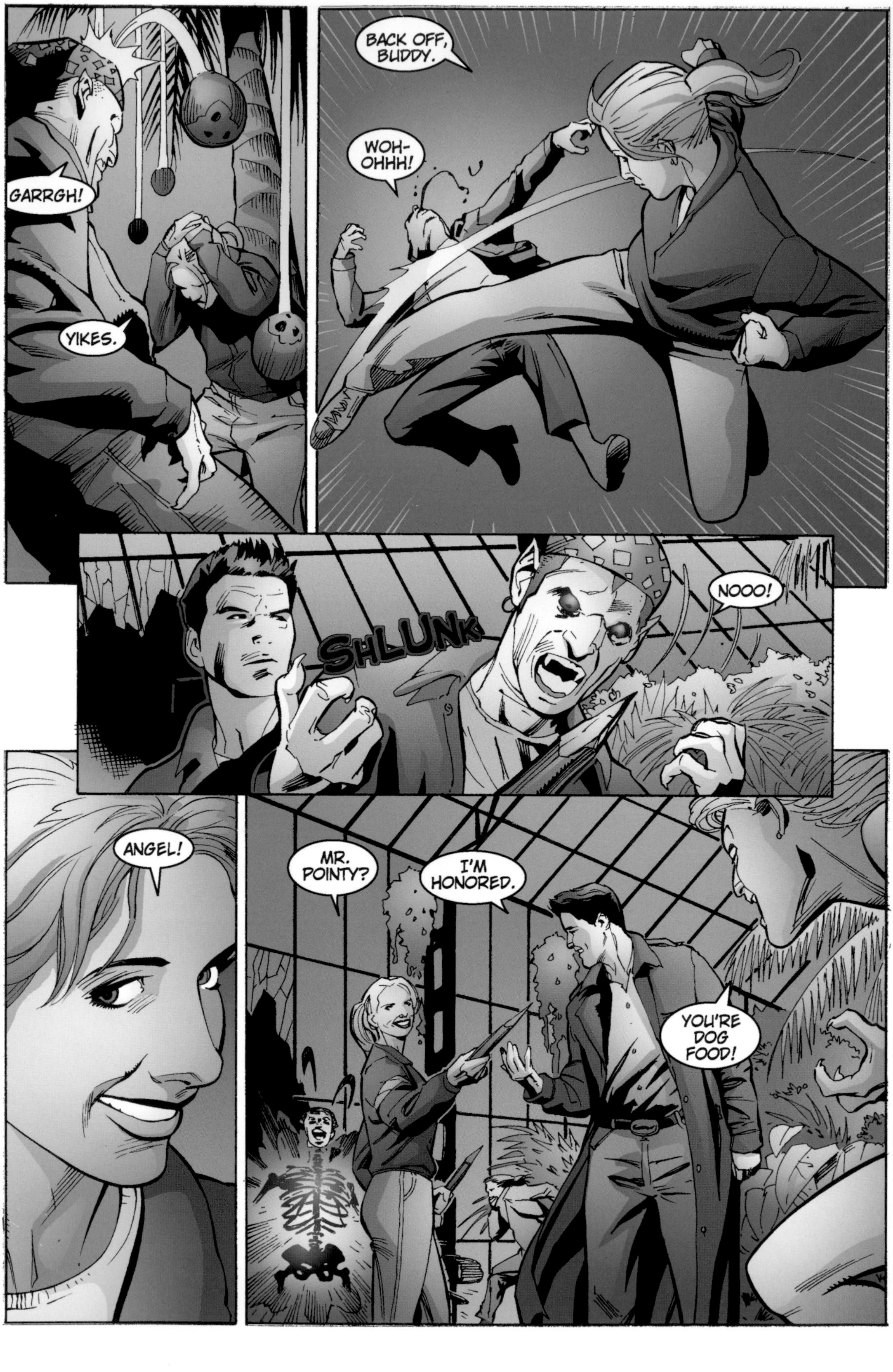
GARRGH!
YIKES.
BACK OFF, BUDDY.
WOH-OHHH!
SHLUNK
NOOO!
ANGEL!
MR. POINTY?
I'M HONORED.
YOU'RE DOG FOOD!

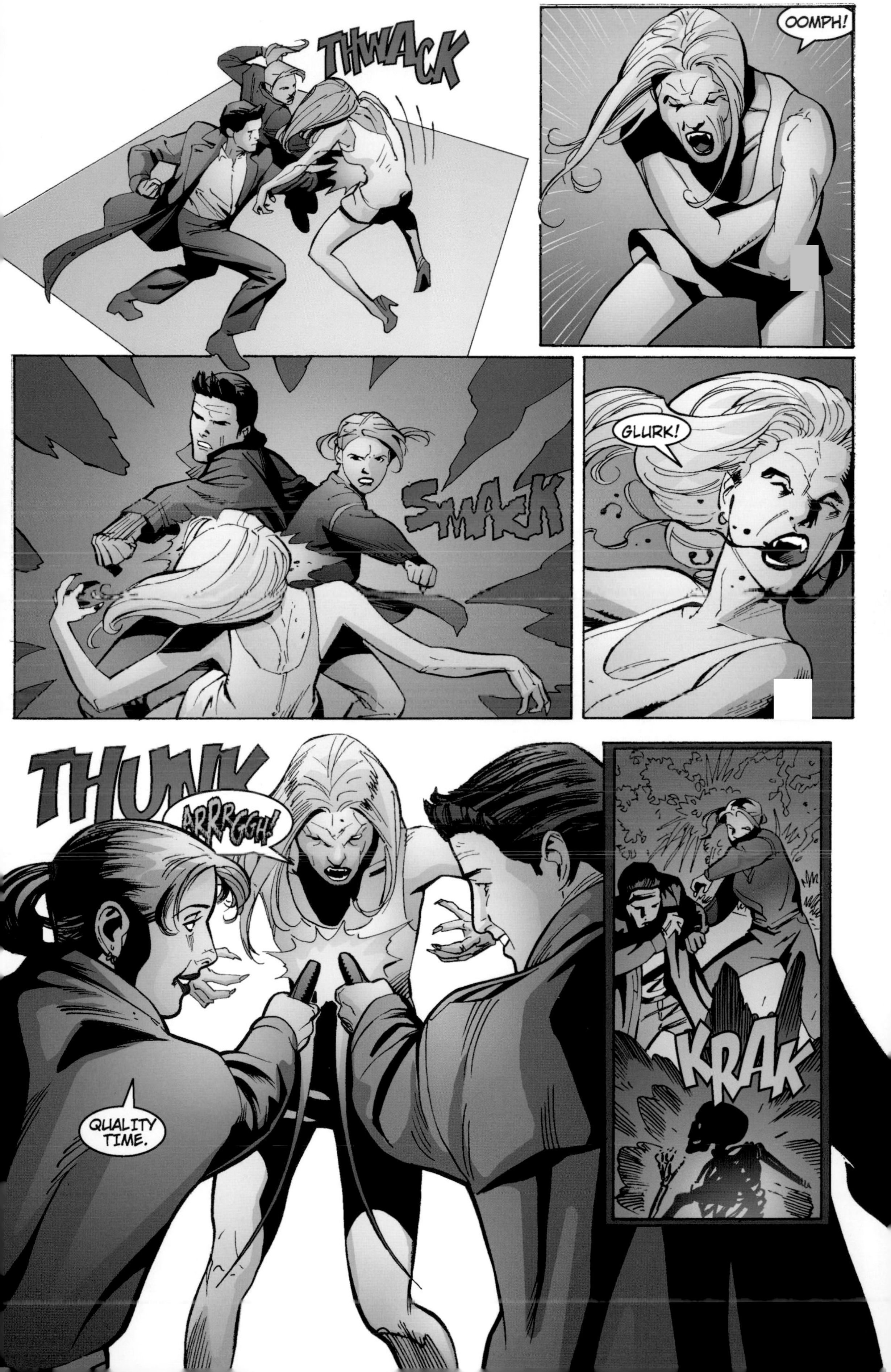
THWACK
OOMPH!
SWACK
GLURK!
THUNK
ARRRGGH!
QUALITY TIME.
KRAK

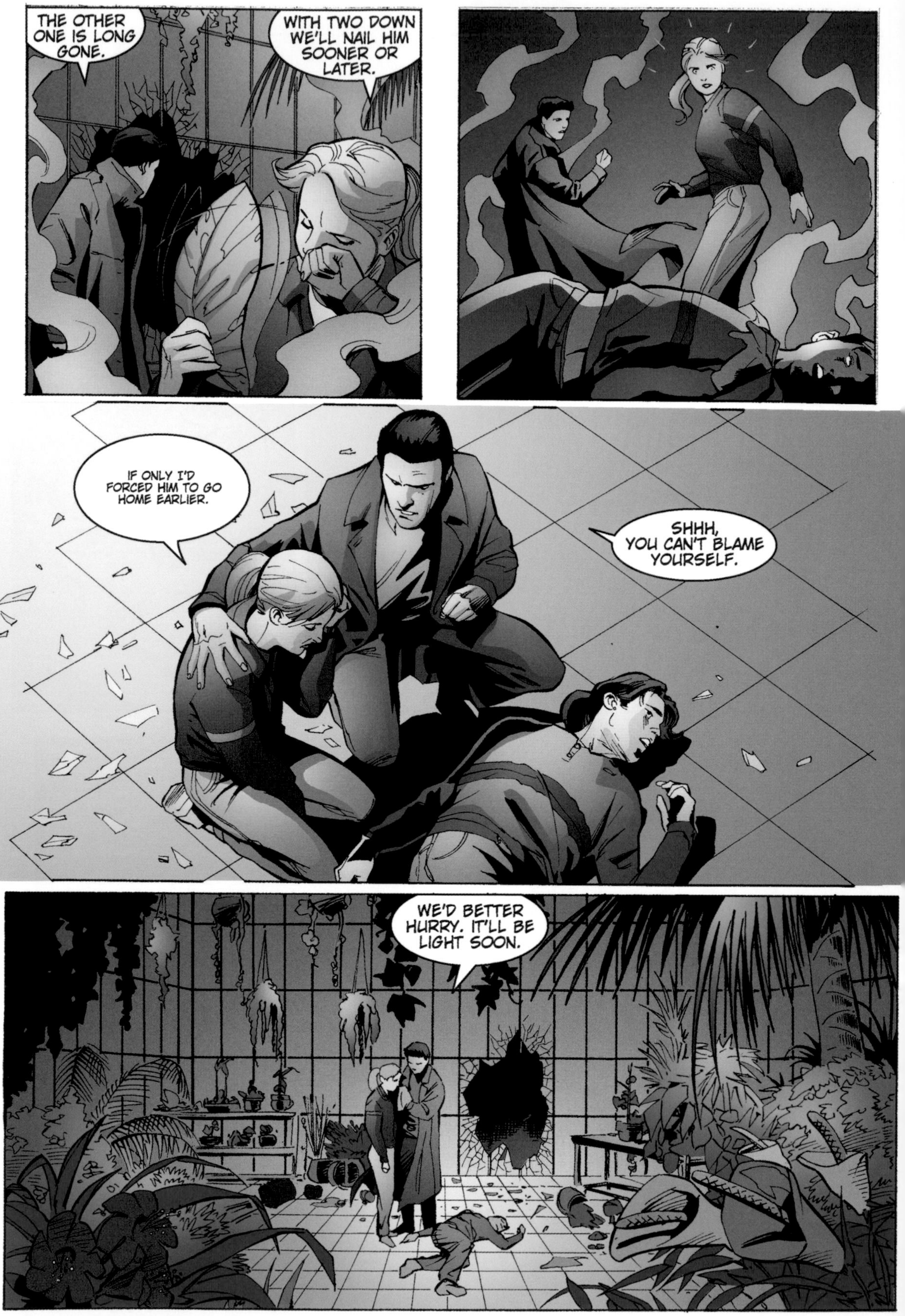
THE OTHER ONE IS LONG GONE.
WITH TWO DOWN WE'LL NAIL HIM SOONER OR LATER.
IF ONLY I'D FORCED HIM TO GO HOME EARLIER.
SHHH, YOU CAN'T BLAME YOURSELF.
WE'D BETTER HURRY. IT'LL BE LIGHT SOON.

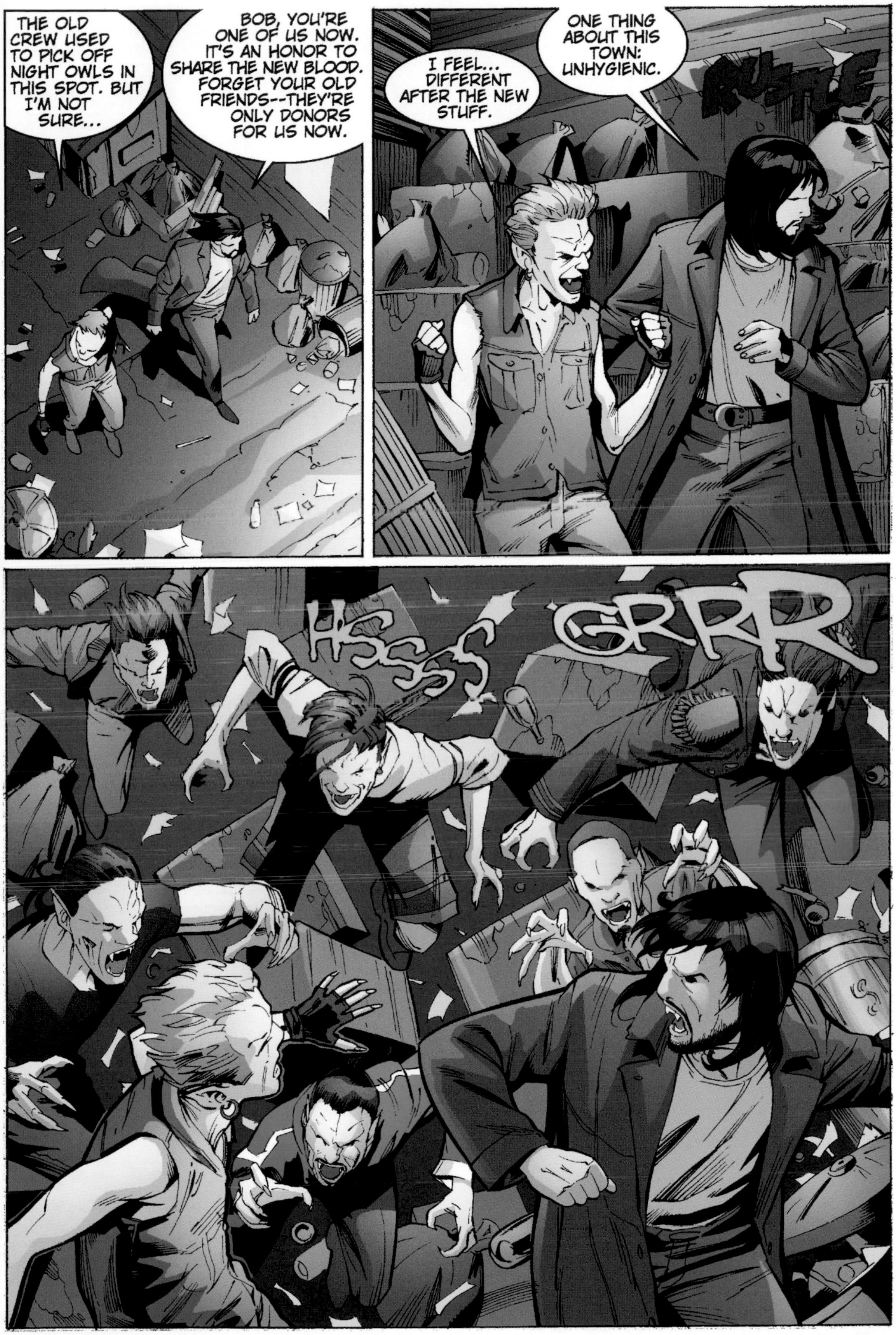
THE OLD CREW USED TO PICK OFF NIGHT OWLS IN THIS SPOT. BUT I'M NOT SURE...
BOB, YOU'RE ONE OF US NOW. IT'S AN HONOR TO SHARE THE NEW BLOOD. FORGET YOUR OLD FRIENDS--THEY'RE ONLY DONORS FOR US NOW.
I FEEL... DIFFERENT AFTER THE NEW STUFF.
ONE THING ABOUT THIS TOWN: UNHYGIENIC.
RUSTLE
HSSSS
GRRR

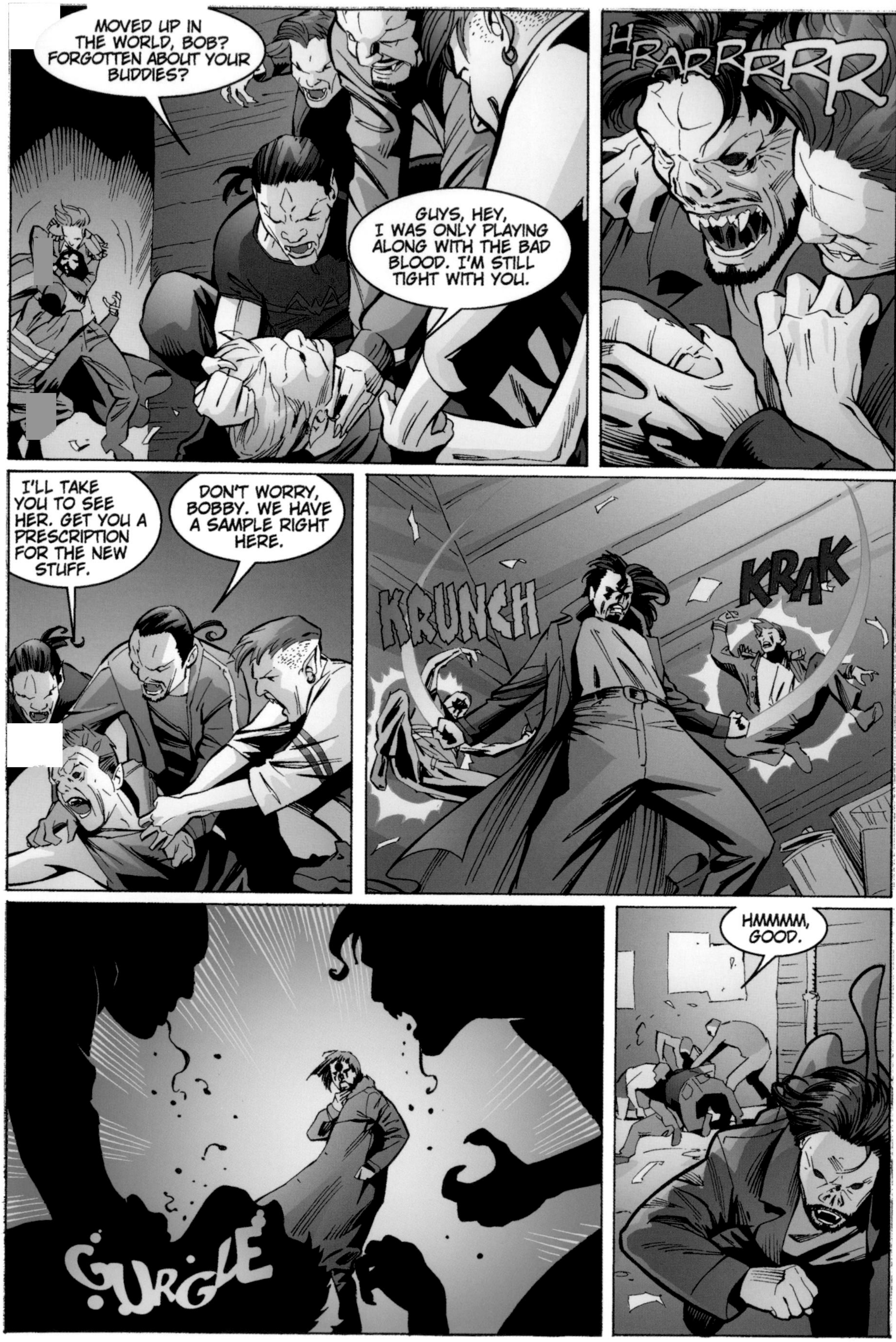
MOVED UP IN THE WORLD, BOB? FORGOTTEN ABOUT YOUR BUDDIES?
GUYS, HEY, I WAS ONLY PLAYING ALONG WITH THE BAD BLOOD. I'M STILL TIGHT WITH YOU.
HRARRRRRR
I'LL TAKE YOU TO SEE HER. GET YOU A PRESCRIPTION FOR THE NEW STUFF.
DON'T WORRY, BOBBY. WE HAVE A SAMPLE RIGHT HERE.
KRUNCH
KRAK
GURGLE
HMMMMM, GOOD.

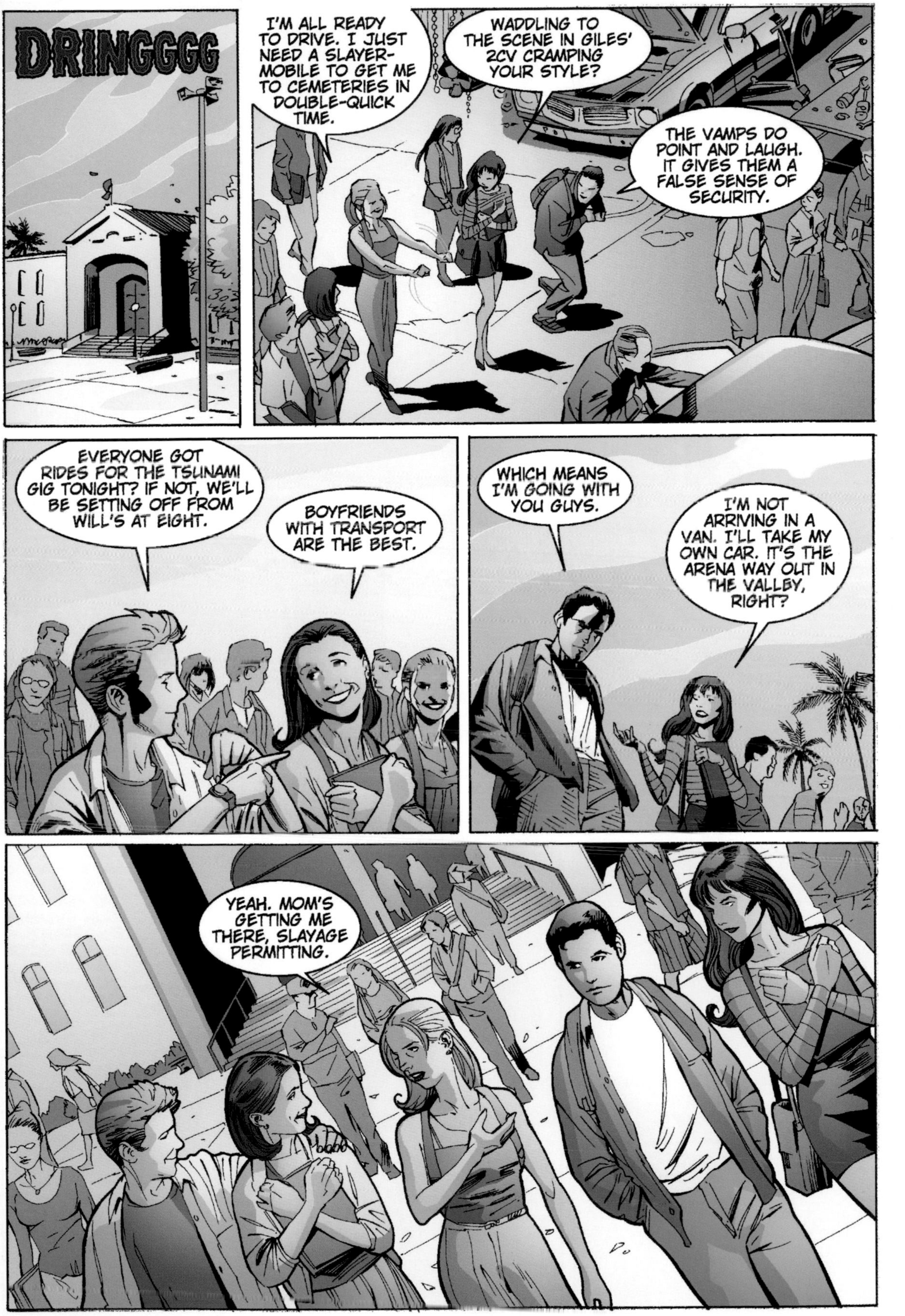
DRINGGGG
I'M ALL READY TO DRIVE. I JUST NEED A SLAYER-MOBILE TO GET ME TO CEMETERIES IN DOUBLE-QUICK TIME.
WADDLING TO THE SCENE IN GILES' 2CV CRAMPING YOUR STYLE?
THE VAMPS DO POINT AND LAUGH. IT GIVES THEM A FALSE SENSE OF SECURITY.
EVERYONE GOT RIDES FOR THE TSUNAMI GIG TONIGHT? IF NOT, WE'LL BE SETTING OFF FROM WILL'S AT EIGHT.
BOYFRIENDS WITH TRANSPORT ARE THE BEST.
WHICH MEANS I'M GOING WITH YOU GUYS.
I'M NOT ARRIVING IN A VAN. I'LL TAKE MY OWN CAR. IT'S THE ARENA WAY OUT IN THE VALLEY, RIGHT?
YEAH. MOM'S GETTING ME THERE, SLAYAGE PERMITTING.

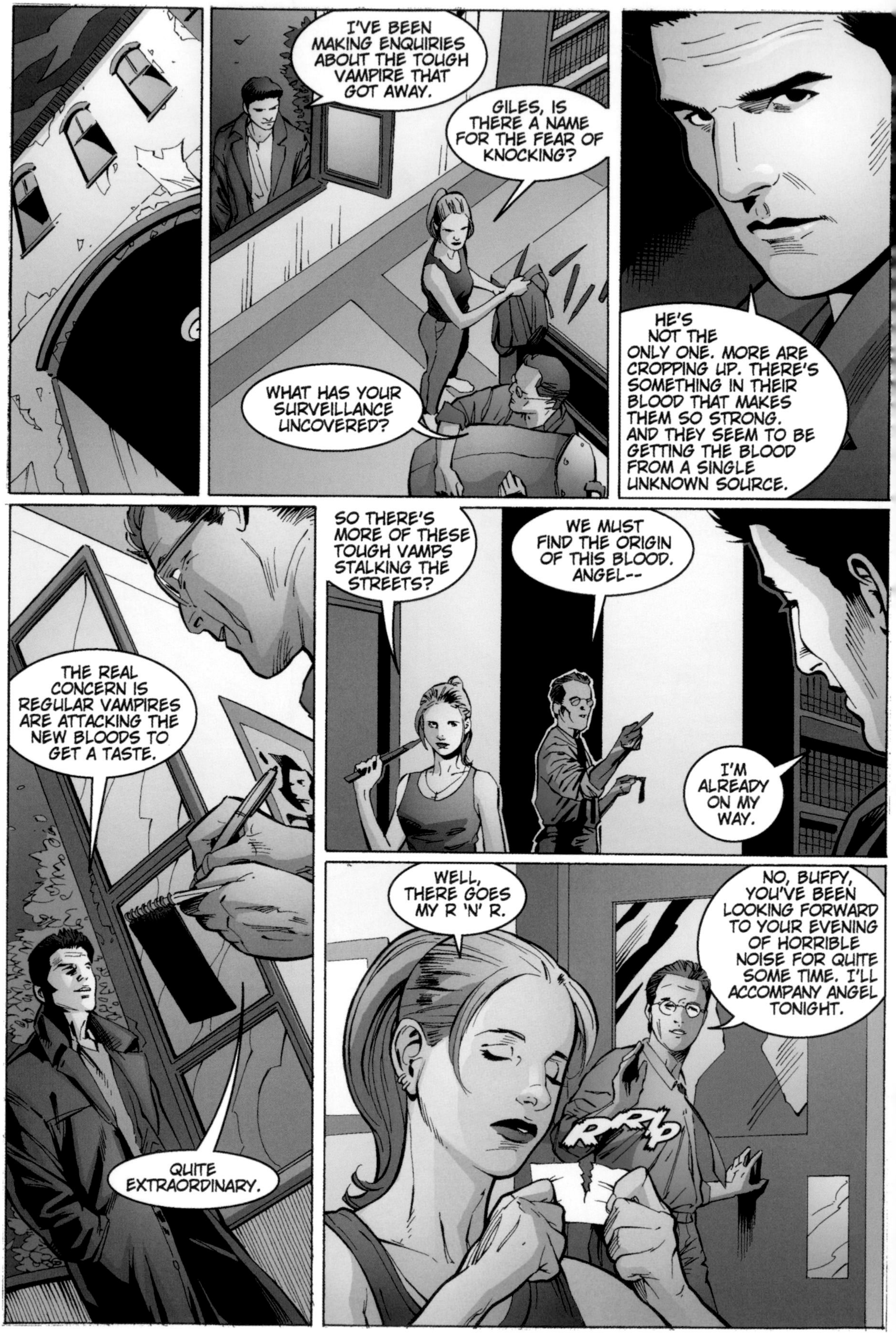
I'VE BEEN MAKING ENQUIRIES ABOUT THE TOUGH VAMPIRE THAT GOT AWAY.
GILES, IS THERE A NAME FOR THE FEAR OF KNOCKING?
WHAT HAS YOUR SURVEILLANCE UNCOVERED?
HE'S NOT THE ONLY ONE. MORE ARE CROPPING UP. THERE'S SOMETHING IN THEIR BLOOD THAT MAKES THEM SO STRONG. AND THEY SEEM TO BE GETTING THE BLOOD FROM A SINGLE UNKNOWN SOURCE.
THE REAL CONCERN IS REGULAR VAMPIRES ARE ATTACKING THE NEW BLOODS TO GET A TASTE.
QUITE EXTRAORDINARY.
SO THERE'S MORE OF THESE TOUGH VAMPS STALKING THE STREETS?
WE MUST FIND THE ORIGIN OF THIS BLOOD. ANGEL--
I'M ALREADY ON MY WAY.
WELL, THERE GOES MY R 'N' R.
NO, BUFFY, YOU'VE BEEN LOOKING FORWARD TO YOUR EVENING OF HORRIBLE NOISE FOR QUITE SOME TIME. I'LL ACCOMPANY ANGEL TONIGHT.
RRRIP

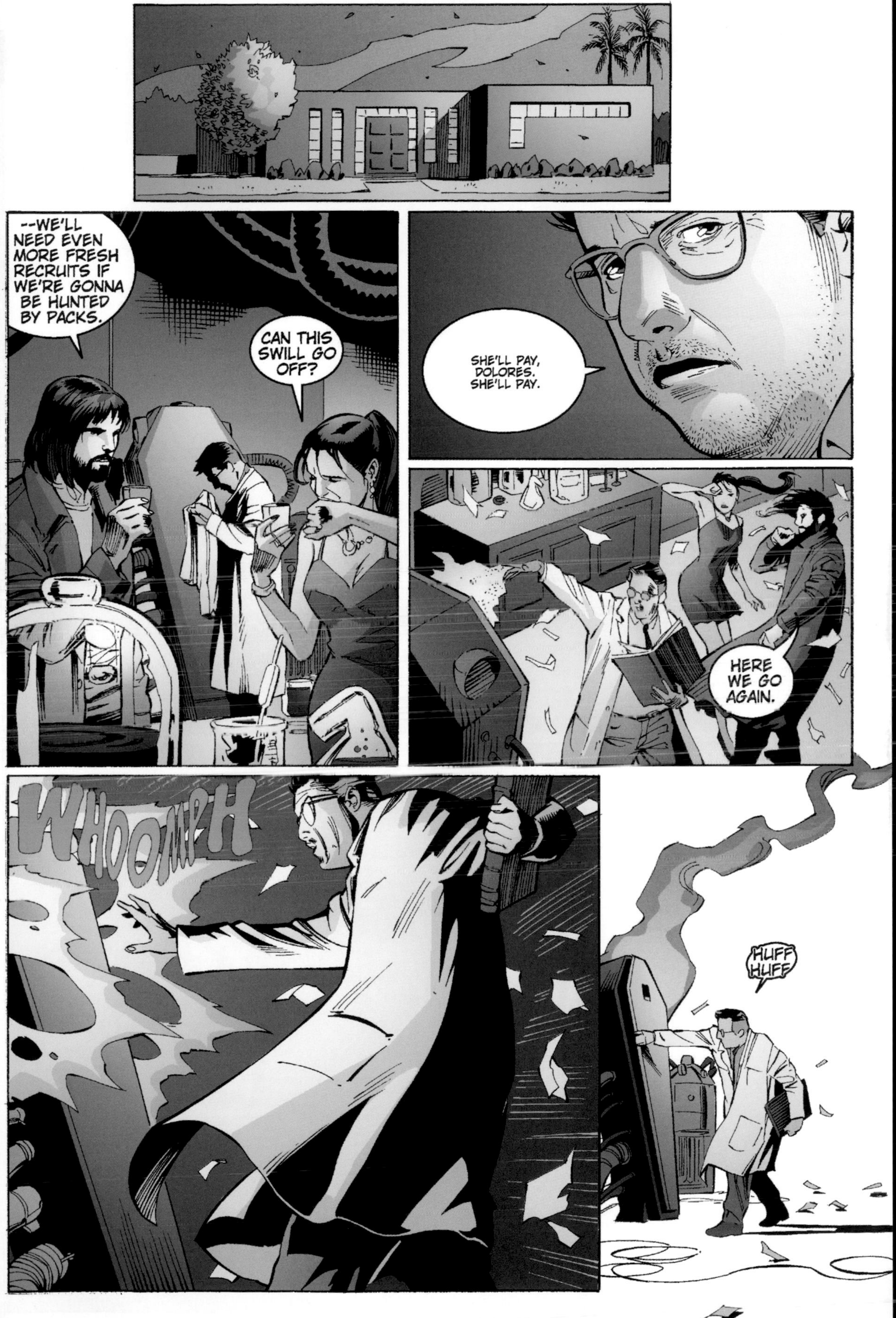
--WE'LL NEED EVEN MORE FRESH RECRUITS IF WE'RE GONNA BE HUNTED BY PACKS.
CAN THIS SWILL GO OFF?
SHE'LL PAY, DOLORES. SHE'LL PAY.
HERE WE GO AGAIN.
WHOOMPH
HUFF HUFF

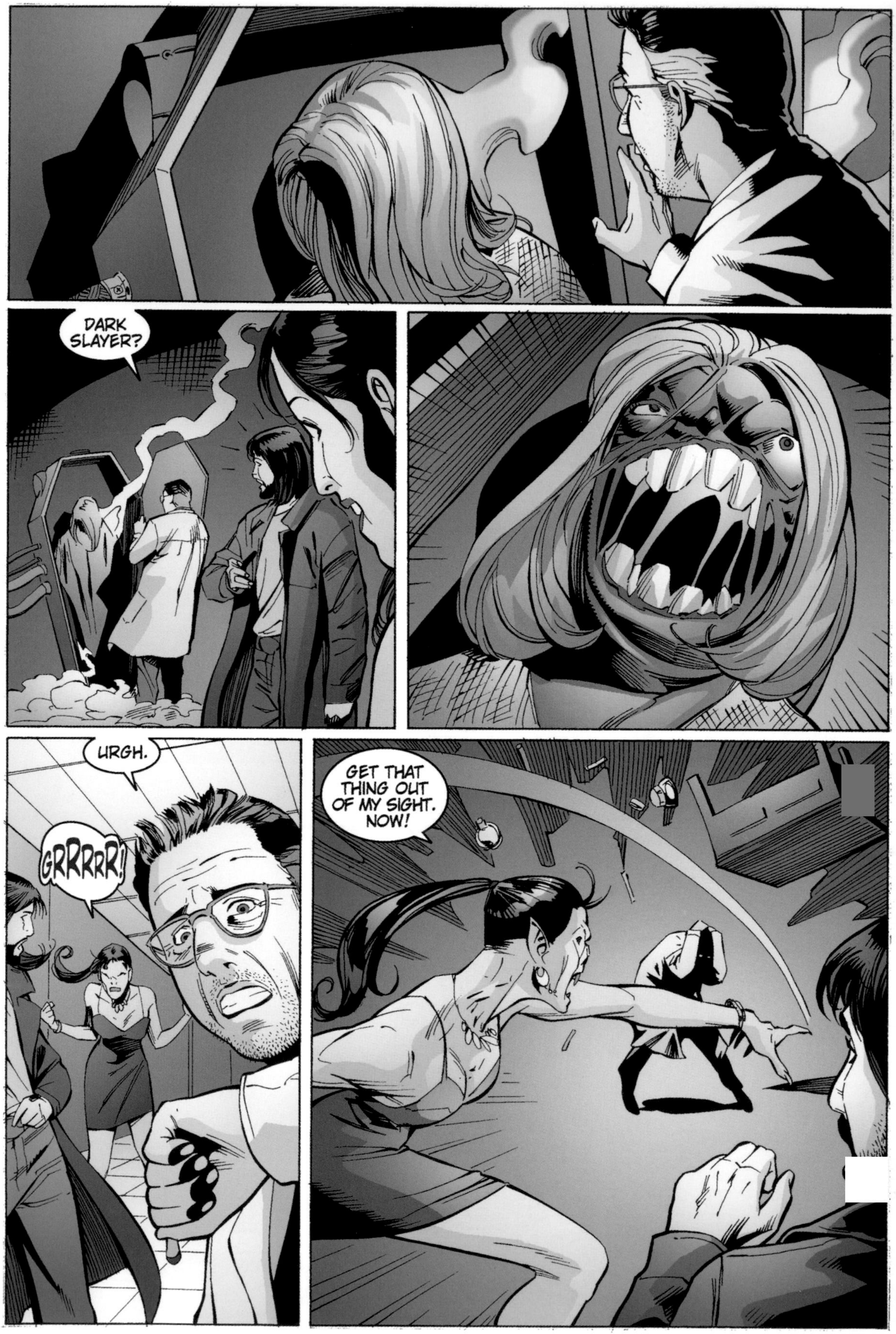
DARK SLAYER?
URGH.
GRRRRR!
GET THAT THING OUT OF MY SIGHT. NOW!

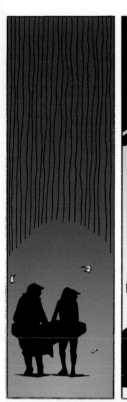

YOU TAKE CARE OF IT. I HAVE OTHER BUSINESS.

WHAT SHOULD I DO?

DUMP IT.

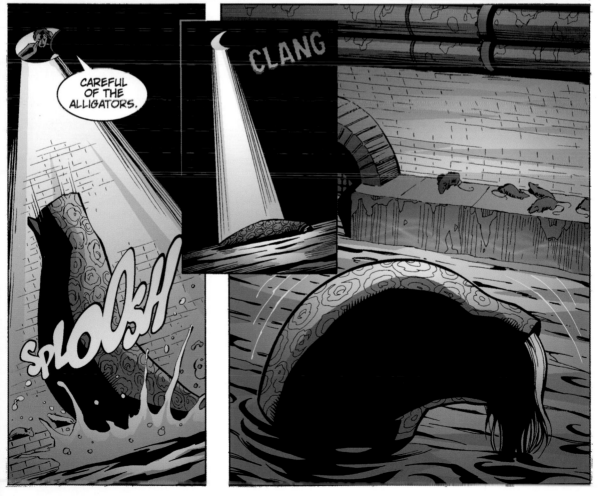

CAREFUL OF THE ALLIGATORS.

CLANG

SPLOOSH

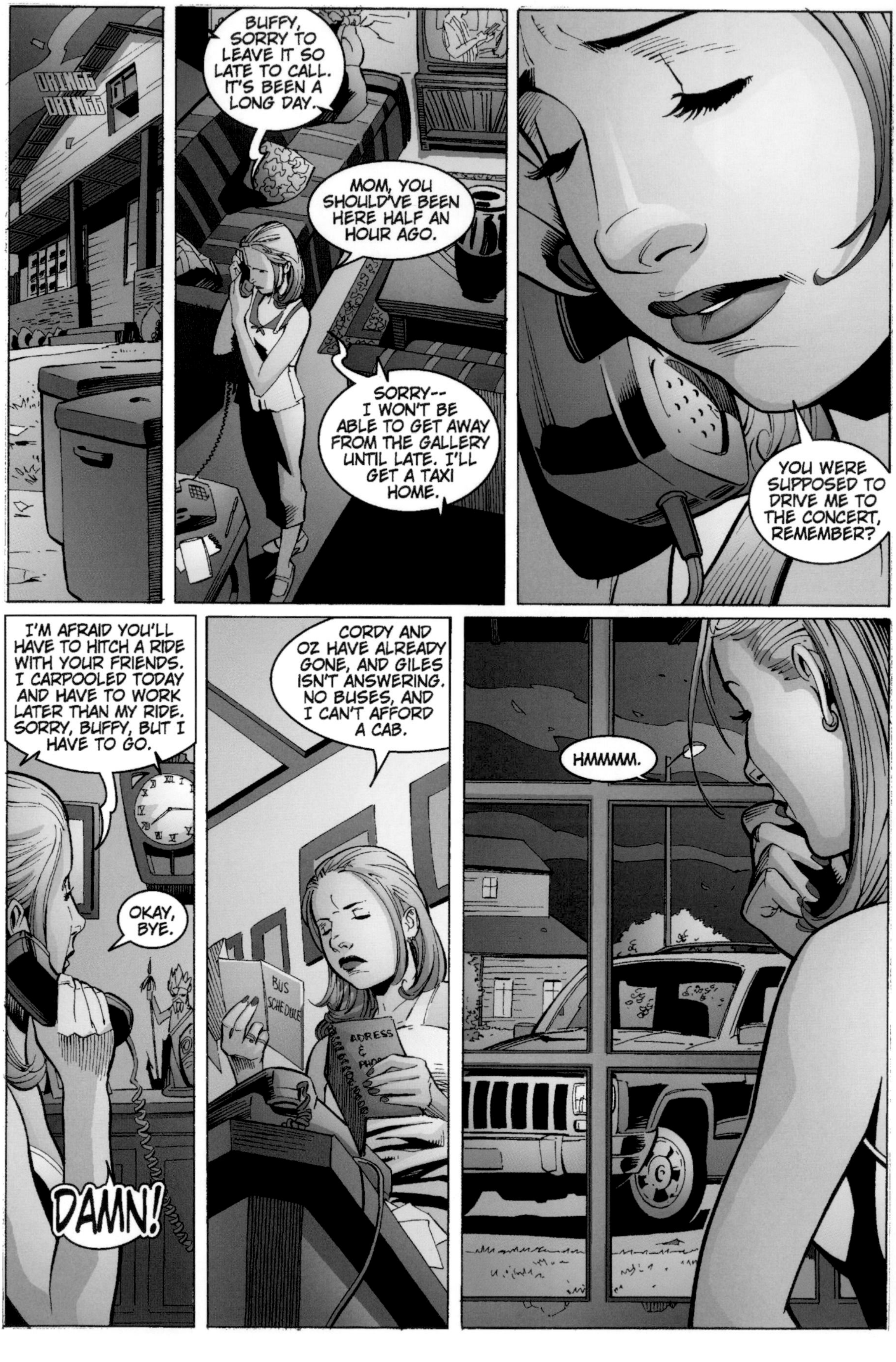
DRINGG DRINGG
BUFFY, SORRY TO LEAVE IT SO LATE TO CALL. IT'S BEEN A LONG DAY.
MOM, YOU SHOULD'VE BEEN HERE HALF AN HOUR AGO.
SORRY-- I WON'T BE ABLE TO GET AWAY FROM THE GALLERY UNTIL LATE. I'LL GET A TAXI HOME.
YOU WERE SUPPOSED TO DRIVE ME TO THE CONCERT, REMEMBER?
I'M AFRAID YOU'LL HAVE TO HITCH A RIDE WITH YOUR FRIENDS. I CARPOOLED TODAY AND HAVE TO WORK LATER THAN MY RIDE. SORRY, BUFFY, BUT I HAVE TO GO.
OKAY, BYE.
DAMN!
CORDY AND OZ HAVE ALREADY GONE, AND GILES ISN'T ANSWERING. NO BUSES, AND I CAN'T AFFORD A CAB.
BUS SCHEDULE
ADRESS &
HMMMM.

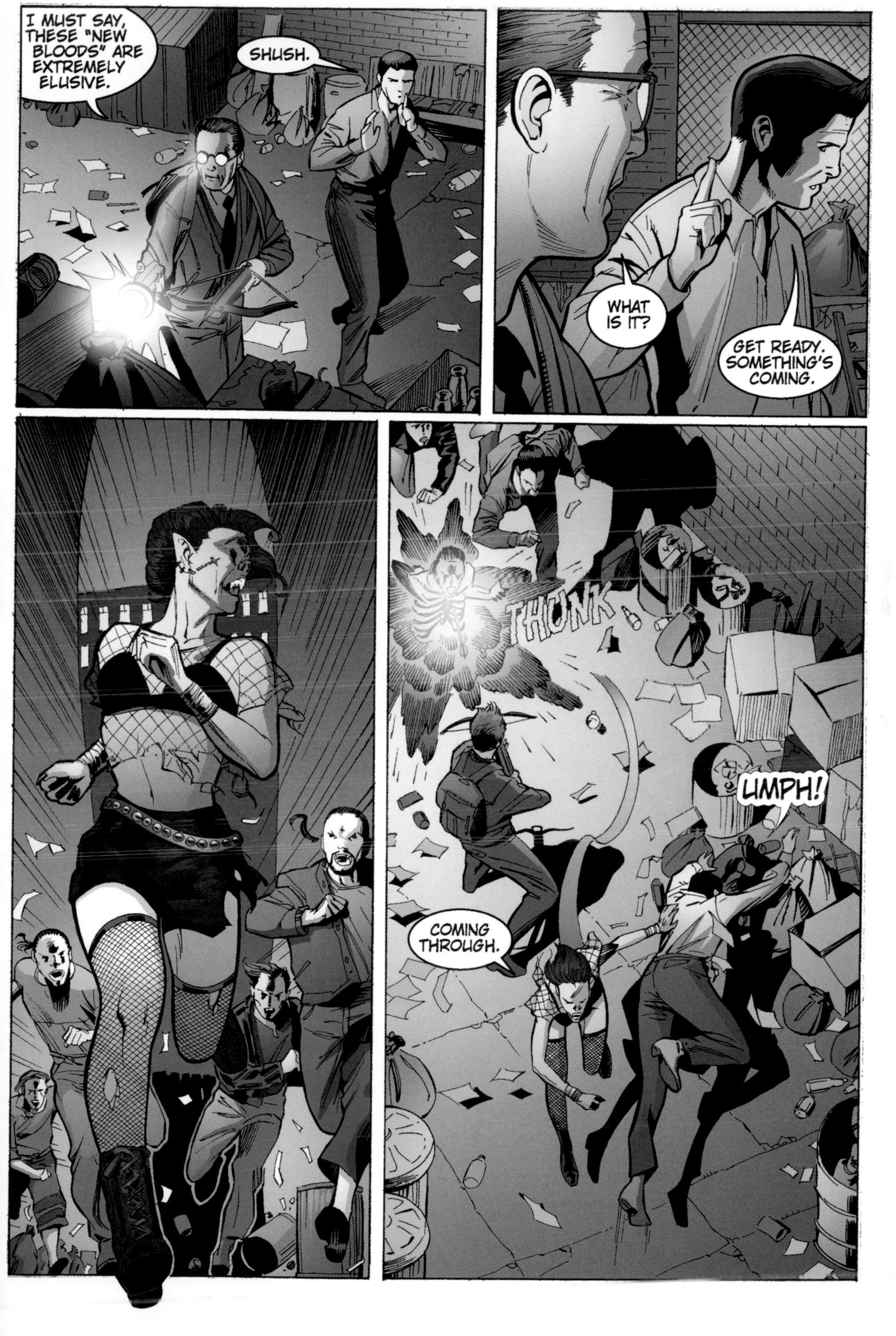
I MUST SAY, THESE "NEW BLOODS" ARE EXTREMELY ELUSIVE.
SHUSH.
WHAT IS IT?
GET READY. SOMETHING'S COMING.
THUNK
UMPH!
COMING THROUGH.

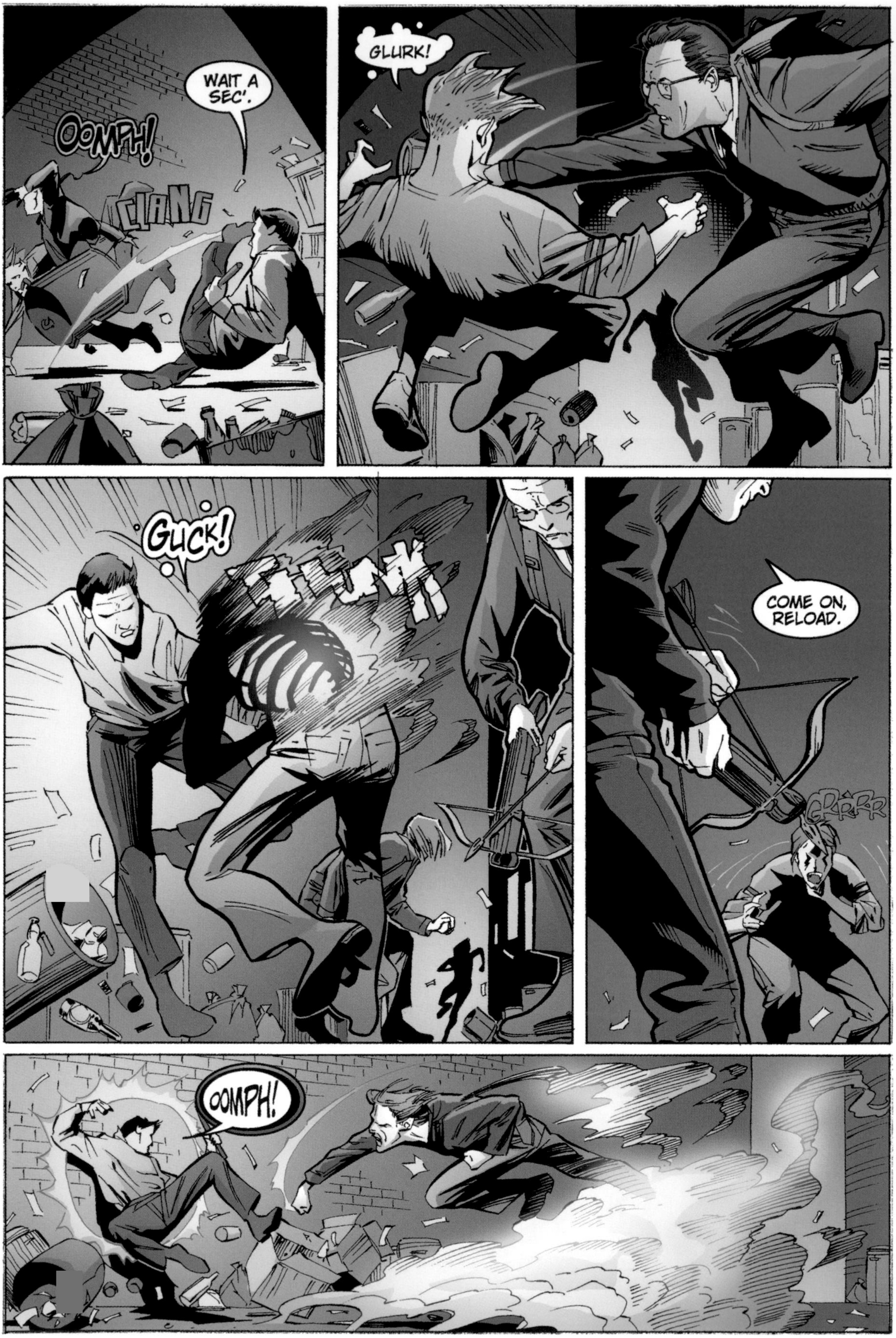
WAIT A SEC'.
OOMPH!
CLANG
GLURK!
GUCK!
COME ON, RELOAD.
GRRRR
OOMPH!

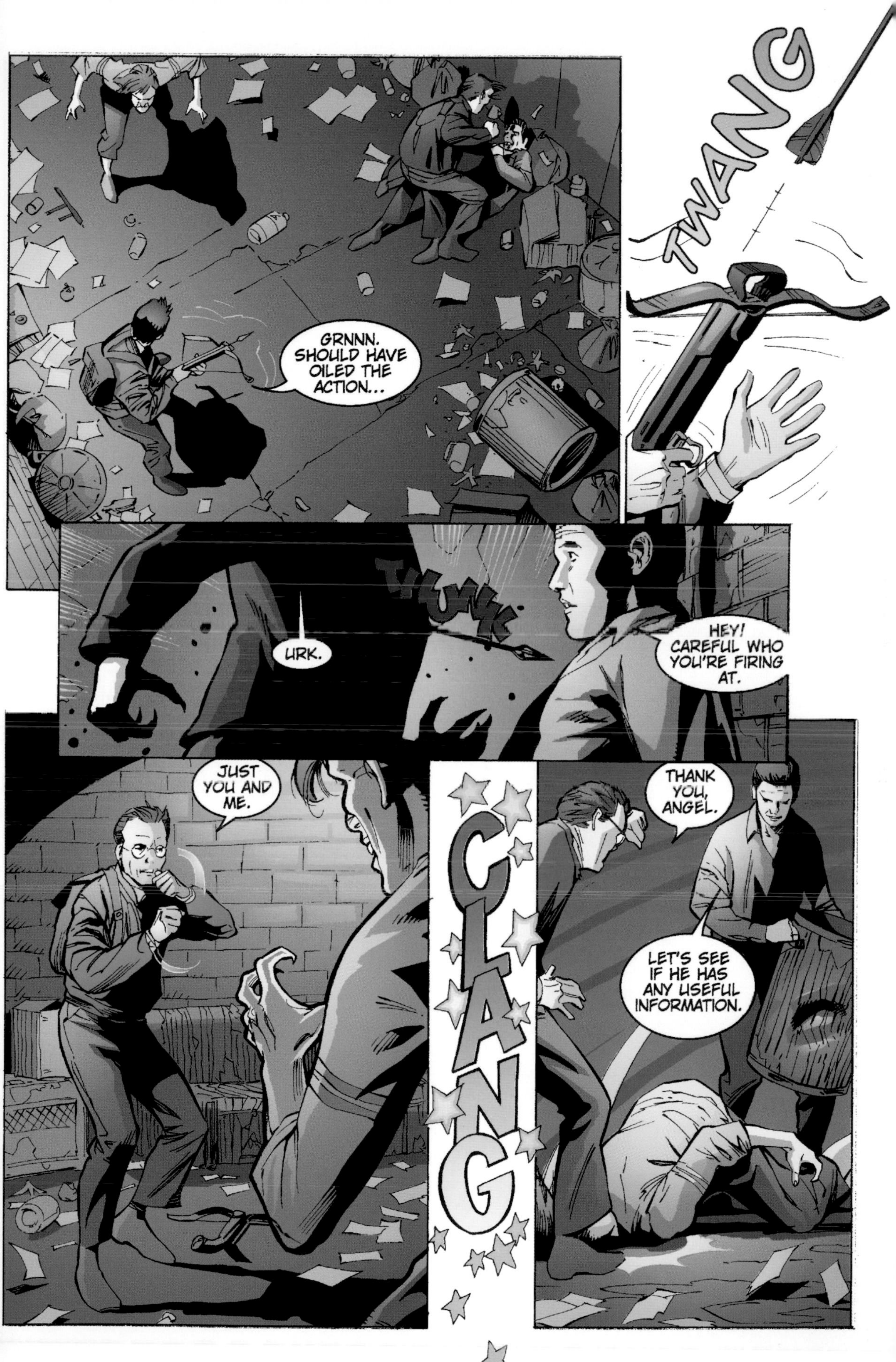
GRNNN. SHOULD HAVE OILED THE ACTION...
TWANG
THUNK
URK.
HEY! CAREFUL WHO YOU'RE FIRING AT.
JUST YOU AND ME.
CLANG
THANK YOU, ANGEL.
LET'S SEE IF HE HAS ANY USEFUL INFORMATION.

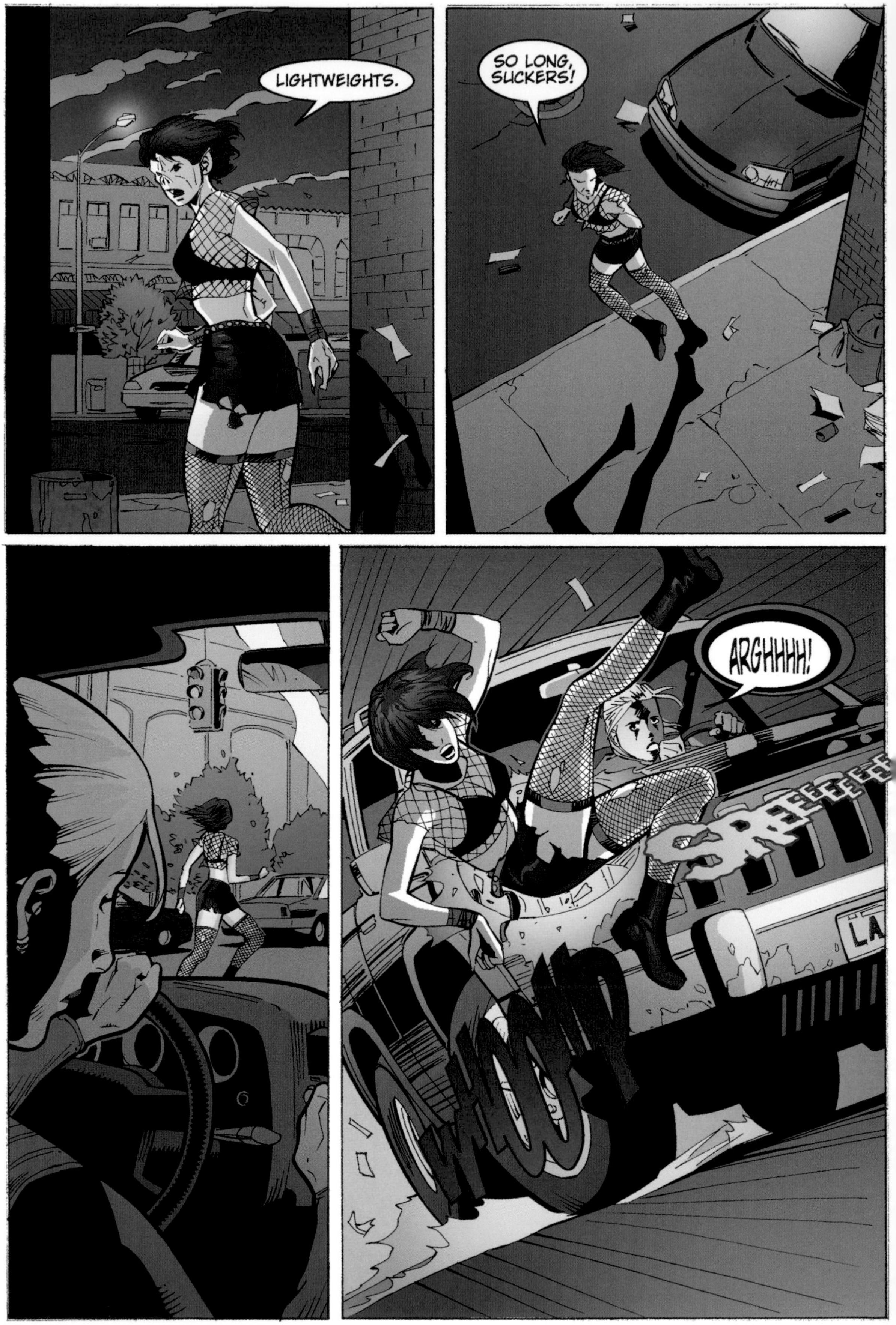
LIGHTWEIGHTS.
SO LONG, SUCKERS!
ARGHHHH!

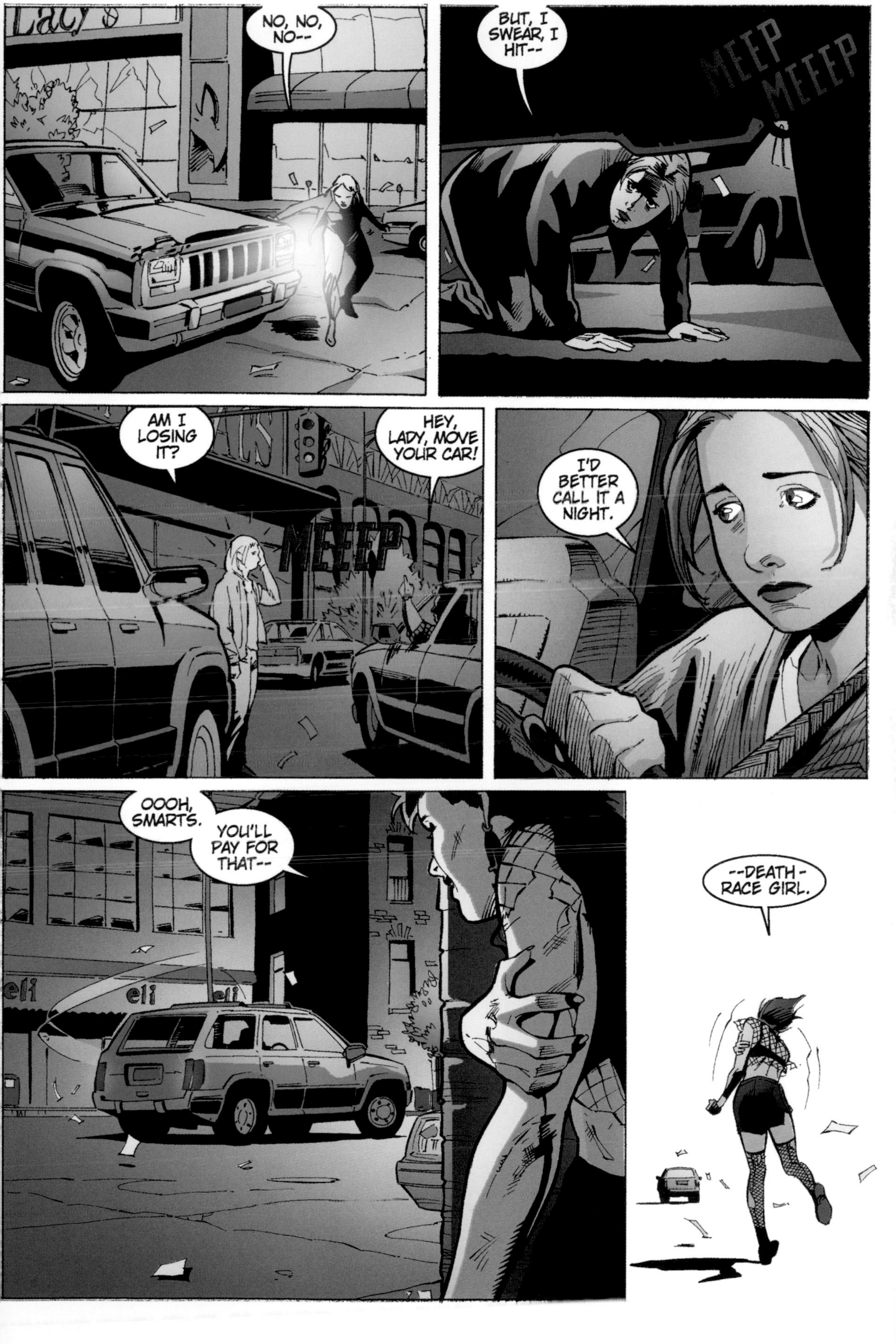
NO, NO, NO--
BUT, I SWEAR, I HIT--
MEEP MEEEP
AM I LOSING IT?
HEY, LADY, MOVE YOUR CAR!
MEEEP
I'D BETTER CALL IT A NIGHT.
OOOH, SMARTS.
YOU'LL PAY FOR THAT--
--DEATH-RACE GIRL.

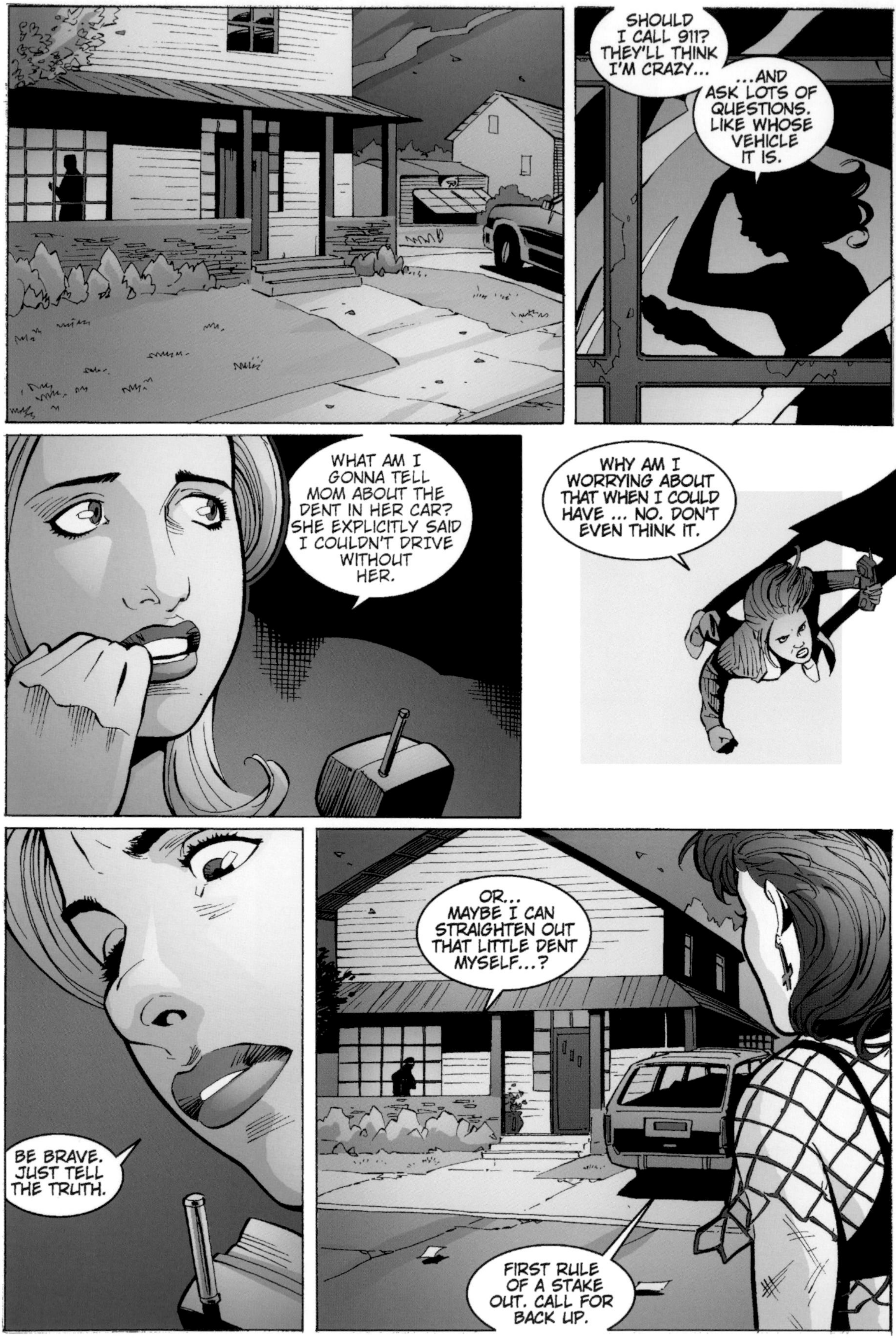
SHOULD I CALL 911? THEY'LL THINK I'M CRAZY...
...AND ASK LOTS OF QUESTIONS. LIKE WHOSE VEHICLE IT IS.
WHAT AM I GONNA TELL MOM ABOUT THE DENT IN HER CAR? SHE EXPLICITLY SAID I COULDN'T DRIVE WITHOUT HER.
WHY AM I WORRYING ABOUT THAT WHEN I COULD HAVE ... NO. DON'T EVEN THINK IT.
BE BRAVE. JUST TELL THE TRUTH.
OR... MAYBE I CAN STRAIGHTEN OUT THAT LITTLE DENT MYSELF...?
FIRST RULE OF A STAKE OUT. CALL FOR BACK UP.

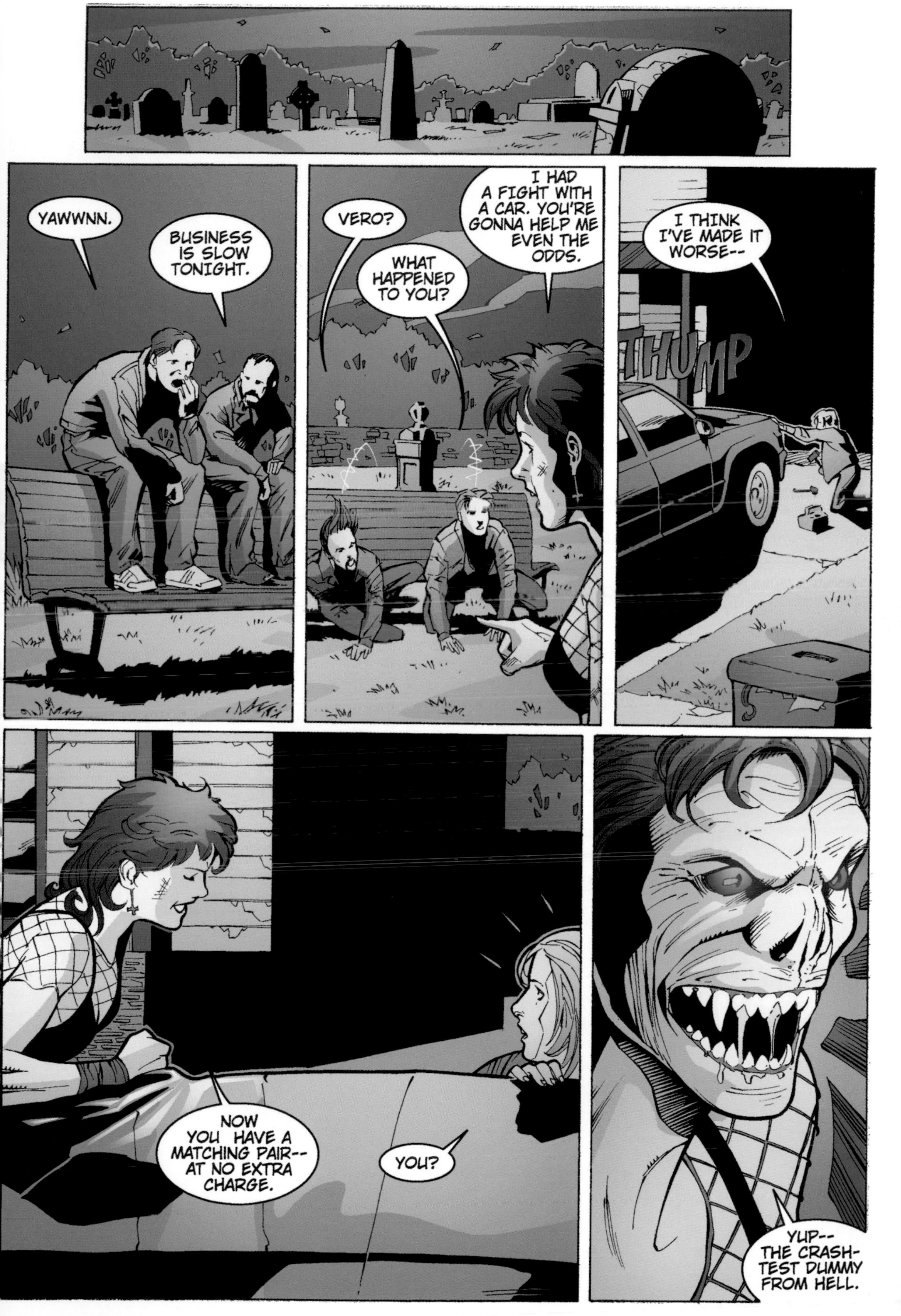
YAWWNN.
BUSINESS IS SLOW TONIGHT.
VERO?
WHAT HAPPENED TO YOU?
I HAD A FIGHT WITH A CAR. YOU'RE GONNA HELP ME EVEN THE ODDS.
I THINK I'VE MADE IT WORSE--
THUMP
NOW YOU HAVE A MATCHING PAIR-- AT NO EXTRA CHARGE.
YOU?
YUP-- THE CRASH-TEST DUMMY FROM HELL.

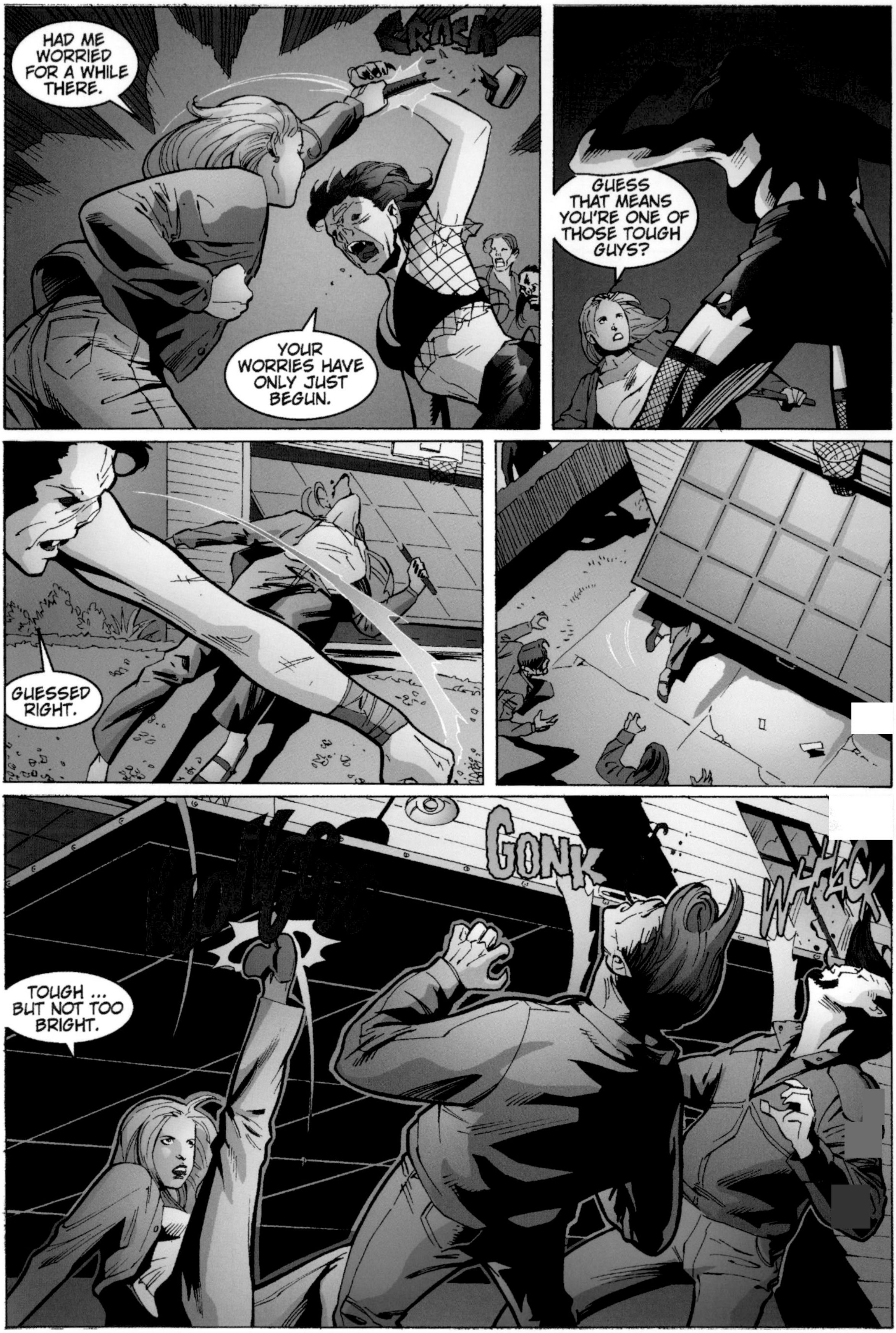

CRACK
HAD ME WORRIED FOR A WHILE THERE.
YOUR WORRIES HAVE ONLY JUST BEGUN.
GUESS THAT MEANS YOU'RE ONE OF THOSE TOUGH GUYS?
GUESSED RIGHT.
GONK
WHACK
TOUGH ... BUT NOT TOO BRIGHT.

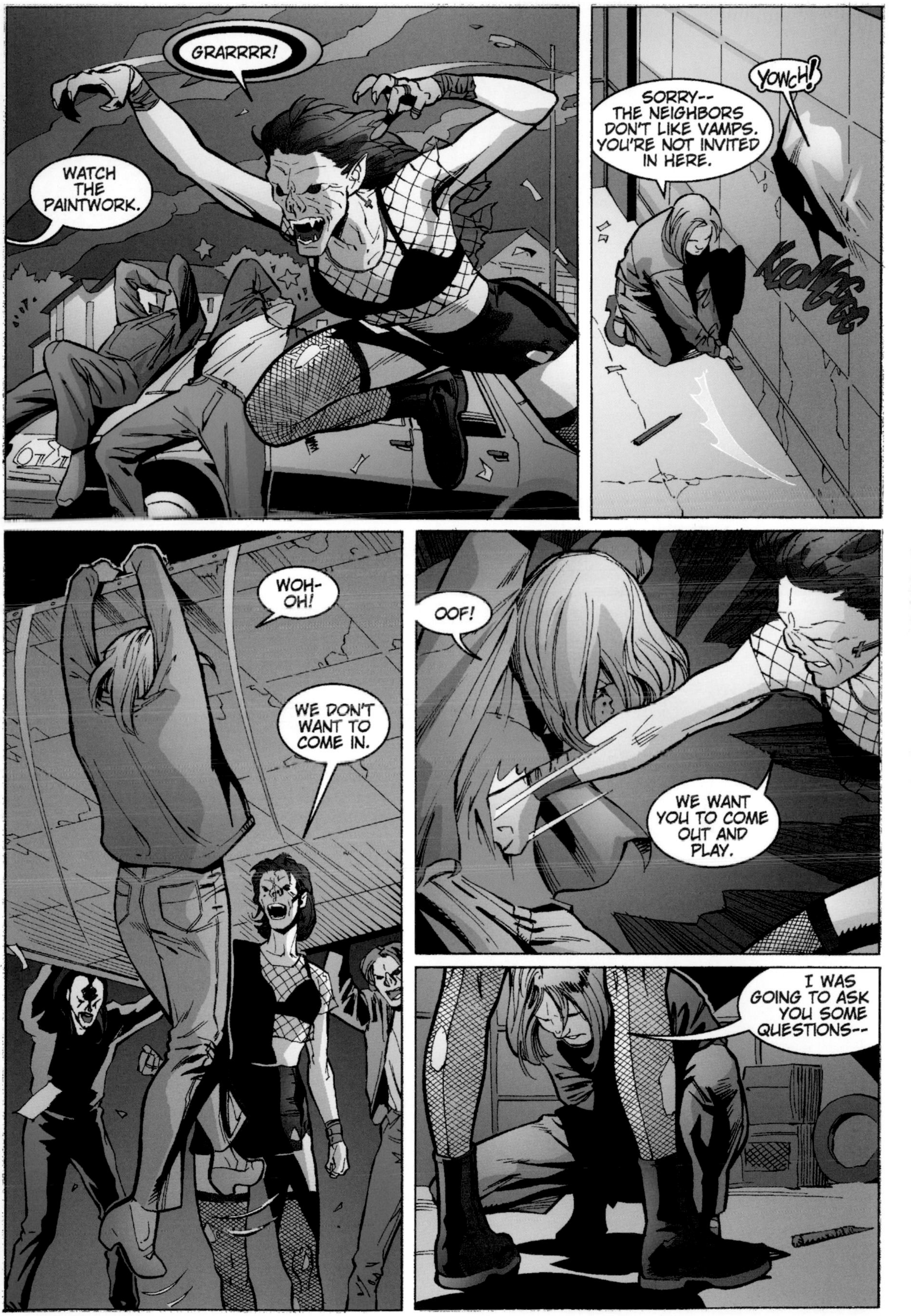
GRARRRR!
WATCH THE PAINTWORK.
SORRY-- THE NEIGHBORS DON'T LIKE VAMPS. YOU'RE NOT INVITED IN HERE.
YOWCH!
WOH- OH!
WE DON'T WANT TO COME IN.
OOF!
WE WANT YOU TO COME OUT AND PLAY.
I WAS GOING TO ASK YOU SOME QUESTIONS--

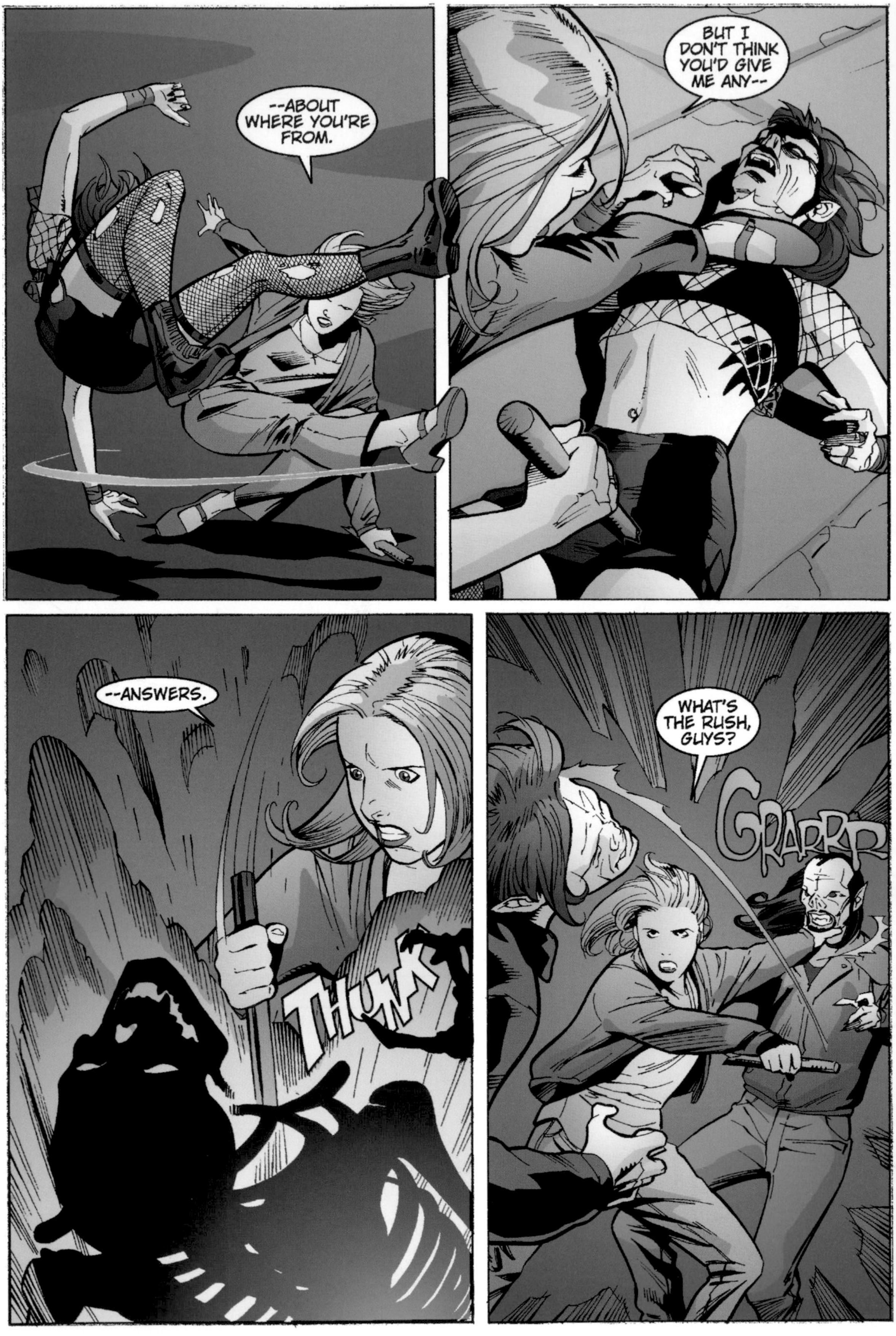
--ABOUT WHERE YOU'RE FROM.
BUT I DON'T THINK YOU'D GIVE ME ANY--
--ANSWERS.
THUNK
WHAT'S THE RUSH, GUYS?
GRARRR

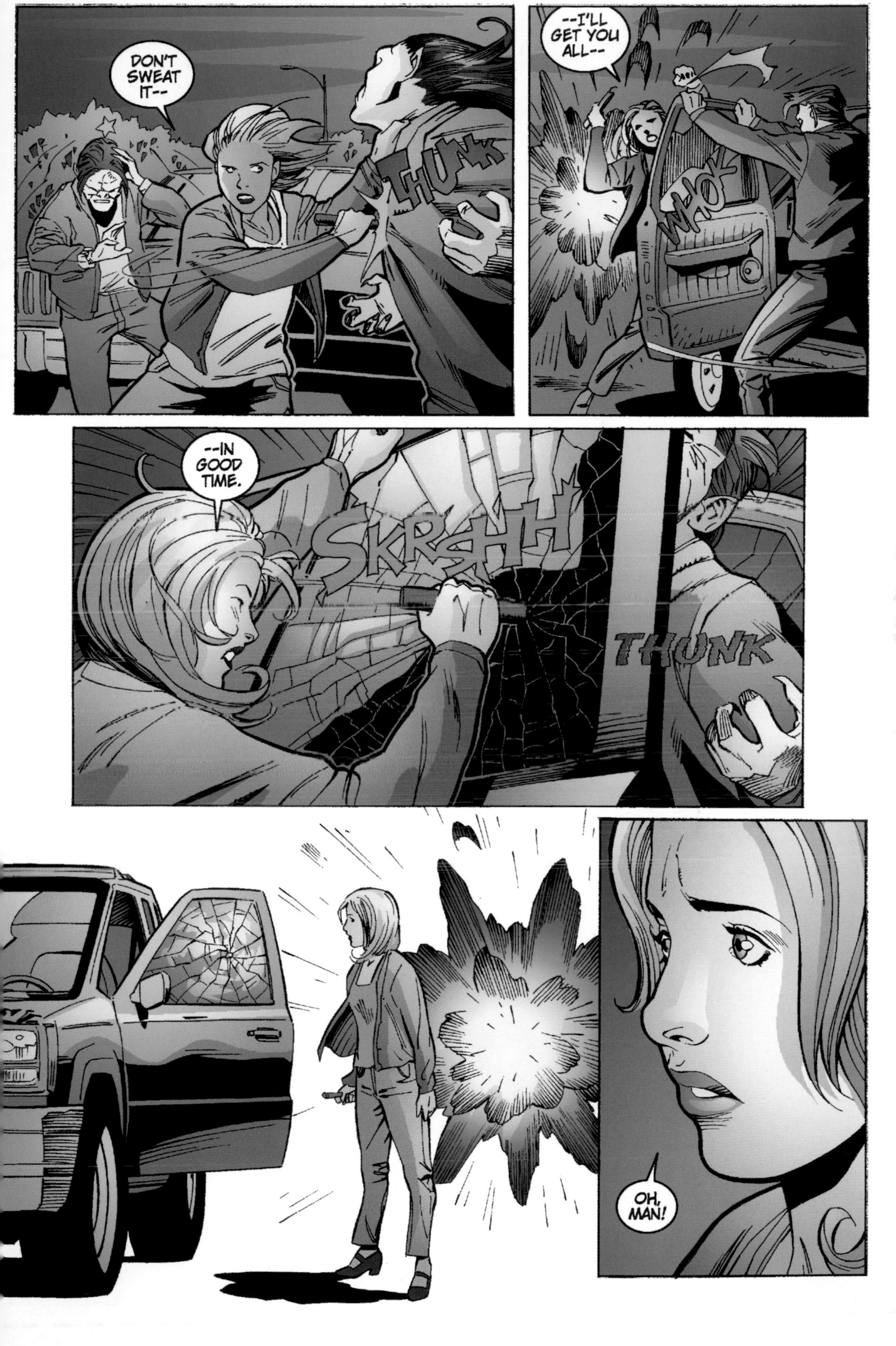
DON'T SWEAT IT--
THUNK
--I'LL GET YOU ALL--
WHOK
--IN GOOD TIME.
SKRSHH
THUNK
OH, MAN!

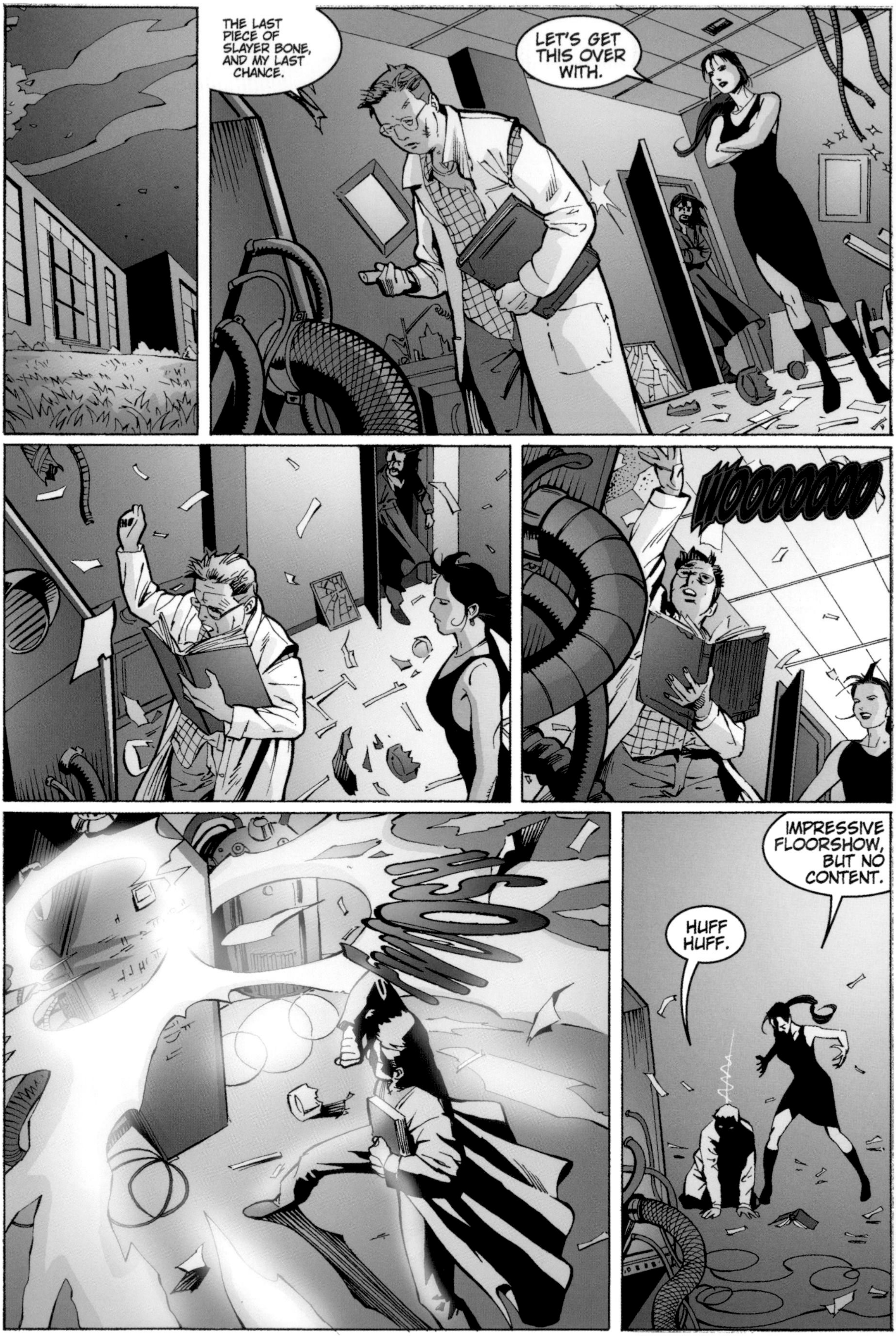
THE LAST PIECE OF SLAYER BONE, AND MY LAST CHANCE.
LET'S GET THIS OVER WITH.
WOOOOOOO
WOOSH
HUFF HUFF.
IMPRESSIVE FLOORSHOW, BUT NO CONTENT.

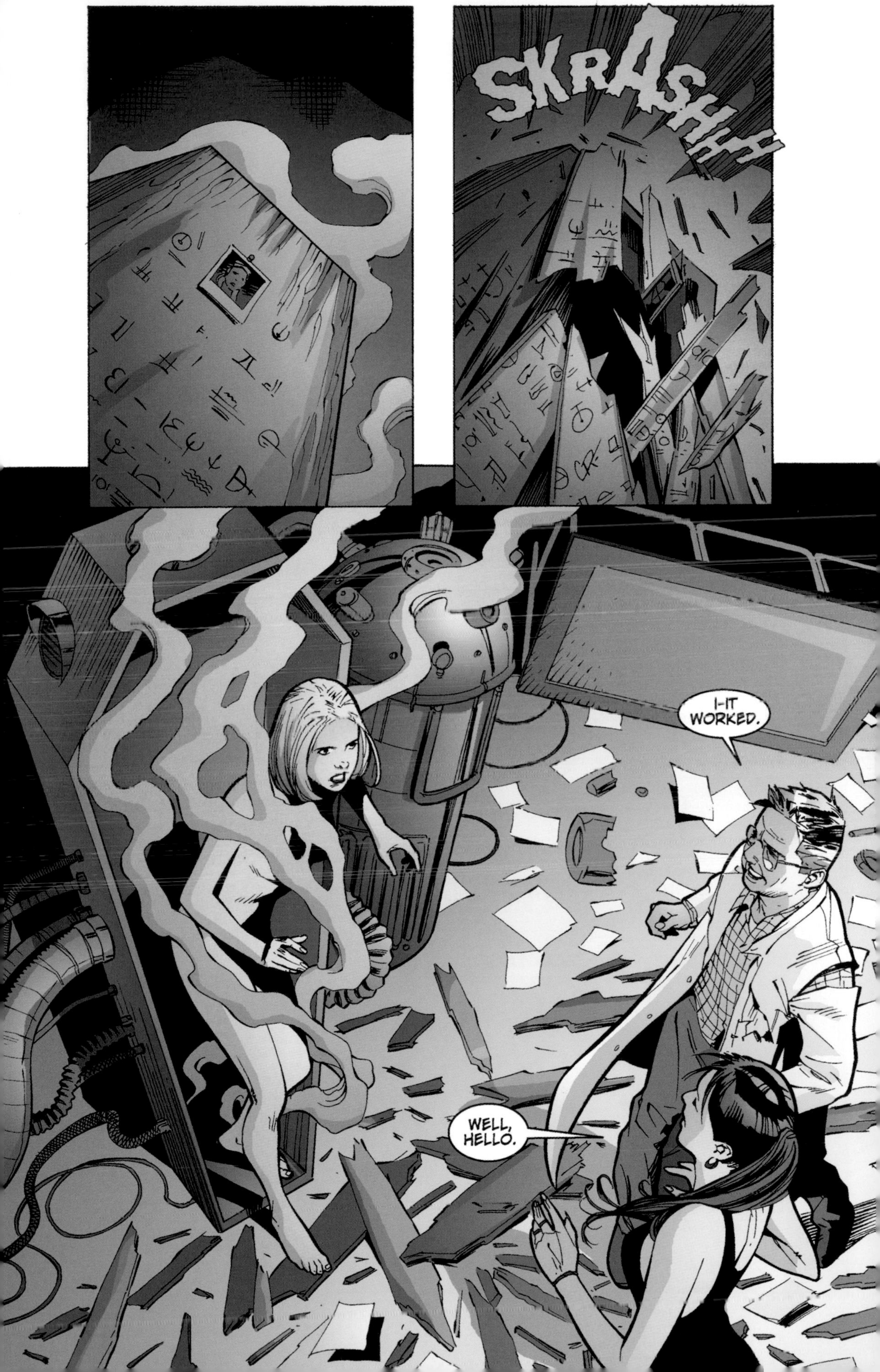
SKRASHH
I-IT WORKED.
WELL, HELLO.

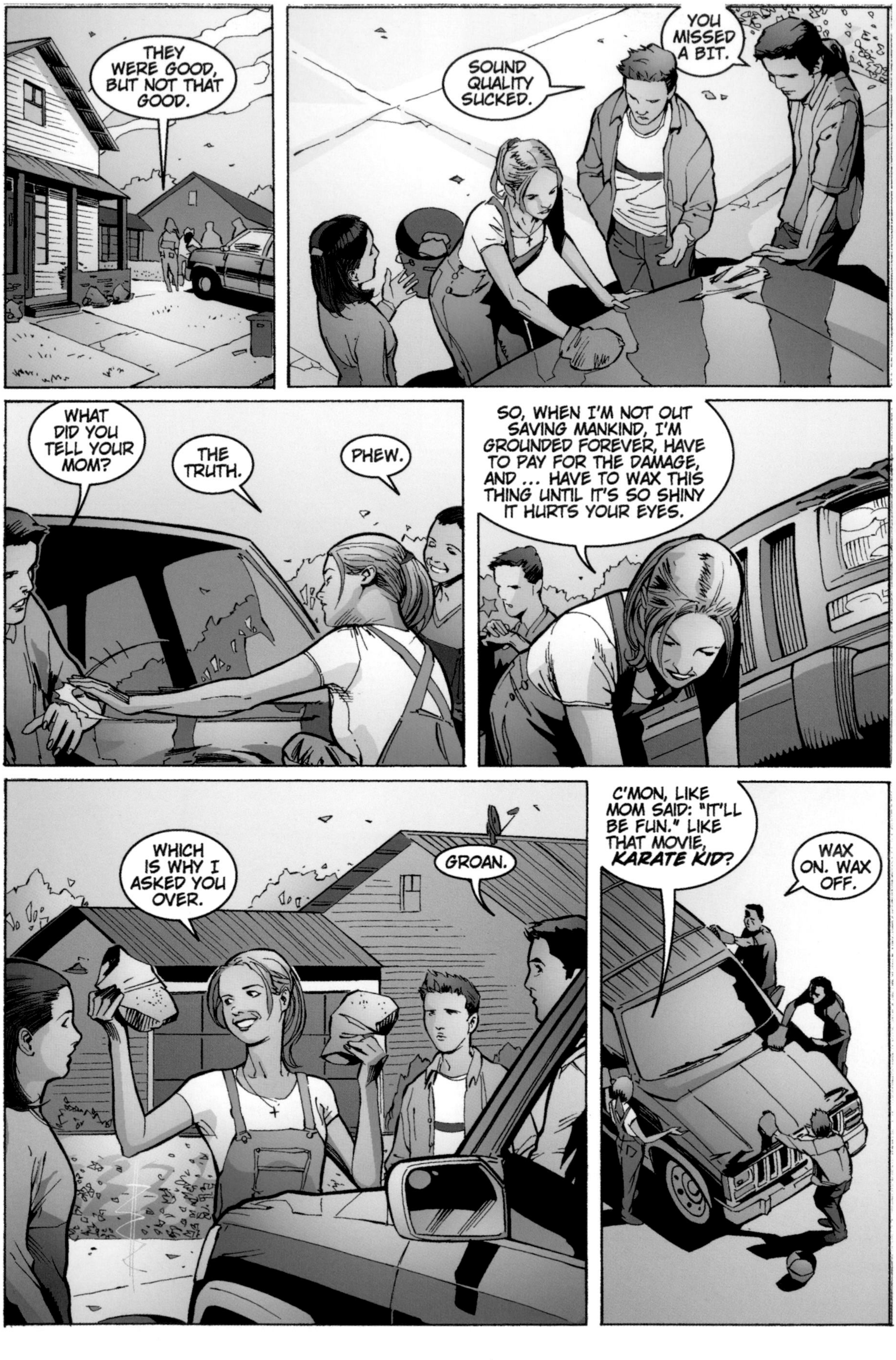
THEY WERE GOOD, BUT NOT THAT GOOD.
SOUND QUALITY SUCKED.
YOU MISSED A BIT.
WHAT DID YOU TELL YOUR MOM?
THE TRUTH.
PHEW.
SO, WHEN I'M NOT OUT SAVING MANKIND, I'M GROUNDED FOREVER, HAVE TO PAY FOR THE DAMAGE, AND ... HAVE TO WAX THIS THING UNTIL IT'S SO SHINY IT HURTS YOUR EYES.
WHICH IS WHY I ASKED YOU OVER.
GROAN.
C'MON, LIKE MOM SAID: "IT'LL BE FUN." LIKE THAT MOVIE, KARATE KID?
WAX ON. WAX OFF.

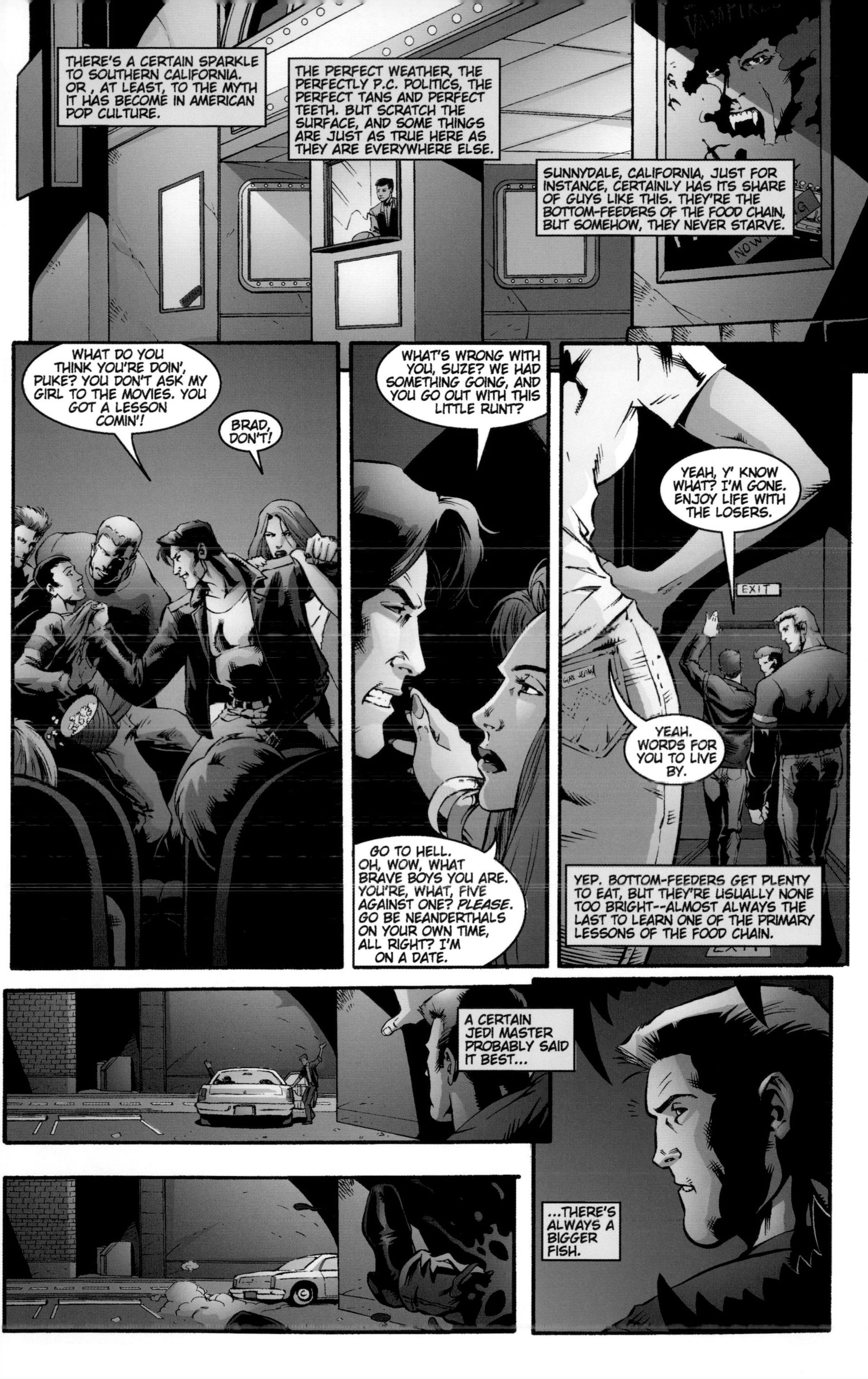

THERE'S A CERTAIN SPARKLE TO SOUTHERN CALIFORNIA. OR, AT LEAST, TO THE MYTH IT HAS BECOME IN AMERICAN POP CULTURE.
THE PERFECT WEATHER, THE PERFECTLY P.C. POLITICS, THE PERFECT TANS AND PERFECT TEETH. BUT SCRATCH THE SURFACE, AND SOME THINGS ARE JUST AS TRUE HERE AS THEY ARE EVERYWHERE ELSE.
SUNNYDALE, CALIFORNIA, JUST FOR INSTANCE, CERTAINLY HAS ITS SHARE OF GUYS LIKE THIS. THEY'RE THE BOTTOM-FEEDERS OF THE FOOD CHAIN, BUT SOMEHOW, THEY NEVER STARVE.
WHAT DO YOU THINK YOU'RE DOIN', PUKE? YOU DON'T ASK MY GIRL TO THE MOVIES. YOU GOT A LESSON COMIN'!
BRAD, DON'T!
WHAT'S WRONG WITH YOU, SUZE? WE HAD SOMETHING GOING, AND YOU GO OUT WITH THIS LITTLE RUNT?
GO TO HELL. OH, WOW, WHAT BRAVE BOYS YOU ARE. YOU'RE, WHAT, FIVE AGAINST ONE? *PLEASE*. GO BE NEANDERTHALS ON YOUR OWN TIME, ALL RIGHT? I'M ON A DATE.
YEAH, Y' KNOW WHAT? I'M GONE. ENJOY LIFE WITH THE LOSERS.
EXIT
YEAH. WORDS FOR YOU TO LIVE BY.
YEP. BOTTOM-FEEDERS GET PLENTY TO EAT, BUT THEY'RE USUALLY NONE TOO BRIGHT--ALMOST ALWAYS THE LAST TO LEARN ONE OF THE PRIMARY LESSONS OF THE FOOD CHAIN.
A CERTAIN JEDI MASTER PROBABLY SAID IT BEST...
...THERE'S ALWAYS A BIGGER FISH.

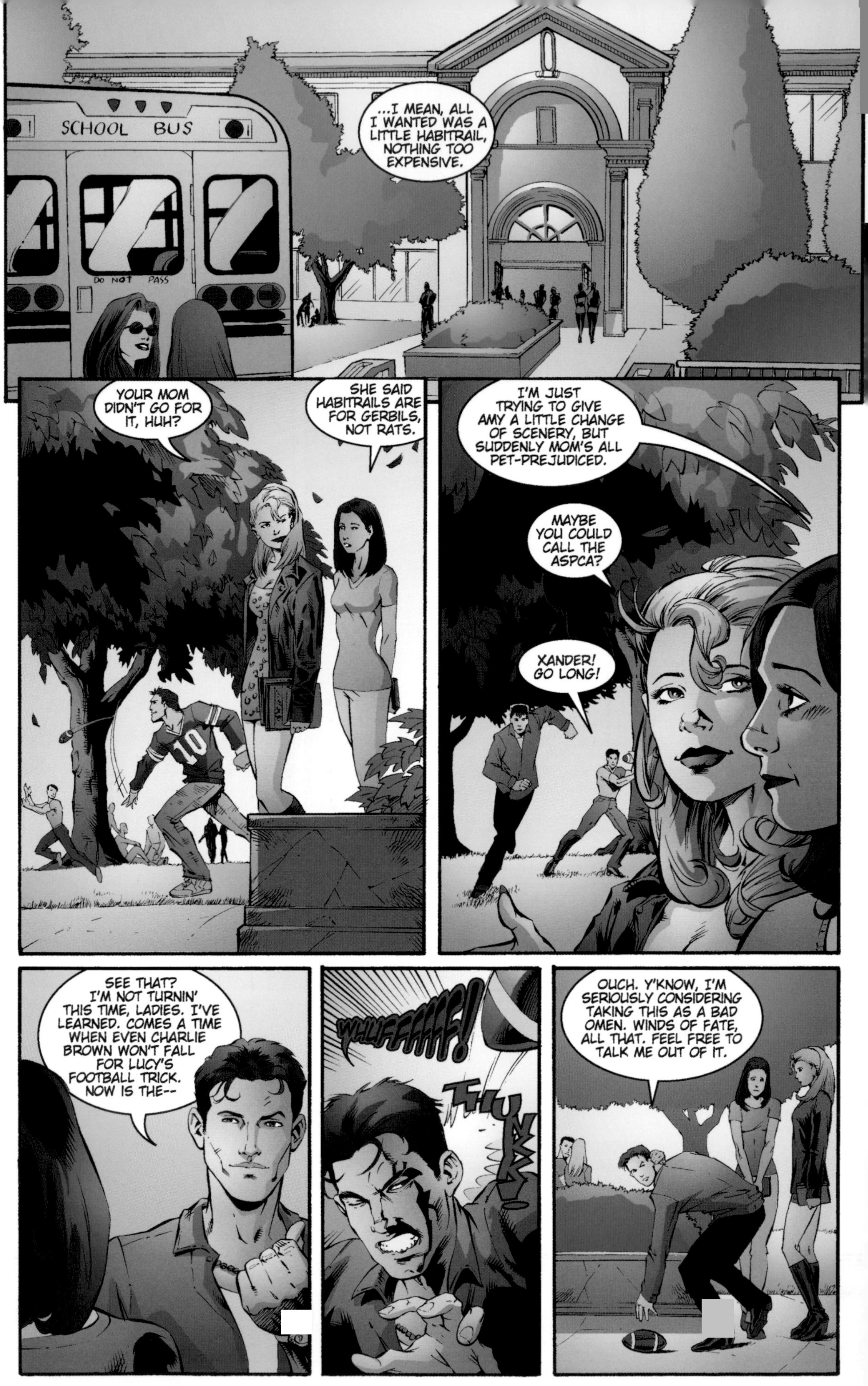
SCHOOL BUS
DO NOT PASS
...I MEAN, ALL I WANTED WAS A LITTLE HABITRAIL, NOTHING TOO EXPENSIVE.
YOUR MOM DIDN'T GO FOR IT, HUH?
SHE SAID HABITRAILS ARE FOR GERBILS, NOT RATS.
I'M JUST TRYING TO GIVE AMY A LITTLE CHANGE OF SCENERY, BUT SUDDENLY MOM'S ALL PET-PREJUDICED.
MAYBE YOU COULD CALL THE ASPCA?
XANDER! GO LONG!
SEE THAT? I'M NOT TURNIN' THIS TIME, LADIES. I'VE LEARNED. COMES A TIME WHEN EVEN CHARLIE BROWN WON'T FALL FOR LUCY'S FOOTBALL TRICK. NOW IS THE--
WHUFFFFFF!
THUNK!
OUCH. Y'KNOW, I'M SERIOUSLY CONSIDERING TAKING THIS AS A BAD OMEN. WINDS OF FATE, ALL THAT. FEEL FREE TO TALK ME OUT OF IT.

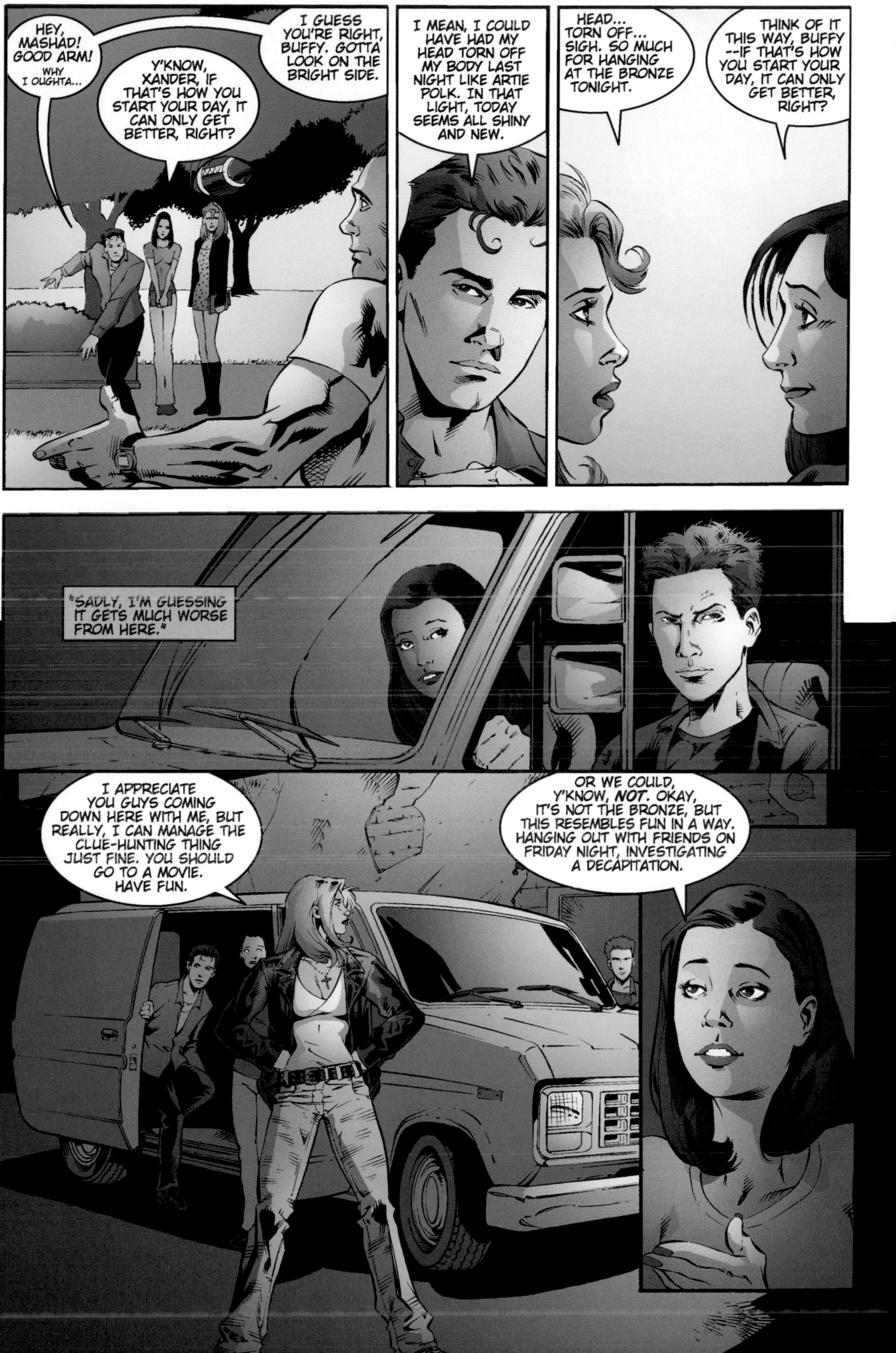

HEY, MASHAD! GOOD ARM!
WHY I OUGHTA...
Y'KNOW, XANDER, IF THAT'S HOW YOU START YOUR DAY, IT CAN ONLY GET BETTER, RIGHT?
I GUESS YOU'RE RIGHT, BUFFY. GOTTA LOOK ON THE BRIGHT SIDE.
I MEAN, I COULD HAVE HAD MY HEAD TORN OFF MY BODY LAST NIGHT LIKE ARTIE POLK. IN THAT LIGHT, TODAY SEEMS ALL SHINY AND NEW.
HEAD... TORN OFF... SIGH. SO MUCH FOR HANGING AT THE BRONZE TONIGHT.
THINK OF IT THIS WAY, BUFFY --IF THAT'S HOW YOU START YOUR DAY, IT CAN ONLY GET BETTER, RIGHT?
"SADLY, I'M GUESSING IT GETS MUCH WORSE FROM HERE."
I APPRECIATE YOU GUYS COMING DOWN HERE WITH ME, BUT REALLY, I CAN MANAGE THE CLUE-HUNTING THING JUST FINE. YOU SHOULD GO TO A MOVIE. HAVE FUN.
OR WE COULD, Y'KNOW, NOT. OKAY, IT'S NOT THE BRONZE, BUT THIS RESEMBLES FUN IN A WAY. HANGING OUT WITH FRIENDS ON FRIDAY NIGHT, INVESTIGATING A DECAPITATION.

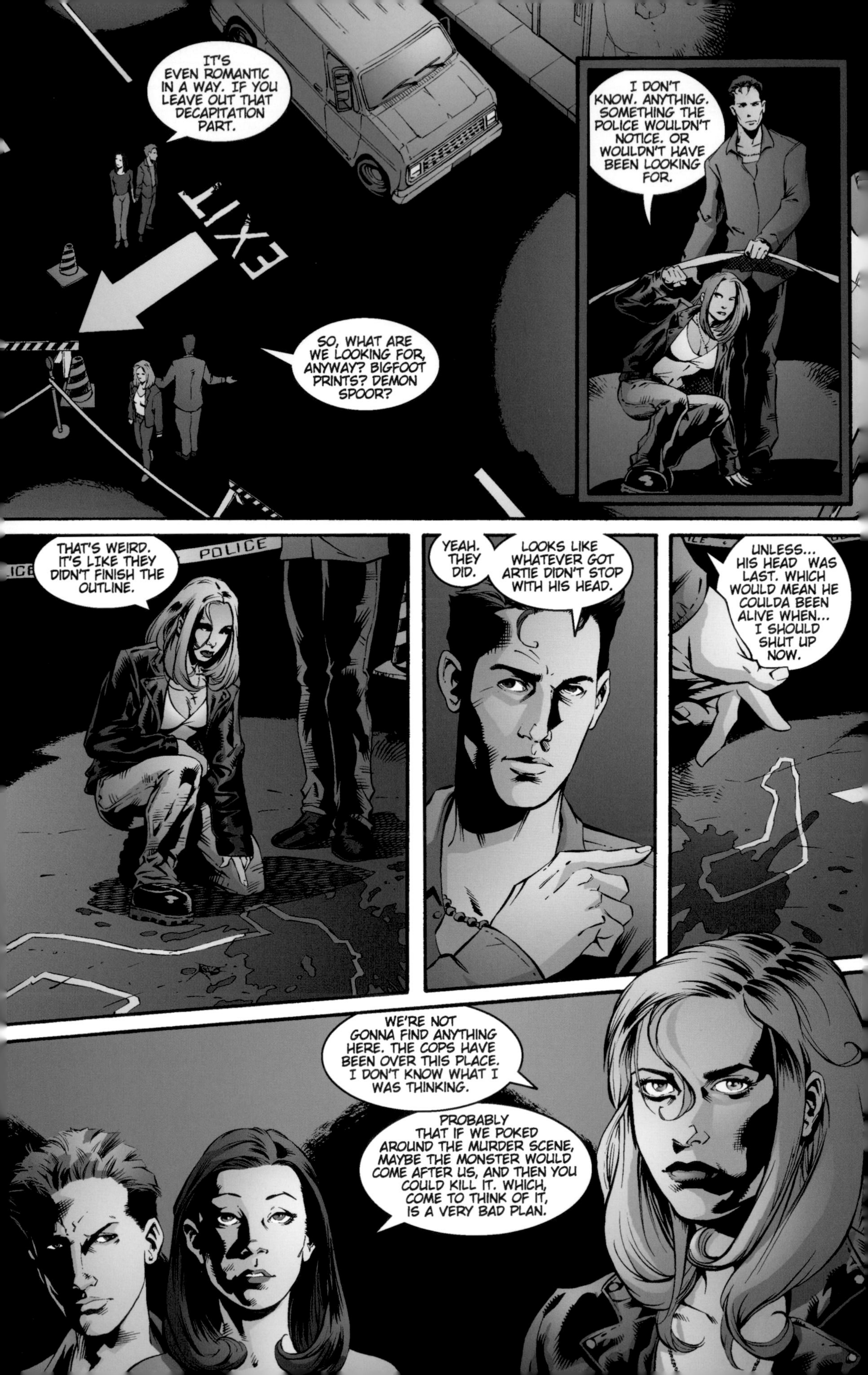
IT'S EVEN ROMANTIC IN A WAY. IF YOU LEAVE OUT THAT DECAPITATION PART.
EXIT
SO, WHAT ARE WE LOOKING FOR, ANYWAY? BIGFOOT PRINTS? DEMON SPOOR?
I DON'T KNOW. ANYTHING. SOMETHING THE POLICE WOULDN'T NOTICE. OR WOULDN'T HAVE BEEN LOOKING FOR.
THAT'S WEIRD. IT'S LIKE THEY DIDN'T FINISH THE OUTLINE.
POLICE
YEAH. THEY DID.
LOOKS LIKE WHATEVER GOT ARTIE DIDN'T STOP WITH HIS HEAD.
UNLESS... HIS HEAD WAS LAST. WHICH WOULD MEAN HE COULDA BEEN ALIVE WHEN... I SHOULD SHUT UP NOW.
WE'RE NOT GONNA FIND ANYTHING HERE. THE COPS HAVE BEEN OVER THIS PLACE. I DON'T KNOW WHAT I WAS THINKING.
PROBABLY THAT IF WE POKED AROUND THE MURDER SCENE, MAYBE THE MONSTER WOULD COME AFTER US, AND THEN YOU COULD KILL IT. WHICH, COME TO THINK OF IT, IS A VERY BAD PLAN.

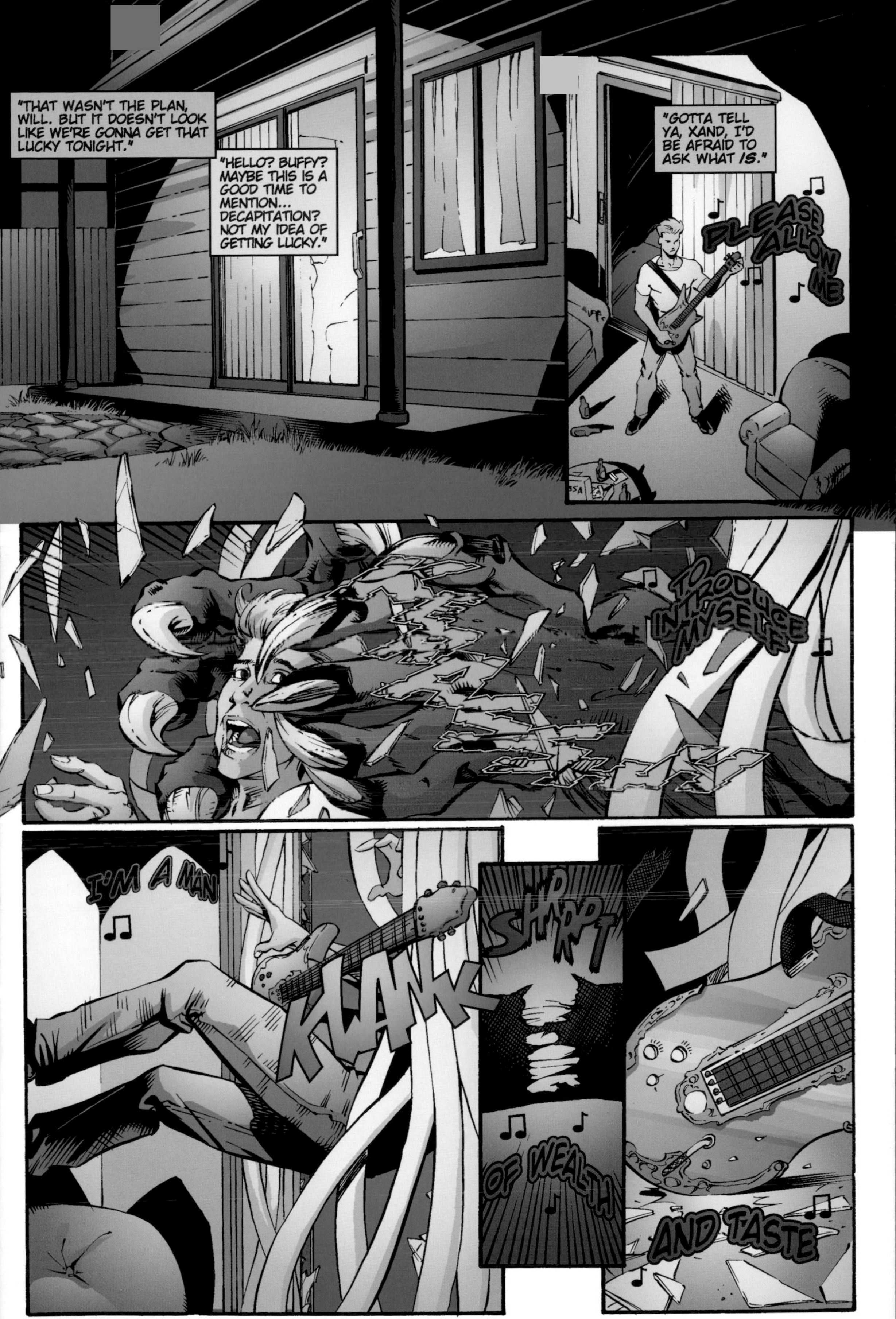
"THAT WASN'T THE PLAN, WILL. BUT IT DOESN'T LOOK LIKE WE'RE GONNA GET THAT LUCKY TONIGHT."
"HELLO? BUFFY? MAYBE THIS IS A GOOD TIME TO MENTION... DECAPITATION? NOT MY IDEA OF GETTING LUCKY."
"GOTTA TELL YA, XAND, I'D BE AFRAID TO ASK WHAT *IS*."
PLEASE ALLOW ME
TO INTRODUCE MYSELF
I'M A MAN
KLANK
OF WEALTH
AND TASTE

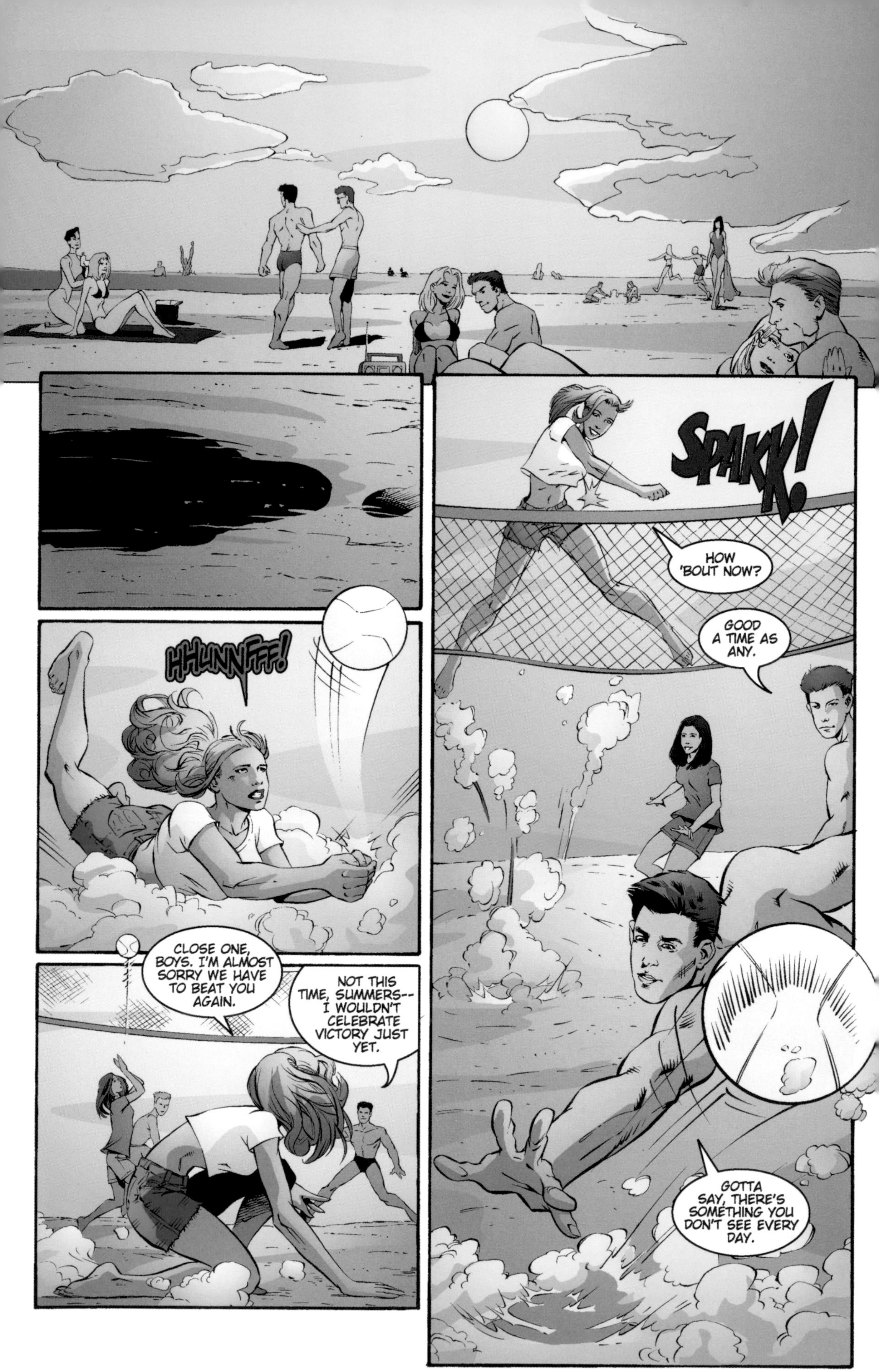
HHUNNFFF!
CLOSE ONE, BOYS. I'M ALMOST SORRY WE HAVE TO BEAT YOU AGAIN.
NOT THIS TIME, SUMMERS-- I WOULDN'T CELEBRATE VICTORY JUST YET.
SPAKK!
HOW 'BOUT NOW?
GOOD A TIME AS ANY.
GOTTA SAY, THERE'S SOMETHING YOU DON'T SEE EVERY DAY.

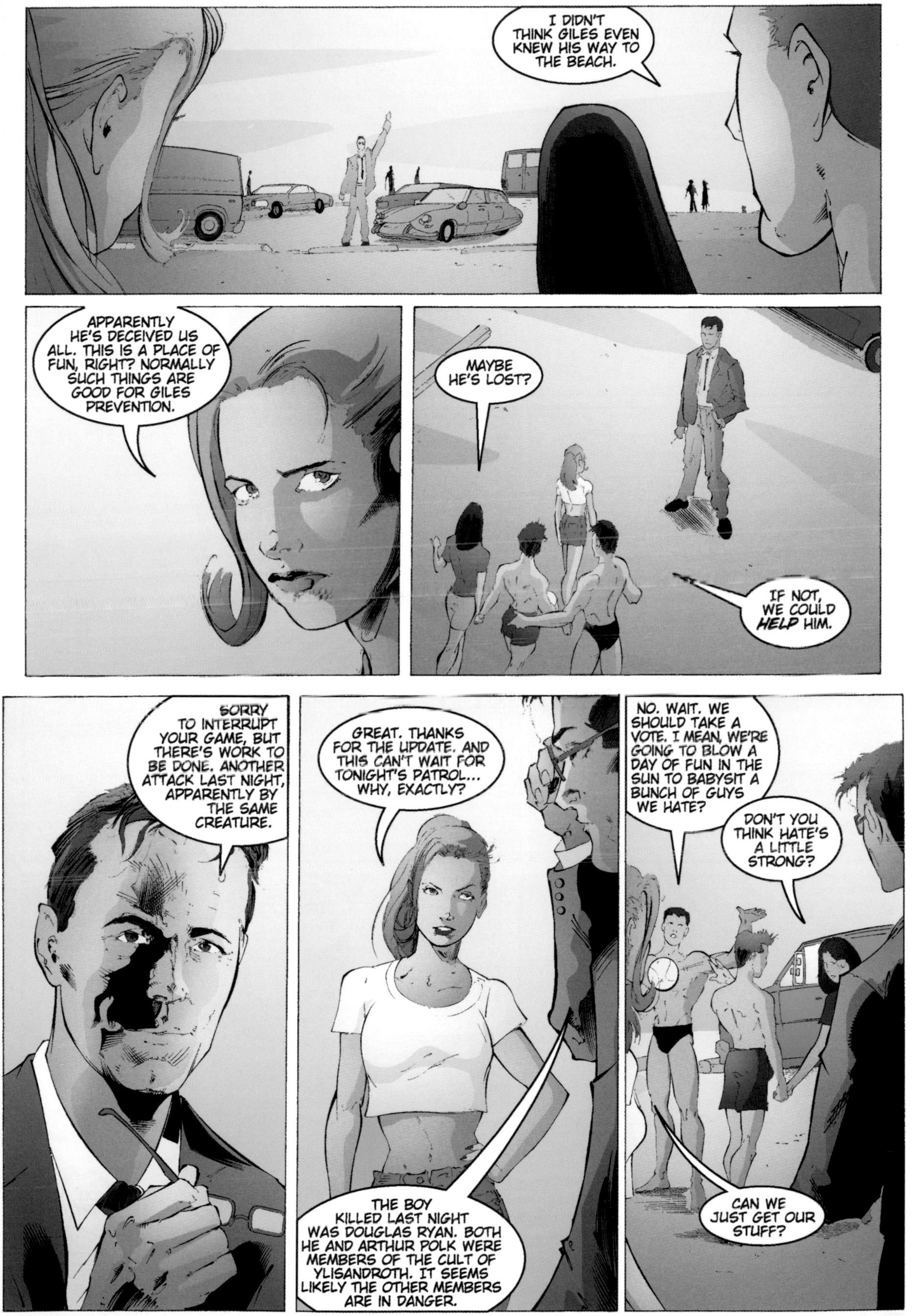
I DIDN'T THINK GILES EVEN KNEW HIS WAY TO THE BEACH.
APPARENTLY HE'S DECEIVED US ALL. THIS IS A PLACE OF FUN, RIGHT? NORMALLY SUCH THINGS ARE GOOD FOR GILES PREVENTION.
MAYBE HE'S LOST?
IF NOT, WE COULD HELP HIM.
SORRY TO INTERRUPT YOUR GAME, BUT THERE'S WORK TO BE DONE. ANOTHER ATTACK LAST NIGHT, APPARENTLY BY THE SAME CREATURE.
GREAT. THANKS FOR THE UPDATE. AND THIS CAN'T WAIT FOR TONIGHT'S PATROL... WHY, EXACTLY?
THE BOY KILLED LAST NIGHT WAS DOUGLAS RYAN. BOTH HE AND ARTHUR POLK WERE MEMBERS OF THE CULT OF YLISANDROTH. IT SEEMS LIKELY THE OTHER MEMBERS ARE IN DANGER.
NO. WAIT. WE SHOULD TAKE A VOTE. I MEAN, WE'RE GOING TO BLOW A DAY OF FUN IN THE SUN TO BABYSIT A BUNCH OF GUYS WE HATE?
DON'T YOU THINK HATE'S A LITTLE STRONG?
CAN WE JUST GET OUR STUFF?

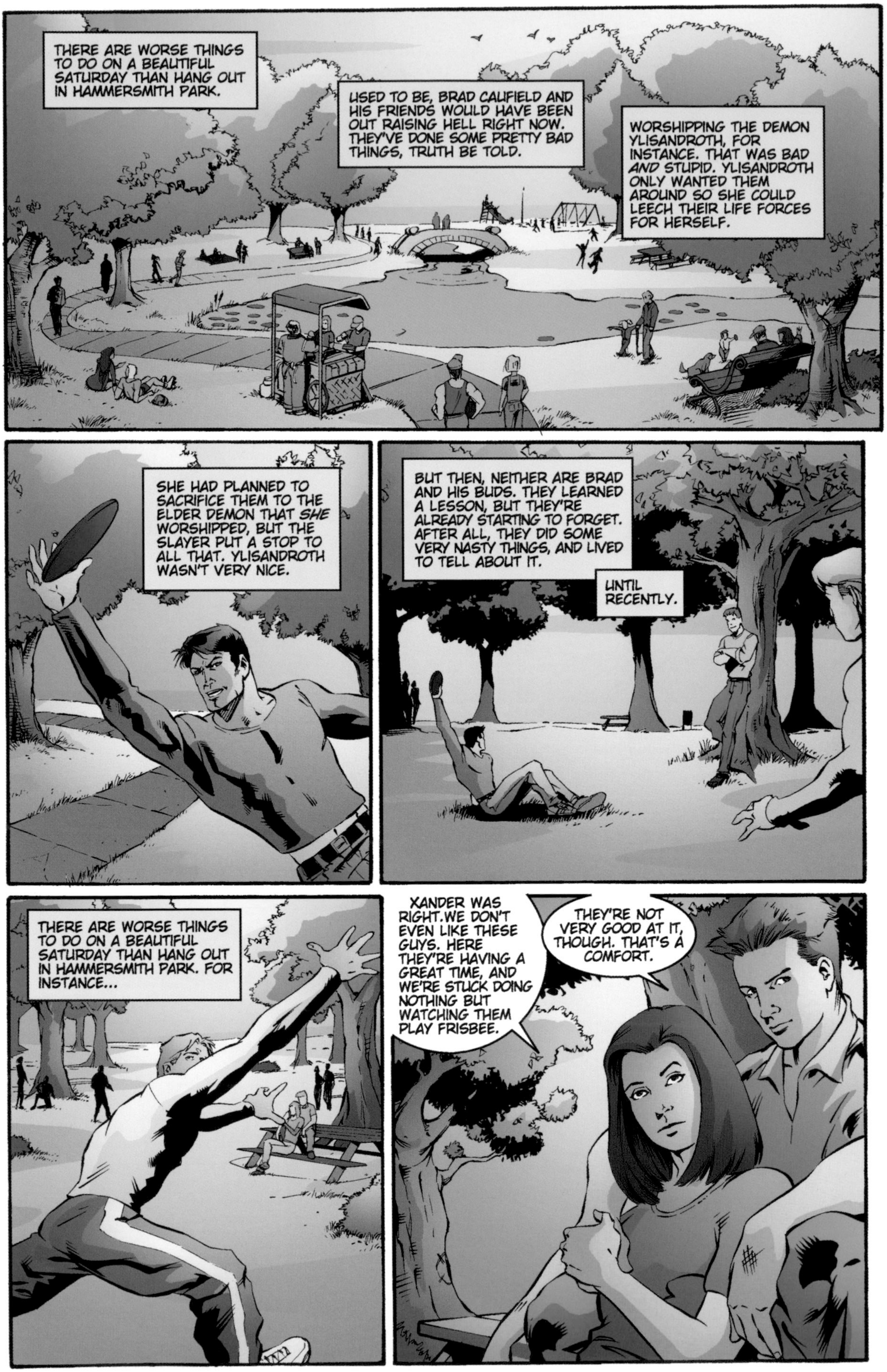
THERE ARE WORSE THINGS TO DO ON A BEAUTIFUL SATURDAY THAN HANG OUT IN HAMMERSMITH PARK.
USED TO BE, BRAD CALFIELD AND HIS FRIENDS WOULD HAVE BEEN OUT RAISING HELL RIGHT NOW. THEY'VE DONE SOME PRETTY BAD THINGS, TRUTH BE TOLD.
WORSHIPPING THE DEMON YLISANDROTH, FOR INSTANCE. THAT WAS BAD *AND* STUPID. YLISANDROTH ONLY WANTED THEM AROUND SO SHE COULD LEECH THEIR LIFE FORCES FOR HERSELF.
SHE HAD PLANNED TO SACRIFICE THEM TO THE ELDER DEMON THAT *SHE* WORSHIPPED, BUT THE SLAYER PUT A STOP TO ALL THAT. YLISANDROTH WASN'T VERY NICE.
BUT THEN, NEITHER ARE BRAD AND HIS BUDS. THEY LEARNED A LESSON, BUT THEY'RE ALREADY STARTING TO FORGET. AFTER ALL, THEY DID SOME VERY NASTY THINGS, AND LIVED TO TELL ABOUT IT.
UNTIL RECENTLY.
THERE ARE WORSE THINGS TO DO ON A BEAUTIFUL SATURDAY THAN HANG OUT IN HAMMERSMITH PARK. FOR INSTANCE...
XANDER WAS RIGHT. WE DON'T EVEN LIKE THESE GUYS. HERE THEY'RE HAVING A GREAT TIME, AND WE'RE STUCK DOING NOTHING BUT WATCHING THEM PLAY FRISBEE.
THEY'RE NOT VERY GOOD AT IT, THOUGH. THAT'S A COMFORT.

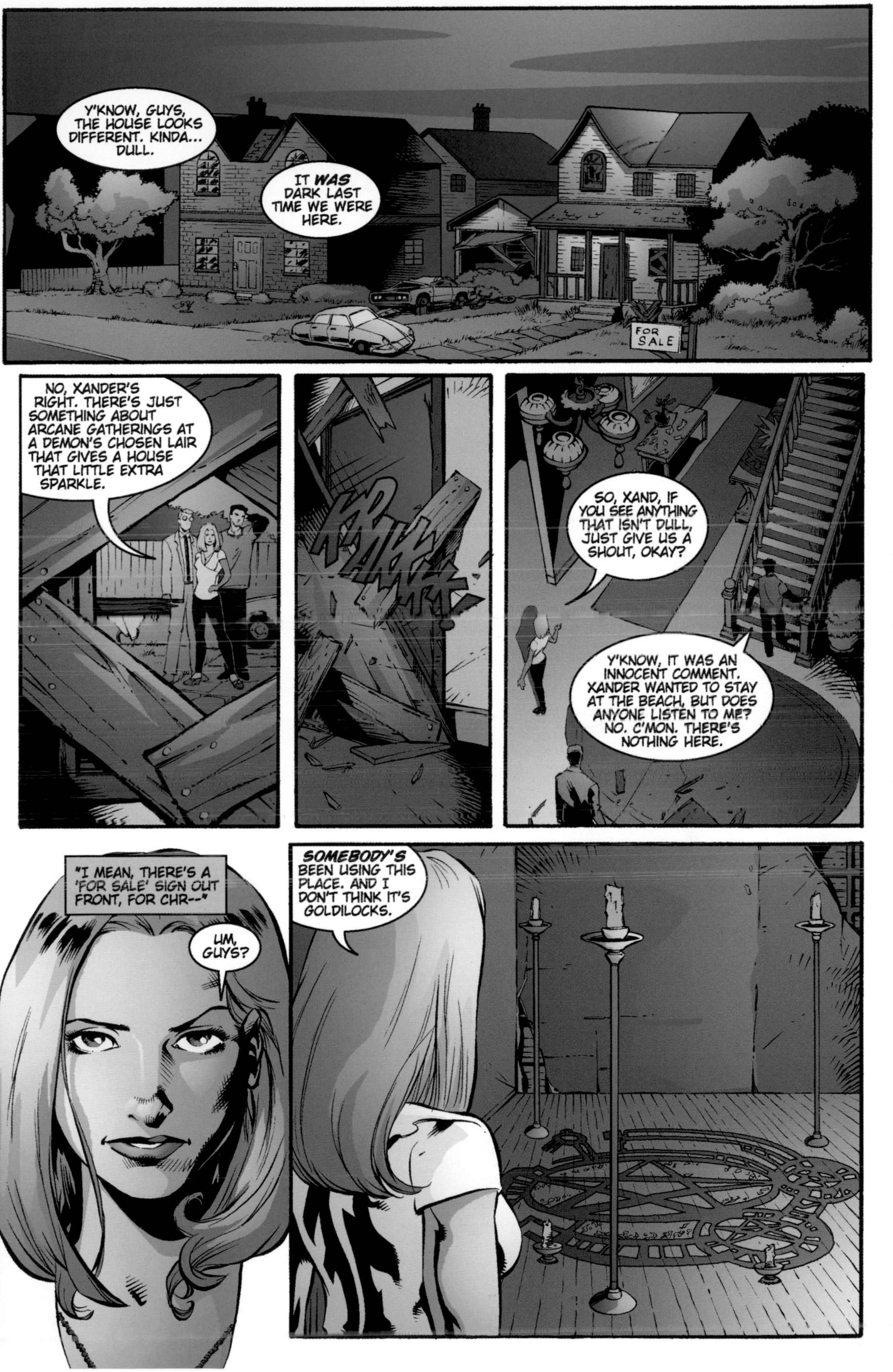
Y'KNOW, GUYS, THE HOUSE LOOKS DIFFERENT. KINDA... DULL.
IT WAS DARK LAST TIME WE WERE HERE.
FOR SALE
NO, XANDER'S RIGHT. THERE'S JUST SOMETHING ABOUT ARCANE GATHERINGS AT A DEMON'S CHOSEN LAIR THAT GIVES A HOUSE THAT LITTLE EXTRA SPARKLE.
KRAKK
SO, XAND, IF YOU SEE ANYTHING THAT ISN'T DULL, JUST GIVE US A SHOUT, OKAY?
Y'KNOW, IT WAS AN INNOCENT COMMENT. XANDER WANTED TO STAY AT THE BEACH, BUT DOES ANYONE LISTEN TO ME? NO. C'MON. THERE'S NOTHING HERE.
"I MEAN, THERE'S A 'FOR SALE' SIGN OUT FRONT, FOR CHR--"
UM, GUYS?
SOMEBODY'S BEEN USING THIS PLACE. AND I DON'T THINK IT'S GOLDILOCKS.

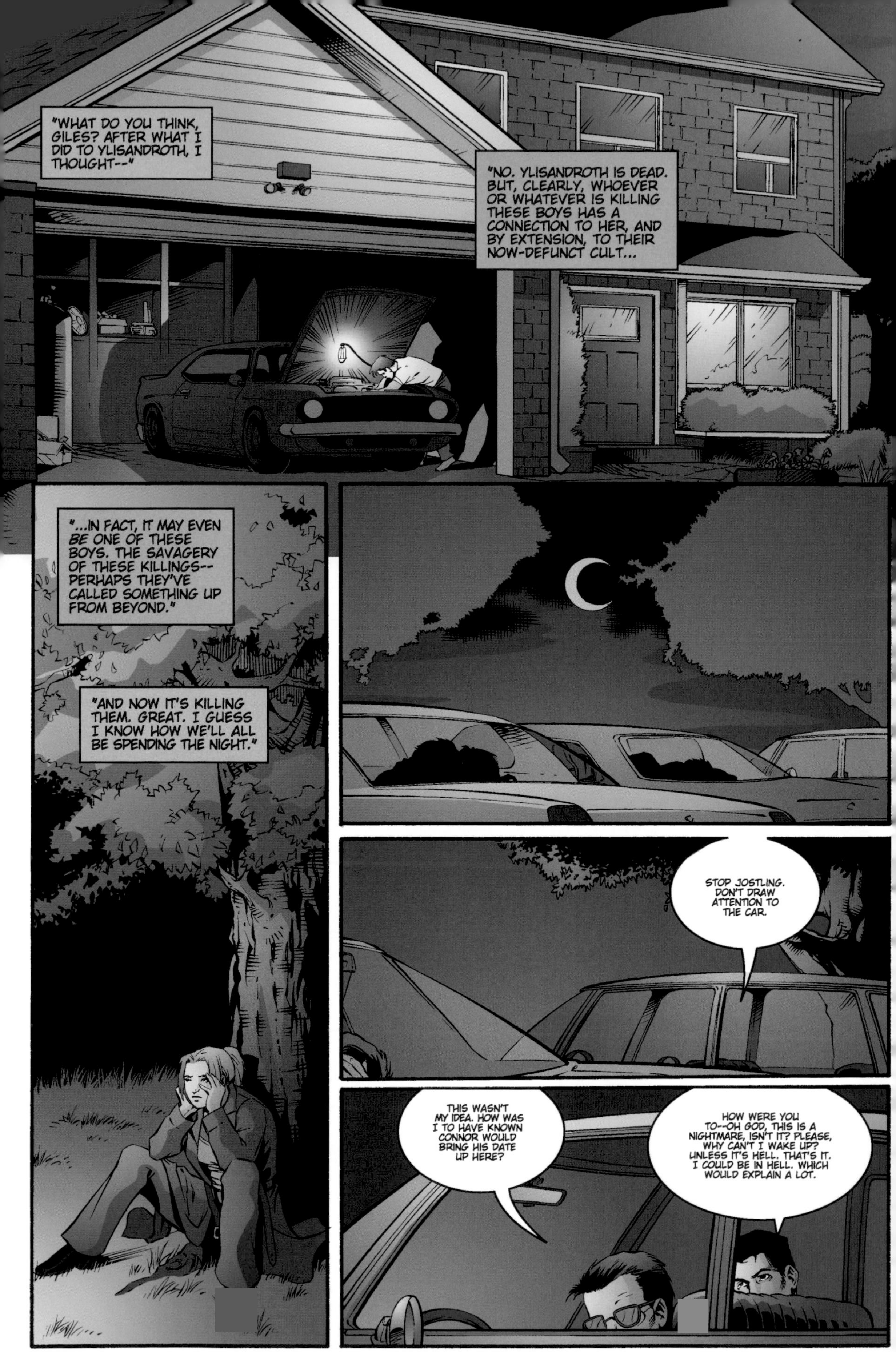
"WHAT DO YOU THINK, GILES? AFTER WHAT I DID TO YLISANDROTH, I THOUGHT--"
"NO. YLISANDROTH IS DEAD. BUT, CLEARLY, WHOEVER OR WHATEVER IS KILLING THESE BOYS HAS A CONNECTION TO HER, AND BY EXTENSION, TO THEIR NOW-DEFUNCT CULT...
"...IN FACT, IT MAY EVEN BE ONE OF THESE BOYS. THE SAVAGERY OF THESE KILLINGS--PERHAPS THEY'VE CALLED SOMETHING UP FROM BEYOND."
"AND NOW IT'S KILLING THEM. GREAT. I GUESS I KNOW HOW WE'LL ALL BE SPENDING THE NIGHT."
STOP JOSTLING. DON'T DRAW ATTENTION TO THE CAR.
THIS WASN'T MY IDEA. HOW WAS I TO HAVE KNOWN CONNOR WOULD BRING HIS DATE UP HERE?
HOW WERE YOU TO--OH GOD, THIS IS A NIGHTMARE, ISN'T IT? PLEASE, WHY CAN'T I WAKE UP? UNLESS IT'S HELL. THAT'S IT. I COULD BE IN HELL. WHICH WOULD EXPLAIN A LOT.

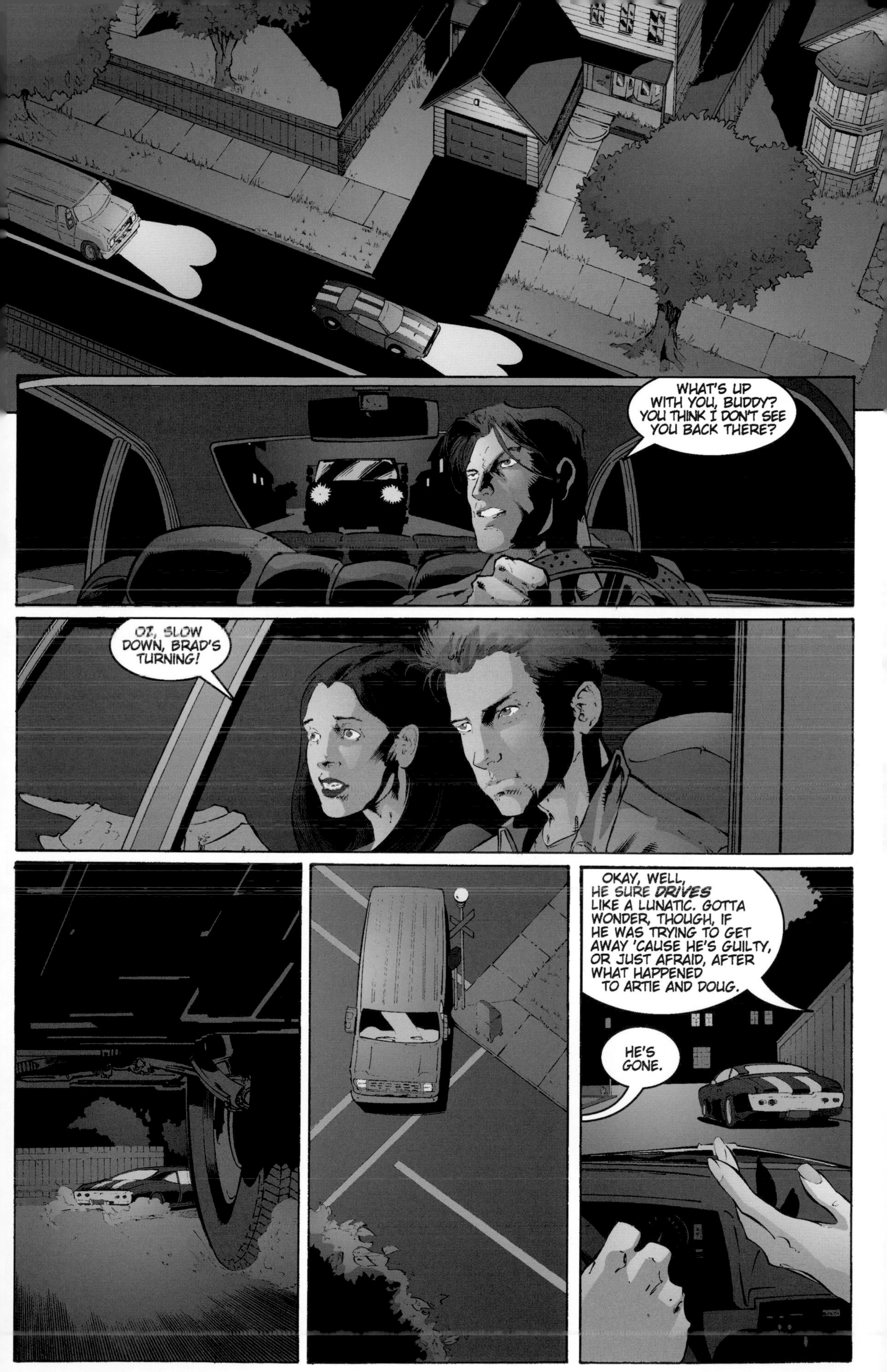
WHAT'S UP WITH YOU, BUDDY? YOU THINK I DON'T SEE YOU BACK THERE?
OZ, SLOW DOWN, BRAD'S TURNING!
OKAY, WELL, HE SURE DRIVES LIKE A LUNATIC. GOTTA WONDER, THOUGH, IF HE WAS TRYING TO GET AWAY 'CAUSE HE'S GUILTY, OR JUST AFRAID, AFTER WHAT HAPPENED TO ARTIE AND DOUG.
HE'S GONE.

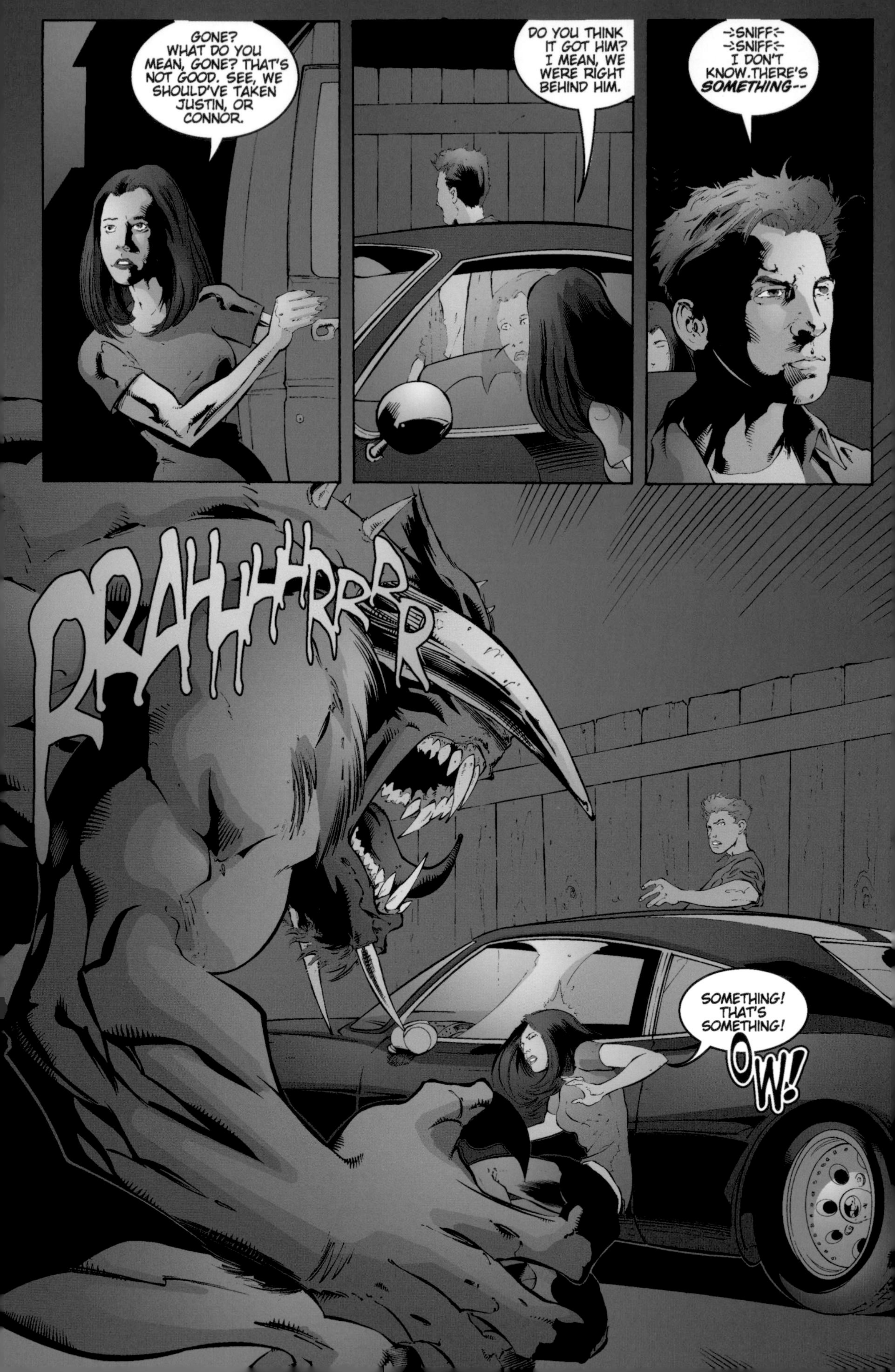
GONE? WHAT DO YOU MEAN, GONE? THAT'S NOT GOOD. SEE, WE SHOULD'VE TAKEN JUSTIN, OR CONNOR.
DO YOU THINK IT GOT HIM? I MEAN, WE WERE RIGHT BEHIND HIM.
-SNIFF- -SNIFF- I DON'T KNOW. THERE'S *SOMETHING*--
RRAHHHRRRR
SOMETHING! THAT'S SOMETHING!
OW!

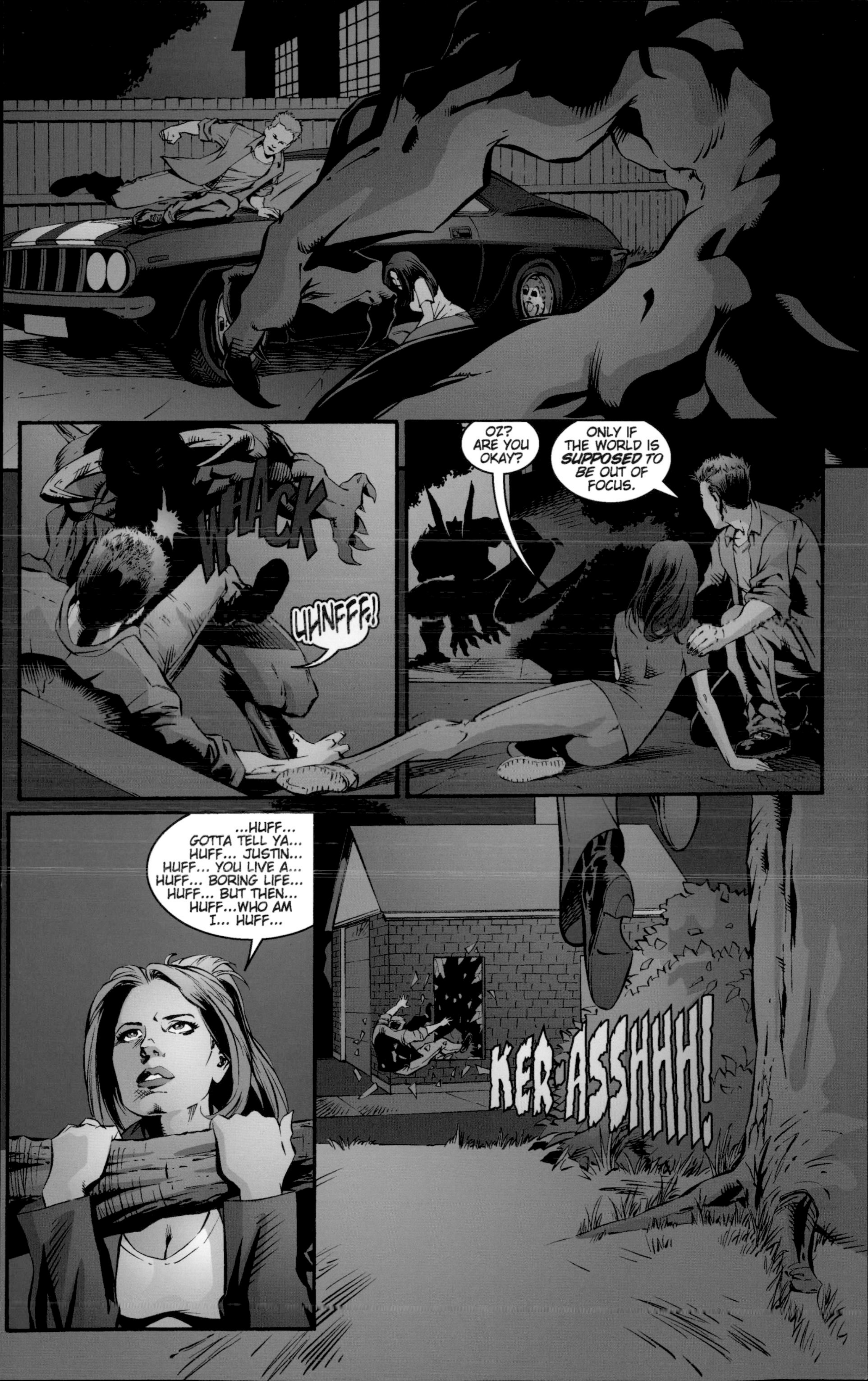
WHACK
UHNFFF!
OZ? ARE YOU OKAY?
ONLY IF THE WORLD IS SUPPOSED TO BE OUT OF FOCUS.
...HUFF... GOTTA TELL YA... HUFF... JUSTIN... HUFF... YOU LIVE A... HUFF... BORING LIFE... HUFF... BUT THEN... HUFF...WHO AM I... HUFF...
KER-ASSHHH!

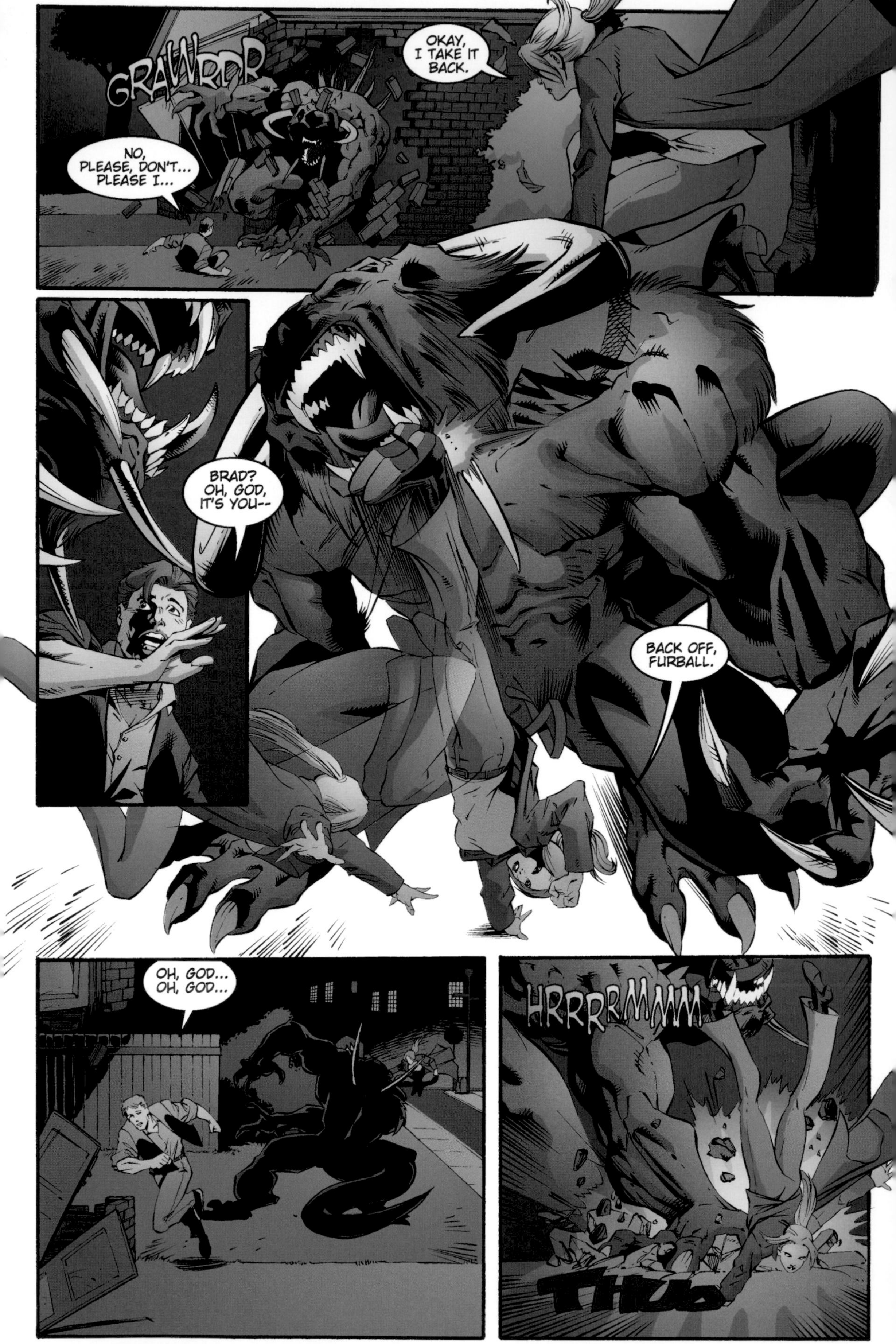
GRAWRDR
OKAY, I TAKE IT BACK.
NO, PLEASE, DON'T... PLEASE I...
BRAD? OH, GOD, IT'S YOU--
BACK OFF, FURBALL.
OH, GOD... OH, GOD...
HRRRRMMMM
THUD

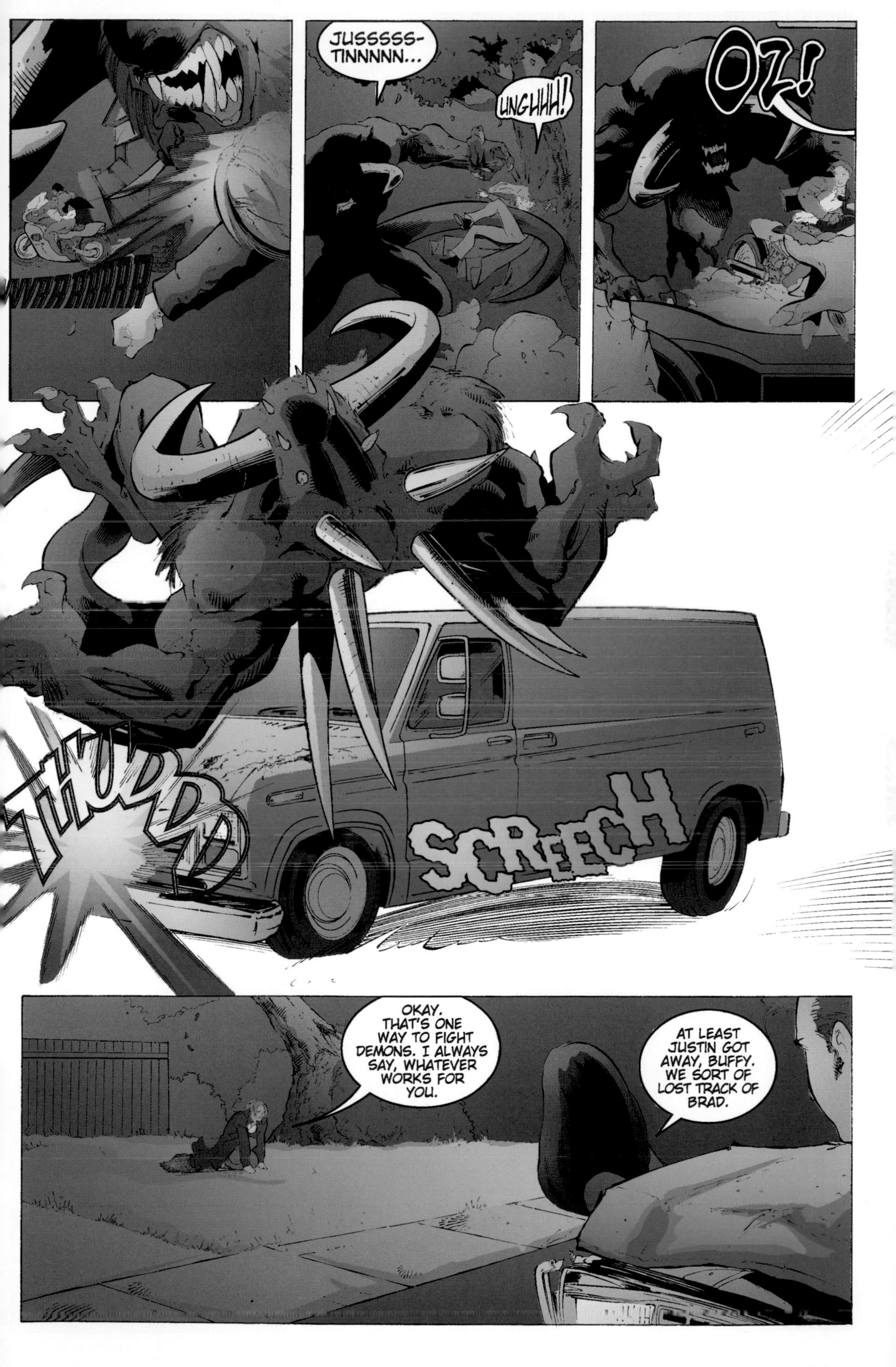
WRRRRRRR
JUSSSSS-TINNNNN...
UNGHHH!
OZ!
THUDDD
SCREECH
OKAY. THAT'S ONE WAY TO FIGHT DEMONS. I ALWAYS SAY, WHATEVER WORKS FOR YOU.
AT LEAST JUSTIN GOT AWAY, BUFFY. WE SORT OF LOST TRACK OF BRAD.

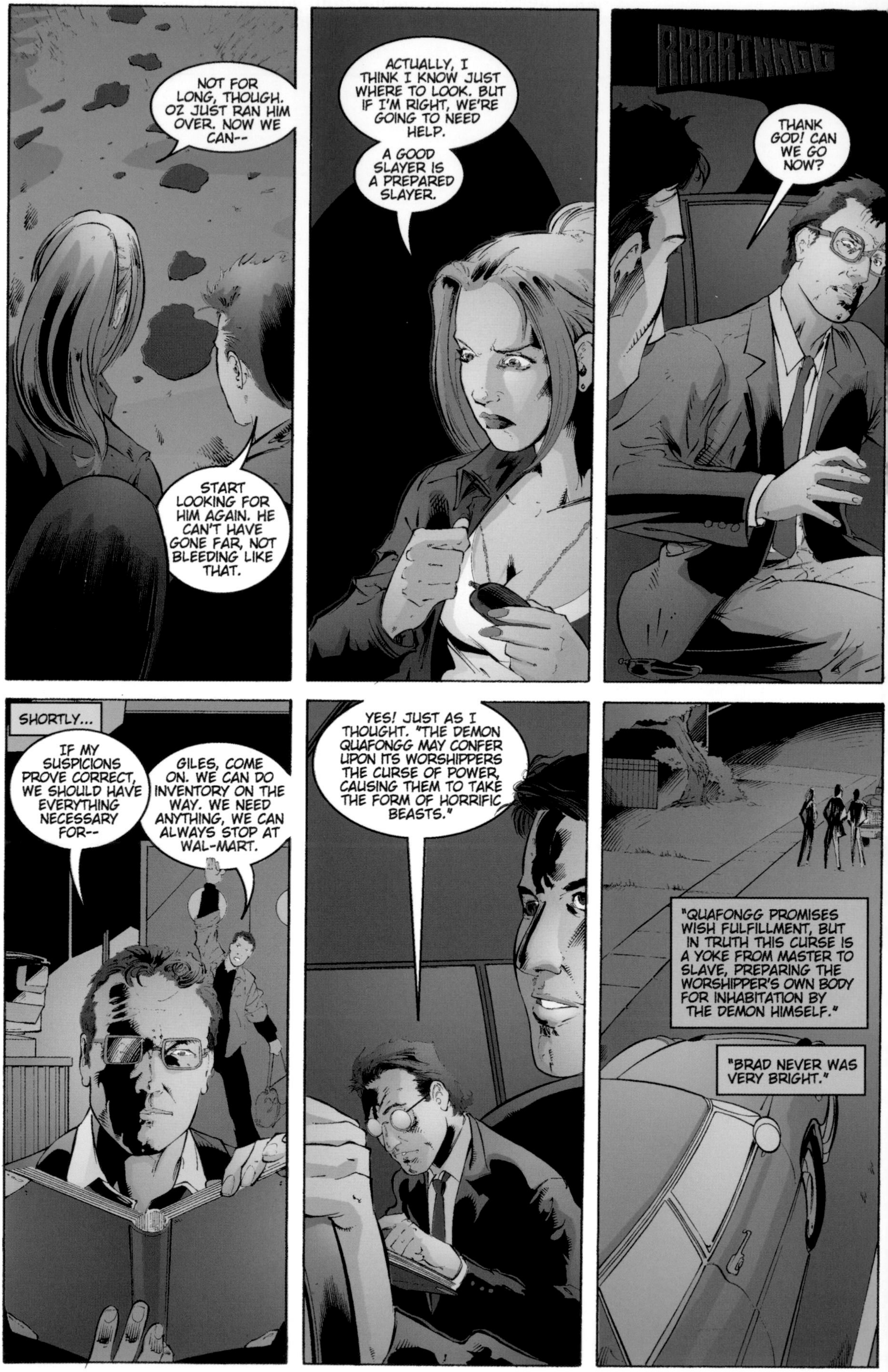
NOT FOR LONG, THOUGH. OZ JUST RAN HIM OVER. NOW WE CAN--
START LOOKING FOR HIM AGAIN. HE CAN'T HAVE GONE FAR, NOT BLEEDING LIKE THAT.
ACTUALLY, I THINK I KNOW JUST WHERE TO LOOK. BUT IF I'M RIGHT, WE'RE GOING TO NEED HELP.
A GOOD SLAYER IS A PREPARED SLAYER.
RRRRINNGG
THANK GOD! CAN WE GO NOW?
SHORTLY...
IF MY SUSPICIONS PROVE CORRECT, WE SHOULD HAVE EVERYTHING NECESSARY FOR--
GILES, COME ON. WE CAN DO INVENTORY ON THE WAY. WE NEED ANYTHING, WE CAN ALWAYS STOP AT WAL-MART.
YES! JUST AS I THOUGHT. "THE DEMON QUAFONGG MAY CONFER UPON ITS WORSHIPPERS THE CURSE OF POWER, CAUSING THEM TO TAKE THE FORM OF HORRIFIC BEASTS."
"QUAFONGG PROMISES WISH FULFILLMENT, BUT IN TRUTH THIS CURSE IS A YOKE FROM MASTER TO SLAVE, PREPARING THE WORSHIPPER'S OWN BODY FOR INHABITATION BY THE DEMON HIMSELF."
"BRAD NEVER WAS VERY BRIGHT."

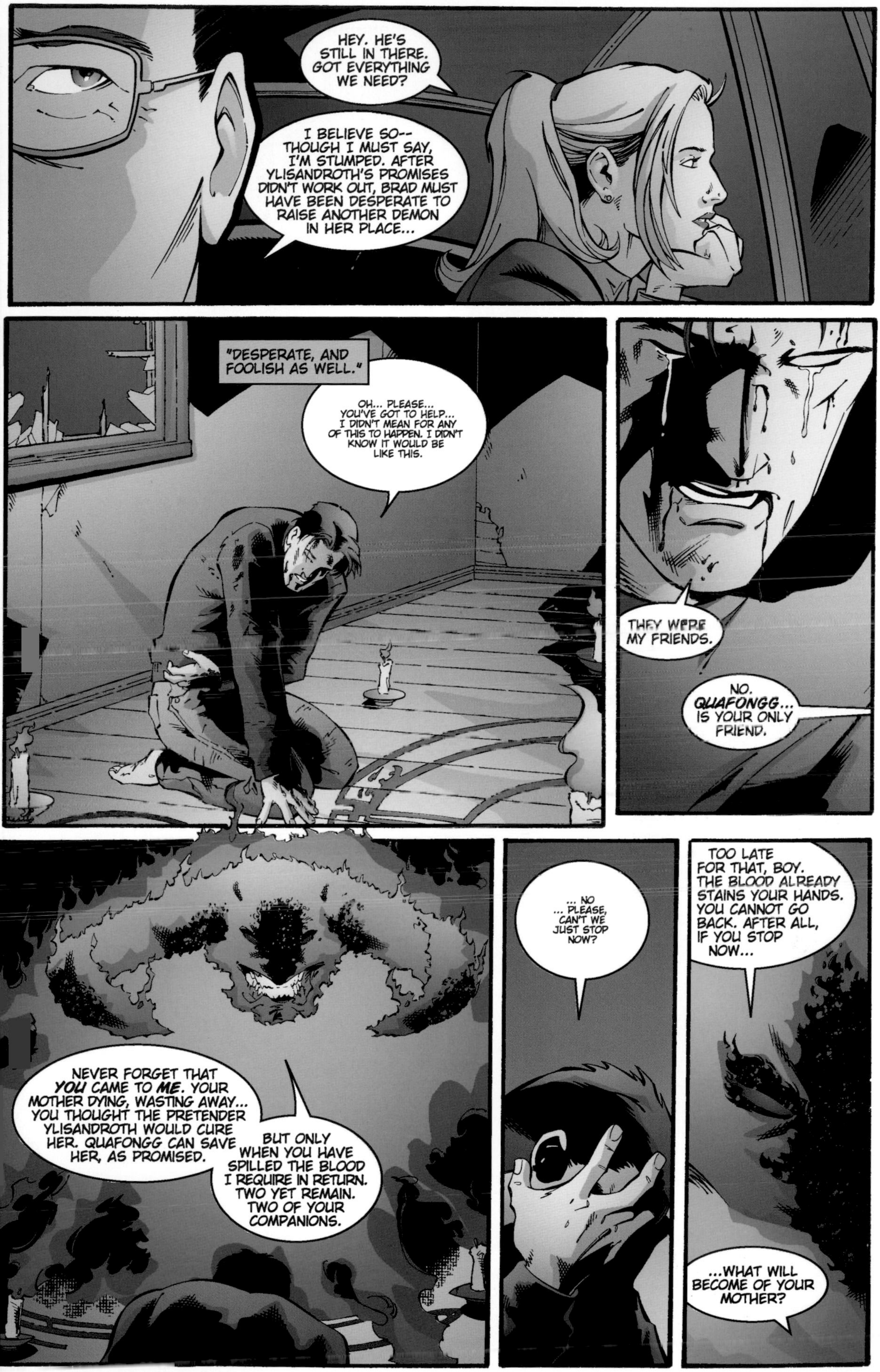
HEY. HE'S STILL IN THERE. GOT EVERYTHING WE NEED?
I BELIEVE SO-- THOUGH I MUST SAY, I'M STUMPED. AFTER YLISANDROTH'S PROMISES DIDN'T WORK OUT, BRAD MUST HAVE BEEN DESPERATE TO RAISE ANOTHER DEMON IN HER PLACE...
"DESPERATE, AND FOOLISH AS WELL."
OH... PLEASE... YOU'VE GOT TO HELP... I DIDN'T MEAN FOR ANY OF THIS TO HAPPEN. I DIDN'T KNOW IT WOULD BE LIKE THIS.
THEY WERE MY FRIENDS.
NO. QUAFONGG... IS YOUR ONLY FRIEND.
NEVER FORGET THAT YOU CAME TO ME. YOUR MOTHER DYING, WASTING AWAY... YOU THOUGHT THE PRETENDER YLISANDROTH WOULD CURE HER. QUAFONGG CAN SAVE HER, AS PROMISED.
BUT ONLY WHEN YOU HAVE SPILLED THE BLOOD I REQUIRE IN RETURN. TWO YET REMAIN. TWO OF YOUR COMPANIONS.
... NO ... PLEASE, CAN'T WE JUST STOP NOW?
TOO LATE FOR THAT, BOY. THE BLOOD ALREADY STAINS YOUR HANDS. YOU CANNOT GO BACK. AFTER ALL, IF YOU STOP NOW...
...WHAT WILL BECOME OF YOUR MOTHER?

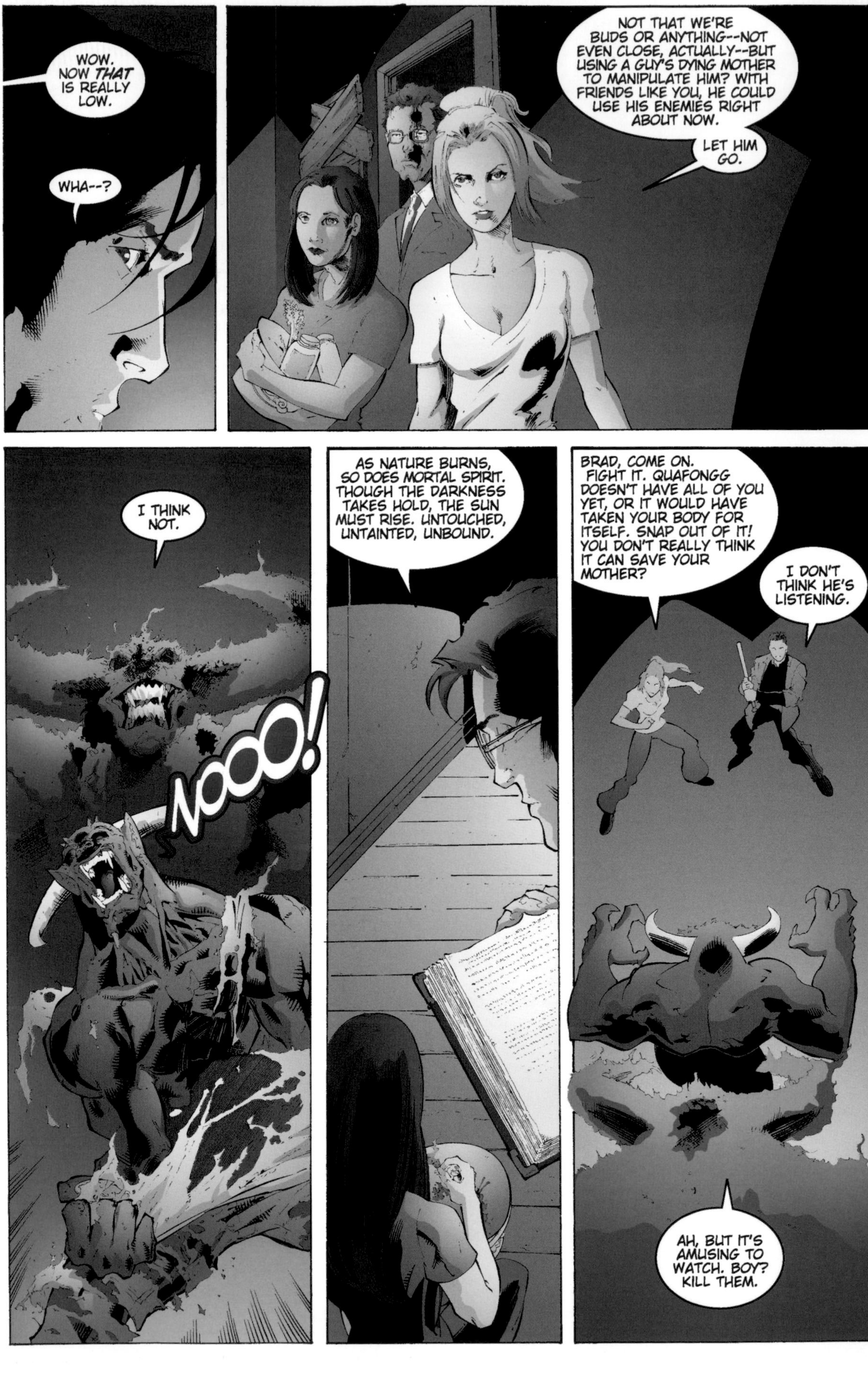
WOW. NOW THAT IS REALLY LOW.
WHA--?
NOT THAT WE'RE BUDS OR ANYTHING--NOT EVEN CLOSE, ACTUALLY--BUT USING A GUY'S DYING MOTHER TO MANIPULATE HIM? WITH FRIENDS LIKE YOU, HE COULD USE HIS ENEMIES RIGHT ABOUT NOW.
LET HIM GO.
I THINK NOT.
NOOO!
AS NATURE BURNS, SO DOES MORTAL SPIRIT. THOUGH THE DARKNESS TAKES HOLD, THE SUN MUST RISE. UNTOUCHED, UNTAINTED, UNBOUND.
BRAD, COME ON. FIGHT IT. QUAFONGG DOESN'T HAVE ALL OF YOU YET, OR IT WOULD HAVE TAKEN YOUR BODY FOR ITSELF. SNAP OUT OF IT! YOU DON'T REALLY THINK IT CAN SAVE YOUR MOTHER?
I DON'T THINK HE'S LISTENING.
AH, BUT IT'S AMUSING TO WATCH. BOY? KILL THEM.

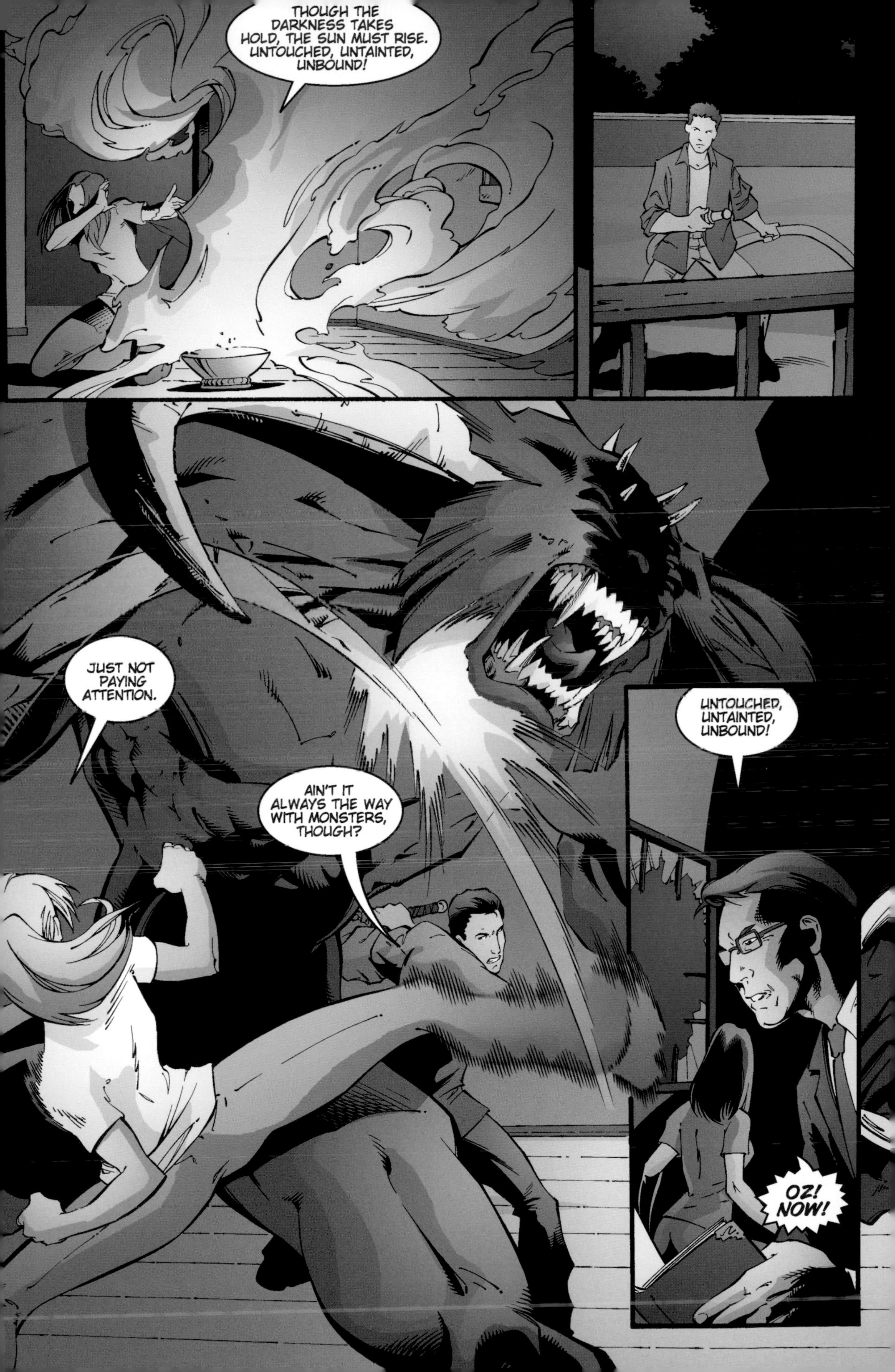
THOUGH THE DARKNESS TAKES HOLD, THE SUN MUST RISE. UNTOUCHED, UNTAINTED, UNBOUND!
JUST NOT PAYING ATTENTION.
AIN'T IT ALWAYS THE WAY WITH MONSTERS, THOUGH?
UNTOUCHED, UNTAINTED, UNBOUND!
OZ! NOW!

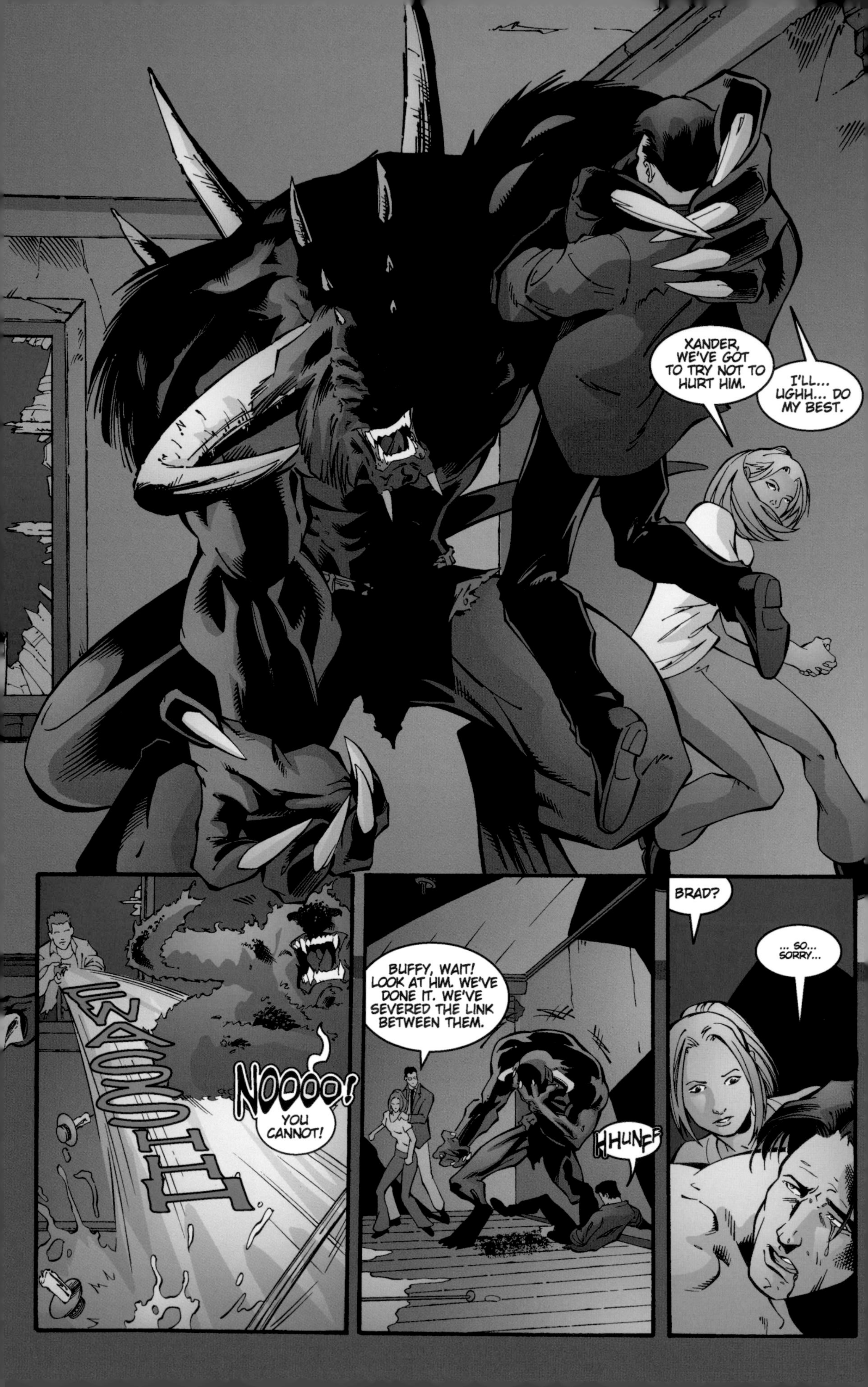
XANDER, WE'VE GOT TO TRY NOT TO HURT HIM.
I'LL... UGHH... DO MY BEST.
WHOOOSH
NOOOO! YOU CANNOT!
BUFFY, WAIT! LOOK AT HIM. WE'VE DONE IT. WE'VE SEVERED THE LINK BETWEEN THEM.
HHUNFF
BRAD?
... SO... SORRY...

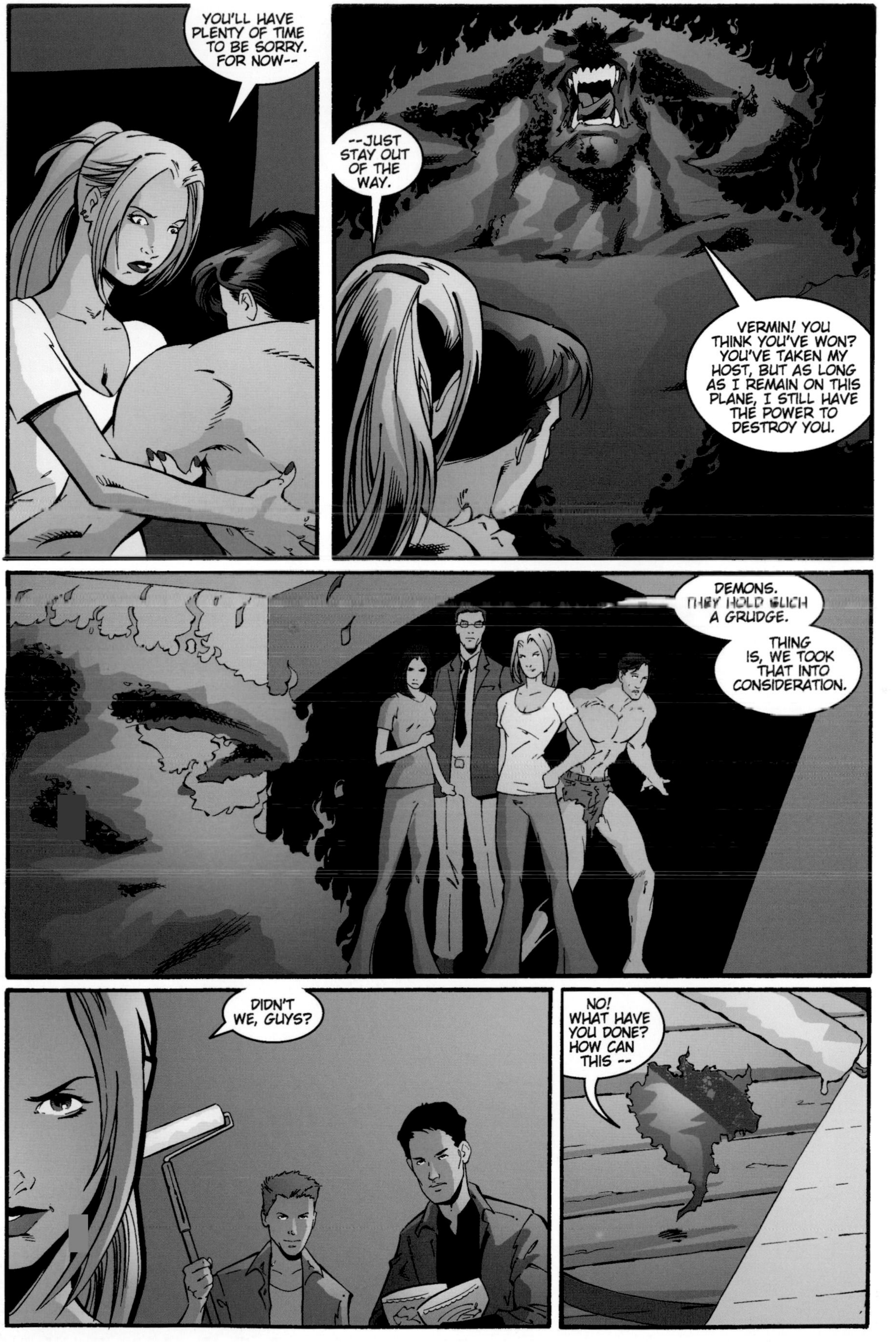
YOU'LL HAVE PLENTY OF TIME TO BE SORRY. FOR NOW--
--JUST STAY OUT OF THE WAY.
VERMIN! YOU THINK YOU'VE WON? YOU'VE TAKEN MY HOST, BUT AS LONG AS I REMAIN ON THIS PLANE, I STILL HAVE THE POWER TO DESTROY YOU.
DEMONS. THEY HOLD SUCH A GRUDGE.
THING IS, WE TOOK THAT INTO CONSIDERATION.
DIDN'T WE, GUYS?
NO! WHAT HAVE YOU DONE? HOW CAN THIS --

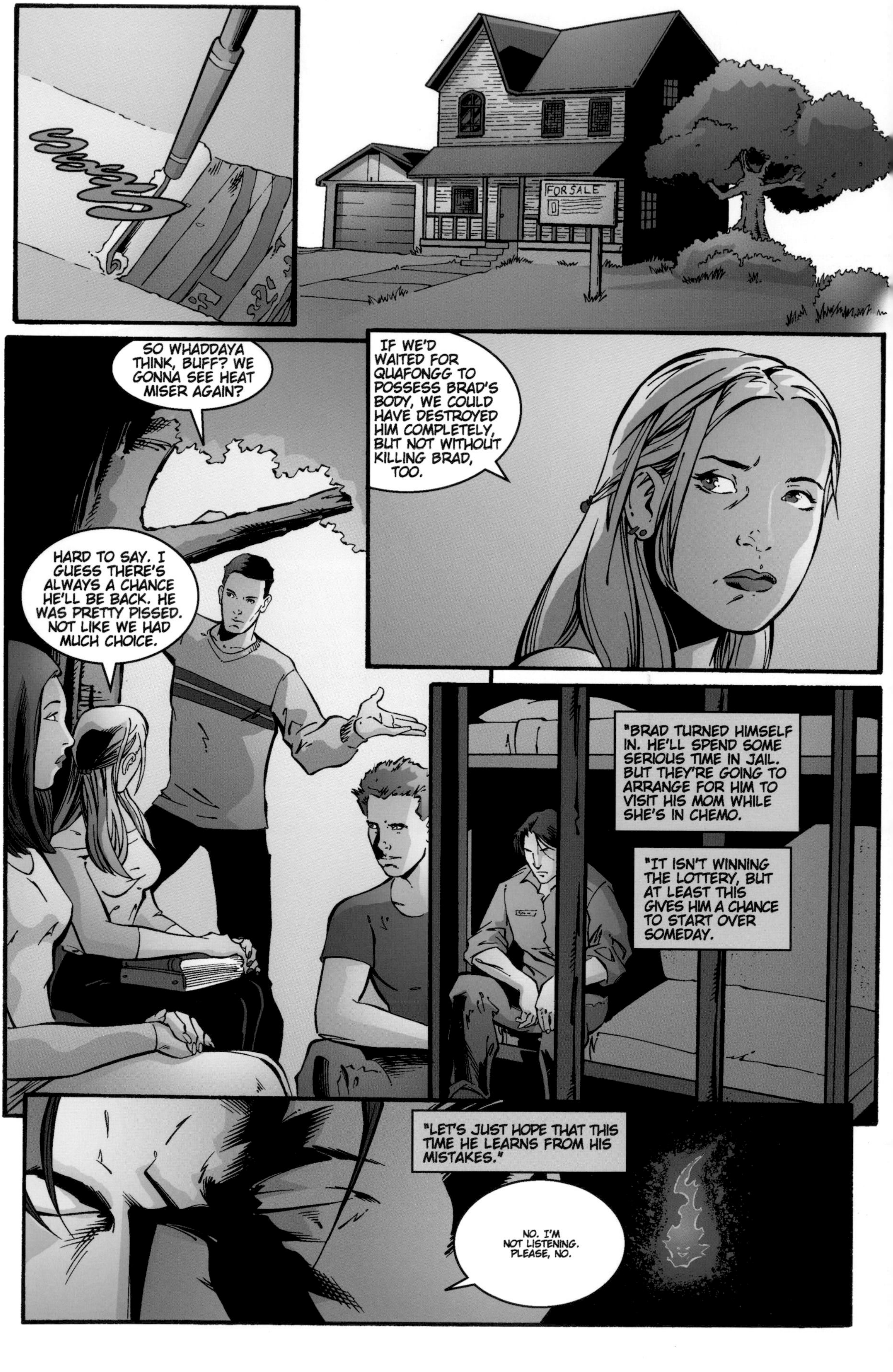
FOR SALE
SO WHADDAYA THINK, BUFF? WE GONNA SEE HEAT MISER AGAIN?
HARD TO SAY. I GUESS THERE'S ALWAYS A CHANCE HE'LL BE BACK. HE WAS PRETTY PISSED. NOT LIKE WE HAD MUCH CHOICE.
IF WE'D WAITED FOR QUAFONGG TO POSSESS BRAD'S BODY, WE COULD HAVE DESTROYED HIM COMPLETELY, BUT NOT WITHOUT KILLING BRAD, TOO.
"BRAD TURNED HIMSELF IN. HE'LL SPEND SOME SERIOUS TIME IN JAIL. BUT THEY'RE GOING TO ARRANGE FOR HIM TO VISIT HIS MOM WHILE SHE'S IN CHEMO.
"IT ISN'T WINNING THE LOTTERY, BUT AT LEAST THIS GIVES HIM A CHANCE TO START OVER SOMEDAY.
"LET'S JUST HOPE THAT THIS TIME HE LEARNS FROM HIS MISTAKES."
NO. I'M NOT LISTENING. PLEASE, NO.

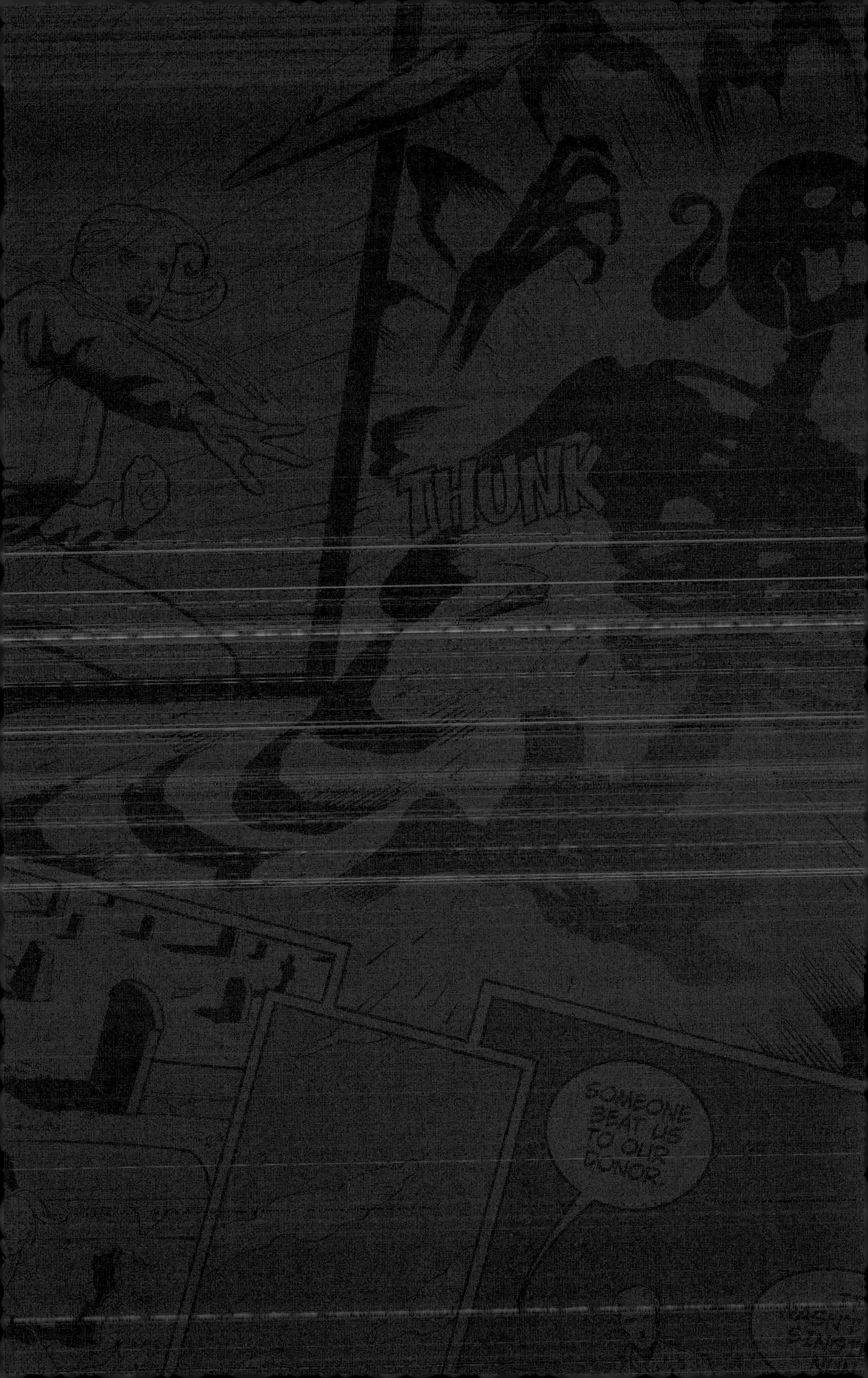
THUNK
SOMEONE BEAT US TO OUR DONOR.

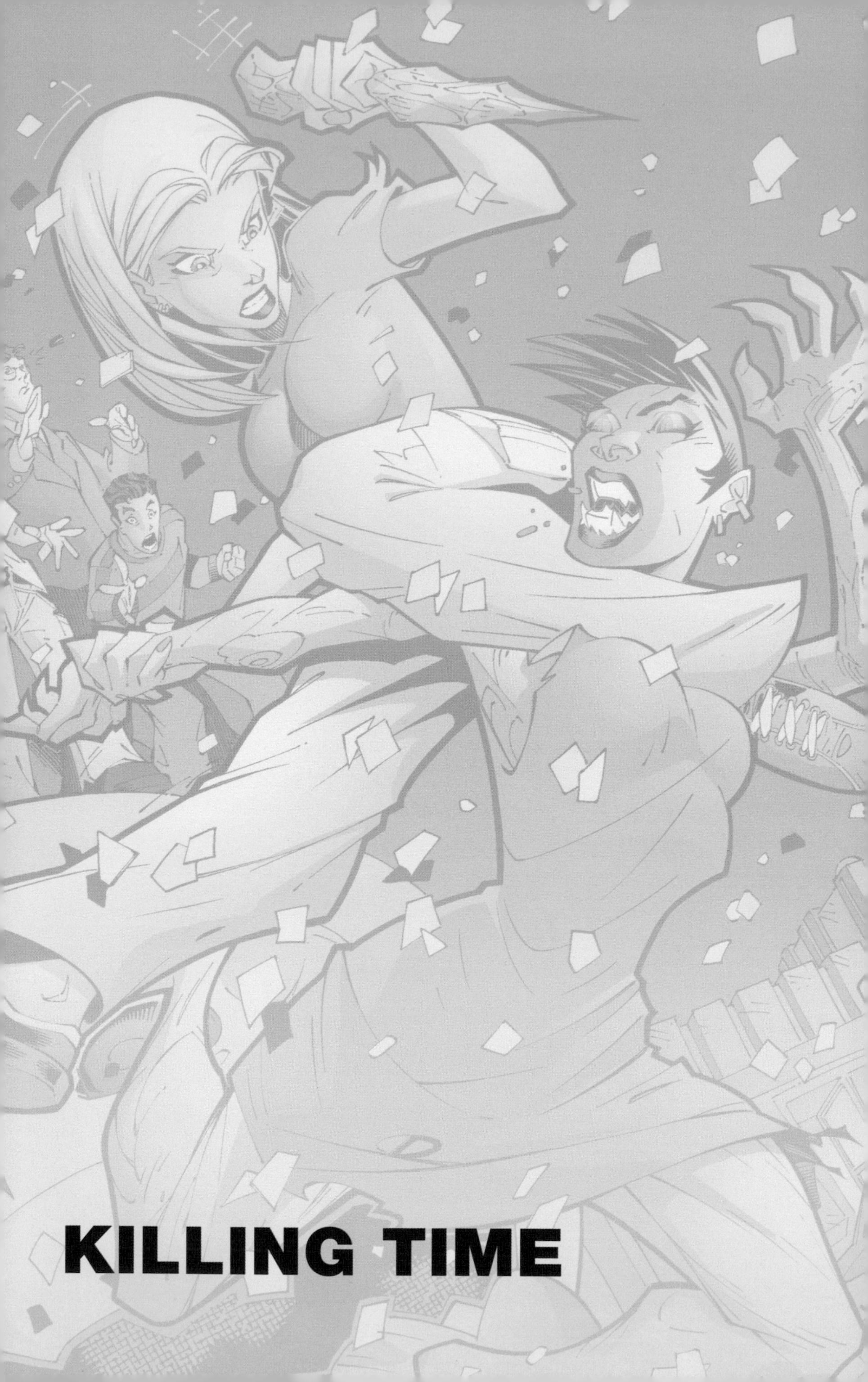

KILLING TIME

Buffy THE VAMPIRE SLAYER

KILLING TIME

TEN MINUTES AGO.

IS THIS LEGAL?

NO, IT'S STEALING. LOOK. THAT MUSEUM'S GOT LOTS OF STUFF--WHAT'S ONE MUSTY OLD NECKLACE?

YOU WANT TO DO THIS OR NOT?

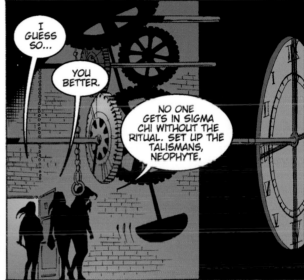

I GUESS SO...

YOU BETTER.

NO ONE GETS IN SIGMA CHI WITHOUT THE RITUAL. SET UP THE TALISMANS, NEOPHYTE.

I CALL UPON THEE RAGGINOR, KILLER OF TIME, ENTER THIS REALM AND FULFILL THE ... ...THIS IS DUMB.

I DON'T NEED YOUR CREEPY SORORITY AND ALL THIS GOTH CRAP. NONE OF THIS STUFF WORKS, ANY--

--WAY?

RRMMMBL!

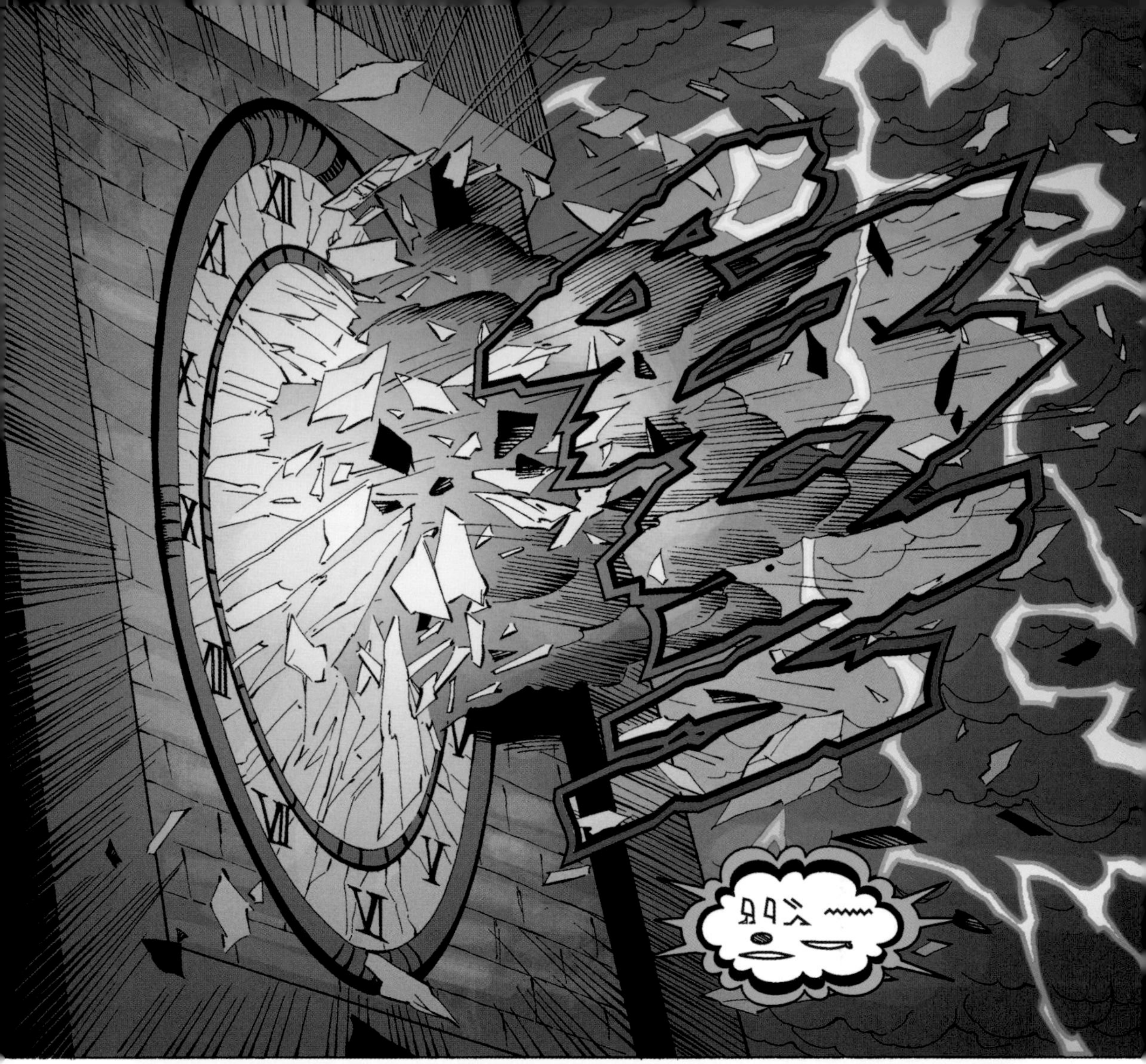

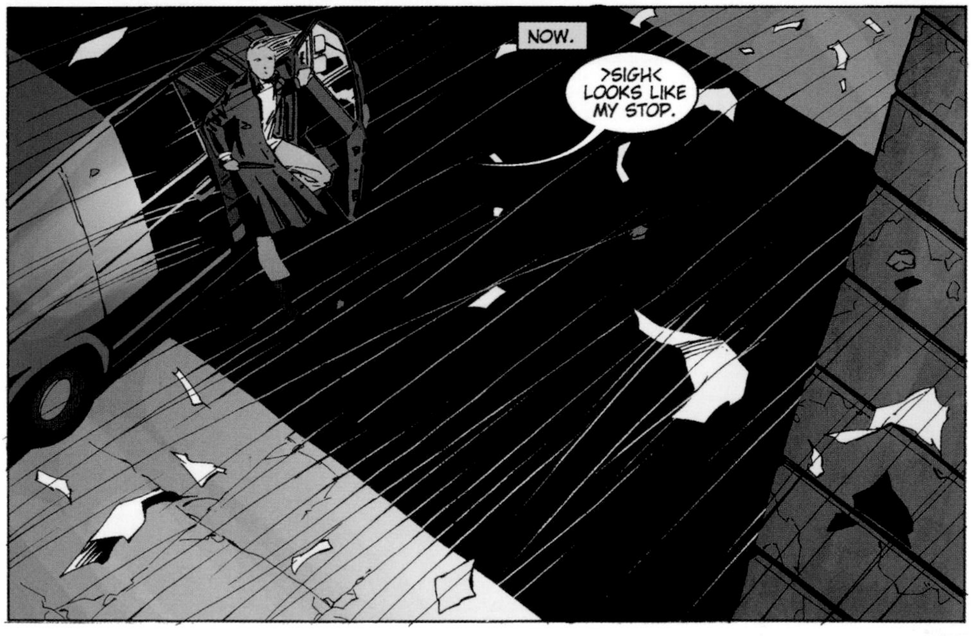
NOW.
>SIGH< LOOKS LIKE MY STOP.

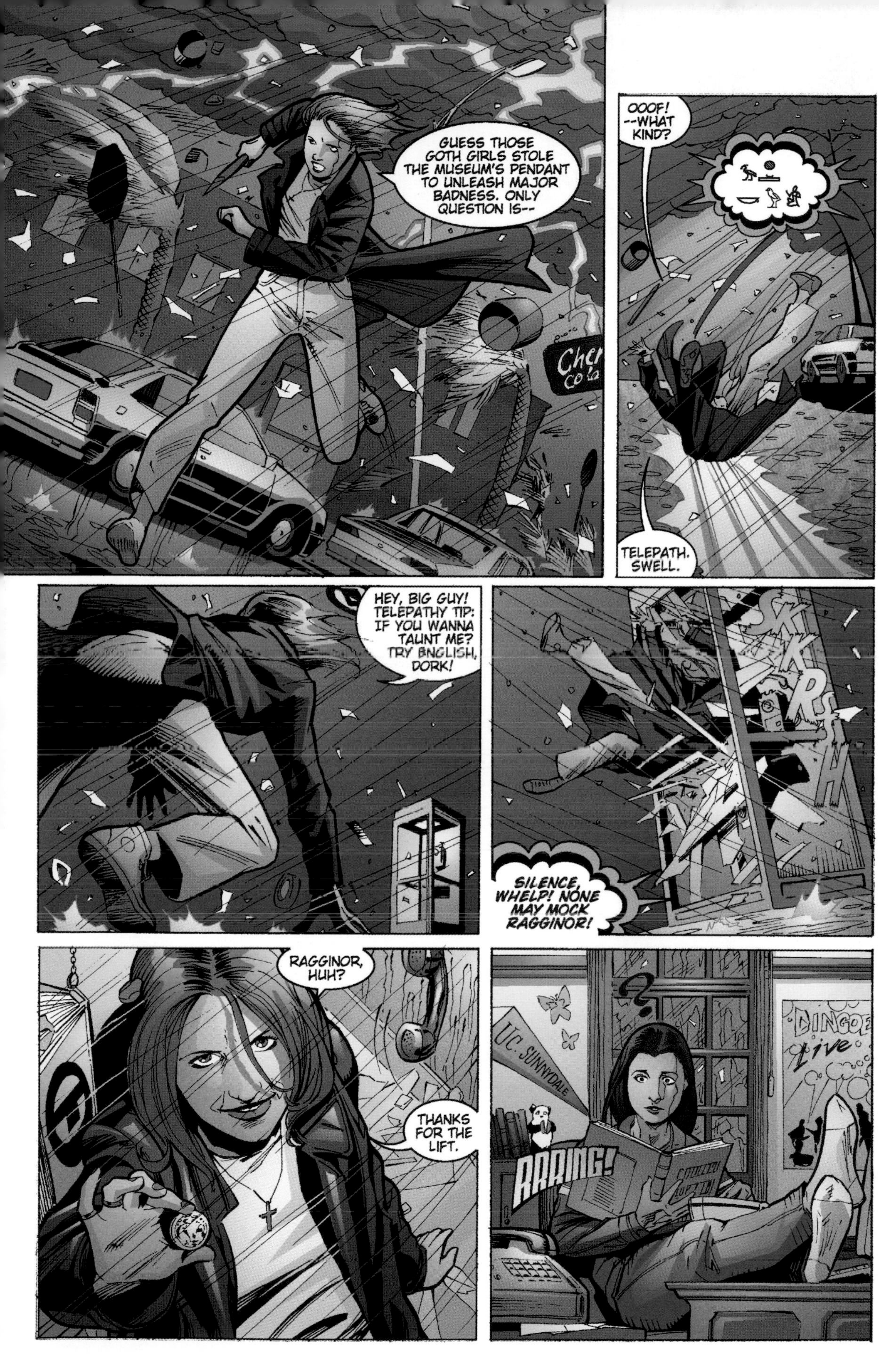
GUESS THOSE GOTH GIRLS STOLE THE MUSEUM'S PENDANT TO UNLEASH MAJOR BADNESS. ONLY QUESTION IS--
OOOF! --WHAT KIND?
TELEPATH. SWELL.
HEY, BIG GUY! TELEPATHY TIP: IF YOU WANNA TAUNT ME? TRY ENGLISH, DORK!
SKKRSSH
SILENCE, WHELP! NONE MAY MOCK RAGGINOR!
RAGGINOR, HUH?
THANKS FOR THE LIFT.
U.C. SUNNYDALE
DINGOES live
RRRING!

WILL? ME. WHAT DO WE KNOW ABOUT A DEMON NAMED RAGGINOR? I'M MORE THAN A LITTLE CURIOUS HERE.

RAGGINOR? OOH. BAD BOY. CONJURE HIM NEAR A CLOCK, HE TAKES FORM AT MIDNIGHT, AND, UH... ENDS ALL TIME AS WE KNOW IT.

FUN. HOW DO I SLAY HIM?

YOU CAN'T.

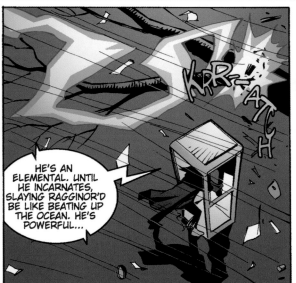

KRR-ATCH

HE'S AN ELEMENTAL. UNTIL HE INCARNATES, SLAYING RAGGINOR'D BE LIKE BEATING UP THE OCEAN. HE'S POWERFUL...

...BUT DUMB. THINKS THE CLOCK IS TIME ITSELF. SO STOP THE CLOCK...

...YOU STOP THE--

SHKWAKK!

KRRASSH!!

--END OF ALL TIME. MAYBE.

11:58 PM

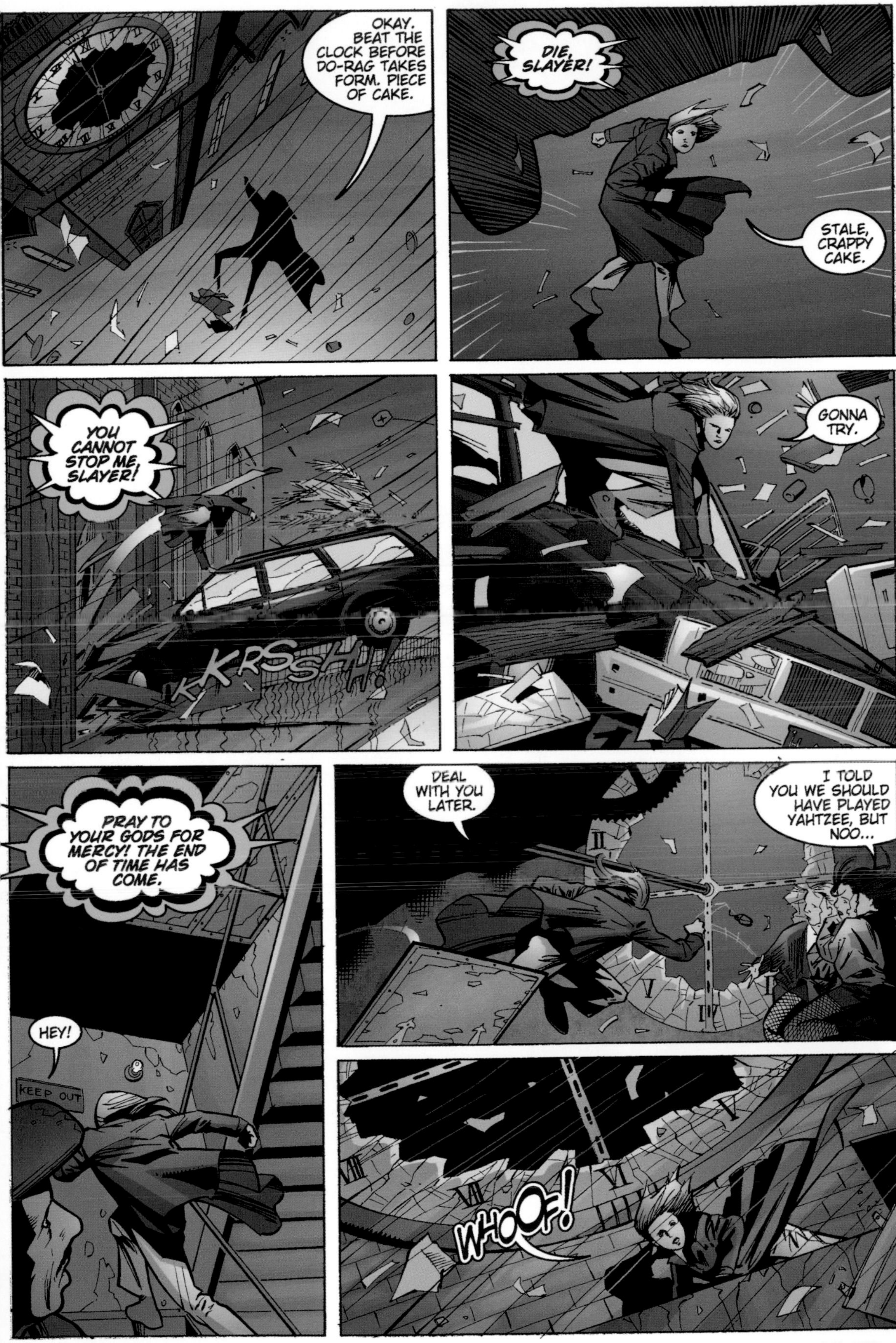
OKAY. BEAT THE CLOCK BEFORE DO-RAG TAKES FORM. PIECE OF CAKE.
DIE, SLAYER!
STALE, CRAPPY CAKE.
YOU CANNOT STOP ME, SLAYER!
KKRSSHH!
GONNA TRY.
PRAY TO YOUR GODS FOR MERCY! THE END OF TIME HAS COME.
HEY!
KEEP OUT
DEAL WITH YOU LATER.
I TOLD YOU WE SHOULD HAVE PLAYED YAHTZEE, BUT NOO...
WHOOF!

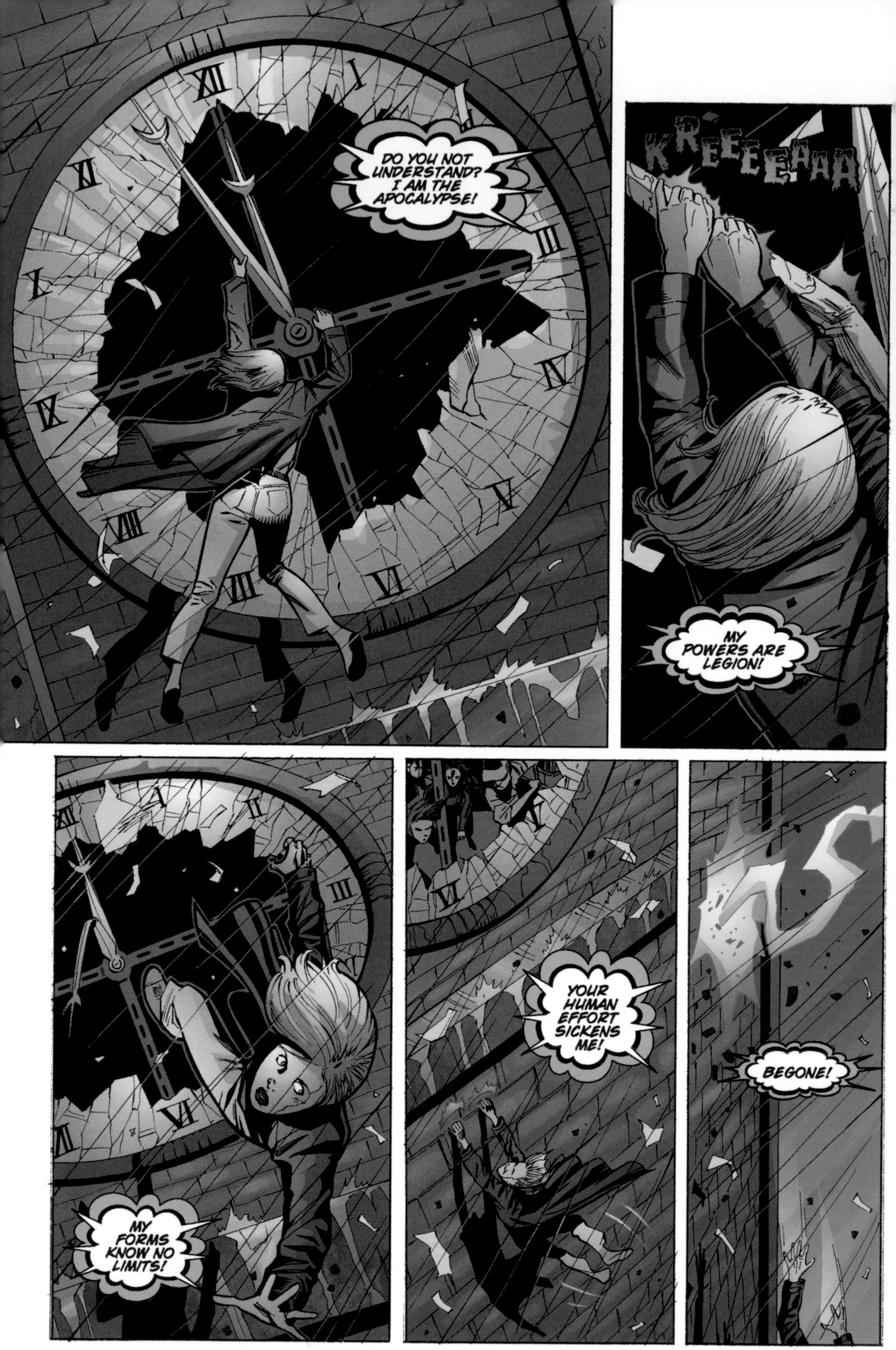
DO YOU NOT UNDERSTAND? I AM THE APOCALYPSE!
KREEEEAAA
MY POWERS ARE LEGION!
MY FORMS KNOW NO LIMITS!
YOUR HUMAN EFFORT SICKENS ME!
BEGONE!

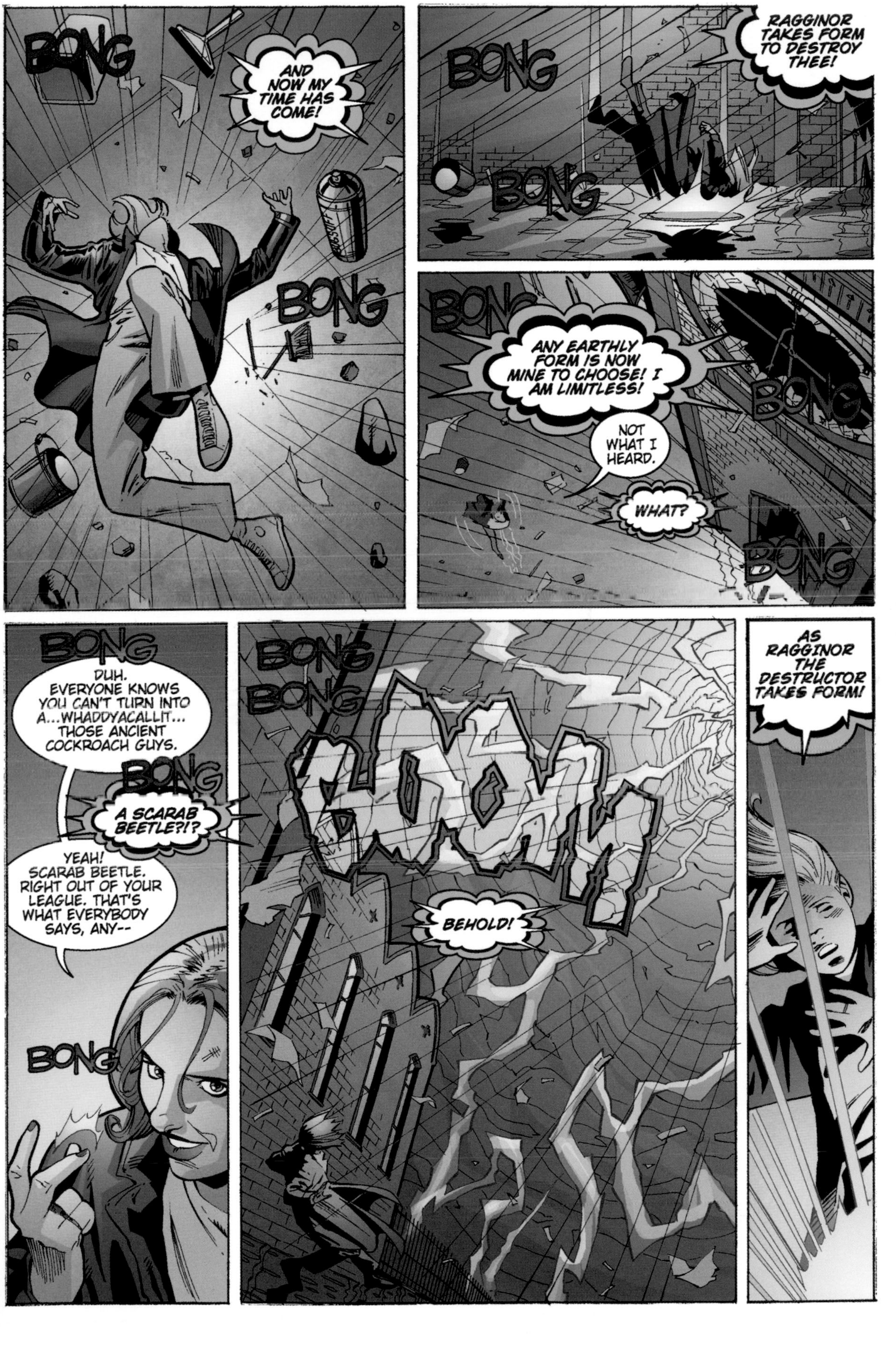
BONG
AND NOW MY TIME HAS COME!
BONG
BONG
BONG
RAGGINOR TAKES FORM TO DESTROY THEE!
BONG
BONG
ANY EARTHLY FORM IS NOW MINE TO CHOOSE! I AM LIMITLESS!
NOT WHAT I HEARD.
WHAT?
BONG
BONG
DUH. EVERYONE KNOWS YOU CAN'T TURN INTO A...WHADDYACALLIT... THOSE ANCIENT COCKROACH GUYS.
BONG
A SCARAB BEETLE?!?
YEAH! SCARAB BEETLE. RIGHT OUT OF YOUR LEAGUE. THAT'S WHAT EVERYBODY SAYS, ANY--
BONG
BONG
BONG
BEHOLD!
AS RAGGINOR THE DESTRUCTOR TAKES FORM!

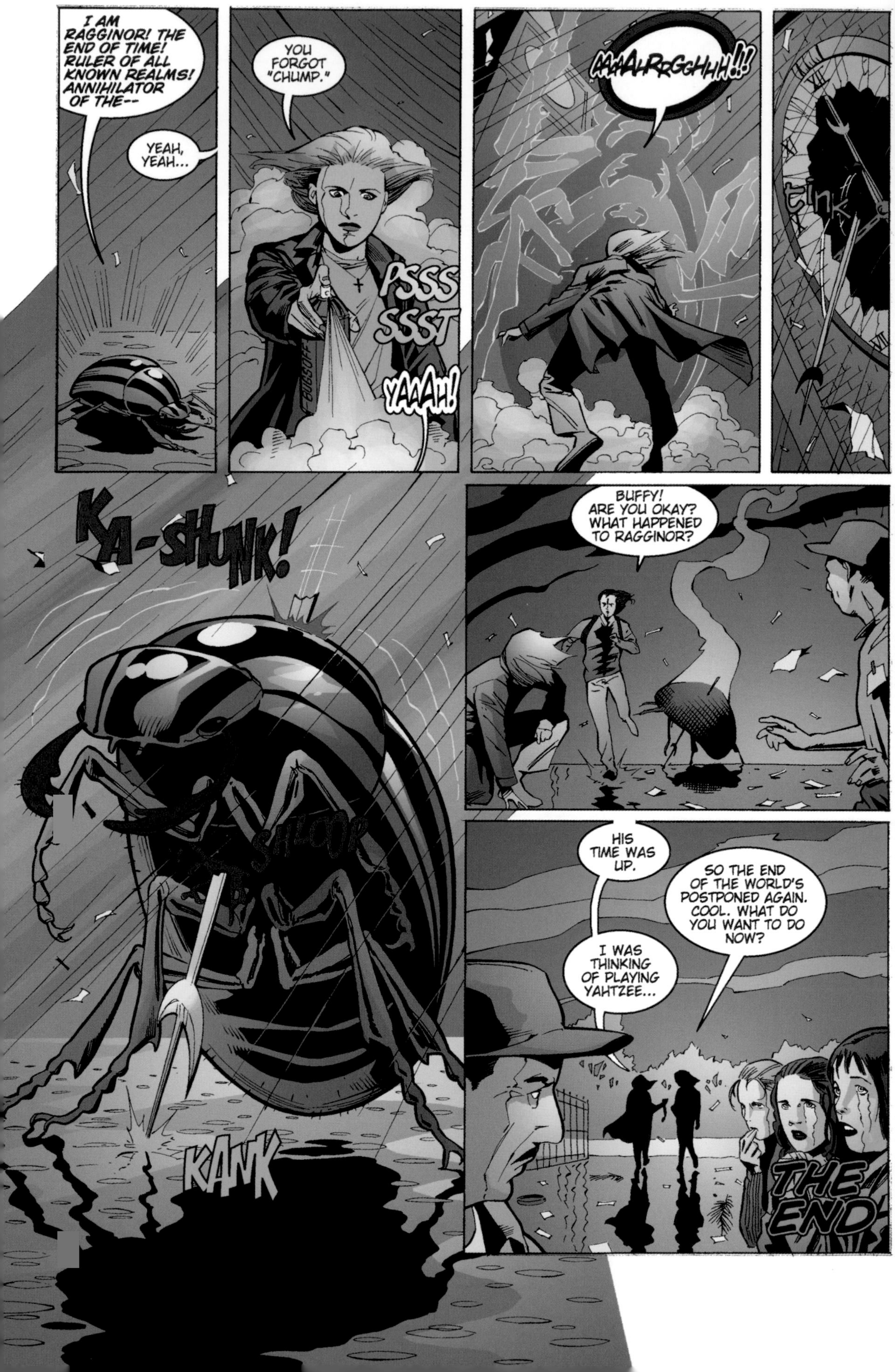
I AM RAGGINOR! THE END OF TIME! RULER OF ALL KNOWN REALMS! ANNIHILATOR OF THE--
YEAH, YEAH...
YOU FORGOT "CHUMP."
PSSSSSST
YAAAH!
AAAAAARRGGHHH!!!
tink
KA-SHUNK!
SHLOOP
KANK
BUFFY! ARE YOU OKAY? WHAT HAPPENED TO RAGGINOR?
HIS TIME WAS UP.
SO THE END OF THE WORLD'S POSTPONED AGAIN. COOL. WHAT DO YOU WANT TO DO NOW?
I WAS THINKING OF PLAYING YAHTZEE...
THE END

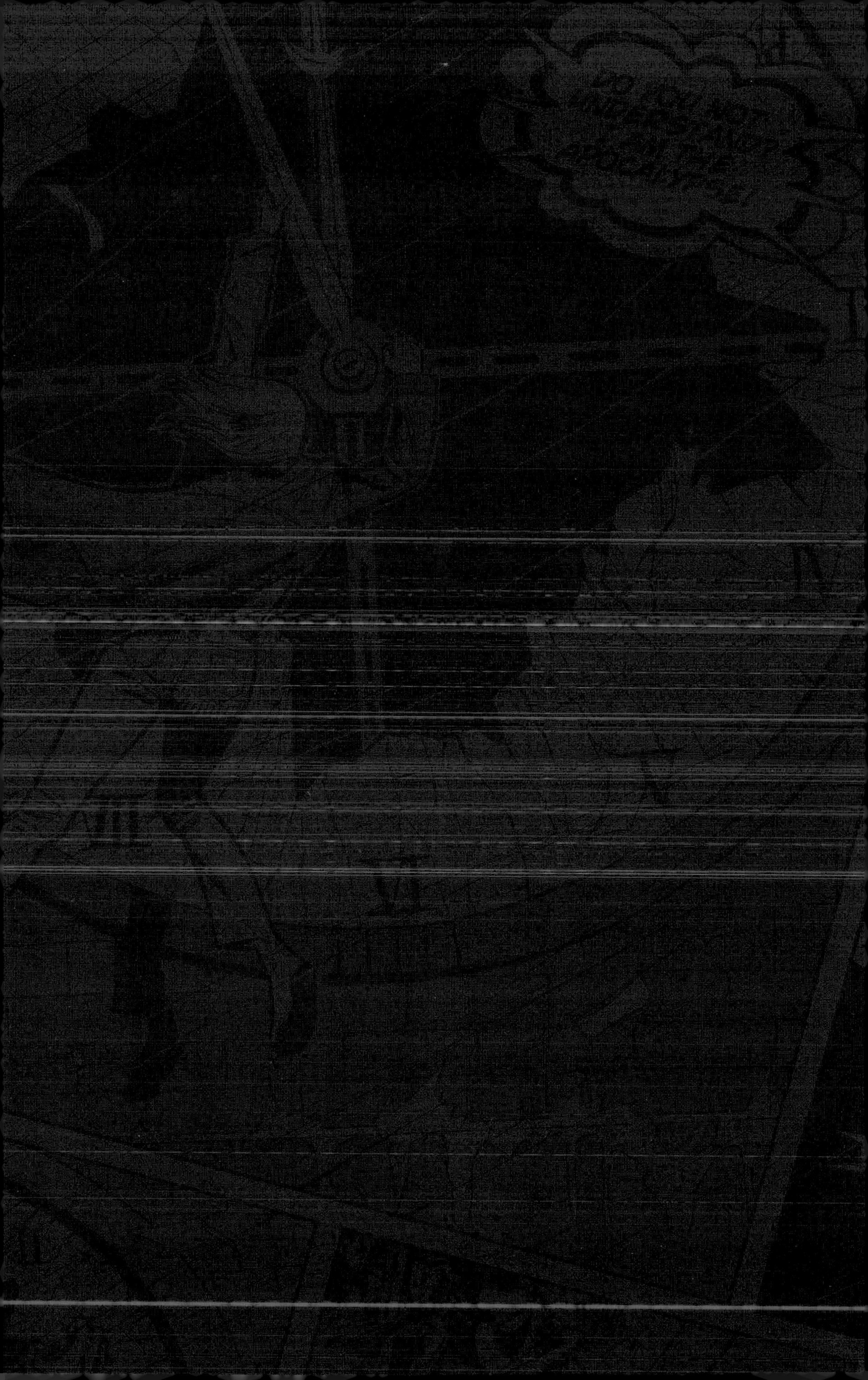

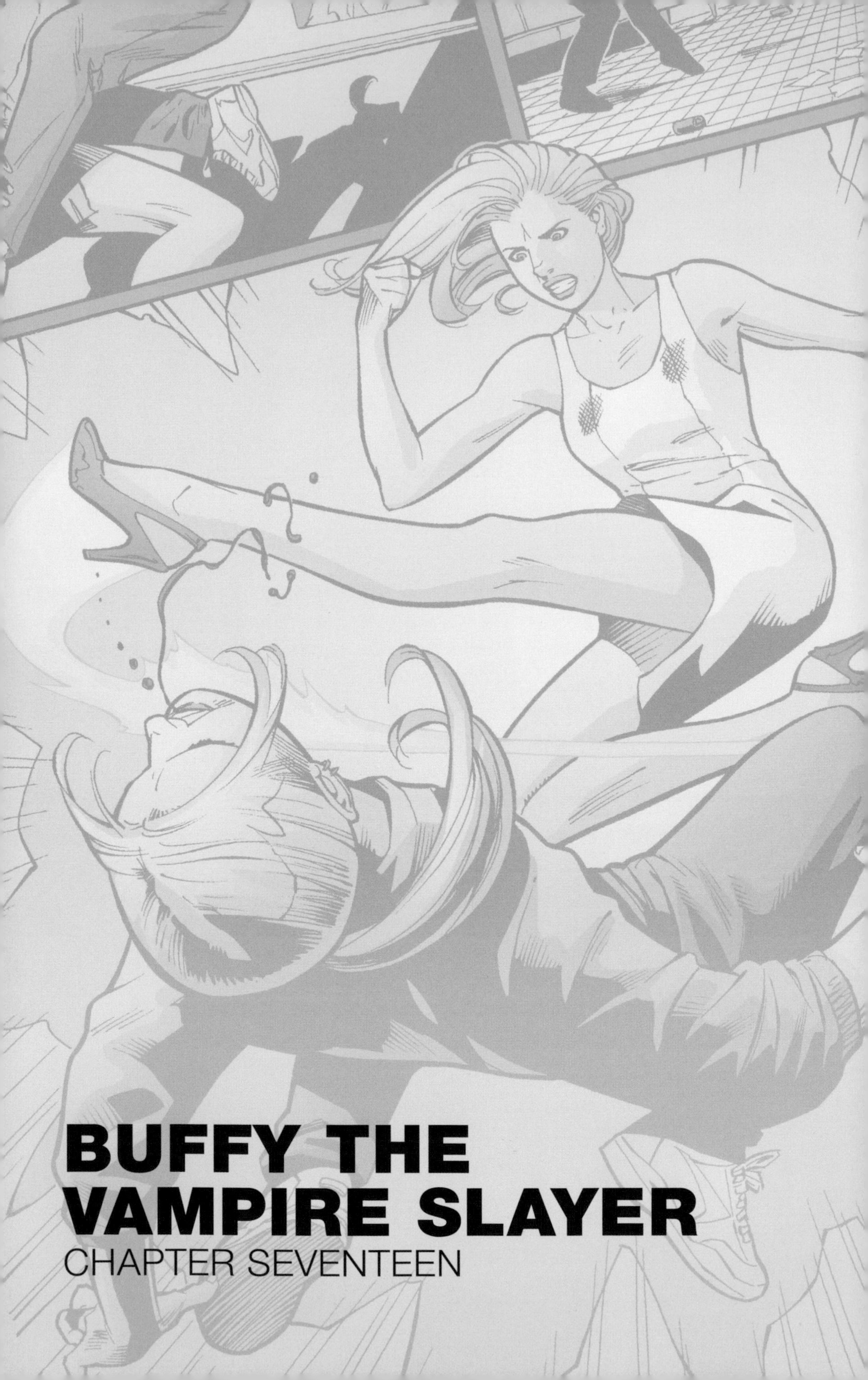

BUFFY THE VAMPIRE SLAYER
CHAPTER SEVENTEEN

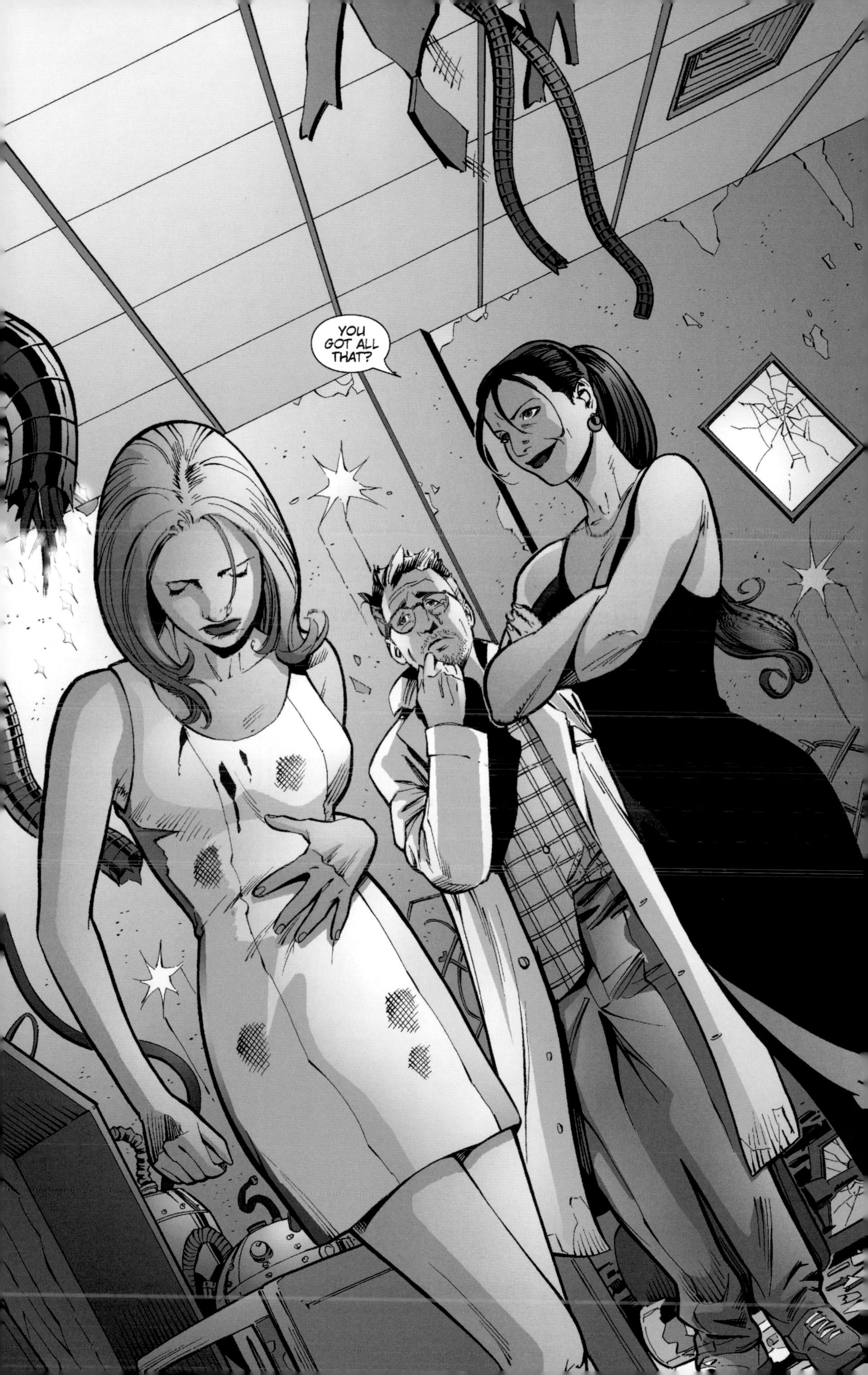
YOU GOT ALL THAT?

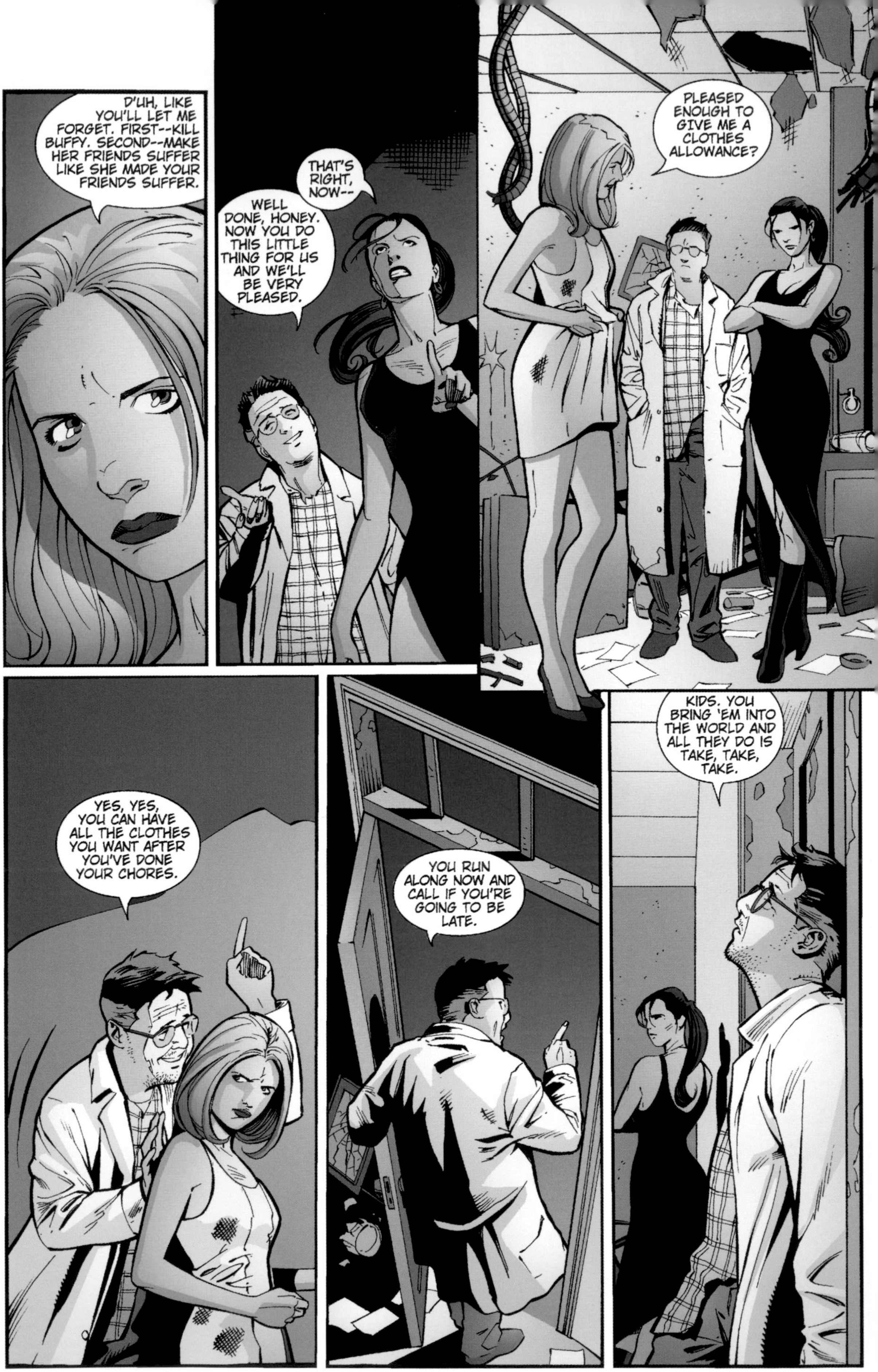
D'UH, LIKE YOU'LL LET ME FORGET. FIRST--KILL BUFFY. SECOND--MAKE HER FRIENDS SUFFER LIKE SHE MADE YOUR FRIENDS SUFFER.
THAT'S RIGHT, NOW--
WELL DONE, HONEY. NOW YOU DO THIS LITTLE THING FOR US AND WE'LL BE VERY PLEASED.
PLEASED ENOUGH TO GIVE ME A CLOTHES ALLOWANCE?
YES, YES, YOU CAN HAVE ALL THE CLOTHES YOU WANT AFTER YOU'VE DONE YOUR CHORES.
YOU RUN ALONG NOW AND CALL IF YOU'RE GOING TO BE LATE.
KIDS. YOU BRING 'EM INTO THE WORLD AND ALL THEY DO IS TAKE, TAKE, TAKE.

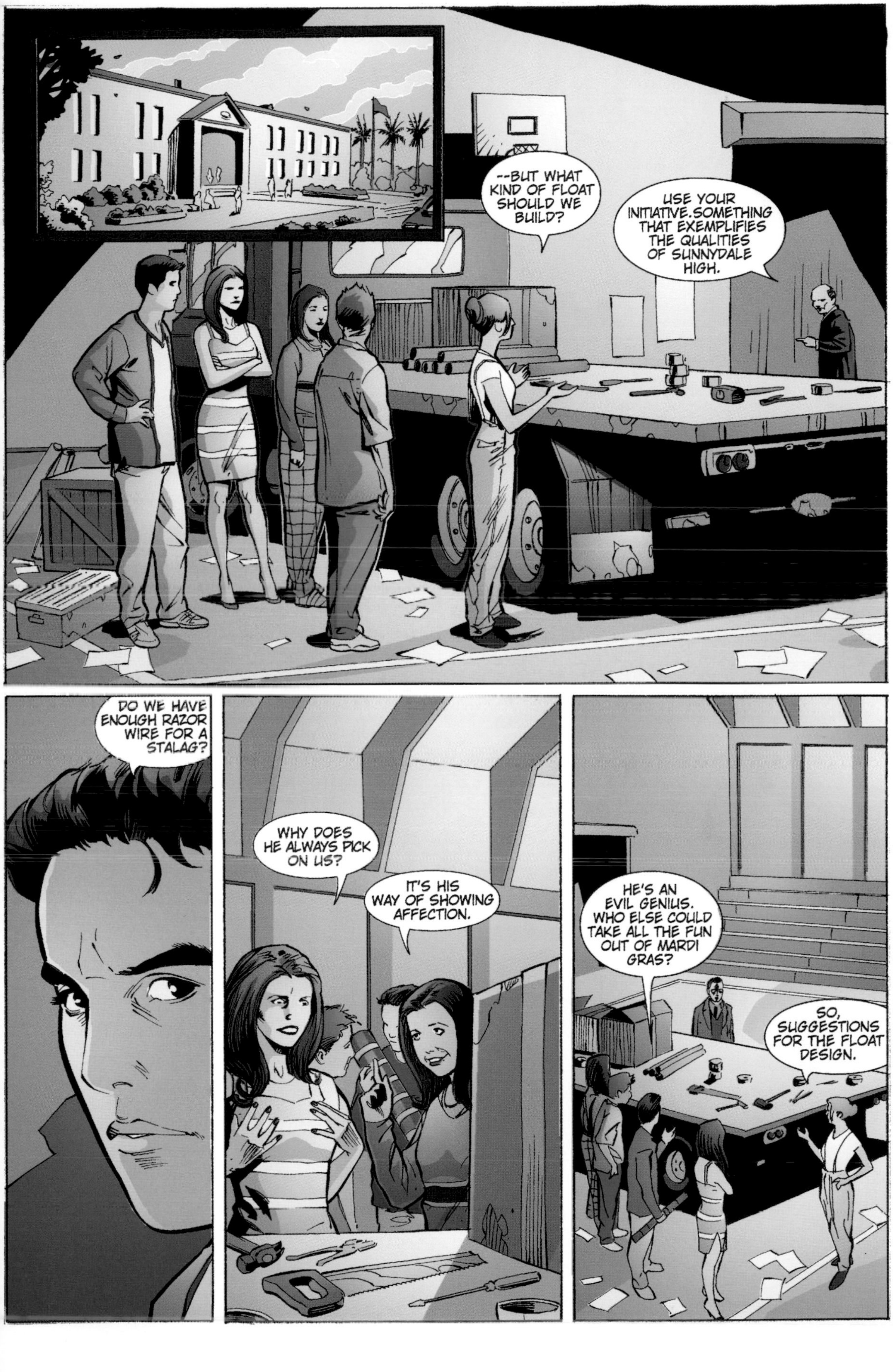
--BUT WHAT KIND OF FLOAT SHOULD WE BUILD?
USE YOUR INITIATIVE.SOMETHING THAT EXEMPLIFIES THE QUALITIES OF SUNNYDALE HIGH.
DO WE HAVE ENOUGH RAZOR WIRE FOR A STALAG?
WHY DOES HE ALWAYS PICK ON US?
IT'S HIS WAY OF SHOWING AFFECTION.
HE'S AN EVIL GENIUS. WHO ELSE COULD TAKE ALL THE FUN OUT OF MARDI GRAS?
SO, SUGGESTIONS FOR THE FLOAT DESIGN.

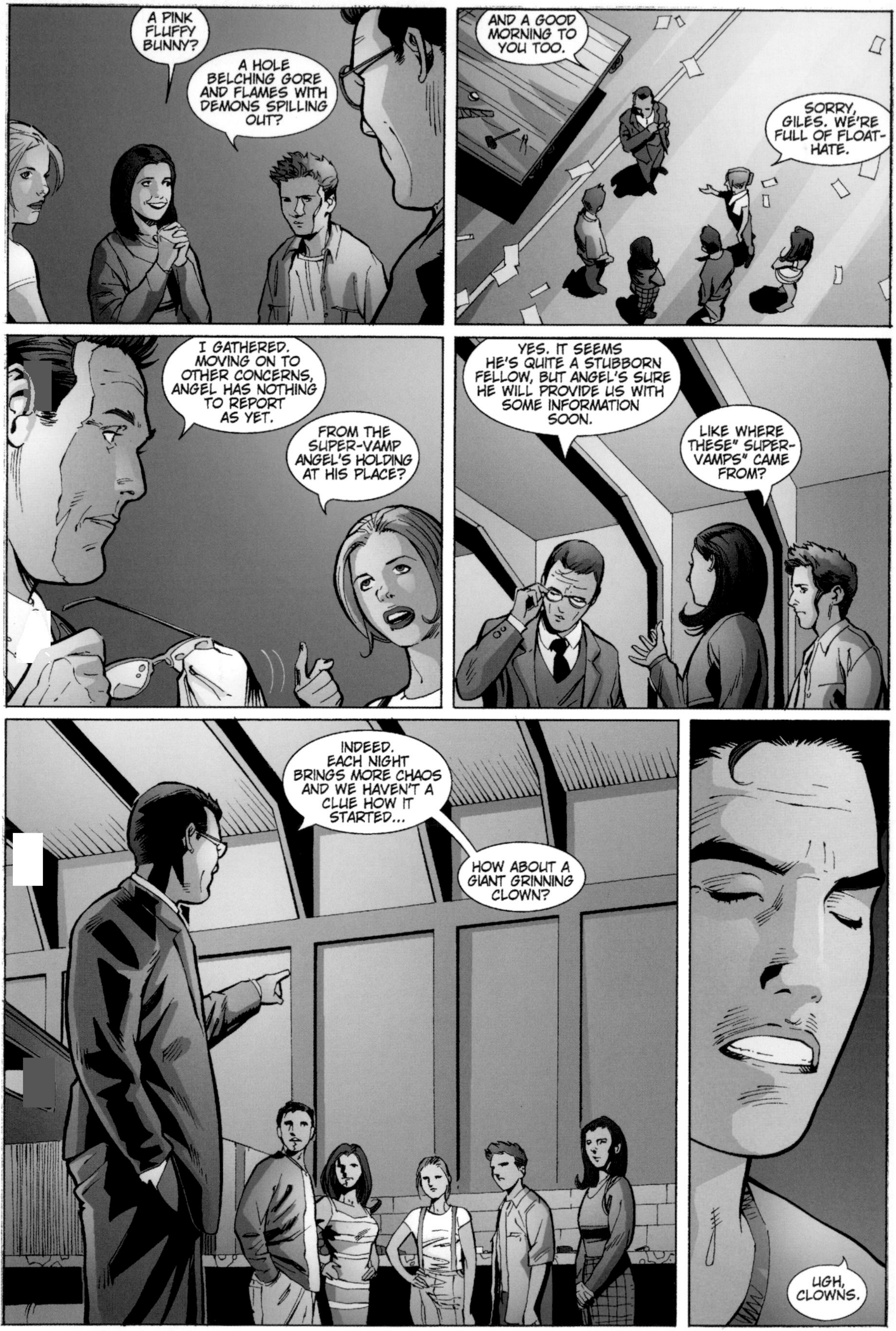

A PINK FLUFFY BUNNY?
A HOLE BELCHING GORE AND FLAMES WITH DEMONS SPILLING OUT?
AND A GOOD MORNING TO YOU TOO.
SORRY, GILES. WE'RE FULL OF FLOAT-HATE.
I GATHERED. MOVING ON TO OTHER CONCERNS, ANGEL HAS NOTHING TO REPORT AS YET.
FROM THE SUPER-VAMP ANGEL'S HOLDING AT HIS PLACE?
YES. IT SEEMS HE'S QUITE A STUBBORN FELLOW, BUT ANGEL'S SURE HE WILL PROVIDE US WITH SOME INFORMATION SOON.
LIKE WHERE THESE" SUPER-VAMPS" CAME FROM?
INDEED. EACH NIGHT BRINGS MORE CHAOS AND WE HAVEN'T A CLUE HOW IT STARTED...
HOW ABOUT A GIANT GRINNING CLOWN?
UGH, CLOWNS.

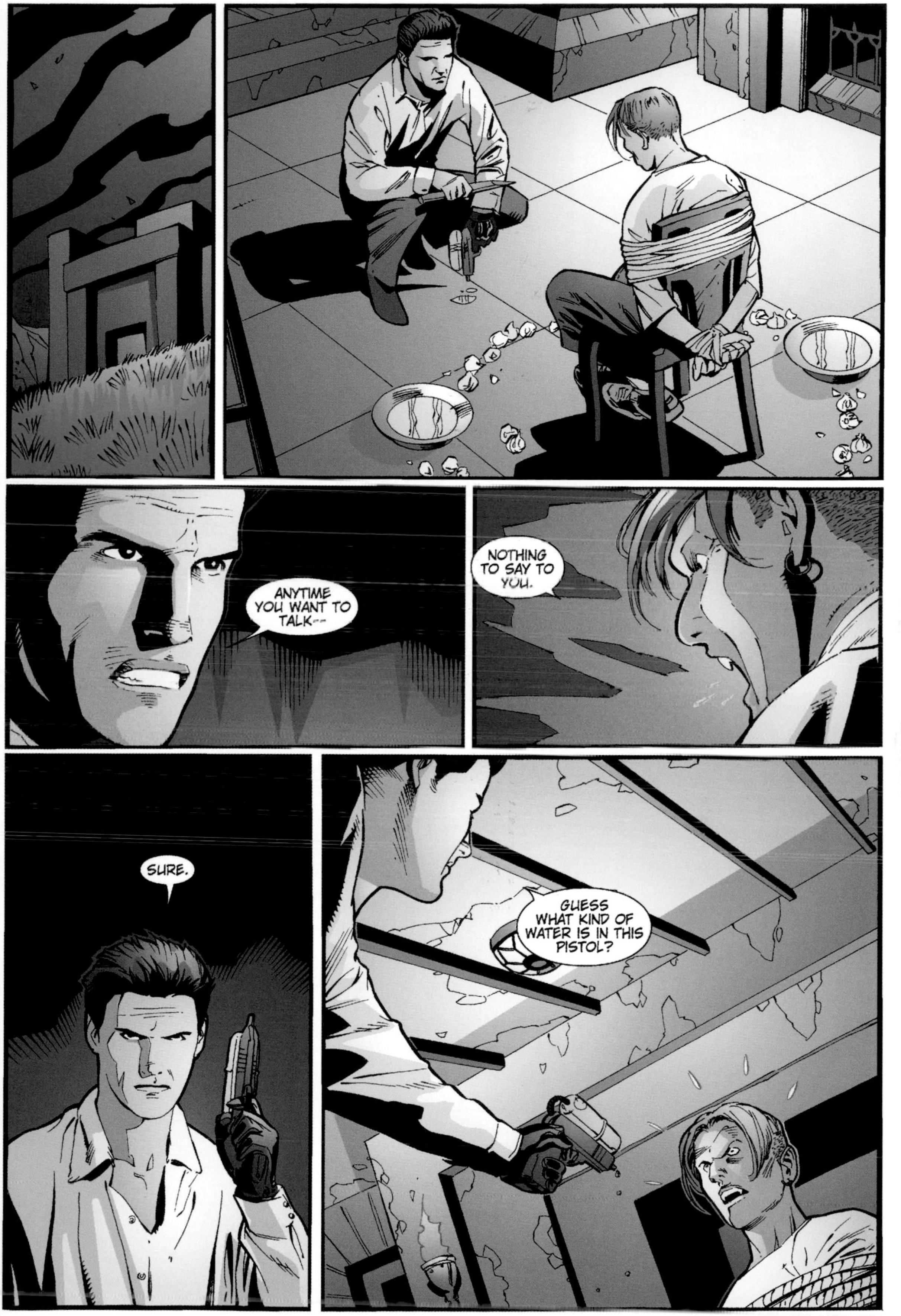
ANYTIME YOU WANT TO TALK--
NOTHING TO SAY TO YOU.
SURE.
GUESS WHAT KIND OF WATER IS IN THIS PISTOL?

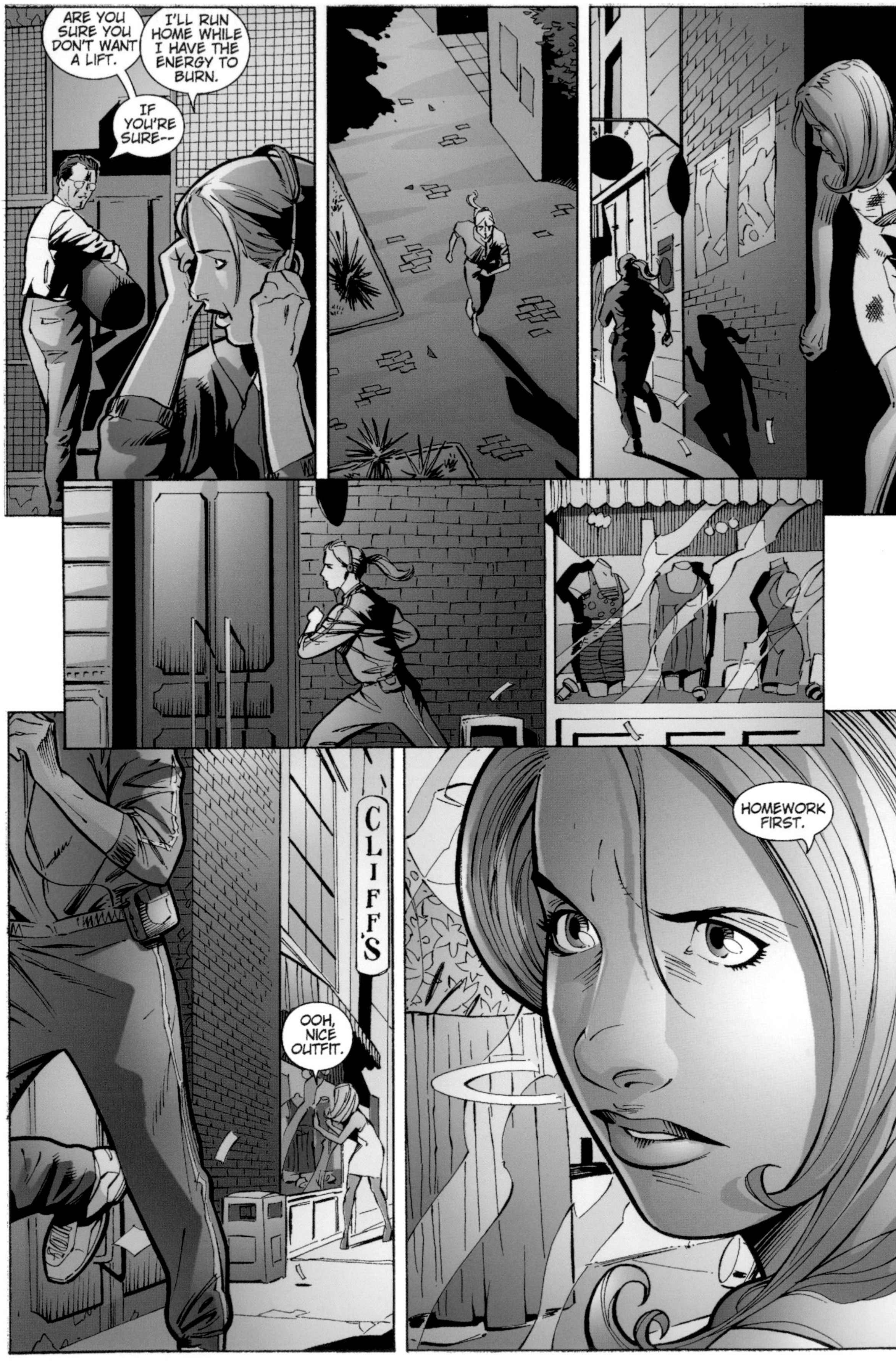
ARE YOU SURE YOU DON'T WANT A LIFT.
I'LL RUN HOME WHILE I HAVE THE ENERGY TO BURN.
IF YOU'RE SURE--
CLIFF'S
OOH, NICE OUTFIT.
HOMEWORK FIRST.

A TOAST TO A DEAD SLAYER.

TASTES LIKE HELL.

SOMETHING ISN'T RIGHT.

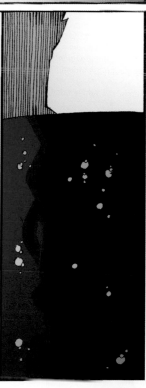

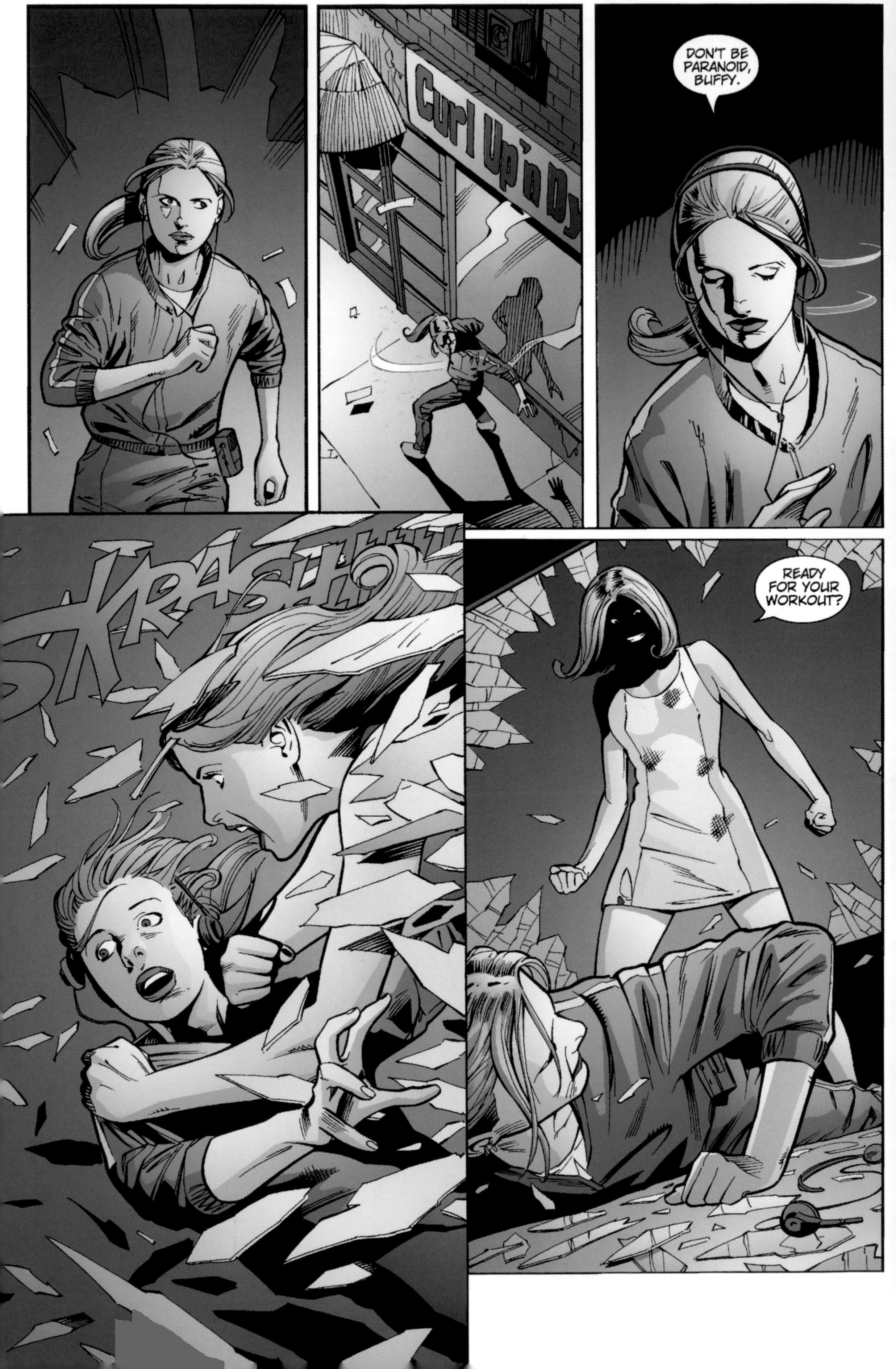
Curl Up 'n Dy
DON'T BE PARANOID, BUFFY.
SKRASH
READY FOR YOUR WORKOUT?

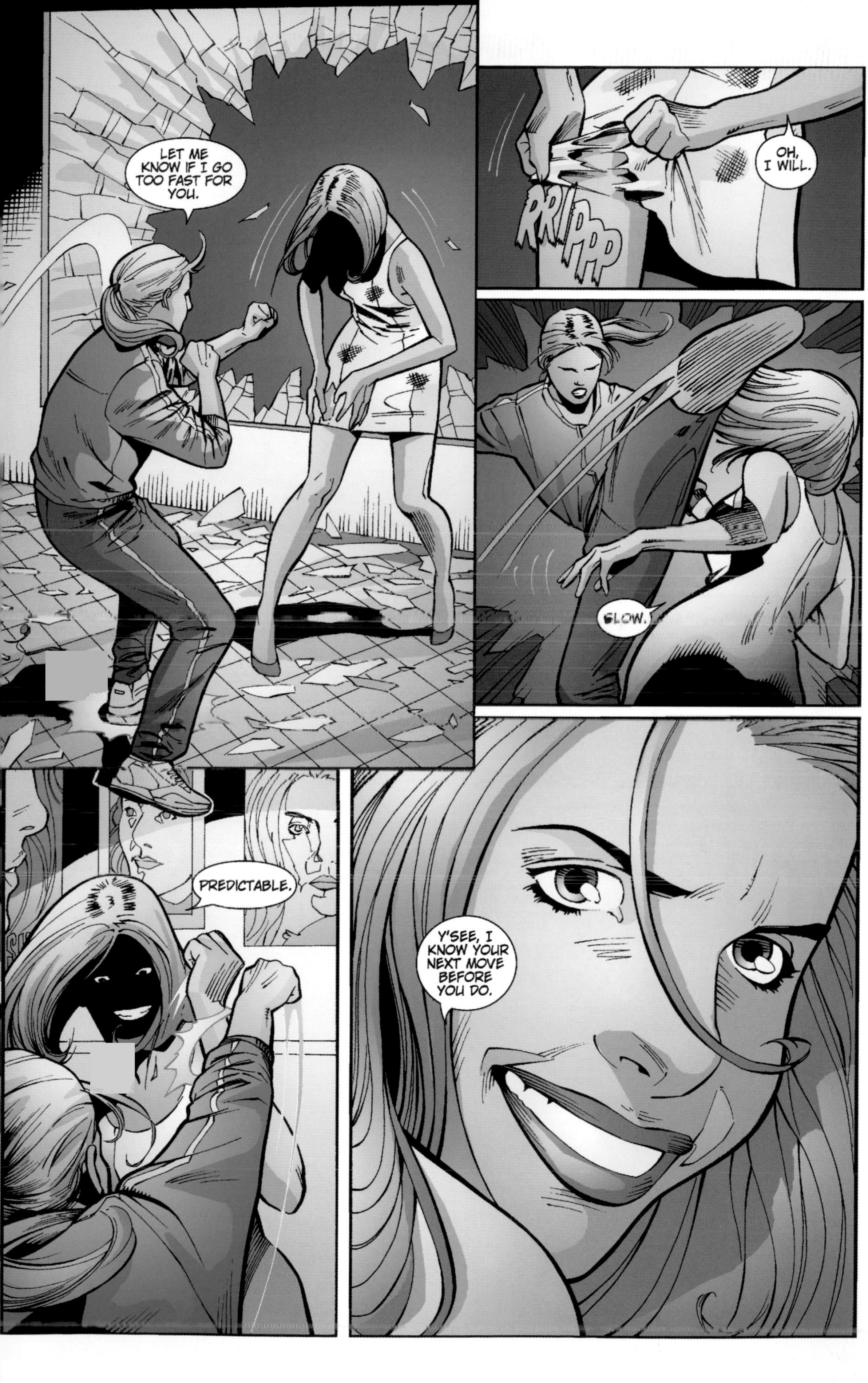
LET ME KNOW IF I GO TOO FAST FOR YOU.
RRIPPP
OH, I WILL.
SLOW.
PREDICTABLE.
Y'SEE, I KNOW YOUR NEXT MOVE BEFORE YOU DO.

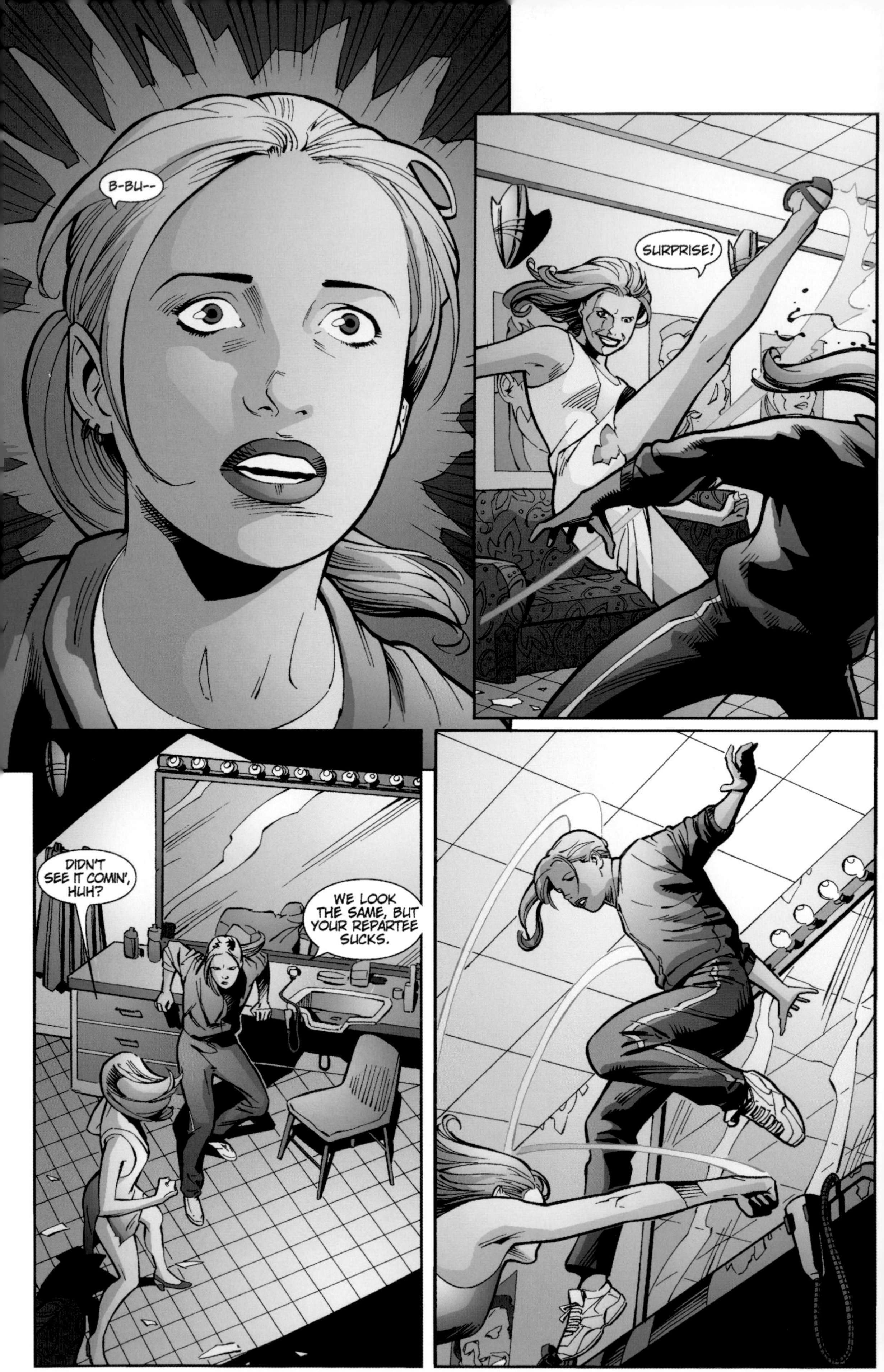
B-BU--
SURPRISE!
DIDN'T SEE IT COMIN', HUH?
WE LOOK THE SAME, BUT YOUR REPARTEE SUCKS.

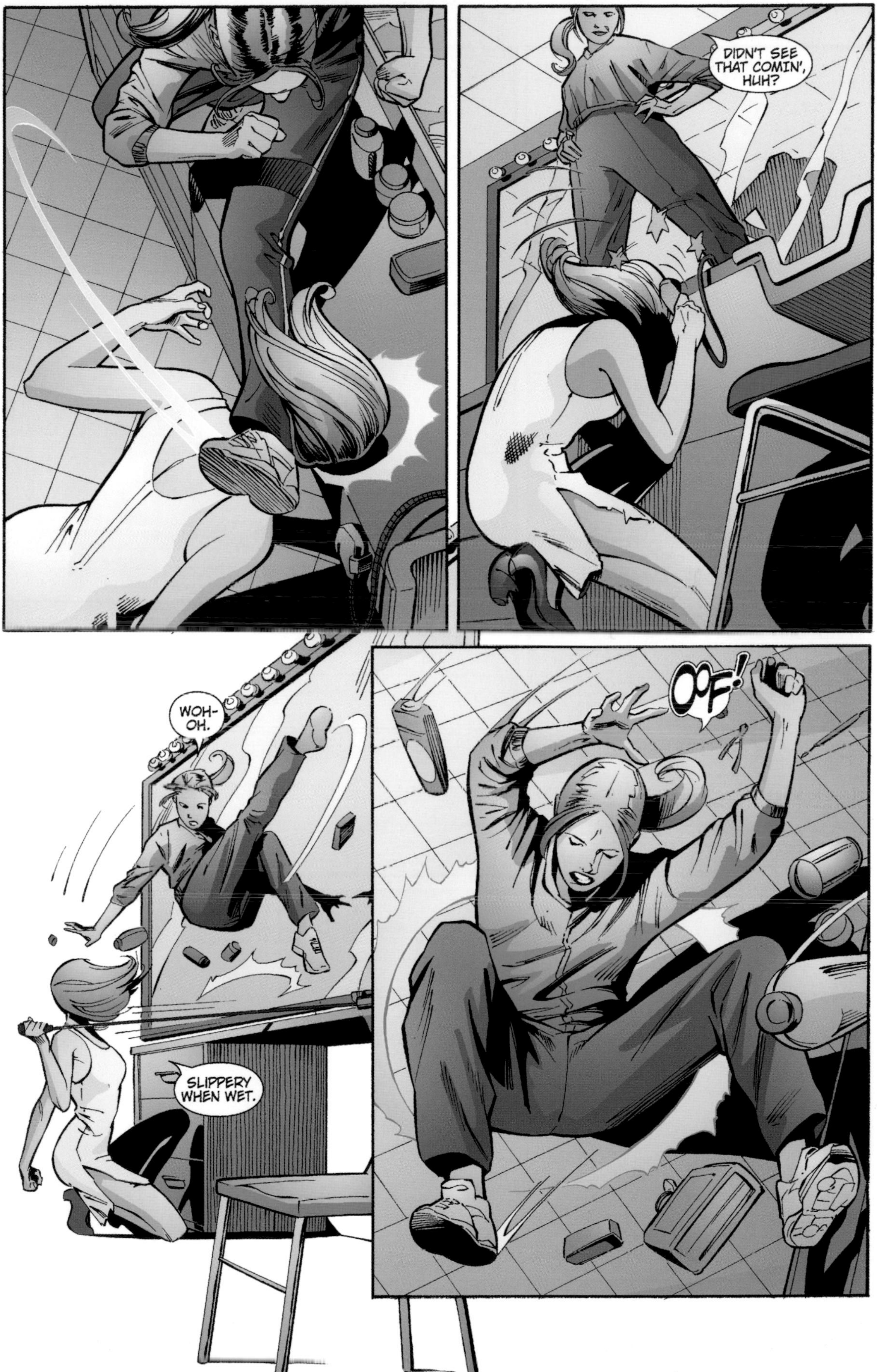
DIDN'T SEE THAT COMIN', HUH?
WOH-OH.
SLIPPERY WHEN WET.
OOF!

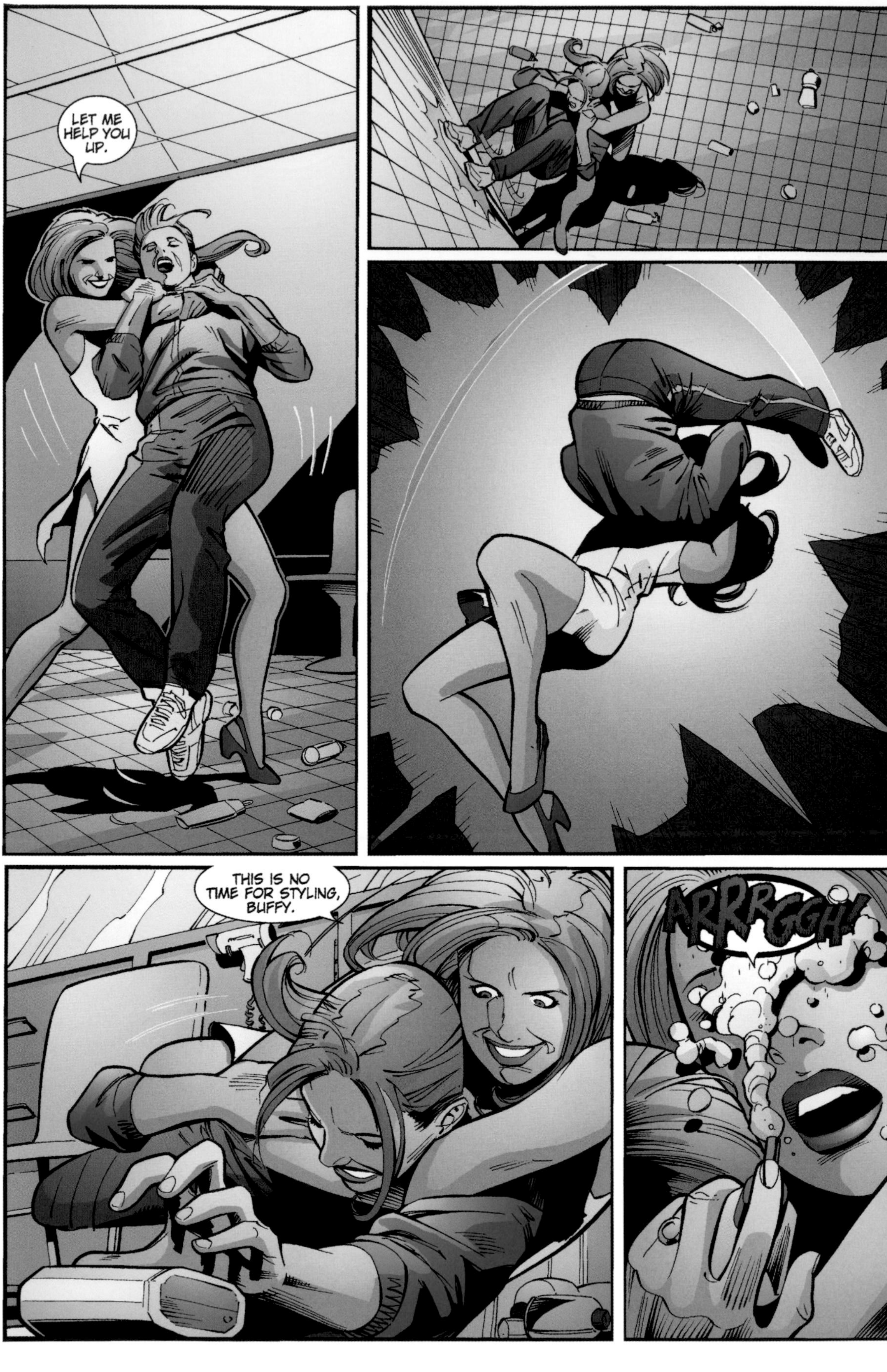
LET ME HELP YOU UP.
THIS IS NO TIME FOR STYLING, BUFFY.
ARRRGGH!

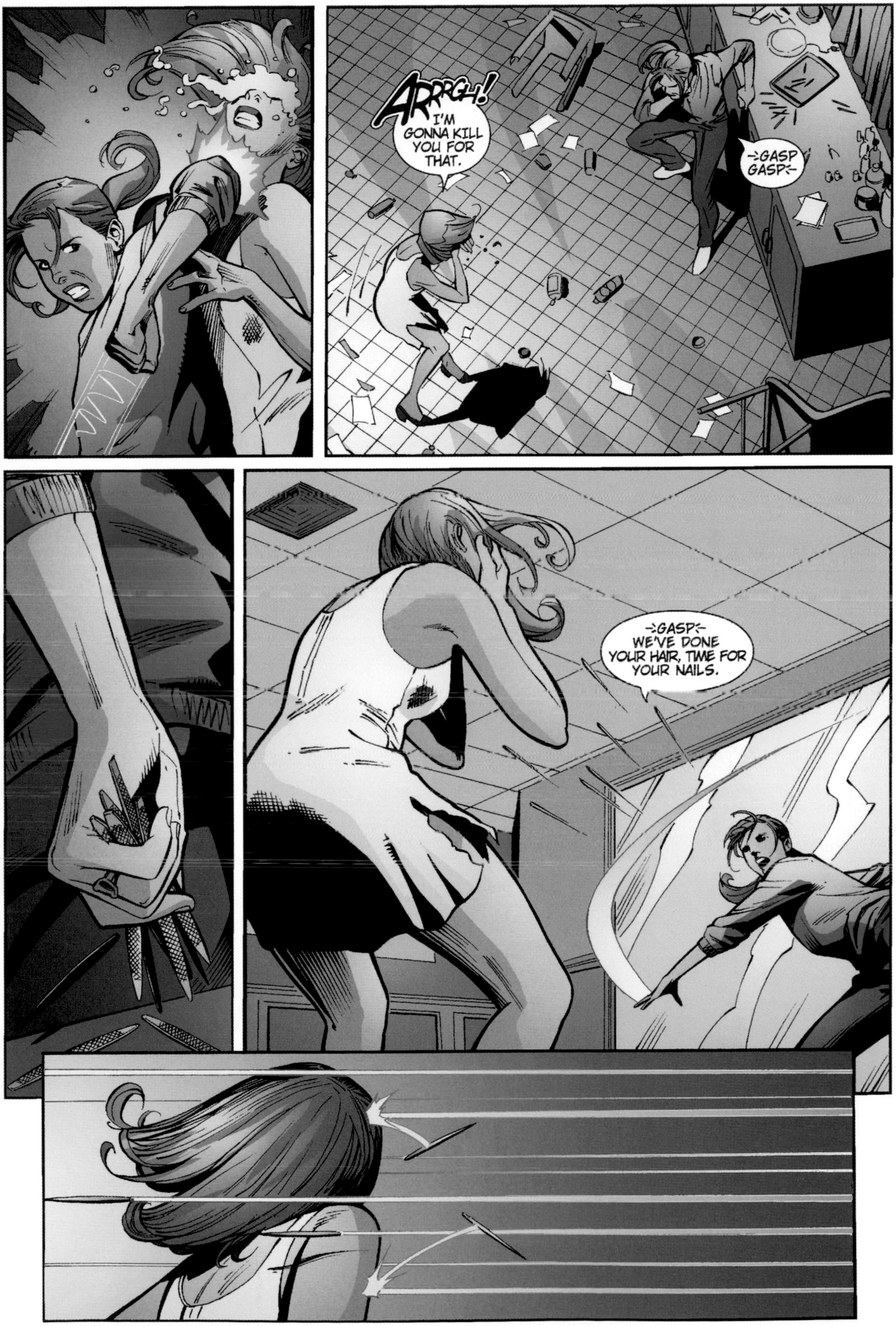
ARRRGH!
I'M GONNA KILL YOU FOR THAT.
-GASP GASP-
-GASP- WE'VE DONE YOUR HAIR, TIME FOR YOUR NAILS.

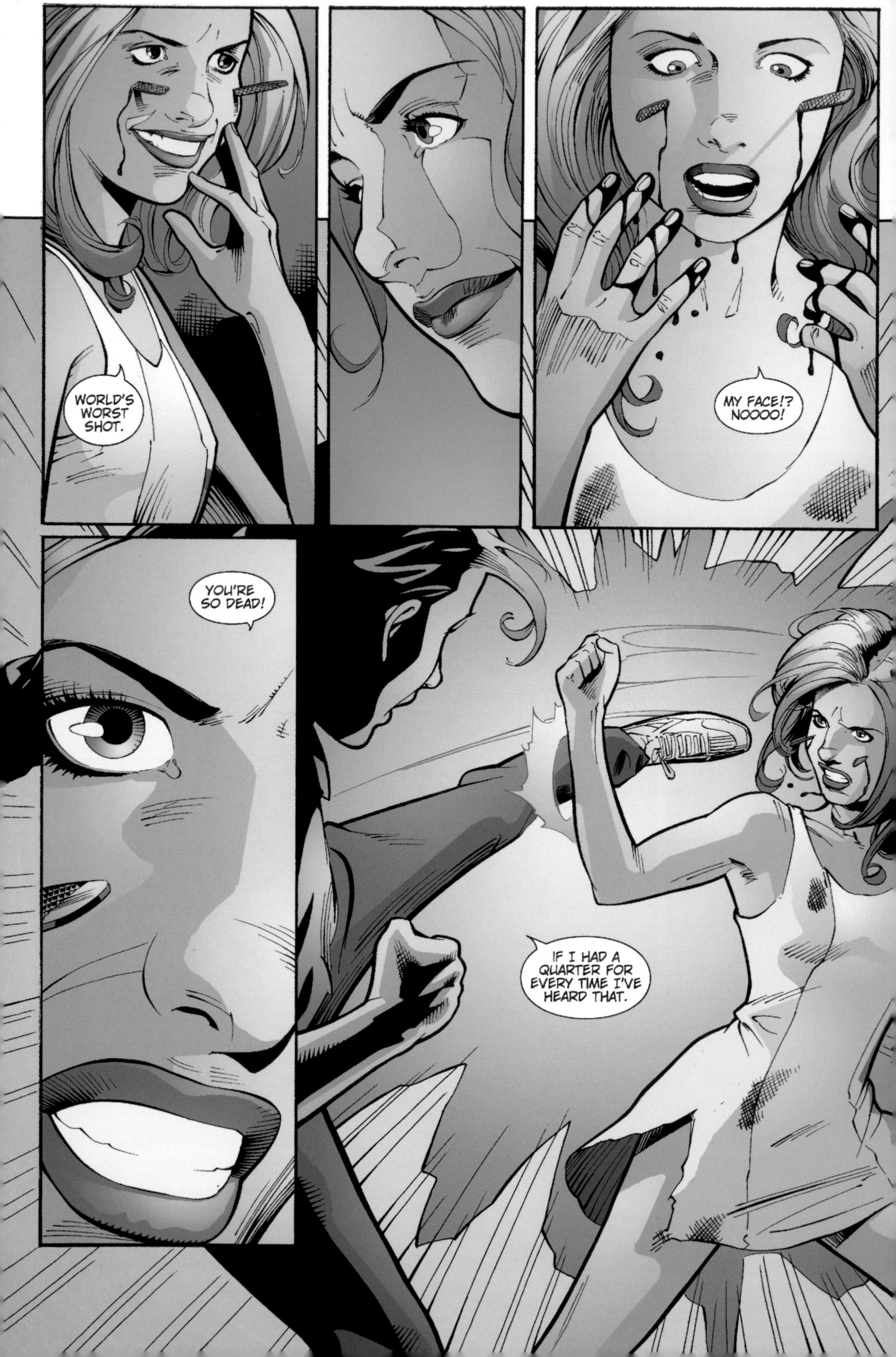
WORLD'S WORST SHOT.
MY FACE!? NOOOO!
YOU'RE SO DEAD!
IF I HAD A QUARTER FOR EVERY TIME I'VE HEARD THAT.

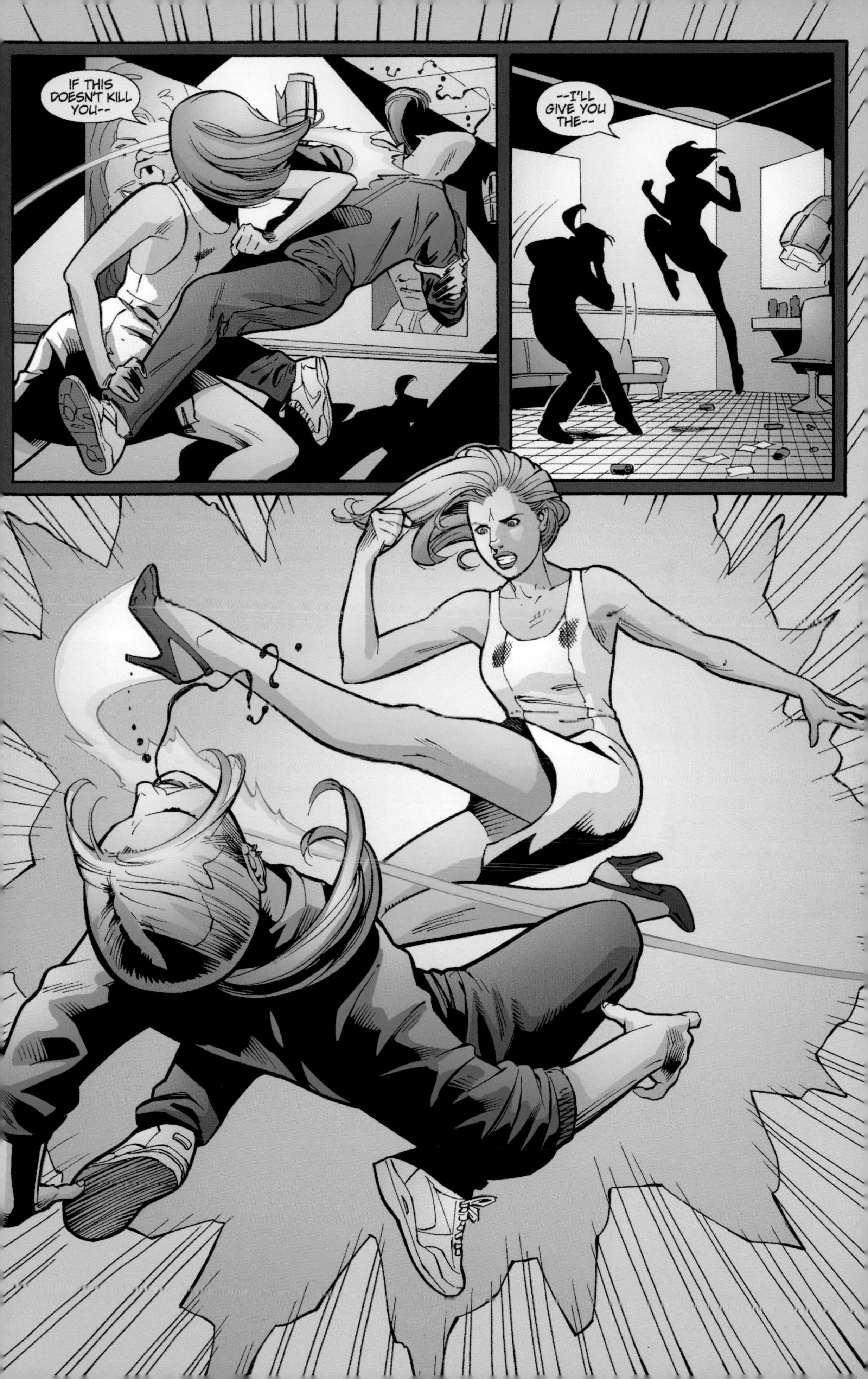
IF THIS DOESN'T KILL YOU--
--I'LL GIVE YOU THE--

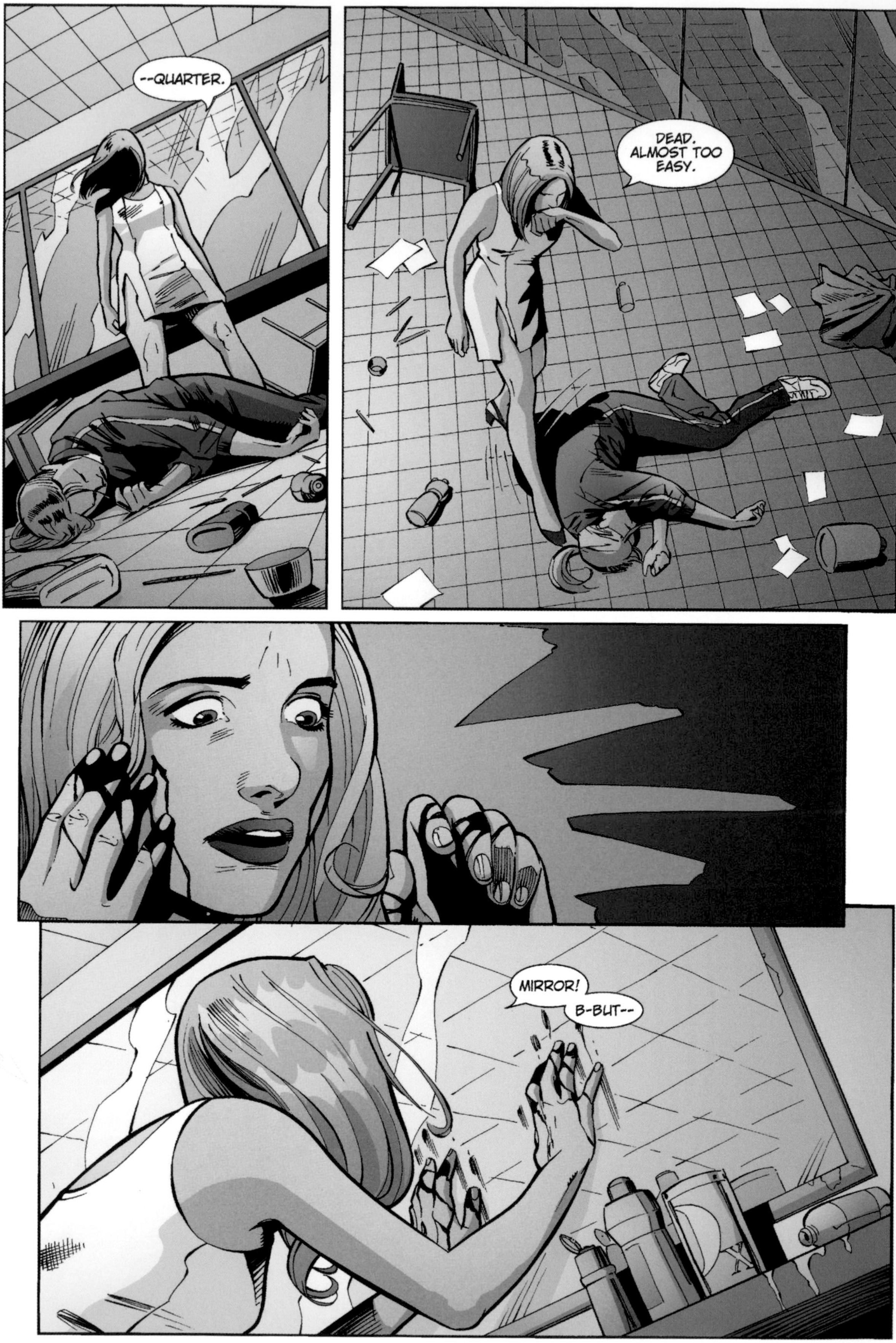
--QUARTER.
DEAD. ALMOST TOO EASY.
MIRROR!
B-BUT--

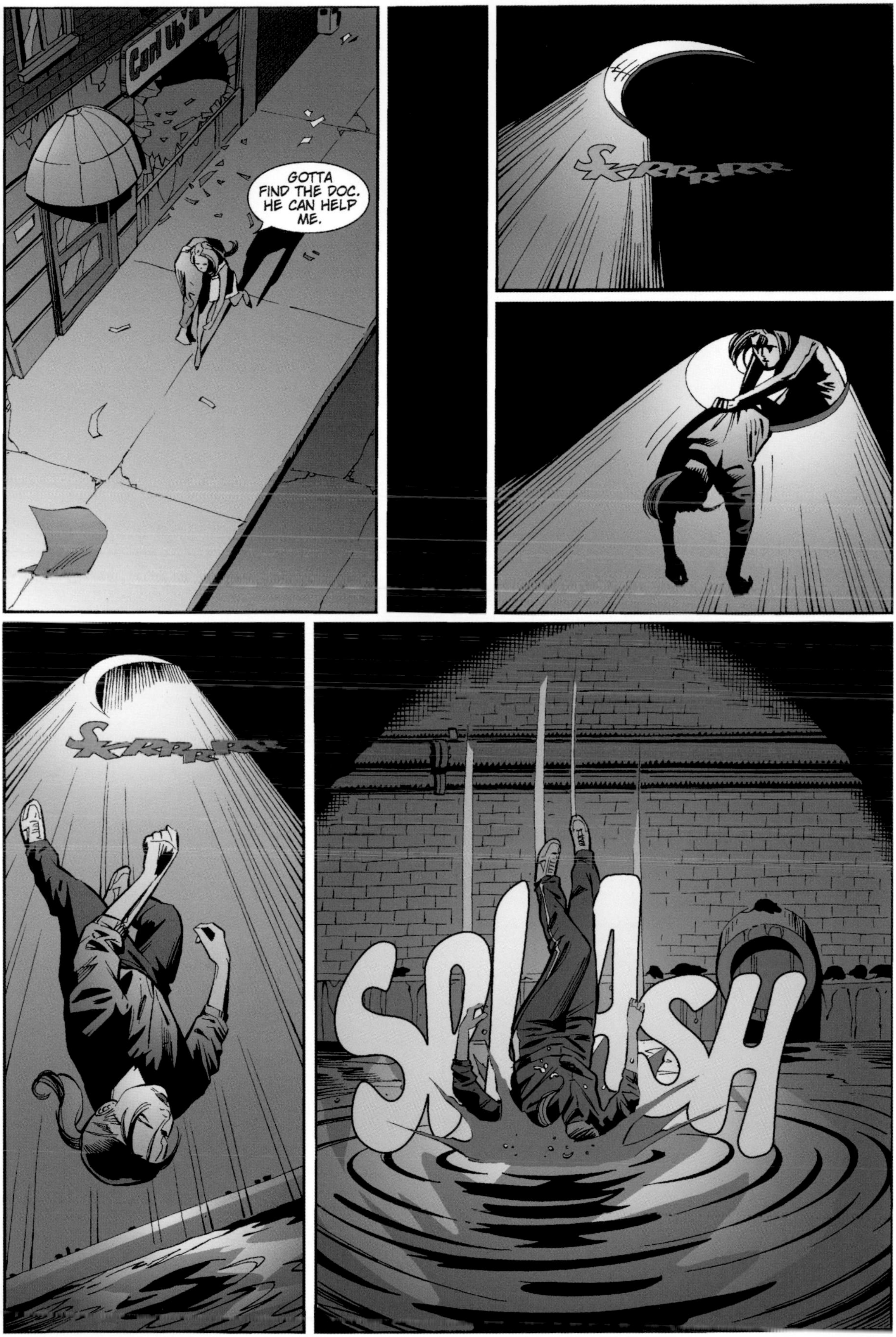
GOTTA FIND THE DOC. HE CAN HELP ME.
SKRRRRRR
SPLASH

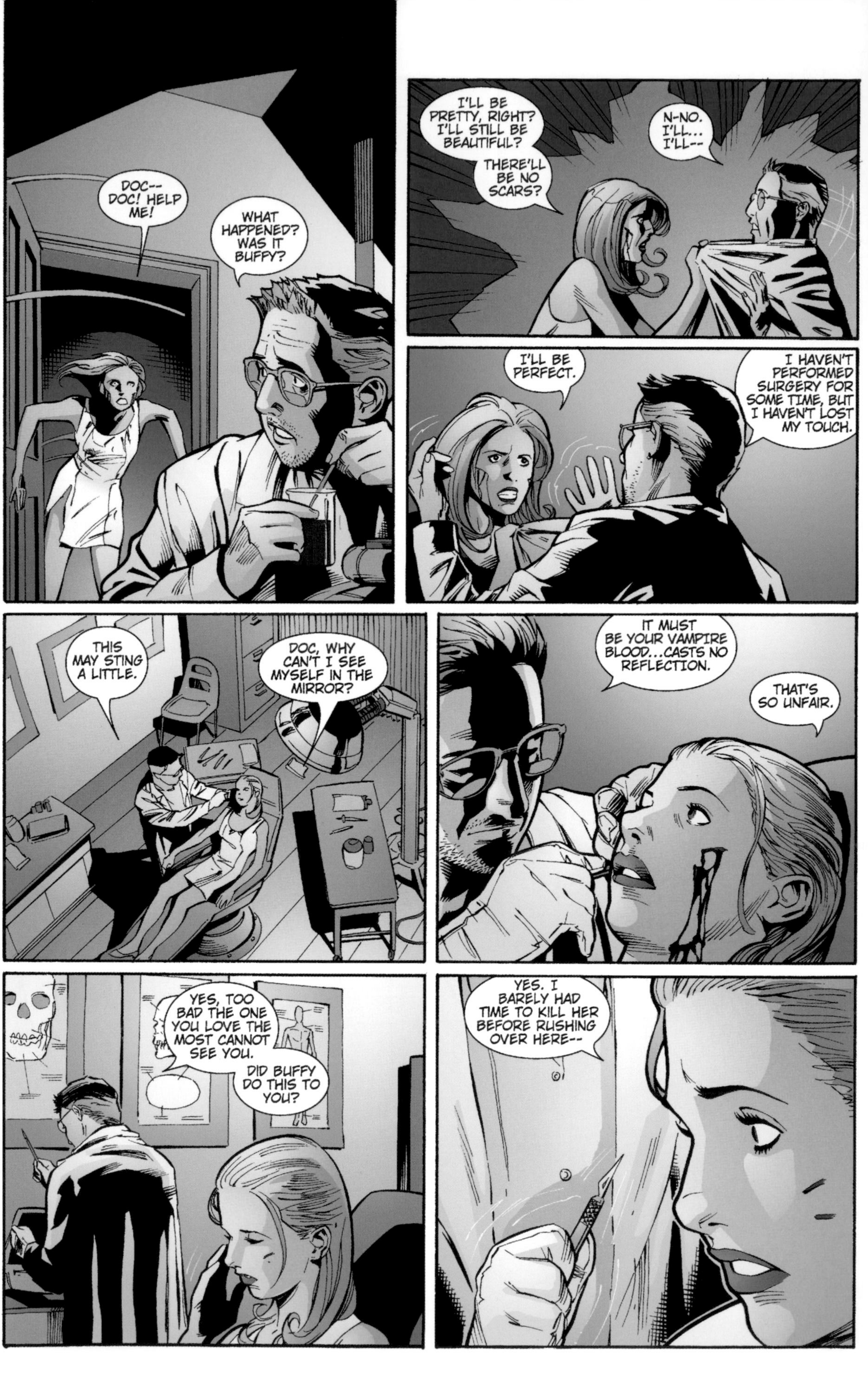
DOC-- DOC! HELP ME!
WHAT HAPPENED? WAS IT BUFFY?
I'LL BE PRETTY, RIGHT? I'LL STILL BE BEAUTIFUL?
THERE'LL BE NO SCARS?
N-NO. I'LL... I'LL--
I'LL BE PERFECT.
I HAVEN'T PERFORMED SURGERY FOR SOME TIME, BUT I HAVEN'T LOST MY TOUCH.
THIS MAY STING A LITTLE.
DOC, WHY CAN'T I SEE MYSELF IN THE MIRROR?
IT MUST BE YOUR VAMPIRE BLOOD...CASTS NO REFLECTION.
THAT'S SO UNFAIR.
YES, TOO BAD THE ONE YOU LOVE THE MOST CANNOT SEE YOU.
DID BUFFY DO THIS TO YOU?
YES. I BARELY HAD TIME TO KILL HER BEFORE RUSHING OVER HERE--

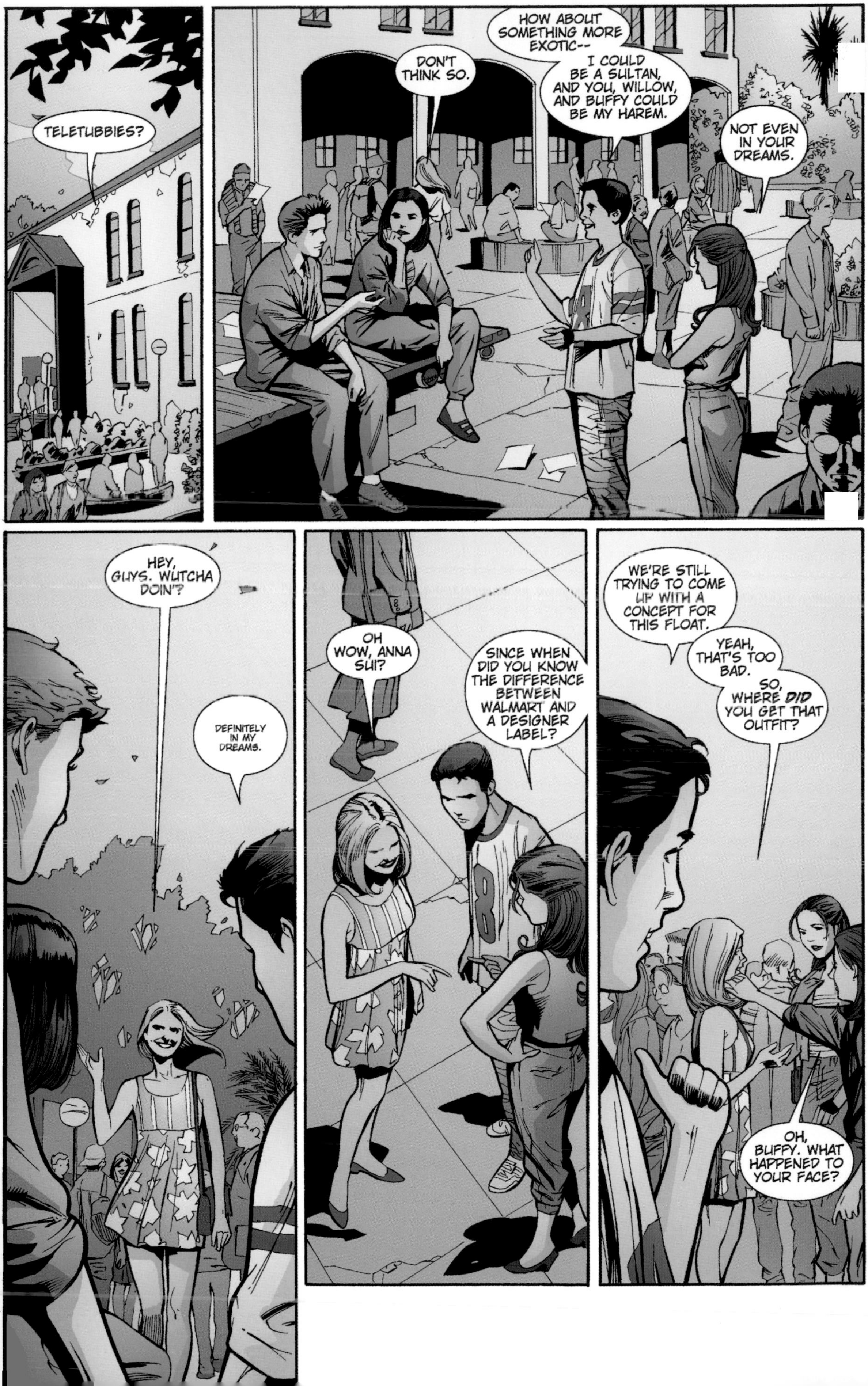
TELETUBBIES?
DON'T THINK SO.
HOW ABOUT SOMETHING MORE EXOTIC--
I COULD BE A SULTAN, AND YOU, WILLOW, AND BUFFY COULD BE MY HAREM.
NOT EVEN IN YOUR DREAMS.
HEY, GUYS. WHTCHA DOIN'?
DEFINITELY IN MY DREAMS.
OH WOW, ANNA SUI?
SINCE WHEN DID YOU KNOW THE DIFFERENCE BETWEEN WALMART AND A DESIGNER LABEL?
WE'RE STILL TRYING TO COME UP WITH A CONCEPT FOR THIS FLOAT.
YEAH, THAT'S TOO BAD.
SO, WHERE DID YOU GET THAT OUTFIT?
OH, BUFFY. WHAT HAPPENED TO YOUR FACE?

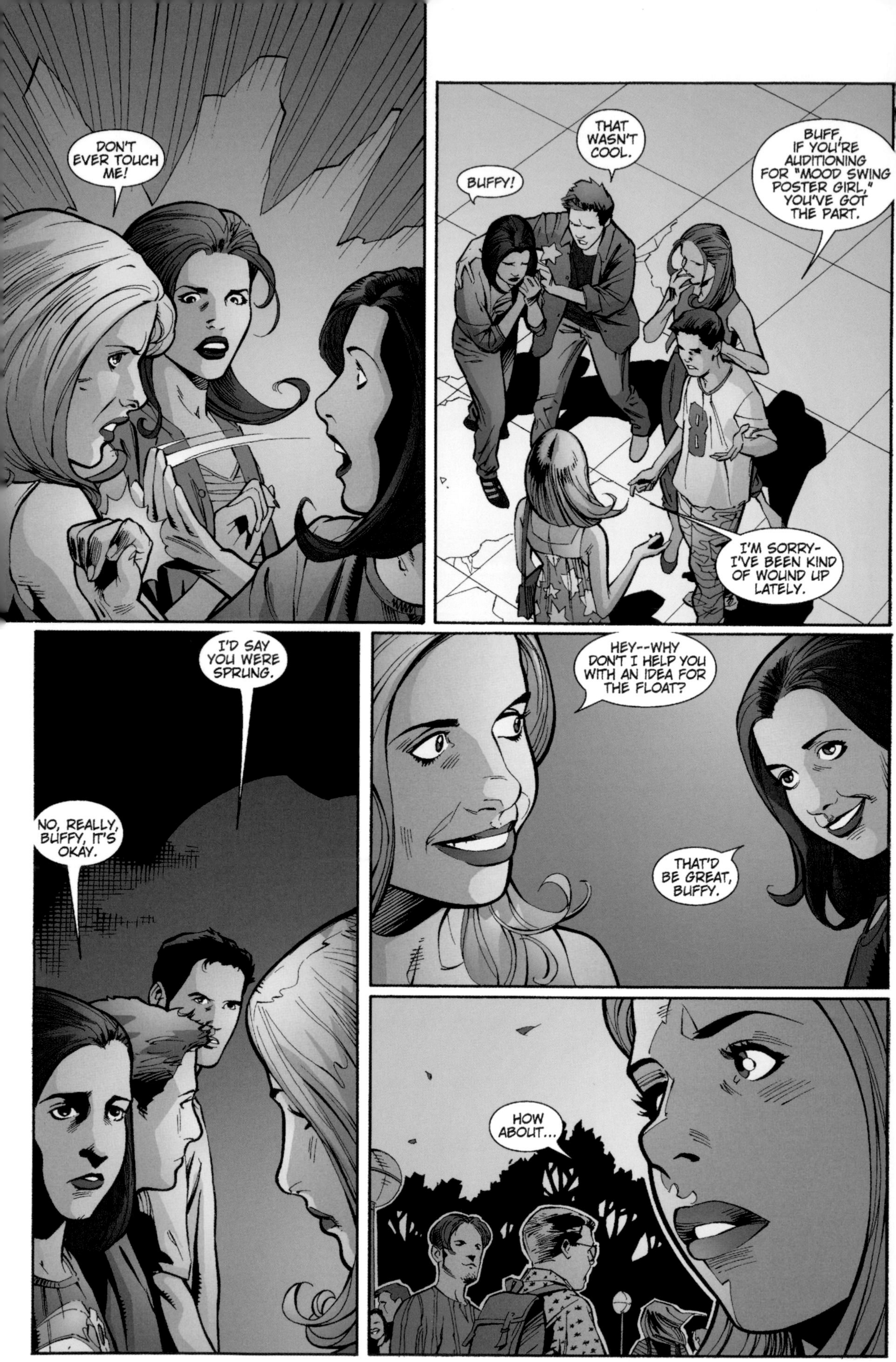
DON'T EVER TOUCH ME!
BUFFY!
THAT WASN'T COOL.
BUFF, IF YOU'RE AUDITIONING FOR "MOOD SWING POSTER GIRL," YOU'VE GOT THE PART.
I'M SORRY-I'VE BEEN KIND OF WOUND UP LATELY.
I'D SAY YOU WERE SPRUNG.
NO, REALLY, BUFFY, IT'S OKAY.
HEY--WHY DON'T I HELP YOU WITH AN IDEA FOR THE FLOAT?
THAT'D BE GREAT, BUFFY.
HOW ABOUT...

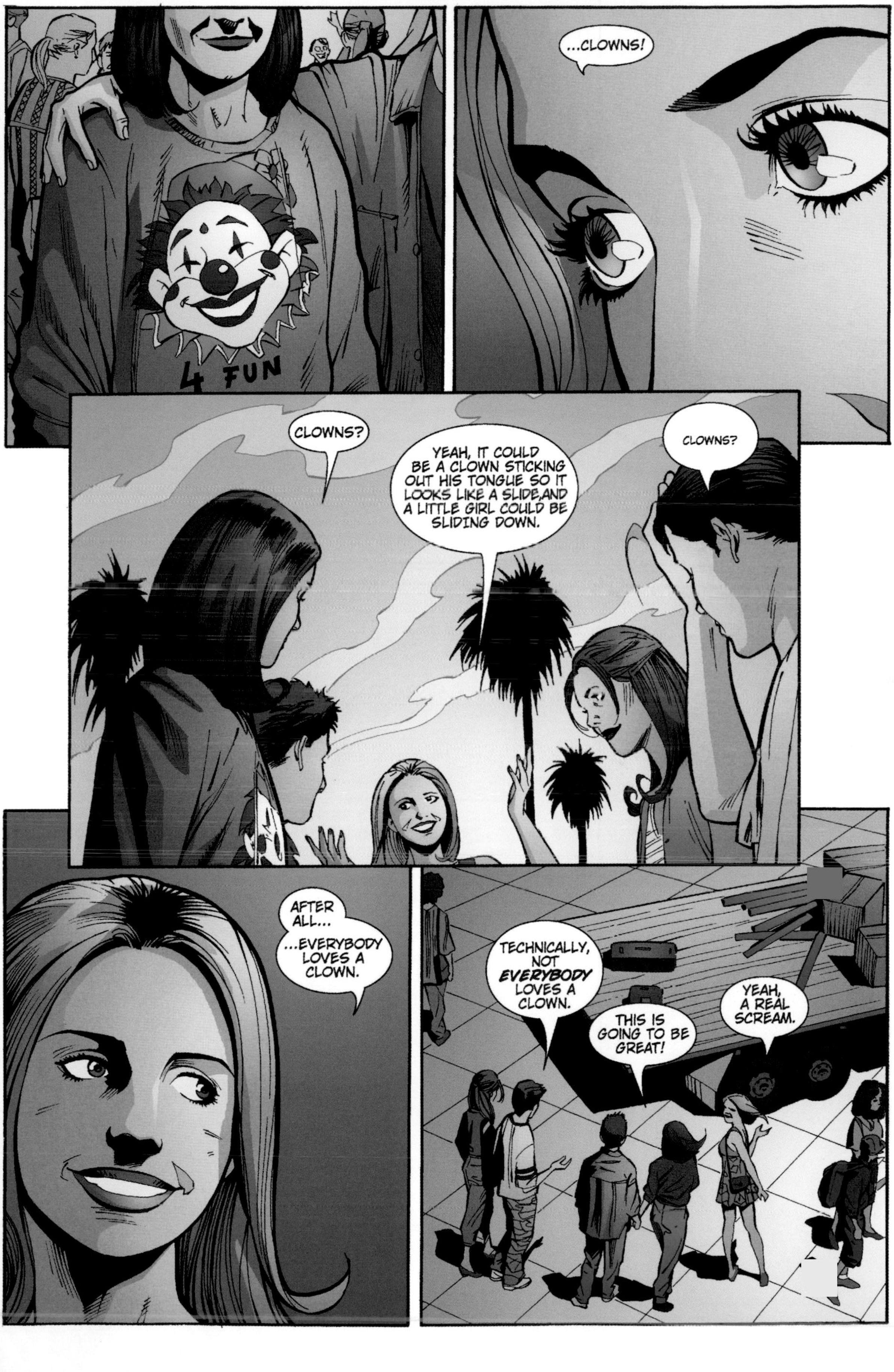
4 FUN
...CLOWNS!
CLOWNS?
YEAH, IT COULD BE A CLOWN STICKING OUT HIS TONGUE SO IT LOOKS LIKE A SLIDE,AND A LITTLE GIRL COULD BE SLIDING DOWN.
CLOWNS?
AFTER ALL...
...EVERYBODY LOVES A CLOWN.
TECHNICALLY, NOT *EVERYBODY* LOVES A CLOWN.
THIS IS GOING TO BE GREAT!
YEAH, A REAL SCREAM.

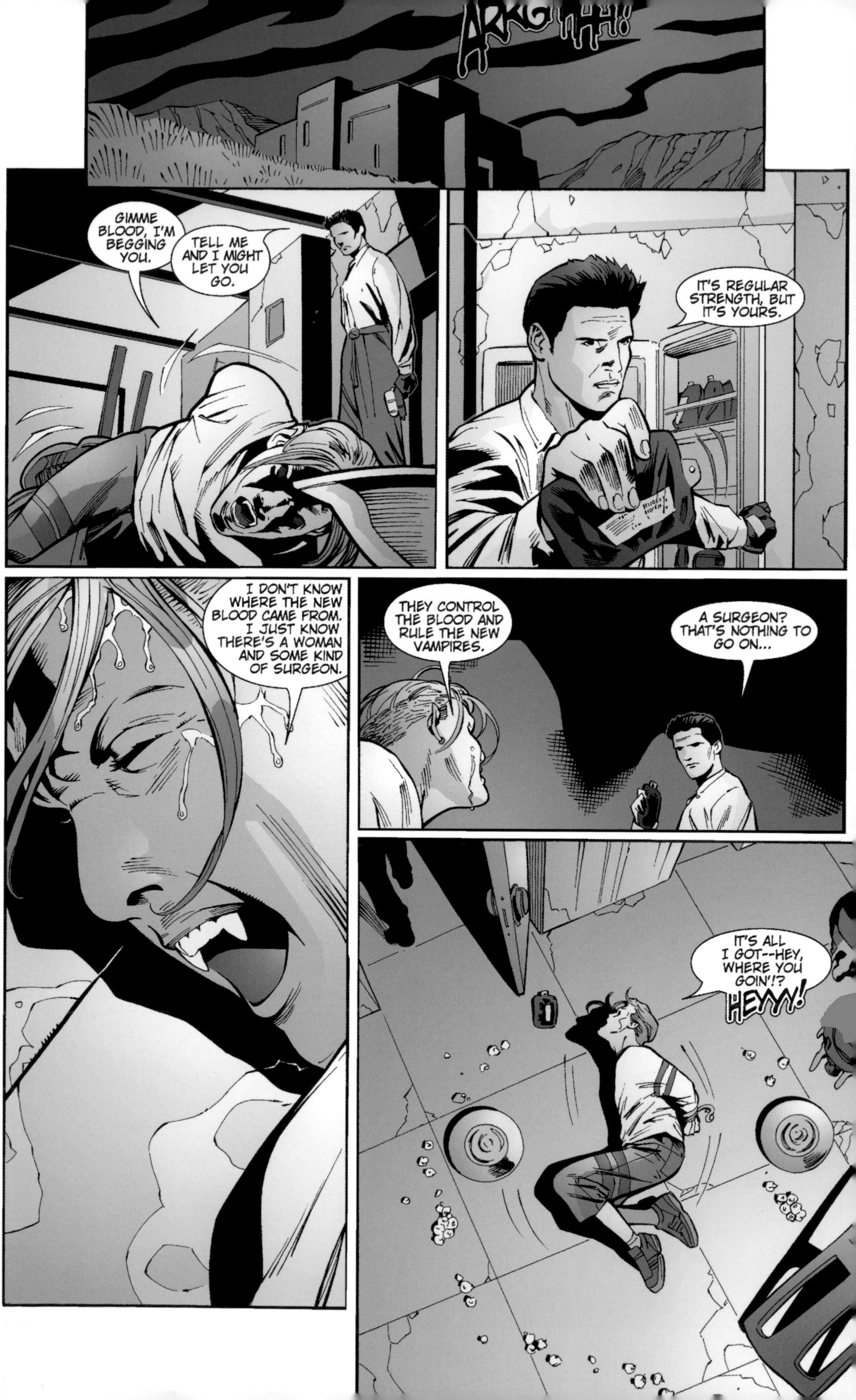
ARKGHHH!
GIMME BLOOD, I'M BEGGING YOU.
TELL ME AND I MIGHT LET YOU GO.
IT'S REGULAR STRENGTH, BUT IT'S YOURS.
I DON'T KNOW WHERE THE NEW BLOOD CAME FROM. I JUST KNOW THERE'S A WOMAN AND SOME KIND OF SURGEON.
THEY CONTROL THE BLOOD AND RULE THE NEW VAMPIRES.
A SURGEON? THAT'S NOTHING TO GO ON...
IT'S ALL I GOT--HEY, WHERE YOU GOIN'!?
HEYYY!

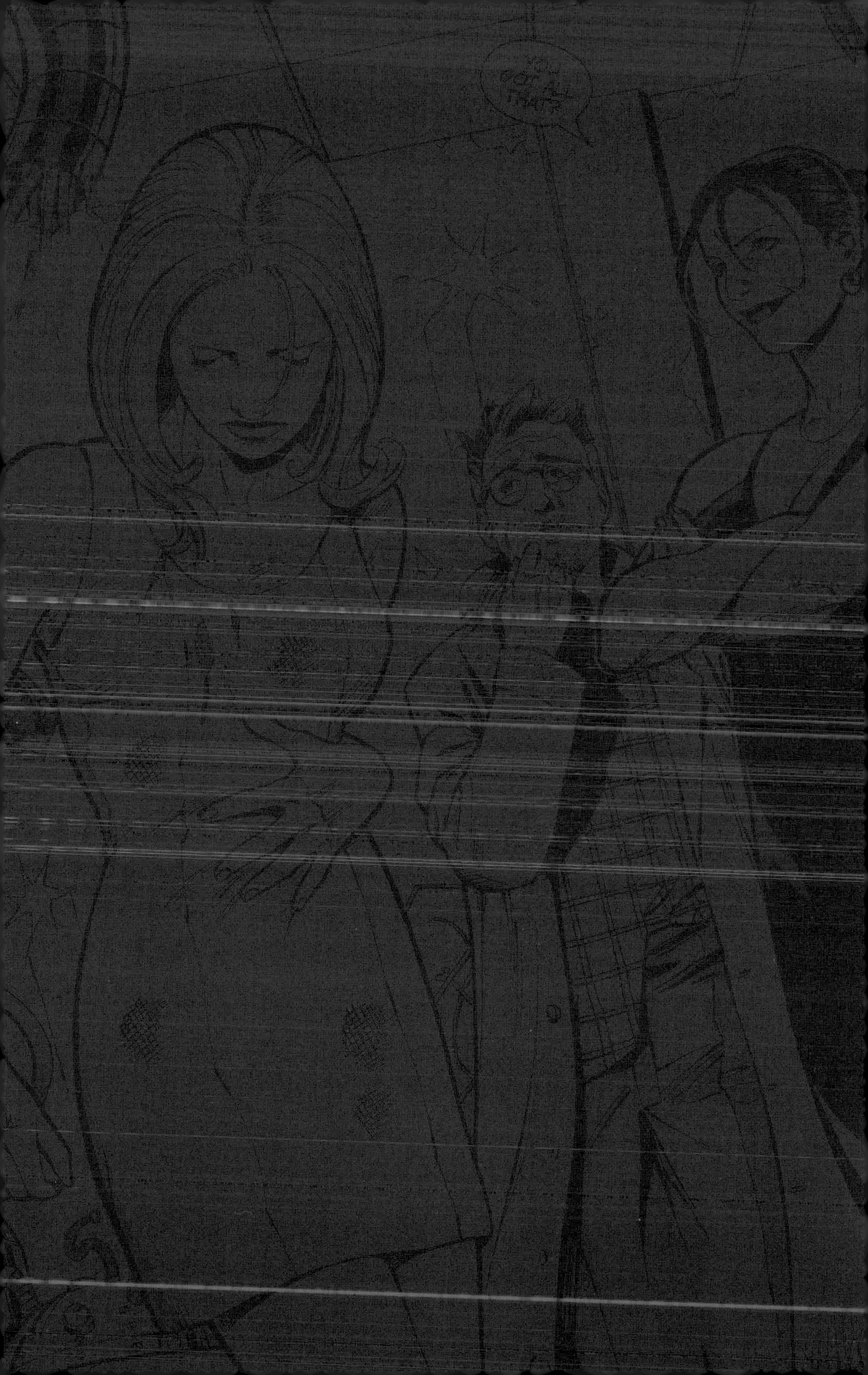

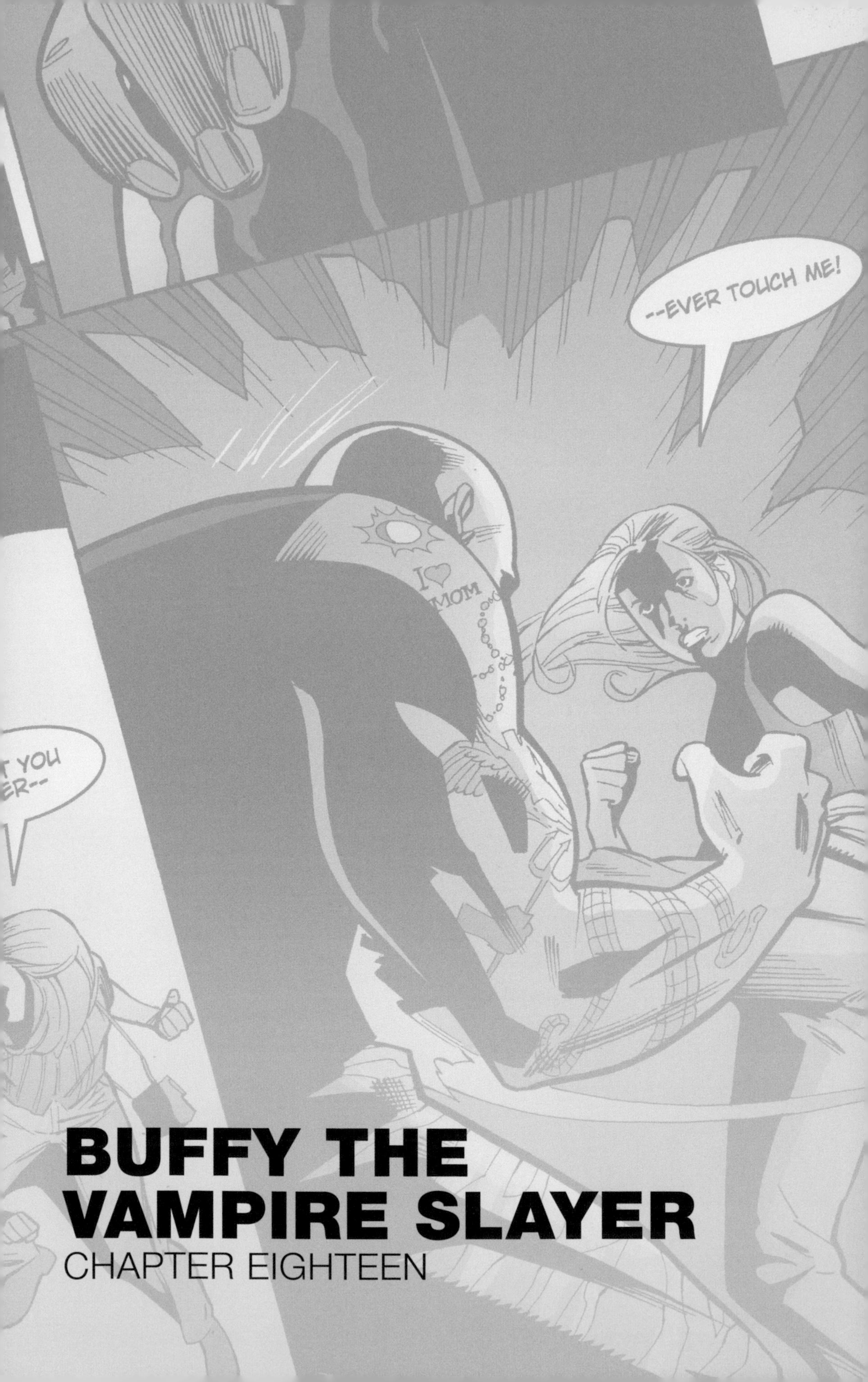
--EVER TOUCH ME!

BUFFY THE VAMPIRE SLAYER
CHAPTER EIGHTEEN

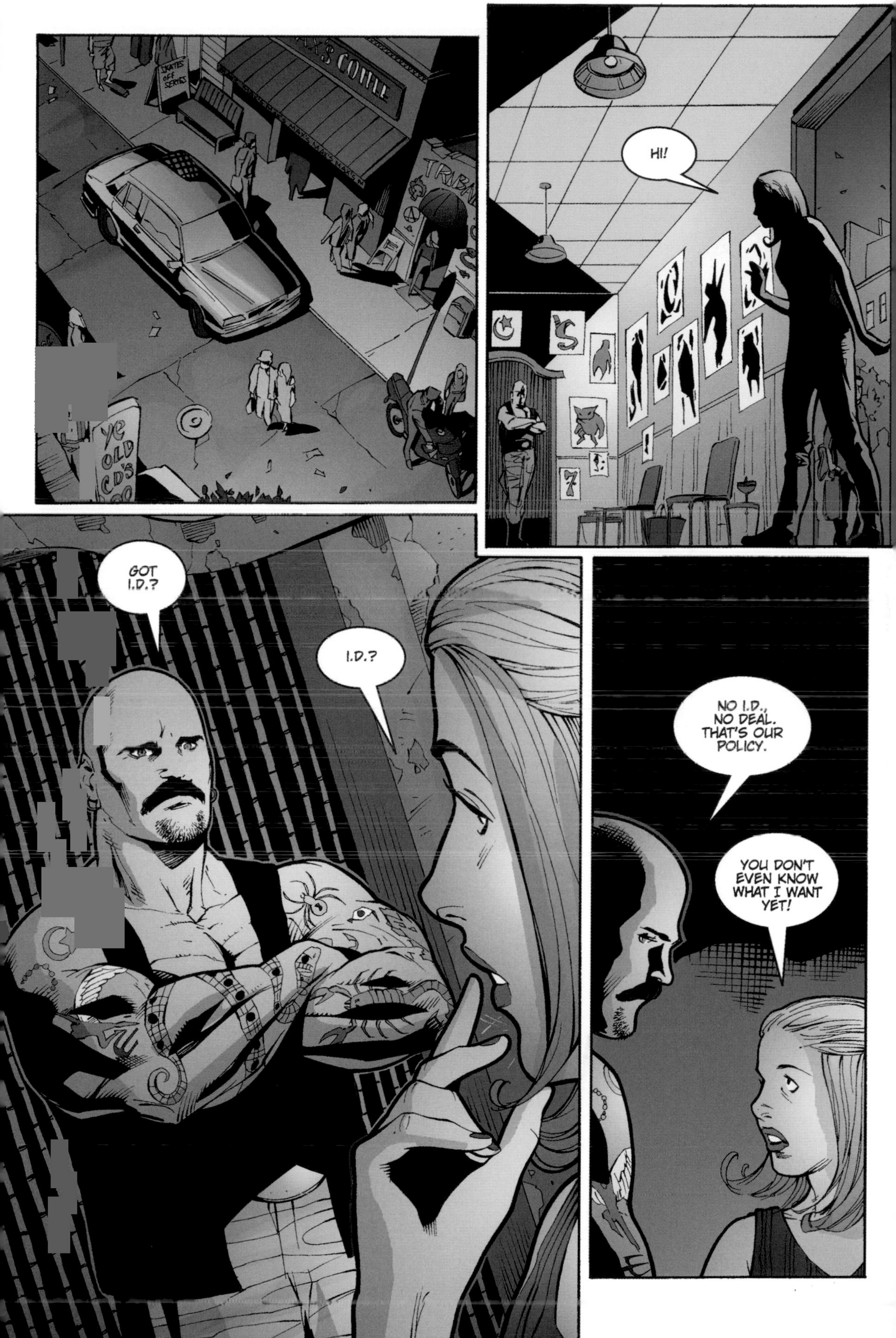
HI!
GOT I.D.?
I.D.?
NO I.D., NO DEAL. THAT'S OUR POLICY.
YOU DON'T EVEN KNOW WHAT I WANT YET!

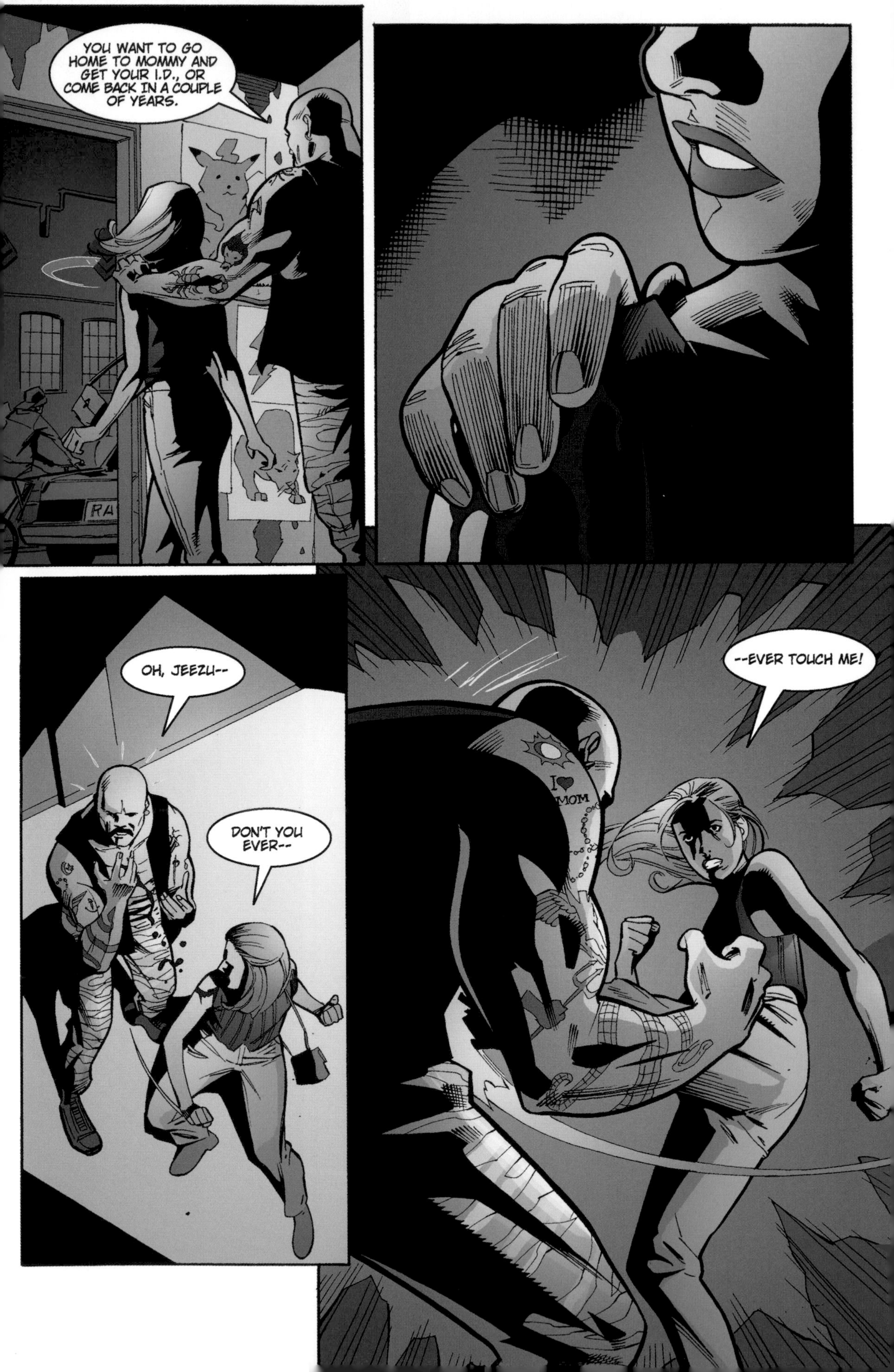
YOU WANT TO GO HOME TO MOMMY AND GET YOUR I.D., OR COME BACK IN A COUPLE OF YEARS.
OH, JEEZU--
DON'T YOU EVER--
--EVER TOUCH ME!

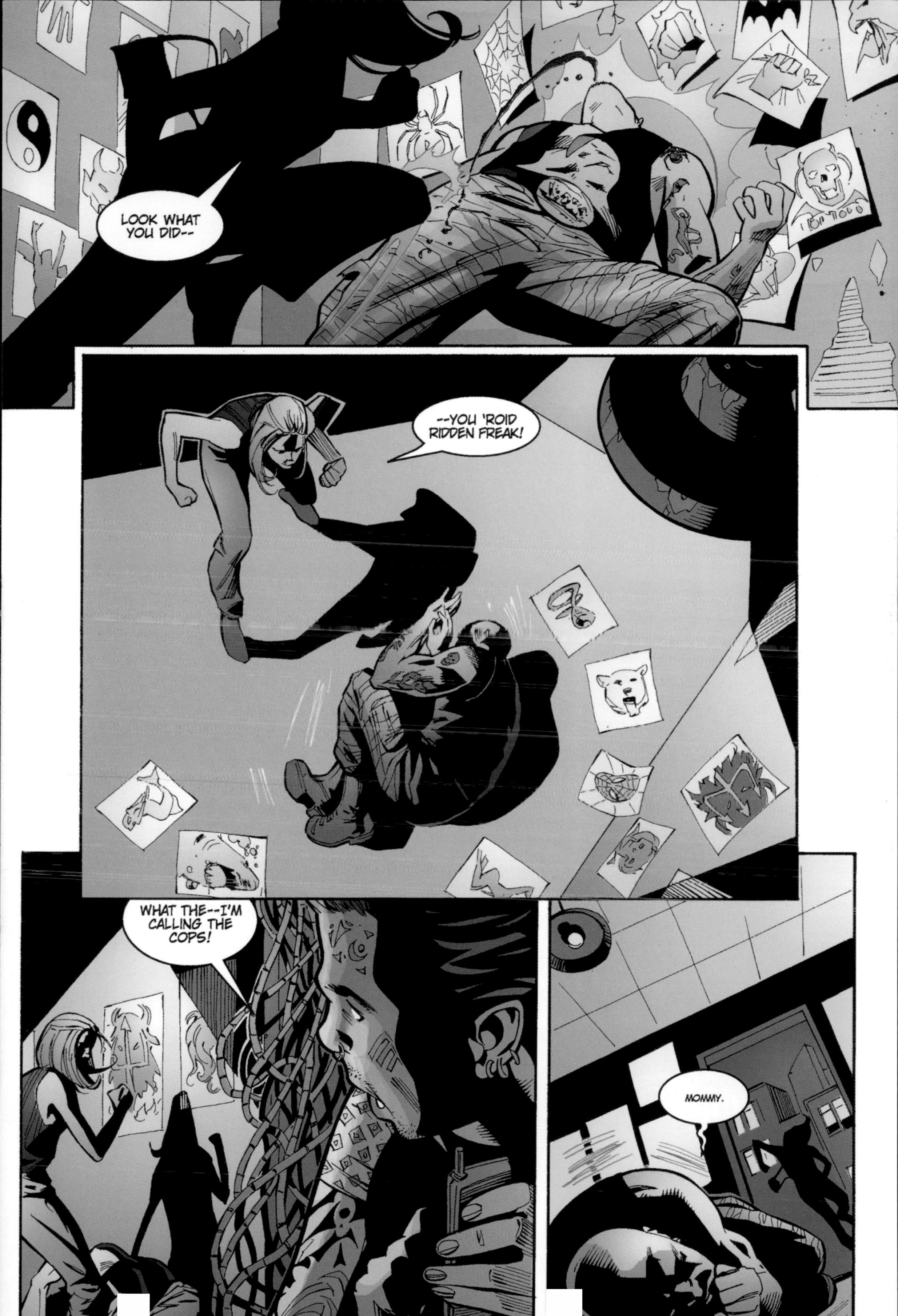
LOOK WHAT YOU DID--
--YOU 'ROID RIDDEN FREAK!
WHAT THE--I'M CALLING THE COPS!
MOMMY.

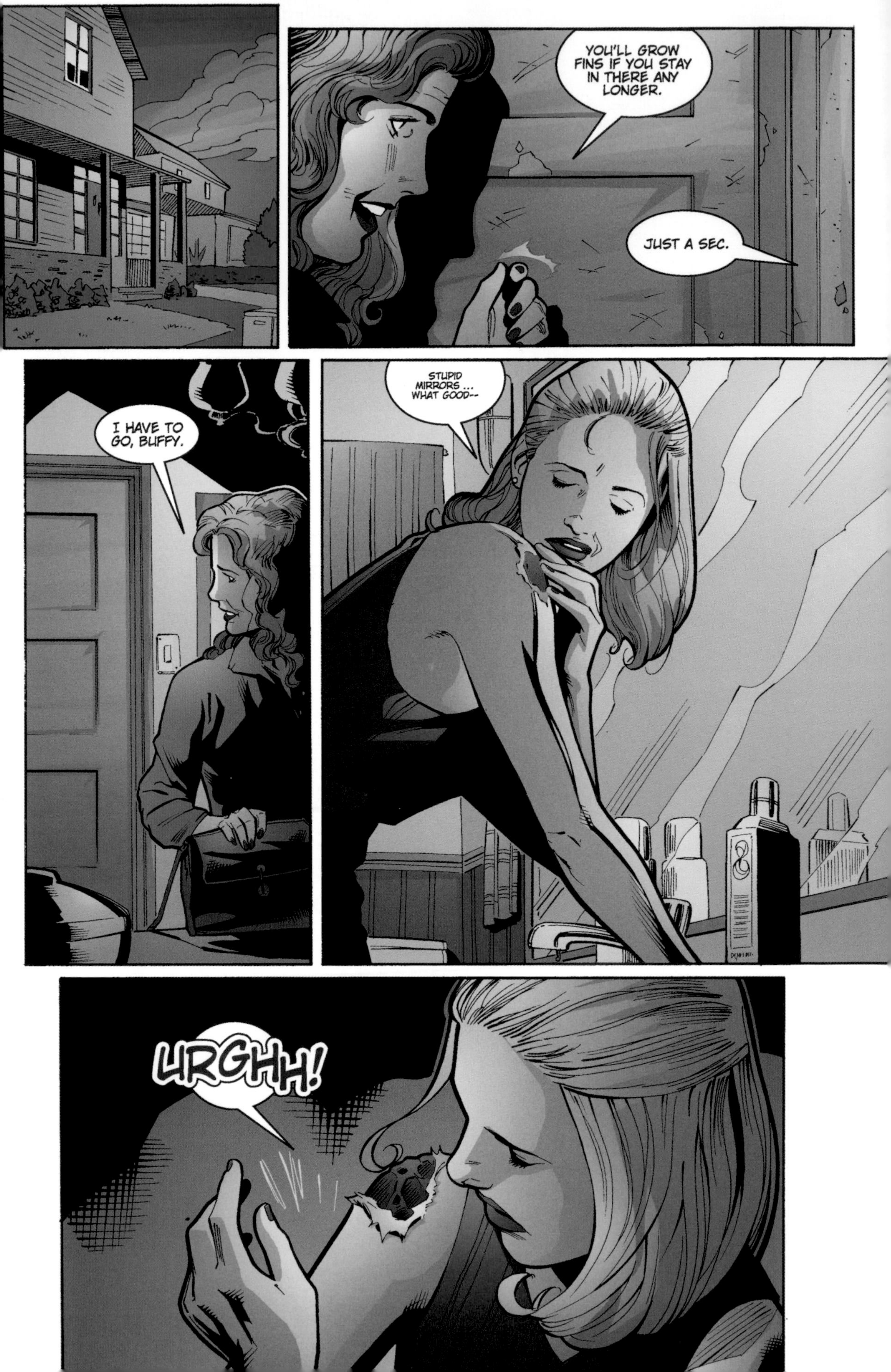
YOU'LL GROW FINS IF YOU STAY IN THERE ANY LONGER.
JUST A SEC.
I HAVE TO GO, BUFFY.
STUPID MIRRORS ... WHAT GOOD--
URGHH!

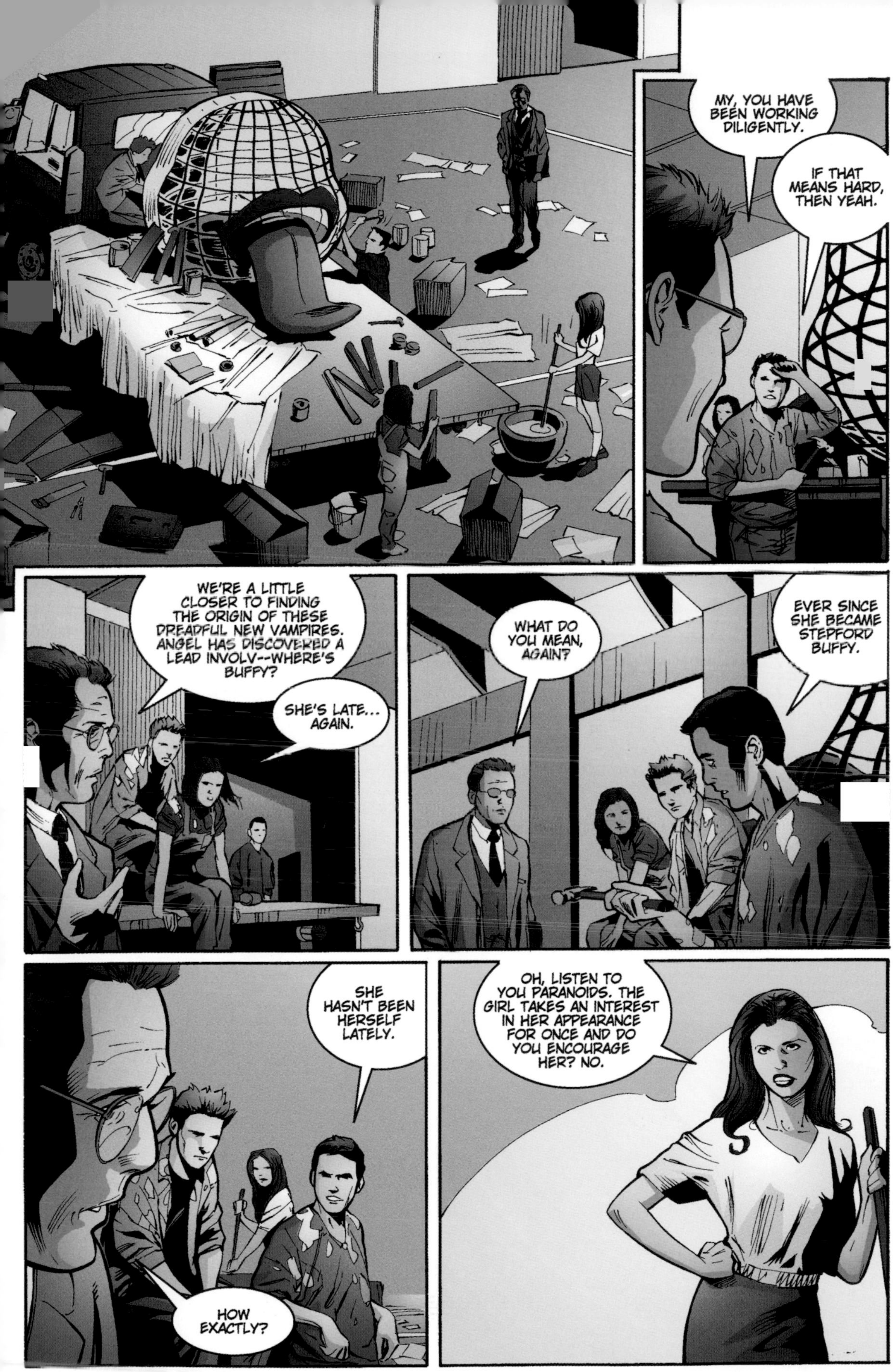
MY, YOU HAVE BEEN WORKING DILIGENTLY.
IF THAT MEANS HARD, THEN YEAH.
WE'RE A LITTLE CLOSER TO FINDING THE ORIGIN OF THESE DREADFUL NEW VAMPIRES. ANGEL HAS DISCOVERED A LEAD INVOLV--WHERE'S BUFFY?
SHE'S LATE... AGAIN.
WHAT DO YOU MEAN, AGAIN?
EVER SINCE SHE BECAME STEPFORD BUFFY.
SHE HASN'T BEEN HERSELF LATELY.
HOW EXACTLY?
OH, LISTEN TO YOU PARANOIDS. THE GIRL TAKES AN INTEREST IN HER APPEARANCE FOR ONCE AND DO YOU ENCOURAGE HER? NO.

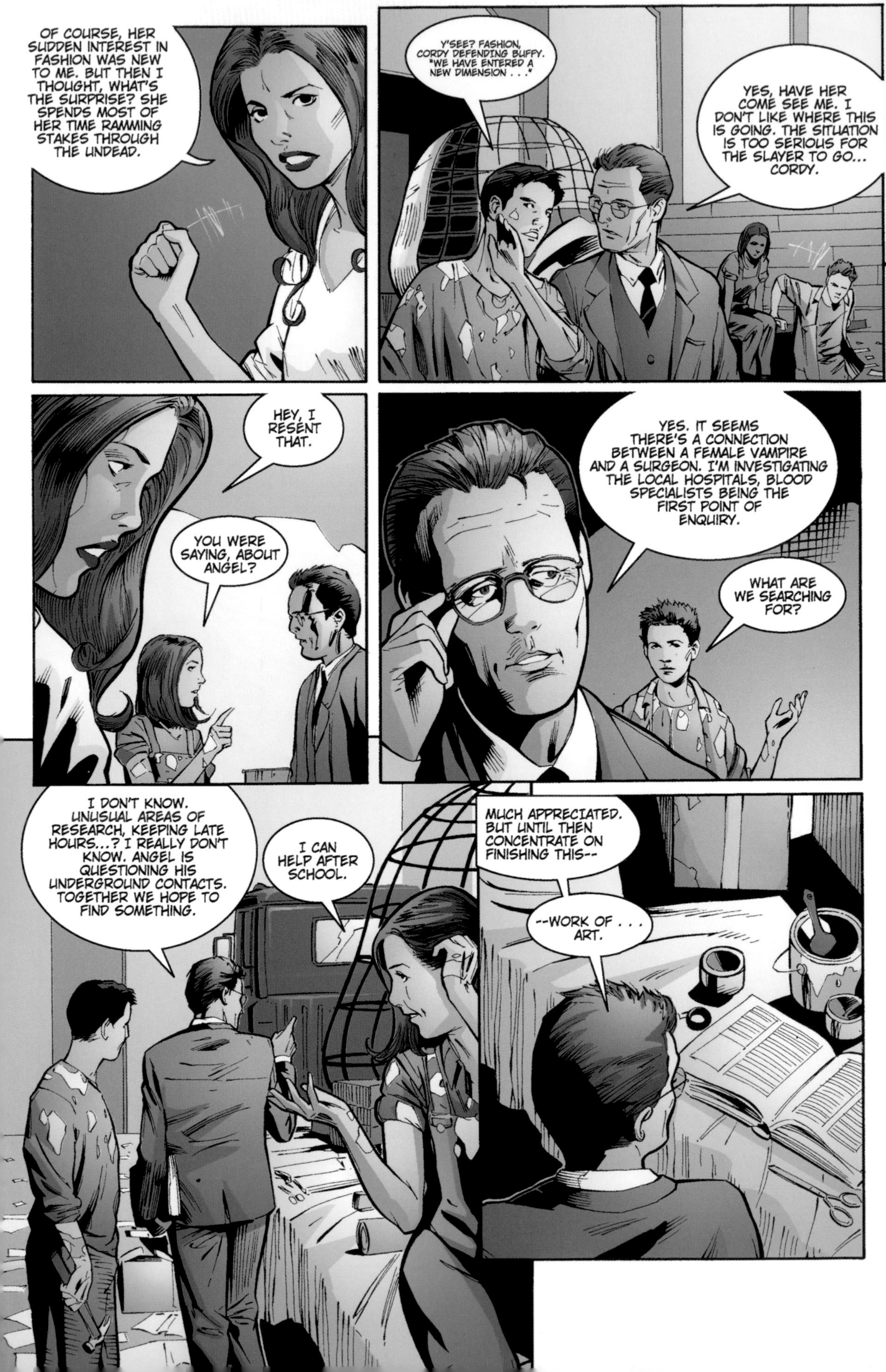
OF COURSE, HER SUDDEN INTEREST IN FASHION WAS NEW TO ME. BUT THEN I THOUGHT, WHAT'S THE SURPRISE? SHE SPENDS MOST OF HER TIME RAMMING STAKES THROUGH THE UNDEAD.
Y'SEE? FASHION, CORDY DEFENDING BUFFY. "WE HAVE ENTERED A NEW DIMENSION . . ."
YES, HAVE HER COME SEE ME. I DON'T LIKE WHERE THIS IS GOING. THE SITUATION IS TOO SERIOUS FOR THE SLAYER TO GO... CORDY.
HEY, I RESENT THAT.
YOU WERE SAYING, ABOUT ANGEL?
YES. IT SEEMS THERE'S A CONNECTION BETWEEN A FEMALE VAMPIRE AND A SURGEON. I'M INVESTIGATING THE LOCAL HOSPITALS, BLOOD SPECIALISTS BEING THE FIRST POINT OF ENQUIRY.
WHAT ARE WE SEARCHING FOR?
I DON'T KNOW. UNUSUAL AREAS OF RESEARCH, KEEPING LATE HOURS...? I REALLY DON'T KNOW. ANGEL IS QUESTIONING HIS UNDERGROUND CONTACTS. TOGETHER WE HOPE TO FIND SOMETHING.
I CAN HELP AFTER SCHOOL.
MUCH APPRECIATED. BUT UNTIL THEN CONCENTRATE ON FINISHING THIS--
--WORK OF . . . ART.

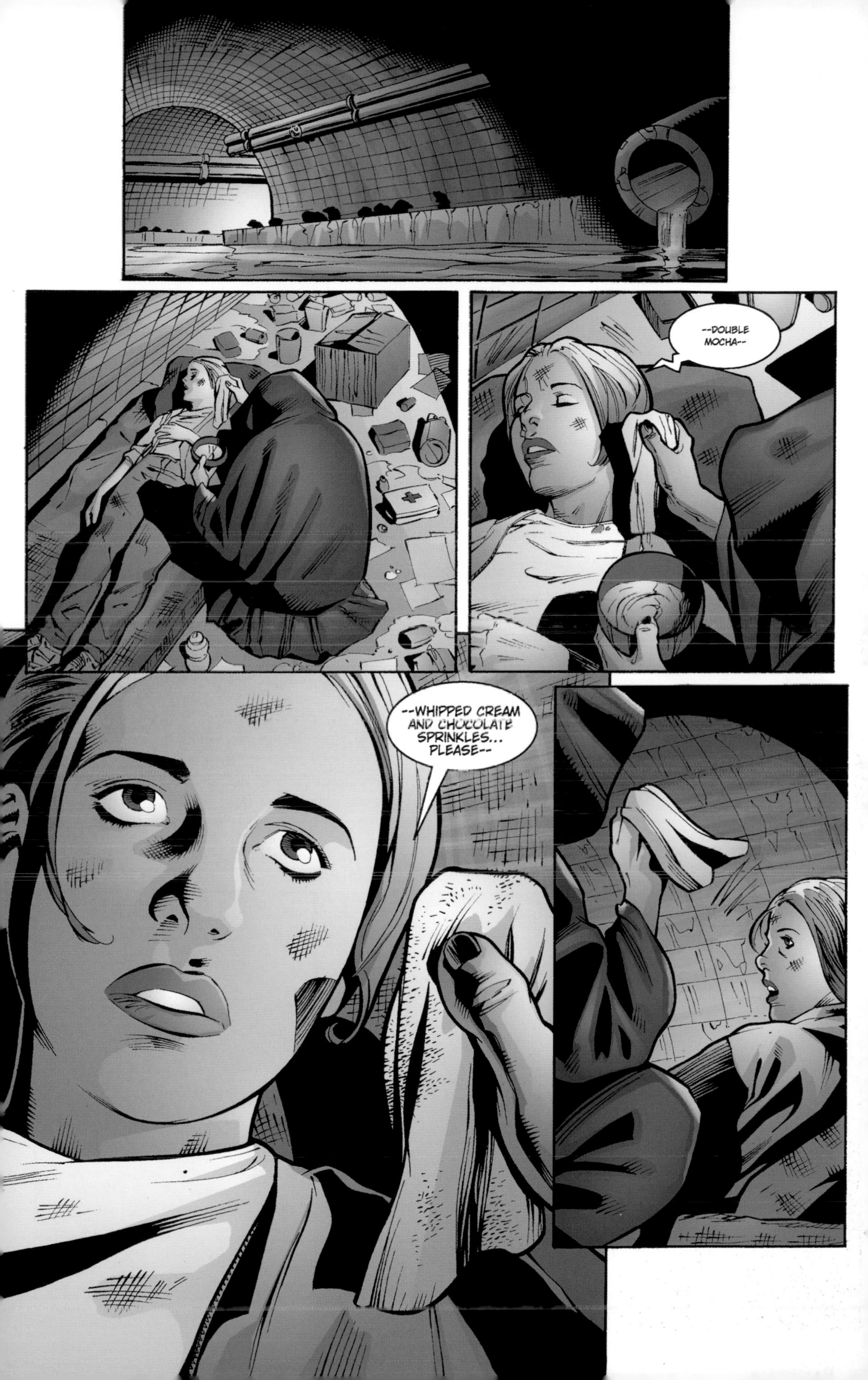
--DOUBLE MOCHA--
--WHIPPED CREAM AND CHOCOLATE SPRINKLES... PLEASE--

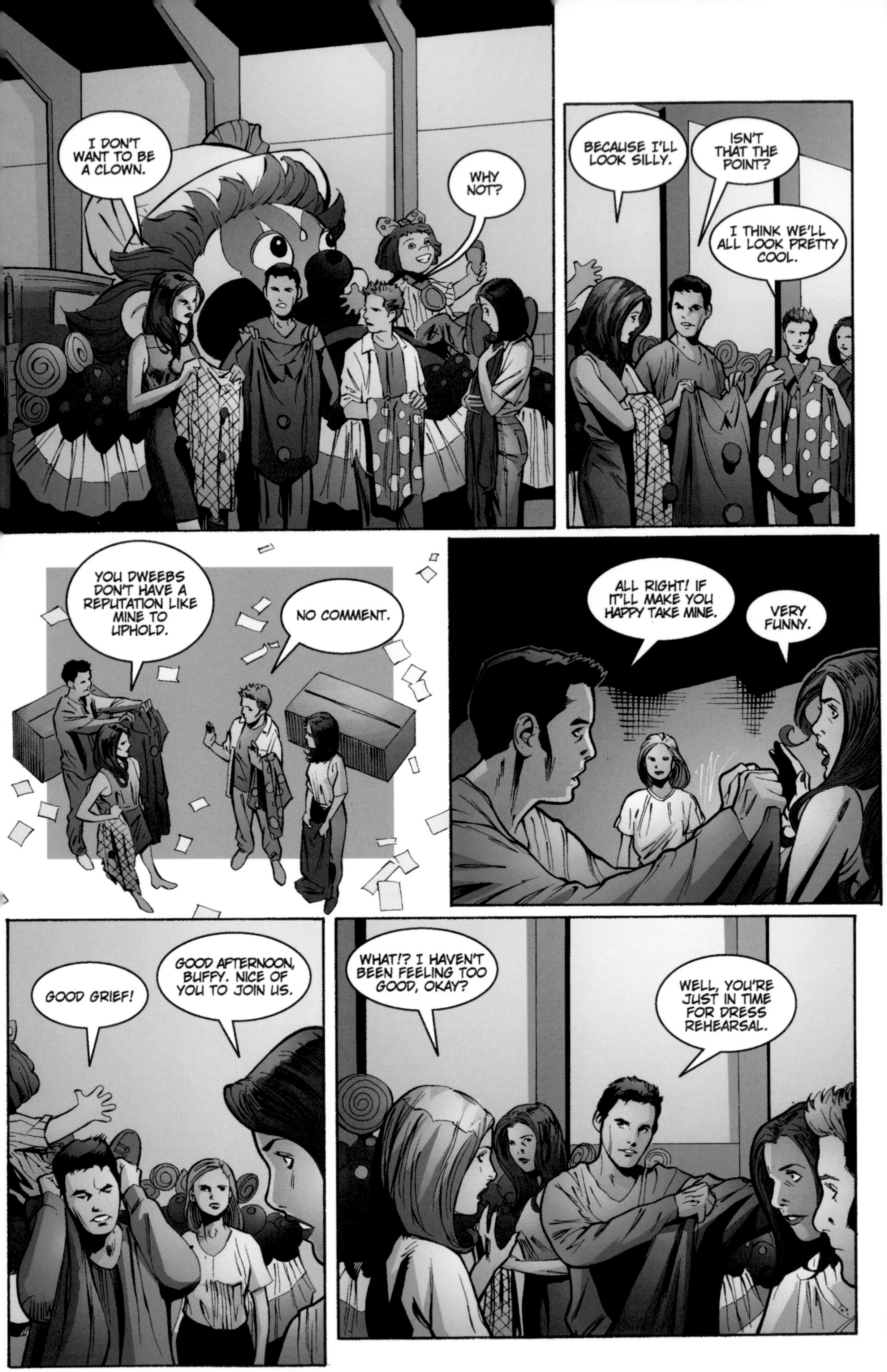
I DON'T WANT TO BE A CLOWN.
WHY NOT?
BECAUSE I'LL LOOK SILLY.
ISN'T THAT THE POINT?
I THINK WE'LL ALL LOOK PRETTY COOL.
YOU DWEEBS DON'T HAVE A REPUTATION LIKE MINE TO UPHOLD.
NO COMMENT.
ALL RIGHT! IF IT'LL MAKE YOU HAPPY TAKE MINE.
VERY FUNNY.
GOOD GRIEF!
GOOD AFTERNOON, BUFFY. NICE OF YOU TO JOIN US.
WHAT!? I HAVEN'T BEEN FEELING TOO GOOD, OKAY?
WELL, YOU'RE JUST IN TIME FOR DRESS REHEARSAL.

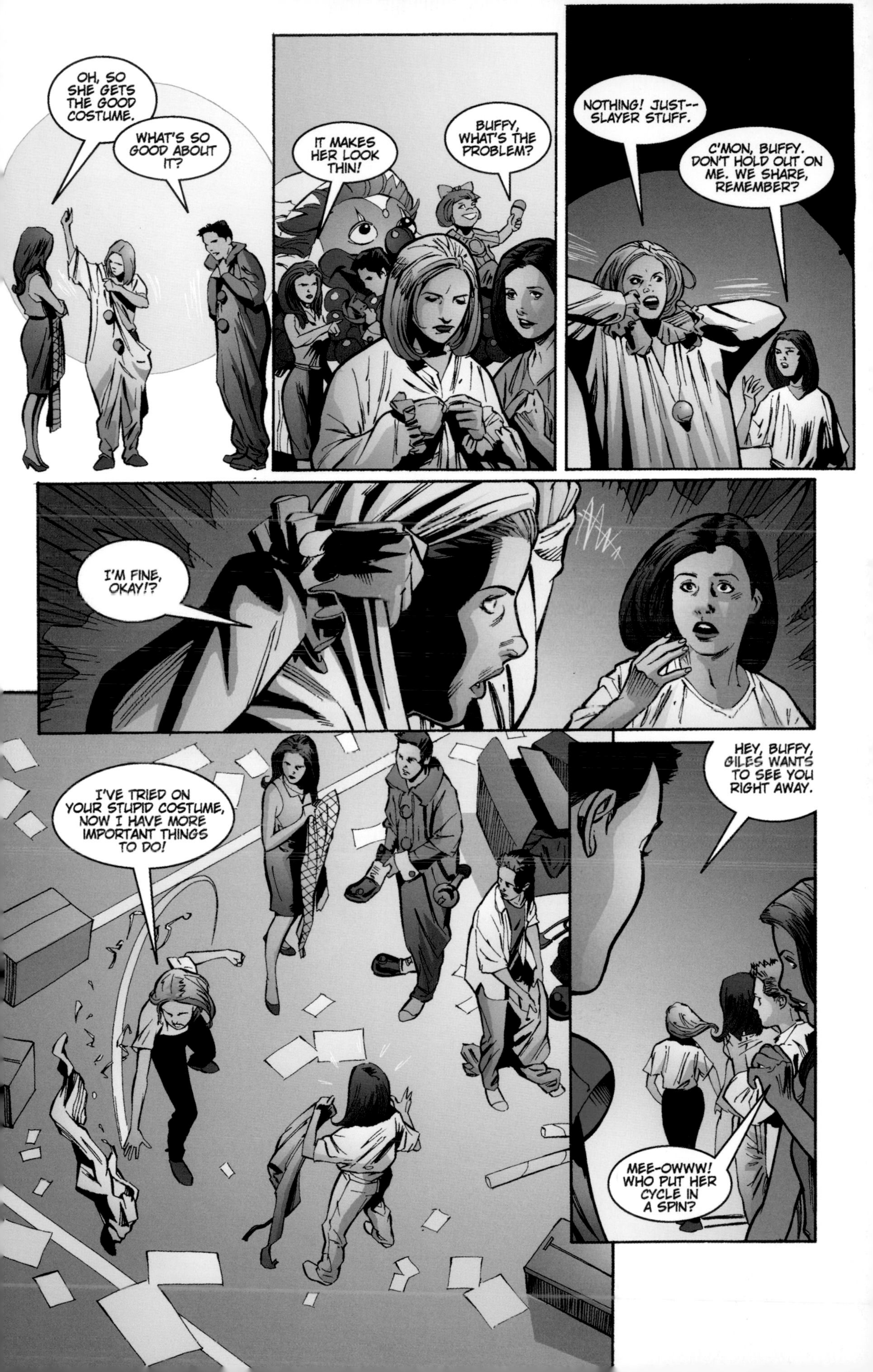
OH, SO SHE GETS THE GOOD COSTUME.
WHAT'S SO GOOD ABOUT IT?
IT MAKES HER LOOK THIN!
BUFFY, WHAT'S THE PROBLEM?
NOTHING! JUST-- SLAYER STUFF.
C'MON, BUFFY. DON'T HOLD OUT ON ME. WE SHARE, REMEMBER?
I'M FINE, OKAY!?
I'VE TRIED ON YOUR STUPID COSTUME, NOW I HAVE MORE IMPORTANT THINGS TO DO!
HEY, BUFFY, GILES WANTS TO SEE YOU RIGHT AWAY.
MEE-OWWW! WHO PUT HER CYCLE IN A SPIN?

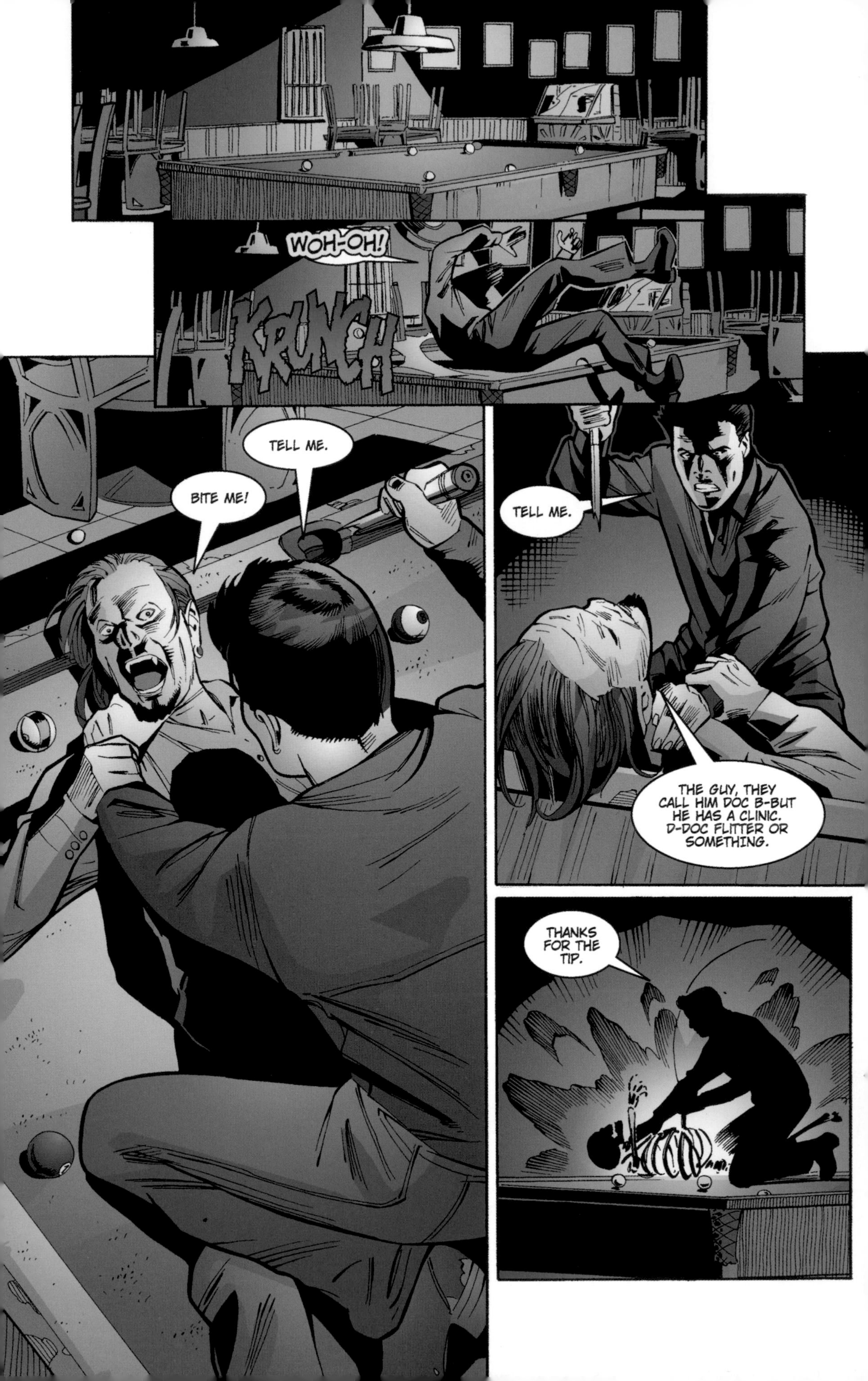
WOH-OH!
KRUNCH
TELL ME.
BITE ME!
TELL ME.
THE GUY, THEY CALL HIM DOC B-BUT HE HAS A CLINIC. D-DOC FLITTER OR SOMETHING.
THANKS FOR THE TIP.

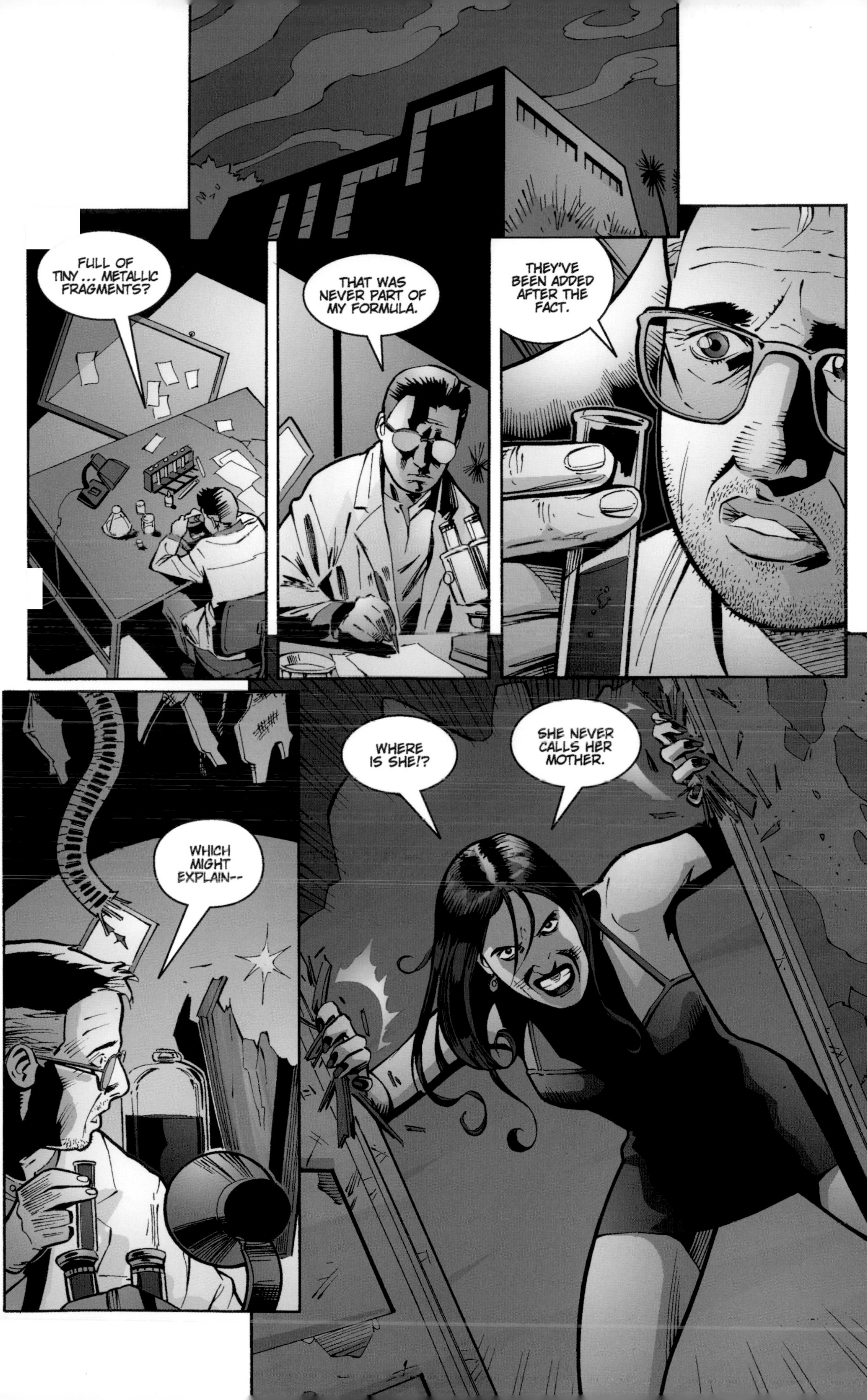
FULL OF TINY ... METALLIC FRAGMENTS?
THAT WAS NEVER PART OF MY FORMULA.
THEY'VE BEEN ADDED AFTER THE FACT.
WHICH MIGHT EXPLAIN--
WHERE IS SHE!?
SHE NEVER CALLS HER MOTHER.

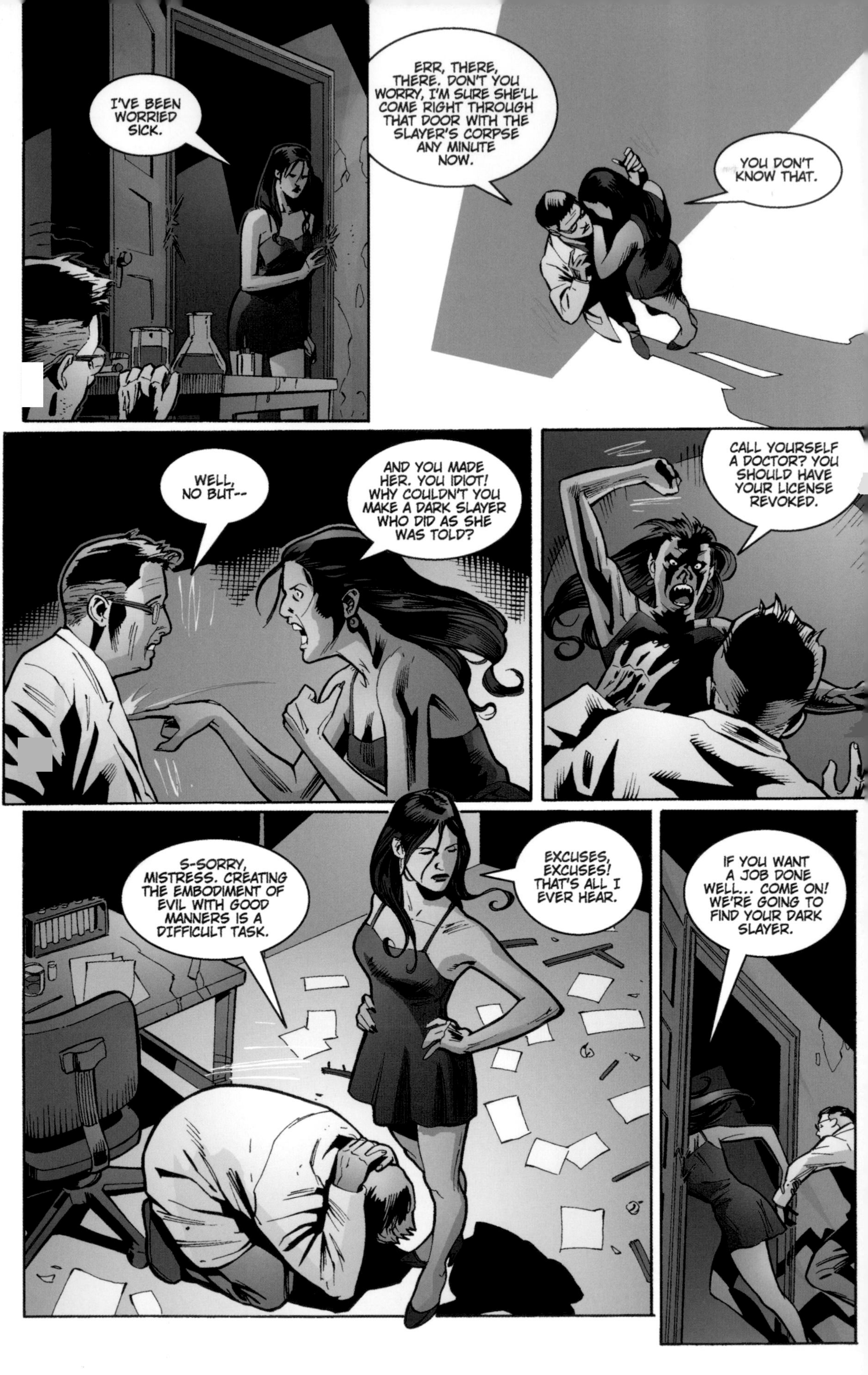
I'VE BEEN WORRIED SICK.
ERR, THERE, THERE. DON'T YOU WORRY, I'M SURE SHE'LL COME RIGHT THROUGH THAT DOOR WITH THE SLAYER'S CORPSE ANY MINUTE NOW.
YOU DON'T KNOW THAT.
WELL, NO BUT--
AND YOU MADE HER. YOU IDIOT! WHY COULDN'T YOU MAKE A DARK SLAYER WHO DID AS SHE WAS TOLD?
CALL YOURSELF A DOCTOR? YOU SHOULD HAVE YOUR LICENSE REVOKED.
S-SORRY, MISTRESS. CREATING THE EMBODIMENT OF EVIL WITH GOOD MANNERS IS A DIFFICULT TASK.
EXCUSES, EXCUSES! THAT'S ALL I EVER HEAR.
IF YOU WANT A JOB DONE WELL... COME ON! WE'RE GOING TO FIND YOUR DARK SLAYER.

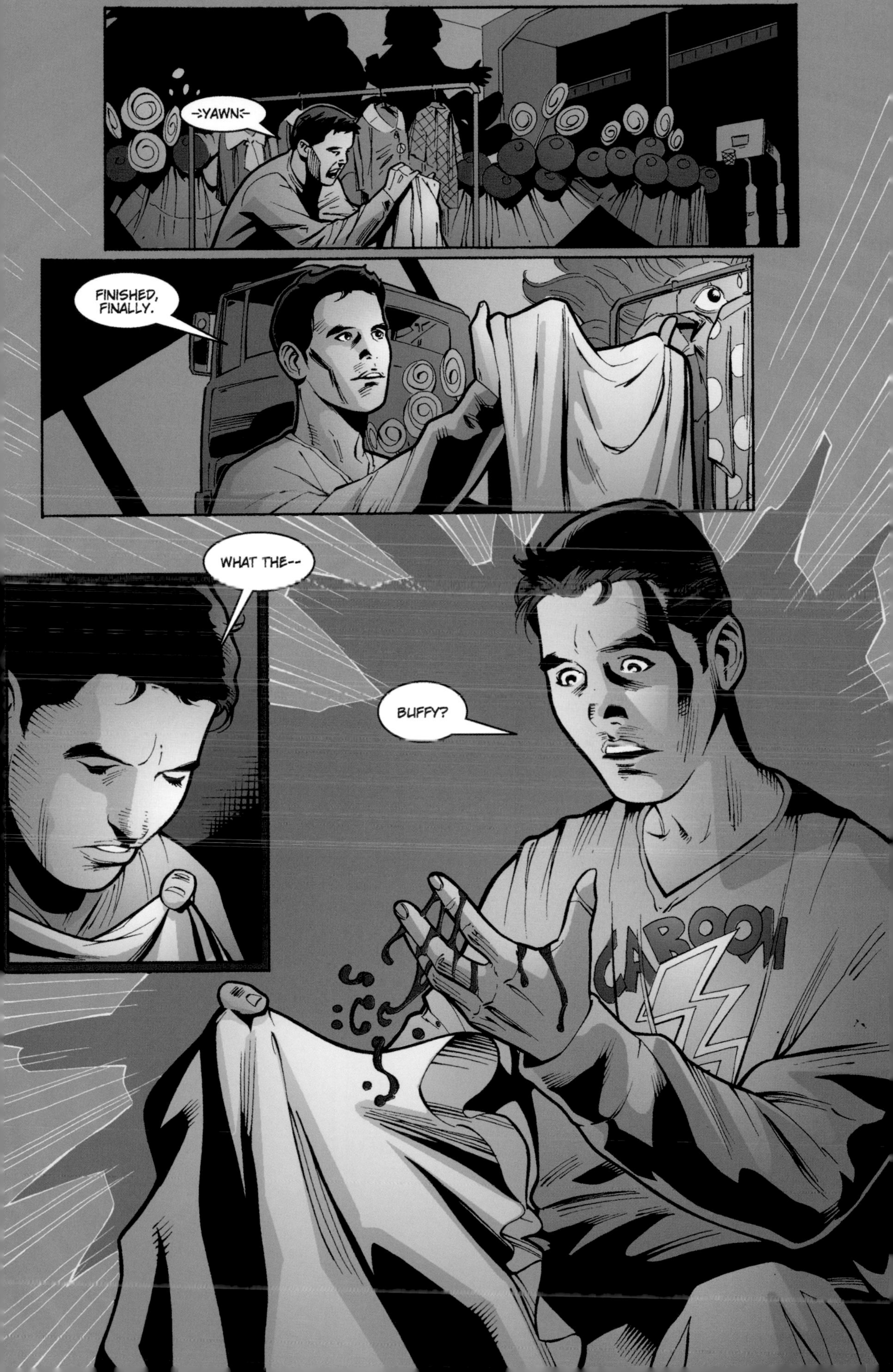
-YAWN-
FINISHED, FINALLY.
WHAT THE--
BUFFY?
CABOOM

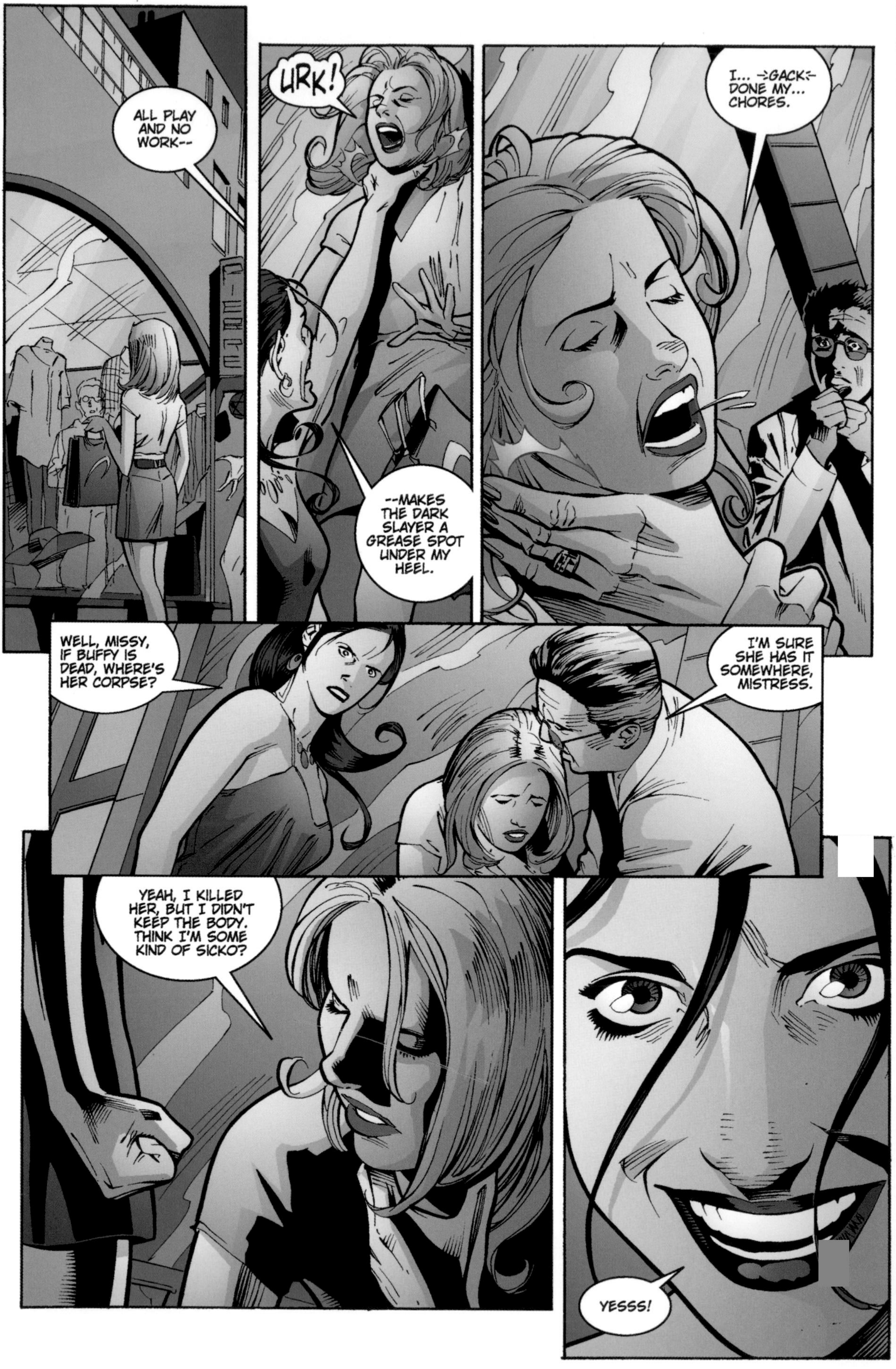
ALL PLAY AND NO WORK--
URK!
--MAKES THE DARK SLAYER A GREASE SPOT UNDER MY HEEL.
I... ⇒GACK⇐ DONE MY... CHORES.
WELL, MISSY, IF BUFFY IS DEAD, WHERE'S HER CORPSE?
I'M SURE SHE HAS IT SOMEWHERE, MISTRESS.
YEAH, I KILLED HER, BUT I DIDN'T KEEP THE BODY. THINK I'M SOME KIND OF SICKO?
YESSS!

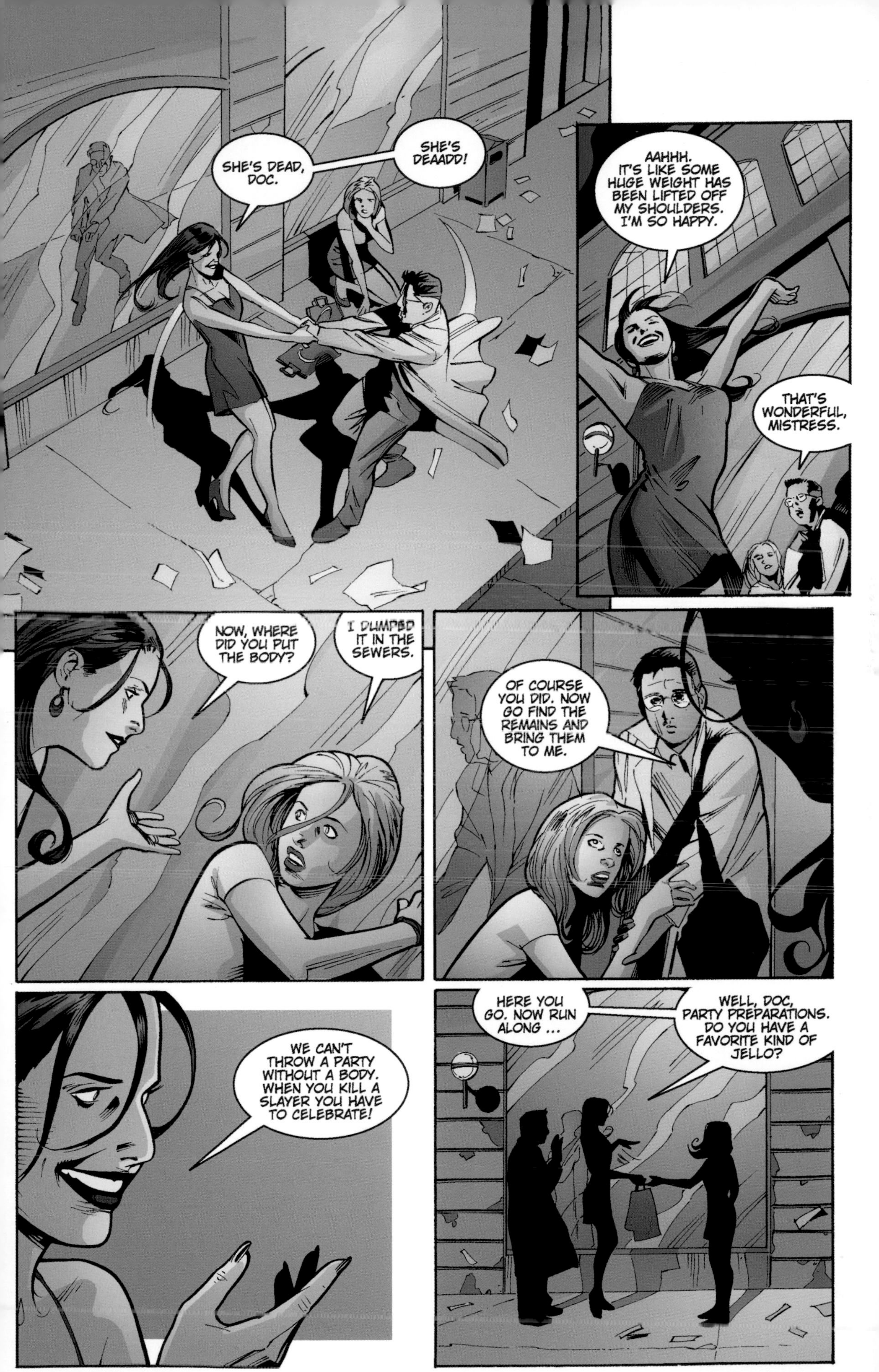
SHE'S DEAD, DOC.
SHE'S DEAADD!
AAHHH. IT'S LIKE SOME HUGE WEIGHT HAS BEEN LIFTED OFF MY SHOULDERS. I'M SO HAPPY.
THAT'S WONDERFUL, MISTRESS.
NOW, WHERE DID YOU PUT THE BODY?
I DUMPED IT IN THE SEWERS.
OF COURSE YOU DID. NOW GO FIND THE REMAINS AND BRING THEM TO ME.
WE CAN'T THROW A PARTY WITHOUT A BODY. WHEN YOU KILL A SLAYER YOU HAVE TO CELEBRATE!
HERE YOU GO. NOW RUN ALONG ...
WELL, DOC, PARTY PREPARATIONS. DO YOU HAVE A FAVORITE KIND OF JELLO?

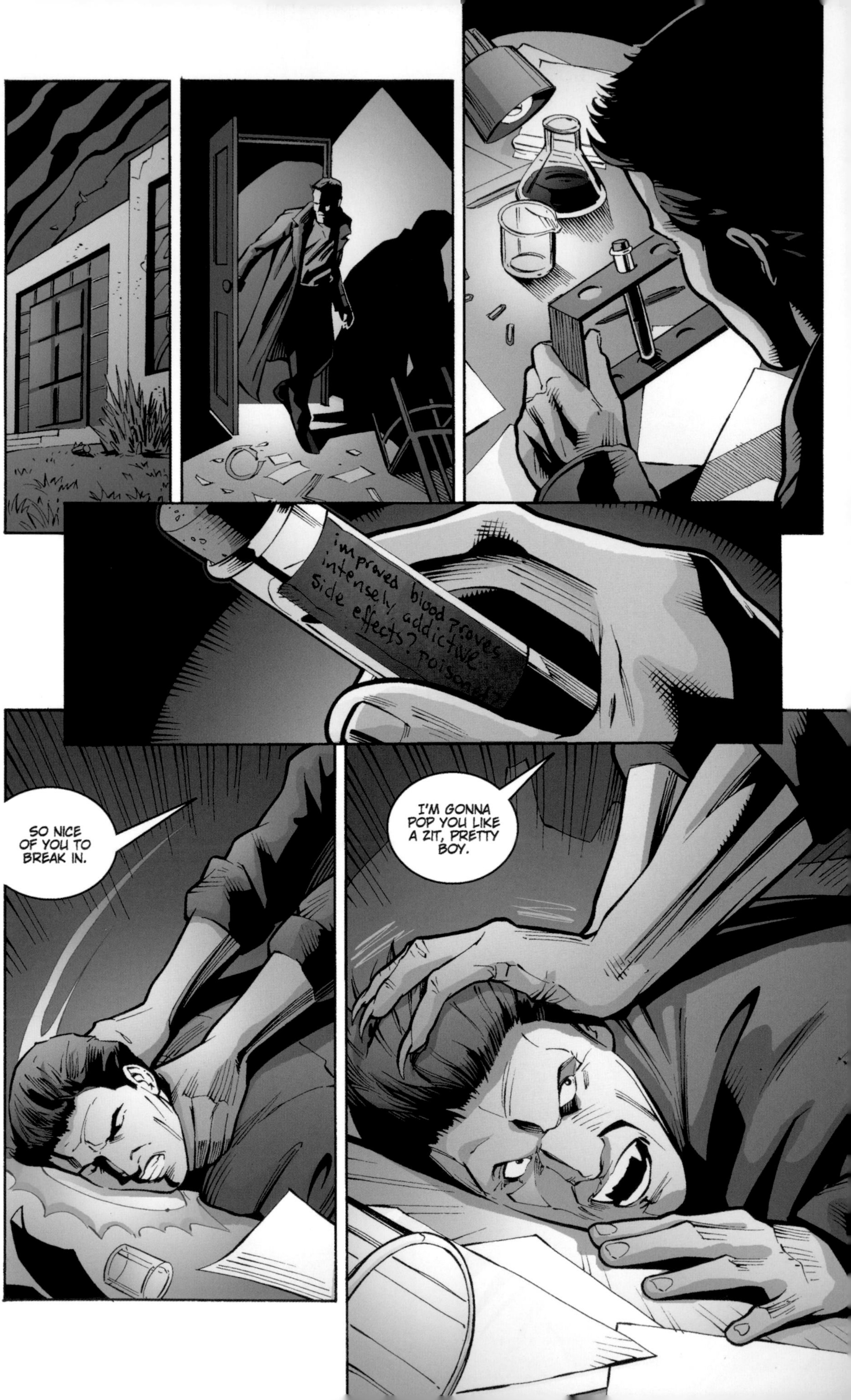
improved blood? proves
intensely addictive.
side effects? poison
SO NICE OF YOU TO BREAK IN.
I'M GONNA POP YOU LIKE A ZIT, PRETTY BOY.

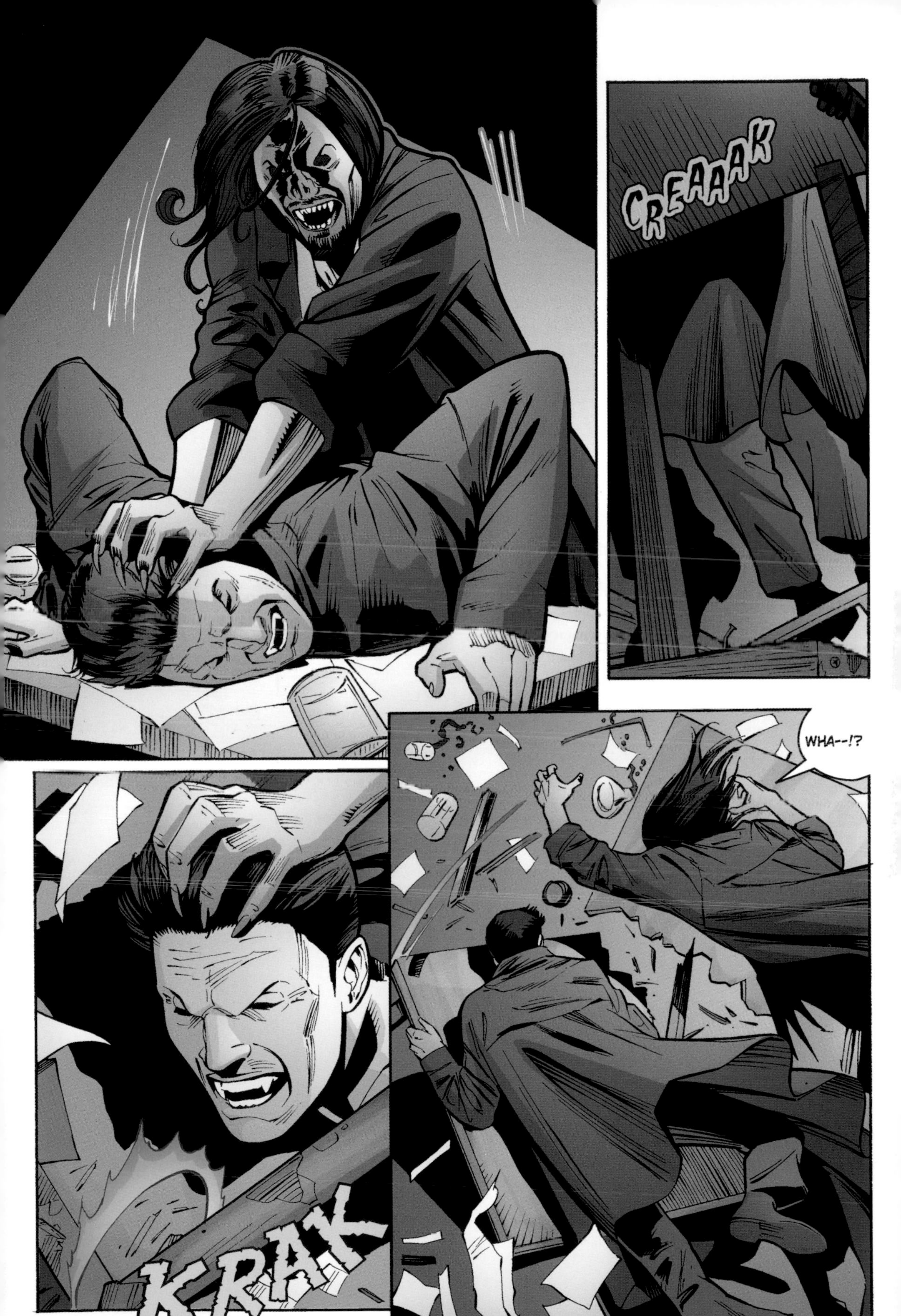
CREAAAK
KRAK
WHA--!?

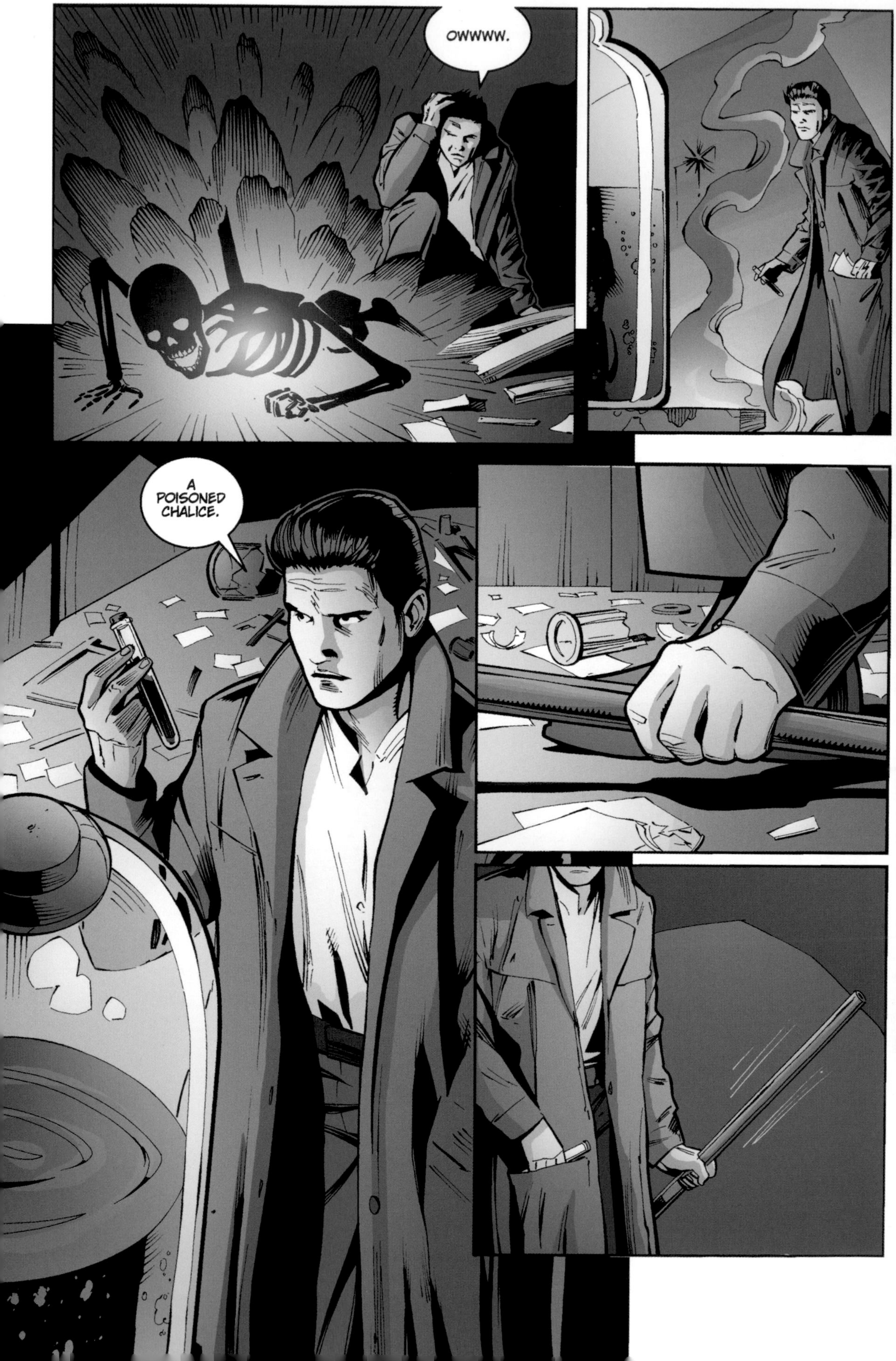
OWWWW.
A POISONED CHALICE.

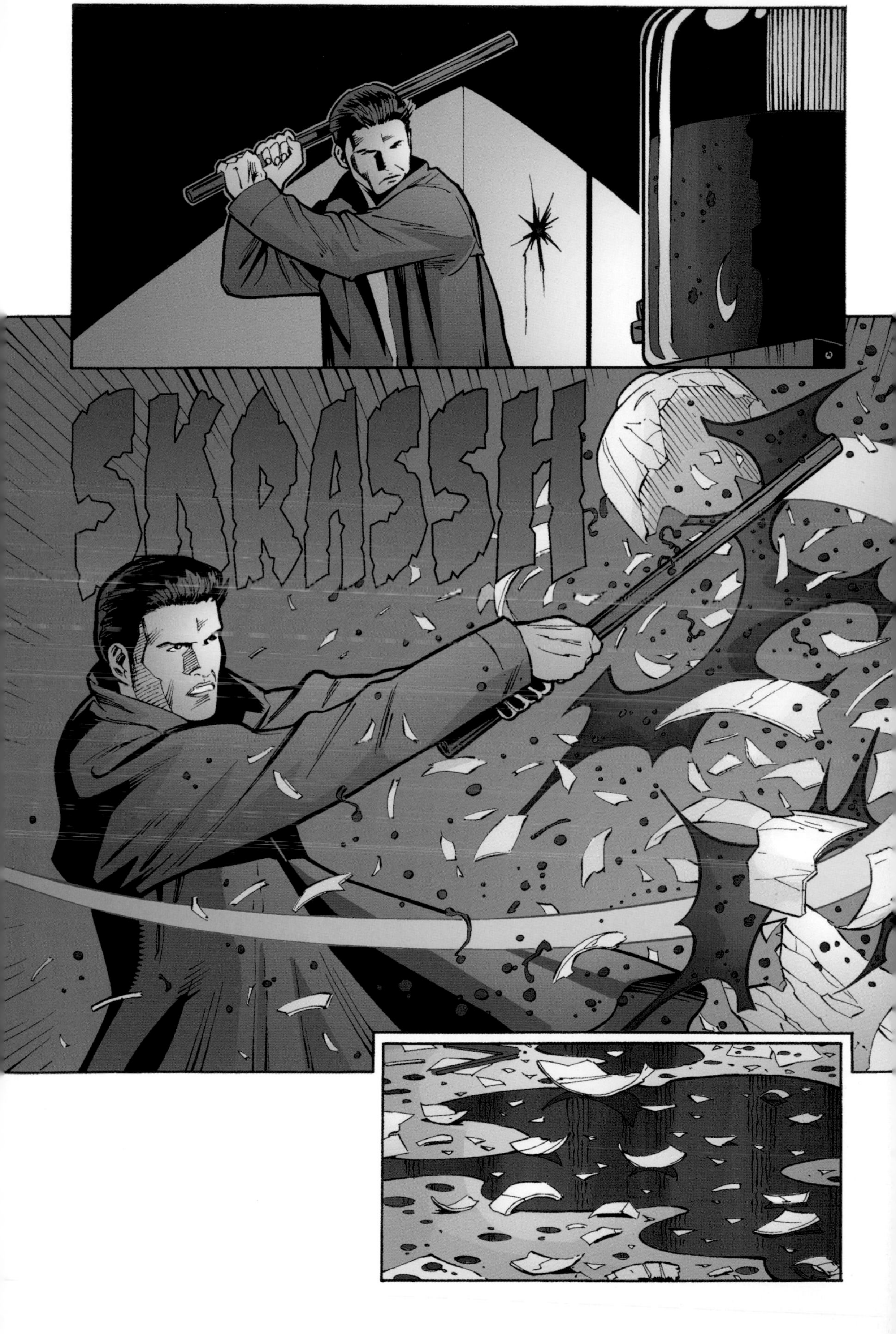
SKRASSH

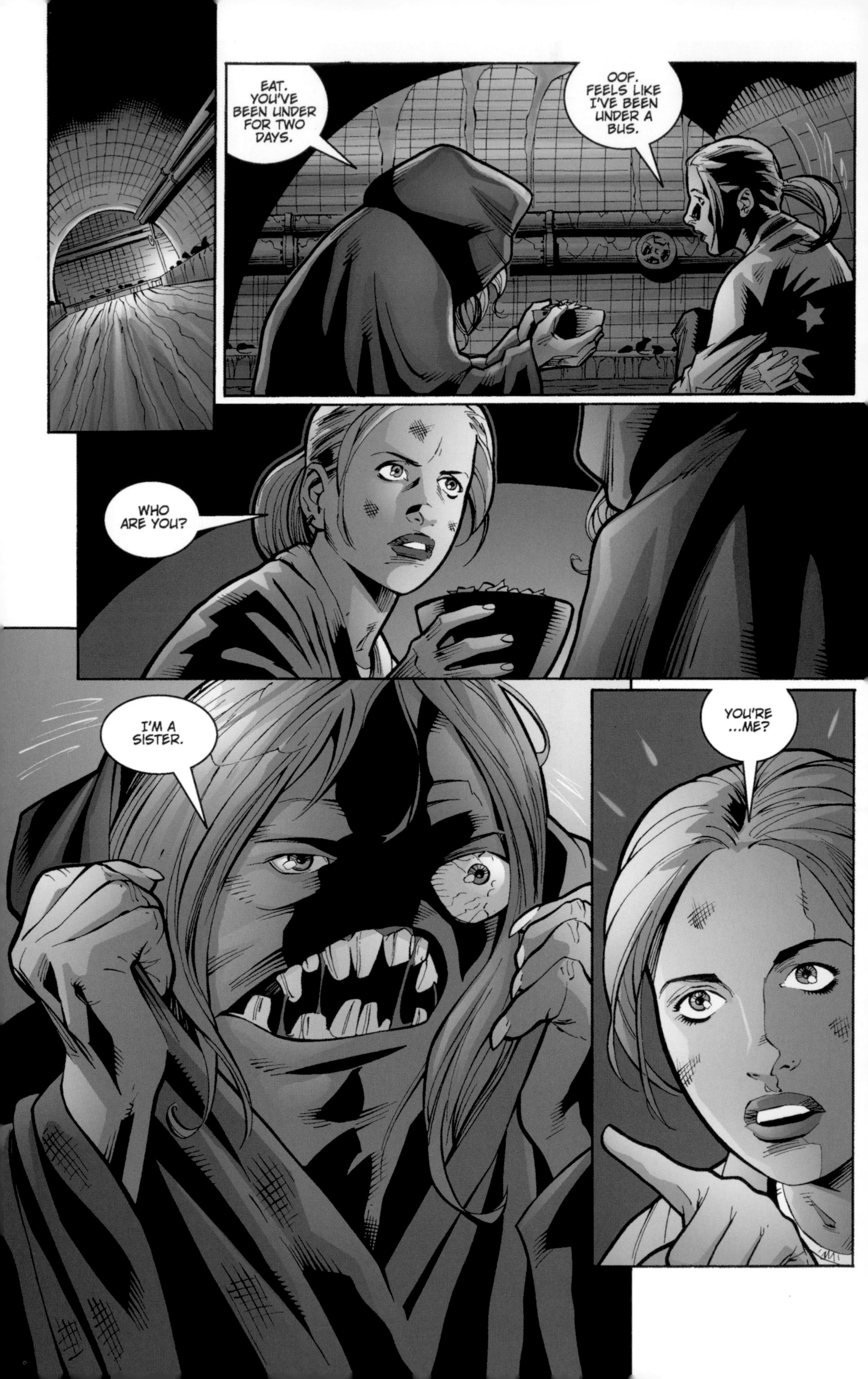
EAT. YOU'VE BEEN UNDER FOR TWO DAYS.
OOF. FEELS LIKE I'VE BEEN UNDER A BUS.
WHO ARE YOU?
I'M A SISTER.
YOU'RE ...ME?

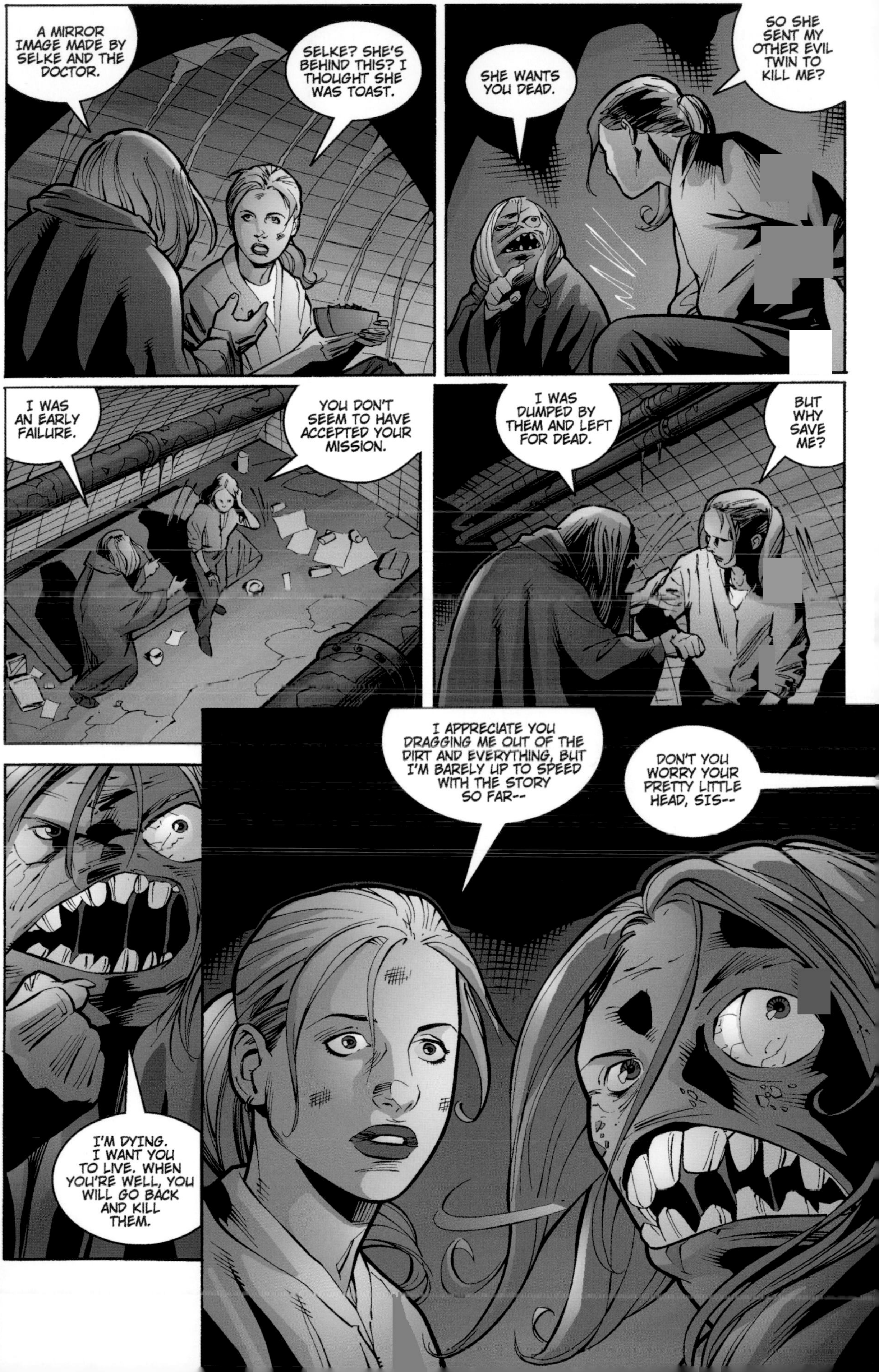
A MIRROR IMAGE MADE BY SELKE AND THE DOCTOR.
SELKE? SHE'S BEHIND THIS? I THOUGHT SHE WAS TOAST.
SHE WANTS YOU DEAD.
SO SHE SENT MY OTHER EVIL TWIN TO KILL ME?
I WAS AN EARLY FAILURE.
YOU DON'T SEEM TO HAVE ACCEPTED YOUR MISSION.
I WAS DUMPED BY THEM AND LEFT FOR DEAD.
BUT WHY SAVE ME?
I'M DYING. I WANT YOU TO LIVE. WHEN YOU'RE WELL, YOU WILL GO BACK AND KILL THEM.
I APPRECIATE YOU DRAGGING ME OUT OF THE DIRT AND EVERYTHING, BUT I'M BARELY UP TO SPEED WITH THE STORY SO FAR--
DON'T YOU WORRY YOUR PRETTY LITTLE HEAD, SIS--

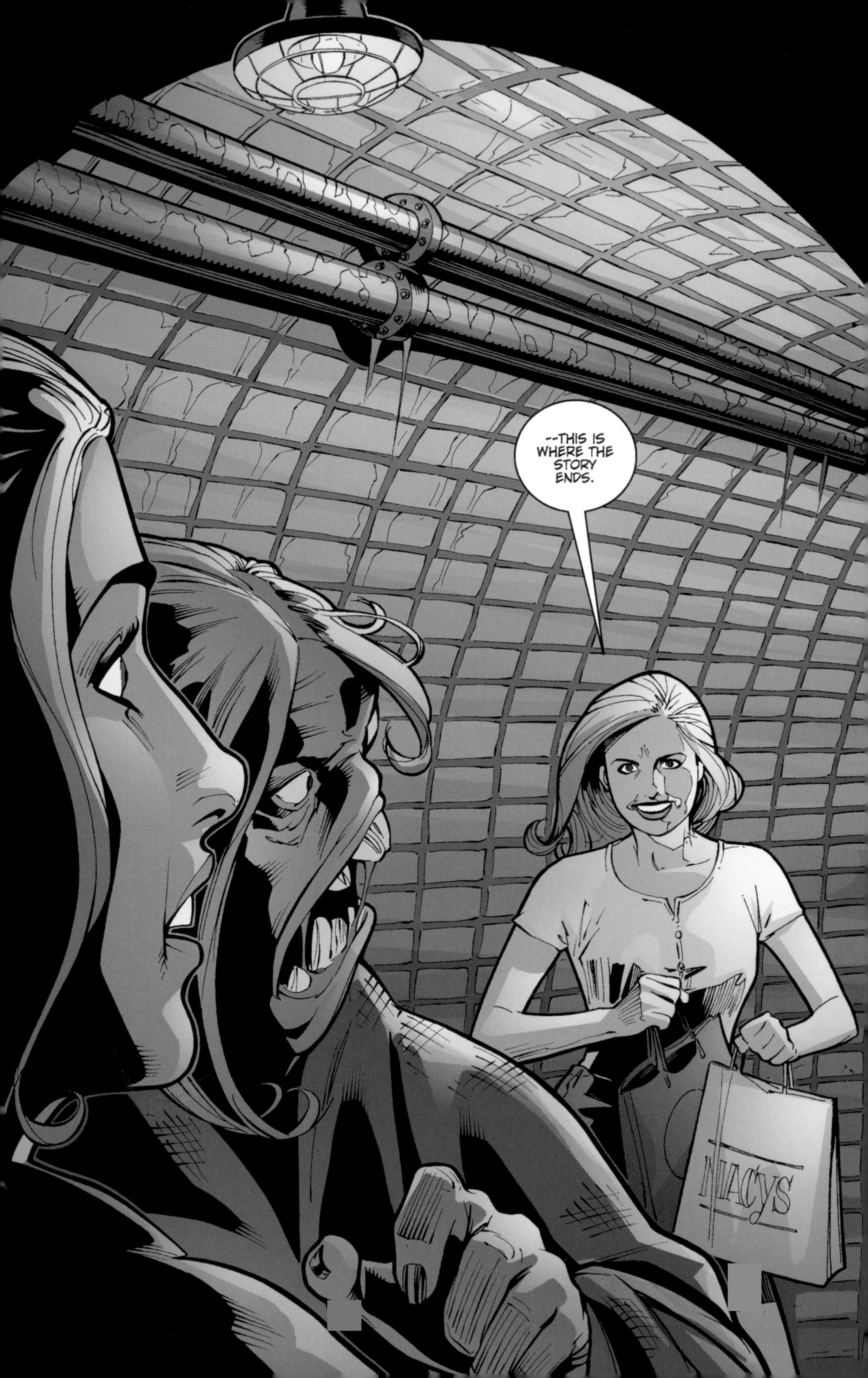
--THIS IS WHERE THE STORY ENDS.
MACYS

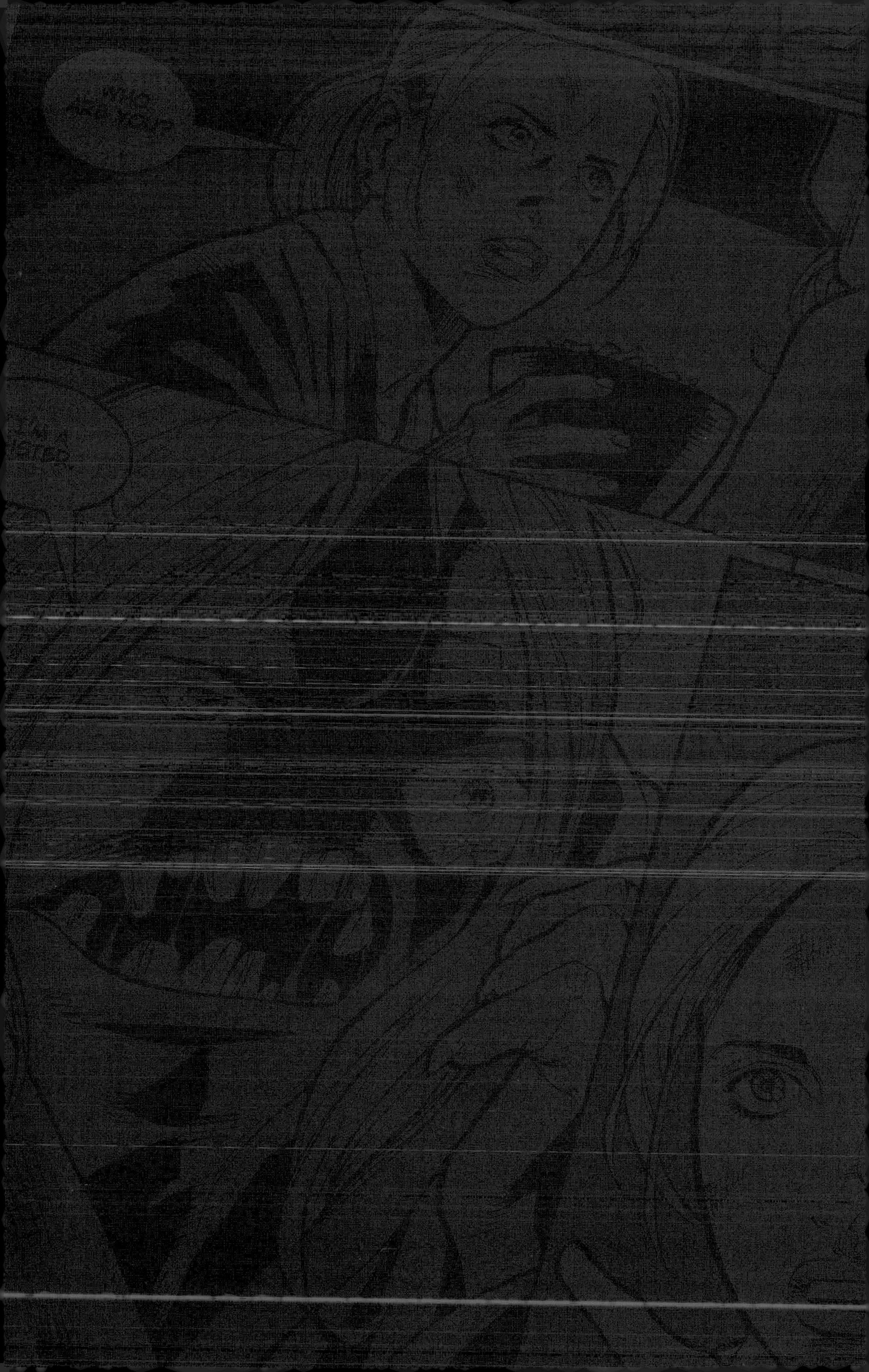

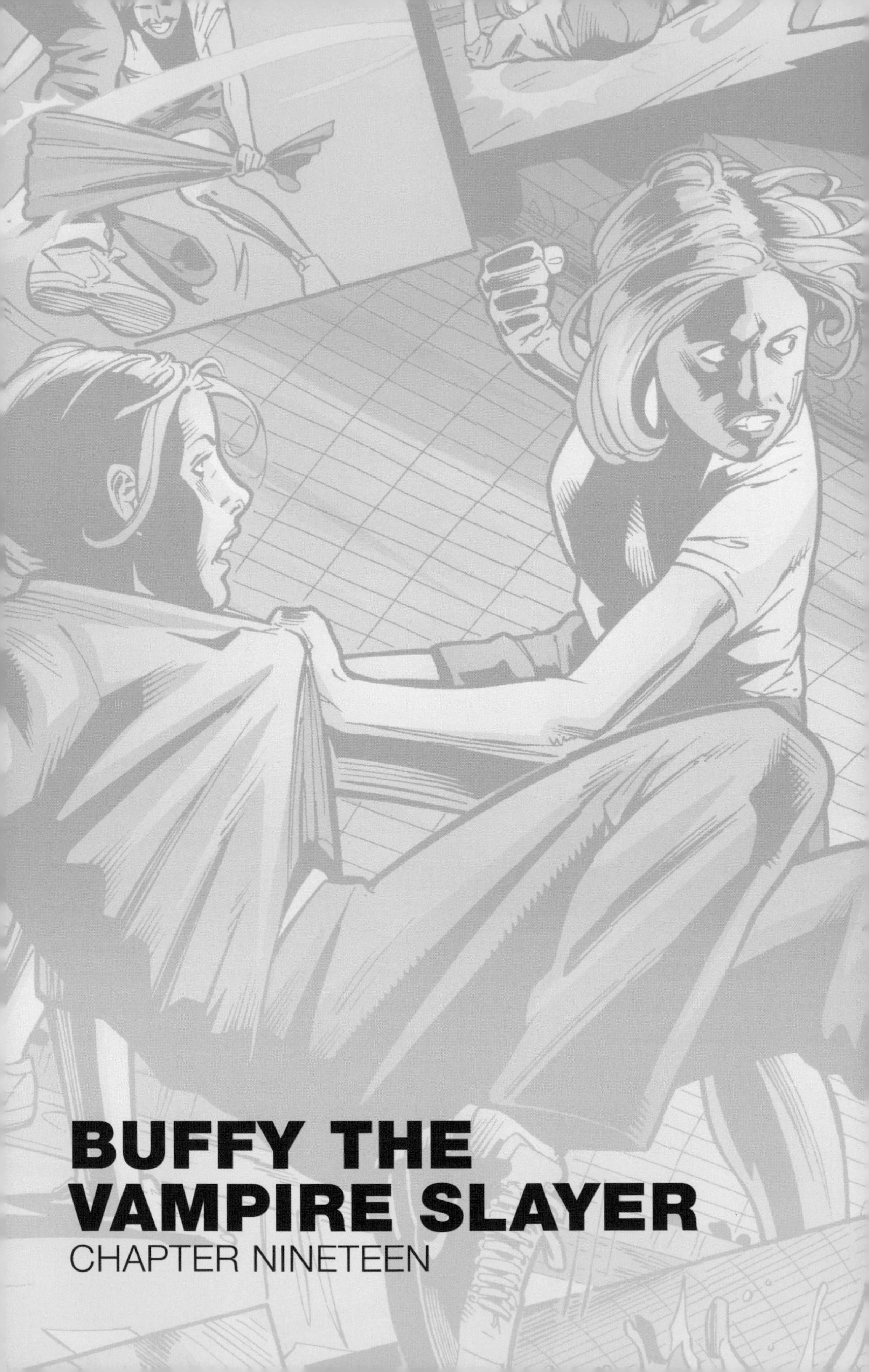

BUFFY THE VAMPIRE SLAYER
CHAPTER NINETEEN

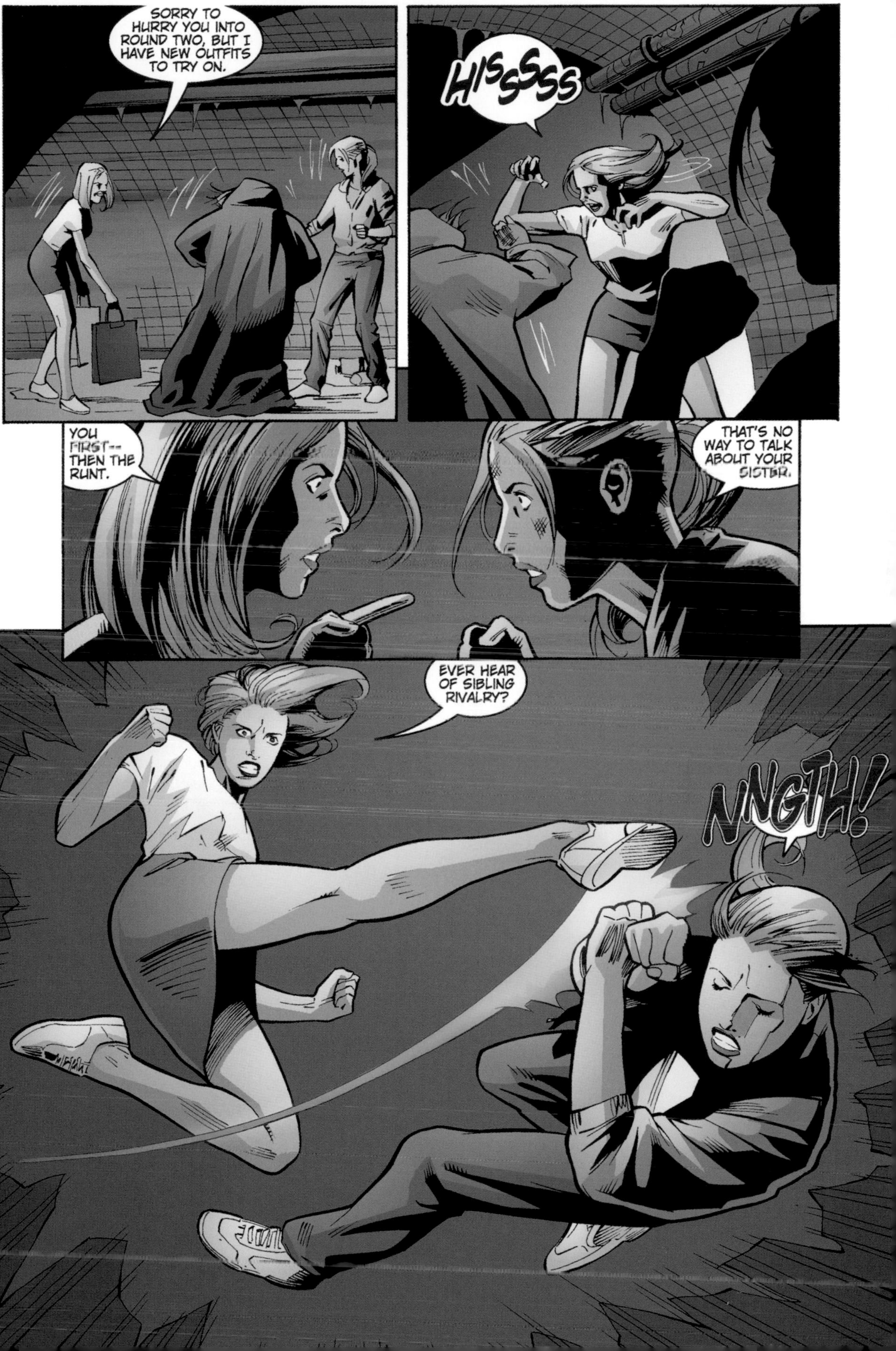
SORRY TO HURRY YOU INTO ROUND TWO, BUT I HAVE NEW OUTFITS TO TRY ON.
HISSSSS
YOU FIRST-- THEN THE RUNT.
THAT'S NO WAY TO TALK ABOUT YOUR SISTER.
EVER HEAR OF SIBLING RIVALRY?
NNGTH!

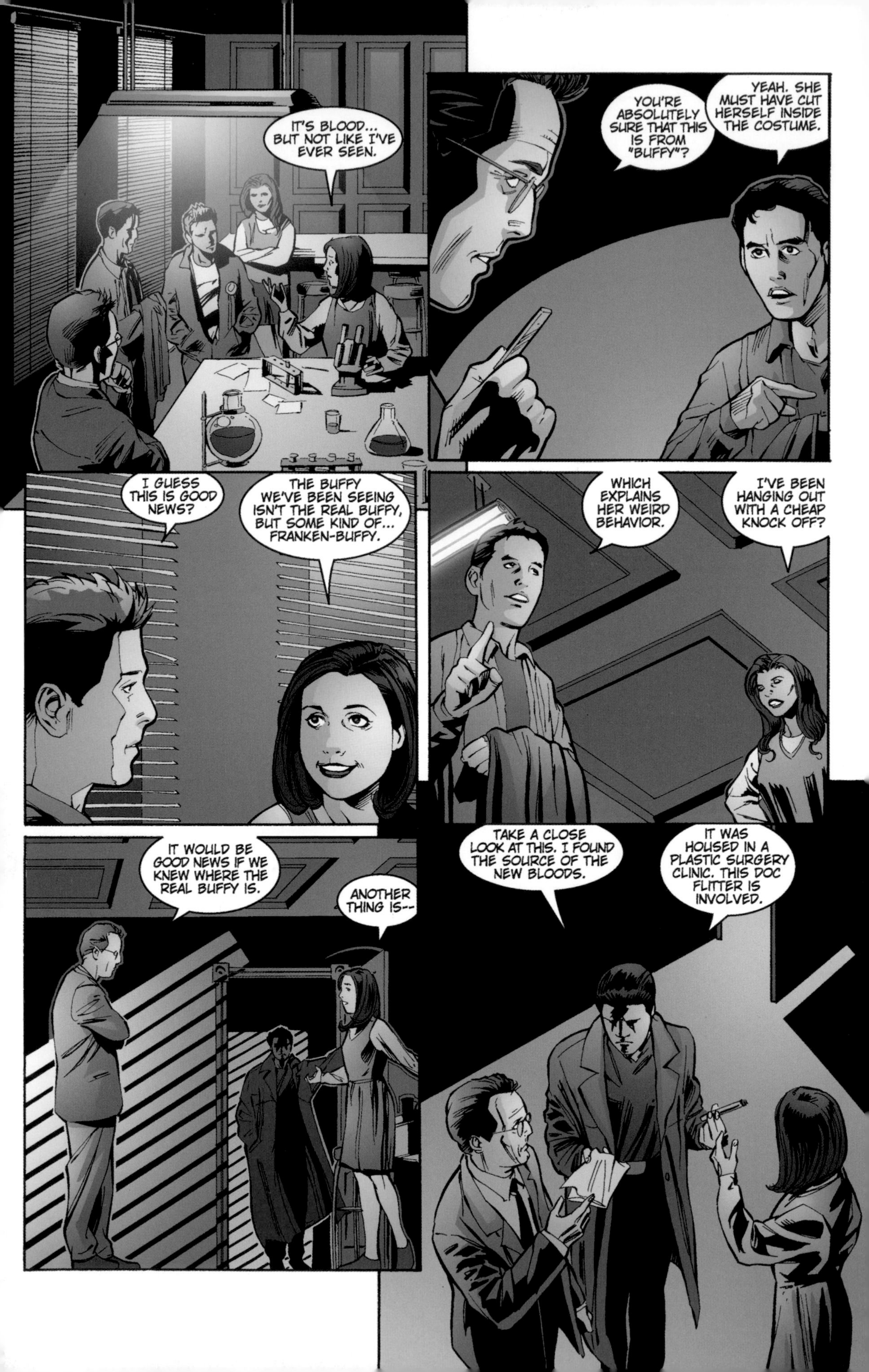
IT'S BLOOD... BUT NOT LIKE I'VE EVER SEEN.
YOU'RE ABSOLUTELY SURE THAT THIS IS FROM "BUFFY"?
YEAH. SHE MUST HAVE CUT HERSELF INSIDE THE COSTUME.
I GUESS THIS IS GOOD NEWS?
THE BUFFY WE'VE BEEN SEEING ISN'T THE REAL BUFFY, BUT SOME KIND OF... FRANKEN-BUFFY.
WHICH EXPLAINS HER WEIRD BEHAVIOR.
I'VE BEEN HANGING OUT WITH A CHEAP KNOCK OFF?
IT WOULD BE GOOD NEWS IF WE KNEW WHERE THE REAL BUFFY IS.
ANOTHER THING IS--
TAKE A CLOSE LOOK AT THIS. I FOUND THE SOURCE OF THE NEW BLOODS.
IT WAS HOUSED IN A PLASTIC SURGERY CLINIC. THIS DOC FLITTER IS INVOLVED.

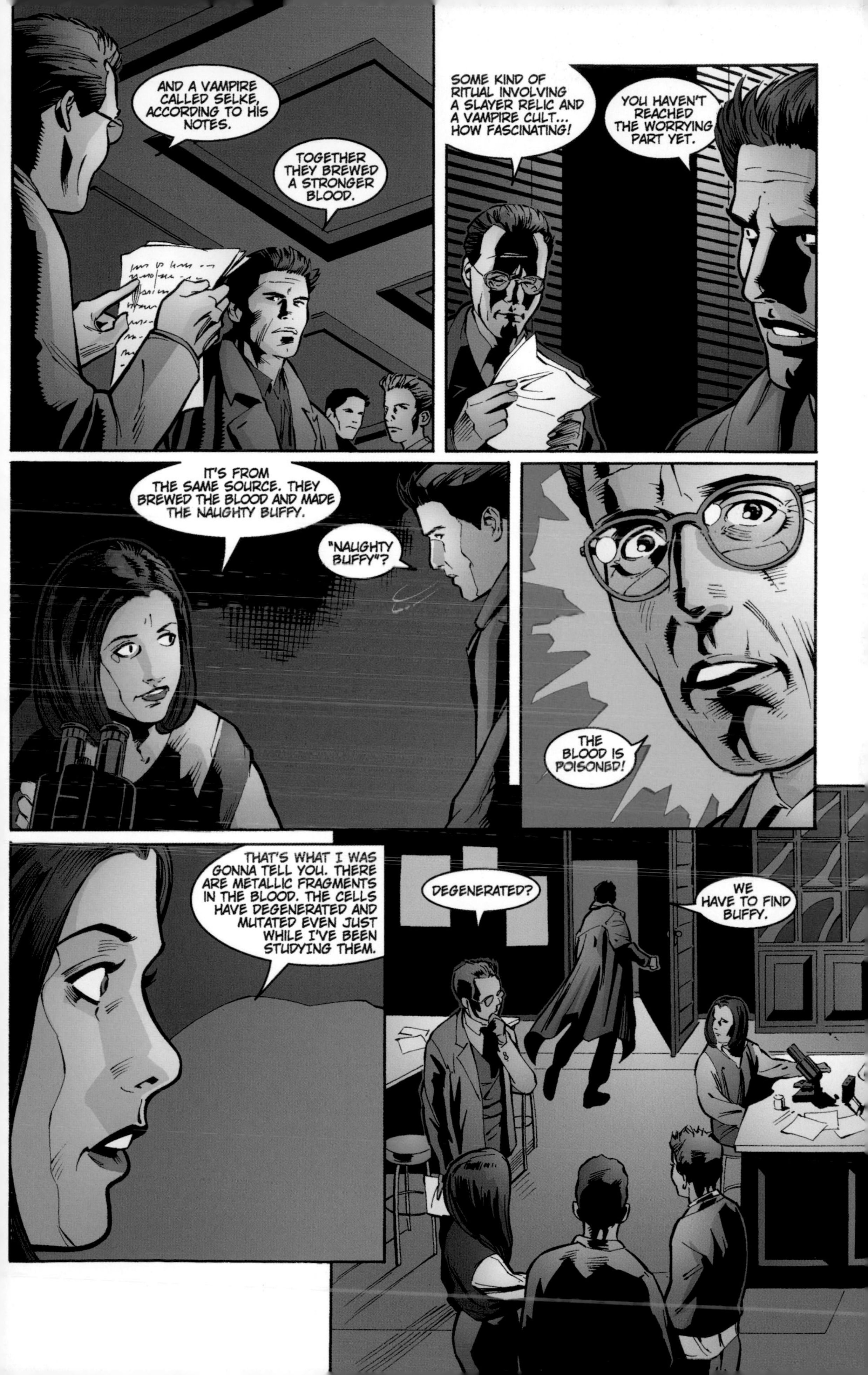
AND A VAMPIRE CALLED SELKE, ACCORDING TO HIS NOTES.
TOGETHER THEY BREWED A STRONGER BLOOD.
SOME KIND OF RITUAL INVOLVING A SLAYER RELIC AND A VAMPIRE CULT... HOW FASCINATING!
YOU HAVEN'T REACHED THE WORRYING PART YET.
IT'S FROM THE SAME SOURCE. THEY BREWED THE BLOOD AND MADE THE NAUGHTY BUFFY.
"NAUGHTY BUFFY"?
THE BLOOD IS POISONED!
THAT'S WHAT I WAS GONNA TELL YOU. THERE ARE METALLIC FRAGMENTS IN THE BLOOD. THE CELLS HAVE DEGENERATED AND MUTATED EVEN JUST WHILE I'VE BEEN STUDYING THEM.
DEGENERATED?
WE HAVE TO FIND BUFFY.

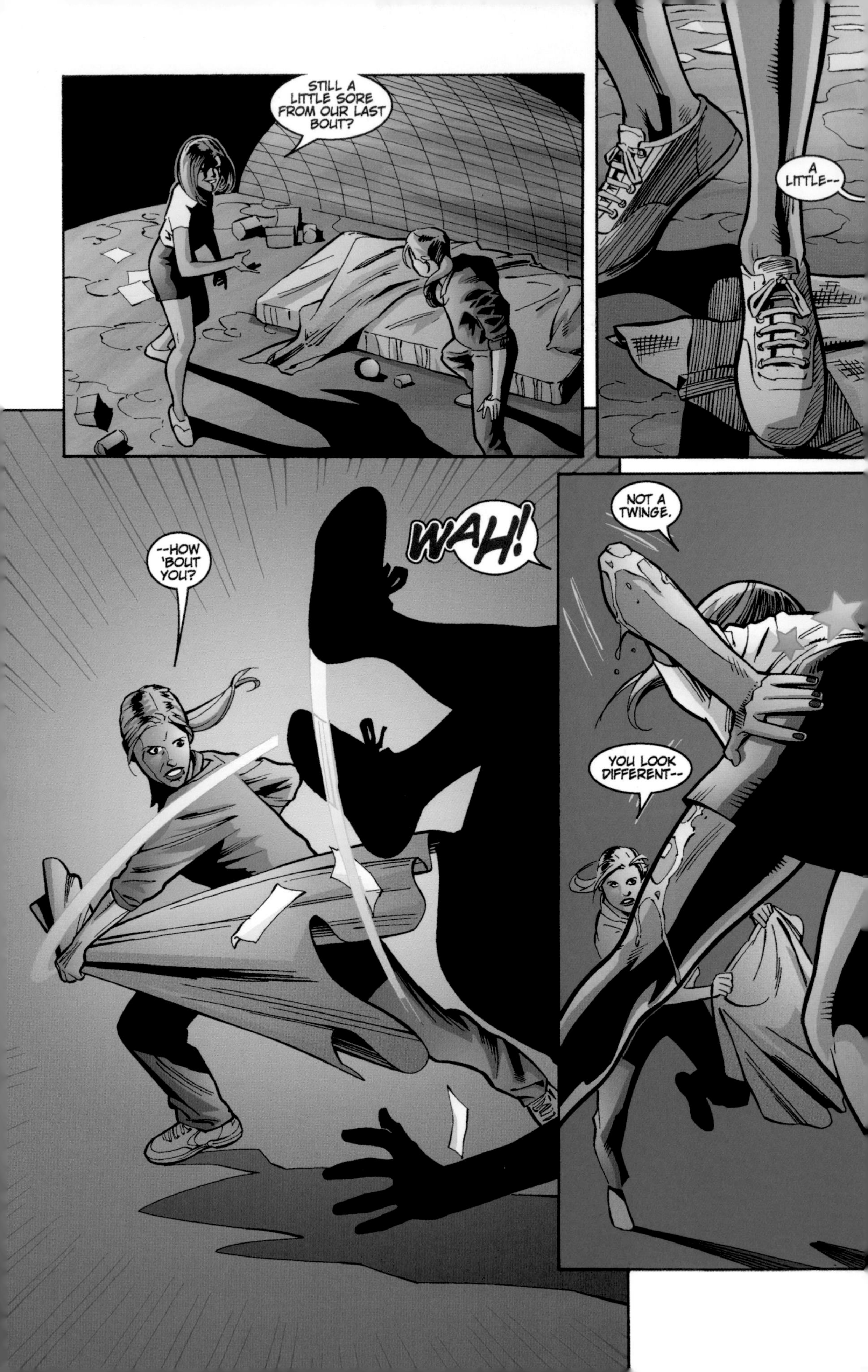
STILL A LITTLE SORE FROM OUR LAST BOUT?
A LITTLE--
--HOW 'BOUT YOU?
WAH!
NOT A TWINGE.
YOU LOOK DIFFERENT--

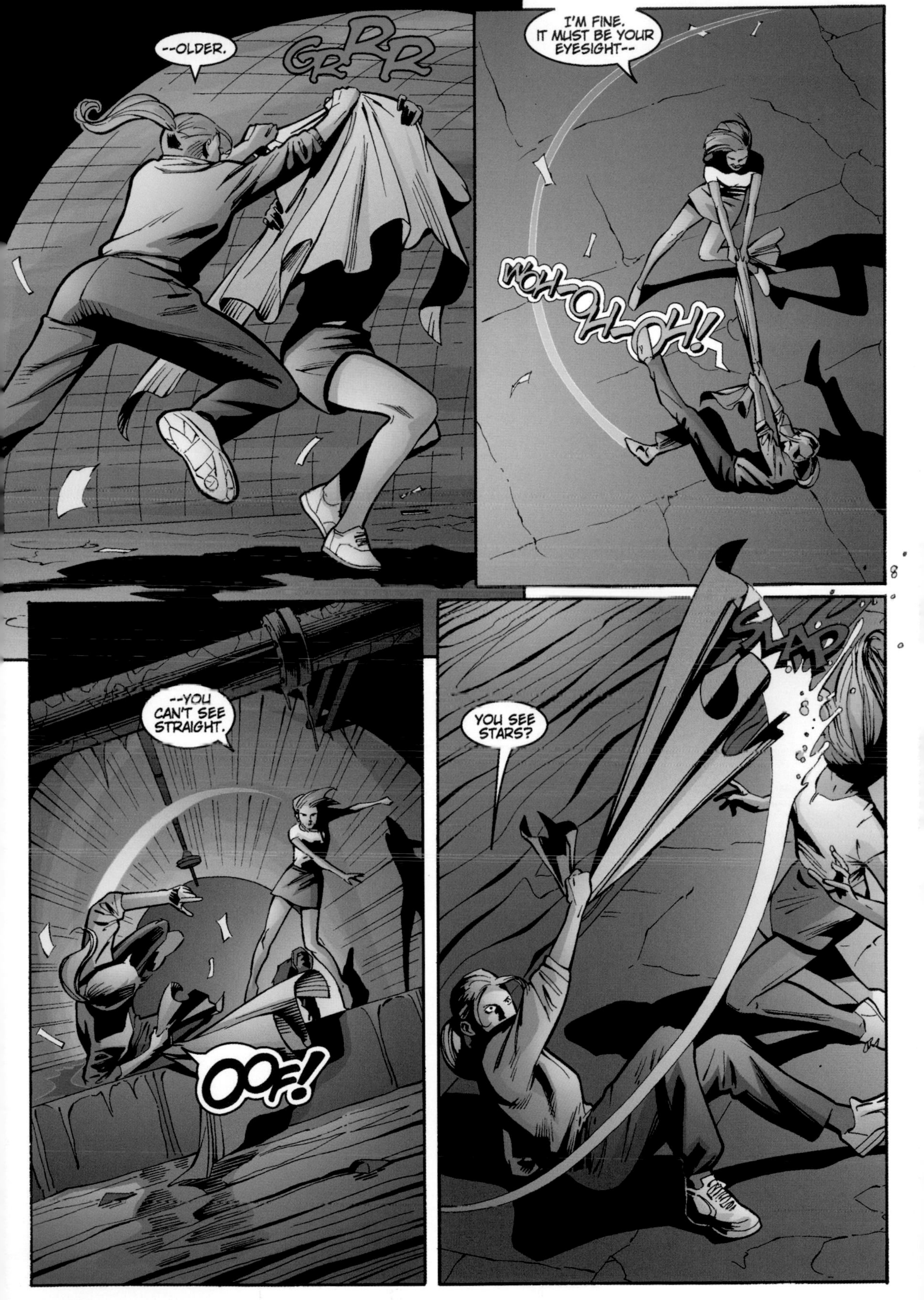
--OLDER.
GRRR
I'M FINE. IT MUST BE YOUR EYESIGHT--
WOH-OH-OH!
--YOU CAN'T SEE STRAIGHT.
OOF!
YOU SEE STARS?
SLAP

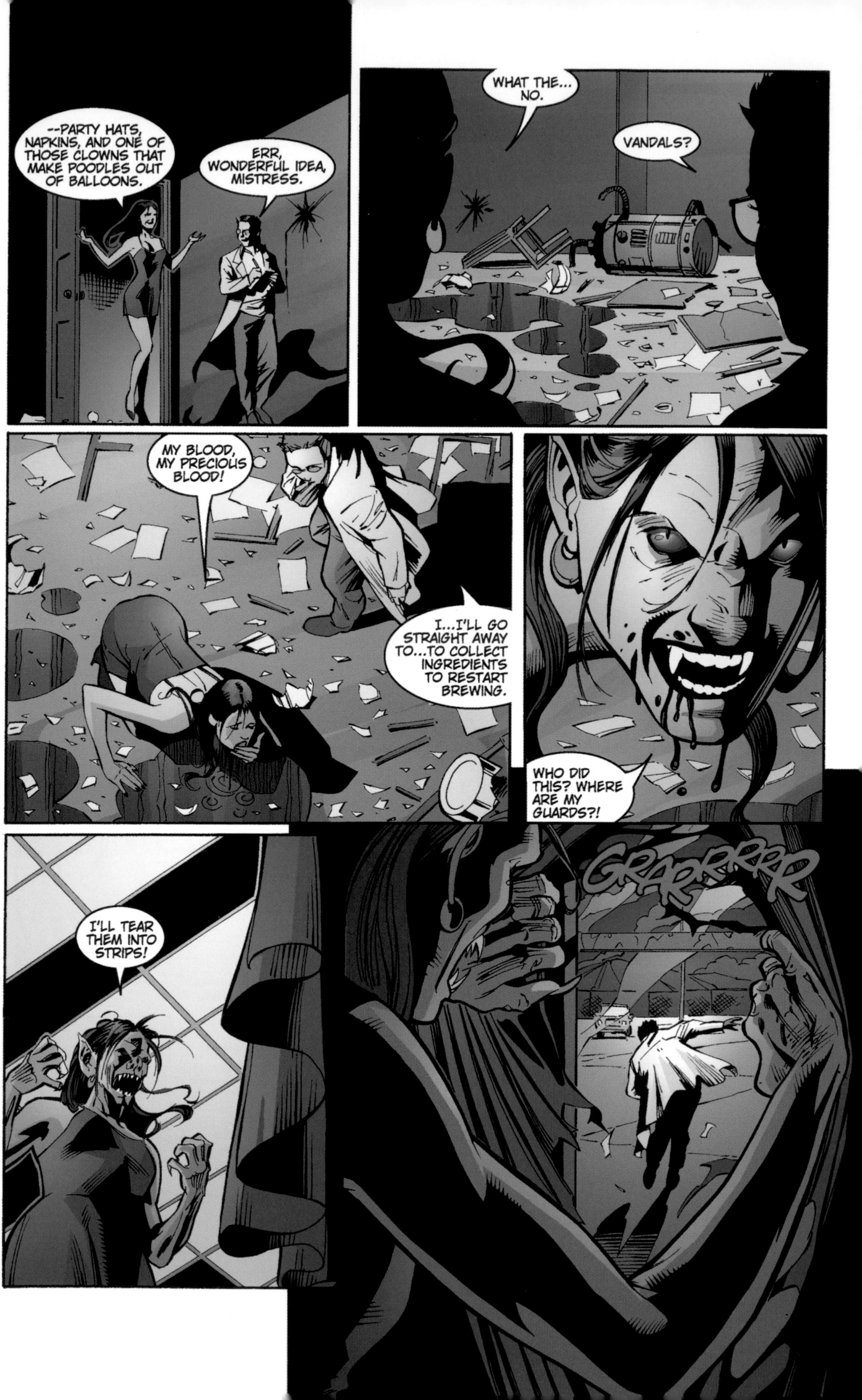
--PARTY HATS, NAPKINS, AND ONE OF THOSE CLOWNS THAT MAKE POODLES OUT OF BALLOONS.
ERR, WONDERFUL IDEA, MISTRESS.
WHAT THE... NO.
VANDALS?
MY BLOOD, MY PRECIOUS BLOOD!
I...I'LL GO STRAIGHT AWAY TO...TO COLLECT INGREDIENTS TO RESTART BREWING.
WHO DID THIS? WHERE ARE MY GUARDS?!
I'LL TEAR THEM INTO STRIPS!
GRARRRRR

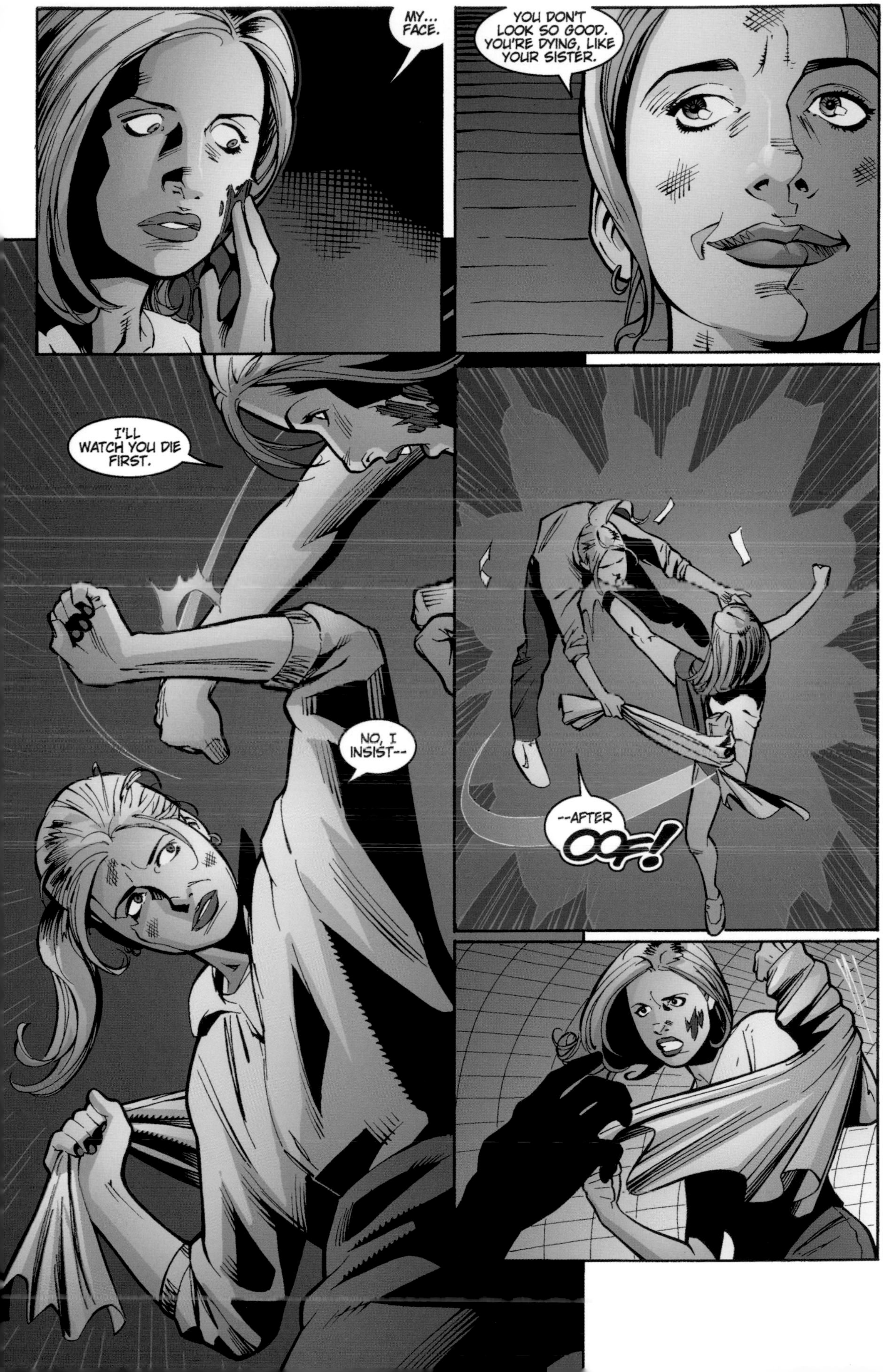
MY... FACE.
YOU DON'T LOOK SO GOOD. YOU'RE DYING, LIKE YOUR SISTER.
I'LL WATCH YOU DIE FIRST.
NO, I INSIST--
--AFTER
OOF!

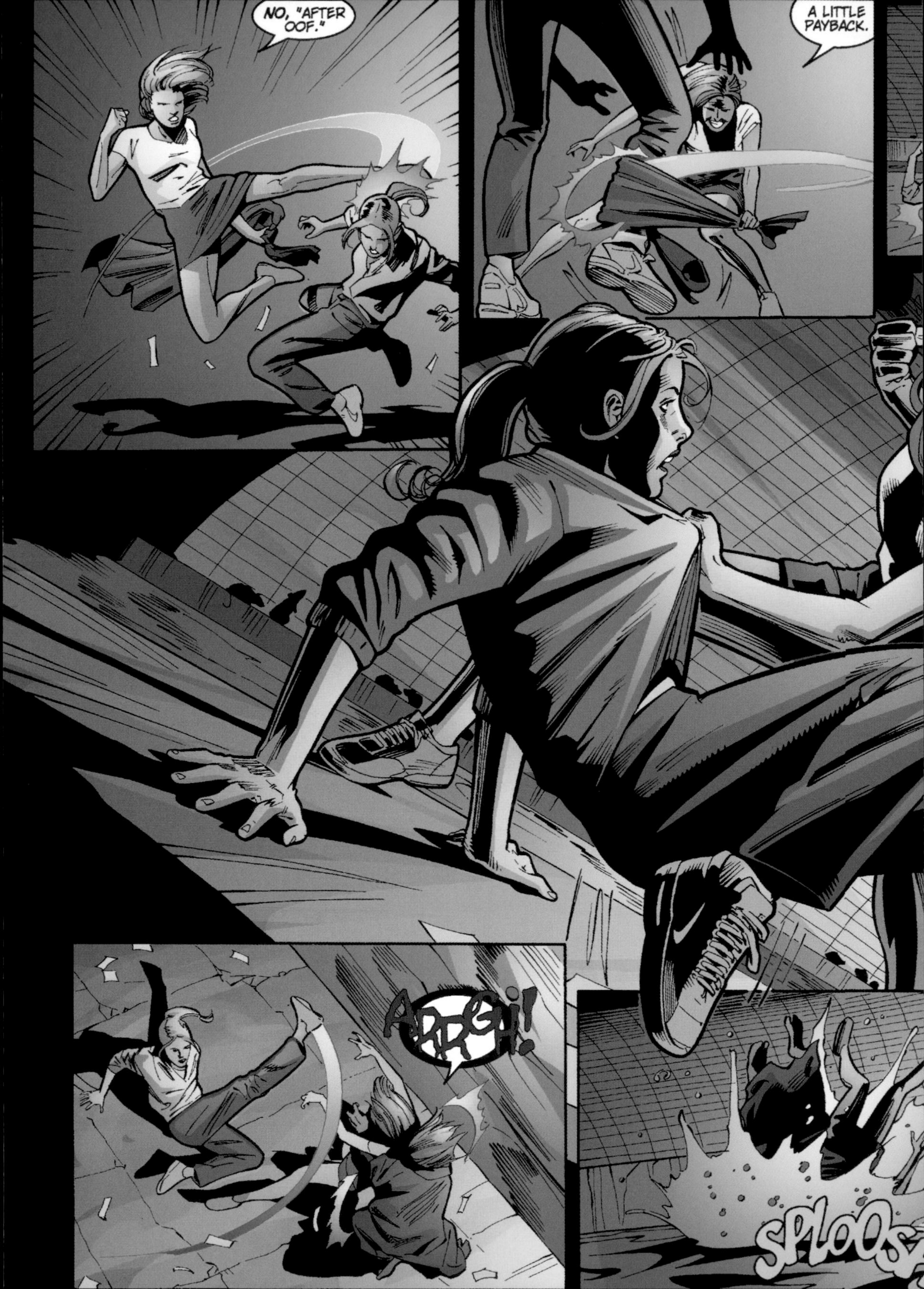
NO, "AFTER OOF."
A LITTLE PAYBACK.
ARRGH!
SPLOOS

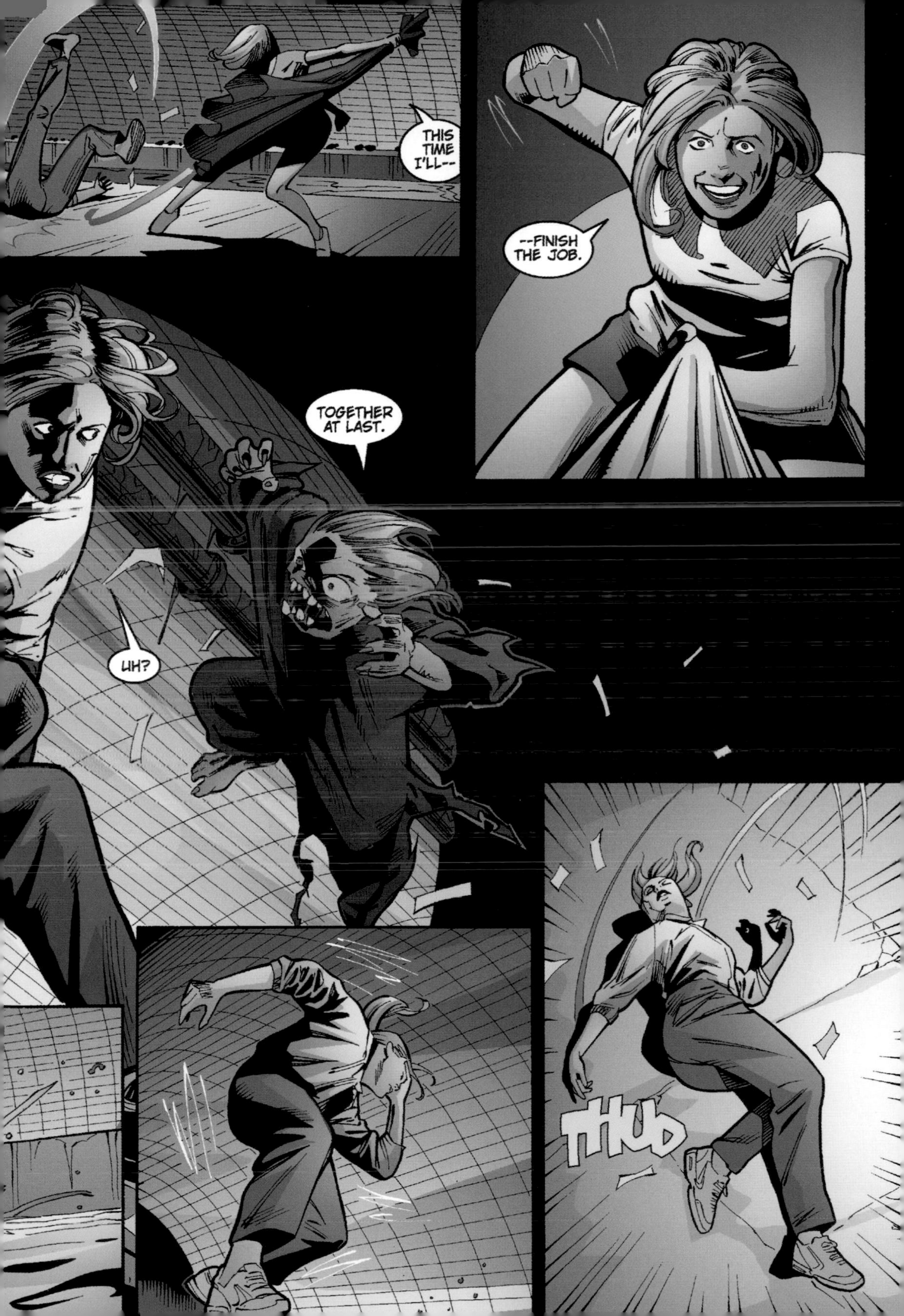
THIS TIME I'LL--
--FINISH THE JOB.
TOGETHER AT LAST.
UH?
THUD

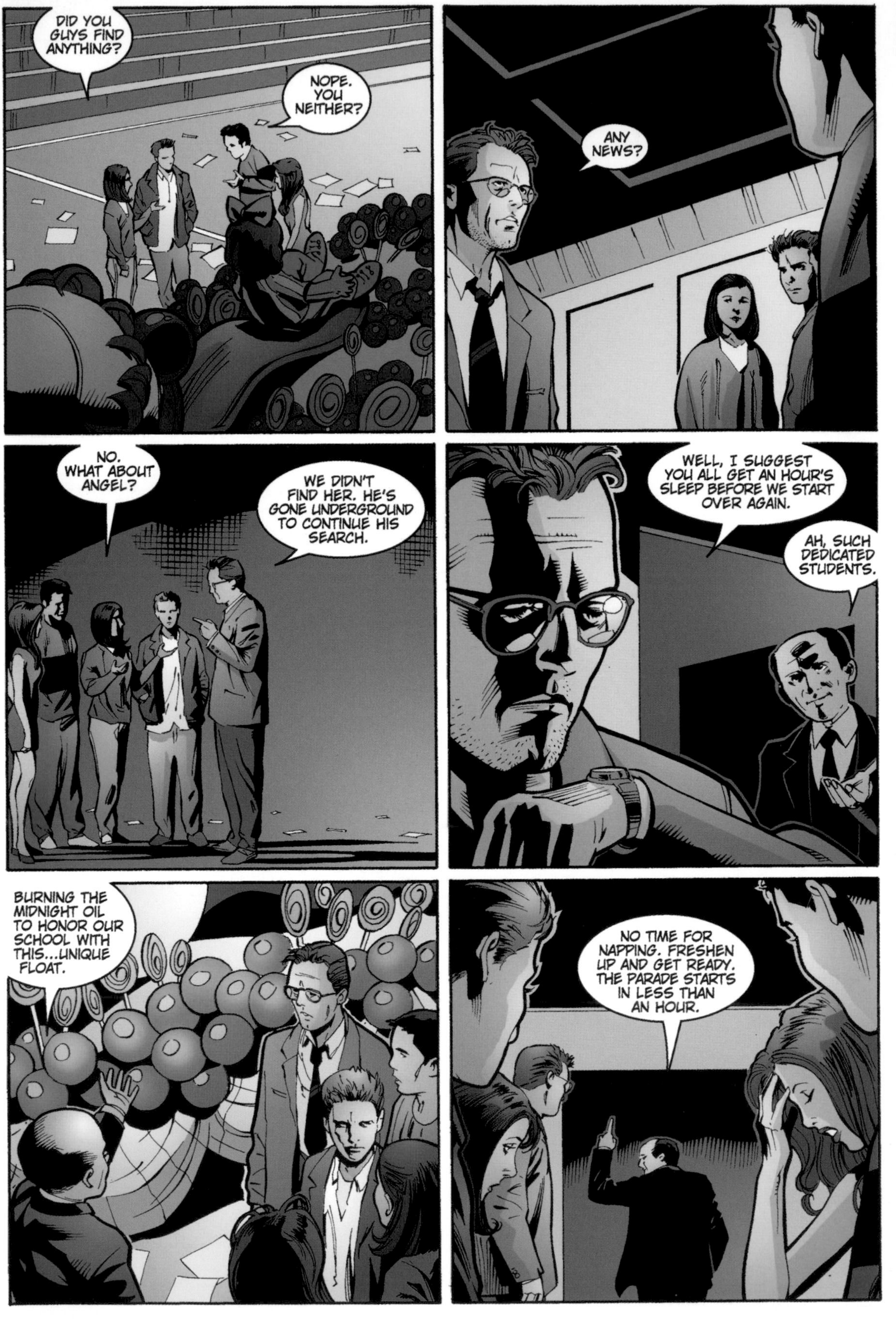
DID YOU GUYS FIND ANYTHING?
NOPE. YOU NEITHER?
ANY NEWS?
NO. WHAT ABOUT ANGEL?
WE DIDN'T FIND HER. HE'S GONE UNDERGROUND TO CONTINUE HIS SEARCH.
WELL, I SUGGEST YOU ALL GET AN HOUR'S SLEEP BEFORE WE START OVER AGAIN.
AH, SUCH DEDICATED STUDENTS.
BURNING THE MIDNIGHT OIL TO HONOR OUR SCHOOL WITH THIS...UNIQUE FLOAT.
NO TIME FOR NAPPING. FRESHEN UP AND GET READY. THE PARADE STARTS IN LESS THAN AN HOUR.

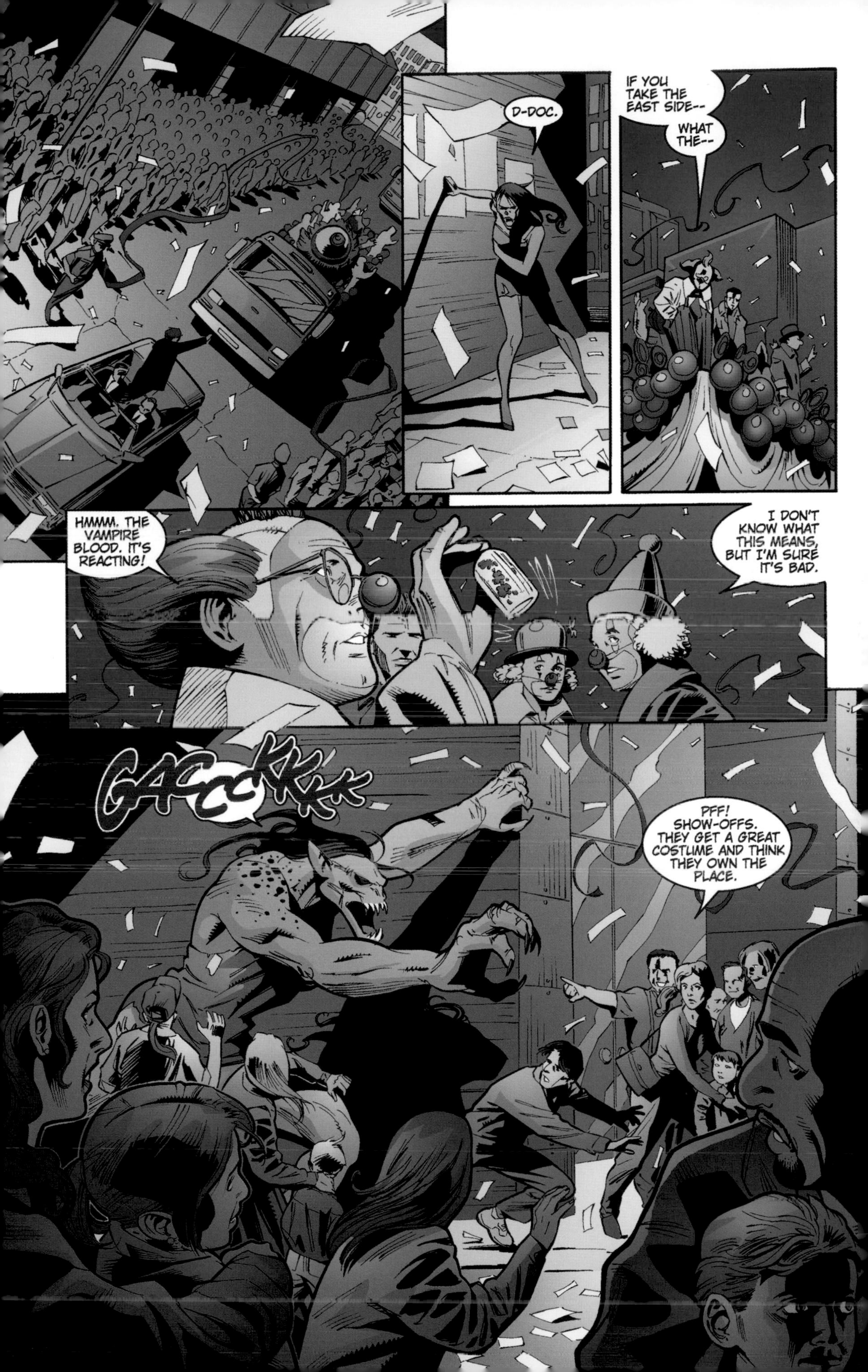
D-DOC.
IF YOU TAKE THE EAST SIDE--
WHAT THE--
HMMM. THE VAMPIRE BLOOD. IT'S REACTING!
I DON'T KNOW WHAT THIS MEANS, BUT I'M SURE IT'S BAD.
GACCCKKKK
PFF! SHOW-OFFS. THEY GET A GREAT COSTUME AND THINK THEY OWN THE PLACE.

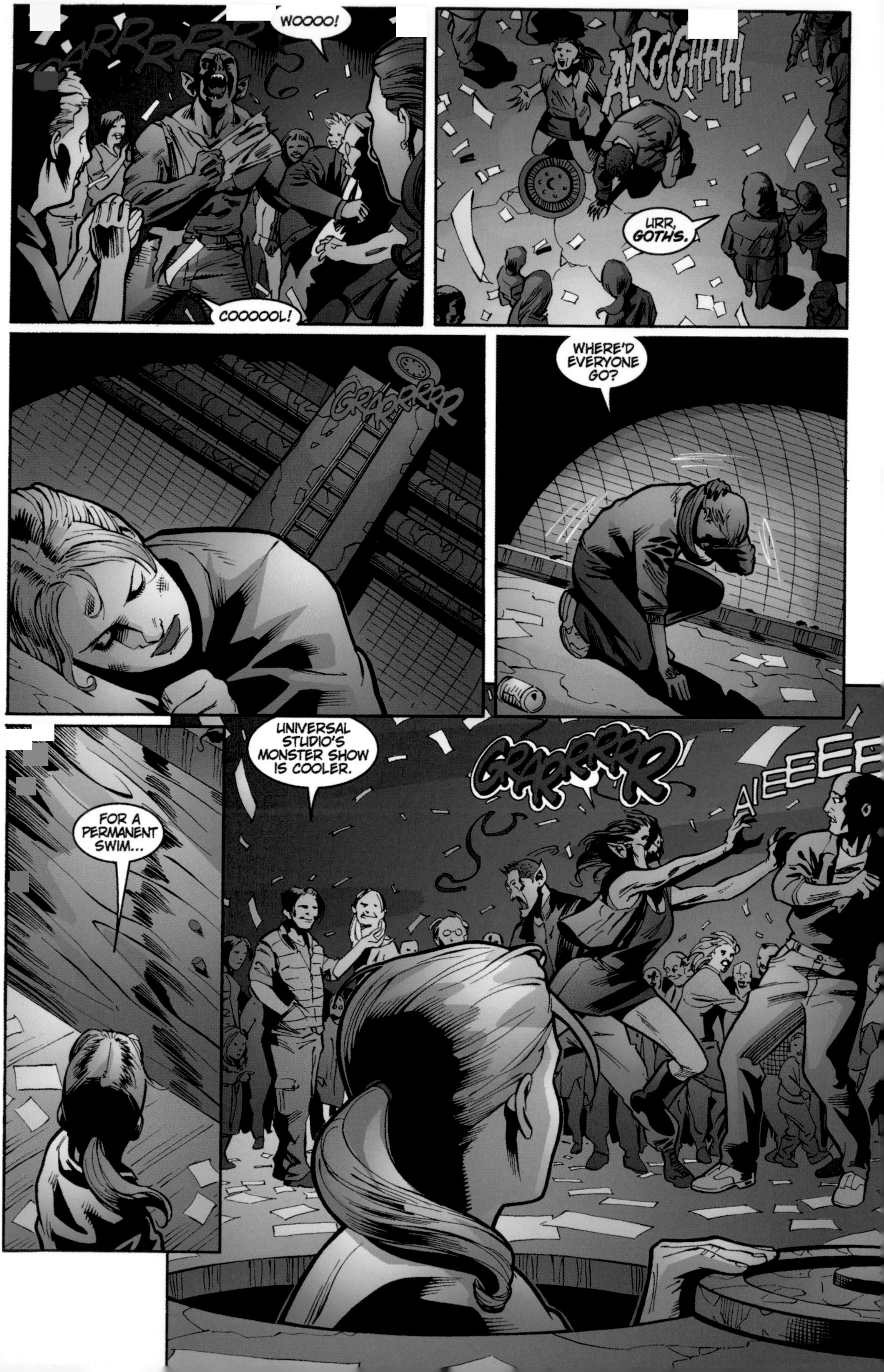
WOOOO!
COOOOOL!
ARGGHHH.
URR, GOTHS.
GRARRRRR
WHERE'D EVERYONE GO?
FOR A PERMANENT SWIM...
UNIVERSAL STUDIO'S MONSTER SHOW IS COOLER.
GRARRRRR
AIEEEEE

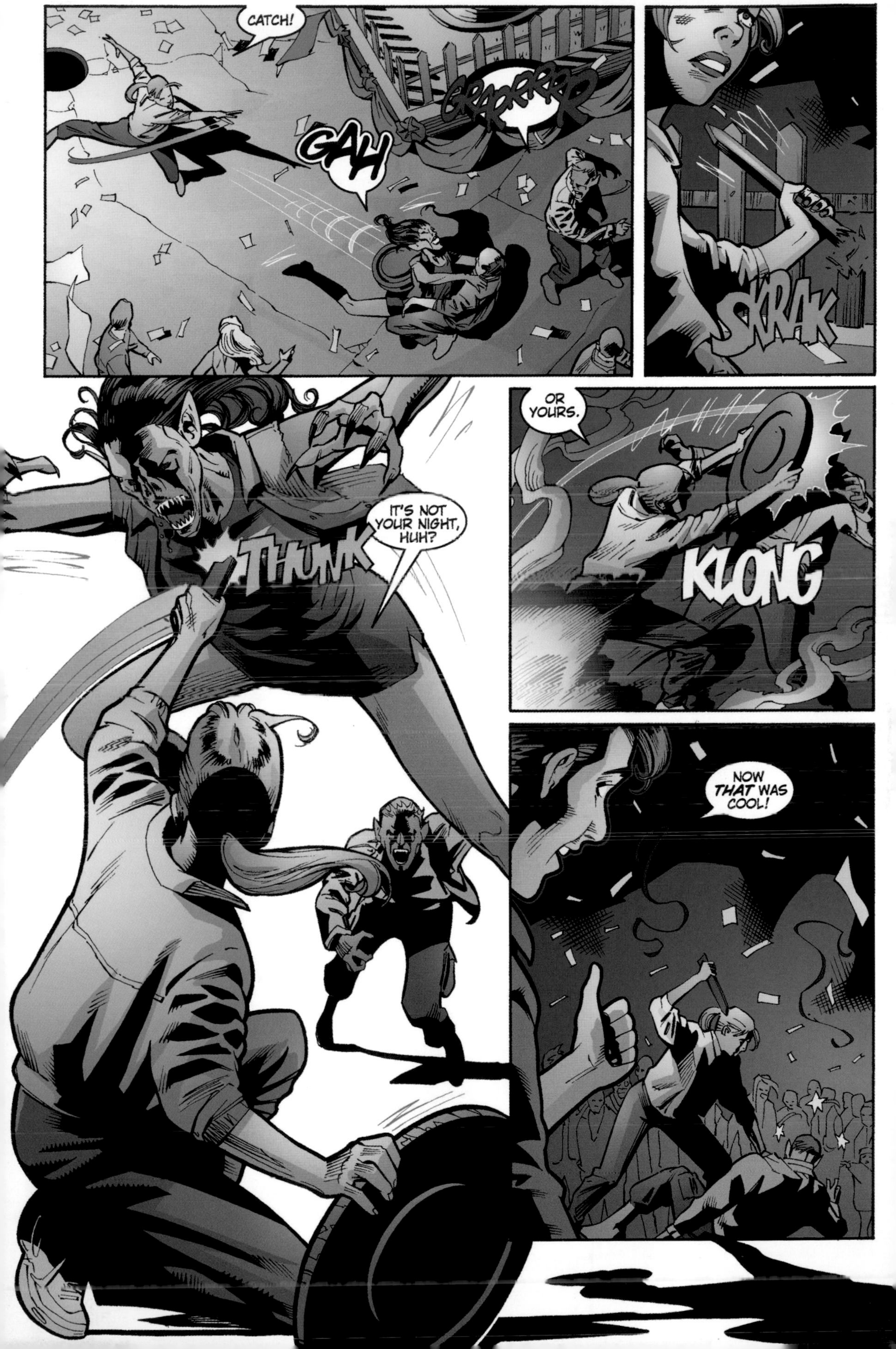
CATCH!
GRARRRR
GAH
SKRAK
IT'S NOT YOUR NIGHT, HUH?
THUNK
OR YOURS.
KLONG
NOW THAT WAS COOL!

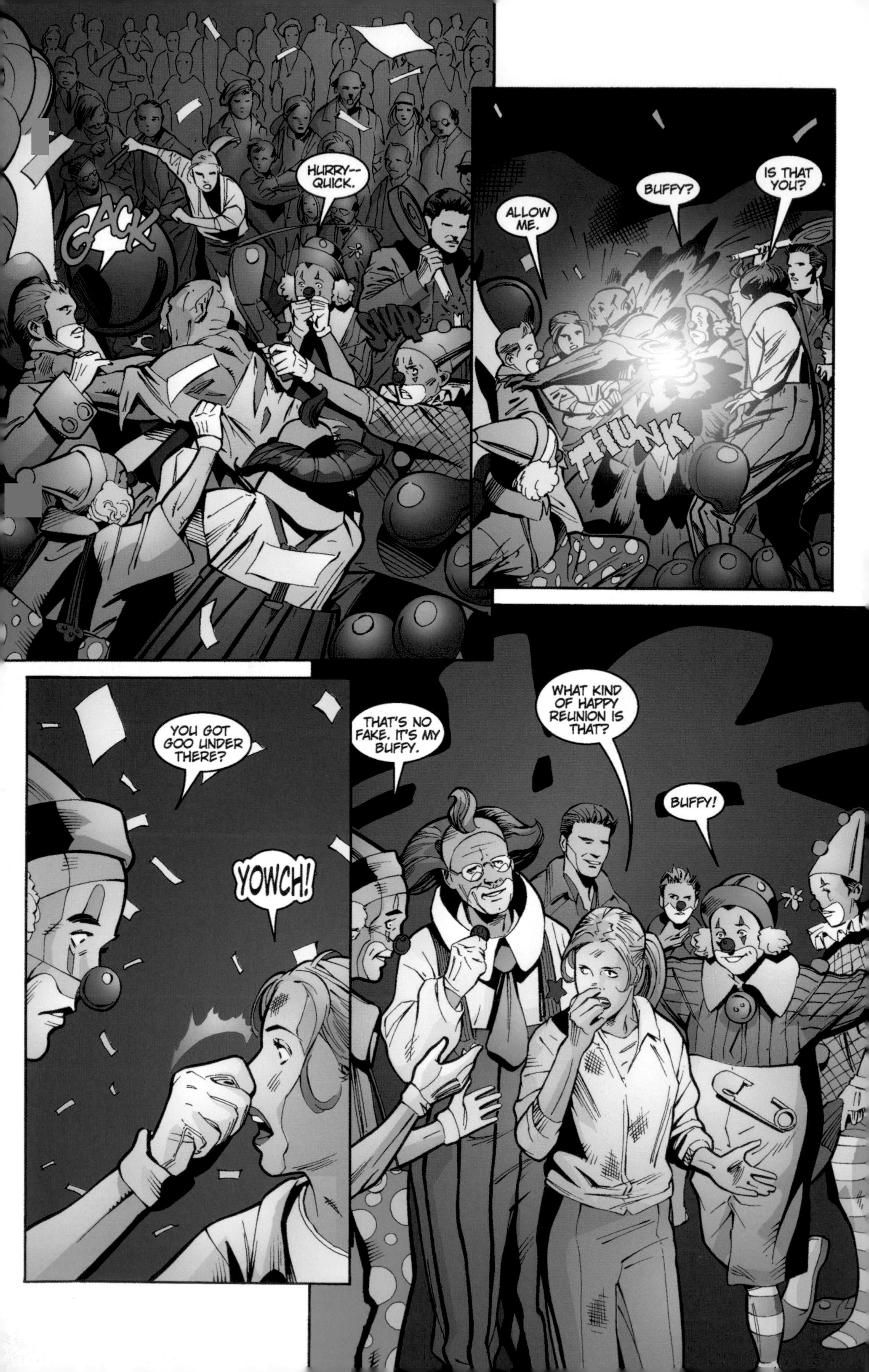
GACK
HURRY-- QUICK.
SNAP
ALLOW ME.
BUFFY?
IS THAT YOU?
THUNK
YOU GOT GOO UNDER THERE?
YOWCH!
THAT'S NO FAKE. IT'S MY BUFFY.
WHAT KIND OF HAPPY REUNION IS THAT?
BUFFY!

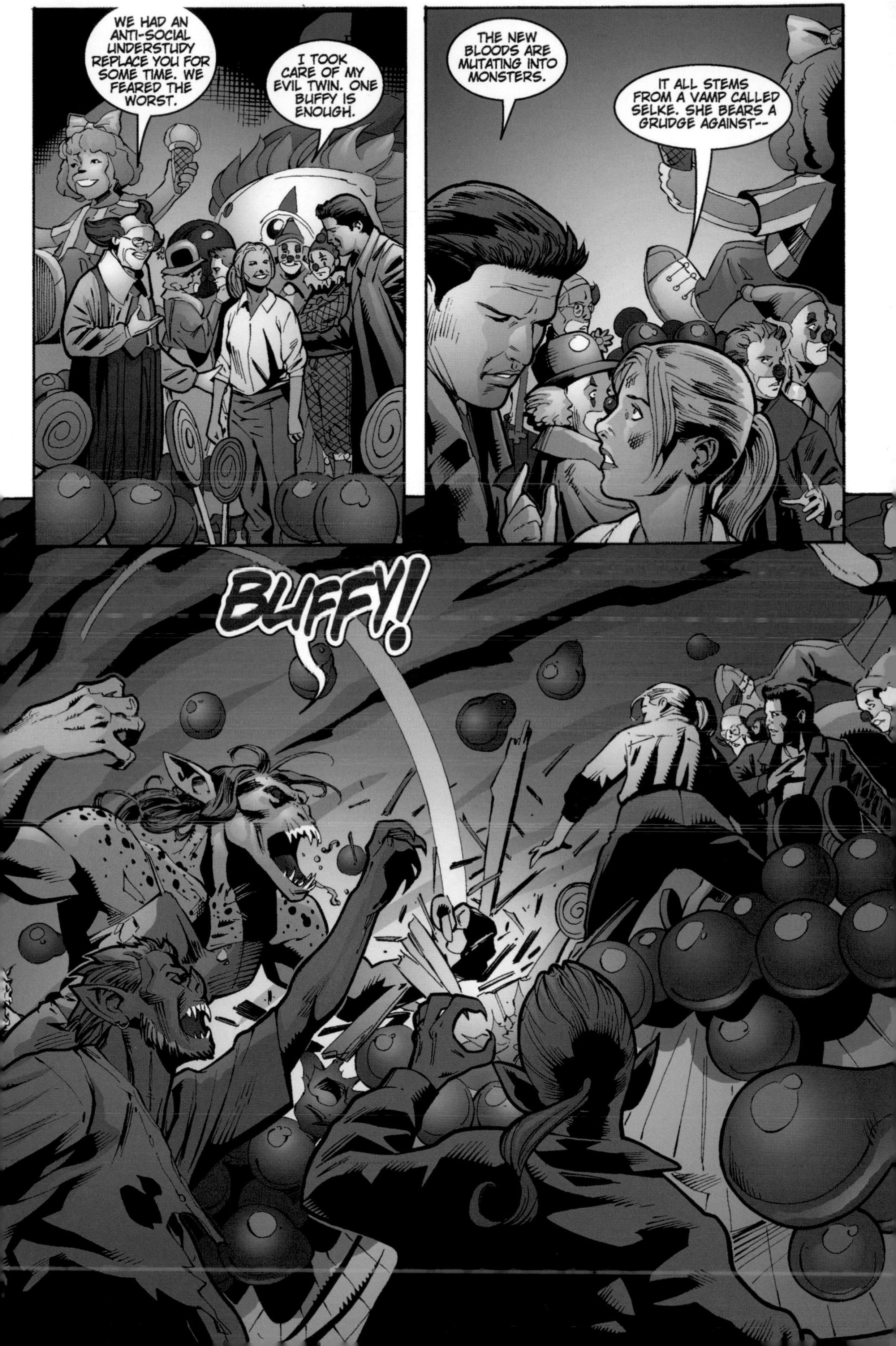
WE HAD AN ANTI-SOCIAL UNDERSTUDY REPLACE YOU FOR SOME TIME. WE FEARED THE WORST.
I TOOK CARE OF MY EVIL TWIN. ONE BUFFY IS ENOUGH.
THE NEW BLOODS ARE MUTATING INTO MONSTERS.
IT ALL STEMS FROM A VAMP CALLED SELKE. SHE BEARS A GRUDGE AGAINST--
BUFFY!

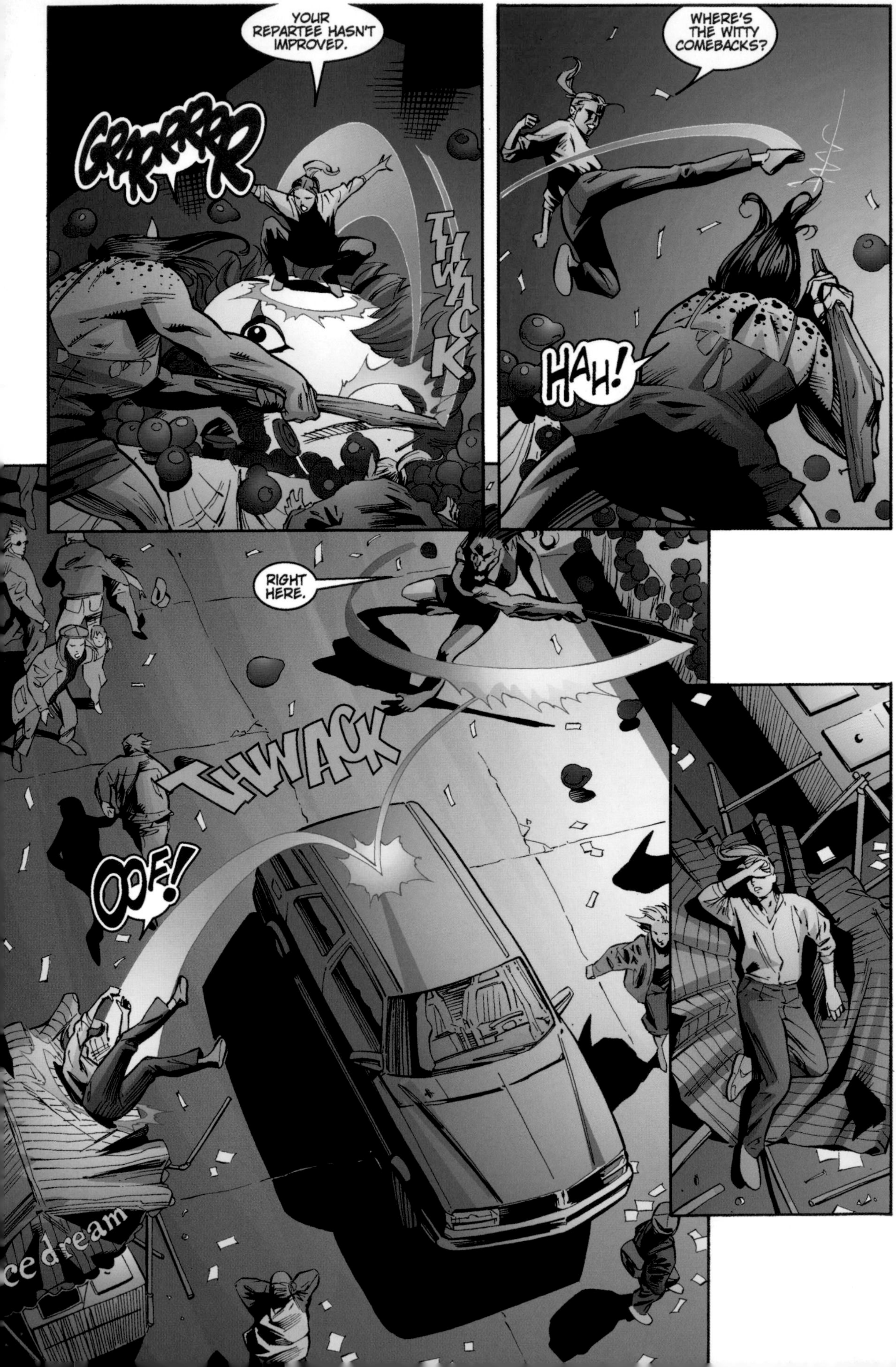
YOUR REPARTEE HASN'T IMPROVED.
GRRRRRR
THWACK
WHERE'S THE WITTY COMEBACKS?
HAH!
RIGHT HERE.
THWACK
OOF!
ce dream

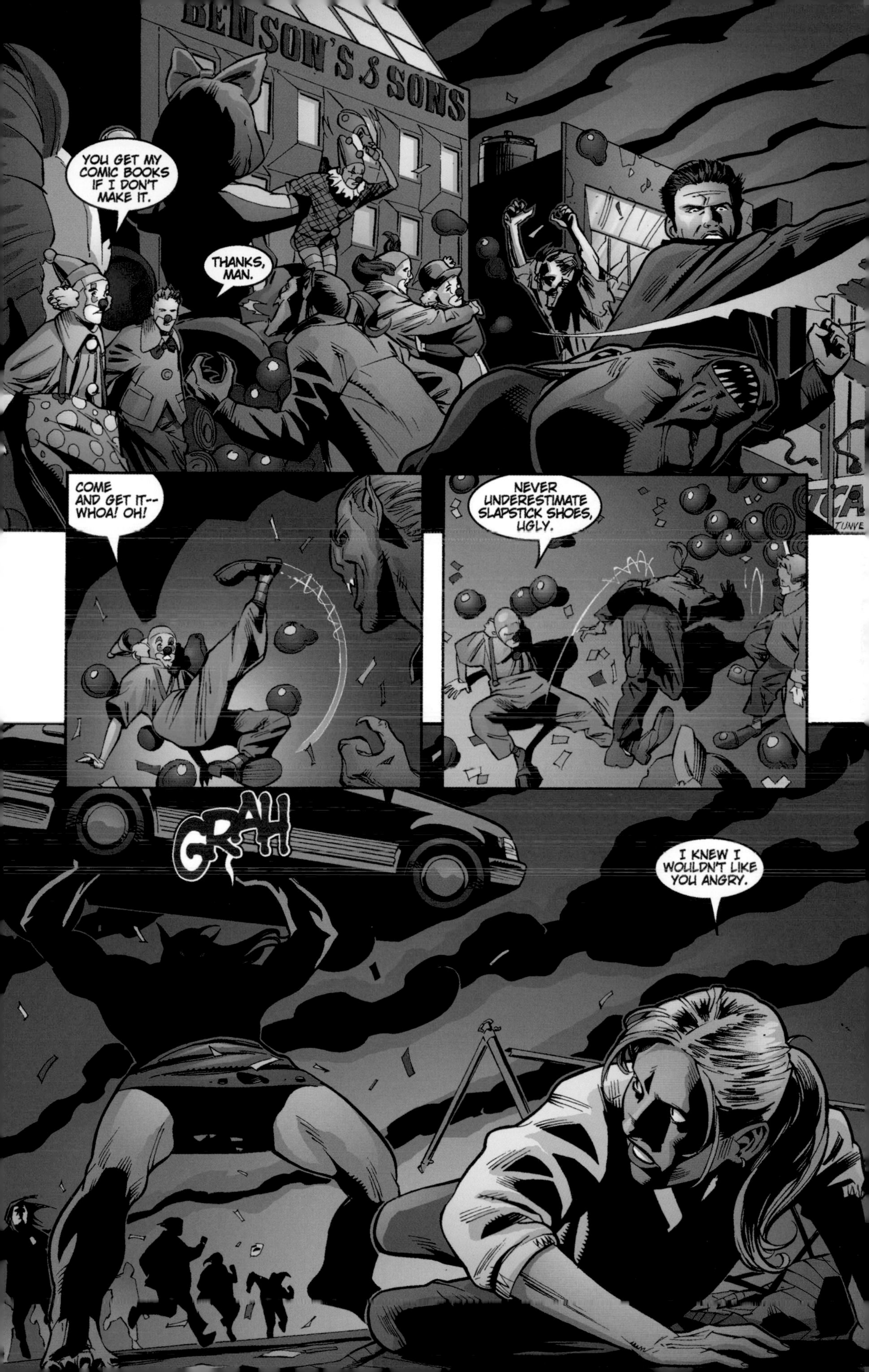
BENSON'S & SONS
YOU GET MY COMIC BOOKS IF I DON'T MAKE IT.
THANKS, MAN.
COME AND GET IT-- WHOA! OH!
NEVER UNDERESTIMATE SLAPSTICK SHOES, UGLY.
GRAH
I KNEW I WOULDN'T LIKE YOU ANGRY.

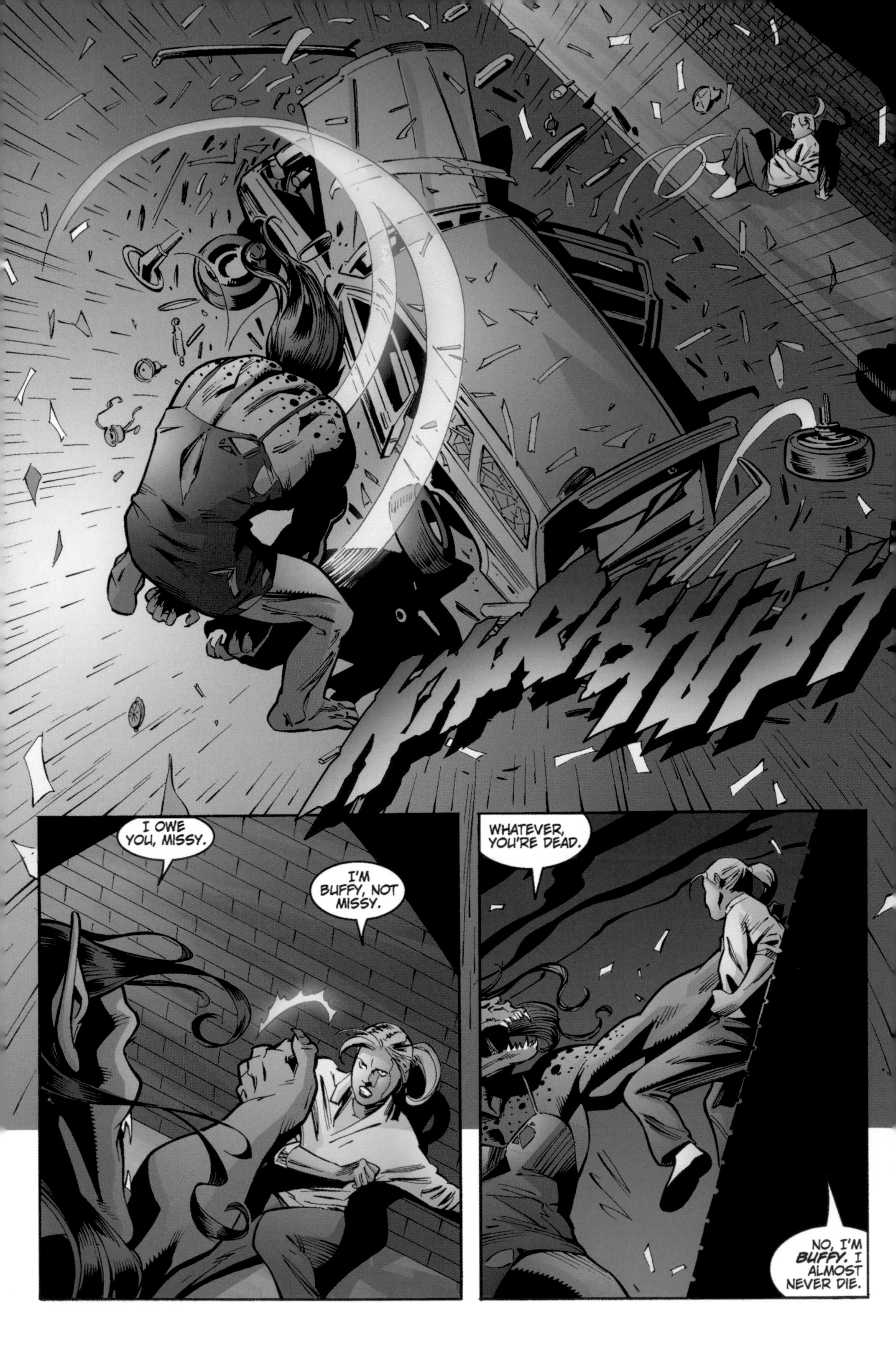

I OWE YOU, MISSY.
I'M BUFFY, NOT MISSY.
WHATEVER, YOU'RE DEAD.
NO, I'M BUFFY. I ALMOST NEVER DIE.

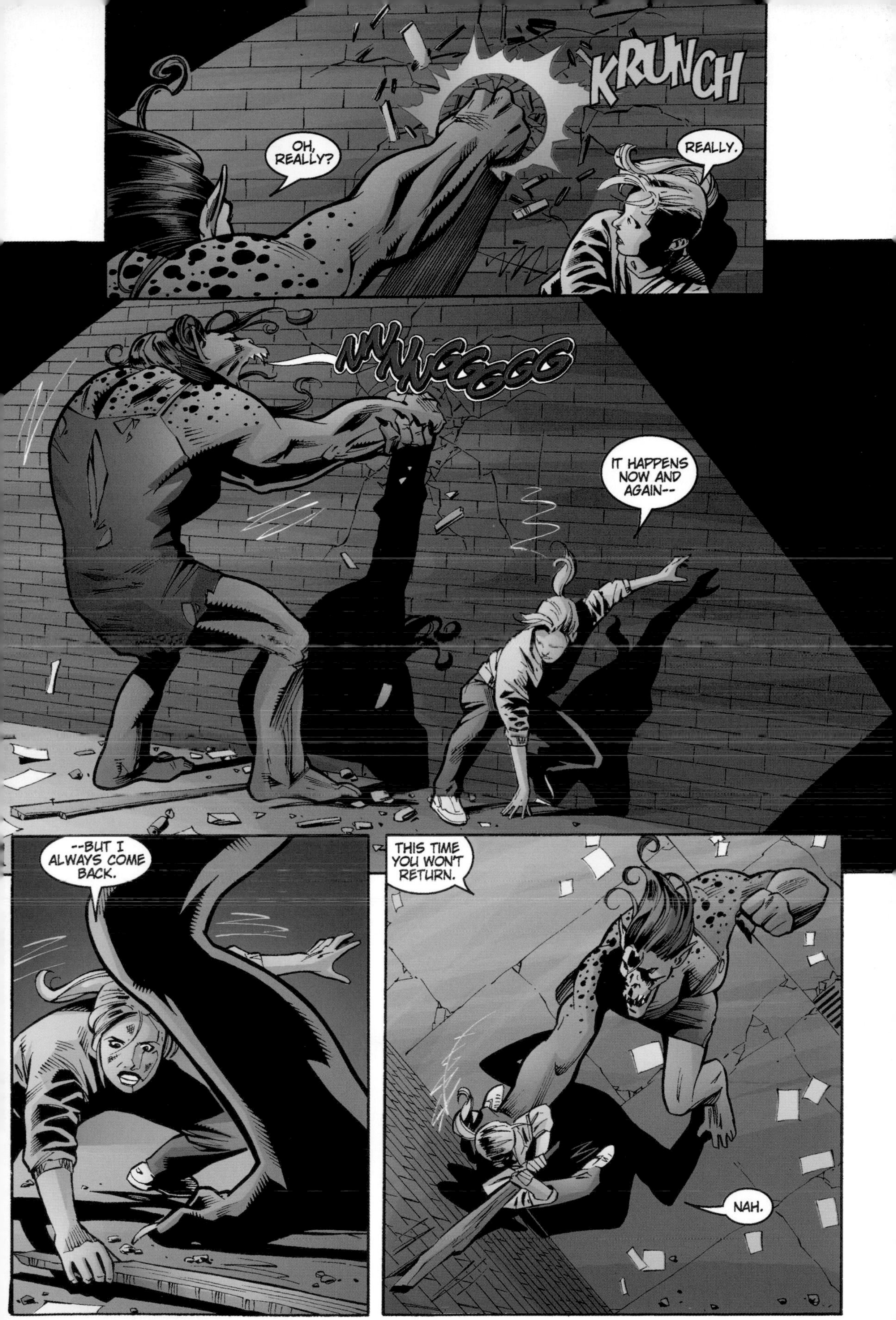
KRUNCH
OH, REALLY?
REALLY.
NNNNGGGGGG
IT HAPPENS NOW AND AGAIN--
--BUT I ALWAYS COME BACK.
THIS TIME YOU WON'T RETURN.
NAH.

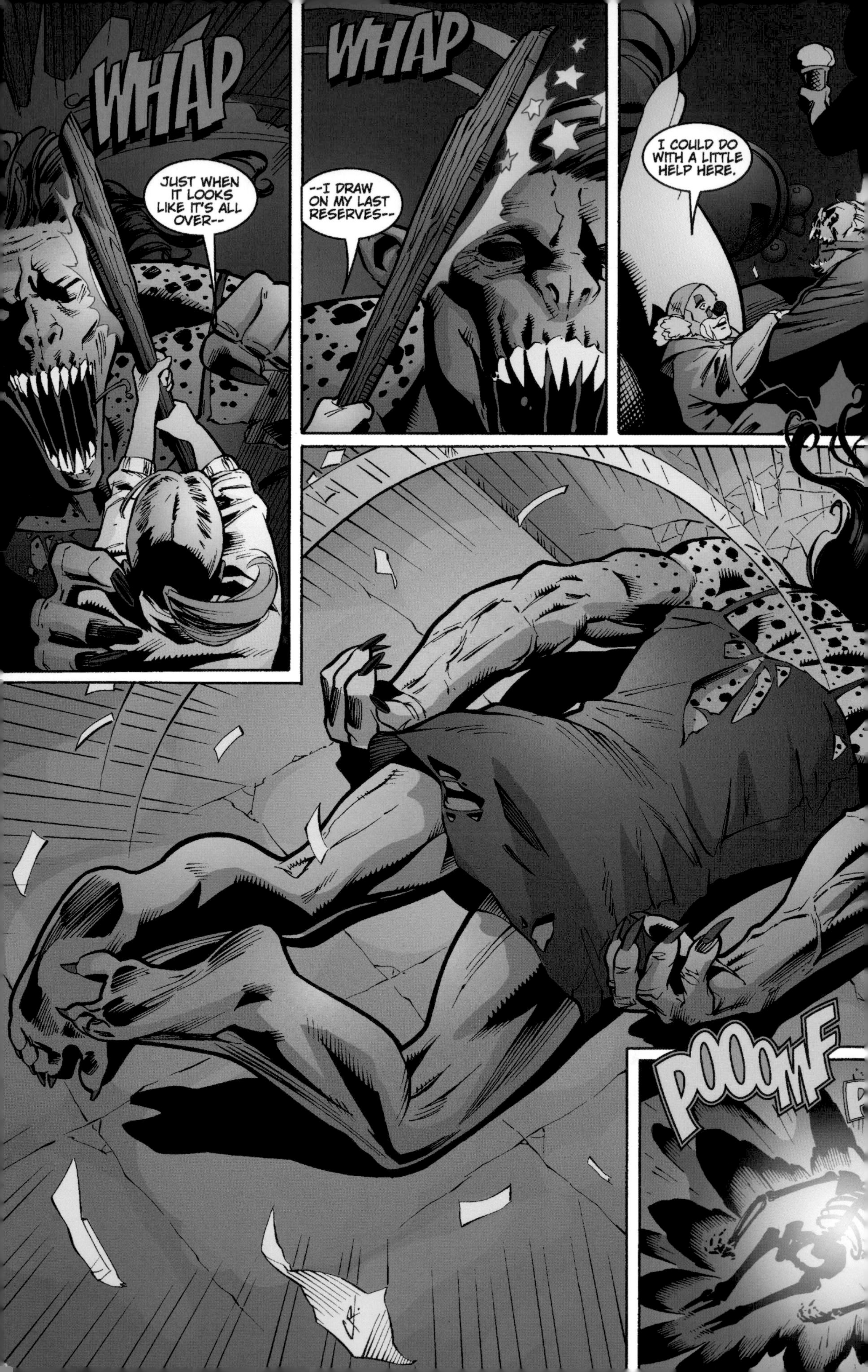
WHAP
JUST WHEN IT LOOKS LIKE IT'S ALL OVER--
WHAP
--I DRAW ON MY LAST RESERVES--
I COULD DO WITH A LITTLE HELP HERE.
POOOMF

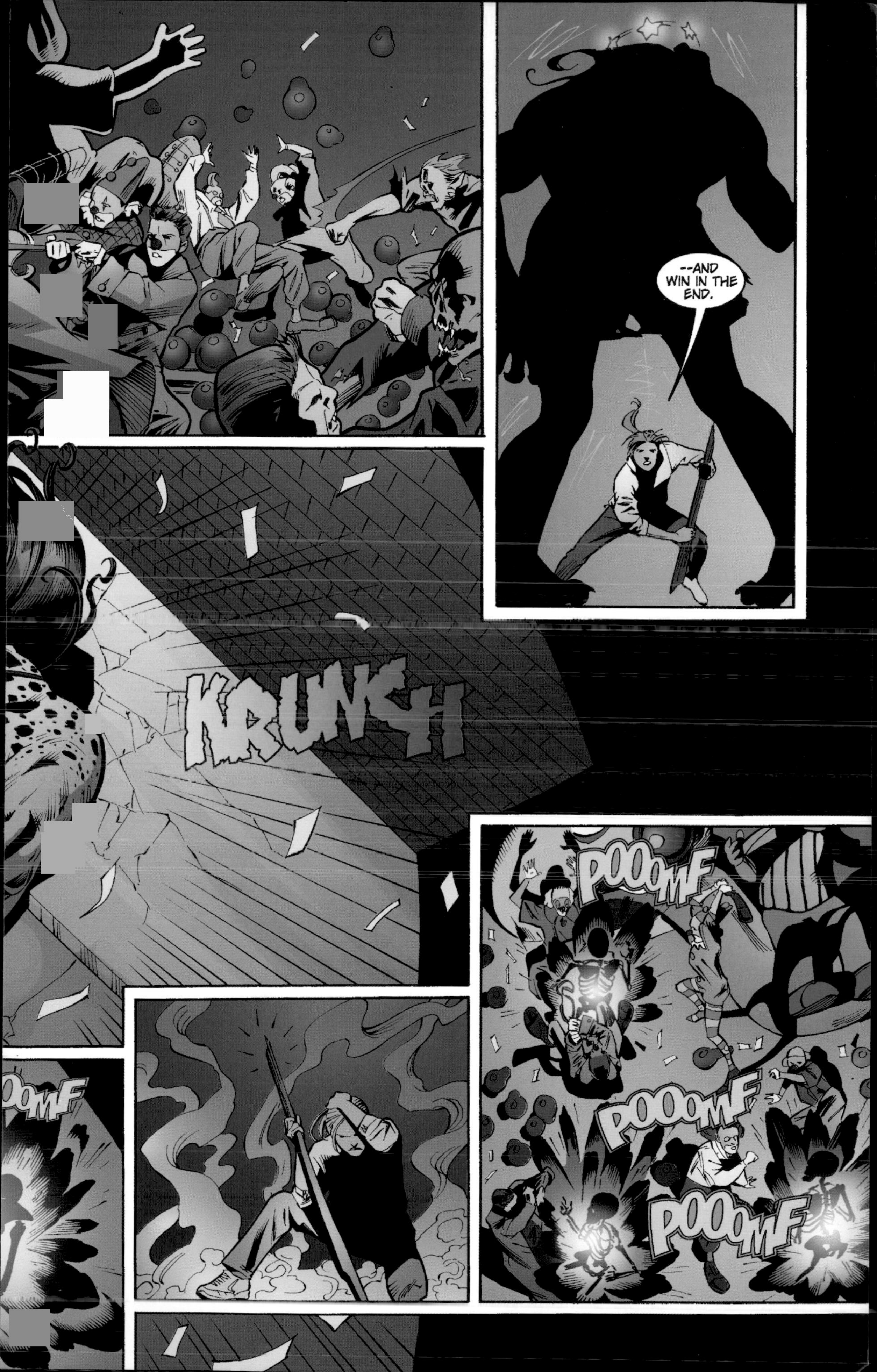
--AND WIN IN THE END.
KRUNCH
POOOMF
POOOMF
POOOMF
OOMF

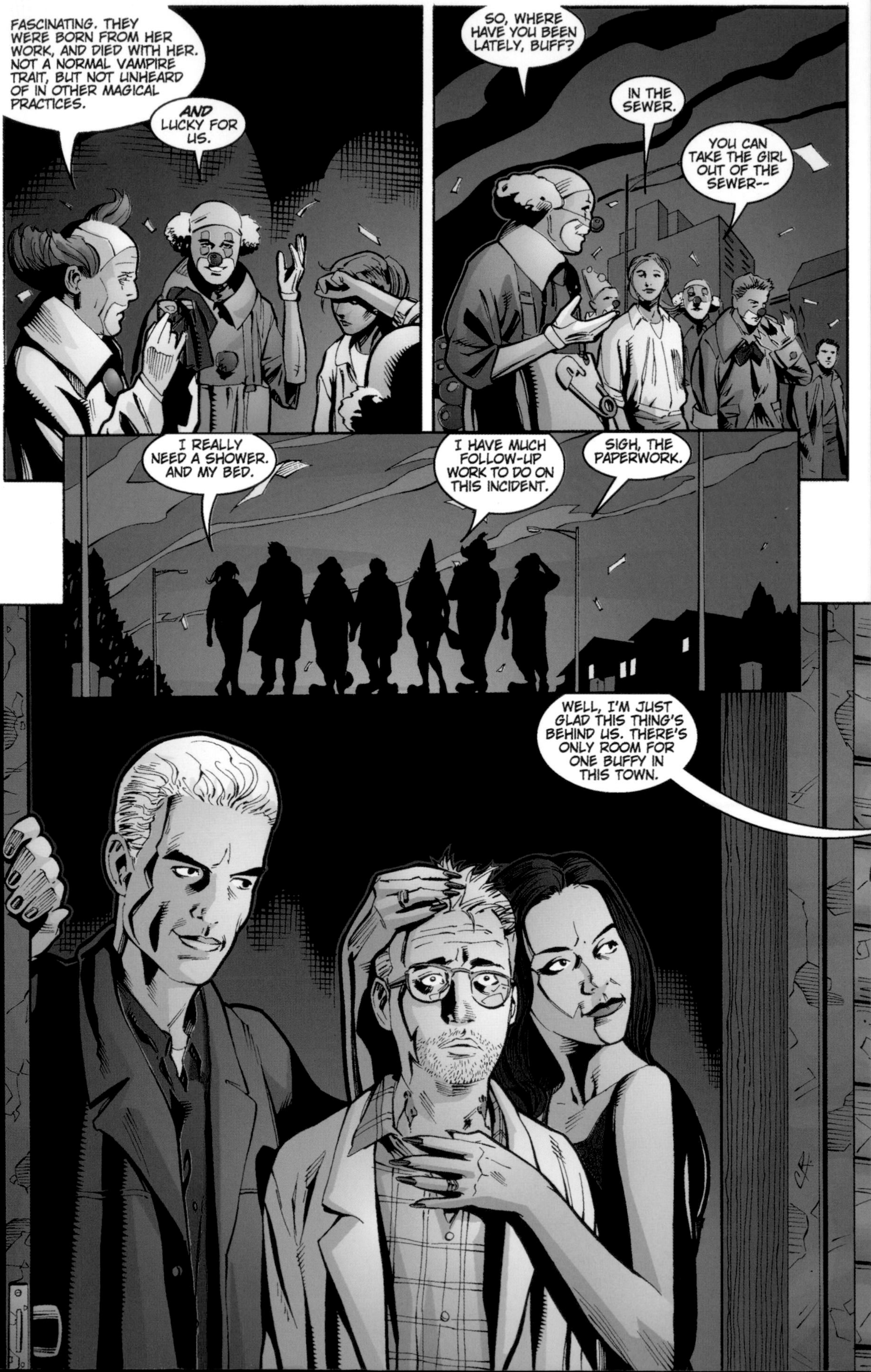
FASCINATING. THEY WERE BORN FROM HER WORK, AND DIED WITH HER. NOT A NORMAL VAMPIRE TRAIT, BUT NOT UNHEARD OF IN OTHER MAGICAL PRACTICES.
AND LUCKY FOR US.
SO, WHERE HAVE YOU BEEN LATELY, BUFF?
IN THE SEWER.
YOU CAN TAKE THE GIRL OUT OF THE SEWER--
I REALLY NEED A SHOWER. AND MY BED.
I HAVE MUCH FOLLOW-UP WORK TO DO ON THIS INCIDENT.
SIGH, THE PAPERWORK.
WELL, I'M JUST GLAD THIS THING'S BEHIND US. THERE'S ONLY ROOM FOR ONE BUFFY IN THIS TOWN.

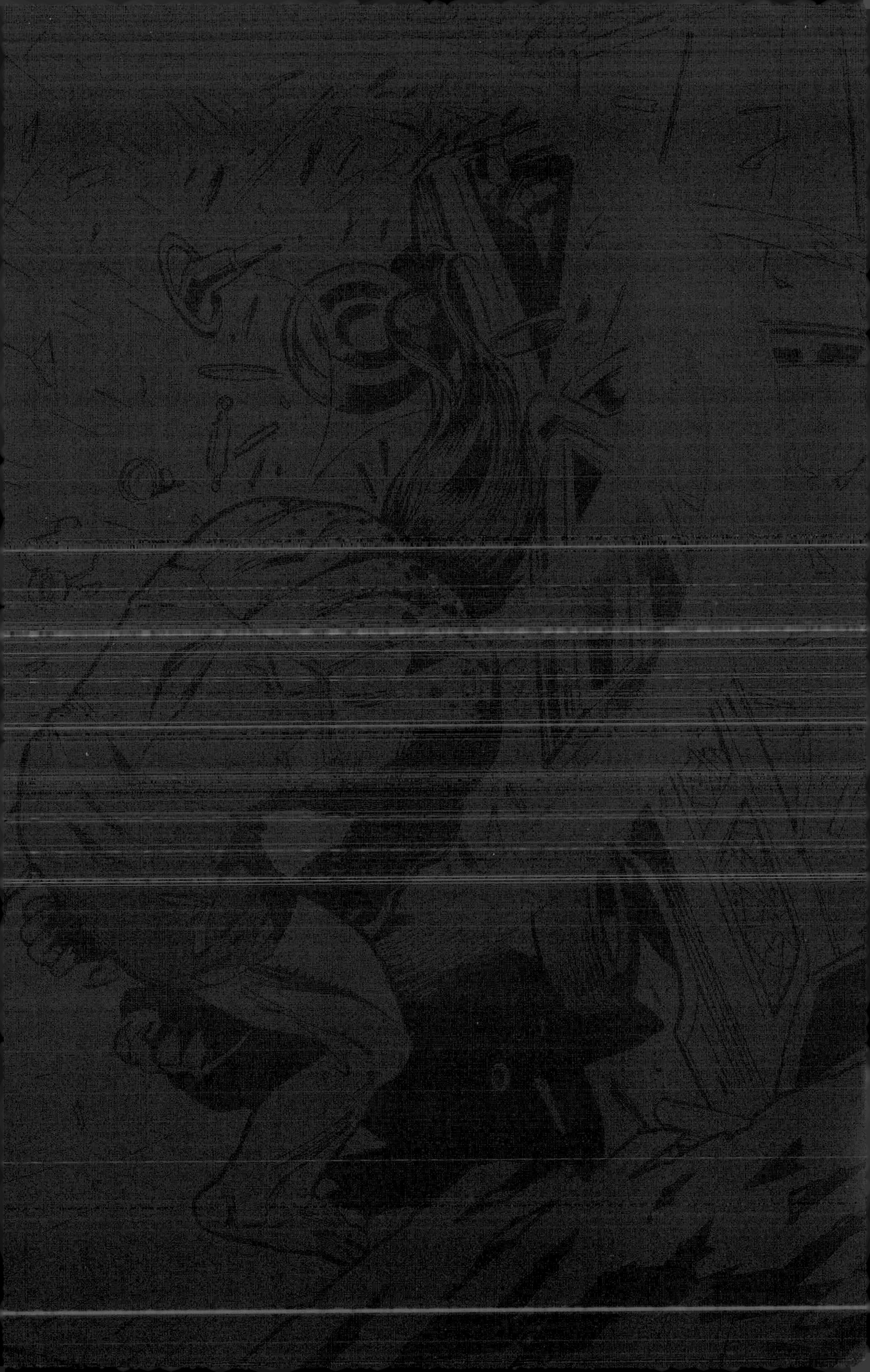

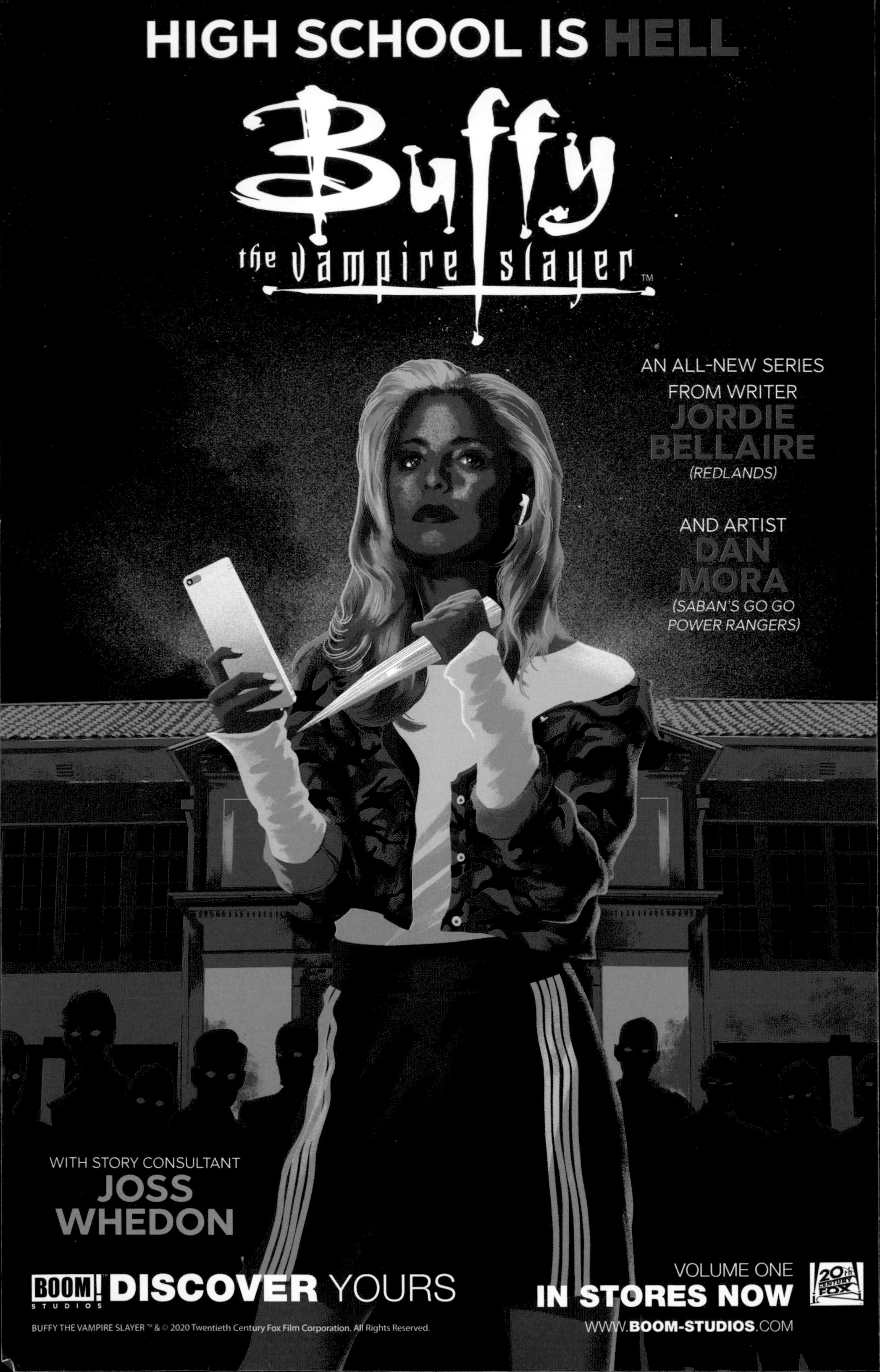

HIGH SCHOOL IS HELL
Buffy the vampire slayer™
AN ALL-NEW SERIES
FROM WRITER
JORDIE
BELLAIRE
(REDLANDS)
AND ARTIST
DAN
MORA
(SABAN'S GO GO
POWER RANGERS)
WITH STORY CONSULTANT
JOSS
WHEDON
BOOM! STUDIOS DISCOVER YOURS
VOLUME ONE
IN STORES NOW
20th CENTURY FOX
WWW.BOOM-STUDIOS.COM
BUFFY THE VAMPIRE SLAYER ™ & © 2020 Twentieth Century Fox Film Corporation. All Rights Reserved.

CAN'T STOP THE SIGNAL...

FIREFLY

LEGACY EDITION BOOK ONE

"...has everything ***Firefly*** fans would expect from the House of Whedon.

—**AIN'T IT COOL NEWS**"

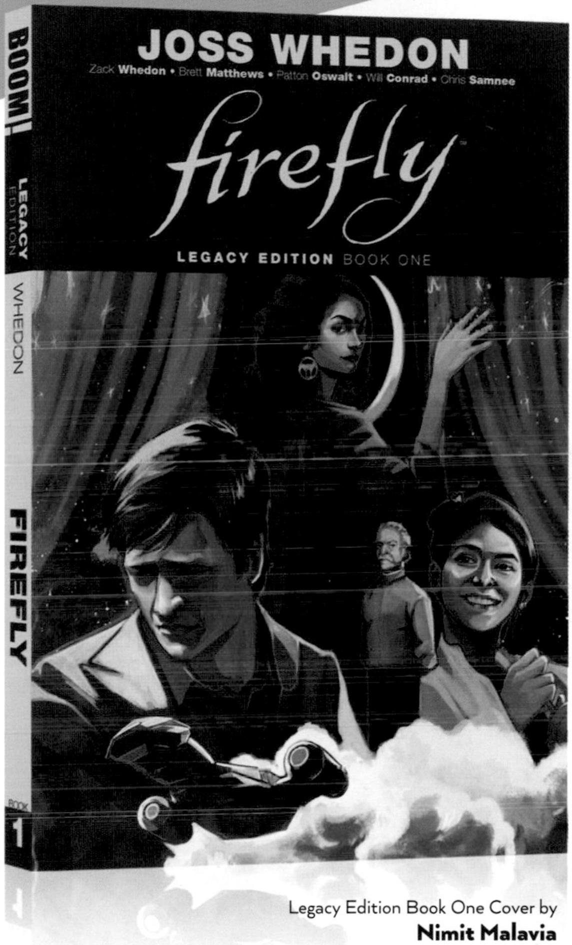
JOSS WHEDON
Zack Whedon • Brett Matthews • Patton Oswalt • Will Conrad • Chris Samnee
firefly
LEGACY EDITION BOOK ONE
BOOM!
LEGACY EDITION
WHEDON
FIREFLY
BOOK 1

Legacy Edition Book One Cover by **Nimit Malavia**

BOOK ONE COLLECTS

Serenity Volume 1: Those Left Behind

Serenity Volume 2: Better Days

Serenity: The Shepherd's Tale OGN

From Joss Whedon (creator of *Buffy the Vampire Slayer*), Serenity rides again, in these official sequels to the critically acclaimed show *Firefly*, collected for the first time under one cover!

Featuring stories by Joss Whedon, Emmy Award-winning comedian Patton Oswalt, and Eisner Award-winning artist Chris Samnee, buried histories and secret identities are revealed, along with all the heist-takin', authority-dodgin', death-defyin' space-cowboyin' you've been missing from your life, as this ragtag crew of mercenaries, outlaws, and fugitives travel the stars in search of their next adventure.

Legacy Editions collect every issue of the most popular BOOM! Studios series in chronological order and in a newly designed, value priced format for the very first time.

AVAILABLE IN STORES NOW

BOOK TWO ALSO AVAILABLE NOW

DISCOVER VISIONARY CREATORS

THE WOODS
JAMES TYNION IV • MICHAEL DIALYNAS
VOL. 1
THE ARROW

"The Spire is fantastic! My kind of genre free-for-all."
—BRIAN K. VAUGHAN (Saga)
THE SPIRE
SIMON SPURRIER
JEFF STOKELY
ANDRÉ MAY

PETER KRAUSE
IRREDEEMABLE
AFTERWORD BY GRANT MORRISON

MARK WAID • JEAN DIAZ
INCORRUPTIBLE

MICHAEL ALAN NELSON
DAN MORA
GABRIEL CASSATA
HEXED
THE HARLOT & THE THIEF VOLUME ONE

ABNETT & CULBARD
WILD'S END
FIRST LIGHT
"IT'S REALLY GREAT!"
JEFF LEMIRE

BOOM! STUDIOS

AVAILABLE AT YOUR LOCAL COMICS SHOP AND BOOKSTORE

To find a comics shop in your area, visit www.comicshoplocator.com

WWW.**BOOM-STUDIOS**.COM

James Tynion IV

The Woods

Volume 1

ISBN: 978-1-60886-454-6 | $9.99 US

Volume 2

ISBN: 978-1-60886-495-9 | $14.99 US

Volume 3

ISBN: 978-1-60886-773-8 | $14.99 US

The Backstagers

Volume 1

ISBN: 978-1-60886-993-0 | $14.99 US

Simon Spurrier

Six-Gun Gorilla

ISBN: 978-1-60886-390-7 | $19.99 US

The Spire

ISBN: 978-1-60886-913-8 | $29.99 US

Weavers

ISBN: 978-1-60886-963-3 | $19.99 US

Mark Waid

Irredeemable

Volume 1

ISBN: 978-1-93450-690-5 | $16.99 US

Volume 2

ISBN: 978-1-60886-000-5 | $16.99 US

Incorruptible

Volume 1

ISBN: 978-1-60886-015-9 | $16.99 US

Volume 2

ISBN: 978-1-60886-028-9 | $16.99 US

Michael Alan Nelson

Hexed The Harlot & The Thief

Volume 1

ISBN: 978-1-60886-718-9 | $14.99 US

Volume 2

ISBN: 978-1-60886-816-2 | $14.99 US

Day Men

Volume 1

ISBN: 978-1-60886-393-8 | $9.99 US

Volume 2

ISBN: 978-1-60886-852-0 | $9.99 US

Dan Abnett

Wild's End

Volume 1: First Light

ISBN: 978-1-60886-735-6 | $19.99 US

Volume 2: The Enemy Within

ISBN: 978-1-60886-877-3 | $19.99 US

Hypernaturals

Volume 1

ISBN: 978-1-60886-298-6 | $16.99 US

Volume 2

ISBN: 978-1-60886-319-8 | $19.99 US

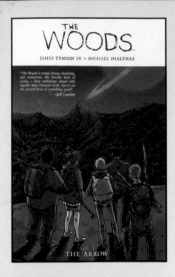

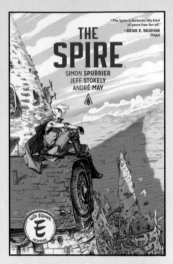

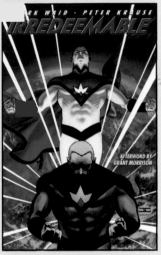

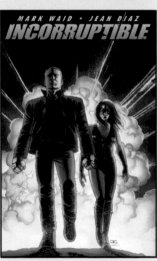

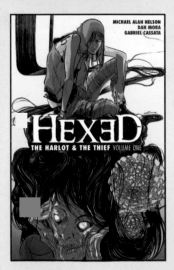

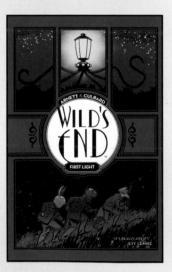

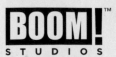